D1526204

International Business Transactions Fundamentals

Documents

International Business Transactions Fundamentals

Documents

Second Edition

Ronald A. Brand

 Wolters Kluwer

Published by:
Kluwer Law International B.V.
PO Box 316
2400 AH Alphen aan den Rijn
The Netherlands
E-mail: international-sales@wolterskluwer.com
Website: lrus.wolterskluwer.com

Sold and distributed in North, Central and South America by:
Wolters Kluwer Legal & Regulatory U.S.
7201 McKinney Circle
Frederick, MD 21704
United States of America
Email: customer.service@wolterskluwer.com

Sold and distributed in all other countries by:
Air Business Subscriptions
Rockwood House
Haywards Heath
West Sussex
RH16 3DH
United Kingdom
Email: international-customerservice@wolterskluwer.com

Printed on acid-free paper.

ISBN 978-90-411-9107-6

e-Book: ISBN 978-90-411-9134-2
web-PDF: ISBN 978-90-411-9135-9

Printed in the United Kingdom.

Table of Contents

SELECTED INTERNATIONAL AND REGIONAL
INSTRUMENTS

A. UNITED NATIONS CONVENTION ON CONTRACTS FOR THE INTERNATIONAL SALE OF GOODS (CISG)

THE STATES PARTIES TO THIS CONVENTION,

BEARING IN MIND the broad objectives in the resolutions adopted by the sixth special session of the General Assembly of the United Nations on the establishment of a New International Economic Order,

CONSIDERING that the development of international trade on the basis of equality and mutual benefit is an important element in promoting friendly relations among States,

BEING OF THE OPINION that the adoption of uniform rules which govern contracts for the international sale of goods and take into account the different social, economic and legal systems would contribute to the removal of legal barriers in international trade and promote the development of international trade,

HAVE AGREED as follows:

PART I
SPHERE OF APPLICATION AND
GENERAL PROVISIONS

Chapter I
SPHERE OF APPLICATION

Article 1

(1) This Convention applies to contracts of sale of goods between parties whose places of business are in different States:
   (a) when the States are Contracting States; or
   (b) when the rules of private international law lead to the application of the law of a Contracting State.
(2) The fact that the parties have their places of business in different States is to be disregarded whenever this fact does not appear either from the contract or from any dealings between, or from information disclosed by, the parties at any time before or at the conclusion of the contract.
(3) Neither the nationality of the parties nor the civil or commercial character of the parties or of the contract is to be taken into consideration in determining the application of this Convention.

Article 2

This Convention does not apply to sales:

(a) of goods bought for personal, family or household use, unless the seller, at any time before or at the conclusion of the contract, neither knew nor ought to have known that the goods were bought for any such use;
(b) by auction;
(c) on execution or otherwise by authority of law;
(d) of stocks, shares, investment securities, negotiable instruments or money;
(e) of ships, vessels, hovercraft or aircraft;
(f) of electricity.

Article 3

(1) Contracts for the supply of goods to be manufactured or produced are to be considered sales unless the party who orders the goods undertakes to supply a substantial part of the materials necessary for such manufacture or production.
(2) This Convention does not apply to contracts in which the preponderant part of the obligations of the party who furnishes the goods consists in the supply of labour or other services.

Article 4

This Convention governs only the formation of the contract of sale and the rights and obligations of the seller and the buyer arising from such a contract. In particular, except as otherwise expressly provided in this Convention, it is not concerned with:

(a) the validity of the contract or of any of its provisions or of any usage;
(b) the effect which the contract may have on the property in the goods sold.

Article 5

This Convention does not apply to the liability of the seller for death or personal injury caused by the goods to any person.

Article 6

The parties may exclude the application of this Convention or, subject to article 12, derogate from or vary the effect of any of its provisions.

Chapter II
GENERAL PROVISIONS

Article 7

(1) In the interpretation of this Convention, regard is to be had to its international character and to the need to promote uniformity in its application and the observance of good faith in international trade.

(2) Questions concerning matters governed by this Convention which are not expressly settled in it are to be settled in conformity with the general principles on which it is based or, in the absence of such principles, in conformity with the law applicable by virtue of the rules of private international law.

Article 8

(1) For the purposes of this Convention statements made by and other conduct of a party are to be interpreted according to his intent where the other party knew or could not have been unaware what that intent was.

(2) If the preceding paragraph is not applicable, statements made by and other conduct of a party are to be interpreted according to the understanding that a reasonable person of the same kind as the other party would have had in the same circumstances.

(3) In determining the intent of a party or the understanding a reasonable person would have had, due consideration is to be given to all relevant circumstances of the case including the negotiations, any practices which the parties have established between themselves, usages and any subsequent conduct of the parties.

Article 9

(1) The parties are bound by any usage to which they have agreed and by any practices which they have established between themselves.

(2) The parties are considered, unless otherwise agreed, to have impliedly made applicable to their contract or its formation a usage of which the parties knew or ought to have known and which in international trade is widely known to, and regularly observed by, parties to contracts of the type involved in the particular trade concerned.

Article 10

For the purposes of this Convention:

(a) if a party has more than one place of business, the place of business is that which has the closest relationship to the contract and its performance, having regard to the circumstances known to or contemplated by the parties at any time before or at the conclusion of the contract;

(b) if a party does not have a place of business, reference is to be made to his habitual residence.

Article 11

A contract of sale need not be concluded in or evidence by writing and is not subject to any other requirements as to form. It may be proved by any means, including witnesses.

Article 12

Any provision of article 11, article 29 or Part II of this Convention that allows a contract of sale or its modification or termination by agreement or any offer, acceptance or other indication of intention to be made in any form other than in writing does not apply where any party has his place of business in a Contracting State which has made a declaration under article 96 of this Convention. The parties may not derogate from or vary the effect of this article.

Article 13

For the purposes of this Convention "writing" includes telegram and telex.

PART II
FORMATION OF THE CONTRACT

Article 14

(1) A proposal for concluding a contract addressed to one or more specific persons constitutes an offer if it is sufficiently definite and indicates the intention of the offeror to be bound in case of acceptance. A proposal is sufficiently definite if it indicates the goods and expressly or implicitly fixes or makes provision for determining the quantity and the price.

(2) A proposal other than one addressed to one or more specific persons is to be considered merely as an invitation to make offers, unless the contrary is clearly indicated by the person making the proposal.

Article 15

(1) An offer becomes effective when it reaches the offeree.
(2) An offer, even if it is irrevocable, may be withdrawn if the withdrawal reaches the offeree before or at the same time as the offer.

Article 16

(1) Until a contract is concluded an offer may be revoked if the revocation reaches the offeree before he has dispatched an acceptance.
(2) However, an offer cannot be revoked:
    (a) if it indicates, whether by stating a fixed time for acceptance or otherwise, that it is irrevocable; or
    (b) if it was reasonable for the offeree to rely on the offer as being irrevocable and the offeree has acted in reliance on the offer.

Article 17

An offer, even if it is irrevocable, is terminated when a rejection reaches the offeror.

Article 18

(1) A statement made by or other conduct of the offeree indicating assent to an offer is an acceptance. Silence or inactivity does not in itself amount to acceptance.
(2) An acceptance of an offer becomes effective at the moment the indication of assent reaches the offeror. An acceptance is not effective if the indication of assent does not reach the offeror within the time he has fixed or, if no time is fixed, within a reasonable time, due account being taken of the circumstances of the transaction, including the rapidity of the means of communication employed by the offeror. An oral offer must be accepted immediately unless the circumstances indicate otherwise.
(3) However, if, by virtue of the offer or as a result of practices which the parties have established between themselves or of usage, the offeree may indicate assent by performing an act, such as one relating to the dispatch of the goods or payment of the price, without notice to the offeror, the acceptance is effective at the moment the act is performed, provided that the act is performed within the period of time laid down in the preceding paragraph.

Article 19

(1) A reply to an offer which purports to be an acceptance but contains additions, limitations or other modifications is a rejection of the offer and constitutes a counter-offer.

(2) However, a reply to an offer which purports to be an acceptance but contains additional or different terms which do not materially alter the terms of the offer constitutes an acceptance, unless the offeror, without undue delay, objects orally to the discrepancy or dispatches a notice to that effect. If he does not so object, the terms of the contract are the terms of the offer with the modifications contained in the acceptance.

(3) Additional or different terms relating, among other things, to the price, payment, quality and quantity of the goods, place and time of delivery, extent of one party's liability to the other or the settlement of disputes are considered to alter the terms of the offer materially.

Article 20

(1) A period of time for acceptance fixed by the offeror in a telegram or a letter begins to run from the moment the telegram is handed in for dispatch or from the date shown on the letter or, if no such date is shown, from the date shown on the envelope. A period of time for acceptance fixed by the offeror by telephone, telex or other means of instantaneous communication, begins to run from the moment that the offer reaches the offeree.

(2) Official holidays or non-business days occurring during the period for acceptance are included in calculating the period. However, if a notice of acceptance cannot be delivered at the address of the offeror on the last day of the period because that day falls on an official holiday or a non-business day at the place of business of the offeror, the period is extended until the first business day which follows.

Article 21

(1) A late acceptance is nevertheless effective as an acceptance if without delay the offeror orally so informs the offeree or dispatches a notice to that effect.

(2) If a letter or other writing containing a late acceptance shows that it has been sent in such circumstances that if its transmission had been normal it would have reached the offeror in due time, the late acceptance is effective as an acceptance unless, without delay, the offeror orally informs the offeree that he considers his offer as having lapsed or dispatches a notice to that effect.

Article 22

An acceptance may be withdrawn if the withdrawal reaches the offeror before or at the same time as the acceptance would have become effective.

Article 23

A contract is concluded at the moment when an acceptance of an offer becomes effective in accordance with the provisions of this Convention.

Article 24

For the purposes of the Part of the Convention, an offer, declaration of acceptance or any other indication of intention "reaches" the addressee when it is made orally to him or delivered by any other means to him personally, to his place of business or mailing address or, if he does not have a place of business or mailing address, to his habitual residence.

PART III
SALE OF GOODS

Chapter I
GENERAL PROVISIONS

Article 25

A breach of contract committed by one of the parties is fundamental if it results in such detriment to the other party as substantially to deprive him of what he is entitled to expect under the contract, unless the party in breach did not foresee and a reasonable person of the same kind in the same circumstances would not have foreseen such a result.

Article 26

A declaration of avoidance of the contract is effective only if made by notice to the other party.

Article 27

Unless otherwise expressly provided in this Part of the Convention, if any notice, request or other communication is given or made by a party in accordance with this Part and by means appropriate in the circumstances, a delay of error in the transmission of the communication or its failure to arrive does not deprive that party of the right to rely on the communication.

Article 28

If, in accordance with the provisions of this Convention, one party is entitled to require performance of any obligation by the other party, a court is not bound to enter a judgement for specific performance unless the court would do so under its own law in respect of similar contracts of sale not governed by this Convention.

Article 29

(1) A contract may be modified or terminated by the mere agreement of the parties.

(2) A contract in writing which contains a provision requiring any modification or termination by agreement to be in writing may not be otherwise modified or terminated by agreement. However, a party may be precluded by his conduct from asserting such a provision to the extent that the other party has relied on that conduct.

Chapter II
OBLIGATIONS OF THE SELLER

Article 30

The seller must deliver the goods, hand over any documents relating to them and transfer the property in the goods, as required by the contract and this Convention.

Section I. Delivery of the goods and handing over of documents

Article 31

If the seller is not bound to deliver the goods at any other particular place, his obligation to deliver consists:

(a) if the contract of sale involves carriage of the goods—in handing the goods over to the first carrier for transmission to the buyer;

(b) if, in cases not within the preceding subparagraph, the contract relates to specific goods, or unidentified goods to be drawn from a specific stock or to be manufactured or produced, and at the time of the conclusion of the contract the parties knew that the goods were at, or were to be manufactured or produced at, a particular place—in placing the goods at the buyer's disposal at that place;

(c) in other cases—in placing the goods at the buyer's disposal at the place where the seller had his place of business at the time of the conclusion of the contract.

Article 32

(1) If the seller, in accordance with the contract or this Convention, hands the goods over to a carrier and if the goods are not clearly identified to the contract by markings on the goods, by shipping documents or otherwise, the seller must give the buyer notice of the consignment specifying the goods.

(2) If the seller is bound to arrange for carriage of the goods, he must make such contracts as are necessary for carriage to the place fixed by means of transportation appropriate in the circumstances and according to the usual terms for such transportation.

(3) If the seller is not bound to effect insurance in respect of the carriage of the goods, he must, at the buyer's request, provide him with all available information necessary to enable him to effect such insurance.

Article 33

The seller must deliver the goods:

(a) if a date is fixed by or determinable from the contract, on that date;

(b) if a period of time is fixed by or determinable from the contract, at any time within that period unless circumstances indicate that the buyer is to choose a date; or

(c) in any other case, within a reasonable time after the conclusion of the contract.

Article 34

If the seller is bound to hand over documents relating to the goods, he must hand them over at the time and place and in the form required by the contract. If the seller has handed over documents before that time, he may, up to that time, cure any lack of conformity in the documents, if the exercise of this right does not cause the buyer unreasonable inconvenience or unreasonable expense. However, the buyer retains any right to claim damages as provided for in this Convention.

Section II. Conformity of the goods and third party claims

Article 35

(1) The seller must deliver goods which are of the quantity, quality and description required by the contract and which are contained or packaged in the manner required by the contract.

(2) Except where the parties have agreed otherwise, the goods do not conform with the contract unless they:

(a) are fit for the purposes for which goods of the same description would ordinarily be used;

(b) are fit for any particular purpose expressly or impliedly made known to the seller at the time of the conclusion of the contract, except where the circumstances show that the buyer did not rely, or that it was unreasonable for him to rely, on the seller's skill and judgement;

(c) possess the qualities of goods which the seller has held out to the buyer as a sample or model;

(d) are contained or packaged in the manner usual for such goods or, where there is no such manner, in a manner adequate to preserve and protect the goods.

(3) The seller is not liable under subparagraphs (a) to (d) of the preceding paragraph for any lack of conformity of the goods if at the time of the conclusion of the contract the buyer knew or could not have been unaware of such lack of conformity.

Article 36

(1) The seller is liable in accordance with the contract and this Convention for any lack of conformity which exists at the time when the risk passes to the buyer, even though the lack of conformity becomes apparent only after that time.

(2) The seller is also liable for any lack of conformity which occurs after the time indicated in the preceding paragraph and which is due to a breach of any of his obligations, including a breach of any guarantee that for a period of time the goods will remain fit for their ordinary purpose or for some particular purpose or will retain specified qualities or characteristics.

Article 37

If the seller has delivered goods before the date for delivery, he may, up to that date, deliver any missing part or make up any deficiency in the quantify of the goods delivered, or deliver goods in replacement of any non-conforming goods delivered or remedy any lack of conformity in the goods delivered, provided that the exercise of this right does not cause the buyer unreasonable inconvenience or unreasonable expense. However, the buyer retains any right to claim damages as provided for in this Convention.

Article 38

(1) The buyer must examine the goods, or cause them to be examined, within as short a period as is practicable in the circumstances.

(2) If the contract involves carriage of the goods, examination may be deferred until after the goods have arrived at their destination.

(3) If the goods are redirected in transit or redispatched by the buyer without a reasonable opportunity for examination by him and at the time of the conclusion of the contract the seller knew or ought to have known of the possibility of such redirection or redispatch, examination may be deferred until after the goods have arrived at the new destination.

Article 39

(1) The buyer loses the right to rely on a lack of conformity of the goods if he does not give notice to the seller specifying the nature of the lack of conformity within a reasonable time after he has discovered it or ought to have discovered it.

(2) In any event, the buyer loses the right to rely on a lack of conformity of the goods if he does not give the seller notice thereof at the latest within a period of two years from the date on which the goods were actually handed over to the buyer, unless this time-limit is inconsistent with a contractual period of guarantee.

Article 40

The seller is not entitled to rely on the provisions of articles 38 and 39 if the lack of conformity relates to facts of which he knew or could not have been unaware and which he did not disclose to the buyer.

Article 41

The seller must deliver goods which are free from any right or claim of a third party, unless the buyer agreed to take the goods subject to that right or claim. However, if such right or claim is based on industrial property or other intellectual property, the seller's obligation is governed by article 42.

Article 42

(1) The seller must deliver goods which are free from any right or claim of a third party based on industrial property or other intellectual property, of which at the time of the conclusion of the contract the seller knew or could not have been unaware, provided that the right or claim is based on industrial property or other intellectual property:

    (a) under the law of the State where the goods will be resold or otherwise used, if it was contemplated by the parties at the time of the conclusion of the contract that the goods would be resold or otherwise used in that State; or

    (b) in any other case, under the law of the State where the buyer has his place of business.

(2) The obligation of the seller under the preceding paragraph does not extend to cases where:

    (a) at the time of the conclusion of the contract the buyer knew or could not have been unaware of the right or claim; or

    (b) the right or claim results from the seller's compliance with technical drawings, designs, formulae or other such specifications furnished by the buyer.

Article 43

(1) The buyer loses the right to rely on the provisions of article 41 or article 42 if he does not give notice to the seller specifying the nature of the right or claim of the third party within a reasonable time after he has become aware or ought to have become aware of the right or claim.

(2) The seller is not entitled to rely on the provisions of the preceding paragraph if he knew of the right or claim of the third party and the nature of it.

Article 44

Notwithstanding the provisions of paragraph (1) of article 39 and paragraph (1) of article 43, the buyer may reduce the price in accordance with article 50 or claim damages, except for loss of profit, if he has a reasonable excuse for his failure to give the required notice.

Section III. Remedies for breach of contract by the seller

Article 45

(1) If the seller fails to perform any of his obligations under the contract or this Convention, the buyer may:
   (a) exercise the rights provided in articles 46 to 52;
   (b) claim damages as provided in articles 74 to 77.

(2) The buyer is not deprived of any right he may have to claim damages by exercising his right to other remedies.

(3) No period of grace may be granted to the seller by a court or arbitral tribunal when the buyer resorts to a remedy for breach of contract.

Article 46

(1) The buyer may require performance by the seller of his obligations unless the buyer has resorted to a remedy which is inconsistent with this requirement.

(2) If the goods do not conform with the contract, the buyer may require delivery of substitute goods only if the lack of conformity constitutes a fundamental breach of contract and a request for substitute goods is made either in conjunction with notice given under article 39 or within a reasonable time thereafter.

(3) If the goods do not conform with the contract, the buyer may require the seller to remedy the lack of conformity by repair, unless this is unreasonable having regard to all the circumstances. A request for repair must be made either in conjunction with notice given under article 39 or within a reasonable time thereafter.

Article 47

(1) The buyer may fix an additional period of time of reasonable length for performance by the seller of his obligations.
(2) Unless the buyer has received notice from the seller that he will not perform within the period so fixed, the buyer may not, during that period, resort to any remedy for breach of contract. However, the buyer is not deprived thereby of any right he may have to claim damages for delay in performance.

Article 48

(1) Subject to article 49, the seller may, even after the date for delivery, remedy at his own expense any failure to perform his obligations, if he can do so without unreasonable delay and without causing the buyer unreasonable inconvenience or uncertainty of reimbursement by the seller of expenses advanced by the buyer. However, the buyer retains any right to claim damages as provided for in this Convention.
(2) If the seller requests the buyer to make known whether he will accept performance and the buyer does not comply with the request within a reasonable time, the seller may perform within the time indicated in his request. The buyer may not, during that period of time, resort to any remedy which is inconsistent with performance by the seller.
(3) A notice by the seller that he will perform within a specified period of time is assumed to include a request, under the preceding paragraph, that the buyer make known his decision.
(4) A request or notice by the seller under paragraph (2) or (3) of this article is not effective unless received by the buyer.

Article 49

(1) The buyer may declare the contract avoided:
   (a) if the failure by the seller to perform any of his obligations under the contract or this Convention amounts to a fundamental breach of contract; or
   (b) in case of non-delivery, if the seller does not deliver the goods within the additional period of time fixed by the buyer in accordance with paragraph (1) or article 47 or declares that he will not deliver within the period so fixed.
(2) However, in cases where the seller has delivered the goods, the buyer loses the right to declare the contract avoided unless he does so:
   (a) in respect of late delivery, within a reasonable time after he has become aware that delivery has been made;
   (b) in respect of any breach other than late delivery, within a reasonable time:

(i) after he knew or ought to have known of the breach;

(ii) after the expiration of any additional period of time fixed by the buyer in accordance with paragraph (1) of article 47, or after the seller has declared that he will not perform his obligations within such an additional period; or

(iii) after the expiration of any additional period of time indicated by the seller in accordance with paragraph (2) of article 48, or after the buyer has declared that he will not accept performance.

Article 50

If the goods do not conform with the contract and whether or not the price has already been paid, the buyer may reduce the price in the same proportion as the value that the goods actually delivered had at the time of the delivery bears to the value that conforming goods would have had at that time. However, if the seller remedies any failure to perform his obligations in accordance with article 37 or article 48 or if the buyer refuses to accept performance by the seller in accordance with those articles, the buyer may not reduce the price.

Article 51

(1) If the seller delivers only a part of the goods or if only a part of the goods delivered is in conformity with the contract, articles 46 to 50 apply in respect of the part which is missing or which does not conform.

(2) The buyer may declare the contract avoided in its entirety only if the failure to make delivery completely or in conformity with the contract amounts to a fundamental breach of the contract.

Article 52

(1) If the seller delivers the goods before the date fixed, the buyer may take delivery or refuse to take delivery.

(2) If the seller delivers a quantity of goods greater than that provided for in the contract, the buyer may take delivery or refuse to take delivery of the excess quantity. If the buyer takes delivery of all or part of the excess quantity, he must pay for it at the contract rate.

Chapter III
OBLIGATIONS OF THE BUYER

Article 53

The buyer must pay the price for the goods and take delivery of them as required by the contract and this Convention.

Section I. Payment of the price

Article 54

The buyer's obligation to pay the price includes taking such steps and complying with such formalities as may be required under the contract or any laws and regulations to enable payment to be made.

Article 55

Where a contract has been validly concluded but does not expressly or implicitly fix or make provision for determining the price, the parties are considered, in the absence of any indication to the contrary, to have impliedly made reference to the price generally charged at the time of the conclusion of the contract for such goods sold under comparable circumstances in the trade concerned.

Article 56

If the price is fixed according to the weight of the goods, in case of doubt it is to be determined by the net weight.

Article 57

(1) If the buyer is not bound to pay the price at any other particular place, he must pay it to the seller:
   (a) at the seller's place of business; or
   (b) if the payment is to be made against the handing over of the goods or of documents, at the place where the handing over takes place.
(2) The seller must bear any increase in the expenses incidental to payment which is caused by a change in his place of business subsequent to the conclusion of the contract.

Article 58

(1) If the buyer is not bound to pay the price at any other specific time, he must pay it when the seller places either the goods or documents controlling their disposition at the buyer's disposal in accordance with the contract and this Convention. The seller may make such payment a condition for handing over the goods or documents.
(2) If the contract involves carriage of the goods, the seller may dispatch the goods on terms whereby the goods, or documents controlling their disposition, will not be handed over to the buyer except against payment of the price.
(3) The buyer is not bound to pay the price until he has had an opportunity to examine the goods, unless the procedures for delivery or payment agreed upon by the parties are inconsistent with his having such an opportunity.

Article 59

The buyer must pay the price on the date fixed by or determinable from the contract and this Convention without the need for any request or compliance with any formality on the part of the seller.

Section II. Taking delivery

Article 60

The buyer's obligation to take delivery consists:

(a) in doing all the acts which could reasonably be expected of him in order to enable the seller to make delivery; and
(b) in taking over the goods.

Section III. Remedies for breach of contract by the buyer

Article 61

(1) If the buyer fails to perform any of his obligations under the contract or this Convention, the seller may:
(a) exercise the rights provided in articles 62 to 65;
(b) claim damages as provided in articles 74 to 77.
(2) The seller is not deprived of any right he may have to claim damages by exercising his right to other remedies.
(3) No period of grace may be granted to the buyer by a court or arbitral tribunal when the seller resorts to a remedy for breach of contract.

Article 62

The seller may require the buyer to pay the price, take delivery or perform his other obligations, unless the seller has resorted to a remedy which is inconsistent with this requirement.

Article 63

(1) The seller may fix an additional period of time of reasonable length for performance by the buyer of his obligations.
(2) Unless the seller has received notice from the buyer that he will not perform within the period so fixed, the seller may not, during that period, resort to any remedy for breach of contract. However, the seller is not deprived thereby of any right he may have to claim damages for delay in performance.

Article 64

(1) The seller may declare the contract avoided:
   (a) if the failure by the buyer to perform any of his obligations under the contract or this Convention amounts to a fundamental breach of contract; or
   (b) if the buyer does not, within the additional period of time fixed by the seller in accordance with paragraph (1) of article 63, perform his obligation to pay the price or take delivery of the goods, or if he declares that he will not do so within the period so fixed.
(2) However, in cases where the buyer has paid the price, the seller loses the right to declare the contract avoided unless he does so:
   (a) in respect of late performance by the buyer, before the seller has become aware that performance has been rendered; or
   (b) in respect of any breach other than late performance by the buyer, within a reasonable time:
      (i) after the seller knew or ought to have known of the breach; or
      (ii) after the expiration of any additional period of time fixed by the seller in accordance with paragraph (1) of article 63, or after the buyer has declared that he will not perform his obligations within such an additional period.

Article 65

(1) If under the contract the buyer is to specify the form, measurement or other features of the goods and he fails to make such specification either on the date agreed upon or within a reasonable time after receipt of a request from the seller, the seller may, without prejudice to any other rights he may have, make the specification himself in accordance with the requirements of the buyer that may be known to him.
(2) If the seller makes the specification himself, he must inform the buyer of the details thereof and must fix a reasonable time within which the buyer may make a different specification. If, after receipt of such a communication, the buyer fails to do so within the time so fixed, the specification made by the seller is binding.

Chapter IV
PASSING OF RISK

Article 66

Loss of or damage to the goods after the risk has passed to the buyer does not discharge him from his obligation to pay the price, unless the loss or damage is due to an act or omission of the seller.

Article 67

(1) If the contract of sale involves carriage of the goods and the seller is not bound to hand them over at a particular place, the risk passes to the buyer when the goods are handed over to the first carrier for transmission to the buyer in accordance with the contract of sale. If the seller is bound to hand the goods over to a carrier at a particular place, the risk does not pass to the buyer until the goods are handed over to the carrier at that place. The fact that the seller is authorized to retain documents controlling the disposition of the goods does not affect the passage of the risk.

(2) Nevertheless, the risk does not pass to the buyer until the goods are clearly identified to the contract, whether by markings on the goods, by shipping documents, by notice given to the buyer or otherwise.

Article 68

The risk in respect of goods sold in transit passes to the buyer from the time of the conclusion of the contract. However, if the circumstances so indicate, the risk is assumed by the buyer from the time the goods were handed over to the carrier who issued the documents embodying the contract of carriage. Nevertheless, if at the time of the conclusion of the contract of sale the seller knew or ought to have known that the goods had been lost or damaged and did not disclose this to the buyer, the loss or damage is at the risk of the seller.

Article 69

(1) In cases not within articles 67 and 68, the risk passes to the buyer when he takes over the goods or, if he does not do so in due time, from the time when the goods are placed at his disposal and he commits a breach of contract by failing to take delivery.

(2) However, if the buyer is bound to take over the goods at a place other than a place of business of the seller, the risk passes when delivery is due and the buyer is aware of the fact that the goods are placed at his disposal at that place.

(3) If the contract relates to goods not then identified, the goods are considered not to be placed at the disposal of the buyer until they are clearly identified to the contract.

Article 70

If the seller has committed a fundamental breach of contract, articles 67, 68 and 69 do not impair the remedies available to the buyer on account of the breach.

Chapter V
PROVISIONS COMMON TO THE OBLIGATIONS OF THE SELLER AND OF THE
BUYER

Section I. Anticipatory breach and instalment contracts

Article 71

(1) A party may suspend the performance of his obligations if, after the conclusion of the contract, it becomes apparent that the other party will not perform a substantial part of his obligations as a result of:
(a) a serious deficiency in his ability to perform or in his creditworthiness; or
(b) his conduct in preparing to perform or in performing the contract.
(2) If the seller has already dispatched the goods before the grounds described in the preceding paragraph become evident, he may prevent the handing over of the goods to the buyer even though the buyer holds a document which entitles him to obtain them. The present paragraph relates only to the rights in the goods as between the buyer and the seller.
(3) A party suspending performance, whether before or after dispatch of the goods, must immediately give notice of the suspension to the other party and must continue with performance if the other party provides adequate assurance of his performance.

Article 72

(1) If prior to the date for performance of the contract it is clear that one of the parties will commit a fundamental breach of contract, the other party may declare the contract avoided.
(2) If time allows, the party intending to declare the contract avoided must give reasonable notice to the other party in order to permit him to provide adequate assurance of his performance.
(3) The requirements of the preceding paragraph do not apply if the other party has declared that he will not perform his obligations.

Article 73

(1) In the case of a contract for delivery of goods by instalments, if the failure of one party to perform any of his obligations in respect of any instalment constitutes a fundamental breach of contract with respect to that instalment, the other party may declare the contract avoided with respect to that instalment.

(2) If one party's failure to perform any of his obligations in respect of any instalment gives the other party good grounds to conclude that a fundamental breach of contract will occur with respect to future instalments, he may declare the contract avoided for the future, provided that he does so within a reasonable time.

(3) A buyer who declares the contract avoided in respect of any delivery may, at the same time, declare it avoided in respect of deliveries already made or of future deliveries if, by reason of their interdependence, those deliveries could not be used for the purpose contemplated by the parties at the time of the conclusion of the contract.

Section II. Damages

Article 74

Damages for breach of contract by one party consist of a sum equal to the loss, including loss of profit, suffered by the other party as a consequence of the breach. Such damages may not exceed the loss which the party in breach foresaw or ought to have foreseen at the time of the conclusion of the contract, in the light of the facts and matters of which he then knew or ought to have known, as a possible consequence of the breach of contract.

Article 75

If the contract is avoided and if, in a reasonable manner and within a reasonable time after avoidance, the buyer has bought goods in replacement or the seller has resold the goods, the party claiming damages may recover the difference between the contract price and the price in the substitute transaction as well as any further damages recoverable under article 74.

Article 76

(1) If the contract is avoided and there is a current price for the goods, the party claiming damages may, if he has not made a purchase or resale under article 75, recover the difference between the price fixed by the contract and the current price at the time of avoidance as well as any further damages recoverable under article 74. If, however, the party claiming damages has avoided the contract after taking over the goods, the current price at the time of such taking over shall be applied instead of the current price at the time of avoidance.

(2) For the purposes of the preceding paragraph, the current price is the price prevailing at the place where delivery of the goods should have been made or, if there is no current price at that place, the price at such other place as serves as a reasonable substitute, making due allowance for differences in the cost of transporting the goods.

Article 77

A party who relies on a breach of contract must take such measures as are reasonable in the circumstances to mitigate the loss, including loss of profit, resulting from the breach. If he fails to take such measures, the party in breach may claim a reduction in the damages in the amount by which the loss should have been mitigated.

Section III. Interest

Article 78

If a party fails to pay the price or any other sum that is in arrears, the other party is entitled to interest on it, without prejudice to any claim for damages recoverable under article 74.

Section IV. Exemptions

Article 79

(1) A party is not liable for a failure to perform any of his obligations if he proves that the failure was due to an impediment beyond his control and that he could not reasonably be expected to have taken the impediment into account at the time of the conclusion of the contract or to have avoided or overcome it or its consequences.

(2) If the party's failure is due to the failure by a third person whom he has engaged to perform the whole or a part of the contract, that party is exempt from liability only if:

   (a) he is exempt under the preceding paragraph; and

   (b) the person whom he has so engaged would be so exempt if the provisions of that paragraph were applied to him.

(3) The exemption provided by this article has effect for the period during which the impediment exists.

(4) The party who fails to perform must give notice to the other party of the impediment and its effect on his ability to perform. If the notice is not received by the other party within a reasonable time after the party who fails to perform knew or ought to have known of the impediment, he is liable for damages resulting form such non-receipt.

(5) Nothing in this article prevents either party from exercising any right other than to claim damages under this Convention.

Article 80

A party may not rely on a failure of the other party to perform, to the extent that such failure was caused by the first party's act or omission.

Section V. Effects of avoidance

Article 81

(1) Avoidance of the contract releases both parties from their obligations under it, subject to any damages which may be due. Avoidance does not affect any provision of the contract for the settlement of disputes or any other provision of the contract governing the rights and obligations of the parties consequent upon the avoidance of the contract.

(2) A party who has performed the contract either wholly or in part may claim restitution from the other party of whatever the first party has supplied or paid under the contract. If both parties are bound to make restitution, they must do so concurrently.

Article 82

(1) The buyer loses the right to declare the contract avoided or to require the seller to deliver substitute goods if it is impossible for him to make restitution of the goods substantially in the condition in which he received them.

(2) The preceding paragraph does not apply:
  (a) if the impossibility of making restitution of the goods or of making restitution of the goods substantially in the condition in which the buyer received them is not due to his act or omission;
  (b) if the goods or part of the goods have perished or deteriorated as a result of the examination provided for in article 38; or
  (c) if the goods or part of the goods have been sold in the normal course of business or have been consumed or transformed by the buyer in the course of normal use before he discovered or ought to have discovered the lack of conformity.

Article 83

A buyer who has lost the right to declare the contract avoided or to require the seller to deliver substitute goods in accordance with article 82 retains all other remedies under the contract and this Convention.

Article 84

(1) If the seller is bound to refund the price, he must also pay interest on it, from the date on which the price was paid.

(2) The buyer must account to the seller for all benefits which he has derived from the goods or part of them:

(a) if he must make restitution of the goods or part of them; or

(b) if it is impossible for him to make restitution of all or part of the goods or to make restitution of all or part of the goods substantially in the condition in which he received them, but he has nevertheless declared the contract avoided or required the seller to deliver substitute goods.

Section VI. Preservation of the goods

Article 85

If the buyer is in delay in taking delivery of the goods or, where payment of the price and delivery of the goods are to be made concurrently, if he fails to pay the price, and the seller is either in possession of the goods or otherwise able to control their disposition, the seller must take such steps as are reasonable in the circumstances to preserve them. He is entitled to retain them until he has been reimbursed his reasonable expenses by the buyer.

Article 86

(1) If the buyer has received the goods and intends to exercise any right under the contract or this Convention to reject them, he must take such steps to preserve them as are reasonable in the circumstances. He is entitled to retain them until he has been reimbursed his reasonable expenses by the seller.

(2) If goods dispatched to the buyer have been placed at his disposal at their destination and he exercises the right to reject them, he must take possession of them on behalf of the seller, provided that this can be done without payment of the price and without unreasonable inconvenience or unreasonable expense. This provision does not apply if the seller or a person authorized to take charge of the goods on his behalf is present at the destination. If the buyer takes possession of the goods under this paragraph, his rights and obligations are governed by the preceding paragraph.

Article 87

A party who is bound to take steps to preserve the goods may deposit them in a warehouse of a third person at the expense of the other party provided that the expense incurred is not unreasonable.

Article 88

(1) A party who is bound to preserve the goods in accordance with article 85 or 86 may sell them by any appropriate means if there has been an unreasonable delay by the other party in taking possession of the goods or in taking them back or in paying the price or the cost of preservation, provided that reasonable notice of the intention to sell has been given to the other party.

(2) If the goods are subject to rapid deterioration or their preservation would involve unreasonable expense, a party who is bound to preserve the goods in accordance with article 85 or 86 must take reasonable measures to sell them. To the extent possible he must give notice to the other party of his intention to sell.

(3) A party selling the goods has the right to retain out of the proceeds of sale an amount equal to the reasonable expenses of preserving the goods and of selling them. He must account to the other party for the balance.

PART IV

FINAL PROVISIONS

Article 89

The Secretary-General of the United Nations is hereby designated as the depositary for this Convention.

Article 90

This Convention does not prevail over any international agreement which has already been or may be entered into and which contains provisions concerning the matters governed by this Convention, provided that the parties have their places of business in States parties to such agreement.

Article 91

(1) This Convention is open for signature at the concluding meeting of the United Nations Conference on Contracts for the International Sale of Goods and will remain open for signature by all States at the Headquarters of the United Nations, New York until 30 September 1981.

(2) This Convention is subject to ratification, acceptance or approval by the signatory States.

(3) This Convention is open for accession by all States which are not signatory States as from the date it is open for signature.

(4) Instruments of ratification, acceptance, approval and accession are to be deposited with the Secretary-General of the United Nations.

Article 92

(1) A Contracting State may declare at the time of signature, ratification, acceptance, approval or accession that it will not be bound by Part II of this Convention or that it will not be bound by Part III of this Convention.

(2) A Contracting State which makes a declaration in accordance with the preceding paragraph in respect of Part II or Part III of this Convention is not to be considered a Contracting State within paragraph (1) of article 1 of this Convention in respect of matters governed by the Part to which the declaration applies.

Article 93

(1) If a Contracting State has two or more territorial units in which, according to its constitution, different systems of law are applicable in relation to the matters dealt with in this Convention, it may, at the time of signature, ratification, acceptance, approval or accession, declare that this Convention is to extend to all its territorial units or only to one or more of them, and may amend its declaration by submitting another declaration at any time.

(2) These declarations are to be notified to the depositary and are to state expressly the territorial units to which the Convention extends.

(3) If, by virtue of a declaration under this article, this Convention extends to one or more but not all of the territorial units of a Contracting State, and if the place of business of a party is located in that State, this place of business, for the purposes of this Convention, is considered not to be in a Contracting State, unless it is in a territorial unit to which the Convention extends.

(4) If a Contracting State makes no declaration under paragraph (1) of this article, the Convention is to extend to all territorial units of that State.

Article 94

(1) Two or more Contracting States which have the same or closely related legal rules on matters governed by this Convention may at any time declare that the Convention is not to apply to contracts of sale or to their formation where the parties have their places of business in those States. Such declarations may be made jointly or by reciprocal unilateral declarations.

(2) A Contracting State which has the same or closely related legal rules on matters governed by this Convention as one or more non-Contracting States may at any time declare that the Convention is not to apply to contracts of sale or to their formation where the parties have their places of business in those States.

(3) If a State which is the object of a declaration under the preceding paragraph subsequently becomes a Contracting State, the declaration made will, as from the date on which the Convention enters into force in respect of the new Contracting State, have the effect of a declaration made under paragraph (1), provided that the new Contracting State joins in such declaration or makes a reciprocal unilateral declaration.

Article 95

Any State may declare at the time of the deposit of its instrument of ratification, acceptance, approval or accession that it will not be bound by subparagraph (1)(b) of article 1 of this Convention.

Article 96

A Contracting State whose legislation requires contracts of sale to be concluded in or evidenced by writing may at any time make a declaration in accordance with article 12 that any provision of article 11, article 29, or Part II of this Convention, that allows a contract of sale or its modification or termination by agreement or any offer, acceptance, or other indication of intention to be made in any form other than in writing, does not apply where any party has his place of business in that State.

Article 97

(1) Declarations made under this Convention at the time of signature are subject to confirmation upon ratification, acceptance or approval.

(2) Declarations and confirmations of declarations are to be in writing and be formally notified to the depositary.

(3) A declaration takes effect simultaneously with the entry into force of this Convention in respect of the State concerned. However, a declaration of which the depositary receives formal notification after such entry into force takes effect on the first day of the month following the expiration of six months after the date of its receipt by the depositary. Reciprocal unilateral declarations under article 94 take effect on the first day of the month following the expiration of six months after the receipt of the latest declaration by the depositary.

(4) Any State which makes a declaration under this Convention may withdraw it at any time by a formal notification in writing addressed to the depositary. Such withdrawal is to take effect on the first day of the month following the expiration of six months after the date of the receipt of the notification by the depositary.

(5) A withdrawal of a declaration made under article 94 renders inoperative, as from the date on which the withdrawal takes effect, any reciprocal declaration made by another State under that article.

Article 98

No reservations are permitted except those expressly authorized in this Convention.

Article 99

(1) This Convention enters into force, subject to the provisions of paragraph (6) of this article, on the first day of the month following the expiration of twelve months after the date of deposit of the tenth instrument of ratification, acceptance, approval or accession, including an instrument which contains a declaration made under article 92.

(2) When a State ratifies, accepts, approves or accedes to this Convention after the deposit of the tenth instrument of ratification, acceptance, approval or accession, this Convention, with the exception of the Part excluded, enters into force in respect of that State, subject to the provisions of paragraph (6) of this article, on the first day of the month following the expiration of twelve months after the date of the deposit of its instrument of ratification, acceptance, approval or accession.

(3) A State which ratifies, accepts, approves or accedes to this Convention and is a party to either or both the Convention relating to a Uniform Law on the Formation of Contracts for the International Sale of Goods done at The Hague on 1 July 1964 (1964 Hague Formation Convention) and the Convention relating to a Uniform Law on the International Sale of Goods done at The Hague on 1 July 1964 (1964 Hague Sales Convention) shall at the same time denounce, as the case may be, either or both the 1964 Hague Sales Convention and the 1964 Hague Formation Convention by notifying the Government of the Netherlands to that effect.

(4) A State party to the 1964 Hague Sales Convention which ratifies, accepts, approves or accedes to the present Convention and declares or has declared under article 92 that it will not be bound by Part II of this Convention shall at the time of ratification, acceptance, approval or accession denounce the 1964 Hague Sales Convention by notifying the Government of the Netherlands to that effect.

(5) A State party to the 1964 Hague Formation Convention which ratifies, accepts, approves or accedes to the present Convention and declares or has declared under article 92 that it will not be bound by Part III of this Convention shall at the time of ratification, acceptance, approval or accession denounce the 1964 Hague Formation Convention by notifying the Government of the Netherlands to that effect.

(6) For the purpose of this article, ratifications, acceptances, approvals and accessions in respect of this Convention by States parties to the 1964 Hague Formation Convention or to the 1964 Hague Sales Convention shall not be effective until such denunciations as may be required on the part of those States in respect of the latter two Conventions have themselves become effective. The depositary of this Convention shall consult with the Government of the Netherlands, as the depositary of the 1964 Conventions, so as to ensure necessary co-ordination in this respect.

Article 100

(1) This Convention applies to the formation of a contract only when the proposal for concluding the contract is made on or after the date when the Convention enters into force in respect of the Contracting States referred to in subparagraph (1)(a) or the Contracting State referred to in subparagraph (1)(b) of article 1.

(2) This Convention applies only to contracts concluded on or after the date when the Convention enters into force in respect of the Contracting States referred to in subparagraph (1)(a) or the Contracting State referred to in subparagraph (1)(b) of article 1.

Article 101

(1) A Contracting State may denounce this Convention, or Part II or Part III of the Convention, by a formal notification in writing addressed to the depositary.

(2) The denunciation takes effect on the first day of the month following the expiration of twelve months after the notification is received by the depositary. Where a longer period for the denunciation to take effect is specified in the notification, the denunciation takes effect upon the expiration of such longer period after the notification is received by the depositary.

DONE at Vienna, this day of eleventh day of April, one thousand nine hundred and eighty, in a single original, of which the Arabic, Chinese, English, French, Russian and Spanish texts are equally authentic.

IN WITNESS WHEREOF the undersigned plenipotentiaries, being duly authorized by their respective Governments, have signed this Convention.

B. REGULATION (EU) NO 1215/2012 OF THE EUROPEAN PARLIAMENT AND OF THE COUNCIL OF 12 DECEMBER 2012 ON JURISDICTION AND THE RECOGNITION AND ENFORCEMENT OF JUDGMENTS IN CIVIL AND COMMERCIAL MATTERS (BRUSSELS I RECAST REGULATION)

THE EUROPEAN PARLIAMENT AND THE COUNCIL OF THE EUROPEAN UNION,

Having regard to the Treaty on the Functioning of the European Union, and in particular Article 67(4) and points (a), (c) and (e) of Article 81(2) thereof,

Having regard to the proposal from the European Commission,

After transmission of the draft legislative act to the national parliaments,

Having regard to the opinion of the European Economic and Social Committee[1],

Acting in accordance with the ordinary legislative procedure[2],

Whereas:

(1) On 21 April 2009, the Commission adopted a report on the application of Council Regulation (EC) No 44/2001 of 22 December 2000 on jurisdiction and the recognition and enforcement of judgments in civil and commercial matters[3]. The report concluded that, in general, the operation of that Regulation is satisfactory, but that it is desirable to improve the application of certain of its provisions, to further facilitate the free circulation of judgments and to further enhance access to justice. Since a number of amendments are to be made to that Regulation it should, in the interests of clarity, be recast.

(2) At its meeting in Brussels on 10 and 11 December 2009, the European Council adopted a new multiannual programme entitled 'The Stockholm Programme – an open and secure Europe serving and protecting citizens'[4]. In the Stockholm Programme the European Council considered that the process of abolishing all intermediate measures (the exequatur) should be continued during the period covered by that Programme. At the same time the abolition of the exequatur should also be accompanied by a series of safeguards.

---

1. OJ C 218, 23.7.2011, p. 78.
2. Position of the European Parliament of 20 November 2012 (not yet published in the Official Journal) and decision of the Council of 6 December 2012.
3. OJ L 12, 16.1.2001, p. 1.
4. OJ C 115, 4.5.2010, p. 1.

(3) The Union has set itself the objective of maintaining and developing an area of freedom, security and justice, inter alia, by facilitating access to justice, in particular through the principle of mutual recognition of judicial and extra-judicial decisions in civil matters. For the gradual establishment of such an area, the Union is to adopt measures relating to judicial cooperation in civil matters having cross-border implications, particularly when necessary for the proper functioning of the internal market.

(4) Certain differences between national rules governing jurisdiction and recognition of judgments hamper the sound operation of the internal market. Provisions to unify the rules of conflict of jurisdiction in civil and commercial matters, and to ensure rapid and simple recognition and enforcement of judgments given in a Member State, are essential.

(5) Such provisions fall within the area of judicial cooperation in civil matters within the meaning of Article 81 of the Treaty on the Functioning of the European Union (TFEU).

(6) In order to attain the objective of free circulation of judgments in civil and commercial matters, it is necessary and appropriate that the rules governing jurisdiction and the recognition and enforcement of judgments be governed by a legal instrument of the Union which is binding and directly applicable.

(7) On 27 September 1968, the then Member States of the European Communities, acting under Article 220, fourth indent, of the Treaty establishing the European Economic Community, concluded the Brussels Convention on Jurisdiction and the Enforcement of Judgments in Civil and Commercial Matters, subsequently amended by conventions on the accession to that Convention of new Member States[5] ('the 1968 Brussels Convention'). On 16 September 1988, the then Member States of the European Communities and certain EFTA States concluded the Lugano Convention on Jurisdiction and the Enforcement of Judgments in Civil and Commercial Matters[6] (2) ('the 1988 Lugano Convention'), which is a parallel convention to the 1968 Brussels Convention. The 1988 Lugano Convention became applicable to Poland on 1 February 2000.

---

5. OJ L 299, 31.12.1972, p. 32, OJ L 304, 30.10.1978, p. 1, OJ L 388, 31.12.1982, p. 1, OJ L 285, 3.10.1989, p. 1, OJ C 15, 15.1.1997, p. 1. For a consolidated text, see OJ C 27, 26.1.1998, p. 1.
6. OJ L 319, 25.11.1988, p. 9.

(8) On 22 December 2000, the Council adopted Regulation (EC) No 44/2001, which replaces the 1968 Brussels Convention with regard to the territories of the Member States covered by the TFEU, as between the Member States except Denmark. By Council Decision 2006/325/EC[7], the Community concluded an agreement with Denmark ensuring the application of the provisions of Regulation (EC) No 44/2001 in Denmark. The 1988 Lugano Convention was revised by the Convention on Jurisdiction and the Recognition and Enforcement of Judgments in Civil and Commercial Matters[8], signed at Lugano on 30 October 2007 by the Community, Denmark, Iceland, Norway and Switzerland ('the 2007 Lugano Convention').

(9) The 1968 Brussels Convention continues to apply to the territories of the Member States which fall within the territorial scope of that Convention and which are excluded from this Regulation pursuant to Article 355 of the TFEU.

(10) The scope of this Regulation should cover all the main civil and commercial matters apart from certain well-defined matters, in particular maintenance obligations, which should be excluded from the scope of this Regulation following the adoption of Council Regulation (EC) No 4/2009 of 18 December 2008 on jurisdiction, applicable law, recognition and enforcement of decisions and cooperation in matters relating to maintenance obligations[9].

(11) For the purposes of this Regulation, courts or tribunals of the Member States should include courts or tribunals common to several Member States, such as the Benelux Court of Justice when it exercises jurisdiction on matters falling within the scope of this Regulation. Therefore, judgments given by such courts should be recognised and enforced in accordance with this Regulation.

(12) This Regulation should not apply to arbitration. Nothing in this Regulation should prevent the courts of a Member State, when seised of an action in a matter in respect of which the parties have entered into an arbitration agreement, from referring the parties to arbitration, from staying or dismissing the proceedings, or from examining whether the arbitration agreement is null and void, inoperative or incapable of being performed, in accordance with their national law.

A ruling given by a court of a Member State as to whether or not an arbitration agreement is null and void, inoperative or incapable of being performed should not be subject to the rules of recognition and enforcement laid down in this Regulation, regardless of whether the court decided on this as a principal issue or as an incidental question.

---

7. OJ L 120, 5.5.2006, p. 22.
8. OJ L 147, 10.6.2009, p. 5.
9. OJ L 7, 10.1.2009, p. 1.

On the other hand, where a court of a Member State, exercising jurisdiction under this Regulation or under national law, has determined that an arbitration agreement is null and void, inoperative or incapable of being performed, this should not preclude that court's judgment on the substance of the matter from being recognised or, as the case may be, enforced in accordance with this Regulation. This should be without prejudice to the competence of the courts of the Member States to decide on the recognition and enforcement of arbitral awards in accordance with the Convention on the Recognition and Enforcement of Foreign Arbitral Awards, done at New York on 10 June 1958 ('the 1958 New York Convention'), which takes precedence over this Regulation.

This Regulation should not apply to any action or ancillary proceedings relating to, in particular, the establishment of an arbitral tribunal, the powers of arbitrators, the conduct of an arbitration procedure or any other aspects of such a procedure, nor to any action or judgment concerning the annulment, review, appeal, recognition or enforcement of an arbitral award.

(13) There must be a connection between proceedings to which this Regulation applies and the territory of the Member States. Accordingly, common rules of jurisdiction should, in principle, apply when the defendant is domiciled in a Member State.

(14) A defendant not domiciled in a Member State should in general be subject to the national rules of jurisdiction applicable in the territory of the Member State of the court seised.

However, in order to ensure the protection of consumers and employees, to safeguard the jurisdiction of the courts of the Member States in situations where they have exclusive jurisdiction and to respect the autonomy of the parties, certain rules of jurisdiction in this Regulation should apply regardless of the defendant's domicile.

(15) The rules of jurisdiction should be highly predictable and founded on the principle that jurisdiction is generally based on the defendant's domicile. Jurisdiction should always be available on this ground save in a few well-defined situations in which the subject-matter of the dispute or the autonomy of the parties warrants a different connecting factor. The domicile of a legal person must be defined autonomously so as to make the common rules more transparent and avoid conflicts of jurisdiction.

(16) In addition to the defendant's domicile, there should be alternative grounds of jurisdiction based on a close connection between the court and the action or in order to facilitate the sound administration of justice. The existence of a close connection should ensure legal certainty and avoid the possibility of the defendant being sued in a court of a Member State which he could not reasonably have foreseen. This is important, particularly in disputes concerning non-contractual obligations arising out of violations of privacy and rights relating to personality, including defamation.

(17) The owner of a cultural object as defined in Article 1(1) of Council Directive 93/7/EEC of 15 March 1993 on the return of cultural objects unlawfully removed from the territory of a Member State[10] should be able under this Regulation to initiate proceedings as regards a civil claim for the recovery, based on ownership, of such a cultural object in the courts for the place where the cultural object is situated at the time the court is seised. Such proceedings should be without prejudice to proceedings initiated under Directive 93/7/EEC.

(18) In relation to insurance, consumer and employment contracts, the weaker party should be protected by rules of jurisdiction more favourable to his interests than the general rules.

(19) The autonomy of the parties to a contract, other than an insurance, consumer or employment contract, where only limited autonomy to determine the courts having jurisdiction is allowed, should be respected subject to the exclusive grounds of jurisdiction laid down in this Regulation.

(20) Where a question arises as to whether a choice-of-court agreement in favour of a court or the courts of a Member State is null and void as to its substantive validity, that question should be decided in accordance with the law of the Member State of the court or courts designated in the agreement, including the conflict-of-laws rules of that Member State.

(21) In the interests of the harmonious administration of justice it is necessary to minimise the possibility of concurrent proceedings and to ensure that irreconcilable judgments will not be given in different Member States. There should be a clear and effective mechanism for resolving cases of *lis pendens* and related actions, and for obviating problems flowing from national differences as to the determination of the time when a case is regarded as pending. For the purposes of this Regulation, that time should be defined autonomously.

---

10. OJ L 74, 27.3.1993, p. 74.

(22) However, in order to enhance the effectiveness of exclusive choice-of-court agreements and to avoid abusive litigation tactics, it is necessary to provide for an exception to the general *lis pendens* rule in order to deal satisfactorily with a particular situation in which concurrent proceedings may arise. This is the situation where a court not designated in an exclusive choice-of-court agreement has been seised of proceedings and the designated court is seised subsequently of proceedings involving the same cause of action and between the same parties. In such a case, the court first seised should be required to stay its proceedings as soon as the designated court has been seised and until such time as the latter court declares that it has no jurisdiction under the exclusive choice-of-court agreement. This is to ensure that, in such a situation, the designated court has priority to decide on the validity of the agreement and on the extent to which the agreement applies to the dispute pending before it. The designated court should be able to proceed irrespective of whether the non-designated court has already decided on the stay of proceedings.

This exception should not cover situations where the parties have entered into conflicting exclusive choice-of-court agreements or where a court designated in an exclusive choice-of-court agreement has been seised first. In such cases, the general *lis pendens* rule of this Regulation should apply.

(23) This Regulation should provide for a flexible mechanism allowing the courts of the Member States to take into account proceedings pending before the courts of third States, considering in particular whether a judgment of a third State will be capable of recognition and enforcement in the Member State concerned under the law of that Member State and the proper administration of justice.

(24) When taking into account the proper administration of justice, the court of the Member State concerned should assess all the circumstances of the case before it. Such circumstances may include connections between the facts of the case and the parties and the third State concerned, the stage to which the proceedings in the third State have progressed by the time proceedings are initiated in the court of the Member State and whether or not the court of the third State can be expected to give a judgment within a reasonable time.

That assessment may also include consideration of the question whether the court of the third State has exclusive jurisdiction in the particular case in circumstances where a court of a Member State would have exclusive jurisdiction.

(25) The notion of provisional, including protective, measures should include, for example, protective orders aimed at obtaining information or preserving evidence as referred to in Articles 6 and 7 of Directive 2004/48/EC of the European Parliament and of the Council of 29 April 2004 on the enforcement of intellectual property rights[11]. It should not include measures which are not of a protective nature, such as measures ordering the hearing of a witness. This should be without prejudice to the application of Council Regulation (EC) No 1206/2001 of 28 May 2001 on cooperation between the courts of the Member States in the taking of evidence in civil or commercial matters[12].

(26) Mutual trust in the administration of justice in the Union justifies the principle that judgments given in a Member State should be recognised in all Member States without the need for any special procedure. In addition, the aim of making cross-border litigation less time-consuming and costly justifies the abolition of the declaration of enforceability prior to enforcement in the Member State addressed. As a result, a judgment given by the courts of a Member State should be treated as if it had been given in the Member State addressed.

(27) For the purposes of the free circulation of judgments, a judgment given in a Member State should be recognised and enforced in another Member State even if it is given against a person not domiciled in a Member State.

(28) Where a judgment contains a measure or order which is not known in the law of the Member State addressed, that measure or order, including any right indicated therein, should, to the extent possible, be adapted to one which, under the law of that Member State, has equivalent effects attached to it and pursues similar aims. How, and by whom, the adaptation is to be carried out should be determined by each Member State.

(29) The direct enforcement in the Member State addressed of a judgment given in another Member State without a declaration of enforceability should not jeopardise respect for the rights of the defence. Therefore, the person against whom enforcement is sought should be able to apply for refusal of the recognition or enforcement of a judgment if he considers one of the grounds for refusal of recognition to be present. This should include the ground that he had not had the opportunity to arrange for his defence where the judgment was given in default of appearance in a civil action linked to criminal proceedings. It should also include the grounds which could be invoked on the basis of an agreement between the Member State addressed and a third State concluded pursuant to Article 59 of the 1968 Brussels Convention.

---

11. OJ L 157, 30.4.2004, p. 45.
12. OJ L 174, 27.6.2001, p. 1.

(30) A party challenging the enforcement of a judgment given in another Member State should, to the extent possible and in accordance with the legal system of the Member State addressed, be able to invoke, in the same procedure, in addition to the grounds for refusal provided for in this Regulation, the grounds for refusal available under national law and within the time-limits laid down in that law.

The recognition of a judgment should, however, be refused only if one or more of the grounds for refusal provided for in this Regulation are present.

(31) Pending a challenge to the enforcement of a judgment, it should be possible for the courts in the Member State addressed, during the entire proceedings relating to such a challenge, including any appeal, to allow the enforcement to proceed subject to a limitation of the enforcement or to the provision of security.

(32) In order to inform the person against whom enforcement is sought of the enforcement of a judgment given in another Member State, the certificate established under this Regulation, if necessary accompanied by the judgment, should be served on that person in reasonable time before the first enforcement measure. In this context, the first enforcement measure should mean the first enforcement measure after such service.

(33) Where provisional, including protective, measures are ordered by a court having jurisdiction as to the substance of the matter, their free circulation should be ensured under this Regulation. However, provisional, including protective, measures which were ordered by such a court without the defendant being summoned to appear should not be recognised and enforced under this Regulation unless the judgment containing the measure is served on the defendant prior to enforcement. This should not preclude the recognition and enforcement of such measures under national law. Where provisional, including protective, measures are ordered by a court of a Member State not having jurisdiction as to the substance of the matter, the effect of such measures should be confined, under this Regulation, to the territory of that Member State.

(34) Continuity between the 1968 Brussels Convention, Regulation (EC) No 44/2001 and this Regulation should be ensured, and transitional provisions should be laid down to that end. The same need for continuity applies as regards the interpretation by the Court of Justice of the European Union of the 1968 Brussels Convention and of the Regulations replacing it.

(35) Respect for international commitments entered into by the Member States means that this Regulation should not affect conventions relating to specific matters to which the Member States are parties.

(36) Without prejudice to the obligations of the Member States under the Treaties, this Regulation should not affect the application of bilateral conventions and agreements between a third State and a Member State concluded before the date of entry into force of Regulation (EC) No 44/2001 which concern matters governed by this Regulation.

(37) In order to ensure that the certificates to be used in connection with the recognition or enforcement of judgments, authentic instruments and court settlements under this Regulation are kept up-to-date, the power to adopt acts in accordance with Article 290 of the TFEU should be delegated to the Commission in respect of amendments to Annexes I and II to this Regulation. It is of particular importance that the Commission carry out appropriate consultations during its preparatory work, including at expert level. The Commission, when preparing and drawing up delegated acts, should ensure a simultaneous, timely and appropriate transmission of relevant documents to the European Parliament and to the Council.

(38) This Regulation respects fundamental rights and observes the principles recognised in the Charter of Fundamental Rights of the European Union, in particular the right to an effective remedy and to a fair trial guaranteed in Article 47 of the Charter.

(39) Since the objective of this Regulation cannot be sufficiently achieved by the Member States and can be better achieved at Union level, the Union may adopt measures in accordance with the principle of subsidiarity as set out in Article 5 of the Treaty on European Union (TEU). In accordance with the principle of proportionality, as set out in that Article, this Regulation does not go beyond what is necessary in order to achieve that objective.

(40) The United Kingdom and Ireland, in accordance with Article 3 of the Protocol on the position of the United Kingdom and Ireland, annexed to the TEU and to the then Treaty establishing the European Community, took part in the adoption and application of Regulation (EC) No 44/2001. In accordance with Article 3 of Protocol No 21 on the position of the United Kingdom and Ireland in respect of the area of freedom, security and justice, annexed to the TEU and to the TFEU, the United Kingdom and Ireland have notified their wish to take part in the adoption and application of this Regulation.

(41) In accordance with Articles 1 and 2 of Protocol No 22 on the position of Denmark annexed to the TEU and to the TFEU, Denmark is not taking part in the adoption of this Regulation and is not bound by it or subject to its application, without prejudice to the possibility for Denmark of applying the amendments to Regulation (EC) No 44/2001 pursuant to Article 3 of the Agreement of 19 October 2005 between the European Community and the Kingdom of Denmark on jurisdiction and the recognition and enforcement of judgments in civil and commercial matters[13],

HAVE ADOPTED THIS REGULATION:

---

13. OJ L 299, 16.11.2005, p. 62.

CHAPTER I
SCOPE AND DEFINITIONS

Article 1

1. This Regulation shall apply in civil and commercial matters whatever the nature of the court or tribunal. It shall not extend, in particular, to revenue, customs or administrative matters or to the liability of the State for acts and omissions in the exercise of State authority (*acta iure imperii*).
2. This Regulation shall not apply to:
   (a) the status or legal capacity of natural persons, rights in property arising out of a matrimonial relationship or out of a relationship deemed by the law applicable to such relationship to have comparable effects to marriage;
   (b) bankruptcy, proceedings relating to the winding-up of insolvent companies or other legal persons, judicial arrangements, compositions and analogous proceedings;
   (c) social security;
   (d) arbitration;
   (e) maintenance obligations arising from a family relationship, parentage, marriage or affinity;
   (f) wills and succession, including maintenance obligations arising by reason of death.

Article 2

For the purposes of this Regulation:

(a) 'judgment' means any judgment given by a court or tribunal of a Member State, whatever the judgment may be called, including a decree, order, decision or writ of execution, as well as a decision on the determination of costs or expenses by an officer of the court.

For the purposes of Chapter III, 'judgment' includes provisional, including protective, measures ordered by a court or tribunal which by virtue of this Regulation has jurisdiction as to the substance of the matter. It does not include a provisional, including protective, measure which is ordered by such a court or tribunal without the defendant being summoned to appear, unless the judgment containing the measure is served on the defendant prior to enforcement;

(b) 'court settlement' means a settlement which has been approved by a court of a Member State or concluded before a court of a Member State in the course of proceedings;

(c) 'authentic instrument' means a document which has been formally drawn up or registered as an authentic instrument in the Member State of origin and the authenticity of which:

> (i) relates to the signature and the content of the instrument; and
>
> (ii) has been established by a public authority or other authority empowered for that purpose;

(d) 'Member State of origin' means the Member State in which, as the case may be, the judgment has been given, the court settlement has been approved or concluded, or the authentic instrument has been formally drawn up or registered;

(e) 'Member State addressed' means the Member State in which the recognition of the judgment is invoked or in which the enforcement of the judgment, the court settlement or the authentic instrument is sought;

(f) 'court of origin' means the court which has given the judgment the recognition of which is invoked or the enforcement of which is sought.

Article 3

For the purposes of this Regulation, 'court' includes the following authorities to the extent that they have jurisdiction in matters falling within the scope of this Regulation:

(a) in Hungary, in summary proceedings concerning orders to pay (fizetési meghagyásos eljárás), the notary (közjegyző);

(b) in Sweden, in summary proceedings concerning orders to pay (betalningsföreläggande) and assistance (handräckning), the Enforcement Authority (Kronofogdemyndigheten).

CHAPTER II
JURISDICTION

SECTION 1
General provisions

Article 4

1. Subject to this Regulation, persons domiciled in a Member State shall, whatever their nationality, be sued in the courts of that Member State.
2. Persons who are not nationals of the Member State in which they are domiciled shall be governed by the rules of jurisdiction applicable to nationals of that Member State.

Article 5

1. Persons domiciled in a Member State may be sued in the courts of another Member State only by virtue of the rules set out in Sections 2 to 7 of this Chapter.

2. In particular, the rules of national jurisdiction of which the Member States are to notify the Commission pursuant to point (a) of Article 76(1) shall not be applicable as against the persons referred to in paragraph 1.

Article 6

1. If the defendant is not domiciled in a Member State, the jurisdiction of the courts of each Member State shall, subject to Article 18(1), Article 21(2) and Articles 24 and 25, be determined by the law of that Member State.
2. As against such a defendant, any person domiciled in a Member State may, whatever his nationality, avail himself in that Member State of the rules of jurisdiction there in force, and in particular those of which the Member States are to notify the Commission pursuant to point (a) of Article 76(1), in the same way as nationals of that Member State.

SECTION 2
Special jurisdiction

Article 7

A person domiciled in a Member State may be sued in another Member State:

(1) (a) in matters relating to a contract, in the courts for the place of performance of the obligation in question;

(b) for the purpose of this provision and unless otherwise agreed, the place of performance of the obligation in question shall be:

— in the case of the sale of goods, the place in a Member State where, under the contract, the goods were delivered or should have been delivered,

— in the case of the provision of services, the place in a Member State where, under the contract, the services were provided or should have been provided;

(c) if point (b) does not apply then point (a) applies;

(2) in matters relating to tort, delict or quasi-delict, in the courts for the place where the harmful event occurred or may occur;

(3) as regards a civil claim for damages or restitution which is based on an act giving rise to criminal proceedings, in the court seised of those proceedings, to the extent that that court has jurisdiction under its own law to entertain civil proceedings;

(4) as regards a civil claim for the recovery, based on ownership, of a cultural object as defined in point 1 of Article 1 of Directive 93/7/EEC initiated by the person claiming the right to recover such an object, in the courts for the place where the cultural object is situated at the time when the court is seised;

(5) as regards a dispute arising out of the operations of a branch, agency or other establishment, in the courts for the place where the branch, agency or other establishment is situated;

(6) as regards a dispute brought against a settlor, trustee or beneficiary of a trust created by the operation of a statute, or by a written instrument, or created orally and evidenced in writing, in the courts of the Member State in which the trust is domiciled;

(7) as regards a dispute concerning the payment of remuneration claimed in respect of the salvage of a cargo or freight, in the court under the authority of which the cargo or freight in question:

(a) has been arrested to secure such payment; or

(b) could have been so arrested, but bail or other security has been given;

provided that this provision shall apply only if it is claimed that the defendant has an interest in the cargo or freight or had such an interest at the time of salvage.

Article 8

A person domiciled in a Member State may also be sued:

(1) where he is one of a number of defendants, in the courts for the place where any one of them is domiciled, provided the claims are so closely connected that it is expedient to hear and determine them together to avoid the risk of irreconcilable judgments resulting from separate proceedings;

(2) as a third party in an action on a warranty or guarantee or in any other third-party proceedings, in the court seised of the original proceedings, unless these were instituted solely with the object of removing him from the jurisdiction of the court which would be competent in his case;

(3) on a counter-claim arising from the same contract or facts on which the original claim was based, in the court in which the original claim is pending;

(4) in matters relating to a contract, if the action may be combined with an action against the same defendant in matters relating to rights *in rem* in immovable property, in the court of the Member State in which the property is situated.

Article 9

Where by virtue of this Regulation a court of a Member State has jurisdiction in actions relating to liability from the use or operation of a ship, that court, or any other court substituted for this purpose by the internal law of that Member State, shall also have jurisdiction over claims for limitation of such liability.

SECTION 3
Jurisdiction in matters relating to insurance

Article 10

In matters relating to insurance, jurisdiction shall be determined by this Section, without prejudice to Article 6 and point 5 of Article 7.

Article 11

1. An insurer domiciled in a Member State may be sued:
   (a) in the courts of the Member State in which he is domiciled;
   (b) in another Member State, in the case of actions brought by the policy-holder, the insured or a beneficiary, in the courts for the place where the claimant is domiciled; or
   (c) if he is a co-insurer, in the courts of a Member State in which proceedings are brought against the leading insurer.
2. An insurer who is not domiciled in a Member State but has a branch, agency or other establishment in one of the Member States shall, in disputes arising out of the operations of the branch, agency or establishment, be deemed to be domiciled in that Member State.

Article 12

In respect of liability insurance or insurance of immovable property, the insurer may in addition be sued in the courts for the place where the harmful event occurred. The same applies if movable and immovable property are covered by the same insurance policy and both are adversely affected by the same contingency.

Article 13

1. In respect of liability insurance, the insurer may also, if the law of the court permits it, be joined in proceedings which the injured party has brought against the insured.
2. Articles 10, 11 and 12 shall apply to actions brought by the injured party directly against the insurer, where such direct actions are permitted.
3. If the law governing such direct actions provides that the policyholder or the insured may be joined as a party to the action, the same court shall have jurisdiction over them.

Article 14

1. Without prejudice to Article 13(3), an insurer may bring proceedings only in the courts of the Member State in which the defendant is domiciled, irrespective of whether he is the policyholder, the insured or a beneficiary.
2. The provisions of this Section shall not affect the right to bring a counter-claim in the court in which, in accordance with this Section, the original claim is pending.

Article 15

The provisions of this Section may be departed from only by an agreement:

(1) which is entered into after the dispute has arisen;
(2) which allows the policyholder, the insured or a beneficiary to bring proceedings in courts other than those indicated in this Section;
(3) which is concluded between a policyholder and an insurer, both of whom are at the time of conclusion of the contract domiciled or habitually resident in the same Member State, and which has the effect of conferring jurisdiction on the courts of that Member State even if the harmful event were to occur abroad, provided that such an agreement is not contrary to the law of that Member State;
(4) which is concluded with a policyholder who is not domiciled in a Member State, except in so far as the insurance is compulsory or relates to immovable property in a Member State; or
(5) which relates to a contract of insurance in so far as it covers one or more of the risks set out in Article 16.

Article 16

The following are the risks referred to in point 5 of Article 15:

(1) any loss of or damage to:
   (a) seagoing ships, installations situated offshore or on the high seas, or aircraft, arising from perils which relate to their use for commercial purposes;
   (b) goods in transit other than passengers' baggage where the transit consists of or includes carriage by such ships or aircraft;
(2) any liability, other than for bodily injury to passengers or loss of or damage to their baggage:
   (a) arising out of the use or operation of ships, installations or aircraft as referred to in point 1(a) in so far as, in respect of the latter, the law of the Member State in which such aircraft are registered does not prohibit agreements on jurisdiction regarding insurance of such risks;
   (b) for loss or damage caused by goods in transit as described in point 1(b);

(3) any financial loss connected with the use or operation of ships, installations or aircraft as referred to in point 1(a), in particular loss of freight or charter-hire;

(4) any risk or interest connected with any of those referred to in points 1 to 3;

(5) notwithstanding points 1 to 4, all 'large risks' as defined in Directive 2009/138/EC of the European Parliament and of the Council of 25 November 2009 on the taking-up and pursuit of the business of Insurance and Reinsurance (Solvency II)[14].

SECTION 4
Jurisdiction over consumer contracts

Article 17

1. In matters relating to a contract concluded by a person, the consumer, for a purpose which can be regarded as being outside his trade or profession, jurisdiction shall be determined by this Section, without prejudice to Article 6 and point 5 of Article 7, if:
   (a) it is a contract for the sale of goods on instalment credit terms;
   (b) it is a contract for a loan repayable by instalments, or for any other form of credit, made to finance the sale of goods; or
   (c) in all other cases, the contract has been concluded with a person who pursues commercial or professional activities in the Member State of the consumer's domicile or, by any means, directs such activities to that Member State or to several States including that Member State, and the contract falls within the scope of such activities.

2. Where a consumer enters into a contract with a party who is not domiciled in a Member State but has a branch, agency or other establishment in one of the Member States, that party shall, in disputes arising out of the operations of the branch, agency or establishment, be deemed to be domiciled in that Member State.

3. This Section shall not apply to a contract of transport other than a contract which, for an inclusive price, provides for a combination of travel and accommodation.

Article 18

1. A consumer may bring proceedings against the other party to a contract either in the courts of the Member State in which that party is domiciled or, regardless of the domicile of the other party, in the courts for the place where the consumer is domiciled.

---

14. OJ L 335, 17.12.2009, p. 1.

2. Proceedings may be brought against a consumer by the other party to the contract only in the courts of the Member State in which the consumer is domiciled.

3. This Article shall not affect the right to bring a counter-claim in the court in which, in accordance with this Section, the original claim is pending.

Article 19

The provisions of this Section may be departed from only by an agreement:

(1) which is entered into after the dispute has arisen;

(2) which allows the consumer to bring proceedings in courts other than those indicated in this Section; or

(3) which is entered into by the consumer and the other party to the contract, both of whom are at the time of conclusion of the contract domiciled or habitually resident in the same Member State, and which confers jurisdiction on the courts of that Member State, provided that such an agreement is not contrary to the law of that Member State.

SECTION 5
Jurisdiction over individual contracts of employment

Article 20

1. In matters relating to individual contracts of employment, jurisdiction shall be determined by this Section, without prejudice to Article 6, point 5 of Article 7 and, in the case of proceedings brought against an employer, point 1 of Article 8.

2. Where an employee enters into an individual contract of employment with an employer who is not domiciled in a Member State but has a branch, agency or other establishment in one of the Member States, the employer shall, in disputes arising out of the operations of the branch, agency or establishment, be deemed to be domiciled in that Member State.

Article 21

1. An employer domiciled in a Member State may be sued:
   (a) in the courts of the Member State in which he is domiciled; or
   (b) in another Member State:
      (i) in the courts for the place where or from where the employee habitually carries out his work or in the courts for the last place where he did so; or
      (ii) if the employee does not or did not habitually carry out his work in any one country, in the courts for the place where the business which engaged the employee is or was situated.

2. An employer not domiciled in a Member State may be sued in a court of a Member State in accordance with point (b) of paragraph 1.

Article 22

1. An employer may bring proceedings only in the courts of the Member State in which the employee is domiciled.
2. The provisions of this Section shall not affect the right to bring a counter-claim in the court in which, in accordance with this Section, the original claim is pending.

Article 23

The provisions of this Section may be departed from only by an agreement:

(1) which is entered into after the dispute has arisen; or
(2) which allows the employee to bring proceedings in courts other than those indicated in this Section.

SECTION 6
Exclusive jurisdiction

Article 24

The following courts of a Member State shall have exclusive jurisdiction, regardless of the domicile of the parties:

(1) in proceedings which have as their object rights *in rem* in immovable property or tenancies of immovable property, the courts of the Member State in which the property is situated.
    However, in proceedings which have as their object tenancies of immovable property concluded for temporary private use for a maximum period of six consecutive months, the courts of the Member State in which the defendant is domiciled shall also have jurisdiction, provided that the tenant is a natural person and that the landlord and the tenant are domiciled in the same Member State;
(2) in proceedings which have as their object the validity of the constitution, the nullity or the dissolution of companies or other legal persons or associations of natural or legal persons, or the validity of the decisions of their organs, the courts of the Member State in which the company, legal person or association has its seat. In order to determine that seat, the court shall apply its rules of private international law;
(3) in proceedings which have as their object the validity of entries in public registers, the courts of the Member State in which the register is kept;

(4) in proceedings concerned with the registration or validity of patents, trade marks, designs, or other similar rights required to be deposited or registered, irrespective of whether the issue is raised by way of an action or as a defence, the courts of the Member State in which the deposit or registration has been applied for, has taken place or is under the terms of an instrument of the Union or an international convention deemed to have taken place.

Without prejudice to the jurisdiction of the European Patent Office under the Convention on the Grant of European Patents, signed at Munich on 5 October 1973, the courts of each Member State shall have exclusive jurisdiction in proceedings concerned with the registration or validity of any European patent granted for that Member State;

(5) in proceedings concerned with the enforcement of judgments, the courts of the Member State in which the judgment has been or is to be enforced.

SECTION 7
Prorogation of jurisdiction

Article 25

1. If the parties, regardless of their domicile, have agreed that a court or the courts of a Member State are to have jurisdiction to settle any disputes which have arisen or which may arise in connection with a particular legal relationship, that court or those courts shall have jurisdiction, unless the agreement is null and void as to its substantive validity under the law of that Member State. Such jurisdiction shall be exclusive unless the parties have agreed otherwise. The agreement conferring jurisdiction shall be either:
   (a) in writing or evidenced in writing;
   (b) in a form which accords with practices which the parties have established between themselves; or
   (c) in international trade or commerce, in a form which accords with a usage of which the parties are or ought to have been aware and which in such trade or commerce is widely known to, and regularly observed by, parties to contracts of the type involved in the particular trade or commerce concerned.

2. Any communication by electronic means which provides a durable record of the agreement shall be equivalent to 'writing'.

3. The court or courts of a Member State on which a trust instrument has conferred jurisdiction shall have exclusive jurisdiction in any proceedings brought against a settlor, trustee or beneficiary, if relations between those persons or their rights or obligations under the trust are involved.

4. Agreements or provisions of a trust instrument conferring jurisdiction shall have no legal force if they are contrary to Articles 15, 19 or 23, or if the courts whose jurisdiction they purport to exclude have exclusive jurisdiction by virtue of Article 24.

5. An agreement conferring jurisdiction which forms part of a contract shall be treated as an agreement independent of the other terms of the contract. The validity of the agreement conferring jurisdiction cannot be contested solely on the ground that the contract is not valid.

Article 26

1. Apart from jurisdiction derived from other provisions of this Regulation, a court of a Member State before which a defendant enters an appearance shall have jurisdiction. This rule shall not apply where appearance was entered to contest the jurisdiction, or where another court has exclusive jurisdiction by virtue of Article 24.
2. In matters referred to in Sections 3, 4 or 5 where the policyholder, the insured, a beneficiary of the insurance contract, the injured party, the consumer or the employee is the defendant, the court shall, before assuming jurisdiction under paragraph 1, ensure that the defendant is informed of his right to contest the jurisdiction of the court and of the consequences of entering or not entering an appearance.

SECTION 8
Examination as to jurisdiction and admissibility

Article 27

Where a court of a Member State is seised of a claim which is principally concerned with a matter over which the courts of another Member State have exclusive jurisdiction by virtue of Article 24, it shall declare of its own motion that it has no jurisdiction.

Article 28

1. Where a defendant domiciled in one Member State is sued in a court of another Member State and does not enter an appearance, the court shall declare of its own motion that it has no jurisdiction unless its jurisdiction is derived from the provisions of this Regulation.
2. The court shall stay the proceedings so long as it is not shown that the defendant has been able to receive the document instituting the proceedings or an equivalent document in sufficient time to enable him to arrange for his defence, or that all necessary steps have been taken to this end.

3. Article 19 of Regulation (EC) No 1393/2007 of the European Parliament and of the Council of 13 November 2007 on the service in the Member States of judicial and extrajudicial documents in civil or commercial matters (service of documents)[15] shall apply instead of paragraph 2 of this Article if the document instituting the proceedings or an equivalent document had to be transmitted from one Member State to another pursuant to that Regulation.

4. Where Regulation (EC) No 1393/2007 is not applicable, Article 15 of the Hague Convention of 15 November 1965 on the Service Abroad of Judicial and Extrajudicial Documents in Civil or Commercial Matters shall apply if the document instituting the proceedings or an equivalent document had to be transmitted abroad pursuant to that Convention.

SECTION 9
Lis pendens — related actions

Article 29

1. Without prejudice to Article 31(2), where proceedings involving the same cause of action and between the same parties are brought in the courts of different Member States, any court other than the court first seised shall of its own motion stay its proceedings until such time as the jurisdiction of the court first seised is established.

2. In cases referred to in paragraph 1, upon request by a court seised of the dispute, any other court seised shall without delay inform the former court of the date when it was seised in accordance with Article 32.

3. Where the jurisdiction of the court first seised is established, any court other than the court first seised shall decline jurisdiction in favour of that court.

Article 30

1. Where related actions are pending in the courts of different Member States, any court other than the court first seised may stay its proceedings.

2. Where the action in the court first seised is pending at first instance, any other court may also, on the application of one of the parties, decline jurisdiction if the court first seised has jurisdiction over the actions in question and its law permits the consolidation thereof.

3. For the purposes of this Article, actions are deemed to be related where they are so closely connected that it is expedient to hear and determine them together to avoid the risk of irreconcilable judgments resulting from separate proceedings.

---

15. OJ L 324, 10.12.2007, p. 79.

Article 31

1. Where actions come within the exclusive jurisdiction of several courts, any court other than the court first seised shall decline jurisdiction in favour of that court.
2. Without prejudice to Article 26, where a court of a Member State on which an agreement as referred to in Article 25 confers exclusive jurisdiction is seised, any court of another Member State shall stay the proceedings until such time as the court seised on the basis of the agreement declares that it has no jurisdiction under the agreement.
3. Where the court designated in the agreement has established jurisdiction in accordance with the agreement, any court of another Member State shall decline jurisdiction in favour of that court.
4. Paragraphs 2 and 3 shall not apply to matters referred to in Sections 3, 4 or 5 where the policyholder, the insured, a beneficiary of the insurance contract, the injured party, the consumer or the employee is the claimant and the agreement is not valid under a provision contained within those Sections.

Article 32

1. For the purposes of this Section, a court shall be deemed to be seised:
    (a) at the time when the document instituting the proceedings or an equivalent document is lodged with the court, provided that the claimant has not subsequently failed to take the steps he was required to take to have service effected on the defendant; or
    (b) if the document has to be served before being lodged with the court, at the time when it is received by the authority responsible for service, provided that the claimant has not subsequently failed to take the steps he was required to take to have the document lodged with the court.

    The authority responsible for service referred to in point (b) shall be the first authority receiving the documents to be served.
2. The court, or the authority responsible for service, referred to in paragraph 1, shall note, respectively, the date of the lodging of the document instituting the proceedings or the equivalent document, or the date of receipt of the documents to be served.

Article 33

1. Where jurisdiction is based on Article 4 or on Articles 7, 8 or 9 and proceedings are pending before a court of a third State at the time when a court in a Member State is seised of an action involving the same cause of action and between the same parties as the proceedings in the court of the third State, the court of the Member State may stay the proceedings if:

(a) it is expected that the court of the third State will give a judgment capable of recognition and, where applicable, of enforcement in that Member State; and

(b) the court of the Member State is satisfied that a stay is necessary for the proper administration of justice.

2. The court of the Member State may continue the proceedings at any time if:

   (a) the proceedings in the court of the third State are themselves stayed or discontinued;

   (b) it appears to the court of the Member State that the proceedings in the court of the third State are unlikely to be concluded within a reasonable time; or

   (c) the continuation of the proceedings is required for the proper administration of justice.

3. The court of the Member State shall dismiss the proceedings if the proceedings in the court of the third State are concluded and have resulted in a judgment capable of recognition and, where applicable, of enforcement in that Member State.

4. The court of the Member State shall apply this Article on the application of one of the parties or, where possible under national law, of its own motion.

Article 34

1. Where jurisdiction is based on Article 4 or on Articles 7, 8 or 9 and an action is pending before a court of a third State at the time when a court in a Member State is seised of an action which is related to the action in the court of the third State, the court of the Member State may stay the proceedings if:

   (a) it is expedient to hear and determine the related actions together to avoid the risk of irreconcilable judgments resulting from separate proceedings;

   (b) it is expected that the court of the third State will give a judgment capable of recognition and, where applicable, of enforcement in that Member State; and

   (c) the court of the Member State is satisfied that a stay is necessary for the proper administration of justice.

2. The court of the Member State may continue the proceedings at any time if:

   (a) it appears to the court of the Member State that there is no longer a risk of irreconcilable judgments;

   (b) the proceedings in the court of the third State are themselves stayed or discontinued;

   (c) it appears to the court of the Member State that the proceedings in the court of the third State are unlikely to be concluded within a reasonable time; or

   (d) the continuation of the proceedings is required for the proper administration of justice.

3. The court of the Member State may dismiss the proceedings if the proceedings in the court of the third State are concluded and have resulted in a judgment capable of recognition and, where applicable, of enforcement in that Member State.

4. The court of the Member State shall apply this Article on the application of one of the parties or, where possible under national law, of its own motion.

SECTION 10
Provisional, including protective, measures

Article 35

Application may be made to the courts of a Member State for such provisional, including protective, measures as may be available under the law of that Member State, even if the courts of another Member State have jurisdiction as to the substance of the matter.

CHAPTER III
RECOGNITION AND ENFORCEMENT

SECTION 1
Recognition

Article 36

1. A judgment given in a Member State shall be recognised in the other Member States without any special procedure being required.

2. Any interested party may, in accordance with the procedure provided for in Subsection 2 of Section 3, apply for a decision that there are no grounds for refusal of recognition as referred to in Article 45.

3. If the outcome of proceedings in a court of a Member State depends on the determination of an incidental question of refusal of recognition, that court shall have jurisdiction over that question.

Article 37

1. A party who wishes to invoke in a Member State a judgment given in another Member State shall produce:
   (a) a copy of the judgment which satisfies the conditions necessary to establish its authenticity; and
   (b) the certificate issued pursuant to Article 53.

2. The court or authority before which a judgment given in another Member State is invoked may, where necessary, require the party invoking it to provide, in accordance with Article 57, a translation or a transliteration of the contents of the certificate referred to in point (b) of paragraph 1. The court or authority may require the party to provide a translation of the judgment instead of a translation of the contents of the certificate if it is unable to proceed without such a translation.

Article 38

The court or authority before which a judgment given in another Member State is invoked may suspend the proceedings, in whole or in part, if:

(a) the judgment is challenged in the Member State of origin; or
(b) an application has been submitted for a decision that there are no grounds for refusal of recognition as referred to in Article 45 or for a decision that the recognition is to be refused on the basis of one of those grounds.

SECTION 2
Enforcement

Article 39

A judgment given in a Member State which is enforceable in that Member State shall be enforceable in the other Member States without any declaration of enforceability being required.

Article 40

An enforceable judgment shall carry with it by operation of law the power to proceed to any protective measures which exist under the law of the Member State addressed.

Article 41

1. Subject to the provisions of this Section, the procedure for the enforcement of judgments given in another Member State shall be governed by the law of the Member State addressed. A judgment given in a Member State which is enforceable in the Member State addressed shall be enforced there under the same conditions as a judgment given in the Member State addressed.
2. Notwithstanding paragraph 1, the grounds for refusal or of suspension of enforcement under the law of the Member State addressed shall apply in so far as they are not incompatible with the grounds referred to in Article 45.

3. The party seeking the enforcement of a judgment given in another Member State shall not be required to have a postal address in the Member State addressed. Nor shall that party be required to have an authorised representative in the Member State addressed unless such a representative is mandatory irrespective of the nationality or the domicile of the parties.

Article 42

1. For the purposes of enforcement in a Member State of a judgment given in another Member State, the applicant shall provide the competent enforcement authority with:
   (a) a copy of the judgment which satisfies the conditions necessary to establish its authenticity; and
   (b) the certificate issued pursuant to Article 53, certifying that the judgment is enforceable and containing an extract of the judgment as well as, where appropriate, relevant information on the recoverable costs of the proceedings and the calculation of interest.
2. For the purposes of enforcement in a Member State of a judgment given in another Member State ordering a provisional, including a protective, measure, the applicant shall provide the competent enforcement authority with:
   (a) a copy of the judgment which satisfies the conditions necessary to establish its authenticity;
   (b) the certificate issued pursuant to Article 53, containing a description of the measure and certifying that:
      (i) the court has jurisdiction as to the substance of the matter;
      (ii) the judgment is enforceable in the Member State of origin; and
   (c) where the measure was ordered without the defendant being summoned to appear, proof of service of the judgment.
3. The competent enforcement authority may, where necessary, require the applicant to provide, in accordance with Article 57, a translation or a transliteration of the contents of the certificate.
4. The competent enforcement authority may require the applicant to provide a translation of the judgment only if it is unable to proceed without such a translation.

Article 43

1. Where enforcement is sought of a judgment given in another Member State, the certificate issued pursuant to Article 53 shall be served on the person against whom the enforcement is sought prior to the first enforcement measure. The certificate shall be accompanied by the judgment, if not already served on that person.

2. Where the person against whom enforcement is sought is domiciled in a Member State other than the Member State of origin, he may request a translation of the judgment in order to contest the enforcement if the judgment is not written in or accompanied by a translation into either of the following languages:

   (a) a language which he understands; or
   (b) the official language of the Member State in which he is domiciled or, where there are several official languages in that Member State, the official language or one of the official languages of the place where he is domiciled.

   Where a translation of the judgment is requested under the first subparagraph, no measures of enforcement may be taken other than protective measures until that translation has been provided to the person against whom enforcement is sought.

   This paragraph shall not apply if the judgment has already been served on the person against whom enforcement is sought in one of the languages referred to in the first subparagraph or is accompanied by a translation into one of those languages.

3. This Article shall not apply to the enforcement of a protective measure in a judgment or where the person seeking enforcement proceeds to protective measures in accordance with Article 40.

Article 44

1. In the event of an application for refusal of enforcement of a judgment pursuant to Subsection 2 of Section 3, the court in the Member State addressed may, on the application of the person against whom enforcement is sought:

   (a) limit the enforcement proceedings to protective measures;
   (b) make enforcement conditional on the provision of such security as it shall determine; or
   (c) suspend, either wholly or in part, the enforcement proceedings.

2. The competent authority in the Member State addressed shall, on the application of the person against whom enforcement is sought, suspend the enforcement proceedings where the enforceability of the judgment is suspended in the Member State of origin.

SECTION 3
Refusal of recognition and enforcement

Subsection 1
Refusal of recognition

Article 45

1. On the application of any interested party, the recognition of a judgment shall be refused:
   (a) if such recognition is manifestly contrary to public policy (ordre public) in the Member State addressed;
   (b) where the judgment was given in default of appearance, if the defendant was not served with the document which instituted the proceedings or with an equivalent document in sufficient time and in such a way as to enable him to arrange for his defence, unless the defendant failed to commence proceedings to challenge the judgment when it was possible for him to do so;
   (c) if the judgment is irreconcilable with a judgment given between the same parties in the Member State addressed;
   (d) if the judgment is irreconcilable with an earlier judgment given in another Member State or in a third State involving the same cause of action and between the same parties, provided that the earlier judgment fulfils the conditions necessary for its recognition in the Member State addressed; or
   (e) if the judgment conflicts with:
      (i) Sections 3, 4 or 5 of Chapter II where the policyholder, the insured, a beneficiary of the insurance contract, the injured party, the consumer or the employee was the defendant; or
      (ii) Section 6 of Chapter II.
2. In its examination of the grounds of jurisdiction referred to in point (e) of paragraph 1, the court to which the application was submitted shall be bound by the findings of fact on which the court of origin based its jurisdiction.
3. Without prejudice to point (e) of paragraph 1, the jurisdiction of the court of origin may not be reviewed. The test of public policy referred to in point (a) of paragraph 1 may not be applied to the rules relating to jurisdiction.
4. The application for refusal of recognition shall be made in accordance with the procedures provided for in Subsection 2 and, where appropriate, Section 4.

Subsection 2
Refusal of enforcement

Article 46

On the application of the person against whom enforcement is sought, the enforcement of a judgment shall be refused where one of the grounds referred to in Article 45 is found to exist.

Article 47

1. The application for refusal of enforcement shall be submitted to the court which the Member State concerned has communicated to the Commission pursuant to point (a) of Article 75 as the court to which the application is to be submitted.
2. The procedure for refusal of enforcement shall, in so far as it is not covered by this Regulation, be governed by the law of the Member State addressed.
3. The applicant shall provide the court with a copy of the judgment and, where necessary, a translation or transliteration of it.
   The court may dispense with the production of the documents referred to in the first subparagraph if it already possesses them or if it considers it unreasonable to require the applicant to provide them. In the latter case, the court may require the other party to provide those documents.
4. The party seeking the refusal of enforcement of a judgment given in another Member State shall not be required to have a postal address in the Member State addressed. Nor shall that party be required to have an authorised representative in the Member State addressed unless such a representative is mandatory irrespective of the nationality or the domicile of the parties.

Article 48

The court shall decide on the application for refusal of enforcement without delay.

Article 49

1. The decision on the application for refusal of enforcement may be appealed against by either party.
2. The appeal is to be lodged with the court which the Member State concerned has communicated to the Commission pursuant to point (b) of Article 75 as the court with which such an appeal is to be lodged.

Article 50

The decision given on the appeal may only be contested by an appeal where the courts with which any further appeal is to be lodged have been communicated by the Member State concerned to the Commission pursuant to point (c) of Article 75.

Article 51

1. The court to which an application for refusal of enforcement is submitted or the court which hears an appeal lodged under Article 49 or Article 50 may stay the proceedings if an ordinary appeal has been lodged against the judgment in the Member State of origin or if the time for such an appeal has not yet expired. In the latter case, the court may specify the time within which such an appeal is to be lodged.
2. Where the judgment was given in Ireland, Cyprus or the United Kingdom, any form of appeal available in the Member State of origin shall be treated as an ordinary appeal for the purposes of paragraph 1.

SECTION 4
Common provisions

Article 52

Under no circumstances may a judgment given in a Member State be reviewed as to its substance in the Member State addressed.

Article 53

The court of origin shall, at the request of any interested party, issue the certificate using the form set out in Annex I.

Article 54

1. If a judgment contains a measure or an order which is not known in the law of the Member State addressed, that measure or order shall, to the extent possible, be adapted to a measure or an order known in the law of that Member State which has equivalent effects attached to it and which pursues similar aims and interests.
   Such adaptation shall not result in effects going beyond those provided for in the law of the Member State of origin.
2. Any party may challenge the adaptation of the measure or order before a court.
3. If necessary, the party invoking the judgment or seeking its enforcement may be required to provide a translation or a transliteration of the judgment.

Article 55

A judgment given in a Member State which orders a payment by way of a penalty shall be enforceable in the Member State addressed only if the amount of the payment has been finally determined by the court of origin.

Article 56

No security, bond or deposit, however described, shall be required of a party who in one Member State applies for the enforcement of a judgment given in another Member State on the ground that he is a foreign national or that he is not domiciled or resident in the Member State addressed.

Article 57

1. When a translation or a transliteration is required under this Regulation, such translation or transliteration shall be into the official language of the Member State concerned or, where there are several official languages in that Member State, into the official language or one of the official languages of court proceedings of the place where a judgment given in another Member State is invoked or an application is made, in accordance with the law of that Member State.
2. For the purposes of the forms referred to in Articles 53 and 60, translations or transliterations may also be into any other official language or languages of the institutions of the Union that the Member State concerned has indicated it can accept.
3. Any translation made under this Regulation shall be done by a person qualified to do translations in one of the Member States.

CHAPTER IV
AUTHENTIC INSTRUMENTS AND COURT SETTLEMENTS

Article 58

1. An authentic instrument which is enforceable in the Member State of origin shall be enforceable in the other Member States without any declaration of enforceability being required. Enforcement of the authentic instrument may be refused only if such enforcement is manifestly contrary to public policy (ordre public) in the Member State addressed.
   The provisions of Section 2, Subsection 2 of Section 3, and Section 4 of Chapter III shall apply as appropriate to authentic instruments.
2. The authentic instrument produced must satisfy the conditions necessary to establish its authenticity in the Member State of origin.

Article 59

A court settlement which is enforceable in the Member State of origin shall be enforced in the other Member States under the same conditions as authentic instruments.

Article 60

The competent authority or court of the Member State of origin shall, at the request of any interested party, issue the certificate using the form set out in Annex II containing a summary of the enforceable obligation recorded in the authentic instrument or of the agreement between the parties recorded in the court settlement.

CHAPTER V
GENERAL PROVISIONS

Article 61

No legalisation or other similar formality shall be required for documents issued in a Member State in the context of this Regulation.

Article 62

1. In order to determine whether a party is domiciled in the Member State whose courts are seised of a matter, the court shall apply its internal law.
2. If a party is not domiciled in the Member State whose courts are seised of the matter, then, in order to determine whether the party is domiciled in another Member State, the court shall apply the law of that Member State.

Article 63

1. For the purposes of this Regulation, a company or other legal person or association of natural or legal persons is domiciled at the place where it has its:
   (a) statutory seat;
   (b) central administration; or
   (c) principal place of business.
2. For the purposes of Ireland, Cyprus and the United Kingdom, 'statutory seat' means the registered office or, where there is no such office anywhere, the place of incorporation or, where there is no such place anywhere, the place under the law of which the formation took place.
3. In order to determine whether a trust is domiciled in the Member State whose courts are seised of the matter, the court shall apply its rules of private international law.

Article 64

Without prejudice to any more favourable provisions of national laws, persons domiciled in a Member State who are being prosecuted in the criminal courts of another Member State of which they are not nationals for an offence which was not intentionally committed may be defended by persons qualified to do so, even if they do not appear in person. However, the court seised of the matter may order appearance in person; in the case of failure to appear, a judgment given in the civil action without the person concerned having had the opportunity to arrange for his defence need not be recognised or enforced in the other Member States.

Article 65

1. The jurisdiction specified in point 2 of Article 8 and Article 13 in actions on a warranty or guarantee or in any other third-party proceedings may be resorted to in the Member States included in the list established by the Commission pursuant to point (b) of Article 76(1) and Article 76(2) only in so far as permitted under national law. A person domiciled in another Member State may be invited to join the proceedings before the courts of those Member States pursuant to the rules on third-party notice referred to in that list.

2. Judgments given in a Member State by virtue of point 2 of Article 8 or Article 13 shall be recognised and enforced in accordance with Chapter III in any other Member State. Any effects which judgments given in the Member States included in the list referred to in paragraph 1 may have, in accordance with the law of those Member States, on third parties by application of paragraph 1 shall be recognised in all Member States.

3. The Member States included in the list referred to in paragraph 1 shall, within the framework of the European Judicial Network in civil and commercial matters established by Council Decision 2001/470/EC[16] ('the European Judicial Network') provide information on how to determine, in accordance with their national law, the effects of the judgments referred to in the second sentence of paragraph 2.

CHAPTER VI
TRANSITIONAL PROVISIONS

Article 66

1. This Regulation shall apply only to legal proceedings instituted, to authentic instruments formally drawn up or registered and to court settlements approved or concluded on or after 10 January 2015.

---

16. OJ L 174, 27.6.2001, p. 25.

2. Notwithstanding Article 80, Regulation (EC) No 44/2001 shall continue to apply to judgments given in legal proceedings instituted, to authentic instruments formally drawn up or registered and to court settlements approved or concluded before 10 January 2015 which fall within the scope of that Regulation.

CHAPTER VII
RELATIONSHIP WITH OTHER INSTRUMENTS

Article 67

This Regulation shall not prejudice the application of provisions governing jurisdiction and the recognition and enforcement of judgments in specific matters which are contained in instruments of the Union or in national legislation harmonised pursuant to such instruments.

Article 68

1. This Regulation shall, as between the Member States, supersede the 1968 Brussels Convention, except as regards the territories of the Member States which fall within the territorial scope of that Convention and which are excluded from this Regulation pursuant to Article 355 of the TFEU.
2. In so far as this Regulation replaces the provisions of the 1968 Brussels Convention between the Member States, any reference to that Convention shall be understood as a reference to this Regulation.

Article 69

Subject to Articles 70 and 71, this Regulation shall, as between the Member States, supersede the conventions that cover the same matters as those to which this Regulation applies. In particular, the conventions included in the list established by the Commission pursuant to point (c) of Article 76(1) and Article 76(2) shall be superseded.

Article 70

1. The conventions referred to in Article 69 shall continue to have effect in relation to matters to which this Regulation does not apply.
2. They shall continue to have effect in respect of judgments given, authentic instruments formally drawn up or registered and court settlements approved or concluded before the date of entry into force of Regulation (EC) No 44/2001.

Article 71

1. This Regulation shall not affect any conventions to which the Member States are parties and which, in relation to particular matters, govern jurisdiction or the recognition or enforcement of judgments.
2. With a view to its uniform interpretation, paragraph 1 shall be applied in the following manner:
   (a) this Regulation shall not prevent a court of a Member State which is party to a convention on a particular matter from assuming jurisdiction in accordance with that convention, even where the defendant is domiciled in another Member State which is not party to that convention. The court hearing the action shall, in any event, apply Article 28 of this Regulation;
   (b) judgments given in a Member State by a court in the exercise of jurisdiction provided for in a convention on a particular matter shall be recognised and enforced in the other Member States in accordance with this Regulation.

   Where a convention on a particular matter to which both the Member State of origin and the Member State addressed are parties lays down conditions for the recognition or enforcement of judgments, those conditions shall apply. In any event, the provisions of this Regulation on recognition and enforcement of judgments may be applied.

Article 72

This Regulation shall not affect agreements by which Member States, prior to the entry into force of Regulation (EC) No 44/2001, undertook pursuant to Article 59 of the 1968 Brussels Convention not to recognise judgments given, in particular in other Contracting States to that Convention, against defendants domiciled or habitually resident in a third State where, in cases provided for in Article 4 of that Convention, the judgment could only be founded on a ground of jurisdiction specified in the second paragraph of Article 3 of that Convention.

Article 73

1. This Regulation shall not affect the application of the 2007 Lugano Convention.
2. This Regulation shall not affect the application of the 1958 New York Convention.
3. This Regulation shall not affect the application of bilateral conventions and agreements between a third State and a Member State concluded before the date of entry into force of Regulation (EC) No 44/2001 which concern matters governed by this Regulation.

CHAPTER VIII
FINAL PROVISIONS

Article 74

The Member States shall provide, within the framework of the European Judicial Network and with a view to making the information available to the public, a description of national rules and procedures concerning enforcement, including authorities competent for enforcement, and information on any limitations on enforcement, in particular debtor protection rules and limitation or prescription periods.

The Member States shall keep this information permanently updated.

Article 75

By 10 January 2014, the Member States shall communicate to the Commission:

(a) the courts to which the application for refusal of enforcement is to be submitted pursuant to Article 47(1);
(b) the courts with which an appeal against the decision on the application for refusal of enforcement is to be lodged pursuant to Article 49(2);
(c) the courts with which any further appeal is to be lodged pursuant to Article 50; and
(d) the languages accepted for translations of the forms as referred to in Article 57(2).

The Commission shall make the information publicly available through any appropriate means, in particular through the European Judicial Network.

Article 76

1. The Member States shall notify the Commission of:
   (a) the rules of jurisdiction referred to in Articles 5(2) and 6(2);
   (b) the rules on third-party notice referred to in Article 65; and
   (c) the conventions referred to in Article 69.
2. The Commission shall, on the basis of the notifications by the Member States referred to in paragraph 1, establish the corresponding lists.
3. The Member States shall notify the Commission of any subsequent amendments required to be made to those lists. The Commission shall amend those lists accordingly.
4. The Commission shall publish the lists and any subsequent amendments made to them in the *Official Journal of the European Union*.
5. The Commission shall make all information notified pursuant to paragraphs 1 and 3 publicly available through any other appropriate means, in particular through the European Judicial Network.

Article 77

The Commission shall be empowered to adopt delegated acts in accordance with Article 78 concerning the amendment of Annexes I and II.

Article 78

1. The power to adopt delegated acts is conferred on the Commission subject to the conditions laid down in this Article.
2. The power to adopt delegated acts referred to in Article 77 shall be conferred on the Commission for an indeterminate period of time from 9 January 2013.
3. The delegation of power referred to in Article 77 may be revoked at any time by the European Parliament or by the Council. A decision to revoke shall put an end to the delegation of the power specified in that decision. It shall take effect the day following the publication of the decision in the *Official Journal of the European Union* or at a later date specified therein. It shall not affect the validity of any delegated acts already in force.
4. As soon as it adopts a delegated act, the Commission shall notify it simultaneously to the European Parliament and to the Council.
5. A delegated act adopted pursuant to Article 77 shall enter into force only if no objection has been expressed either by the European Parliament or the Council within a period of two months of notification of that act to the European Parliament and the Council or if, before the expiry of that period, the European Parliament and the Council have both informed the Commission that they will not object. That period shall be extended by two months at the initiative of the European Parliament or of the Council.

Article 79

By 11 January 2022 the Commission shall present a report to the European Parliament, to the Council and to the European Economic and Social Committee on the application of this Regulation. That report shall include an evaluation of the possible need for a further extension of the rules on jurisdiction to defendants not domiciled in a Member State, taking into account the operation of this Regulation and possible developments at international level. Where appropriate, the report shall be accompanied by a proposal for amendment of this Regulation.

Article 80

This Regulation shall repeal Regulation (EC) No 44/2001. References to the repealed Regulation shall be construed as references to this Regulation and shall be read in accordance with the correlation table set out in Annex III.

Article 81

This Regulation shall enter into force on the twentieth day following that of its publication in the *Official Journal of the European Union*.

It shall apply from 10 January 2015, with the exception of Articles 75 and 76, which shall apply from 10 January 2014.

This Regulation shall be binding in its entirety and directly applicable in the Member States in accordance with the Treaties.

Done at Strasbourg, 12 December 2012.

For the European Parliament
The President
M. SCHULZ

For the Council
The President
A. D. MAVROYIANNIS

———

C. UNITED NATIONS CONVENTION ON THE RECOGNITION AND ENFORCEMENT OF FOREIGN ARBITRAL AWARDS (NEW YORK ARBITRATION CONVENTION)

Article I

1. This Convention shall apply to the recognition and enforcement of arbitral awards made in the territory of a State other than the State where the recognition and enforcement of such awards are sought, and arising out of differences between persons, whether physical or legal. It shall also apply to arbitral awards not considered as domestic awards in the State where their recognition and enforcement are sought.
2. The term "arbitral awards" shall include not only awards made by arbitrators appointed for each case but also those made by permanent arbitral bodies to which the parties have submitted.
3. When signing, ratifying or acceding to this Convention, or notifying extension under Article X hereof, any State may on the basis of reciprocity declare that it will apply the Convention to the recognition and enforcement of awards made only in the territory of another Contracting State. It may also declare that it will apply the Convention only to differences arising out of legal relationships, whether contractual or not, which are considered as commercial under the national law of the State making such declaration.

Article II

1. Each Contracting State shall recognize an agreement in writing under which the parties undertake to submit to arbitration all or any differences which have arisen or which may arise between them in respect of a defined legal relationship, whether contractual or not, concerning a subject matter capable of settlement by arbitration.
2. The term "agreement in writing" shall include an arbitral clause in a contract or an arbitration agreement, signed by the parties or contained in an exchange of letters or telegrams.
3. The court of a Contracting State, when seized of an action in a matter in respect of which the parties have made an agreement within the meaning of this article, shall, at the request of one of the parties, refer the parties to arbitration, unless it finds that the said agreement is null and void, inoperative or incapable of being performed.

Article III

Each Contracting State shall recognize arbitral awards as binding and enforce them in accordance with the rules of procedure of the territory where the award is relied upon, under the conditions laid down in the following articles. There shall not be imposed substantially more onerous conditions or higher fees or charges on the recognition or enforcement of arbitral awards to which this Convention applies than are imposed on the recognition or enforcement of domestic arbitral awards.

Article IV

1. To obtain the recognition and enforcement mentioned in the preceding article, the party applying for recognition and enforcement shall, at the time of the application, supply:
   (a) The duly authenticated original award or a duly certified copy thereof;
   (b) The original agreement referred to in Article II or a duly certified copy thereof.
2. If the said award or agreement is not made in an official language of the country in which the award is relied upon, the party applying for recognition and enforcement of the award shall produce a translation of these documents into such language. The translation shall be certified by an official or sworn translator or by a diplomatic or consular agent.

Article V

1. Recognition and enforcement of the award may be refused, at the request of the party against whom it is invoked, only if that party furnishes to the competent authority where the recognition and enforcement is sought, proof that:
   (a) The parties to the agreement referred to in Article II were, under the law applicable to them, under some incapacity, or the said agreement is not valid under the law to which the parties have subjected it or, failing any indication thereon, under the law of the country where the award was made; or
   (b) The party against whom the award is invoked was not given proper notice of the appointment of the arbitrator or of the arbitration proceedings or was otherwise unable to present his case; or
   (c) The award deals with a difference not contemplated by or not falling within the terms of the submission to arbitration, or it contains decisions on matters beyond the scope of the submission to arbitration, provided that, if the decisions on matters submitted to arbitration can be separated

from those not so submitted, that part of the award which contains decisions on matters submitted to arbitration may be recognized and enforced; or

(d) The composition of the arbitral authority or the arbitral procedure was not in accordance with the agreement of the parties, or, failing such agreement, was not in accordance with the law of the country where the arbitration took place; or

(e) The award has not yet become binding on the parties, or has been set aside or suspended by a competent authority of the country in which, or under the law of which, that award was made.

2. Recognition and enforcement of an arbitral award may also be refused if the competent authority in the country where recognition and enforcement is sought finds that:

(a) The subject matter of the difference is not capable of settlement by arbitration under the law of that country; or

(b) The recognition or enforcement of the award would be contrary to the public policy of that country.

Article VI

If an application for the setting aside or suspension of the award has been made to a competent authority referred to in Article V(1)(e), the authority before which the award is sought to be relied upon may, if it considers it proper, adjourn the decision on the enforcement of the award and may also, on the application of the party claiming enforcement of the award, order the other party to give suitable security.

Article VII

1. The provisions of the present Convention shall not affect the validity of multilateral or bilateral agreements concerning the recognition and enforcement of arbitral awards entered into by the Contracting States nor deprive any interested party of any right he may have to avail himself of an arbitral award in the manner and to the extent allowed by the law or the treaties of the country where such award is sought to be relied upon.

2. The Geneva Protocol on Arbitration Clauses of 1923 and the Geneva Convention on the Execution of Foreign Arbitral Awards of 1927 shall cease to have effect between Contracting States on their becoming bound and to the extent that they become bound, by this Convention.

Article VIII

1. This Convention shall be open until 31 December 1958 for signature on behalf of any Member of the United Nations and also on behalf of any other State which is or hereafter becomes a member of any specialized agency of the United Nations, or which is or hereafter becomes a party to the Statute of the International Court of Justice, or any other State to which an invitation has been addressed by the General Assembly of the United Nations.
2. This Convention shall be ratified and the instrument of ratification shall be deposited with the Secretary-General of the United Nations.

Article IX

1. This Convention shall be open for accession to all States referred to in Article VIII.
2. Accession shall be effected by the deposit of an instrument of accession with the Secretary-General of the United Nations.

Article X

1. Any State may, at the time of signature, ratification or accession, declare that this Convention shall extend to all or any of the territories for the international relations of which it is responsible. Such a declaration shall take effect when the Convention enters into force for the State concerned.
2. At any time thereafter any such extension shall be made by notification addressed to the Secretary-General of the United Nations and shall take effect as from the 90th day after the day of receipt by the Secretary-General of the United Nations of this notification, or as from the date of entry into force of the Convention for the State concerned, whichever is the later.
3. With respect to those territories to which this Convention is not extended at the time of signature, ratification or accession, each State concerned shall consider the possibility of taking the necessary steps in order to extend the application of this Convention to such territories, subject, where necessary for constitutional reasons, to the consent of the Governments of such territories.

Article XI

In the case of a federal or non-unitary State the following provisions shall apply:

(a) With respect to those articles of this Convention that come within the legislative jurisdiction of the federal authority, the obligations of the federal Government shall to this extent be the same as those of Contracting States which are not federal States;

(b) With respect to those articles of this Convention that come within the legislative jurisdiction of constituent states or provinces which are not, under the constitutional system of the federation, bound to take legislative action, the federal Government shall bring such articles with a favourable recommendation to the notice of the appropriate authorities of constituent states or provinces at the earliest possible moment;

(c) A federal State Party to this Convention shall, at the request of any other Contracting State transmitted through the Secretary-General of the United Nations, supply a statement of the law and practice of the federation and its constituent units in regard to any particular provision of this Convention, showing the extent to which effect has been given to that provision by legislative or other action.

Article XII

1. This Convention shall come into force on the 90th day following the date of deposit of the third instrument of ratification or accession.

2. For each State ratifying or acceding to this Convention after the deposit of the third instrument of ratification or accession, this Convention shall enter into force on the 90th day after deposit by such State of its instrument of ratification or accession.

Article XIII

1. Any Contracting State may denounce this Convention by a written notification to the Secretary-General of the United Nations. Denunciation shall take effect one year after the date of receipt of the notification by the Secretary-General.

2. Any State which has made a declaration or notification under Article X may, at any time thereafter, by notification to the Secretary-General of the United Nations, declare that this Convention shall cease to extend to the territory concerned one year after the date of the receipt of the notification by the Secretary-General.

3. This Convention shall continue to be applicable to arbitral awards in respect of which recognition or enforcement proceedings have been instituted before the denunciation takes effect.

Article XIV

A Contracting State shall not be entitled to avail itself of the present Convention against other Contracting States except to the extent that it is itself bound to apply the Convention.

Article XV

The Secretary-General of the United Nations shall notify the States contemplated in Article VIII of the following:

(a) Signatures and ratifications in accordance with Article VIII;

(b) Accessions in accordance with Article IX;

(c) Declarations and notifications under Articles I, X and XI;

(d) The date upon which this Convention enters into force in accordance with Article XII;

(e) Denunciations and notifications in accordance with Article XIII.

Article XVI

1. This Convention, of which the Chinese, English, French, Russian and Spanish texts shall be equally authentic, shall be deposited in the archives of the United Nations.

2. The Secretary-General of the United Nations shall transmit a certified copy of this Convention to the States contemplated in Article VIII.

D. 2005 HAGUE CONVENTION ON CHOICE OF COURT AGREEMENTS

The States Parties to the present Convention,

Desiring to promote international trade and investment through enhanced judicial co-operation,

Believing that such co-operation can be enhanced by uniform rules on jurisdiction and on recognition and enforcement of foreign judgments in civil or commercial matters,

Believing that such enhanced co-operation requires in particular an international legal regime that provides certainty and ensures the effectiveness of exclusive choice of court agreements between parties to commercial transactions and that governs the recognition and enforcement of judgments resulting from proceedings based on such agreements,

Have resolved to conclude this Convention and have agreed upon the following provisions –

CHAPTER I – SCOPE AND DEFINITIONS

Article 1 Scope

1. This Convention shall apply in international cases to exclusive choice of court agreements concluded in civil or commercial matters.
2. For the purposes of Chapter II, a case is international unless the parties are resident in the same Contracting State and the relationship of the parties and all other elements relevant to the dispute, regardless of the location of the chosen court, are connected only with that State.
3. For the purposes of Chapter III, a case is international where recognition or enforcement of a foreign judgment is sought.

Article 2 Exclusions from scope

1. This Convention shall not apply to exclusive choice of court agreements –
    a) to which a natural person acting primarily for personal, family or house-hold purposes (a consumer) is a party;
    b) relating to contracts of employment, including collective agreements.
2. This Convention shall not apply to the following matters –
    a) the status and legal capacity of natural persons;
    b) maintenance obligations;
    c) other family law matters, including matrimonial property regimes and other rights or obligations arising out of marriage or similar relationships;
    d) wills and succession;
    e) insolvency, composition and analogous matters;

    f) the carriage of passengers and goods;

    g) marine pollution, limitation of liability for maritime claims, general average, and emergency towage and salvage;

    h) anti-trust (competition) matters;

    i) liability for nuclear damage;

    j) claims for personal injury brought by or on behalf of natural persons;

    k) tort or delict claims for damage to tangible property that do not arise from a contractual relationship;

    l) rights *in rem* in immovable property, and tenancies of immovable property;

    m) the validity, nullity, or dissolution of legal persons, and the validity of decisions of their organs;

    n) the validity of intellectual property rights other than copyright and related rights;

    o) infringement of intellectual property rights other than copyright and related rights, except where infringement proceedings are brought for breach of a contract between the parties relating to such rights, or could have been brought for breach of that contract;

    p) the validity of entries in public registers.

3. Notwithstanding paragraph 2, proceedings are not excluded from the scope of this Convention where a matter excluded under that paragraph arises merely as a preliminary question and not as an object of the proceedings. In particular, the mere fact that a matter excluded under paragraph 2 arises by way of defence does not exclude proceedings from the Convention, if that matter is not an object of the proceedings.

4. This Convention shall not apply to arbitration and related proceedings.

5. Proceedings are not excluded from the scope of this Convention by the mere fact that a State, including a government, a governmental agency or any person acting for a State, is a party thereto.

6. Nothing in this Convention shall affect privileges and immunities of States or of international organisations, in respect of themselves and of their property.

Article 3 Exclusive choice of court agreements

For the purposes of this Convention –

    a) "exclusive choice of court agreement" means an agreement concluded by two or more parties that meets the requirements of paragraph *c)* and designates, for the purpose of deciding disputes which have arisen or may arise in connection with a particular legal relationship, the courts of one Contracting State or one or more specific courts of one Contracting State to the exclusion of the jurisdiction of any other courts;

    b) a choice of court agreement which designates the courts of one Contracting State or one or more specific courts of one Contracting State shall be deemed to be exclusive unless the parties have expressly provided otherwise;

c) an exclusive choice of court agreement must be concluded or documented –
   i) in writing; or
   ii) by any other means of communication which renders information accessible so as to be usable for subsequent reference;
d) an exclusive choice of court agreement that forms part of a contract shall be treated as an agreement independent of the other terms of the contract. The validity of the exclusive choice of court agreement cannot be contested solely on the ground that the contract is not valid.

Article 4 Other definitions

1. In this Convention, "judgment" means any decision on the merits given by a court, whatever it may be called, including a decree or order, and a determination of costs or expenses by the court (including an officer of the court), provided that the determination relates to a decision on the merits which may be recognised or enforced under this Convention. An interim measure of protection is not a judgment.
2. For the purposes of this Convention, an entity or person other than a natural person shall be considered to be resident in the State –
   a) where it has its statutory seat;
   b) under whose law it was incorporated or formed;
   c) where it has its central administration; or
   d) where it has its principal place of business.

CHAPTER II – JURISDICTION

Article 5 Jurisdiction of the chosen court

1. The court or courts of a Contracting State designated in an exclusive choice of court agreement shall have jurisdiction to decide a dispute to which the agreement applies, unless the agreement is null and void under the law of that State.
2. A court that has jurisdiction under paragraph 1 shall not decline to exercise jurisdiction on the ground that the dispute should be decided in a court of another State.
3. The preceding paragraphs shall not affect rules –
   a) on jurisdiction related to subject matter or to the value of the claim;
   b) on the internal allocation of jurisdiction among the courts of a Contracting State. However, where the chosen court has discretion as to whether to transfer a case, due consideration should be given to the choice of the parties.

Article 6 Obligations of a court not chosen

A court of a Contracting State other than that of the chosen court shall suspend or dismiss proceedings to which an exclusive choice of court agreement applies unless –

a) the agreement is null and void under the law of the State of the chosen court;
b) a party lacked the capacity to conclude the agreement under the law of the State of the court seised;
c) giving effect to the agreement would lead to a manifest injustice or would be manifestly contrary to the public policy of the State of the court seised;
d) for exceptional reasons beyond the control of the parties, the agreement cannot reasonably be performed; or
e) the chosen court has decided not to hear the case.

Article 7 Interim measures of protection

Interim measures of protection are not governed by this Convention. This Convention neither requires nor precludes the grant, refusal or termination of interim measures of protection by a court of a Contracting State and does not affect whether or not a party may request or a court should grant, refuse or terminate such measures.

CHAPTER III – RECOGNITION AND ENFORCEMENT

Article 8 Recognition and enforcement

1. A judgment given by a court of a Contracting State designated in an exclusive choice of court agreement shall be recognised and enforced in other Contracting States in accordance with this Chapter. Recognition or enforcement may be refused only on the grounds specified in this Convention.
2. Without prejudice to such review as is necessary for the application of the provisions of this Chapter, there shall be no review of the merits of the judgment given by the court of origin. The court addressed shall be bound by the findings of fact on which the court of origin based its jurisdiction, unless the judgment was given by default.
3. A judgment shall be recognised only if it has effect in the State of origin, and shall be enforced only if it is enforceable in the State of origin.
4. Recognition or enforcement may be postponed or refused if the judgment is the subject of review in the State of origin or if the time limit for seeking ordinary review has not expired. A refusal does not prevent a subsequent application for recognition or enforcement of the judgment.

5. This Article shall also apply to a judgment given by a court of a Contracting State pursuant to a transfer of the case from the chosen court in that Contracting State as permitted by Article 5, paragraph 3. However, where the chosen court had discretion as to whether to transfer the case to another court, recognition or enforcement of the judgment may be refused against a party who objected to the transfer in a timely manner in the State of origin.

Article 9 Refusal of recognition or enforcement

Recognition or enforcement may be refused if –

a) the agreement was null and void under the law of the State of the chosen court, unless the chosen court has determined that the agreement is valid;

b) a party lacked the capacity to conclude the agreement under the law of the requested State;

c) the document which instituted the proceedings or an equivalent document, including the essential elements of the claim,
   i) was not notified to the defendant in sufficient time and in such a way as to enable him to arrange for his defence, unless the defendant entered an appearance and presented his case without contesting notification in the court of origin, provided that the law of the State of origin permitted notification to be contested; or
   ii) was notified to the defendant in the requested State in a manner that is incompatible with fundamental principles of the requested State concerning service of documents;

d) the judgment was obtained by fraud in connection with a matter of procedure;

e) recognition or enforcement would be manifestly incompatible with the public policy of the requested State, including situations where the specific proceedings leading to the judgment were incompatible with fundamental principles of procedural fairness of that State;

f) the judgment is inconsistent with a judgment given in the requested State in a dispute between the same parties; or

g) the judgment is inconsistent with an earlier judgment given in another State between the same parties on the same cause of action, provided that the earlier judgment fulfils the conditions necessary for its recognition in the requested State.

Article 10 Preliminary questions

1. Where a matter excluded under Article 2, paragraph 2, or under Article 21, arose as a preliminary question, the ruling on that question shall not be recognised or enforced under this Convention.

2. Recognition or enforcement of a judgment may be refused if, and to the extent that, the judgment was based on a ruling on a matter excluded under Article 2, paragraph 2.

3. However, in the case of a ruling on the validity of an intellectual property right other than copyright or a related right, recognition or enforcement of a judgment may be refused or postponed under the preceding paragraph only where –

   a) that ruling is inconsistent with a judgment or a decision of a competent authority on that matter given in the State under the law of which the intellectual property right arose; or

   b) proceedings concerning the validity of the intellectual property right are pending in that State.

4. Recognition or enforcement of a judgment may be refused if, and to the extent that, the judgment was based on a ruling on a matter excluded pursuant to a declaration made by the requested State under Article 21.

Article 11 Damages

1. Recognition or enforcement of a judgment may be refused if, and to the extent that, the judgment awards damages, including exemplary or punitive damages, that do not compensate a party for actual loss or harm suffered.

2. The court addressed shall take into account whether and to what extent the damages awarded by the court of origin serve to cover costs and expenses relating to the proceedings.

Article 12 Judicial settlements (transactions judiciaires)

Judicial settlements (*transactions judiciaires*) which a court of a Contracting State designated in an exclusive choice of court agreement has approved, or which have been concluded before that court in the course of proceedings, and which are enforceable in the same manner as a judgment in the State of origin, shall be enforced under this Convention in the same manner as a judgment.

Article 13 Documents to be produced

1. The party seeking recognition or applying for enforcement shall produce –

   a) a complete and certified copy of the judgment;

   b) the exclusive choice of court agreement, a certified copy thereof, or other evidence of its existence;

   c) if the judgment was given by default, the original or a certified copy of a document establishing that the document which instituted the proceedings or an equivalent document was notified to the defaulting party;

   d) any documents necessary to establish that the judgment has effect or, where applicable, is enforceable in the State of origin;

e) in the case referred to in Article 12, a certificate of a court of the State of origin that the judicial settlement or a part of it is enforceable in the same manner as a judgment in the State of origin.

2. If the terms of the judgment do not permit the court addressed to verify whether the conditions of this Chapter have been complied with, that court may require any necessary documents.

3. An application for recognition or enforcement may be accompanied by a document, issued by a court (including an officer of the court) of the State of origin, in the form recommended and published by the Hague Conference on Private International Law.

4. If the documents referred to in this Article are not in an official language of the requested State, they shall be accompanied by a certified translation into an official language, unless the law of the requested State provides otherwise.

Article 14 Procedure

The procedure for recognition, declaration of enforceability or registration for enforcement, and the enforcement of the judgment, are governed by the law of the requested State unless this Convention provides otherwise. The court addressed shall act expeditiously.

Article 15 Severability

Recognition or enforcement of a severable part of a judgment shall be granted where recognition or enforcement of that part is applied for, or only part of the judgment is capable of being recognised or enforced under this Convention.

CHAPTER IV – GENERAL CLAUSES

Article 16 Transitional provisions

1. This Convention shall apply to exclusive choice of court agreements concluded after its entry into force for the State of the chosen court.

2. This Convention shall not apply to proceedings instituted before its entry into force for the State of the court seised.

Article 17 Contracts of insurance and reinsurance

1. Proceedings under a contract of insurance or reinsurance are not excluded from the scope of this Convention on the ground that the contract of insurance or reinsurance relates to a matter to which this Convention does not apply.

2. Recognition and enforcement of a judgment in respect of liability under the terms of a contract of insurance or reinsurance may not be limited or refused on the ground that the liability under that contract includes liability to indemnify the insured or reinsured in respect of –

    a) a matter to which this Convention does not apply; or

    b) an award of damages to which Article 11 might apply.

Article 18 No legalisation

All documents forwarded or delivered under this Convention shall be exempt from legalisation or any analogous formality, including an Apostille.

Article 19 Declarations limiting jurisdiction

A State may declare that its courts may refuse to determine disputes to which an exclusive choice of court agreement applies if, except for the location of the chosen court, there is no connection between that State and the parties or the dispute.

Article 20 Declarations limiting recognition and enforcement

A State may declare that its courts may refuse to recognise or enforce a judgment given by a court of another Contracting State if the parties were resident in the requested State, and the relationship of the parties and all other elements relevant to the dispute, other than the location of the chosen court, were connected only with the requested State.

Article 21 Declarations with respect to specific matters

1. Where a State has a strong interest in not applying this Convention to a specific matter, that State may declare that it will not apply the Convention to that matter. The State making such a declaration shall ensure that the declaration is no broader than necessary and that the specific matter excluded is clearly and precisely defined.

2. With regard to that matter, the Convention shall not apply –

    a) in the Contracting State that made the declaration;

    b) in other Contracting States, where an exclusive choice of court agreement designates the courts, or one or more specific courts, of the State that made the declaration.

Article 22 Reciprocal declarations on non-exclusive choice of court agreements

1. A Contracting State may declare that its courts will recognise and enforce judgments given by courts of other Contracting States designated in a choice of court agreement concluded by two or more parties that meets the requirements of Article 3, paragraph *c)*, and designates, for the purpose of deciding disputes which have arisen or may arise in connection with a particular legal relationship, a court or courts of one or more Contracting States (a non-exclusive choice of court agreement).

2. Where recognition or enforcement of a judgment given in a Contracting State that has made such a declaration is sought in another Contracting State that has made such a declaration, the judgment shall be recognised and enforced under this Convention, if –

a) the court of origin was designated in a non-exclusive choice of court agreement;

b) there exists neither a judgment given by any other court before which proceedings could be brought in accordance with the non-exclusive choice of court agreement, nor a proceeding pending between the same parties in any other such court on the same cause of action; and

c) the court of origin was the court first seised.

Article 23 Uniform interpretation

In the interpretation of this Convention, regard shall be had to its international character and to the need to promote uniformity in its application.

Article 24 Review of operation of the Convention

The Secretary General of the Hague Conference on Private International Law shall at regular intervals make arrangements for –

a) review of the operation of this Convention, including any declarations; and

b) consideration of whether any amendments to this Convention are desirable.

Article 25 Non-unified legal systems

1. In relation to a Contracting State in which two or more systems of law apply in different territorial units with regard to any matter dealt with in this Convention –

a) any reference to the law or procedure of a State shall be construed as referring, where appropriate, to the law or procedure in force in the relevant territorial unit;

b) any reference to residence in a State shall be construed as referring, where appropriate, to residence in the relevant territorial unit;

c) any reference to the court or courts of a State shall be construed as referring, where appropriate, to the court or courts in the relevant territorial unit;

d) any reference to a connection with a State shall be construed as referring, where appropriate, to a connection with the relevant territorial unit.

2. Notwithstanding the preceding paragraph, a Contracting State with two or more territorial units in which different systems of law apply shall not be bound to apply this Convention to situations which involve solely such different territorial units.

3. A court in a territorial unit of a Contracting State with two or more territorial units in which different systems of law apply shall not be bound to recognise or enforce a judgment from another Contracting State solely because the judgment has been recognised or enforced in another territorial unit of the same Contracting State under this Convention.

4. This Article shall not apply to a Regional Economic Integration Organisation.

Article 26 Relationship with other international instruments

1. This Convention shall be interpreted so far as possible to be compatible with other treaties in force for Contracting States, whether concluded before or after this Convention.

2. This Convention shall not affect the application by a Contracting State of a treaty, whether concluded before or after this Convention, in cases where none of the parties is resident in a Contracting State that is not a Party to the treaty.

3. This Convention shall not affect the application by a Contracting State of a treaty that was concluded before this Convention entered into force for that Contracting State, if applying this Convention would be inconsistent with the obligations of that Contracting State to any non-Contracting State. This paragraph shall also apply to treaties that revise or replace a treaty concluded before this Convention entered into force for that Contracting State, except to the extent that the revision or replacement creates new inconsistencies with this Convention.

4. This Convention shall not affect the application by a Contracting State of a treaty, whether concluded before or after this Convention, for the purposes of obtaining recognition or enforcement of a judgment given by a court of a Contracting State that is also a Party to that treaty. However, the judgment shall not be recognised or enforced to a lesser extent than under this Convention.

5. This Convention shall not affect the application by a Contracting State of a treaty which, in relation to a specific matter, governs jurisdiction or the recognition or enforcement of judgments, even if concluded after this Convention and even if all States concerned are Parties to this Convention. This paragraph shall apply only if the Contracting State has made a declaration in respect of the treaty under this paragraph. In the case of such a declaration, other Contracting States shall not be obliged to apply this Convention to that specific matter to the extent of any inconsistency, where an exclusive choice of court agreement designates the courts, or one or more specific courts, of the Contracting State that made the declaration.

6. This Convention shall not affect the application of the rules of a Regional Economic Integration Organisation that is a Party to this Convention, whether adopted before or after this Convention –

   a) where none of the parties is resident in a Contracting State that is not a Member State of the Regional Economic Integration Organisation;

b) as concerns the recognition or enforcement of judgments as between Member States of the Regional Economic Integration Organisation.

CHAPTER V – FINAL CLAUSES

Article 27 Signature, ratification, acceptance, approval or accession

1. This Convention is open for signature by all States.
2. This Convention is subject to ratification, acceptance or approval by the signatory States.
3. This Convention is open for accession by all States.
4. Instruments of ratification, acceptance, approval or accession shall be deposited with the Ministry of Foreign Affairs of the Kingdom of the Netherlands, depositary of the Convention.

Article 28 Declarations with respect to non-unified legal systems

1. If a State has two or more territorial units in which different systems of law apply in relation to matters dealt with in this Convention, it may at the time of signature, ratification, acceptance, approval or accession declare that the Convention shall extend to all its territorial units or only to one or more of them and may modify this declaration by submitting another declaration at any time.
2. A declaration shall be notified to the depositary and shall state expressly the territorial units to which the Convention applies.
3. If a State makes no declaration under this Article, the Convention shall extend to all territorial units of that State.
4. This Article shall not apply to a Regional Economic Integration Organisation.

Article 29 Regional Economic Integration Organisations

1. A Regional Economic Integration Organisation which is constituted solely by sovereign States and has competence over some or all of the matters governed by this Convention may similarly sign, accept, approve or accede to this Convention. The Regional Economic Integration Organisation shall in that case have the rights and obligations of a Contracting State, to the extent that the Organisation has competence over matters governed by this Convention.
2. The Regional Economic Integration Organisation shall, at the time of signature, acceptance, approval or accession, notify the depositary in writing of the matters governed by this Convention in respect of which competence has been transferred to that Organisation by its Member States. The Organisation shall promptly notify the depositary in writing of any changes to its competence as specified in the most recent notice given under this paragraph.

3. For the purposes of the entry into force of this Convention, any instrument deposited by a Regional Economic Integration Organisation shall not be counted unless the Regional Economic Integration Organisation declares in accordance with Article 30 that its Member States will not be Parties to this Convention.

4. Any reference to a "Contracting State" or "State" in this Convention shall apply equally, where appropriate, to a Regional Economic Integration Organisation that is a Party to it.

Article 30 Accession by a Regional Economic Integration Organisation without its Member States

1. At the time of signature, acceptance, approval or accession, a Regional Economic Integration Organisation may declare that it exercises competence over all the matters governed by this Convention and that its Member States will not be Parties to this Convention but shall be bound by virtue of the signature, acceptance, approval or accession of the Organisation.

2. In the event that a declaration is made by a Regional Economic Integration Organisation in accordance with paragraph 1, any reference to a "Contracting State" or "State" in this Convention shall apply equally, where appropriate, to the Member States of the Organisation.

Article 31 Entry into force

1. This Convention shall enter into force on the first day of the month following the expiration of three months after the deposit of the second instrument of ratification, acceptance, approval or accession referred to in Article 27.

2. Thereafter this Convention shall enter into force –
   a) for each State or Regional Economic Integration Organisation subsequently ratifying, accepting, approving or acceding to it, on the first day of the month following the expiration of three months after the deposit of its instrument of ratification, acceptance, approval or accession;
   b) for a territorial unit to which this Convention has been extended in accordance with Article 28, paragraph 1, on the first day of the month following the expiration of three months after the notification of the declaration referred to in that Article.

Article 32 Declarations

1. Declarations referred to in Articles 19, 20, 21, 22 and 26 may be made upon signature, ratification, acceptance, approval or accession or at any time thereafter, and may be modified or withdrawn at any time.

2. Declarations, modifications and withdrawals shall be notified to the depositary.

3. A declaration made at the time of signature, ratification, acceptance, approval or accession shall take effect simultaneously with the entry into force of this Convention for the State concerned.

4. A declaration made at a subsequent time, and any modification or withdrawal of a declaration, shall take effect on the first day of the month following the expiration of three months after the date on which the notification is received by the depositary.

5. A declaration under Articles 19, 20, 21 and 26 shall not apply to exclusive choice of court agreements concluded before it takes effect.

Article 33 Denunciation

1. This Convention may be denounced by notification in writing to the depositary. The denunciation may be limited to certain territorial units of a non-unified legal system to which this Convention applies.

2. The denunciation shall take effect on the first day of the month following the expiration of twelve months after the date on which the notification is received by the depositary. Where a longer period for the denunciation to take effect is specified in the notification, the denunciation shall take effect upon the expiration of such longer period after the date on which the notification is received by the depositary.

Article 34 Notifications by the depositary

The depositary shall notify the Members of the Hague Conference on Private International Law, and other States and Regional Economic Integration Organisations which have signed, ratified, accepted, approved or acceded in accordance with Articles 27, 29 and 30 of the following –

   a) the signatures, ratifications, acceptances, approvals and accessions referred to in Articles 27, 29 and 30;

   b) the date on which this Convention enters into force in accordance with Article 31;

   c) the notifications, declarations, modifications and withdrawals of declarations referred to in Articles 19, 20, 21, 22, 26, 28, 29 and 30;

   d) the denunciations referred to in Article 33.

In witness whereof the undersigned, being duly authorised thereto, have signed this Convention.

Done at The Hague, on 30 June 2005, in the English and French languages, both texts being equally authentic, in a single copy which shall be deposited in the archives of the Government of the Kingdom of the Netherlands, and of which a certified copy shall be sent, through diplomatic channels, to each of the Member States of the Hague Conference on Private International Law as of the date of its Twentieth Session and to each State which participated in that Session.

B The following Recommendation relating to the Convention on Choice of Court Agreements –

The Twentieth Session

Recommends to the States Parties to the *Convention on Choice of Court Agreements* to use the following form confirming the issuance and content of a judgment given by the court of origin for the purposes of recognition and enforcement under the Convention –

RECOMMENDED FORM UNDER THE CONVENTION ON CHOICE OF COURT AGREEMENTS ("THE CONVENTION")
(Sample form confirming the issuance and content of a judgment given by the court of origin for the purposes of recognition and enforcement under the Convention)
1. (THE COURT OF ORIGIN).....................
ADDRESS...................
TEL...............
FAX....................
E-MAIL......................
2. CASE / DOCKET NUMBER...............
3. .... (PLAINTIFF)
v.
.... (DEFENDANT)
4. (THE COURT OF ORIGIN) gave a judgment in the above-captioned matter on (DATE) in (CITY, STATE).
5. This court was designated in an exclusive choice of court agreement within the meaning of Article 3 of the Convention:
YES   NO
UNABLE TO CONFIRM
6. If yes, the exclusive choice of court agreement was concluded or documented in the following manner:
7. This court awarded the following payment of money *(please indicate, where applicable, any relevant categories of damages included)*:
8. This court awarded interest as follows *(please specify the rate(s) of interest, the portion(s) of the award to which interest applies, the date from which interest is computed, and any further information regarding interest that would assist the court addressed)*:
9. This court included within the judgment the following costs and expenses relating to the proceedings *(please specify the amounts of any such awards, including, where applicable, any amount(s) within a monetary award intended to cover costs and expenses relating to the proceedings)*:

10. This court awarded the following non-monetary relief *(please describe the nature of such relief)*:
11. This judgment is enforceable in the State of origin:
YES   NO
UNABLE TO CONFIRM
12. This judgment (or a part thereof) is currently the subject of review in the State of origin:
YES   NO
UNABLE TO CONFIRM
If "yes" please specify the nature and status of such review:
13. Any other relevant information:
14. Attached to this form are the documents marked in the following list *(if available)*:a complete and certified copy of the judgment;   the exclusive choice of court agreement, a certified copy thereof, or other evidence of its existence;   if the judgment was given by default, the original or a certified copy of a document establishing that the document which instituted the proceedings or an equivalent document was notified to the defaulting party;   any documents necessary to establish that the judgment has effect or, where applicable, is enforceable in the State of origin;
*(list if applicable):*in the case referred to in Article 12 of the Convention, a certificate of a court of the State of origin that the judicial settlement or a part of it is enforceable in the same manner as a judgment in the State of origin;   other documents:
15. Dated this ....day of ...., 20... at ....
16. Signature and / or stamp by the court or officer of the court:
CONTACT PERSON:
TEL.:
FAX:
E-MAIL:

E. OECD CONVENTION ON COMBATING BRIBERY OF FOREIGN PUBLIC OFFICIALS IN INTERNATIONAL BUSINESS TRANSACTIONS

Adopted by the Negotiating Conference on 20 November 1997

Preamble

The Parties,

Considering that bribery is a widespread phenomenon in international business transactions, including trade and investment, which raises serious moral and political concerns, undermines good governance and economic development, and distorts international competitive conditions;

Considering that all countries share a responsibility to combat bribery in international business transactions;

Having regard to the Revised Recommendation on Combating Bribery in International Business Transactions, adopted by the Council of the Organisation for Economic Co-operation and Development (OECD) on 23 May 1997, C(97)123/FINAL, which, inter alia, called for effective measures to deter, prevent and combat the bribery of foreign public officials in connection with international business transactions, in particular the prompt criminalisation of such bribery in an effective and co-ordinated manner and in conformity with the agreed common elements set out in that Recommendation and with the jurisdictional and other basic legal principles of each country;

Welcoming other recent developments which further advance international understanding and co-operation in combating bribery of public officials, including actions of the United Nations, the World Bank, the International Monetary Fund, the World Trade Organisation, the Organisation of American States, the Council of Europe and the European Union;

Welcoming the efforts of companies, business organisations and trade unions as well as other non-governmental organisations to combat bribery;

Recognising the role of governments in the prevention of solicitation of bribes from individuals and enterprises in international business transactions;

Recognising that achieving progress in this field requires not only efforts on a national level but also multilateral co-operation, monitoring and follow-up;

Recognising that achieving equivalence among the measures to be taken by the Parties is an essential object and purpose of the Convention, which requires that the Convention be ratified without derogations affecting this equivalence;

Have agreed as follows:

Article 1 - The Offence of Bribery of Foreign Public Officials

1. Each Party shall take such measures as may be necessary to establish that it is a criminal offence under its law for any person intentionally to offer, promise or give any undue pecuniary or other advantage, whether directly or through intermediaries, to a foreign public official, for that official or for a third party, in order that the official act or refrain from acting in relation to the performance of official duties, in order to obtain or retain business or other improper advantage in the conduct of international business.

2. Each Party shall take any measures necessary to establish that complicity in, including incitement, aiding and abetting, or authorisation of an act of bribery of a foreign public official shall be a criminal offence. Attempt and conspiracy to bribe a foreign public official shall be criminal offences to the same extent as attempt and conspiracy to bribe a public official of that Party.

3. The offences set out in paragraphs 1 and 2 above are hereinafter referred to as "bribery of a foreign public official".

4. For the purpose of this Convention:

   a. "foreign public official" means any person holding a legislative, administrative or judicial office of a foreign country, whether appointed or elected; any person exercising a public function for a foreign country, including for a public agency or public enterprise; and any official or agent of a public international organisation;

   b. "foreign country" includes all levels and subdivisions of government, from national to local;

   c. "act or refrain from acting in relation to the performance of official duties" includes any use of the public official's position, whether or not within the official's authorised competence.

Article 2 - Responsibility of Legal Persons

Each Party shall take such measures as may be necessary, in accordance with its legal principles, to establish the liability of legal persons for the bribery of a foreign public official.

Article 3 - Sanctions

1. The bribery of a foreign public official shall be punishable by effective, proportionate and dissuasive criminal penalties. The range of penalties shall be comparable to that applicable to the bribery of the Party's own public officials and shall, in the case of natural persons, include deprivation of liberty sufficient to enable effective mutual legal assistance and extradition.

2. In the event that, under the legal system of a Party, criminal responsibility is not applicable to legal persons, that Party shall ensure that legal persons shall be subject to effective, proportionate and dissuasive non-criminal sanctions, including monetary sanctions, for bribery of foreign public officials.

3. Each Party shall take such measures as may be necessary to provide that the bribe and the proceeds of the bribery of a foreign public official, or property the value of which corresponds to that of such proceeds, are subject to seizure and confiscation or that monetary sanctions of comparable effect are applicable.

4. Each Party shall consider the imposition of additional civil or administrative sanctions upon a person subject to sanctions for the bribery of a foreign public official.

Article 4 - Jurisdiction

1. Each Party shall take such measures as may be necessary to establish its jurisdiction over the bribery of a foreign public official when the offence is committed in whole or in part in its territory.

2. Each Party which has jurisdiction to prosecute its nationals for offences committed abroad shall take such measures as may be necessary to establish its jurisdiction to do so in respect of the bribery of a foreign public official, according to the same principles.

3. When more than one Party has jurisdiction over an alleged offence described in this Convention, the Parties involved shall, at the request of one of them, consult with a view to determining the most appropriate jurisdiction for prosecution.

4. Each Party shall review whether its current basis for jurisdiction is effective in the fight against the bribery of foreign public officials and, if it is not, shall take remedial steps.

Article 5 - Enforcement

Investigation and prosecution of the bribery of a foreign public official shall be subject to the applicable rules and principles of each Party. They shall not be influenced by considerations of national economic interest, the potential effect upon relations with another State or the identity of the natural or legal persons involved.

Article 6 - Statute of Limitations

Any statute of limitations applicable to the offence of bribery of a foreign public official shall allow an adequate period of time for the investigation and prosecution of this offence.

Article 7 - Money Laundering

Each Party which has made bribery of its own public official a predicate offence for the purpose of the application of its money laundering legislation shall do so on the same terms for the bribery of a foreign public official, without regard to the place where the bribery occurred.

Article 8 - Accounting

1. In order to combat bribery of foreign public officials effectively, each Party shall take such measures as may be necessary, within the framework of its laws and regulations regarding the maintenance of books and records, financial statement disclosures, and accounting and auditing standards, to prohibit the establishment of off-the-books accounts, the making of off-the-books or inadequately identified transactions, the recording of non-existent expenditures, the entry of liabilities with incorrect identification of their object, as well as the use of false documents, by companies subject to those laws and regulations, for the purpose of bribing foreign public officials or of hiding such bribery.

2. Each Party shall provide effective, proportionate and dissuasive civil, administrative or criminal penalties for such omissions and falsifications in respect of the books, records, accounts and financial statements of such companies.

Article 9 - Mutual Legal Assistance

1. Each Party shall, to the fullest extent possible under its laws and relevant treaties and arrangements, provide prompt and effective legal assistance to another Party for the purpose of criminal investigations and proceedings brought by a Party concerning offences within the scope of this Convention and for non-criminal proceedings within the scope of this Convention brought by a Party against a legal person. The requested Party shall inform the requesting Party, without delay, of any additional information or documents needed to support the request for assistance and, where requested, of the status and outcome of the request for assistance.

2. Where a Party makes mutual legal assistance conditional upon the existence of dual criminality, dual criminality shall be deemed to exist if the offence for which the assistance is sought is within the scope of this Convention.

3. A Party shall not decline to render mutual legal assistance for criminal matters within the scope of this Convention on the ground of bank secrecy.

Article 10 - Extradition

1. Bribery of a foreign public official shall be deemed to be included as an extraditable offence under the laws of the Parties and the extradition treaties between them.

2. If a Party which makes extradition conditional on the existence of an extradition treaty receives a request for extradition from another Party with which it has no extradition treaty, it may consider this Convention to be the legal basis for extradition in respect of the offence of bribery of a foreign public official.

3. Each Party shall take any measures necessary to assure either that it can extradite its nationals or that it can prosecute its nationals for the offence of bribery of a foreign public official. A Party which declines a request to extradite a person for bribery of a foreign public official solely on the ground that the person is its national shall submit the case to its competent authorities for the purpose of prosecution.

4. Extradition for bribery of a foreign public official is subject to the conditions set out in the domestic law and applicable treaties and arrangements of each Party. Where a Party makes extradition conditional upon the existence of dual criminality, that condition shall be deemed to be fulfilled if the offence for which extradition is sought is within the scope of Article 1 of this Convention.

Article 11 - Responsible Authorities

For the purposes of Article 4, paragraph 3, on consultation, Article 9, on mutual legal assistance and Article 10, on extradition, each Party shall notify to the Secretary-General of the OECD an authority or authorities responsible for making and receiving requests, which shall serve as channel of communication for these matters for that Party, without prejudice to other arrangements between Parties.

Article 12 - Monitoring and Follow-up

The Parties shall co-operate in carrying out a programme of systematic follow-up to monitor and promote the full implementation of this Convention. Unless otherwise decided by consensus of the Parties, this shall be done in the framework of the OECD Working Group on Bribery in International Business Transactions and according to its terms of reference, or within the framework and terms of reference of any successor to its functions, and Parties shall bear the costs of the programme in accordance with the rules applicable to that body.

Article 13 - Signature and Accession

1. Until its entry into force, this Convention shall be open for signature by OECD members and by non-members which have been invited to become full participants in its Working Group on Bribery in International Business Trans-actions.

2. Subsequent to its entry into force, this Convention shall be open to accession by any non-signatory which is a member of the OECD or has become a full participant in the Working Group on Bribery in International Business Transactions or any successor to its functions. For each such non-signatory, the Convention shall enter into force on the sixtieth day following the date of deposit of its instrument of accession.

Article 14 - Ratification and Depositary

1. This Convention is subject to acceptance, approval or ratification by the Signatories, in accordance with their respective laws.
2. Instruments of acceptance, approval, ratification or accession shall be deposited with the Secretary-General of the OECD, who shall serve as Depositary of this Convention.

Article 15 - Entry into Force

1. This Convention shall enter into force on the sixtieth day following the date upon which five of the ten countries which have the ten largest export shares (see annex), and which represent by themselves at least sixty per cent of the combined total exports of those ten countries, have deposited their instruments of acceptance, approval, or ratification. For each signatory depositing its instrument after such entry into force, the Convention shall enter into force on the sixtieth day after deposit of its instrument.
2. If, after 31 December 1998, the Convention has not entered into force under paragraph 1 above, any signatory which has deposited its instrument of acceptance, approval or ratification may declare in writing to the Depositary its readiness to accept entry into force of this Convention under this paragraph 2. The Convention shall enter into force for such a signatory on the sixtieth day following the date upon which such declarations have been deposited by at least two signatories. For each signatory depositing its declaration after such entry into force, the Convention shall enter into force on the sixtieth day following the date of deposit.

Article 16 - Amendment

Any Party may propose the amendment of this Convention. A proposed amendment shall be submitted to the Depositary which shall communicate it to the other Parties at least sixty days before convening a meeting of the Parties to consider the proposed amendment. An amendment adopted by consensus of the Parties, or by such other means as the Parties may determine by consensus, shall enter into force sixty days after the deposit of an instrument of ratification, acceptance or approval by all of the Parties, or in such other circumstances as may be specified by the Parties at the time of adoption of the amendment.

Article 17 - Withdrawal

A Party may withdraw from this Convention by submitting written notification to the Depositary. Such withdrawal shall be effective one year after the date of the receipt of the notification. After withdrawal, co-operation shall continue between the Parties and the Party which has withdrawn on all requests for assistance or extradition made before the effective date of withdrawal which remain pending.

F. CONVENTION ESTABLISHING THE MULTILATERAL INVESTMENT GUARANTEE AGENCY (MIGA)

PREAMBLE

The Contracting States

Considering the need to strengthen international cooperation for economic development and to foster the contribution to such development of foreign investment in general and private foreign investment in particular;

Recognizing that the flow of foreign investment to developing countries would be facilitated and further encouraged by alleviating concerns related to non-commercial risks;

Desiring to enhance the flow to developing countries of capital and technology for productive purposes under conditions consistent with their development needs, policies and objectives, on the basis of fair and stable standards for the treatment of foreign investment;

Convinced that the Multilateral Investment Guarantee Agency can play an important role in the encouragement of foreign investment complementing national and regional investment guarantee programs and private insurers of non-commercial risk; and

Realizing that such Agency should, to the extent possible, meet its obligations without resort to its callable capital and that such an objective would be served by continued improvement in investment conditions,

Have agreed as follows:

CHAPTER I: ESTABLISHMENT, STATUS, PURPOSES AND DEFINITIONS

Article 1. Establishment and Status of the Agency

(a) There is hereby established the Multilateral Investment Guarantee Agency (hereinafter called the Agency).

(b) The Agency shall possess full juridical personality and, in particular, the capacity to:
   (i)   contract;
   (ii) acquire and dispose of movable and immovable property; and
   (iii) institute legal proceedings.

Article 2. Objective and Purposes

The objective of the Agency shall be to encourage the flow of investments for productive purposes among member countries, and in particular to developing member countries, thus supplementing the activities of the International Bank for Reconstruction and Development (hereinafter referred to as the Bank), the International Finance Corporation and other international development finance institutions.

To serve its objective, the Agency shall:

(a) issue guarantees, including coinsurance and reinsurance, against noncommercial risks in respect of investments in a member country which flow from other member countries;

(b) carry out appropriate complementary activities to promote the flow of investments to and among developing member countries; and

(c) exercise such other incidental powers as shall be necessary or desirable in the furtherance of its objective.

The Agency shall be guided in all its decisions by the provisions of this Article.

Article 3. Definitions

For the purposes of this Convention:

(a) "Member" means a State with respect to which this Convention has entered into force in accordance with Article 61.

(b) "Host country" or "host government" means a member, its government, or any public authority of a member in whose territories, as defined in Article 66, an investment which has been guaranteed or reinsured, or is considered for guarantee or reinsurance, by the Agency is to be located.

(c) A "developing member country" means a member which is listed as such in Schedule A hereto as this Schedule may be amended from time to time by the Council of Governors referred to in Article 30 (hereinafter called the Council).

(d) A "special majority" means an affirmative vote of not less than two-thirds of the total voting power representing not less than fifty-five percent of the subscribed shares of the capital stock of the Agency.

(e) A "freely usable currency" means (i) any currency designated as such by the International Monetary Fund from time to time and (ii) any other freely available and effectively usable currency which the Board of Directors referred to in Article 30 (hereinafter called the Board) may designate for the purposes of this Convention after consultation with the International Monetary Fund and with the approval of the country of such currency.

CHAPTER II: MEMBERSHIP AND CAPITAL

Article 4. Membership

(a) Membership in the Agency shall be open to all members of the Bank and to Switzerland.

(b) Original members shall be the States which are listed in Schedule A hereto and become parties to this Convention on or before October 30, 1987.

Article 5. Capital

(a) The authorized capital stock of the Agency shall be one billion Special Drawing Rights (SDR 1,000,000,000). The capital stock shall be divided into 100,000 shares having a par value of SDR 10,000 each, which shall be available for subscription by members. All payment obligations of members with respect to capital stock shall be settled on the basis of the average value of the SDR in terms of United States dollars for the period January 1, 1981 to June 30, 1985, such value being 1.082 United States dollars per SDR.

(b) The capital stock shall increase on the admission of a new member to the extent that the then authorized shares are insufficient to provide the shares to be subscribed by such member pursuant to Article 6.

(c) The Council, by special majority, may at any time increase the capital stock of the Agency.

Article 6. Subscription of Shares

Each original member of the Agency shall subscribe at par to the number of shares of capital stock set forth opposite its name in Schedule A hereto. Each other member shall subscribe to such number of shares of capital stock on such terms and conditions as may be determined by the Council, but in no event at an issue price of less than par. No member shall subscribe to less than fifty shares. The Council may prescribe rules by which members may subscribe to additional shares of the authorized capital stock.

Article 7. Division and Calls of Subscribed Capital

The initial subscription of each member shall be paid as follows:

(i) Within ninety days from the date on which this Convention enters into force with respect to such member, ten percent of the price of each share shall be paid in cash as stipulated in Section (a) of Article 8 and an additional ten percent in the form of non-negotiable, non-interest-bearing promissory notes or similar obligations to be encashed pursuant to a decision of the Board in order to meet the Agency's obligations.

(ii) The remainder shall be subject to call by the Agency when required to meet its obligations.

Article 8. Payment of Subscription of Shares

(a) Payments of subscriptions shall be made in freely usable currencies except that payments by developing member countries may be made in their own currencies up to twenty-five percent of the paid-in cash portion of their subscriptions payable under Article 7(i).

(b) Calls on any portion of unpaid subscriptions shall be uniform on all shares.

(c) If the amount received by the Agency on a call shall be insufficient to meet the obligations which have necessitated the call, the Agency may make further successive calls on unpaid subscriptions until the aggregate amount received by it shall be sufficient to meet such obligations.

(d) Liability on shares shall be limited to the unpaid portion of the issue price.

Article 9. Valuation of Currencies

Whenever it shall be necessary for the purposes of this Convention to determine the value of one currency in terms of another, such value shall be as reasonably determined by the Agency, after consultation with the International Monetary Fund.

Article 10. Refunds

(a) The Agency shall, as soon as practicable, return to members amounts paid on calls on subscribed capital if and to the extent that:

   (i) the call shall have been made to pay a claim resulting from a guarantee or reinsurance contract and thereafter the Agency shall have recovered its payment, in whole or in part, in a freely usable currency; or

   (ii) the call shall have been made because of a default in payment by a member and thereafter such member shall have made good such default in whole or in part; or

   (iii) the Council, by special majority, determines that the financial position of the Agency permits all or part of such amounts to be returned out of the Agency's revenues.

(b) Any refund effected under this Article to a member shall be made in freely usable currency in the proportion of the payments made by that member to the total amount paid pursuant to calls made prior to such refund.

(c) The equivalent of amounts refunded under this Article to a member shall become part of the callable capital obligations of the member under Article 7 (ii).

CHAPTER III: OPERATIONS

Article 11. Covered Risks

(a) Subject to the provisions of Sections (b) and (c) below, the Agency may guarantee eligible investments against a loss resulting from one or more of the following types of risk:

    (i) Currency Transfer: any introduction attributable to the host government of restrictions on the transfer outside the host country of its currency into a freely usable currency or another currency acceptable to the holder of the guarantee, including a failure of the host government to act within a reasonable period of time on an application by such holder for such transfer;

    (ii) Expropriation and Similar Measures: any legislative action or administrative action or omission attributable to the host government which has the effect of depriving the holder of a guarantee of his ownership or control of, or a substantial benefit from, his investment, with the exception of non-discriminatory measures of general application which governments normally take for the purpose of regulating economic activity in their territories;

    (iii) Breach of Contract: any repudiation or breach by the host government of a contract with the holder of a guarantee, when (a) the holder of a guarantee does not have recourse to a judicial or arbitral forum to determine the claim of repudiation or breach, or (b) a decision by such forum is not rendered within such reasonable period of time as shall be prescribed in the contracts of guarantee pursuant to the Agency's regulations, or (c) such a decision cannot be enforced; and

    (iv) War and Civil Disturbance: any military action or civil disturbance in any territory of the host country to which this Convention shall be applicable as provided in Article 66.

(b) In addition the Board, by special majority, may approve the extension of coverage under this Article to specific non-commercial risks other than those referred to in Section (a) above, but in no case to the risk of devaluation or depreciation of currency.

(c) Losses resulting from the following shall not be covered:

    (i) any host government action or omission to which the holder of the guarantee has agreed or for which he has been responsible; and

    (ii) any host government action or omission or any other event occurring before the conclusion of the contract of guarantee.

Article 12. Eligible Investments

(a) Eligible investments shall include equity interests, including medium- or long-term loans made or guaranteed by holders of equity in the enterprise concerned, and such forms of direct investment as may be determined by the Board.

(b) Loans other than those mentioned in Section (a) above are eligible for coverage

    (i) if they are made to finance or are otherwise related to a specific investment or project in which some other form of direct investment is present, whether or not guaranteed by the Agency and regardless of when such other investment was made, or

    (ii) as may be otherwise approved by the Board by special majority.

(c) The Board, by special majority, may extend eligibility to any other medium- or long-term form of investment.

(d) Guarantees shall generally be restricted to investments the implementation of which begins subsequent to the registration of the application for the guarantee by the Agency or receipt by the agency of other satisfactory evidence of investor intent to obtain guarantees from the Agency. Such investments may include:

    (i) a transfer of foreign exchange made to modernize, expand, or develop an existing investment, in which case both the original investment and the additional investment may be considered eligible for coverage;

    (ii) the use of earnings from existing investments which could otherwise be transferred outside the host country.

    (iii) the acquisition of an existing investment by a new eligible investor;

    (iv) existing investments where an eligible investor is seeking to insure a pool of existing and new investments;

    (v) existing investment owned by an eligible investor where there is an improvement or enhancement of the underlying project or the investor otherwise demonstrates medium- or long-term commitment to the project, and the Agency is satisfied that the project continues to have a high developmental impact in the host country; and

    (vi) such other investments as may be approved by the Boad by special majority.

(e) In guaranteeing an investment, the Agency shall satisfy itself as to:

    (i) the economic soundness of the investment and its contribution to the development of the host country;

    (ii) compliance of the investment with the host country's laws and regulations;

    (iii) consistency of the investment with the declared development objectives and priorities of the host country; and

(iv) the investment conditions in the host country, including the availability of fair and equitable treatment and legal protection for the investment.

Article 13. Eligible Investors

(a) Any natural person and any juridical person may be eligible to receive the Agency's guarantee provided that:
  (i) such natural person is a national of a member other than the host country;
  (ii) such juridical person is incorporated and has its principal place of business in a member or the majority of its capital is owned by a member or members or nationals thereof, provided that such member is not the host country in any of the above cases; and
  (iii) such juridical person, whether or not it is privately owned, operates on a commercial basis.
(b) In case the investor has more than one nationality, for the purposes of Section (a) above the nationality of a member shall prevail over the nationality of a non-member, and the nationality of the host country shall prevail over the nationality of any other member.
(c) Upon the joint application of the investor and the host country, the Board, by special majority, may extend eligibility to a natural person who is a national of the host country or a juridical person which is incorporated in the host country or the majority of whose capital is owned by its nationals, provided that the assets invested are transferred from outside the host country.

Article 14. Eligible Host Countries

Investments shall be guaranteed under this Chapter only if they are to be made in the territory of a developing member country.

Article 15. Host Country Approval

The Agency shall not conclude any contract of guarantee before the host government has approved the issuance of the guarantee by the Agency against the risks designated for cover.

Article 16. Terms and Conditions

The terms and conditions of each contract of guarantee shall be determined by the Agency subject to such rules and regulations as the Board shall issue, provided that the Agency shall not cover the total loss of the guaranteed investment. Contracts of guarantee shall be approved by the President under the direction of the Board.

Article 17. Payment of Claims

The President under the direction of the Board shall decide on the payment of claims to a holder of a guarantee in accordance with the contract of guarantee and such policies as the Board may adopt. Contracts of guarantee shall require holders of guarantees to seek, before a payment is made by the Agency, such administrative remedies as may be appropriate under the circumstances, provided that they are readily available to them under the laws of the host country. Such contracts may require the lapse of certain reasonable periods between the occurrence of events giving rise to claims and payments of claims.

Article 18. Subrogation

(a) Upon paying or agreeing to pay compensation to a holder of a guarantee, the Agency shall be subrogated to such rights or claims related to the guaranteed investment as the holder of a guarantee may have had against the host country and other obligors. The contract of guarantee shall provide the terms and conditions of such subrogation.

(b) The rights of the Agency pursuant to Section (a) above shall be recognized by all members.

(c) Amounts in the currency of the host country acquired by the Agency as subrogee pursuant to Section (a) above shall be accorded, with respect to use and conversion, treatment by the host country as favorable as the treatment to which such funds would be entitled in the hands of the holder of the guarantee. In any case, such amounts may be used by the Agency for the payment of its administrative expenditures and other costs. The Agency shall also seek to enter into arrangements with host countries on other uses of such currencies to the extent that they are not freely usable.

Article 19. Relationship to National and Regional Entities

The Agency shall cooperate with, and seek to complement the operations of, national entities of members and regional entities the majority of whose capital is owned by members, which carry out activities similar to those of the Agency, with a view to maximizing both the efficiency of their respective services and their contribution to increased flows of foreign investment. To this end, the Agency may enter into arrangements with such entities on the details of such cooperation, including in particular the modalities of reinsurance and coinsurance.

Article 20. Reinsurance of National and Regional Entities

(a) The Agency may issue reinsurance in respect of a specific investment against a loss resulting from one or more of the non-commercial risks underwritten by a member or agency thereof or by a regional investment guarantee agency the majority of whose capital is owned by members. The Board, by special majority, shall from time to time prescribe maximum amounts of contingent liability which may be assumed by the Agency with respect to reinsurance contracts. In respect of specific investments which have been completed more than twelve months prior to receipt of the application for reinsurance by the Agency, the maximum amount shall initially be set at ten percent of the aggregate contingent liability of the Agency under this Chapter. The conditions of eligibility specified in Articles 11 and 14 shall apply to reinsurance operations, except that the reinsured investments need not be implemented subsequent to the application for reinsurance.

(b) The mutual rights and obligations of the Agency and a reinsured member or agency shall be stated in contracts of reinsurance subject to such rules and regulations as the Board shall issue. The Board shall approve each contract for reinsurance covering an investment which has been made prior to receipt of the application for reinsurance by the Agency, with a view to minimizing risks, assuring that the Agency receives premiums commensurate with its risk, and assuring that the reinsured entity is appropriately committed toward promoting new investment in developing member countries.

(c) The Agency shall, to the extent possible, assure that it or the reinsured entity shall have the rights of subrogation and arbitration equivalent to those the Agency would have if it were the primary guarantor. The terms and conditions of reinsurance shall require that administrative remedies are sought in accordance with Article 17 before a payment is made by the Agency. Subrogation shall be effective with respect to the host country concerned only after its approval of the reinsurance by the Agency. The Agency shall include in the contracts of reinsurance provisions requiring the reinsured to pursue with due diligence the rights or claims related to the reinsured investment.

Article 21. Cooperation with Private Insurers and with Reinsurers

(a) The Agency may enter into arrangements with private insurers in member countries to enhance its own operations and encourage such insurers to provide coverage of non-commercial risks in developing member countries on conditions similar to those applied by the Agency. Such arrangements may include the provision of reinsurance by the Agency under the conditions and procedures specified in Article 20.

(b) The Agency may reinsure with any appropriate reinsurance entity, in whole or in part, any guarantee or guarantees issued by it.

(c) The Agency will in particular seek to guarantee investments for which comparable coverage on reasonable terms is not available from private insurers and reinsurers.

Article 22. Limits of Guarantee

(a) Unless determined otherwise by the Council by special majority, the aggregate amount of contingent liabilities which may be assumed by the Agency under this Chapter shall not exceed one hundred and 50 percent of the amount of the Agency's unimpaired subscribed capital and its reserves plus such portion of its reinsurance cover as the Board may determine. The Board shall from time to time review the risk profile of the Agency's portfolio in the light of its experience with claims, degree of risk diversification, reinsurance cover and other relevant factors with a view to ascertaining whether changes in the maximum aggregate amount of contingent liabilities should be recommended to the Council. The maximum amount determined by the Council shall not under any circumstances exceed five times the amount of the Agency's unimpaired subscribed capital, its reserves and such portion of its reinsurance cover as may be deemed appropriate.

(b) Without prejudice to the general limit of guarantee referred to in Section (a) above, the Board may prescribe:

    (i) maximum aggregate amounts of contingent liability which may be assumed by the Agency under this Chapter for all guarantees issued to investors of each individual member. In determining such maximum amounts, the Board shall give due consideration to the share of the respective member in the capital of the Agency and the need to apply more liberal limitations in respect of investments originating in developing member countries; and

    (ii) maximum aggregate amounts of contingent liability which may be assumed by the Agency with respect to such risk diversification factors as individual projects, individual host countries and types of investment or risk.

Article 23. Investment Promotion

(a) The Agency shall carry out research, undertake activities to promote investment flows and disseminate information on investment opportunities in developing member countries, with a view to improving the environment for foreign investment flows to such countries. The Agency may, upon the request of a member, provide technical advice and assistance to improve the investment conditions in the territories of that member. In performing these activities, the Agency shall:

    (i) be guided by relevant investment agreements among member countries;

    (ii) seek to remove impediments, in both developed and developing member countries, to the flow of investment to developing member countries; and

    (iii) coordinate with other agencies concerned with the promotion of foreign investment, and in particular the International Finance Corporation.

(b) The Agency also shall:

    (i) encourage the amicable settlement of disputes between investors and host countries;

    (ii) endeavor to conclude agreements with developing member countries, and in particular with prospective host countries, which will assure that the Agency, with respect to investment guaranteed by it, has treatment at least as favorable as that agreed by the member concerned for the most favored investment guarantee agency or State in an agreement relating to investment, such agreements to be approved by special majority of the Board; and

    (iii) promote and facilitate the conclusion of agreements, among its members, on the promotion and protection of investments.

(c) The Agency shall give particular attention in its promotional efforts to the importance of increasing the flow of investments among developing member countries.

Article 24. Guarantees of Sponsored Investments

In addition to the guarantee operations undertaken by the Agency under this Chapter, the Agency may guarantee investments under the sponsorship arrangements provided for in Annex I to this Convention.

CHAPTER IV: FINANCIAL PROVISIONS

Article 25. Financial Management

The Agency shall carry out its activities in accordance with sound business and prudent financial management practices with a view to maintaining under all circumstances its ability to meet its financial obligations.

Article 26. Premiums and Fees

The Agency shall establish and periodically review the rates of premiums, fees and other charges, if any, applicable to each type of risk.

Article 27. Allocation of Net Income

(a) Without prejudice to the provisions of Section (a)(iii) of Article 10, the Agency shall allocate net income to reserves until such reserves reach five times the subscribed capital of the Agency.

(b) After the reserves of the Agency have reached the level prescribed in Section (a) above, the Council shall decide whether, and to what extent, the Agency's net income shall be allocated to reserves, be distributed to the Agency's members or be used otherwise. Any distribution of net income to the Agency's members shall be made in proportion to the share of each member in the capital of the Agency in accordance with a decision of the Council acting by special majority.

Article 28. Budget

The President shall prepare an annual budget of revenues and expenditures of the Agency for approval by the Board.

Article 29. Accounts

The Agency shall publish an Annual Report which shall include statements of its accounts and of the accounts of the Sponsorship Trust Fund referred to in Annex I to this Convention, as audited by independent auditors. The Agency shall circulate to members at appropriate intervals a summary statement of its financial position and a profit and loss statement showing the results of its operations.

CHAPTER V: ORGANIZATION AND MANAGEMENT

Article 30. Structure of the Agency

The Agency shall have a Council of Governors, a Board of Directors, a President and staff to perform such duties as the Agency may determine.

Article 31. The Council

(a) All the powers of the Agency shall be vested in the Council, except such powers as are, by the terms of this Convention, specifically conferred upon another organ of the Agency. The Council may delegate to the Board the exercise of any of its powers, except the power to:
    (i) admit new members and determine the conditions of their admission;
    (ii) suspend a member;
    (iii) decide on any increase or decrease in capital;
    (iv) increase the limit of the aggregate amount of contingent liabilities pursuant to Section (a) of Article 22;

(v) designate a member as a developing member country pursuant to Section (c) of Article 3;

(vi) classify a new member as belonging to Category One or Category Two for voting purposes pursuant to Section (a) of Article 39 or reclassify an existing member for the same purpose;

(vii) determine the compensation of Directors and their Alternates;

(viii) cease operations and liquidate the Agency;

(ix) distribute assets to members upon liquidation; and

(x) amend this Convention, its Annexes and Schedules.

(b) The Council shall be composed of one Governor and one Alternate appointed by each member in such manner as it may determine. No Alternate may vote except in the absence of his principal. The Council shall select one of the Governors as Chairman.

(c) The Council shall hold an annual meeting and such other meetings as may be determined by the Council or called by the Board. The Board shall call a meeting of the Council whenever requested by five members or by members having 25 percent of the total voting power.

Article 32. The Board

(a) The Board shall be responsible for the general operations of the Agency and shall take, in the fulfillment of this responsibility, any action required or permitted under this Convention.

(b) The Board shall consist of not less than twelve Directors. The number of Directors may be adjusted by the Council to take into account changes in membership. Each Director may appoint an Alternate with full power to act for him in case of the Director's absence or inability to act. The President of the Bank shall be *ex officio* Chairman of the Board, but shall have no vote except a deciding vote in case of an equal division.

(c) The Council shall determine the term of office of the Directors. The first Board shall be constituted by the Council at its inaugural meeting.

(d) The Board shall meet at the call of its Chairman acting on his own initiative or upon request of three Directors.

(e) Until such time as the Council may decide that the Agency shall have a resident Board which functions in continuous session, the Directors and Alternates shall receive compensation only for the cost of attendance at the meetings of the Board and the discharge of other official functions on behalf of the Agency. Upon the establishment of a Board in continuous session, the Directors and Alternates shall receive such remuneration as may be determined by the Council.

Article 33. President and Staff

(a) The President shall, under the general control of the Board, conduct the ordinary business of the Agency. He shall be responsible for the organization, appointment and dismissal of the staff.

(b) The President shall be appointed by the Board on the nomination of its Chairman. The Council shall determine the salary and terms of the contract of service of the President.

(c) In the discharge of their offices, the President and the staff owe their duty entirely to the Agency and to no other authority. Each member of the Agency shall respect the international character of this duty and shall refrain from all attempts to influence the President or the staff in the discharge of their duties.

(d) In appointing the staff, the President shall, subject to the paramount importance of securing the highest standards of efficiency and of technical competence, pay due regard to the importance of recruiting personnel on as wide a geographical basis as possible.

(e) The President and staff shall maintain at all times the confidentiality of information obtained in carrying out the Agency's operations.

Article 34. Political Activity Prohibited

The Agency, its President and staff shall not interfere in the political affairs of any member. Without prejudice to the right of the Agency to take into account all the circumstances surrounding an investment, they shall not be influenced in their decisions by the political character of the member or members concerned. Considerations relevant to their decisions shall be weighed impartially in order to achieve the purposes stated in Article 2.

Article 35. Relations with International Organizations

The Agency shall, within the terms of this Convention, cooperate with the United Nations and with other inter-governmental organizations having specialized responsibilities in related fields, including in particular the Bank and the International Finance Corporation.

Article 36. Location of Principal Office

(a) The principal office of the Agency shall be located in Washington, D.C., unless the Council, by special majority, decides to establish it in another location.

(b) The Agency may establish other offices as may be necessary for its work.

Article 37. Depositories for Assets

Each member shall designate its central bank as a depository in which the Agency may keep holdings of such member's currency or other assets of the Agency or, if it has no central bank, it shall designate for such purpose such other institution as may be acceptable to the Agency.

Article 38. Channel of Communication

(a) Each member shall designate an appropriate authority with which the Agency may communicate in connection with any matter arising under this Convention. The Agency may rely on statements of such authority as being statements of the member. The Agency, upon the request of a member, shall consult with that member with respect to matters dealt with in Articles 19 to 21 and related to entities or insurers of that member.

(b) Whenever the approval of any member is required before any act may be done by the Agency, approval shall be deemed to have been given unless the member presents an objection within such reasonable period as the Agency may fix in notifying the member of the proposed act.

CHAPTER VI: VOTING, ADJUSTMENTS OF SUBSCRIPTIONS AND REPRESENTATION

Article 39. Voting and Adjustments of Subscriptions

(a) In order to provide for voting arrangements that reflect the equal interest in the Agency of the two Categories of States listed in Schedule A of this Convention, as well as the importance of each member's financial participation, each member shall have 177 membership votes plus one subscription vote for each share of stock held by that member.

(b) If at any time within three years after the entry into force of this Convention the aggregate sum of membership and subscription votes of members which belong to either of the two Categories of States listed in Schedule A of this Convention is less than 40 percent of the total voting power, members from such a Category shall have such number of supplementary votes as shall be necessary for the aggregate voting power of the Category to equal such a percentage of the total voting power. Such supplementary votes shall be distributed among the members of such Category in the proportion that the subscription votes of each bears to the aggregate of subscription votes of the Category. Such supplementary votes shall be subject to automatic adjustment to ensure that such percentage is maintained and shall be canceled at the end of the above-mentioned three-year period.

(c) During the third year following the entry into force of this Convention, the Council shall review the allocation of shares and shall be guided in its decision by the following principles:

    (i) the votes of members shall reflect actual subscriptions to the Agency's capital and the membership votes as set out in Section (a) of this Article;

    (ii) shares allocated to countries which shall not have signed the Convention shall be made available for reallocation to such members and in such manner as to make possible voting parity between the above-mentioned Categories; and

    (iii) the Council will take measures that will facilitate members' ability to subscribe to shares allocated to them.

(d) Within the three-year period provided for in Section (b) of this Article, all decisions of the Council and Board shall be taken by special majority, except that decisions requiring a higher majority under this Convention shall be taken by such higher majority.

(e) In case the capital stock of the Agency is increased pursuant to Section (c) of Article 5, each member which so requests shall be authorized to subscribe a proportion of the increase equivalent to the proportion which its stock theretofore subscribed bears to the total capital stock of the Agency, but no member shall be obligated to subscribe any part of the increased capital.

(f) The Council shall issue regulations regarding the making of additional subscriptions under Section (e) of this Article. Such regulations shall prescribe reasonable time limits for the submission by members of requests to make such subscriptions.

Article 40. Voting in the Council

(a) Each Governor shall be entitled to cast the votes of the member he represents. Except as otherwise specified in this Convention, decisions of the Council shall be taken by a majority of the votes cast.

(b) A quorum for any meeting of the Council shall be constituted by a majority of the Governors exercising not less than two-thirds of the total voting power.

(c) The Council may by regulation establish a procedure whereby the Board, when it deems such action to be in the best interests of the Agency, may request a decision of the Council on a specific question without calling a meeting of the Council.

Article 41. Election of Directors

(a) Directors shall be elected in accordance with Schedule B.

(b) Directors shall continue in office until their successors are elected. If the office of a Director becomes vacant more than ninety days before the end of his term, another Director shall be elected for the remainder of the term by the Governors who elected the former Director. A majority of the votes cast shall be required for election. While the office remains vacant, the Alternate of the former Director shall exercise his powers, except that of appointing an Alternate.

Article 42. Voting in the Board

(a) Each Director shall be entitled to cast the number of votes of the members whose votes counted towards his election. All the votes which a Director is entitled to cast shall be cast as a unit. Except as otherwise specified in this Convention, decisions of the Board shall be taken by a majority of the votes cast.

(b) A quorum for a meeting of the Board shall be constituted by a majority of the Directors exercising not less than one-half of the total voting power.

(c) The Board may by regulation establish a procedure whereby its Chairman, when he deems such action to be in the best interests of the Agency, may request a decision of the Board on a specific question without calling a meeting of the Board.

CHAPTER VII: PRIVILEGES AND IMMUNITIES

Article 43. Purposes of Chapter

To enable the Agency to fulfill its functions, the immunities and privileges set forth in this Chapter shall be accorded to the Agency in the territories of each member.

Article 44. Legal Process

Actions other than those within the scope of Articles 57 and 58 may be brought against the Agency only in a court of competent jurisdiction in the territories of a member in which the Agency has an office or has appointed an agent for the purpose of accepting service or notice of process. No such action against the Agency shall be brought:

(i) by members or persons acting for or deriving claims from members or

(ii) in respect of personnel matters.

The property and assets of the Agency shall, wherever located and by whomsoever held, be immune from all forms of seizure, attachment or execution before the delivery of the final judgment or award against the Agency.

Article 45. Assets

(a) The property and assets of the Agency, wherever located and by whomsoever held, shall be immune from search, requisition, confiscation, expropriation or any other form of seizure by executive or legislative action.

(b) To the extent necessary to carry out its operations under this Convention, all property and assets of the Agency shall be free from restrictions, regulations, controls and moratoria of any nature; provided that property and assets acquired by the Agency as successor to or subrogee of a holder of a guarantee, a reinsured entity or an investor insured by a reinsured entity shall be free from applicable foreign exchange restrictions, regulations and controls in force in the territories of the member concerned to the extent that the holder, entity or investor to whom the Agency was subrogated was entitled to such treatment.

(c) For purposes of this Chapter, the term "assets" shall include the assets of the Sponsorship Trust Fund referred to in Annex I to this Convention and other assets administered by the Agency in furtherance of its objective.

Article 46. Archives and Communications

(a) The archives of the Agency shall be inviolable, wherever they may be.

(b) The official communications of the Agency shall be accorded by each member the same treatment that is accorded to the official communications of the Bank.

Article 47. Taxes

(a) The Agency, its assets, property and income, and its operations and transactions authorized by this Convention, shall be immune from all taxes and customs duties. The Agency shall also be immune from liability for the collection or payment of any tax or duty.

(b) Except in the case of local nationals, no tax shall be levied on or in respect of expense allowances paid by the Agency to Governors and their Alternates or on or in respect of salaries, expense allowances or other emoluments paid by the Agency to the Chairman of the Board, Directors, their Alternates, the President or staff of the Agency.

(c) No taxation of any kind shall be levied on any investment guaranteed or reinsured by the Agency (including any earnings therefrom) or any insurance policies reinsured by the Agency (including any premiums and other revenues therefrom) by whomsoever held:

  (i) which discriminates against such investment or insurance policy solely because it is guaranteed or reinsured by the Agency; or
  (ii) if the sole jurisdictional basis for such taxation is the location of any office or place of business maintained by the Agency.

Article 48. Officials of the Agency

All Governors, Directors, Alternates, the President and staff of the Agency:

   (i) shall be immune from legal process with respect to acts performed by them in their official capacity;

  (ii) not being local nationals, shall be accorded the same immunities from immigration restrictions, alien registration requirements and national service obligations, and the same facilities as regards exchange restrictions as are accorded by the members concerned to the representatives, officials and employees of comparable rank of other members; and

 (iii) shall be granted the same treatment in respect of travelling facilities as is accorded by the members concerned to representatives, officials and employees of comparable rank of other members.

Article 49. Application of the Chapter

Each member shall take such action as is necessary in its own territories for the purpose of making effective in terms of its own law the principles set forth in this Chapter and shall inform the Agency of the detailed action which it has taken.

Article 50. Waiver

The immunities, exemptions and privileges provided in this Chapter are granted in the interests of the Agency and may be waived, to such extent and upon such conditions as the Agency may determine, in cases where such a waiver would not prejudice its interests. The Agency shall waive the immunity of any of its staff in cases where, in its opinion, the immunity would impede the course of justice and can be waived without prejudice to the interests of the Agency.

CHAPTER VIII: WITHDRAWAL, SUSPENSION OF MEMBERSHIP AND CESSATION OF OPERATIONS

Article 51. Withdrawal

Any member may, after the expiration of three years following the date upon which this Convention has entered into force with respect to such member, withdraw from the Agency at any time by giving notice in writing to the Agency at its principal office. The Agency shall notify the Bank, as depository of this Convention, of the receipt of such notice. Any withdrawal shall become effective ninety days following the date of the receipt of such notice by the Agency. A member may revoke such notice as long as it has not become effective.

Article 52. Suspension of Membership

(a) If a member fails to fulfill any of its obligations under this Convention, the Council may, by a majority of its members exercising a majority of the total voting power, suspend its membership.

(b) While under suspension a member shall have no rights under this Convention, except for the right of withdrawal and other rights provided in this Chapter and Chapter IX, but shall remain subject to all its obligations.

(c) For purposes of determining eligibility for a guarantee or reinsurance to be issued under Chapter III or Annex I to this Convention, a suspended member shall not be treated as a member of the Agency.

(d) The suspended member shall automatically cease to be a member one year from the date of its suspension unless the Council decides to extend the period of suspension or to restore the member to good standing.

Article 53. Rights and Duties of States Ceasing to be Members

(a) When a State ceases to be a member, it shall remain liable for all its obligations, including its contingent obligations, under this Convention which shall have been in effect before the cessation of its membership.

(b) Without prejudice to Section (a) above, the Agency shall enter into an arrangement with such State for the settlement of their respective claims and obligations. Any such arrangement shall be approved by the Board.

Article 54. Suspension of Operations

(a) The Board may, whenever it deems it justified, suspend the issuance of new guarantees for a specified period.

(b) In an emergency, the Board may suspend all activities of the Agency for a period not exceeding the duration of such emergency, provided that necessary arrangements shall be made for the protection of the interests of the Agency and of third parties.

(c) The decision to suspend operations shall have no effect on the obligations of the members under this Convention or on the obligations of the Agency towards holders of a guarantee or reinsurance policy or towards third parties.

Article 55. Liquidation

(a) The Council, by special majority, may decide to cease operations and to liquidate the Agency. Thereupon the Agency shall forthwith cease all activities, except those incident to the orderly realization, conservation and preservation of assets and settlement of obligations. Until final settlement and distribution of assets, the Agency shall remain in existence and all rights and obligations of members under this Convention shall continue unimpaired.

(b) No distribution of assets shall be made to members until all liabilities to holders of guarantees and other creditors shall have been discharged or provided for and until the Council shall have decided to make such distribution.

(c) Subject to the foregoing, the Agency shall distribute its remaining assets to members in proportion to each member's share in the subscribed capital. The Agency shall also distribute any remaining assets of the Sponsorship Trust Fund referred to in Annex I to this Convention to sponsoring members in the proportion which the investments sponsored by each bears to the total of sponsored investments. No member shall be entitled to its share in the assets of the Agency or the Sponsorship Trust Fund unless that member has settled all outstanding claims by the Agency against it. Every distribution of assets shall be made at such times as the Council shall determine and in such manner as it shall deem fair and equitable.

CHAPTER IX: SETTLEMENT OF DISPUTES

Article 56. Interpretation and Application of the Convention

(a) Any question of interpretation or application of the provisions of this Convention arising between any member of the Agency and the Agency or among members of the Agency shall be submitted to the Board for its decision. Any member which is particularly affected by the question and which is not otherwise represented by a national in the Board may send a representative to attend any meeting of the Board at which such question is considered.

(b) In any case where the Board has given a decision under Section (a) above, any member may require that the question be referred to the Council, whose decision shall be final. Pending the result of the referral to the Council, the Agency may, so far as it deems necessary, act on the basis of the decision of the Board.

Article 57. Disputes between the Agency and Members

(a) Without prejudice to the provisions of Article 56 and of Section (b) of this Article, any dispute between the Agency and a member or an agency thereof and any dispute between the Agency and a country (or agency thereof) which has ceased to be a member, shall be settled in accordance with the procedure set out in Annex II to this Convention.

(b) Disputes concerning claims of the Agency acting as subrogee of an investor shall be settled in accordance with either

(i) the procedure set out in Annex II to this Convention, or

(ii) an agreement to be entered into between the Agency and the member concerned on an alternative method or methods for the settlement of such disputes.

In the latter case, Annex II to this Convention shall serve as a basis for such an agreement which shall, in each case, be approved by the Board by special majority prior to the undertaking by the Agency of operations in the territories of the member concerned.

Article 58. Disputes Involving Holders of a Guarantee or Reinsurance

Any dispute arising under a contract of guarantee or reinsurance between the parties thereto shall be submitted to arbitration for final determination in accordance with such rules as shall be provided for or referred to in the contract of guarantee or reinsurance.

CHAPTER X: AMENDMENTS

Article 59. Amendment by Council

(a) This Convention and its Annexes may be amended by vote of three-fifths of the Governors exercising four-fifths of the total voting power, provided that:

(i) any amendment modifying the right to withdraw from the Agency provided in Article 51 or the limitation on liability provided in Section (d) of Article 8 shall require the affirmative vote of all Governors; and

(ii) any amendment modifying the loss-sharing arrangement provided in Articles 1 and 3 of Annex I to this Convention which will result in an increase in any member's liability thereunder shall require the affirmative vote of the Governor of each such member.

(b) Schedules A and B to this Convention may be amended by the Council by special majority.

(c) If an amendment affects any provision of Annex I to this Convention, total votes shall include the additional votes alloted under Article 7 of such Annex to sponsoring members and countries hosting sponsored investments.

Article 60. Procedure

Any proposal to amend this Convention, whether emanating from a member or a Governor or a Director, shall be communicated to the Chairman of the Board who shall bring the proposal before the Board. If the proposed amendment is recommended by the Board, it shall be submitted to the Council for approval in accordance with Article 59. When an amendment has been duly approved by the Council, the Agency shall so certify by formal communication addressed to all members. Amendments shall enter into force for all members ninety days after the date of the formal communication unless the Council shall specify a different date.

CHAPTER XI: FINAL PROVISIONS

Article 61. Entry into Force

(a) This Convention shall be open for signature on behalf of all members of the Bank and Switzerland and shall be subject to ratification, acceptance or approval by the signatory States in accordance with their constitutional procedures.

(b) This Convention shall enter into force on the day when not less than five instruments of ratification, acceptance or approval shall have been deposited on behalf of signatory States in Category One, and not less than fifteen such instruments shall have been deposited on behalf of signatory States in Category Two; provided that total subscriptions of these States amount to not less than one-third of the authorized capital of the Agency as prescribed in Article 5.

(c) For each State which deposits its instrument of ratification, acceptance or approval after this Convention shall have entered into force, this Convention shall enter into force on the date of such deposit.

(d) If this Convention shall not have entered into force within two years after its opening for signature, the President of the Bank shall convene a conference of interested countries to determine the future course of action.

Article 62. Inaugural Meeting

Upon entry into force of this Convention, the President of the Bank shall call the inaugural meeting of the Council. This meeting shall be held at the principal office of the Agency within sixty days from the date on which this Convention has entered into force or as soon as practicable thereafter.

Article 63. Depository

Instruments of ratification, acceptance or approval of this Convention and amendments thereto shall be deposited with the Bank which shall act as the depository of this Convention. The depository shall transmit certified copies of this Convention to States members of the Bank and to Switzerland.

Article 64. Registration

The depository shall register this Convention with the Secretariat of the United Nations in accordance with Article 102 of the Charter of the United Nations and the Regulations thereunder adopted by the General Assembly.

Article 65. Notification

The depository shall notify all signatory States and, upon the entry into force of this Convention, the Agency of the following:

(a) signatures of this Convention;
(b) deposits of instruments of ratification, acceptance and approval in accordance with Article 63;
(c) the date on which this Convention enters into force in accordance with Article 61;
(d) exclusions from territorial application pursuant to Article 66; and
(e) withdrawal of a member from the Agency pursuant to Article 51.

Article 66. Territorial Application

This Convention shall apply to all territories under the jurisdiction of a member including the territories for whose international relations a member is responsible, except those which are excluded by such member by written notice to the depository of this Convention either at the time of ratification, acceptance or approval or subsequently.

Article 67. Periodic Reviews

(a) The Council shall periodically undertake comprehensive reviews of the activities of the Agency as well as the results achieved with a view to introducing any changes required to enhance the Agency's ability to serve its objectives.
(b) The first such review shall take place five years after the entry into force of this Convention. The dates of subsequent reviews shall be determined by the Council.

DONE at Seoul, in a single copy which shall remain deposited in the archives of the International Bank for Reconstruction and Development, which has indicated by its signature below its agreement to fulfill the functions with which it is charged under this Convention.

G. CONVENTION ON THE SETTLEMENT OF INVESTMENT DISPUTES BETWEEN STATES AND NATIONALS OF OTHER STATES (ICSID)

PREAMBLE

The Contracting States

Considering the need for international cooperation for economic development, and the role of private international investment therein;

Bearing in mind the possibility that from time to time disputes may arise in connection with such investment between Contracting States and nationals of other Contracting States;

Recognizing that while such disputes would usually be subject to national legal processes, international methods of settlement may be appropriate in certain cases;

Attaching particular importance to the availability of facilities for international conciliation or arbitration to which Contracting States and nationals of other Contracting States may submit such disputes if they so desire;

Desiring to establish such facilities under the auspices of the International Bank for Reconstruction and Development;

Recognizing that mutual consent by the parties to submit such disputes to conciliation or to arbitration through such facilities constitutes a binding agreement which requires in particular that due consideration be given to any recommendation of conciliators, and that any arbitral award be complied with; and

Declaring that no Contracting State shall by the mere fact of its ratification, acceptance or approval of this Convention and without its consent be deemed to be under any obligation to submit any particular dispute to conciliation or arbitration,

Have agreed as follows:

CHAPTER I
International Centre for Settlement of Investment Disputes

Section 1
Establishment and Organization

Article 1

(1) There is hereby established the International Centre for Settlement of Investment Disputes (hereinafter called the Centre).

(2) The purpose of the Centre shall be to provide facilities for conciliation and arbitration of investment disputes between Contracting States and nationals of other Contracting States in accordance with the provisions of this Convention.

Article 2

The seat of the Centre shall be at the principal office of the International Bank for Reconstruction and Development (hereinafter called the Bank). The seat may be moved to another place by decision of the Administrative Council adopted by a majority of two-thirds of its members.

Article 3

The Centre shall have an Administrative Council and a Secretariat and shall maintain a Panel of Conciliators and a Panel of Arbitrators.

Section 2
The Administrative Council

Article 4

(1) The Administrative Council shall be composed of one representative of each Contracting State. An alternate may act as representative in case of his principal's absence from a meeting or inability to act.
(2) In the absence of a contrary designation, each governor and alternate governor of the Bank appointed by a Contracting State shall be ex officio its representative and its alternate respectively.

Article 5

The President of the Bank shall be ex officio Chairman of the Administrative Council (hereinafter called the Chairman) but shall have no vote. During his absence or inability to act and during any vacancy in the office of President of the Bank, the person for the time being acting as President shall act as Chairman of the Administrative Council.

Article 6

(1) Without prejudice to the powers and functions vested in it by other provisions of this Convention, the Administrative Council shall
  (a) adopt the administrative and financial regulations of the Centre;
  (b) adopt the rules of procedure for the institution of conciliation and arbitration proceedings;
  (c) adopt the rules of procedure for conciliation and arbitration proceedings (hereinafter called the Conciliation Rules and the Arbitration Rules);

(d) approve arrangements with the Bank for the use of the Bank's administrative facilities and services;

(e) determine the conditions of service of the Secretary-General and of any Deputy Secretary-General;

(f) adopt the annual budget of revenues and expenditures of the Centre;

(g) approve the annual report on the operation of the Centre.

The decisions referred to in sub-paragraphs (a), (b), (c) and (f) above shall be adopted by a majority of two-thirds of the members of the Administrative Council.

(2) The Administrative Council may appoint such committees as it considers necessary.

(3) The Administrative Council shall also exercise such other powers and perform such other functions as it shall determine to be necessary for the implementation of the provisions of this Convention.

Article 7

(1) The Administrative Council shall hold an annual meeting and such other meetings as may be determined by the Council, or convened by the Chairman, or convened by the Secretary-General at the request of not less than five members of the Council.

(2) Each member of the Administrative Council shall have one vote and, except as otherwise herein provided, all matters before the Council shall be decided by a majority of the votes cast.

(3) A quorum for any meeting of the Administrative Council shall be a majority of its members.

(4) The Administrative Council may establish, by a majority of two-thirds of its members, a procedure whereby the Chairman may seek a vote of the Council without convening a meeting of the Council. The vote shall be considered valid only if the majority of the members of the Council cast their votes within the time limit fixed by the said procedure.

Article 8

Members of the Administrative Council and the Chairman shall serve without remuneration from the Centre.

Section 3
The Secretariat

Article 9

The Secretariat shall consist of a Secretary-General, one or more Deputy Secretaries-General and staff.

Article 10

(1) The Secretary-General and any Deputy Secretary-General shall be elected by the Administrative Council by a majority of two-thirds of its members upon the nomination of the Chairman for a term of service not exceeding six years and shall be eligible for re-election. After consulting the members of the Administrative Council, the Chairman shall propose one or more candidates for each such office.

(2) The offices of Secretary-General and Deputy Secretary-General shall be incompatible with the exercise of any political function. Neither the Secretary-General nor any Deputy Secretary-General may hold any other employment or engage in any other occupation except with the approval of the Administrative Council.

(3) During the Secretary-General's absence or inability to act, and during any vacancy of the office of Secretary-General, the Deputy Secretary-General shall act as Secretary-General. If there shall be more than one Deputy Secretary-General, the Administrative Council shall determine in advance the order in which they shall act as Secretary-General.

Article 11

The Secretary-General shall be the legal representative and the principal officer of the Centre and shall be responsible for its administration, including the appointment of staff, in accordance with the provisions of this Convention and the rules adopted by the Administrative Council. He shall perform the function of registrar and shall have the power to authenticate arbitral awards rendered pursuant to this Convention, and to certify copies thereof.

Section 4
The Panels

Article 12

The Panel of Conciliators and the Panel of Arbitrators shall each consist of qualified persons, designated as hereinafter provided, who are willing to serve thereon.

Article 13

(1) Each Contracting State may designate to each Panel four persons who may but need not be its nationals.

(2) The Chairman may designate ten persons to each Panel. The persons so designated to a Panel shall each have a different nationality.

Article 14

(1) Persons designated to serve on the Panels shall be persons of high moral character and recognized competence in the fields of law, commerce, industry or finance, who may be relied upon to exercise independent judgment. Competence in the field of law shall be of particular importance in the case of persons on the Panel of Arbitrators.

(2) The Chairman, in designating persons to serve on the Panels, shall in addition pay due regard to the importance of assuring representation on the Panels of the principal legal systems of the world and of the main forms of economic activity.

Article 15

(1) Panel members shall serve for renewable periods of six years.

(2) In case of death or resignation of a member of a Panel, the authority which designated the member shall have the right to designate another person to serve for the remainder of that member's term.

(3) Panel members shall continue in office until their successors have been designated.

Article 16

(1) A person may serve on both Panels.

(2) If a person shall have been designated to serve on the same Panel by more than one Contracting State, or by one or more Contracting States and the Chairman, he shall be deemed to have been designated by the authority which first designated him or, if one such authority is the State of which he is a national, by that State.

(3) All designations shall be notified to the Secretary-General and shall take effect from the date on which the notification is received.

Section 5
Financing the Centre

Article 17

If the expenditure of the Centre cannot be met out of charges for the use of its facilities, or out of other receipts, the excess shall be borne by Contracting States which are members of the Bank in proportion to their respective subscriptions to the capital stock of the Bank, and by Contracting States which are not members of the Bank in accordance with rules adopted by the Administrative Council.

Section 6
Status, Immunities and Privileges

Article 18

The Centre shall have full international legal personality. The legal capacity of the Centre shall include the capacity

(a) to contract;
(b) to acquire and dispose of movable and immovable property;
(c) to institute legal proceedings.

Article 19

To enable the Centre to fulfil its functions, it shall enjoy in the territories of each Contracting State the immunities and privileges set forth in this Section.

Article 20

The Centre, its property and assets shall enjoy immunity from all legal process, except when the Centre waives this immunity.

Article 21

The Chairman, the members of the Administrative Council, persons acting as concili-ators or arbitrators or members of a Committee appointed pursuant to paragraph (3) of Article 52, and the officers and employees of the Secretariat

(a) shall enjoy immunity from legal process with respect to acts performed by them in the exercise of their functions, except when the Centre waives this immunity;
(b) not being local nationals, shall enjoy the same immunities from immigration restrictions, alien registration requirements and national service obligations, the same facilities as regards exchange restrictions and the same treatment in respect of travelling facilities as are accorded by Contracting States to the representatives, officials and employees of comparable rank of other Con-tracting States.

Article 22

The provisions of Article 21 shall apply to persons appearing in proceedings under this Convention as parties, agents, counsel, advocates, witnesses or experts; provided, however, that sub-paragraph (b) thereof shall apply only in connection with their travel to and from, and their stay at, the place where the proceedings are held.

Article 23

(1) The archives of the Centre shall be inviolable, wherever they may be.

(2) With regard to its official communications, the Centre shall be accorded by each Contracting State treatment not less favourable than that accorded to other international organizations.

Article 24

(1) The Centre, its assets, property and income, and its operations and transactions authorized by this Convention shall be exempt from all taxation and customs duties. The Centre shall also be exempt from liability for the collection or payment of any taxes or customs duties.

(2) Except in the case of local nationals, no tax shall be levied on or in respect of expense allowances paid by the Centre to the Chairman or members of the Administrative Council, or on or in respect of salaries, expense allowances or other emoluments paid by the Centre to officials or employees of the Secretariat.

(3) No tax shall be levied on or in respect of fees or expense allowances received by persons acting as conciliators, or arbitrators, or members of a Committee appointed pursuant to paragraph (3) of Article 52, in proceedings under this Convention, if the sole jurisdictional basis for such tax is the location of the Centre or the place where such proceedings are conducted or the place where such fees or allowances are paid.

CHAPTER II
Jurisdiction of the Centre

Article 25

(1) The jurisdiction of the Centre shall extend to any legal dispute arising directly out of an investment, between a Contracting State (or any constituent subdivision or agency of a Contracting State designated to the Centre by that State) and a national of another Contracting State, which the parties to the dispute consent in writing to submit to the Centre. When the parties have given their consent, no party may withdraw its consent unilaterally.

(2) 'National of another Contracting State' means:

    (a) any natural person who had the nationality of a Contracting State other than the State party to the dispute on the date on which the parties consented to submit such dispute to conciliation or arbitration as well as on the date on which the request was registered pursuant to paragraph (3) of Article 28 or paragraph (3) of Article 36, but does not include any person who on either date also had the nationality of the Contracting State party to the dispute; and

(b) any juridical person which had the nationality of a Contracting State other than the State party to the dispute on the date on which the parties consented to submit such dispute to conciliation or arbitration and any juridical person which had the nationality of the Contracting State party to the dispute on that date and which, because of foreign control, the parties have agreed should be treated as a national of another Contracting State for the purposes of this Convention.

(3) Consent by a constituent subdivision or agency of a Contracting State shall require the approval of that State unless that State notifies the Centre that no such approval is required.

(4) Any Contracting State may, at the time of ratification, acceptance or approval of this Convention or at any time thereafter, notify the Centre of the class or classes of disputes which it would or would not consider submitting to the jurisdiction of the Centre. The Secretary-General shall forthwith transmit such notification to all Contracting States. Such notification shall not constitute the consent required by paragraph (1).

Article 26

Consent of the parties to arbitration under this Convention shall, unless otherwise stated, be deemed consent to such arbitration to the exclusion of any other remedy. A Contracting State may require the exhaustion of local administrative or judicial remedies as a condition of its consent to arbitration under this Convention.

Article 27

(1) No Contracting State shall give diplomatic protection, or bring an international claim, in respect of a dispute which one of its nationals and another Contracting State shall have consented to submit or shall have submitted to arbitration under this Convention, unless such other Contracting State shall have failed to abide by and comply with the award rendered in such dispute.

(2) Diplomatic protection, for the purposes of paragraph (1), shall not include informal diplomatic exchanges for the sole purpose of facilitating a settlement of the dispute.

CHAPTER III
Conciliation

Section 1
Request for Conciliation

Article 28

(1) Any Contracting State or any national of a Contracting State wishing to institute conciliation proceedings shall address a request to that effect in writing to the Secretary-General who shall send a copy of the request to the other party.

(2) The request shall contain information concerning the issues in dispute, the identity of the parties and their consent to conciliation in accordance with the rules of procedure for the institution of conciliation and arbitration proceedings.

(3) The Secretary-General shall register the request unless he finds, on the basis of the information contained in the request, that the dispute is manifestly outside the jurisdiction of the Centre. He shall forthwith notify the parties of registration or refusal to register.

Section 2
Constitution of the Conciliation Commission

Article 29

(1) The Conciliation Commission (hereinafter called the Commission) shall be constituted as soon as possible after registration of a request pursuant to Article 28.

(2) (a) The Commission shall consist of a sole conciliator or any uneven number of conciliators appointed as the parties shall agree.

　　(b) Where the parties do not agree upon the number of conciliators and the method of their appointment, the Commission shall consist of three conciliators, one conciliator appointed by each party and the third, who shall be the president of the Commission, appointed by agreement of the parties.

Article 30

If the Commission shall not have been constituted within 90 days after notice of registration of the request has been dispatched by the Secretary-General in accordance with paragraph (3) of Article 28, or such other period as the parties may agree, the Chairman shall, at the request of either party and after consulting both parties as far as possible, appoint the conciliator or conciliators not yet appointed.

Article 31

(1) Conciliators may be appointed from outside the Panel of Conciliators, except in the case of appointments by the Chairman pursuant to Article 30.
(2) Conciliators appointed from outside the Panel of Conciliators shall possess the qualities stated in paragraph (1) of Article 14.

Section 3
Conciliation Proceedings

Article 32

(1) The Commission shall be the judge of its own competence.
(2) Any objection by a party to the dispute that that dispute is not within the jurisdiction of the Centre, or for other reasons is not within the competence of the Commission, shall be considered by the Commission which shall determine whether to deal with it as a preliminary question or to join it to the merits of the dispute.

Article 33

Any conciliation proceeding shall be conducted in accordance with the provisions of this Section and, except as the parties otherwise agree, in accordance with the Conciliation Rules in effect on the date on which the parties consented to conciliation. If any question of procedure arises which is not covered by this Section or the Conciliation Rules or any rules agreed by the parties, the Commission shall decide the question.

Article 34

(1) It shall be the duty of the Commission to clarify the issues in dispute between the parties and to endeavour to bring about agreement between them upon mutually acceptable terms. To that end, the Commission may at any stage of the proceedings and from time to time recommend terms of settlement to the parties. The parties shall cooperate in good faith with the Commission in order to enable the Commission to carry out its functions, and shall give their most serious consideration to its recommendations.
(2) If the parties reach agreement, the Commission shall draw up a report noting the issues in dispute and recording that the parties have reached agreement. If, at any stage of the proceedings, it appears to the Commission that there is no likelihood of agreement between the parties, it shall close the proceedings and shall draw up a report noting the submission of the dispute and recording the failure of the parties to reach agreement. If one party fails to appear or participate in the proceedings, the Commission shall close the proceedings and shall draw up a report noting that party's failure to appear or participate.

Article 35

Except as the parties to the dispute shall otherwise agree, neither party to a conciliation proceeding shall be entitled in any other proceeding, whether before arbitrators or in a court of law or otherwise, to invoke or rely on any views expressed or statements or admissions or offers of settlement made by the other party in the conciliation proceedings, or the report or any recommendations made by the Commission.

CHAPTER IV
Arbitration

Section 1
Request for Arbitration

Article 36

(1) Any Contracting State or any national of a Contracting State wishing to institute arbitration proceedings shall address a request to that effect in writing to the Secretary-General who shall send a copy of the request to the other party.

(2) The request shall contain information concerning the issues in dispute, the identity of the parties and their consent to arbitration in accordance with the rules of procedure for the institution of conciliation and arbitration proceedings.

(3) The Secretary-General shall register the request unless he finds, on the basis of the information contained in the request, that the dispute is manifestly outside the jurisdiction of the Centre. He shall forthwith notify the parties of registration or refusal to register.

Section 2
Constitution of the Tribunal

Article 37

(1) The Arbitral Tribunal (hereinafter called the Tribunal) shall be constituted as soon as possible after registration of a request pursuant to Article 36.

(2) (a) The Tribunal shall consist of a sole arbitrator or any uneven number of arbitrators appointed as the parties shall agree.

(b) Where the parties do not agree upon the number of arbitrators and the method of their appointment, the Tribunal shall consist of three arbitrators, one arbitrator appointed by each party and the third, who shall be the president of the Tribunal, appointed by agreement of the parties.

Article 38

If the Tribunal shall not have been constituted within 90 days after notice of registration of the request has been dispatched by the Secretary-General in accordance with paragraph (3) of Article 36, or such other period as the parties may agree, the Chairman shall, at the request of either party and after consulting both parties as far as possible, appoint the arbitrator or arbitrators not yet appointed. Arbitrators appointed by the Chairman pursuant to this Article shall not be nationals of the Contracting State party to the dispute or of the Contracting State whose national is a party to the dispute.

Article 39

The majority of the arbitrators shall be nationals of States other than the Contracting State party to the dispute and the Contracting State whose national is a party to the dispute; provided, however, that the foregoing provisions of this Article shall not apply if the sole arbitrator or each individual member of the Tribunal has been appointed by agreement of the parties.

Article 40

(1) Arbitrators may be appointed from outside the Panel of Arbitrators, except in the case of appointments by the Chairman pursuant to Article 38.
(2) Arbitrators appointed from outside the Panel of Arbitrators shall possess the qualities stated in paragraph (1) of Article 14.

Section 3
Powers and Functions of the Tribunal

Article 41

(1) The Tribunal shall be the judge of its own competence.
(2) Any objection by a party to the dispute that that dispute is not within the jurisdiction of the Centre, or for other reasons is not within the competence of the Tribunal, shall be considered by the Tribunal which shall determine whether to deal with it as a preliminary question or to join it to the merits of the dispute.

Article 42

(1) The Tribunal shall decide a dispute in accordance with such rules of law as may be agreed by the parties. In the absence of such agreement, the Tribunal shall apply the law of the Contracting State party to the dispute (including its rules on the conflict of laws) and such rules of international law as may be applicable.

(2) The Tribunal may not bring in a finding of non liquet on the ground of silence or obscurity of the law.

(3) The provisions of paragraphs (1) and (2) shall not prejudice the power of the Tribunal to decide a dispute ex aequo et bono if the parties so agree.

Article 43

Except as the parties otherwise agree, the Tribunal may, if it deems it necessary at any stage of the proceedings,

(a) call upon the parties to produce documents or other evidence, and
(b) visit the scene connected with the dispute, and conduct such inquiries there as it may deem appropriate.

Article 44

Any arbitration proceeding shall be conducted in accordance with the provisions of this Section and, except as the parties otherwise agree, in accordance with the Arbitration Rules in effect on the date on which the parties consented to arbitration. If any question of procedure arises which is not covered by this Section or the Arbitration Rules or any rules agreed by the parties, the Tribunal shall decide the question.

Article 45

(1) Failure of a party to appear or to present his case shall not be deemed an admission of the other party's assertions.

(2) If a party fails to appear or to present his case at any stage of the proceedings the other party may request the Tribunal to deal with the questions submitted to it and to render an award. Before rendering an award, the Tribunal shall notify, and grant a period of grace to, the party failing to appear or to present its case, unless it is satisfied that that party does not intend to do so.

Article 46

Except as the parties otherwise agree, the Tribunal shall, if requested by a party, determine any incidental or additional claims or counter-claims arising directly out of the subject-matter of the dispute provided that they are within the scope of the consent of the parties and are otherwise within the jurisdiction of the Centre.

Article 47

Except as the parties otherwise agree, the Tribunal may, if it considers that the circumstances so require, recommend any provisional measures which should be taken to preserve the respective rights of either party.

Section 4
The Award

Article 48

(1) The Tribunal shall decide questions by a majority of the votes of all its members.
(2) The award of the Tribunal shall be in writing and shall be signed by the members of the Tribunal who voted for it.
(3) The award shall deal with every question submitted to the Tribunal, and shall state the reasons upon which it is based.
(4) Any member of the Tribunal may attach his individual opinion to the award, whether he dissents from the majority or not, or a statement of his dissent.
(5) The Centre shall not publish the award without the consent of the parties.

Article 49

(1) The Secretary-General shall promptly dispatch certified copies of the award to the parties. The award shall be deemed to have been rendered on the date on which the certified copies were dispatched.
(2) The Tribunal upon the request of a party made within 45 days after the date on which the award was rendered may after notice to the other party decide any question which it had omitted to decide in the award, and shall rectify any clerical, arithmetical or similar error in the award. Its decision shall become part of the award and shall be notified to the parties in the same manner as the award. The periods of time provided for under paragraph (2) of Article 51 and paragraph (2) and Article 52 shall run from the date on which the decision was rendered.

Section 5
Interpretation, Revision and Annulment of the Award

Article 50

(1) If any dispute shall arise between the parties as to the meaning or scope of an award, either party may request interpretation of the award by an application in writing addressed to the Secretary-General.
(2) The request shall, if possible, be submitted to the Tribunal which rendered the award. If this shall not be possible, a new Tribunal shall be constituted in accordance with Section 2 of this Chapter. The Tribunal may, if it considers that the circumstances so require, stay enforcement of the award pending its decision.

Article 51

(1) Either party may request revision of the award by an application in writing addressed to the Secretary-General on the ground of discovery of some fact of such a nature as decisively to affect the award, provided that when the award was rendered that fact was unknown to the Tribunal and to the applicant and that the applicant's ignorance of that fact was not due to negligence.

(2) The application shall be made within 90 days after the discovery of such fact and in any event within three years after the date on which the award was rendered.

(3) The request shall, if possible, be submitted to the Tribunal which rendered the award. If this shall not be possible, a new Tribunal shall be constituted in accordance with Section 2 of this Chapter.

(4) The Tribunal may, if it considers that the circumstances so require, stay enforcement of the award pending its decision. If the applicant requests a stay of enforcement of the award in his application, enforcement shall be stayed provisionally until the Tribunal rules on such request.

Article 52

(1) Either party may request annulment of the award by an application in writing addressed to the Secretary-General on one or more of the following grounds:
  (a) that the Tribunal was not properly constituted;
  (b) that the Tribunal has manifestly exceeded it powers;
  (c) that there was corruption on the part of a member of the Tribunal;
  (d) that there has been a serious departure from a fundamental rule of procedure; or
  (e) that the award has failed to state the reasons on which it is based.

(2) The application shall be made within 120 days after the date on which the award was rendered except that when annulment is requested on the ground of corruption such application shall be made within 120 days after discovery of the corruption and in any event within three years after the date on which the award was rendered.

(3) On receipt of the request the Chairman shall forthwith appoint from the Panel of Arbitrators an ad hoc Committee of three persons. None of the members of the Committee shall have been a member of the Tribunal which rendered the award, shall be of the same nationality as any such member, shall be a national of the State party to the dispute or of the State whose national is a party to the dispute, shall have been designated to the Panel of Arbitrators by either of those States, or shall have acted as a conciliator in the same dispute. The Committee shall have the authority to annul the award or any part thereof on any of the grounds set forth in paragraph (1).

(4) The provisions of Articles 41-45, 48, 49, 53 and 54, and of Chapters VI and VII shall apply mutatis mutandis to proceedings before the Committee.

(5) The Committee may, if it considers that the circumstances so require, stay enforcement of the award pending its decision. If the applicant requests a stay of enforcement of the award in his application, enforcement shall be stayed provisionally until the Committee rules on such request.

(6) If the award is annulled the dispute shall, at the request of either party, be submitted to a new Tribunal constituted in accordance with Section 2 of this Chapter.

Section 6
Recognition and Enforcement of the Award

Article 53

(1) The award shall be binding on the parties and shall not be subject to any appeal or to any other remedy except those provided for in this Convention. Each party shall abide by and comply with the terms of the award except to the extent that enforcement shall have been stayed pursuant to the relevant provisions of this Convention.

(2) For the purposes of this Section, 'award' shall include any decision interpreting, revising or annulling such award pursuant to Articles 50, 51 or 52.

Article 54

(1) Each Contracting State shall recognize an award rendered pursuant to this Convention as binding and enforce the pecuniary obligations imposed by that award within its territories as if it were a final judgment of a court in that State. A Contracting State with a federal constitution may enforce such an award in or through its federal courts and may provide that such courts shall treat the award as if it were a final judgment of the courts of a constituent state.

(2) A party seeking recognition or enforcement in the territories of a Contracting State shall furnish to a competent court or other authority which such State shall have designated for this purpose a copy of the award certified by the Secretary-General. Each Contracting State shall notify the Secretary-General of the designation of the competent court or other authority for this purpose and of any subsequent change in such designation.

(3) Execution of the award shall be governed by the laws concerning the execution of judgments in force in the State in whose territories such execution is sought.

Article 55

Nothing in Article 54 shall be construed as derogating from the law in force in any Contracting State relating to immunity of that State or of any foreign State from execution.

CHAPTER V
Replacement and Disqualification of Conciliators
and Arbitrators

Article 56

(1) After a Commission or a Tribunal has been constituted and proceedings have begun, its composition shall remain unchanged; provided, however, that if a conciliator or an arbitrator should die, become incapacitated, or resign, the resulting vacancy shall be filled in accordance with the provisions of Section 2 of Chapter III or Section 2 of Chapter IV.

(2) A member of a Commission or Tribunal shall continue to serve in that capacity notwithstanding that he shall have ceased to be a member of the Panel.

(3) If a conciliator or arbitrator appointed by a party shall have resigned without the consent of the Commission or Tribunal of which he was a member, the Chairman shall appoint a person from the appropriate Panel to fill the resulting vacancy.

Article 57

A party may propose to a Commission or Tribunal the disqualification of any of its members on account of any fact indicating a manifest lack of the qualities required by paragraph (1) of Article 14. A party to arbitration proceedings may, in addition, propose the disqualification of an arbitrator on the ground that he was ineligible for appointment to the Tribunal under Section 2 of Chapter IV.

Article 58

The decision on any proposal to disqualify a conciliator or arbitrator shall be taken by the other members of the Commission or Tribunal as the case may be, provided that where those members are equally divided, or in the case of a proposal to disqualify a sole conciliator or arbitrator, or a majority of the conciliators or arbitrators, the Chairman shall take that decision. If it is decided that the proposal is well-founded the conciliator or arbitrator to whom the decision relates shall be replaced in accordance with the provisions of Section 2 of Chapter III or Section 2 of Chapter IV.

CHAPTER VI
Cost of Proceedings

Article 59

The charges payable by the parties for the use of the facilities of the Centre shall be determined by the Secretary-General in accordance with the regulations adopted by the Administrative Council.

Article 60

(1) Each Commission and each Tribunal shall determine the fees and expenses of its members within limits established from time to time by the Administrative Council and after consultation with the Secretary-General.

(2) Nothing in paragraph (1) of this Article shall preclude the parties from agreeing in advance with the Commission or Tribunal concerned upon the fees and expenses of its members.

Article 61

(1) In the case of conciliation proceedings the fees and expenses of members of the Commission as well as the charges for the use of the facilities of the Centre, shall be borne equally by the parties. Each party shall bear any other expenses it incurs in connection with the proceedings.

(2) In the case of arbitration proceedings the Tribunal shall, except as the parties otherwise agree, assess the expenses incurred by the parties in connection with the proceedings, and shall decide how and by whom those expenses, the fees and expenses of the members of the tribunal and the charges for the use of the facilities of the Centre shall be paid. Such decision shall form part of the award.

CHAPTER VII
Place of Proceedings

Article 62

Conciliation and arbitration proceedings shall be held at the seat of the Centre except as hereinafter provided.

Article 63

Conciliation and arbitration proceedings may be held, if the parties so agree,

(a) at the seat of the Permanent Court of Arbitration or of any other appropriate institution, whether private or public, with which the Centre may make arrangements for that purpose; or

(b) at any other place approved by the Commission or Tribunal after consultation with the Secretary-General.

CHAPTER VIII
Disputes between Contracting States

Article 64

Any dispute arising between Contracting States concerning the interpretation or application of this Convention which is not settled by negotiation shall be referred to the International Court of Justice by the application of any party to such dispute, unless the States concerned agree to another method of settlement.

CHAPTER IX
Amendment

Article 65

Any Contracting State may propose amendment of this Convention. The text of a proposed amendment shall be communicated to the Secretary-General not less than 90 days prior to the meeting of the Administrative Council at which such amendment is to be considered and shall forthwith be transmitted by him to all the members of the Administrative Council.

Article 66

(1) If the Administrative Council shall so decide by a majority of two-thirds of its members, the proposed amendment shall be circulated to all Contracting States for ratification, acceptance or approval. Each amendment shall enter into force 30 days after dispatch by the depositary of this Convention of a notification to Contracting States that all Contracting States have ratified, accepted or approved the amendment.

(2) No amendment shall affect the rights and obligations under this Convention of any Contracting State or of any of its constituent subdivisions or agencies, or of any national of such State arising out of consent to the jurisdiction of the Centre given before the date of entry into force of the amendment.

CHAPTER X
Final Provisions

Article 67

This Convention shall be open for signature on behalf of States members of the Bank. It shall also be open for signature on behalf of any other State which is a party to the Statute of the International Court of Justice and which the Administrative Council, by a vote of two-thirds of its members, shall have invited to sign the Convention.

Article 68

(1) This Convention shall be subject to ratification, acceptance or approval by the signatory States in accordance with their respective constitutional procedures.

(2) This Convention shall enter into force 30 days after the date of deposit of the twentieth instrument of ratification, acceptance or approval. It shall enter into force for each State which subsequently deposits its instrument of ratification, acceptance or approval 30 days after the date of such deposit.

Article 69

Each Contracting State shall take such legislative or other measures as may be necessary for making the provisions of this Convention effective in its territories.

Article 70

This Convention shall apply to all territories for whose international relations a Contracting State is responsible, except those which are excluded by such State by written notice to the depositary of this Convention either at the time of ratification, acceptance or approval or subsequently.

Article 71

Any Contracting State may denounce this Convention by written notice to the depositary of this Convention. The denunciation shall take effect six months after receipt of such notice.

Article 72

Notice by a Contracting State pursuant to Articles 70 or 71 shall not affect the rights or obligations under this Convention of that State or of any of its constituent subdivisions or agencies or of any national of that State arising out of consent to the jurisdiction of the Centre given by one of them before such notice was received by the depositary.

Article 73

Instruments of ratification, acceptance or approval of this Convention and of amendments thereto shall be deposited with the Bank which shall act as the depositary of this Convention. The depositary shall transmit certified copies of this Convention to States members of the Bank and to any other State invited to sign the Convention.

Article 74

The depositary shall register this Convention with the Secretariat of the United Nations in accordance with Article 102 of the Charter of the United Nations and the Regulations thereunder adopted by the General Assembly.

Article 75

The depositary shall notify all signatory States of the following:

(a) signatures in accordance with Article 67;
(b) deposits of instruments of ratification, acceptance and approval in accordance with Article 73;
(c) the date on which this Convention enters into force in accordance with Article 68;
(d) exclusions from territorial application pursuant to Article 70;
(e) the date on which any amendment of this Convention enters into force in accordance with Article 66; and
(f) denunciations in accordance with Article 71.

H. 2012 UNITED STATES MODEL BILATERAL INVESTMENT TREATY

TREATY BETWEEN
THE GOVERNMENT OF THE UNITED STATES OF AMERICA
AND THE GOVERNMENT OF [Country]
CONCERNING THE ENCOURAGEMENT
AND RECIPROCAL PROTECTION OF INVESTMENT

The Government of the United States of America and the Government of [Country] (hereinafter the "Parties");

Desiring to promote greater economic cooperation between them with respect to investment by nationals and enterprises of one Party in the territory of the other Party;

Recognizing that agreement on the treatment to be accorded such investment will stimulate the flow of private capital and the economic development of the Parties;

Agreeing that a stable framework for investment will maximize effective utilization of economic resources and improve living standards;

Recognizing the importance of providing effective means of asserting claims and enforcing rights with respect to investment under national law as well as through international arbitration;

Desiring to achieve these objectives in a manner consistent with the protection of health, safety, and the environment, and the promotion of internationally recognized labor rights;

Having resolved to conclude a Treaty concerning the encouragement and reciprocal protection of investment;

Have agreed as follows:

SECTION A

Article 1: Definitions

For purposes of this Treaty:

"central level of government" means:

  (a) for the United States, the federal level of government; and
  (b) for [Country], [_____].
    "Centre" means the International Centre for Settlement of Investment Disputes ("ICSID") established by the ICSID Convention.
    "claimant" means an investor of a Party that is a party to an investment dispute with the other Party.

"**covered investment**" means, with respect to a Party, an investment in its territory of an investor of the other Party in existence as of the date of entry into force of this Treaty or established, acquired, or expanded thereafter.

"**disputing parties**" means the claimant and the respondent.

"**disputing party**" means either the claimant or the respondent.

"**enterprise**" means any entity constituted or organized under applicable law, whether or not for profit, and whether privately or governmentally owned or controlled, including a corporation, trust, partnership, sole proprietorship, joint venture, association, or similar organization; and a branch of an enterprise.

"**enterprise of a Party**" means an enterprise constituted or organized under the law of a Party, and a branch located in the territory of a Party and carrying out business activities there.

"**existing**" means in effect on the date of entry into force of this Treaty.

"**freely usable currency**" means "freely usable currency" as determined by the International Monetary Fund under its *Articles of Agreement*.

"**GATS**" means the *General Agreement on Trade in Services*, contained in Annex 1B to the WTO Agreement.

"**government procurement**" means the process by which a government obtains the use of or acquires goods or services, or any combination thereof, for governmental purposes and not with a view to commercial sale or resale, or use in the production or supply of goods or services for commercial sale or resale.

"**ICSID Additional Facility Rules**" means the *Rules Governing the Additional Facility for the Administration of Proceedings by the Secretariat of the International Centre for Settlement of Investment Disputes*.

"**ICSID Convention**" means the *Convention on the Settlement of Investment Disputes between States and Nationals of Other States*, done at Washington, March 18, 1965.

["**Inter-American Convention**" means the *Inter-American Convention on International Commercial Arbitration*, done at Panama, January 30, 1975.]

"**investment**" means every asset that an investor owns or controls, directly or indirectly, that has the characteristics of an investment, including such characteristics as the commitment of capital or other resources, the expectation of gain or profit, or the assumption of risk. Forms that an investment may take include:

(a) an enterprise;

(b) shares, stock, and other forms of equity participation in an enterprise;

(c) bonds, debentures, other debt instruments, and loans;[1]

(d) futures, options, and other derivatives;

(e) turnkey, construction, management, production, concession, revenue-sharing, and other similar contracts;

(f) intellectual property rights;

(g) licenses, authorizations, permits, and similar rights conferred pursuant to domestic law;[2, 3] and

(h) other tangible or intangible, movable or immovable property, and related property rights, such as leases, mortgages, liens, and pledges.

"investment agreement" means a written agreement[4] between a national authority[5] of a Party and a covered investment or an investor of the other Party, on which the covered investment or the investor relies in establishing or acquiring a covered investment other than the written agreement itself, that grants rights to the covered investment or investor:

(a) with respect to natural resources that a national authority controls, such as for their exploration, extraction, refining, transportation, distribution, or sale;

(b) to supply services to the public on behalf of the Party, such as power generation or distribution, water treatment or distribution, or telecommunications; or

(c) to undertake infrastructure projects, such as the construction of roads, bridges, canals, dams, or pipelines, that are not for the exclusive or predominant use and benefit of the government.

---

1. Some forms of debt, such as bonds, debentures, and long-term notes, are more likely to have the characteristics of an investment, while other forms of debt, such as claims to payment that are immediately due and result from the sale of goods or services, are less likely to have such characteristics.

2. Whether a particular type of license, authorization, permit, or similar instrument (including a concession, to the extent that it has the nature of such an instrument) has the characteristics of an investment depends on such factors as the nature and extent of the rights that the holder has under the law of the Party. Among the licenses, authorizations, permits, and similar instruments that do not have the characteristics of an investment are those that do not create any rights protected under domestic law. For greater certainty, the foregoing is without prejudice to whether any asset associated with the license, authorization, permit, or similar instrument has the characteristics of an investment.

3. The term "investment" does not include an order or judgment entered in a judicial or administrative action.

4. "Written agreement" refers to an agreement in writing, executed by both parties, whether in a single instrument or in multiple instruments, that creates an exchange of rights and obligations, binding on both parties under the law applicable under Article 30[Governing Law](2). For greater certainty, (a) a unilateral act of an administrative or judicial authority, such as a permit, license, or authorization issued by a Party solely in its regulatory capacity, or a decree, order, or judgment, standing alone; and (b) an administrative or judicial consent decree or order, shall not be considered a written agreement.

5. For purposes of this definition, "national authority" means (a) for the United States, an authority at the central level of government; and (b) for [Country], [ ].

"investment authorization"[6] means an authorization that the foreign investment authority of a Party grants to a covered investment or an investor of the other Party.

"investor of a non-Party" means, with respect to a Party, an investor that attempts to make, is making, or has made an investment in the territory of that Party, that is not an investor of either Party.

"investor of a Party" means a Party or state enterprise thereof, or a national or an enterprise of a Party, that attempts to make, is making, or has made an investment in the territory of the other Party; provided, however, that a natural person who is a dual national shall be deemed to be exclusively a national of the State of his or her dominant and effective nationality.

"measure" includes any law, regulation, procedure, requirement, or practice.

"national" means:

(a) for the United States, a natural person who is a national of the United States as defined in Title III of the Immigration and Nationality Act; and

(b) for [Country], [_____].

"New York Convention" means the *United Nations Convention on the Recognition and Enforcement of Foreign Arbitral Awards*, done at New York, June 10, 1958.

"non-disputing Party" means the Party that is not a party to an investment dispute.

"person" means a natural person or an enterprise.

"person of a Party" means a national or an enterprise of a Party.

"protected information" means confidential business information or information that is privileged or otherwise protected from disclosure under a Party's law.

"regional level of government" means:

(a) for the United States, a state of the United States, the District of Columbia, or Puerto Rico; and

(b) for [Country], [_____].

"respondent" means the Party that is a party to an investment dispute.

"Secretary-General" means the Secretary-General of ICSID.

"state enterprise" means an enterprise owned, or controlled through ownership interests, by a Party.

"territory" means:

(a) with respect to the United States,

    (i) the customs territory of the United States, which includes the 50 states, the District of Columbia, and Puerto Rico;

---

6. For greater certainty, actions taken by a Party to enforce laws of general application, such as competition laws, are not encompassed within this definition.

> (ii) the foreign trade zones located in the United States and Puerto Rico.

(b) with respect to [Country,] [_____].

(c) with respect to each Party, the territorial sea and any area beyond the territorial sea of the Party within which, in accordance with customary international law as reflected in the United Nations Convention on the Law of the Sea, the Party may exercise sovereign rights or jurisdiction.

"TRIPS Agreement" means the *Agreement on Trade-Related Aspects of Intellectual Property Rights*, contained in Annex 1C to the WTO Agreement.[7]

"UNCITRAL Arbitration Rules" means the arbitration rules of the United Nations Commission on International Trade Law.

"WTO Agreement" means the *Marrakesh Agreement Establishing the World Trade Organization*, done on April 15, 1994.

Article 2: Scope and Coverage

1. This Treaty applies to measures adopted or maintained by a Party relating to:
   (a) investors of the other Party;
   (b) covered investments; and
   (c) with respect to Articles 8 [Performance Requirements], 12 [Investment and Environment], and 13 [Investment and Labor], all investments in the territory of the Party.

2. A Party's obligations under Section A shall apply:
   (a) to a state enterprise or other person when it exercises any regulatory, administrative, or other governmental authority delegated to it by that Party;[8] and
   (b) to the political subdivisions of that Party.

3. For greater certainty, this Treaty does not bind either Party in relation to any act or fact that took place or any situation that ceased to exist before the date of entry into force of this Treaty.

Article 3: National Treatment

1. Each Party shall accord to investors of the other Party treatment no less favorable than that it accords, in like circumstances, to its own investors with respect to the establishment, acquisition, expansion, management, conduct, operation, and sale or other disposition of investments in its territory.

---

7. For greater certainty, "TRIPS Agreement" includes any waiver in force between the Parties of any provision of the TRIPS Agreement granted by WTO Members in accordance with the WTO Agreement.
8. For greater certainty, government authority that has been delegated includes a legislative grant, and a government order, directive or other action transferring to the state enterprise or other person, or authorizing the exercise by the state enterprise or other person of, governmental authority.

2. Each Party shall accord to covered investments treatment no less favorable than that it accords, in like circumstances, to investments in its territory of its own investors with respect to the establishment, acquisition, expansion, management, conduct, operation, and sale or other disposition of investments.

3. The treatment to be accorded by a Party under paragraphs 1 and 2 means, with respect to a regional level of government, treatment no less favorable than the treatment accorded, in like circumstances, by that regional level of government to natural persons resident in and enterprises constituted under the laws of other regional levels of government of the Party of which it forms a part, and to their respective investments.

Article 4: Most-Favored-Nation Treatment

1. Each Party shall accord to investors of the other Party treatment no less favorable than that it accords, in like circumstances, to investors of any non-Party with respect to the establishment, acquisition, expansion, management, conduct, operation, and sale or other disposition of investments in its territory.

2. Each Party shall accord to covered investments treatment no less favorable than that it accords, in like circumstances, to investments in its territory of investors of any non-Party with respect to the establishment, acquisition, expansion, management, conduct, operation, and sale or other disposition of investments.

Article 5: Minimum Standard of Treatment[9]

1. Each Party shall accord to covered investments treatment in accordance with customary international law, including fair and equitable treatment and full protection and security.

2. For greater certainty, paragraph 1 prescribes the customary international law minimum standard of treatment of aliens as the minimum standard of treatment to be afforded to covered investments. The concepts of "fair and equitable treatment" and "full protection and security" do not require treatment in addition to or beyond that which is required by that standard, and do not create additional substantive rights. The obligation in paragraph 1 to provide:

    (a) "fair and equitable treatment" includes the obligation not to deny justice in criminal, civil, or administrative adjudicatory proceedings in accordance with the principle of due process embodied in the principal legal systems of the world; and

    (b) "full protection and security" requires each Party to provide the level of police protection required under customary international law.

---

9. Article 5 [Minimum Standard of Treatment] shall be interpreted in accordance with Annex A.

3. A determination that there has been a breach of another provision of this Treaty, or of a separate international agreement, does not establish that there has been a breach of this Article.

4. Notwithstanding Article 14 [Non-Conforming Measures](5)(b) [subsidies and grants], each Party shall accord to investors of the other Party, and to covered investments, non-discriminatory treatment with respect to measures it adopts or maintains relating to losses suffered by investments in its territory owing to armed conflict or civil strife.

5. Notwithstanding paragraph 4, if an investor of a Party, in the situations referred to in paragraph 4, suffers a loss in the territory of the other Party resulting from:

   (a) requisitioning of its covered investment or part thereof by the latter's forces or authorities; or

   (b) destruction of its covered investment or part thereof by the latter's forces or authorities, which was not required by the necessity of the situation, the latter Party shall provide the investor restitution, compensation, or both, as appropriate, for such loss. Any compensation shall be prompt, adequate, and effective in accordance with Article 6 [Expropriation and Compensation](2) through (4), *mutatis mutandis.*

6. Paragraph 4 does not apply to existing measures relating to subsidies or grants that would be inconsistent with Article 3 [National Treatment] but for Article 14 [Non-Conforming Measures](5)(b) [subsidies and grants].

Article 6: Expropriation and Compensation[10]

1. Neither Party may expropriate or nationalize a covered investment either directly or indirectly through measures equivalent to expropriation or nationalization ("expropriation"), except:

   (a) for a public purpose;

   (b) in a non-discriminatory manner;

   (c) on payment of prompt, adequate, and effective compensation; and

   (d) in accordance with due process of law and Article 5 [Minimum Standard of Treatment](1) through (3).

2. The compensation referred to in paragraph 1(c) shall:

   (a) be paid without delay;

   (b) be equivalent to the fair market value of the expropriated investment immediately before the expropriation took place ("the date of expropriation");

   (c) not reflect any change in value occurring because the intended expropriation had become known earlier; and

   (d) be fully realizable and freely transferable.

10. Article 6 [Expropriation] shall be interpreted in accordance with Annexes A and B.

3. If the fair market value is denominated in a freely usable currency, the compensation referred to in paragraph 1(c) shall be no less than the fair market value on the date of expropriation, plus interest at a commercially reasonable rate for that currency, accrued from the date of expropriation until the date of payment.

4. If the fair market value is denominated in a currency that is not freely usable, the compensation referred to in paragraph 1(c) – converted into the currency of payment at the market rate of exchange prevailing on the date of payment – shall be no less than:

   (a) the fair market value on the date of expropriation, converted into a freely usable currency at the market rate of exchange prevailing on that date, plus

   (b) interest, at a commercially reasonable rate for that freely usable currency, accrued from the date of expropriation until the date of payment.

5. This Article does not apply to the issuance of compulsory licenses granted in relation to intellectual property rights in accordance with the TRIPS Agreement, or to the revocation, limitation, or creation of intellectual property rights, to the extent that such issuance, revocation, limitation, or creation is consistent with the TRIPS Agreement.

Article 7: Transfers

1. Each Party shall permit all transfers relating to a covered investment to be made freely and without delay into and out of its territory. Such transfers include:

   (a) contributions to capital;

   (b) profits, dividends, capital gains, and proceeds from the sale of all or any part of the covered investment or from the partial or complete liquidation of the covered investment;

   (c) interest, royalty payments, management fees, and technical assistance and other fees;

   (d) payments made under a contract, including a loan agreement;

   (e) payments made pursuant to Article 5 [Minimum Standard of Treatment](4) and (5) and Article 6 [Expropriation and Compensation]; and

   (f) payments arising out of a dispute.

2. Each Party shall permit transfers relating to a covered investment to be made in a freely usable currency at the market rate of exchange prevailing at the time of transfer.

3. Each Party shall permit returns in kind relating to a covered investment to be made as authorized or specified in a written agreement between the Party and a covered investment or an investor of the other Party.

4. Notwithstanding paragraphs 1 through 3, a Party may prevent a transfer through the equitable, non-discriminatory, and good faith application of its laws relating to:

(a) bankruptcy, insolvency, or the protection of the rights of creditors;

(b) issuing, trading, or dealing in securities, futures, options, or derivatives;

(c) criminal or penal offenses;

(d) financial reporting or record keeping of transfers when necessary to assist law enforcement or financial regulatory authorities; or

(e) ensuring compliance with orders or judgments in judicial or administrative proceedings.

Article 8: Performance Requirements

1. Neither Party may, in connection with the establishment, acquisition, expansion, management, conduct, operation, or sale or other disposition of an investment of an investor of a Party or of a non-Party in its territory, impose or enforce any requirement or enforce any commitment or undertaking:[11]

   (a) to export a given level or percentage of goods or services;

   (b) to achieve a given level or percentage of domestic content;

   (c) to purchase, use, or accord a preference to goods produced in its territory, or to purchase goods from persons in its territory;

   (d) to relate in any way the volume or value of imports to the volume or value of exports or to the amount of foreign exchange inflows associated with such investment;

   (e) to restrict sales of goods or services in its territory that such investment produces or supplies by relating such sales in any way to the volume or value of its exports or foreign exchange earnings;

   (f) to transfer a particular technology, a production process, or other proprietary knowledge to a person in its territory;

   (g) to supply exclusively from the territory of the Party the goods that such investment produces or the services that it supplies to a specific regional market or to the world market; or

   (h) (i) to purchase, use, or accord a preference to, in its territory, technology of the Party or of persons of the Party;[12] or

   (ii) that prevents the purchase or use of, or the according of a preference to, in its territory, particular technology,

   so as to afford protection on the basis of nationality to its own investors or investments or to technology of the Party or of persons of the Party.

2. Neither Party may condition the receipt or continued receipt of an advantage, in connection with the establishment, acquisition, expansion, management,

---

11. For greater certainty, a condition for the receipt or continued receipt of an advantage referred to in paragraph 2 does not constitute a "commitment or undertaking" for the purposes of paragraph 1.

12. For purposes of this Article, the term "technology of the Party or of persons of the Party" includes technology that is owned by the Party or persons of the Party, and technology for which the Party holds, or persons of the Party hold, an exclusive license.

conduct, operation, or sale or other disposition of an investment in its territory of an investor of a Party or of a non-Party, on compliance with any requirement:

(a) to achieve a given level or percentage of domestic content;

(b) to purchase, use, or accord a preference to goods produced in its territory, or to purchase goods from persons in its territory;

(c) to relate in any way the volume or value of imports to the volume or value of exports or to the amount of foreign exchange inflows associated with such investment; or

(d) to restrict sales of goods or services in its territory that such investment produces or supplies by relating such sales in any way to the volume or value of its exports or foreign exchange earnings.

3. (a) Nothing in paragraph 2 shall be construed to prevent a Party from conditioning the receipt or continued receipt of an advantage, in connection with an investment in its territory of an investor of a Party or of a non-Party, on compliance with a requirement to locate production, supply a service, train or employ workers, construct or expand particular facilities, or carry out research and development, in its territory.

(b) Paragraphs 1(f) and (h) do not apply:

(i) when a Party authorizes use of an intellectual property right in accordance with Article 31 of the TRIPS Agreement, or to measures requiring the disclosure of proprietary information that fall within the scope of, and are consistent with, Article 39 of the TRIPS Agreement; or

(ii) when the requirement is imposed or the commitment or undertaking is enforced by a court, administrative tribunal, or competition authority to remedy a practice determined after judicial or administrative process to be anticompetitive under the Party's competition laws.[13]

(c) Provided that such measures are not applied in an arbitrary or unjustifiable manner, and provided that such measures do not constitute a disguised restriction on international trade or investment, paragraphs 1(b), (c), (f), and (h), and 2(a) and (b), shall not be construed to prevent a Party from adopting or maintaining measures, including environmental measures:

(i) necessary to secure compliance with laws and regulations that are not inconsistent with this Treaty;

(ii) necessary to protect human, animal, or plant life or health; or

(iii) related to the conservation of living or non-living exhaustible natural resources.

---

13. The Parties recognize that a patent does not necessarily confer market power.

(d) Paragraphs 1(a), (b), and (c), and 2(a) and (b), do not apply to qualification requirements for goods or services with respect to export promotion and foreign aid programs.

(e) Paragraphs 1(b), (c), (f), and (g), and 2(a) and (b), do not apply to government procurement.

(f) Paragraphs 2(a) and (b) do not apply to requirements imposed by an importing Party relating to the content of goods necessary to qualify for preferential tariffs or preferential quotas.

4. For greater certainty, paragraphs 1 and 2 do not apply to any commitment, undertaking, or requirement other than those set out in those paragraphs.

5. This Article does not preclude enforcement of any commitment, undertaking, or requirement between private parties, where a Party did not impose or require the commitment, undertaking, or requirement.

Article 9: Senior Management and Boards of Directors

1. Neither Party may require that an enterprise of that Party that is a covered investment appoint to senior management positions natural persons of any particular nationality.

2. A Party may require that a majority of the board of directors, or any committee thereof, of an enterprise of that Party that is a covered investment, be of a particular nationality, or resident in the territory of the Party, provided that the requirement does not materially impair the ability of the investor to exercise control over its investment.

Article 10: Publication of Laws and Decisions Respecting Investment

1. Each Party shall ensure that its:
   (a) laws, regulations, procedures, and administrative rulings of general application; and
   (b) adjudicatory decisions
   respecting any matter covered by this Treaty are promptly published or otherwise made publicly available.

2. For purposes of this Article, "administrative ruling of general application" means an administrative ruling or interpretation that applies to all persons and fact situations that fall generally within its ambit and that establishes a norm of conduct but does not include:
   (a) a determination or ruling made in an administrative or quasi-judicial proceeding that applies to a particular covered investment or investor of the other Party in a specific case; or
   (b) a ruling that adjudicates with respect to a particular act or practice.

Article 11: Transparency

1. The Parties agree to consult periodically on ways to improve the transparency practices set out in this Article, Article 10 and Article 29.
2. Publication
   To the extent possible, each Party shall:
   (a) publish in advance any measure referred to in Article 10(1)(a) that it proposes to adopt; and
   (b) provide interested persons and the other Party a reasonable opportunity to comment on such proposed measures.
3. With respect to proposed regulations of general application of its central level of government respecting any matter covered by this Treaty that are published in accordance with paragraph 2(a), each Party:
   (a) shall publish the proposed regulations in a single official journal of national circulation and shall encourage their distribution through additional outlets;
   (b) should in most cases publish the proposed regulations not less than 60 days before the date public comments are due;
   (c) shall include in the publication an explanation of the purpose of and rationale for the proposed regulations; and
   (d) shall, at the time it adopts final regulations, address significant, substantive comments received during the comment period and explain substantive revisions that it made to the proposed regulations in its official journal or in a prominent location on a government Internet site.
4. With respect to regulations of general application that are adopted by its central level of government respecting any matter covered by this Treaty, each Party:
   (a) shall publish the regulations in a single official journal of national circulation and shall encourage their distribution through additional outlets; and
   (b) shall include in the publication an explanation of the purpose of and rationale for the regulations.
5. Provision of Information
   (a) On request of the other Party, a Party shall promptly provide information and respond to questions pertaining to any actual or proposed measure that the requesting Party considers might materially affect the operation of this Treaty or otherwise substantially affect its interests under this Treaty.
   (b) Any request or information under this paragraph shall be provided to the other Party through the relevant contact points.
   (c) Any information provided under this paragraph shall be without prejudice as to whether the measure is consistent with this Treaty.

6. Administrative Proceedings

With a view to administering in a consistent, impartial, and reasonable manner all measures referred to in Article 10(1)(a), each Party shall ensure that in its administrative proceedings applying such measures to particular covered investments or investors of the other Party in specific cases:

(a) wherever possible, covered investments or investors of the other Party that are directly affected by a proceeding are provided reasonable notice, in accordance with domestic procedures, when a proceeding is initiated, including a description of the nature of the proceeding, a statement of the legal authority under which the proceeding is initiated, and a general description of any issues in controversy;

(b) such persons are afforded a reasonable opportunity to present facts and arguments in support of their positions prior to any final administrative action, when time, the nature of the proceeding, and the public interest permit; and

(c) its procedures are in accordance with domestic law.

7. Review and Appeal

(a) Each Party shall establish or maintain judicial, quasi-judicial, or administrative tribunals or procedures for the purpose of the prompt review and, where warranted, correction of final administrative actions regarding matters covered by this Treaty. Such tribunals shall be impartial and independent of the office or authority entrusted with administrative enforcement and shall not have any substantial interest in the outcome of the matter.

(b) Each Party shall ensure that, in any such tribunals or procedures, the parties to the proceeding are provided with the right to:

(i) a reasonable opportunity to support or defend their respective positions; and

(ii) a decision based on the evidence and submissions of record or, where required by domestic law, the record compiled by the administrative authority.

(c) Each Party shall ensure, subject to appeal or further review as provided in its domestic law, that such decisions shall be implemented by, and shall govern the practice of, the offices or authorities with respect to the administrative action at issue.

8. Standards-Setting

    (a) Each Party shall allow persons of the other Party to participate in the development of standards and technical regulations by its central government bodies.[14] Each Party shall allow persons of the other Party to participate in the development of these measures, and the development of conformity assessment procedures by its central government bodies, on terms no less favorable than those it accords to its own persons.

    (b) Each Party shall recommend that non-governmental standardizing bodies in its territory allow persons of the other Party to participate in the development of standards by those bodies. Each Party shall recommend that non-governmental standardizing bodies in its territory allow persons of the other Party to participate in the development of these standards, and the development of conformity assessment procedures by those bodies, on terms no less favorable than those they accord to persons of the Party.

    (c) Subparagraphs 8(a) and 8(b) do not apply to:

        (i) sanitary and phytosanitary measures as defined in Annex A of the World Trade Organization (WTO) Agreement on the Application of Sanitary and Phytosanitary Measures; or

        (ii) purchasing specifications prepared by a governmental body for its production or consumption requirements.

    (d) For purposes of subparagraphs 8(a) and 8(b), "central government body", "standards", "technical regulations" and "conformity assessment procedures" have the meanings assigned to those terms in Annex 1 of the WTO Agreement on Technical Barriers to Trade. Consistent with Annex 1, the three latter terms do not include standards, technical regulations or conformity assessment procedures for the supply of a service.

Article 12: Investment and Environment

1. The Parties recognize that their respective environmental laws and policies, and multilateral environmental agreements to which they are both party, play an important role in protecting the environment.

---

14. A Party may satisfy this obligation by, for example, providing interested persons a reasonable opportunity to provide comments on the measure it proposes to develop and taking those comments into account in the development of the measure.

2. The Parties recognize that it is inappropriate to encourage investment by weakening or reducing the protections afforded in domestic environmental laws. Accordingly, each Party shall ensure that it does not waive or otherwise derogate from or offer to waive or otherwise derogate from its environmental laws[15] in a manner that weakens or reduces the protections afforded in those laws, or fail to effectively enforce those laws through a sustained or recurring course of action or inaction, as an encouragement for the establishment, acquisition, expansion, or retention of an investment in its territory.

3. The Parties recognize that each Party retains the right to exercise discretion with respect to regulatory, compliance, investigatory, and prosecutorial matters, and to make decisions regarding the allocation of resources to enforcement with respect to other environmental matters determined to have higher priorities. Accordingly, the Parties understand that a Party is in compliance with paragraph 2 where a course of action or inaction reflects a reasonable exercise of such discretion, or results from a *bona fide* decision regarding the allocation of resources.

4. For purposes of this Article, "environmental law" means each Party's statutes or regulations,[16] or provisions thereof, the primary purpose of which is the protection of the environment, or the prevention of a danger to human, animal, or plant life or health, through the:

   (a) prevention, abatement, or control of the release, discharge, or emission of pollutants or environmental contaminants;

   (b) control of environmentally hazardous or toxic chemicals, substances, materials, and wastes, and the dissemination of information related thereto; or

   (c) protection or conservation of wild flora or fauna, including endangered species, their habitat, and specially protected natural areas,

   in the Party's territory, but does not include any statute or regulation, or provision thereof, directly related to worker safety or health.

5. Nothing in this Treaty shall be construed to prevent a Party from adopting, maintaining, or enforcing any measure otherwise consistent with this Treaty that it considers appropriate to ensure that investment activity in its territory is undertaken in a manner sensitive to environmental concerns.

6. A Party may make a written request for consultations with the other Party regarding any matter arising under this Article. The other Party shall respond to a request for consultations within thirty days of receipt of such request. Thereafter, the Parties shall consult and endeavor to reach a mutually satisfactory resolution.

---

15. Paragraph 2 shall not apply where a Party waives or derogates from an environmental law pursuant to a provision in law providing for waivers or derogations.
16. For the United States, "statutes or regulations" for the purposes of this Article means an act of the United States Congress or regulations promulgated pursuant to an act of the United States Congress that is enforceable by action of the central level of government.

7. The Parties confirm that each Party may, as appropriate, provide opportunities for public participation regarding any matter arising under this Article.

Article 13: Investment and Labor

1. The Parties reaffirm their respective obligations as members of the International Labor Organization ("ILO") and their commitments under the *ILO Declaration on Fundamental Principles and Rights at Work and its Follow-Up*.
2. The Parties recognize that it is inappropriate to encourage investment by weakening or reducing the protections afforded in domestic labor laws. Accordingly, each Party shall ensure that it does not waive or otherwise derogate from or offer to waive or otherwise derogate from its labor laws where the waiver or derogation would be inconsistent with the labor rights referred to in subparagraphs (a) through (e) of paragraph 3, or fail to effectively enforce its labor laws through a sustained or recurring course of action or inaction, as an encouragement for the establishment, acquisition, expansion, or retention of an investment in its territory.
3. For purposes of this Article, "labor laws" means each Party's statutes or regulations,[17] or provisions thereof, that are directly related to the following:
   (a) freedom of association;
   (b) the effective recognition of the right to collective bargaining;
   (c) the elimination of all forms of forced or compulsory labor;
   (d) the effective abolition of child labor and a prohibition on the worst forms of child labor;
   (e) the elimination of discrimination in respect of employment and occupation; and
   (f) acceptable conditions of work with respect to minimum wages, hours of work, and occupational safety and health.
4. A Party may make a written request for consultations with the other Party regarding any matter arising under this Article. The other Party shall respond to a request for consultations within thirty days of receipt of such request. Thereafter, the Parties shall consult and endeavor to reach a mutually satisfactory resolution.
5. The Parties confirm that each Party may, as appropriate, provide opportunities for public participation regarding any matter arising under this Article.

Article 14: Non-Conforming Measures

1. Articles 3 [National Treatment], 4 [Most-Favored-Nation Treatment], 8 [Performance Requirements], and 9 [Senior Management and Boards of Directors] do not apply to:

---

17. For the United States, "statutes or regulations" for purposes of this Article means an act of the United States Congress or regulations promulgated pursuant to an act of the United States Congress that is enforceable by action of the central level of government.

(a) any existing non-conforming measure that is maintained by a Party at:
    (i) the central level of government, as set out by that Party in its Schedule to Annex I or Annex III,
    (ii) a regional level of government, as set out by that Party in its Schedule to Annex I or Annex III, or
    (iii) a local level of government;
(b) the continuation or prompt renewal of any non-conforming measure referred to in subparagraph (a); or
(c) an amendment to any non-conforming measure referred to in subparagraph (a) to the extent that the amendment does not decrease the conformity of the measure, as it existed immediately before the amendment, with Article 3 [National Treatment], 4 [Most-Favored-Nation Treatment], 8 [Performance Requirements], or 9 [Senior Management and Boards of Directors].

2. Articles 3 [National Treatment], 4 [Most-Favored-Nation Treatment], 8 [Performance Requirements], and 9 [Senior Management and Boards of Directors] do not apply to any measure that a Party adopts or maintains with respect to sectors, subsectors, or activities, as set out in its Schedule to Annex II.

3. Neither Party may, under any measure adopted after the date of entry into force of this Treaty and covered by its Schedule to Annex II, require an investor of the other Party, by reason of its nationality, to sell or otherwise dispose of an investment existing at the time the measure becomes effective.

4. Articles 3 [National Treatment] and 4 [Most-Favored-Nation Treatment] do not apply to any measure covered by an exception to, or derogation from, the obligations under Article 3 or 4 of the TRIPS Agreement, as specifically provided in those Articles and in Article 5 of the TRIPS Agreement.

5. Articles 3 [National Treatment], 4 [Most-Favored-Nation Treatment], and 9 [Senior Management and Boards of Directors] do not apply to:
    (a) government procurement; or
    (b) subsidies or grants provided by a Party, including government-supported loans, guarantees, and insurance.

Article 15: Special Formalities and Information Requirements

1. Nothing in Article 3 [National Treatment] shall be construed to prevent a Party from adopting or maintaining a measure that prescribes special formalities in connection with covered investments, such as a requirement that investors be residents of the Party or that covered investments be legally constituted under the laws or regulations of the Party, provided that such formalities do not materially impair the protections afforded by a Party to investors of the other Party and covered investments pursuant to this Treaty.

2. Notwithstanding Articles 3 [National Treatment] and 4 [Most-Favored-Nation Treatment], a Party may require an investor of the other Party or its covered investment to provide information concerning that investment solely for informational or statistical purposes. The Party shall protect any confidential business information from any disclosure that would prejudice the competitive position of the investor or the covered investment. Nothing in this paragraph shall be construed to prevent a Party from otherwise obtaining or disclosing information in connection with the equitable and good faith application of its law.

Article 16: Non-Derogation

This Treaty shall not derogate from any of the following that entitle an investor of a Party or a covered investment to treatment more favorable than that accorded by this Treaty:
1. laws or regulations, administrative practices or procedures, or administrative or adjudicatory decisions of a Party;
2. international legal obligations of a Party; or
3. obligations assumed by a Party, including those contained in an investment authorization or an investment agreement.

Article 17: Denial of Benefits

1. A Party may deny the benefits of this Treaty to an investor of the other Party that is an enterprise of such other Party and to investments of that investor if persons of a non-Party own or control the enterprise and the denying Party:
   (a) does not maintain diplomatic relations with the non-Party; or
   (b) adopts or maintains measures with respect to the non-Party or a person of the non-Party that prohibit transactions with the enterprise or that would be violated or circumvented if the benefits of this Treaty were accorded to the enterprise or to its investments.
2. A Party may deny the benefits of this Treaty to an investor of the other Party that is an enterprise of such other Party and to investments of that investor if the enterprise has no substantial business activities in the territory of the other Party and persons of a non-Party, or of the denying Party, own or control the enterprise.

Article 18: Essential Security

Nothing in this Treaty shall be construed:
1. to require a Party to furnish or allow access to any information the disclosure of which it determines to be contrary to its essential security interests; or

2. to preclude a Party from applying measures that it considers necessary for the fulfillment of its obligations with respect to the maintenance or restoration of international peace or security, or the protection of its own essential security interests.

Article 19: Disclosure of Information

Nothing in this Treaty shall be construed to require a Party to furnish or allow access to confidential information the disclosure of which would impede law enforcement or otherwise be contrary to the public interest, or which would prejudice the legitimate commercial interests of particular enterprises, public or private.

Article 20: Financial Services

1. Notwithstanding any other provision of this Treaty, a Party shall not be prevented from adopting or maintaining measures relating to financial services for prudential reasons, including for the protection of investors, depositors, policy holders, or persons to whom a fiduciary duty is owed by a financial services supplier, or to ensure the integrity and stability of the financial system.[18] Where such measures do not conform with the provisions of this Treaty, they shall not be used as a means of avoiding the Party's commitments or obligations under this Treaty.

2. (a) Nothing in this Treaty applies to non-discriminatory measures of general application taken by any public entity in pursuit of monetary and related credit policies or exchange rate policies. This paragraph shall not affect a Party's obligations under Article 7 [Transfers] or Article 8 [Performance Requirements].[19]

   (b) For purposes of this paragraph, "public entity" means a central bank or monetary authority of a Party.

3. Where a claimant submits a claim to arbitration under Section B [Investor-State Dispute Settlement], and the respondent invokes paragraph 1 or 2 as a defense, the following provisions shall apply:

---

18. It is understood that the term "prudential reasons" includes the maintenance of the safety, soundness, integrity, or financial responsibility of individual financial institutions, as well as the maintenance of the safety and financial and operational integrity of payment and clearing systems.

19. For greater certainty, measures of general application taken in pursuit of monetary and related credit policies or exchange rate policies do not include measures that expressly nullify or amend contractual provisions that specify the currency of denomination or the rate of exchange of currencies.

(a) The respondent shall, within 120 days of the date the claim is submitted to arbitration under Section B, submit in writing to the competent financial authorities[20] of both Parties a request for a joint determination on the issue of whether and to what extent paragraph 1 or 2 is a valid defense to the claim. The respondent shall promptly provide the tribunal, if constituted, a copy of such request. The arbitration may proceed with respect to the claim only as provided in subparagraph (d).

(b) The competent financial authorities of both Parties shall make themselves available for consultations with each other and shall attempt in good faith to make a determination as described in subparagraph (a). Any such determination shall be transmitted promptly to the disputing parties and, if constituted, to the tribunal. The determination shall be binding on the tribunal.

(c) If the competent financial authorities of both Parties, within 120 days of the date by which they have both received the respondent's written request for a joint determination under subparagraph (a), have not made a determination as described in that subparagraph, the tribunal shall decide the issue left unresolved by the competent financial authorities. The provisions of Section B shall apply, except as modified by this subparagraph.

  (i) In the appointment of all arbitrators not yet appointed to the tribunal, each disputing party shall take appropriate steps to ensure that the tribunal has expertise or experience in financial services law or practice. The expertise of particular candidates with respect to the particular sector of financial services in which the dispute arises shall be taken into account in the appointment of the presiding arbitrator.

  (ii) If, before the respondent submits the request for a joint determination in conformance with subparagraph (a), the presiding arbitrator has been appointed pursuant to Article 27(3), such arbitrator shall be replaced on the request of either disputing party and the tribunal shall be reconstituted consistent with subparagraph (c)(i). If, within 30 days of the date the arbitration proceedings are resumed under subparagraph (d), the disputing parties have not agreed on the appointment of a new presiding arbitrator, the Secretary-General, on the request of a disputing party, shall appoint the presiding arbitrator consistent with subparagraph (c)(i).

---

20. For purposes of this Article, "competent financial authorities" means, for the United States, the Department of the Treasury for banking and other financial services, and the Office of the United States Trade Representative, in coordination with the Department of Commerce and other agencies, for insurance; and for [Country], [____].

   (iii) The tribunal shall draw no inference regarding the application of paragraph 1 or 2 from the fact that the competent financial authorities have not made a determination as described in sub-paragraph (a).

   (iv) The non-disputing Party may make oral and written submissions to the tribunal regarding the issue of whether and to what extent paragraph 1 or 2 is a valid defense to the claim. Unless it makes such a submission, the non-disputing Party shall be presumed, for purposes of the arbitration, to take a position on paragraph 1 or 2 not inconsistent with that of the respondent.

  (d) The arbitration referred to in subparagraph (a) may proceed with respect to the claim:

   (i) 10 days after the date the competent financial authorities' joint determination has been received by both the disputing parties and, if constituted, the tribunal; or

   (ii) 10 days after the expiration of the 120-day period provided to the competent financial authorities in subparagraph (c).

  (e) On the request of the respondent made within 30 days after the expiration of the 120-day period for a joint determination referred to in subpara-graph (c), or, if the tribunal has not been constituted as of the expiration of the 120-day period, within 30 days after the tribunal is constituted, the tribunal shall address and decide the issue or issues left unresolved by the competent financial authorities as referred to in subparagraph (c) prior to deciding the merits of the claim for which paragraph 1 or 2 has been invoked by the respondent as a defense. Failure of the respondent to make such a request is without prejudice to the right of the respondent to invoke paragraph 1 or 2 as a defense at any appropriate phase of the arbitration.

4. Where a dispute arises under Section C and the competent financial authorities of one Party provide written notice to the competent financial authorities of the other Party that the dispute involves financial services, Section C shall apply except as modified by this paragraph and paragraph 5.

  (a) The competent financial authorities of both Parties shall make themselves available for consultations with each other regarding the dispute, and shall have 180 days from the date such notice is received to transmit a report on their consultations to the Parties. A Party may submit the dispute to arbitration under Section C only after the expiration of that 180-day period.

  (b) Either Party may make any such report available to a tribunal constituted under Section C to decide the dispute referred to in this paragraph or a similar dispute, or to a tribunal constituted under Section B to decide a claim arising out of the same events or circumstances that gave rise to the dispute under Section C.

5. Where a Party submits a dispute involving financial services to arbitration under Section C in conformance with paragraph 4, and on the request of either Party within 30 days of the date the dispute is submitted to arbitration, each Party shall, in the appointment of all arbitrators not yet appointed, take appropriate steps to ensure that the tribunal has expertise or experience in financial services law or practice. The expertise of particular candidates with respect to financial services shall be taken into account in the appointment of the presiding arbitrator.

6. Notwithstanding Article 11(2)-(4) [Transparency – Publication], each Party shall, to the extent practicable,

   (a) shall publish in advance any regulations of general application relating to financial services that it proposes to adopt and the purpose of the regulation;

   (b) shall provide interested persons and the other Party a reasonable opportunity to comment on such proposed regulations, and

   (c) should at the time it adopts final regulations, address in writing significant substantive comments received from interested persons with respect to the proposed regulations.

7. The terms "financial service" or "financial services" shall have the same meaning as in subparagraph 5(a) of the Annex on Financial Services of the GATS.

8. For greater certainty, nothing in this Treaty shall be construed to prevent the adoption or enforcement by a party of measures relating to investors of the other Party, or covered investments, in financial institutions that are necessary to secure compliance with laws or regulations that are not inconsistent with this Treaty, including those related to the prevention of deceptive and fraudulent practices or that deal with the effects of a default on financial services contracts, subject to the requirement that such measures are not applied in a manner which would constitute a means of arbitrary or unjustifiable discrimination between countries where like conditions prevail, or a disguised restriction on investment in financial institutions.

Article 21: Taxation

1. Except as provided in this Article, nothing in Section A shall impose obligations with respect to taxation measures.

2. Article 6 [Expropriation] shall apply to all taxation measures, except that a claimant that asserts that a taxation measure involves an expropriation may submit a claim to arbitration under Section B only if:

   (a) the claimant has first referred to the competent tax authorities[21] of both Parties in writing the issue of whether that taxation measure involves an expropriation; and

---

21. For the purposes of this Article, the "competent tax authorities" means:

(b) within 180 days after the date of such referral, the competent tax authorities of both Parties fail to agree that the taxation measure is not an expropriation.

3. Subject to paragraph 4, Article 8 [Performance Requirements] (2) through (4) shall apply to all taxation measures.

4. Nothing in this Treaty shall affect the rights and obligations of either Party under any tax convention. In the event of any inconsistency between this Treaty and any such convention, that convention shall prevail to the extent of the inconsistency. In the case of a tax convention between the Parties, the competent authorities under that convention shall have sole responsibility for determining whether any inconsistency exists between this Treaty and that convention.

Article 22: Entry into Force, Duration, and Termination

1. This Treaty shall enter into force thirty days after the date the Parties exchange instruments of ratification. It shall remain in force for a period of ten years and shall continue in force thereafter unless terminated in accordance with paragraph 2.

2. A Party may terminate this Treaty at the end of the initial ten-year period or at any time thereafter by giving one year's written notice to the other Party.

3. For ten years from the date of termination, all other Articles shall continue to apply to covered investments established or acquired prior to the date of termination, except insofar as those Articles extend to the establishment or acquisition of covered investments.

SECTION B

Article 23: Consultation and Negotiation

In the event of an investment dispute, the claimant and the respondent should initially seek to resolve the dispute through consultation and negotiation, which may include the use of non-binding, third-party procedures.

Article 24: Submission of a Claim to Arbitration

1. In the event that a disputing party considers that an investment dispute cannot be settled by consultation and negotiation:
   (a) the claimant, on its own behalf, may submit to arbitration under this Section a claim

---

(a) for the United States, the Assistant Secretary of the Treasury (Tax Policy), Department of the Treasury; and
(b) for [Country], [_____].

        (i) that the respondent has breached
            (A) an obligation under Articles 3 through 10,
            (B) an investment authorization, or
            (C) an investment agreement;
               and
        (ii) that the claimant has incurred loss or damage by reason of, or arising out of, that breach; and

(b) the claimant, on behalf of an enterprise of the respondent that is a juridical person that the claimant owns or controls directly or indirectly, may submit to arbitration under this Section a claim

        (i) that the respondent has breached
            (A) an obligation under Articles 3 through 10,
            (B) an investment authorization, or
            (C) an investment agreement;
               and
        (ii) that the enterprise has incurred loss or damage by reason of, or arising out of, that breach,

provided that a claimant may submit pursuant to subparagraph (a)(i)(C) or (b)(i)(C) a claim for breach of an investment agreement only if the subject matter of the claim and the claimed damages directly relate to the covered investment that was established or acquired, or sought to be established or acquired, in reliance on the relevant investment agreement.

2. At least 90 days before submitting any claim to arbitration under this Section, a claimant shall deliver to the respondent a written notice of its intention to submit the claim to arbitration ("notice of intent"). The notice shall specify:

    (a) the name and address of the claimant and, where a claim is submitted on behalf of an enterprise, the name, address, and place of incorporation of the enterprise;

    (b) for each claim, the provision of this Treaty, investment authorization, or investment agreement alleged to have been breached and any other relevant provisions;

    (c) the legal and factual basis for each claim; and

    (d) the relief sought and the approximate amount of damages claimed.

3. Provided that six months have elapsed since the events giving rise to the claim, a claimant may submit a claim referred to in paragraph 1:

    (a) under the ICSID Convention and the ICSID Rules of Procedure for Arbitration Proceedings, provided that both the respondent and the non-disputing Party are parties to the ICSID Convention;

    (b) under the ICSID Additional Facility Rules, provided that either the respondent or the non-disputing Party is a party to the ICSID Convention;

    (c) under the UNCITRAL Arbitration Rules; or

    (d) if the claimant and respondent agree, to any other arbitration institution or under any other arbitration rules.

4. A claim shall be deemed submitted to arbitration under this Section when the claimant's notice of or request for arbitration ("notice of arbitration"):

    (a) referred to in paragraph 1 of Article 36 of the ICSID Convention is received by the Secretary-General;

    (b) referred to in Article 2 of Schedule C of the ICSID Additional Facility Rules is received by the Secretary-General;

    (c) referred to in Article 3 of the UNCITRAL Arbitration Rules, together with the statement of claim referred to in Article 18 of the UNCITRAL Arbitration Rules, are received by the respondent; or

    (d) referred to under any arbitral institution or arbitral rules selected under paragraph 3(d) is received by the respondent.

        A claim asserted by the claimant for the first time after such notice of arbitration is submitted shall be deemed submitted to arbitration under this Section on the date of its receipt under the applicable arbitral rules.

5. The arbitration rules applicable under paragraph 3, and in effect on the date the claim or claims were submitted to arbitration under this Section, shall govern the arbitration except to the extent modified by this Treaty.

6. The claimant shall provide with the notice of arbitration:

    (a) the name of the arbitrator that the claimant appoints; or

    (b) the claimant's written consent for the Secretary-General to appoint that arbitrator.

Article 25: Consent of Each Party to Arbitration

1. Each Party consents to the submission of a claim to arbitration under this Section in accordance with this Treaty.

2. The consent under paragraph 1 and the submission of a claim to arbitration under this Section shall satisfy the requirements of:

    (a) Chapter II of the ICSID Convention (Jurisdiction of the Centre) and the ICSID Additional Facility Rules for written consent of the parties to the dispute; [and]

    (b) Article II of the New York Convention for an "agreement in writing[."] [;" and

    (c) Article I of the Inter-American Convention for an "agreement."]

Article 26: Conditions and Limitations on Consent of Each Party

1. No claim may be submitted to arbitration under this Section if more than three years have elapsed from the date on which the claimant first acquired, or should have first acquired, knowledge of the breach alleged under Article 24(1) and knowledge that the claimant (for claims brought under Article 24(1)(a)) or the enterprise (for claims brought under Article 24(1)(b)) has incurred loss or damage.

2. No claim may be submitted to arbitration under this Section unless:
   (a) the claimant consents in writing to arbitration in accordance with the procedures set out in this Treaty; and
   (b) the notice of arbitration is accompanied,
       (i) for claims submitted to arbitration under Article 24(1)(a), by the claimant's written waiver, and
       (ii) for claims submitted to arbitration under Article 24(1)(b), by the claimant's and the enterprise's written waivers

   of any right to initiate or continue before any administrative tribunal or court under the law of either Party, or other dispute settlement procedures, any proceeding with respect to any measure alleged to constitute a breach referred to in Article 24.

3. Notwithstanding paragraph 2(b), the claimant (for claims brought under Article 24(1)(a)) and the claimant or the enterprise (for claims brought under Article 24(1)(b)) may initiate or continue an action that seeks interim injunctive relief and does not involve the payment of monetary damages before a judicial or administrative tribunal of the respondent, provided that the action is brought for the sole purpose of preserving the claimant's or the enterprise's rights and interests during the pendency of the arbitration.

Article 27: Selection of Arbitrators

1. Unless the disputing parties otherwise agree, the tribunal shall comprise three arbitrators, one arbitrator appointed by each of the disputing parties and the third, who shall be the presiding arbitrator, appointed by agreement of the disputing parties.

2. The Secretary-General shall serve as appointing authority for an arbitration under this Section.

3. Subject to Article 20(3), if a tribunal has not been constituted within 75 days from the date that a claim is submitted to arbitration under this Section, the Secretary-General, on the request of a disputing party, shall appoint, in his or her discretion, the arbitrator or arbitrators not yet appointed.

4. For purposes of Article 39 of the ICSID Convention and Article 7 of Schedule C to the ICSID Additional Facility Rules, and without prejudice to an objection to an arbitrator on a ground other than nationality:

    (a) the respondent agrees to the appointment of each individual member of a tribunal established under the ICSID Convention or the ICSID Additional Facility Rules;

    (b) a claimant referred to in Article 24(1)(a) may submit a claim to arbitration under this Section, or continue a claim, under the ICSID Convention or the ICSID Additional Facility Rules, only on condition that the claimant agrees in writing to the appointment of each individual member of the tribunal; and

    (c) a claimant referred to in Article 24(1)(b) may submit a claim to arbitration under this Section, or continue a claim, under the ICSID Convention or the ICSID Additional Facility Rules, only on condition that the claimant and the enterprise agree in writing to the appointment of each individual member of the tribunal.

Article 28: Conduct of the Arbitration

1. The disputing parties may agree on the legal place of any arbitration under the arbitral rules applicable under Article 24(3). If the disputing parties fail to reach agreement, the tribunal shall determine the place in accordance with the applicable arbitral rules, provided that the place shall be in the territory of a State that is a party to the New York Convention.

2. The non-disputing Party may make oral and written submissions to the tribunal regarding the interpretation of this Treaty.

3. The tribunal shall have the authority to accept and consider *amicus curiae* submissions from a person or entity that is not a disputing party.

4. Without prejudice to a tribunal's authority to address other objections as a preliminary question, a tribunal shall address and decide as a preliminary question any objection by the respondent that, as a matter of law, a claim submitted is not a claim for which an award in favor of the claimant may be made under Article 34.

    (a) Such objection shall be submitted to the tribunal as soon as possible after the tribunal is constituted, and in no event later than the date the tribunal fixes for the respondent to submit its counter-memorial (or, in the case of an amendment to the notice of arbitration, the date the tribunal fixes for the respondent to submit its response to the amendment).

    (b) On receipt of an objection under this paragraph, the tribunal shall suspend any proceedings on the merits, establish a schedule for considering the objection consistent with any schedule it has established for considering any other preliminary question, and issue a decision or award on the objection, stating the grounds therefor.

(c) In deciding an objection under this paragraph, the tribunal shall assume to be true claimant's factual allegations in support of any claim in the notice of arbitration (or any amendment thereof) and, in disputes brought under the UNCITRAL Arbitration Rules, the statement of claim referred to in Article 18 of the UNCITRAL Arbitration Rules. The tribunal may also consider any relevant facts not in dispute.

(d) The respondent does not waive any objection as to competence or any argument on the merits merely because the respondent did or did not raise an objection under this paragraph or make use of the expedited procedure set out in paragraph 5.

5. In the event that the respondent so requests within 45 days after the tribunal is constituted, the tribunal shall decide on an expedited basis an objection under paragraph 4 and any objection that the dispute is not within the tribunal's competence. The tribunal shall suspend any proceedings on the merits and issue a decision or award on the objection(s), stating the grounds therefor, no later than 150 days after the date of the request. However, if a disputing party requests a hearing, the tribunal may take an additional 30 days to issue the decision or award. Regardless of whether a hearing is requested, a tribunal may, on a showing of extraordinary cause, delay issuing its decision or award by an additional brief period, which may not exceed 30 days.

6. When it decides a respondent's objection under paragraph 4 or 5, the tribunal may, if warranted, award to the prevailing disputing party reasonable costs and attorney's fees incurred in submitting or opposing the objection. In determining whether such an award is warranted, the tribunal shall consider whether either the claimant's claim or the respondent's objection was frivolous, and shall provide the disputing parties a reasonable opportunity to comment.

7. A respondent may not assert as a defense, counterclaim, right of set-off, or for any other reason that the claimant has received or will receive indemnification or other compensation for all or part of the alleged damages pursuant to an insurance or guarantee contract.

8. A tribunal may order an interim measure of protection to preserve the rights of a disputing party, or to ensure that the tribunal's jurisdiction is made fully effective, including an order to preserve evidence in the possession or control of a disputing party or to protect the tribunal's jurisdiction. A tribunal may not order attachment or enjoin the application of a measure alleged to constitute a breach referred to in Article 24. For purposes of this paragraph, an order includes a recommendation.

9. (a) In any arbitration conducted under this Section, at the request of a disputing party, a tribunal shall, before issuing a decision or award on liability, transmit its proposed decision or award to the disputing parties and to the non-disputing Party. Within 60 days after the tribunal transmits its proposed decision or award, the disputing parties may submit written comments to the tribunal concerning any aspect of its proposed decision or award. The tribunal shall consider any such comments and issue its decision or award not later than 45 days after the expiration of the 60-day comment period.

(b) Subparagraph (a) shall not apply in any arbitration conducted pursuant to this Section for which an appeal has been made available pursuant to paragraph 10.

10. In the event that an appellate mechanism for reviewing awards rendered by investor-State dispute settlement tribunals is developed in the future under other institutional arrangements, the Parties shall consider whether awards rendered under Article 34 should be subject to that appellate mechanism. The Parties shall strive to ensure that any such appellate mechanism they consider adopting provides for transparency of proceedings similar to the transparency provisions established in Article 29.

Article 29: Transparency of Arbitral Proceedings

1. Subject to paragraphs 2 and 4, the respondent shall, after receiving the following documents, promptly transmit them to the non-disputing Party and make them available to the public:

(a) the notice of intent;

(b) the notice of arbitration;

(c) pleadings, memorials, and briefs submitted to the tribunal by a disputing party and any written submissions submitted pursuant to Article 28(2) [Non-Disputing Party submissions] and (3) [*Amicus* Submissions] and Article 33 [Consolidation];

(d) minutes or transcripts of hearings of the tribunal, where available; and

(e) orders, awards, and decisions of the tribunal.

2. The tribunal shall conduct hearings open to the public and shall determine, in consultation with the disputing parties, the appropriate logistical arrangements. However, any disputing party that intends to use information designated as protected information in a hearing shall so advise the tribunal. The tribunal shall make appropriate arrangements to protect the information from disclosure.

3. Nothing in this Section requires a respondent to disclose protected information or to furnish or allow access to information that it may withhold in accordance with Article 18 [Essential Security Article] or Article 19 [Disclosure of Information Article].

4. Any protected information that is submitted to the tribunal shall be protected from disclosure in accordance with the following procedures:

(a) Subject to subparagraph (d), neither the disputing parties nor the tribunal shall disclose to the non-disputing Party or to the public any protected information where the disputing party that provided the information clearly designates it in accordance with subparagraph (b);

(b) Any disputing party claiming that certain information constitutes protected information shall clearly designate the information at the time it is submitted to the tribunal;

(c) A disputing party shall, at the time it submits a document containing information claimed to be protected information, submit a redacted version of the document that does not contain the information. Only the redacted version shall be provided to the non-disputing Party and made public in accordance with paragraph 1; and

(d) The tribunal shall decide any objection regarding the designation of information claimed to be protected information. If the tribunal determines that such information was not properly designated, the disputing party that submitted the information may (i) withdraw all or part of its submission containing such information, or (ii) agree to resubmit complete and redacted documents with corrected designations in accordance with the tribunal's determination and subparagraph (c). In either case, the other disputing party shall, whenever necessary, resubmit complete and redacted documents which either remove the information withdrawn under (i) by the disputing party that first submitted the information or redesignate the information consistent with the designation under (ii) of the disputing party that first submitted the information.

5. Nothing in this Section requires a respondent to withhold from the public information required to be disclosed by its laws.

Article 30: Governing Law

1. Subject to paragraph 3, when a claim is submitted under Article 24(1)(a)(i)(A) or Article 24(1)(b)(i)(A), the tribunal shall decide the issues in dispute in accordance with this Treaty and applicable rules of international law.

2. Subject to paragraph 3 and the other terms of this Section, when a claim is submitted under Article 24(1)(a)(i)(B) or (C), or Article 24(1)(b)(i)(B) or (C), the tribunal shall apply:

(a) the rules of law specified in the pertinent investment authorization or investment agreement, or as the disputing parties may otherwise agree; or

(b) if the rules of law have not been specified or otherwise agreed:

    (i) the law of the respondent, including its rules on the conflict of laws;[22] and

    (ii) such rules of international law as may be applicable.

3. A joint decision of the Parties, each acting through its representative designated for purposes of this Article, declaring their interpretation of a provision of this Treaty shall be binding on a tribunal, and any decision or award issued by a tribunal must be consistent with that joint decision.

Article 31: Interpretation of Annexes

1. Where a respondent asserts as a defense that the measure alleged to be a breach is within the scope of an entry set out in Annex I, II, or III, the tribunal shall, on request of the respondent, request the interpretation of the Parties on the issue. The Parties shall submit in writing any joint decision declaring their interpretation to the tribunal within 90 days of delivery of the request.

2. A joint decision issued under paragraph 1 by the Parties, each acting through its representative designated for purposes of this Article, shall be binding on the tribunal, and any decision or award issued by the tribunal must be consistent with that joint decision. If the Parties fail to issue such a decision within 90 days, the tribunal shall decide the issue.

Article 32: Expert Reports

Without prejudice to the appointment of other kinds of experts where authorized by the applicable arbitration rules, a tribunal, at the request of a disputing party or, unless the disputing parties disapprove, on its own initiative, may appoint one or more experts to report to it in writing on any factual issue concerning environmental, health, safety, or other scientific matters raised by a disputing party in a proceeding, subject to such terms and conditions as the disputing parties may agree.

Article 33: Consolidation

1. Where two or more claims have been submitted separately to arbitration under Article 24(1) and the claims have a question of law or fact in common and arise out of the same events or circumstances, any disputing party may seek a consolidation order in accordance with the agreement of all the disputing parties sought to be covered by the order or the terms of paragraphs 2 through 10.

2. A disputing party that seeks a consolidation order under this Article shall deliver, in writing, a request to the Secretary-General and to all the disputing parties sought to be covered by the order and shall specify in the request:

---

22. The "law of the respondent" means the law that a domestic court or tribunal of proper jurisdiction would apply in the same case.

(a) the names and addresses of all the disputing parties sought to be covered by the order;

(b) the nature of the order sought; and

(c) the grounds on which the order is sought.

3. Unless the Secretary-General finds within 30 days after receiving a request under paragraph 2 that the request is manifestly unfounded, a tribunal shall be established under this Article.

4. Unless all the disputing parties sought to be covered by the order otherwise agree, a tribunal established under this Article shall comprise three arbitrators:

(a) one arbitrator appointed by agreement of the claimants;

(b) one arbitrator appointed by the respondent; and

(c) the presiding arbitrator appointed by the Secretary-General, provided, however, that the presiding arbitrator shall not be a national of either Party.

5. If, within 60 days after the Secretary-General receives a request made under paragraph 2, the respondent fails or the claimants fail to appoint an arbitrator in accordance with paragraph 4, the Secretary-General, on the request of any disputing party sought to be covered by the order, shall appoint the arbitrator or arbitrators not yet appointed. If the respondent fails to appoint an arbitrator, the Secretary-General shall appoint a national of the disputing Party, and if the claimants fail to appoint an arbitrator, the Secretary-General shall appoint a national of the nondisputing Party.

6. Where a tribunal established under this Article is satisfied that two or more claims that have been submitted to arbitration under Article 24(1) have a question of law or fact in common, and arise out of the same events or circumstances, the tribunal may, in the interest of fair and efficient resolution of the claims, and after hearing the disputing parties, by order:

(a) assume jurisdiction over, and hear and determine together, all or part of the claims;

(b) assume jurisdiction over, and hear and determine one or more of the claims, the determination of which it believes would assist in the resolution of the others; or

(c) instruct a tribunal previously established under Article 27 [Selection of Arbitrators] to assume jurisdiction over, and hear and determine together, all or part of the claims, provided that

(i) that tribunal, at the request of any claimant not previously a disputing party before that tribunal, shall be reconstituted with its original members, except that the arbitrator for the claimants shall be appointed pursuant to paragraphs 4(a) and 5; and

(ii) that tribunal shall decide whether any prior hearing shall be repeated.

7. Where a tribunal has been established under this Article, a claimant that has submitted a claim to arbitration under Article 24(1) and that has not been named in a request made under paragraph 2 may make a written request to the tribunal that it be included in any order made under paragraph 6, and shall specify in the request:
   (a) the name and address of the claimant;
   (b) the nature of the order sought; and
   (c) the grounds on which the order is sought.
   The claimant shall deliver a copy of its request to the Secretary-General.

8. A tribunal established under this Article shall conduct its proceedings in accordance with the UNCITRAL Arbitration Rules, except as modified by this Section.

9. A tribunal established under Article 27 [Selection of Arbitrators] shall not have jurisdiction to decide a claim, or a part of a claim, over which a tribunal established or instructed under this Article has assumed jurisdiction.

10. On application of a disputing party, a tribunal established under this Article, pending its decision under paragraph 6, may order that the proceedings of a tribunal established under Article 27 [Selection of Arbitrators] be stayed, unless the latter tribunal has already adjourned its proceedings.

Article 34: Awards

1. Where a tribunal makes a final award against a respondent, the tribunal may award, separately or in combination, only:
   (a) monetary damages and any applicable interest; and
   (b) restitution of property, in which case the award shall provide that the respondent may pay monetary damages and any applicable interest in lieu of restitution.
   A tribunal may also award costs and attorney's fees in accordance with this Treaty and the applicable arbitration rules.

2. Subject to paragraph 1, where a claim is submitted to arbitration under Article 24(1)(b):
   (a) an award of restitution of property shall provide that restitution be made to the enterprise;
   (b) an award of monetary damages and any applicable interest shall provide that the sum be paid to the enterprise; and
   (c) the award shall provide that it is made without prejudice to any right that any person may have in the relief under applicable domestic law.

3. A tribunal may not award punitive damages.

4. An award made by a tribunal shall have no binding force except between the disputing parties and in respect of the particular case.

5. Subject to paragraph 6 and the applicable review procedure for an interim award, a disputing party shall abide by and comply with an award without delay.

6. A disputing party may not seek enforcement of a final award until:
   (a) in the case of a final award made under the ICSID Convention,
      (i) 120 days have elapsed from the date the award was rendered and no disputing party has requested revision or annulment of the award; or
      (ii) revision or annulment proceedings have been completed; and
   (b) in the case of a final award under the ICSID Additional Facility Rules, the UNCITRAL Arbitration Rules, or the rules selected pursuant to Article 24(3)(d),
      (i) 90 days have elapsed from the date the award was rendered and no disputing party has commenced a proceeding to revise, set aside, or annul the award; or
      (ii) a court has dismissed or allowed an application to revise, set aside, or annul the award and there is no further appeal.

7. Each Party shall provide for the enforcement of an award in its territory.

8. If the respondent fails to abide by or comply with a final award, on delivery of a request by the non-disputing Party, a tribunal shall be established under Article 37 [State-State Dispute Settlement]. Without prejudice to other remedies available under applicable rules of international law, the requesting Party may seek in such proceedings:
   (a) a determination that the failure to abide by or comply with the final award is inconsistent with the obligations of this Treaty; and
   (b) a recommendation that the respondent abide by or comply with the final award.

9. A disputing party may seek enforcement of an arbitration award under the ICSID Convention or the New York Convention [or the Inter-American Convention] regardless of whether proceedings have been taken under paragraph 8.

10. A claim that is submitted to arbitration under this Section shall be considered to arise out of a commercial relationship or transaction for purposes of Article I of the New York Convention [and Article I of the Inter-American Convention].

Article 35: Annexes and Footnotes

The Annexes and footnotes shall form an integral part of this Treaty.

Article 36: Service of Documents

Delivery of notice and other documents on a Party shall be made to the place named for that Party in Annex C.

SECTION C

Article 37: State-State Dispute Settlement

1. Subject to paragraph 5, any dispute between the Parties concerning the interpretation or application of this Treaty, that is not resolved through consultations or other diplomatic channels, shall be submitted on the request of either Party to arbitration for a binding decision or award by a tribunal in accordance with applicable rules of international law. In the absence of an agreement by the Parties to the contrary, the UNCITRAL Arbitration Rules shall govern, except as modified by the Parties or this Treaty.

2. Unless the Parties otherwise agree, the tribunal shall comprise three arbitrators, one arbitrator appointed by each Party and the third, who shall be the presiding arbitrator, appointed by agreement of the Parties. If a tribunal has not been constituted within 75 days from the date that a claim is submitted to arbitration under this Section, the Secretary-General, on the request of either Party, shall appoint, in his or her discretion, the arbitrator or arbitrators not yet appointed.

3. Expenses incurred by the arbitrators, and other costs of the proceedings, shall be paid for equally by the Parties. However, the tribunal may, in its discretion, direct that a higher proportion of the costs be paid by one of the Parties.

4. Articles 28(3) [*Amicus Curiae* Submissions], 29 [Investor-State Transparency], 30(1) and (3) [Governing Law], and 31 [Interpretation of Annexes] shall apply *mutatis mutandis* to arbitrations under this Article.

5. Paragraphs 1 through 4 shall not apply to a matter arising under Article 12 or Article 13.

IN WITNESS WHEREOF, the respective plenipotentiaries have signed this Treaty.

DONE in duplicate at [city] this [number] day of [month, year], in the English and [foreign] languages, each text being equally authentic.

FOR THE GOVERNMENT OF   FOR THE GOVERNMENT OF

THE UNITED STATES OF AMERICA: [Country]:

Annex A
Customary International Law

The Parties confirm their shared understanding that "customary international law" generally and as specifically referenced in Article 5 [Minimum Standard of Treatment] and Annex B [Expropriation] results from a general and consistent practice of States that they follow from a sense of legal obligation. With regard to Article 5 [Minimum Standard of Treatment], the customary international law minimum standard of treatment of aliens refers to all customary international law principles that protect the economic rights and interests of aliens.

Annex B
Expropriation

The Parties confirm their shared understanding that:

1. Article 6 [Expropriation and Compensation](1) is intended to reflect customary international law concerning the obligation of States with respect to expropriation.
2. An action or a series of actions by a Party cannot constitute an expropriation unless it interferes with a tangible or intangible property right or property interest in an investment.
3. Article 6 [Expropriation and Compensation](1) addresses two situations. The first is direct expropriation, where an investment is nationalized or otherwise directly expropriated through formal transfer of title or outright seizure.
4. The second situation addressed by Article 6 [Expropriation and Compensation](1) is indirect expropriation, where an action or series of actions by a Party has an effect equivalent to direct expropriation without formal transfer of title or outright seizure.
   (a) The determination of whether an action or series of actions by a Party, in a specific fact situation, constitutes an indirect expropriation, requires a case-by-case, fact-based inquiry that considers, among other factors:
      (i) the economic impact of the government action, although the fact that an action or series of actions by a Party has an adverse effect on the economic value of an investment, standing alone, does not establish that an indirect expropriation has occurred;
      (ii) the extent to which the government action interferes with distinct, reasonable investment-backed expectations; and
      (iii) the character of the government action.
   (b) Except in rare circumstances, non-discriminatory regulatory actions by a Party that are designed and applied to protect legitimate public welfare objectives, such as public health, safety, and the environment, do not constitute indirect expropriations.

Annex C
Service of Documents on a Party
United States

Notices and other documents shall be served on the United States by delivery to:

Executive Director (L/EX)

Office of the Legal Adviser

Department of State

Washington, D.C. 20520

United States of America

[Country]

Notices and other documents shall be served on [Country] by delivery to:
    [insert place of delivery of notices and other documents for [Country]]

I. EUROPEAN PARLIAMENT AND COUNCIL REGULATION (EC) NO 593/2008 OF 17 JUNE 2008 ON THE LAW APPLICABLE TO CONTRACTUAL OBLIGATIONS (ROME I REGULATION)

REGULATION (EC) No 593/2008 OF THE EUROPEAN PARLIAMENT AND OF THE COUNCIL
of 17 June 2008
on the law applicable to contractual obligations (Rome I)

THE EUROPEAN PARLIAMENT AND THE COUNCIL OF THE EUROPEAN UNION,

Having regard to the Treaty establishing the European Community, and in particular Article 61(c) and the second indent of Article 67(5) thereof,

Having regard to the proposal from the Commission,

Having regard to the opinion of the European Economic and Social Committee([1]),

Acting in accordance with the procedure laid down in Article 251 of the Treaty([2]),

Whereas:

(1) The Community has set itself the objective of maintaining and developing an area of freedom, security and justice. For the progressive establishment of such an area, the Community is to adopt measures relating to judicial cooperation in civil matters with a cross-border impact to the extent necessary for the proper functioning of the internal market.

(2) According to Article 65, point (b) of the Treaty, these measures are to include those promoting the compatibility of the rules applicable in the Member States concerning the conflict of laws and of jurisdiction.

(3) The European Council meeting in Tampere on 15 and 16 October 1999 endorsed the principle of mutual recognition of judgments and other decisions of judicial authorities as the cornerstone of judicial cooperation in civil matters and invited the Council and the Commission to adopt a programme of measures to implement that principle.

(4) On 30 November 2000 the Council adopted a joint Commission and Council programme of measures for implementation of the principle of mutual recognition of decisions in civil and commercial matters([3]). The programme identifies measures relating to the harmonisation of conflict-of-law rules as those facilitating the mutual recognition of judgments.

---

1. OJ C 318, 23.12.2006, p. 56.
2. Opinion of the European Parliament of 29 November 2007 (not yet published in the Official Journal) and Council Decision of 5 June 2008.
3. OJ C 12, 15.1.2001, p. 1.

(5) The Hague Programme([4]), adopted by the European Council on 5 November 2004, called for work to be pursued actively on the conflict-of-law rules regarding contractual obligations (Rome I).

(6) The proper functioning of the internal market creates a need, in order to improve the predictability of the outcome of litigation, certainty as to the law applicable and the free movement of judgments, for the conflict-of-law rules in the Member States to designate the same national law irrespective of the country of the court in which an action is brought.

(7) The substantive scope and the provisions of this Regulation should be consistent with Council Regulation (EC) No 44/2001 of 22 December 2000 on jurisdiction and the recognition and enforcement of judgments in civil and commercial matters([5]) (Brussels I) and Regulation (EC) No 864/2007 of the European Parliament and of the Council of 11 July 2007 on the law applicable to non-contractual obligations (Rome II)([6]).

(8) Family relationships should cover parentage, marriage, affinity and collateral relatives. The reference in Article 1(2) to relationships having comparable effects to marriage and other family relationships should be interpreted in accordance with the law of the Member State in which the court is seised.

(9) Obligations under bills of exchange, cheques and promissory notes and other negotiable instruments should also cover bills of lading to the extent that the obligations under the bill of lading arise out of its negotiable character.

(10) Obligations arising out of dealings prior to the conclusion of the contract are covered by Article 12 of Regulation (EC) No 864/2007. Such obligations should therefore be excluded from the scope of this Regulation.

(11) The parties' freedom to choose the applicable law should be one of the cornerstones of the system of conflict-of-law rules in matters of contractual obligations.

(12) An agreement between the parties to confer on one or more courts or tribunals of a Member State exclusive jurisdiction to determine disputes under the contract should be one of the factors to be taken into account in determining whether a choice of law has been clearly demonstrated.

(13) This Regulation does not preclude parties from incorporating by reference into their contract a non-State body of law or an international convention.

(14) Should the Community adopt, in an appropriate legal instrument, rules of substantive contract law, including standard terms and conditions, such instrument may provide that the parties may choose to apply those rules.

---

4. OJ C 53, 3.3.2005, p. 1.
5. OJ L 12, 16.1.2001, p. 1. Regulation as last amended by Regulation (EC) No 1791/2006 (OJ L 363, 20.12.2006, p. 1).
6. OJ L 199, 31.7.2007, p. 40.

(15) Where a choice of law is made and all other elements relevant to the situation are located in a country other than the country whose law has been chosen, the choice of law should not prejudice the application of provisions of the law of that country which cannot be derogated from by agreement. This rule should apply whether or not the choice of law was accompanied by a choice of court or tribunal. Whereas no substantial change is intended as compared with Article 3(3) of the 1980 Convention on the Law Applicable to Contractual Obligations([1]) (the Rome Convention), the wording of this Regulation is aligned as far as possible with Article 14 of Regulation (EC) No 864/2007.

(16) To contribute to the general objective of this Regulation, legal certainty in the European judicial area, the conflict-of-law rules should be highly foreseeable. The courts should, however, retain a degree of discretion to determine the law that is most closely connected to the situation.

(17) As far as the applicable law in the absence of choice is concerned, the concept of 'provision of services' and 'sale of goods' should be interpreted in the same way as when applying Article 5 of Regulation (EC) No 44/2001 in so far as sale of goods and provision of services are covered by that Regulation. Although franchise and distribution contracts are contracts for services, they are the subject of specific rules.

(18) As far as the applicable law in the absence of choice is concerned, multilateral systems should be those in which trading is conducted, such as regulated markets and multilateral trading facilities as referred to in Article 4 of Directive 2004/39/EC of the European Parliament and of the Council of 21 April 2004 on markets in financial instruments([2]), regardless of whether or not they rely on a central counterparty.

(19) Where there has been no choice of law, the applicable law should be determined in accordance with the rule specified for the particular type of contract. Where the contract cannot be categorised as being one of the specified types or where its elements fall within more than one of the specified types, it should be governed by the law of the country where the party required to effect the characteristic performance of the contract has his habitual residence. In the case of a contract consisting of a bundle of rights and obligations capable of being categorised as falling within more than one of the specified types of contract, the characteristic performance of the contract should be determined having regard to its centre of gravity.

(20) Where the contract is manifestly more closely connected with a country other than that indicated in Article 4(1) or (2), an escape clause should provide that the law of that other country is to apply. In order to determine that country, account should be taken, inter alia, of whether the contract in question has a very close relationship with another contract or contracts.

1. OJ C 334, 30.12.2005, p. 1.
2. OJ L 145, 30.4.2004, p. 1. Directive as last amended by Directive 2008/10/EC (OJ L 76, 19.3.2008, p. 33).

(21) In the absence of choice, where the applicable law cannot be determined either on the basis of the fact that the contract can be categorised as one of the specified types or as being the law of the country of habitual residence of the party required to effect the characteristic performance of the contract, the contract should be governed by the law of the country with which it is most closely connected. In order to determine that country, account should be taken, inter alia, of whether the contract in question has a very close relationship with another contract or contracts.

(22) As regards the interpretation of contracts for the carriage of goods, no change in substance is intended with respect to Article 4(4), third sentence, of the Rome Convention. Consequently, single-voyage charter parties and other contracts the main purpose of which is the carriage of goods should be treated as contracts for the carriage of goods. For the purposes of this Regulation, the term 'consignor' should refer to any person who enters into a contract of carriage with the carrier and the term 'the carrier' should refer to the party to the contract who undertakes to carry the goods, whether or not he performs the carriage himself.

(23) As regards contracts concluded with parties regarded as being weaker, those parties should be protected by conflict-of-law rules that are more favourable to their interests than the general rules.

(24) With more specific reference to consumer contracts, the conflict-of-law rule should make it possible to cut the cost of settling disputes concerning what are commonly relatively small claims and to take account of the development of distance-selling techniques. Consistency with Regulation (EC) No 44/2001 requires both that there be a reference to the concept of directed activity as a condition for applying the consumer protection rule and that the concept be interpreted harmoniously in Regulation (EC) No 44/2001 and this Regulation, bearing in mind that a joint declaration by the Council and the Commission on Article 15 of Regulation (EC) No 44/2001 states that 'for Article 15(1)(c) to be applicable it is not sufficient for an undertaking to target its activities at the Member State of the consumer's residence, or at a number of Member States including that Member State; a contract must also be concluded within the framework of its activities'. The declaration also states that 'the mere fact that an Internet site is accessible is not sufficient for Article 15 to be applicable, although a factor will be that this Internet site solicits the conclusion of distance contracts and that a contract has actually been concluded at a distance, by whatever means. In this respect, the language or currency which a website uses does not constitute a relevant factor.'.

(25) Consumers should be protected by such rules of the country of their habitual residence that cannot be derogated from by agreement, provided that the consumer contract has been concluded as a result of the professional pursuing his commercial or professional activities in that particular country. The same protection should be guaranteed if the professional, while not pursuing his commercial or professional activities in the country where the consumer has his habitual residence, directs his activities by any means to that country or to several countries, including that country, and the contract is concluded as a result of such activities.

(26) For the purposes of this Regulation, financial services such as investment services and activities and ancillary services provided by a professional to a consumer, as referred to in sections A and B of Annex I to Directive 2004/39/EC, and contracts for the sale of units in collective investment undertakings, whether or not covered by Council Directive 85/611/EEC of 20 December 1985 on the coordination of laws, regulations and administrative provisions relating to undertakings for collective investment in transferable securities (UCITS)([1]), should be subject to Article 6 of this Regulation. Consequently, when a reference is made to terms and conditions governing the issuance or offer to the public of transferable securities or to the subscription and redemption of units in collective investment undertakings, that reference should include all aspects binding the issuer or the offeror to the consumer, but should not include those aspects involving the provision of financial services.

(27) Various exceptions should be made to the general conflict-of-law rule for consumer contracts. Under one such exception the general rule should not apply to contracts relating to rights *in rem* in immovable property or tenancies of such property unless the contract relates to the right to use immovable property on a timeshare basis within the meaning of Directive 94/47/EC of the European Parliament and of the Council of 26 October 1994 on the protection of purchasers in respect of certain aspects of contracts relating to the purchase of the right to use immovable properties on a timeshare basis([2]).

---

1. OJ L 375, 31.12.1985, p. 3. Directive as last amended by Directive 2008/18/EC of the European Parliament and of the Council (OJ L 76, 19.3.2008, p. 42).
2. OJ L 280, 29.10.1994, p. 83.

(28) It is important to ensure that rights and obligations which constitute a financial instrument are not covered by the general rule applicable to consumer contracts, as that could lead to different laws being applicable to each of the instruments issued, therefore changing their nature and preventing their fungible trading and offering. Likewise, whenever such instruments are issued or offered, the contractual relationship established between the issuer or the offeror and the consumer should not necessarily be subject to the mandatory application of the law of the country of habitual residence of the consumer, as there is a need to ensure uniformity in the terms and conditions of an issuance or an offer. The same rationale should apply with regard to the multilateral systems covered by Article 4(1)(h), in respect of which it should be ensured that the law of the country of habitual residence of the consumer will not interfere with the rules applicable to contracts concluded within those systems or with the operator of such systems.

(29) For the purposes of this Regulation, references to rights and obligations constituting the terms and conditions governing the issuance, offers to the public or public take-over bids of transferable securities and references to the subscription and redemption of units in collective investment undertakings should include the terms governing, inter alia, the allocation of securities or units, rights in the event of over-subscription, withdrawal rights and similar matters in the context of the offer as well as those matters referred to in Articles 10, 11, 12 and 13, thus ensuring that all relevant contractual aspects of an offer binding the issuer or the offeror to the consumer are governed by a single law.

(30) For the purposes of this Regulation, financial instruments and transferable securities are those instruments referred to in Article 4 of Directive 2004/39/EC.

(31) Nothing in this Regulation should prejudice the operation of a formal arrangement designated as a system under Article 2(a) of Directive 98/26/EC of the European Parliament and of the Council of 19 May 1998 on settlement finality in payment and securities settlement systems([3]).

(32) Owing to the particular nature of contracts of carriage and insurance contracts, specific provisions should ensure an adequate level of protection of passengers and policy holders. Therefore, Article 6 should not apply in the context of those particular contracts.

(33) Where an insurance contract not covering a large risk covers more than one risk, at least one of which is situated in a Member State and at least one of which is situated in a third country, the special rules on insurance contracts in this Regulation should apply only to the risk or risks situated in the relevant Member State or Member States.

---

3. OJ L 166, 11.6.1998, p. 45.

(34) The rule on individual employment contracts should not prejudice the application of the overriding mandatory provisions of the country to which a worker is posted in accordance with Directive 96/71/EC of the European Parliament and of the Council of 16 December 1996 concerning the posting of workers in the framework of the provision of services([4]).

(35) Employees should not be deprived of the protection afforded to them by provisions which cannot be derogated from by agreement or which can only be derogated from to their benefit.

(36) As regards individual employment contracts, work carried out in another country should be regarded as temporary if the employee is expected to resume working in the country of origin after carrying out his tasks abroad. The conclusion of a new contract of employment with the original employer or an employer belonging to the same group of companies as the original employer should not preclude the employee from being regarded as carrying out his work in another country temporarily.

(37) Considerations of public interest justify giving the courts of the Member States the possibility, in exceptional circumstances, of applying exceptions based on public policy and overriding mandatory provisions. The concept of 'overriding mandatory provisions' should be distinguished from the expression 'provisions which cannot be derogated from by agreement' and should be construed more restrictively.

(38) In the context of voluntary assignment, the term 'relationship' should make it clear that Article 14(1) also applies to the property aspects of an assignment, as between assignor and assignee, in legal orders where such aspects are treated separately from the aspects under the law of obligations. However, the term 'relationship' should not be understood as relating to any relationship that may exist between assignor and assignee. In particular, it should not cover preliminary questions as regards a voluntary assignment or a contractual subrogation. The term should be strictly limited to the aspects which are directly relevant to the voluntary assignment or contractual subrogation in question.

(39) For the sake of legal certainty there should be a clear definition of habitual residence, in particular for companies and other bodies, corporate or unincorporated. Unlike Article 60(1) of Regulation (EC) No 44/2001, which establishes three criteria, the conflict-of-law rule should proceed on the basis of a single criterion; otherwise, the parties would be unable to foresee the law applicable to their situation.

(40) A situation where conflict-of-law rules are dispersed among several instruments and where there are differences between those rules should be avoided. This Regulation, however, should not exclude the possibility of inclusion of conflict-of-law rules relating to contractual obligations in provisions of Community law with regard to particular matters.

---

4. OJ L 18, 21.1.1997, p. 1.

This Regulation should not prejudice the application of other instruments laying down provisions designed to contribute to the proper functioning of the internal market application of provisions of the applicable law designated by the rules of this Regulation should not restrict the free movement of goods and services as regulated by Community instruments, such as Directive 2000/31/EC of the European Parliament and of the Council of 8 June 2000 on certain legal aspects of information society services, in particular electronic commerce, in the Internal Market (Directive on electronic commerce)([1]).

(41) Respect for international commitments entered into by the Member States means that this Regulation should not affect international conventions to which one or more Member States are parties at the time when this Regulation is adopted. To make the rules more accessible, the Commission should publish the list of the relevant conventions in the *Official Journal of the European Union* on the basis of information supplied by the Member States.

(42) The Commission will make a proposal to the European Parliament and to the Council concerning the procedures and conditions according to which Member States would be entitled to negotiate and conclude, on their own behalf, agreements with third countries in individual and exceptional cases, concerning sectoral matters and containing provisions on the law applicable to contractual obligations.

(43) Since the objective of this Regulation cannot be sufficiently achieved by the Member States and can therefore, by reason of the scale and effects of this Regulation, be better achieved at Community level, the Community may adopt measures, in accordance with the principle of subsidiarity as set out in Article 5 of the Treaty. In accordance with the principle of proportionality, as set out in that Article, this Regulation does not go beyond what is necessary to attain its objective.

(44) In accordance with Article 3 of the Protocol on the position of the United Kingdom and Ireland, annexed to the Treaty on European Union and to the Treaty establishing the European Community, Ireland has notified its wish to take part in the adoption and application of the present Regulation.

(45) In accordance with Articles 1 and 2 of the Protocol on the position of the United Kingdom and Ireland, annexed to the Treaty on European Union and to the Treaty establishing the European Community, and without prejudice to Article 4 of the said Protocol, the United Kingdom is not taking part in the adoption of this Regulation and is not bound by it or subject to its application.

---

1. OJ L 178, 17.7.2000, p. 1.

(46) In accordance with Articles 1 and 2 of the Protocol on the position of Denmark, annexed to the Treaty on European Union and to the Treaty establishing the European Community, Denmark is not taking part in the adoption of this Regulation and is not bound by it or subject to its application,

HAVE ADOPTED THIS REGULATION:

CHAPTER I
SCOPE

Article 1
Material scope

1. This Regulation shall apply, in situations involving a conflict of laws, to contractual obligations in civil and commercial matters.
   It shall not apply, in particular, to revenue, customs or administrative matters.
2. The following shall be excluded from the scope of this Regulation:
   (a) questions involving the status or legal capacity of natural persons, without prejudice to Article 13;
   (b) obligations arising out of family relationships and relationships deemed by the law applicable to such relationships to have comparable effects, including maintenance obligations;
   (c) obligations arising out of matrimonial property regimes, property regimes of relationships deemed by the law applicable to such relationships to have comparable effects to marriage, and wills and succession;
   (d) obligations arising under bills of exchange, cheques and promissory notes and other negotiable instruments to the extent that the obligations under such other negotiable instruments arise out of their negotiable character;
   (e) arbitration agreements and agreements on the choice of court;
   (f) questions governed by the law of companies and other bodies, corporate or unincorporated, such as the creation, by registration or otherwise, legal capacity, internal organisation or winding-up of companies and other bodies, corporate or unincorporated, and the personal liability of officers and members as such for the obligations of the company or body;
   (g) the question whether an agent is able to bind a principal, or an organ to bind a company or other body corporate or unincorporated, in relation to a third party;
   (h) the constitution of trusts and the relationship between settlors, trustees and beneficiaries;
   (i) obligations arising out of dealings prior to the conclusion of a contract;

(j) insurance contracts arising out of operations carried out by organisations other than undertakings referred to in Article 2 of Directive
2002/83/EC of the European Parliament and of the Council of 5
November 2002 concerning life assurance([1]) the object of which is to
provide benefits for employed or self-employed persons belonging to
an undertaking or group of undertakings, or to a trade or group of
trades, in the event of death or survival or of discontinuance or
curtailment of activity, or of sickness related to work or accidents at
work.

3. This Regulation shall not apply to evidence and procedure, without
prejudice to Article 18.

4. In this Regulation, the term 'Member State' shall mean Member States to
which this Regulation applies. However, in Article 3(4) and Article 7 the
term shall mean all the Member States.

Article 2
Universal application

Any law specified by this Regulation shall be applied whether or not it is the law of a
Member State.

CHAPTER II
UNIFORM RULES

Article 3
Freedom of choice

1. A contract shall be governed by the law chosen by the parties. The choice
shall be made expressly or clearly demonstrated by the terms of the
contract or the circumstances of the case. By their choice the parties can
select the law applicable to the whole or to part only of the contract.

2. The parties may at any time agree to subject the contract to a law other than
that which previously governed it, whether as a result of an earlier choice
made under this Article or of other provisions of this Regulation. Any
change in the law to be applied that is made after the conclusion of the
contract shall not prejudice its formal validity under Article 11 or adversely
affect the rights of third parties.

3. Where all other elements relevant to the situation at the time of the choice
are located in a country other than the country whose law has been chosen,
the choice of the parties shall not prejudice the application of provisions of
the law of that other country which cannot be derogated from by agreement.

---

1. OJ L 345, 19.12.2002, p. 1. Directive as last amended by Directive 2008/19/EC (OJ L 76,
19.3.2008, p. 44).

4. Where all other elements relevant to the situation at the time of the choice are located in one or more Member States, the parties' choice of applicable law other than that of a Member State shall not prejudice the application of provisions of Community law, where appropriate as implemented in the Member State of the forum, which cannot be derogated from by agreement.
5. The existence and validity of the consent of the parties as to the choice of the applicable law shall be determined in accordance with the provisions of Articles 10, 11 and 13.

Article 4
Applicable law in the absence of choice

1. To the extent that the law applicable to the contract has not been chosen in accordance with Article 3 and without prejudice to Articles 5 to 8, the law governing the contract shall be determined as follows:
   (a) a contract for the sale of goods shall be governed by the law of the country where the seller has his habitual residence;
   (b) a contract for the provision of services shall be governed by the law of the country where the service provider has his habitual residence;
   (c) a contract relating to a right *in rem* in immovable property or to a tenancy of immovable property shall be governed by the law of the country where the property is situated;
   (d) notwithstanding point (c), a tenancy of immovable property concluded for temporary private use for a period of no more than six consecutive months shall be governed by the law of the country where the landlord has his habitual residence, provided that the tenant is a natural person and has his habitual residence in the same country;
   (e) a franchise contract shall be governed by the law of the country where the franchisee has his habitual residence;
   (f) a distribution contract shall be governed by the law of the country where the distributor has his habitual residence;
   (g) a contract for the sale of goods by auction shall be governed by the law of the country where the auction takes place, if such a place can be determined;
   (h) a contract concluded within a multilateral system which brings together or facilitates the bringing together of multiple third-party buying and selling interests in financial instruments, as defined by Article 4(1), point (17) of Directive 2004/39/EC, in accordance with non-discretionary rules and governed by a single law, shall be governed by that law.

191

2. Where the contract is not covered by paragraph 1 or where the elements of the contract would be covered by more than one of points (a) to (h) of paragraph 1, the contract shall be governed by the law of the country where the party required to effect the characteristic performance of the contract has his habitual residence.

3. Where it is clear from all the circumstances of the case that the contract is manifestly more closely connected with a country other than that indicated in paragraphs 1 or 2, the law of that other country shall apply.

4. Where the law applicable cannot be determined pursuant to paragraphs 1 or 2, the contract shall be governed by the law of the country with which it is most closely connected.

Article 5
Contracts of carriage

1. To the extent that the law applicable to a contract for the carriage of goods has not been chosen in accordance with Article 3, the law applicable shall be the law of the country of habitual residence of the carrier, provided that the place of receipt or the place of delivery or the habitual residence of the consignor is also situated in that country. If those requirements are not met, the law of the country where the place of delivery as agreed by the parties is situated shall apply.

2. To the extent that the law applicable to a contract for the carriage of passengers has not been chosen by the parties in accordance with the second subparagraph, the law applicable shall be the law of the country where the passenger has his habitual residence, provided that either the place of departure or the place of destination is situated in that country. If these requirements are not met, the law of the country where the carrier has his habitual residence shall apply.

   The parties may choose as the law applicable to a contract for the carriage of passengers in accordance with Article 3 only the law of the country where:

   (a) the passenger has his habitual residence; or
   (b) the carrier has his habitual residence; or
   (c) the carrier has his place of central administration; or
   (d) the place of departure is situated; or
   (e) the place of destination is situated.

3. Where it is clear from all the circumstances of the case that the contract, in the absence of a choice of law, is manifestly more closely connected with a country other than that indicated in paragraphs 1 or 2, the law of that other country shall apply.

Article 6
Consumer contracts

1 Without prejudice to Articles 5 and 7, a contract concluded by a natural person for a purpose which can be regarded as being outside his trade or profession (the consumer) with another person acting in the exercise of his trade or profession (the professional) shall be governed by the law of the country where the consumer has his habitual residence, provided that the professional:

(a) pursues his commercial or professional activities in the country where the consumer has his habitual residence, or

(b) by any means, directs such activities to that country or to several countries including that country,

and the contract falls within the scope of such activities.

2. Notwithstanding paragraph 1, the parties may choose the law applicable to a contract which fulfils the requirements of paragraph 1, in accordance with Article 3. Such a choice may not, however, have the result of depriving the consumer of the protection afforded to him by provisions that cannot be derogated from by agreement by virtue of the law which, in the absence of choice, would have been applicable on the basis of paragraph 1.

3. If the requirements in points (a) or (b) of paragraph 1 are not fulfilled, the law applicable to a contract between a consumer and a professional shall be determined pursuant to Articles 3 and 4.

4. Paragraphs 1 and 2 shall not apply to:

(a) a contract for the supply of services where the services are to be supplied to the consumer exclusively in a country other than that in which he has his habitual residence;

(b) a contract of carriage other than a contract relating to package travel within the meaning of Council Directive 90/314/EEC of 13 June 1990 on package travel, package holidays and package tours([1]);

(c) a contract relating to a right *in rem* in immovable property or a tenancy of immovable property other than a contract relating to the right to use immovable properties on a timeshare basis within the meaning of Directive 94/47/EC;

(d) rights and obligations which constitute a financial instrument and rights and obligations constituting the terms and conditions governing the issuance or offer to the public and public take-over bids of transferable securities, and the subscription and redemption of units in collective investment undertakings in so far as these activities do not constitute provision of a financial service;

(e) a contract concluded within the type of system falling within the scope of Article 4(1)(h).

---

1. OJ L 158, 23.6.1990, p. 59.

Article 7
Insurance contracts

1. This Article shall apply to contracts referred to in paragraph 2, whether or not the risk covered is situated in a Member State, and to all other insurance contracts covering risks situated inside the territory of the Member States. It shall not apply to reinsurance contracts.

2. An insurance contract covering a large risk as defined in Article 5(d) of the First Council Directive 73/239/EEC of 24 July 1973 on the coordination of laws, regulations and administrative provisions relating to the taking-up and pursuit of the business of direct insurance other than life assurance([2]) shall be governed by the law chosen by the parties in accordance with Article 3 of this Regulation.

   To the extent that the applicable law has not been chosen by the parties, the insurance contract shall be governed by the law of the country where the insurer has his habitual residence. Where it is clear from all the circumstances of the case that the contract is manifestly more closely connected with another country, the law of that other country shall apply.

3. In the case of an insurance contract other than a contract falling within paragraph 2, only the following laws may be chosen by the parties in accordance with Article 3:

   (a) the law of any Member State where the risk is situated at the time of conclusion of the contract;

   (b) the law of the country where the policy holder has his habitual residence;

   (c) in the case of life assurance, the law of the Member State of which the policy holder is a national;

   (d) for insurance contracts covering risks limited to events occurring in one Member State other than the Member State where the risk is situated, the law of that Member State;

   (e) where the policy holder of a contract falling under this paragraph pursues a commercial or industrial activity or a liberal profession and the insurance contract covers two or more risks which relate to those activities and are situated in different Member States, the law of any of the Member States concerned or the law of the country of habitual residence of the policy holder.

   Where, in the cases set out in points (a), (b) or (e), the Member States referred to grant greater freedom of choice of the law applicable to the insurance contract, the parties may take advantage of that freedom.

---

2. OJ L 228, 16.8.1973, p. 3. Directive as last amended by Directive 2005/68/EC of the European Parliament and of the Council (OJ L 323, 9.12.2005, p. 1).

To the extent that the law applicable has not been chosen by the parties in accordance with this paragraph, such a contract shall be governed by the law of the Member State in which the risk is situated at the time of conclusion of the contract.

4. The following additional rules shall apply to insurance contracts covering risks for which a Member State imposes an obligation to take out insurance:

(a) the insurance contract shall not satisfy the obligation to take out insurance unless it complies with the specific provisions relating to that insurance laid down by the Member State that imposes the obligation. Where the law of the Member State in which the risk is situated and the law of the Member State imposing the obligation to take out insurance contradict each other, the latter shall prevail;

(b) by way of derogation from paragraphs 2 and 3, a Member State may lay down that the insurance contract shall be governed by the law of the Member State that imposes the obligation to take out insurance.

5. For the purposes of paragraph 3, third subparagraph, and paragraph 4, where the contract covers risks situated in more than one Member State, the contract shall be considered as constituting several contracts each relating to only one Member State.

6. For the purposes of this Article, the country in which the risk is situated shall be determined in accordance with Article 2(d) of the Second Council Directive 88/357/EEC of 22 June 1988 on the coordination of laws, regulations and administrative provisions relating to direct insurance other than life assurance and laying down provisions to facilitate the effective exercise of freedom to provide services([1]) and, in the case of life assurance, the country in which the risk is situated shall be the country of the commitment within the meaning of Article 1(1) (g) of Directive 2002/83/EC.

Article 8
Individual employment contracts

1. An individual employment contract shall be governed by the law chosen by the parties in accordance with Article 3. Such a choice of law may not, however, have the result of depriving the employee of the protection afforded to him by provisions that cannot be derogated from by agreement under the law that, in the absence of choice, would have been applicable pursuant to paragraphs 2, 3 and 4 of this Article.

---

1. OJ L 172, 4.7.1988, p. 1. Directive as last amended by Directive 2005/14/EC of the European Parliament and of the Council (OJ L 149, 11.6.2005, p. 14).

2. To the extent that the law applicable to the individual employment contract has not been chosen by the parties, the contract shall be governed by the law of the country in which or, failing that, from which the employee habitually carries out his work in performance of the contract. The country where the work is habitually carried out shall not be deemed to have changed if he is temporarily employed in another country.

3. Where the law applicable cannot be determined pursuant to paragraph 2, the contract shall be governed by the law of the country where the place of business through which the employee was engaged is situated.

4. Where it appears from the circumstances as a whole that the contract is more closely connected with a country other than that indicated in paragraphs 2 or 3, the law of that other country shall apply.

Article 9
Overriding mandatory provisions

1. Overriding mandatory provisions are provisions the respect for which is regarded as crucial by a country for safeguarding its public interests, such as its political, social or economic organisation, to such an extent that they are applicable to any situation falling within their scope, irrespective of the law otherwise applicable to the contract under this Regulation.

2. Nothing in this Regulation shall restrict the application of the overriding mandatory provisions of the law of the forum.

3. Effect may be given to the overriding mandatory provisions of the law of the country where the obligations arising out of the contract have to be or have been performed, in so far as those overriding mandatory provisions render the performance of the contract unlawful. In considering whether to give effect to those provisions, regard shall be had to their nature and purpose and to the consequences of their application or non-application.

Article 10
Consent and material validity

1. The existence and validity of a contract, or of any term of a contract, shall be determined by the law which would govern it under this Regulation if the contract or term were valid.

2. Nevertheless, a party, in order to establish that he did not consent, may rely upon the law of the country in which he has his habitual residence if it appears from the circumstances that it would not be reasonable to determine the effect of his conduct in accordance with the law specified in paragraph 1.

Article 11
Formal validity

1. A contract concluded between persons who, or whose agents, are in the same country at the time of its conclusion is formally valid if it satisfies the formal requirements of the law which governs it in substance under this Regulation or of the law of the country where it is concluded.
2. A contract concluded between persons who, or whose agents, are in different countries at the time of its conclusion is formally valid if it satisfies the formal requirements of the law which governs it in substance under this Regulation, or of the law of either of the countries where either of the parties or their agent is present at the time of conclusion, or of the law of the country where either of the parties had his habitual residence at that time.
3. A unilateral act intended to have legal effect relating to an existing or contemplated contract is formally valid if it satisfies the formal requirements of the law which governs or would govern the contract in substance under this Regulation, or of the law of the country where the act was done, or of the law of the country where the person by whom it was done had his habitual residence at that time.
4. Paragraphs 1, 2 and 3 of this Article shall not apply to contracts that fall within the scope of Article 6. The form of such contracts shall be governed by the law of the country where the consumer has his habitual residence.
5. Notwithstanding paragraphs 1 to 4, a contract the subject matter of which is a right *in rem* in immovable property or a tenancy of immovable property shall be subject to the requirements of form of the law of the country where the property is situated if by that law:
   (a) those requirements are imposed irrespective of the country where the contract is concluded and irrespective of the law governing the contract; and
   (b) those requirements cannot be derogated from by agreement.

Article 12
Scope of the law applicable

1. The law applicable to a contract by virtue of this Regulation shall govern in particular:
   (a) interpretation;
   (b) performance;
   (c) within the limits of the powers conferred on the court by its procedural law, the consequences of a total or partial breach of obligations, including the assessment of damages in so far as it is governed by rules of law;
   (d) the various ways of extinguishing obligations, and prescription and limitation of actions;
   (e) the consequences of nullity of the contract.

2. In relation to the manner of performance and the steps to be taken in the event of defective performance, regard shall be had to the law of the country in which performance takes place.

Article 13
Incapacity

In a contract concluded between persons who are in the same country, a natural person who would have capacity under the law of that country may invoke his incapacity resulting from the law of another country, only if the other party to the contract was aware of that incapacity at the time of the conclusion of the contract or was not aware thereof as a result of negligence.

Article 14
Voluntary assignment and contractual subrogation

1. The relationship between assignor and assignee under a voluntary assignment or contractual subrogation of a claim against another person (the debtor) shall be governed by the law that applies to the contract between the assignor and assignee under this Regulation.
2. The law governing the assigned or subrogated claim shall determine its assignability, the relationship between the assignee and the debtor, the conditions under which the assignment or subrogation can be invoked against the debtor and whether the debtor's obligations have been discharged.
3. The concept of assignment in this Article includes outright transfers of claims, transfers of claims by way of security and pledges or other security rights over claims.

Article 15
Legal subrogation

Where a person (the creditor) has a contractual claim against another (the debtor) and a third person has a duty to satisfy the creditor, or has in fact satisfied the creditor in discharge of that duty, the law which governs the third person's duty to satisfy the creditor shall determine whether and to what extent the third person is entitled to exercise against the debtor the rights which the creditor had against the debtor under the law governing their relationship.

Article 16
Multiple liability

If a creditor has a claim against several debtors who are liable for the same claim, and one of the debtors has already satisfied the claim in whole or in part, the law governing the debtor's obligation towards the creditor also governs the debtor's right to claim recourse from the other debtors. The other debtors may rely on the defences they had against the creditor to the extent allowed by the law governing their obligations towards the creditor.

Article 17
Set-off

Where the right to set-off is not agreed by the parties, set-off shall be governed by the law applicable to the claim against which the right to set-off is asserted.

Article 18
Burden of proof

1. The law governing a contractual obligation under this Regulation shall apply to the extent that, in matters of contractual obligations, it contains rules which raise presumptions of law or determine the burden of proof.
2. A contract or an act intended to have legal effect may be proved by any mode of proof recognised by the law of the forum or by any of the laws referred to in Article 11 under which that contract or act is formally valid, provided that such mode of proof can be administered by the forum.

CHAPTER III
OTHER PROVISIONS

Article 19
Habitual residence

1. For the purposes of this Regulation, the habitual residence of companies and other bodies, corporate or unincorporated, shall be the place of central administration.
   The habitual residence of a natural person acting in the course of his business activity shall be his principal place of business.
2. Where the contract is concluded in the course of the operations of a branch, agency or any other establishment, or if, under the contract, performance is the responsibility of such a branch, agency or establishment, the place where the branch, agency or any other establishment is located shall be treated as the place of habitual residence.
3. For the purposes of determining the habitual residence, the relevant point in time shall be the time of the conclusion of the contract.

Article 20
Exclusion of *renvoi*

The application of the law of any country specified by this Regulation means the application of the rules of law in force in that country other than its rules of private international law, unless provided otherwise in this Regulation.

Article 21
Public policy of the forum

The application of a provision of the law of any country specified by this Regulation may be refused only if such application is manifestly incompatible with the public policy (*ordre public*) of the forum.

Article 22
States with more than one legal system

1. Where a State comprises several territorial units, each of which has its own rules of law in respect of contractual obligations, each territorial unit shall be considered as a country for the purposes of identifying the law applicable under this Regulation.
2. A Member State where different territorial units have their own rules of law in respect of contractual obligations shall not be required to apply this Regulation to conflicts solely between the laws of such units.

Article 23
Relationship with other provisions of Community law

With the exception of Article 7, this Regulation shall not prejudice the application of provisions of Community law which, in relation to particular matters, lay down conflict-of-law rules relating to contractual obligations.

Article 24
Relationship with the Rome Convention

1. This Regulation shall replace the Rome Convention in the Member States, except as regards the territories of the Member States which fall within the territorial scope of that Convention and to which this Regulation does not apply pursuant to Article 299 of the Treaty.
2. In so far as this Regulation replaces the provisions of the Rome Convention, any reference to that Convention shall be understood as a reference to this Regulation.

Article 25
Relationship with existing international conventions

1. This Regulation shall not prejudice the application of international conventions to which one or more Member States are parties at the time when this Regulation is adopted and which lay down conflict-of-law rules relating to contractual obligations.
2. However, this Regulation shall, as between Member States, take precedence over conventions concluded exclusively between two or more of them in so far as such conventions concern matters governed by this Regulation.

Article 26
List of Conventions

1. By 17 June 2009, Member States shall notify the Commission of the conventions referred to in Article 25(1). After that date, Member States shall notify the Commission of all denunciations of such conventions.
2. Within six months of receipt of the notifications referred to in paragraph 1, the Commission shall publish in the *Official Journal of the European Union*:
   (a) a list of the conventions referred to in paragraph 1;
   (b) the denunciations referred to in paragraph 1.

Article 27
Review clause

1. By 17 June 2013, the Commission shall submit to the European Parliament, the Council and the European Economic and Social Committee a report on the application of this Regulation. If appropriate, the report shall be accompanied by proposals to amend this Regulation. The report shall include:
   (a) a study on the law applicable to insurance contracts and an assessment of the impact of the provisions to be introduced, if any; and
   (b) an evaluation on the application of Article 6, in particular as regards the coherence of Community law in the field of consumer protection.
2. By 17 June 2010, the Commission shall submit to the European Parliament, the Council and the European Economic and Social Committee a report on the question of the effectiveness of an assignment or subrogation of a claim against third parties and the priority of the assigned or subrogated claim over a right of another person. The report shall be accompanied, if appropriate, by a proposal to amend this Regulation and an assessment of the impact of the provisions to be introduced.

Article 28
Application in time

This Regulation shall apply to contracts concluded after 17 December 2009.

CHAPTER IV
FINAL PROVISIONS

Article 29
Entry into force and application

This Regulation shall enter into force on the 20th day following its publication in the Official Journal of the European Union.

It shall apply from 17 December 2009 except for Article 26 which shall apply from 17 June 2009.

This Regulation shall be binding in its entirety and directly applicable in the Member States in accordance with the Treaty establishing the European Community.

Done at Strasbourg, 17 June 2008.

For the European Parliament	*For the Council*
The President	*The President*
H.-G. PÖTTERING	J. LENARČI

OTHER INTERNATIONAL DOCUMENTS

A. INTERNATIONAL CHAMBER OF COMMERCE INCOTERMS 2010 (SUMMARY)

Source: Incoterms 2010 (ICC Publication No. 715E, 2010)

Website information:

http://www.iccwbo.org/

This is the website of the International Chamber of Commerce (ICC). It provides a general introduction to the ICC, and contains information on the work, structure and role of the ICC. The website does not contain the text of the Incoterms, but does provide details on purchasing information about the Incoterms from the ICC.

The Text of the Incoterms is not available online

Introduction

"Incoterms" or "international commercial terms" are a product of the International Chamber of Commerce (ICC), a non-governmental organization established in 1919 and headquartered in Paris. The ICC has published eight versions of the Incoterms since beginning a study of the meaning of trade terms in 1921. Each version has updated the terms to more closely reflect actual commercial practice; the 2010 version recognizes the growth of multimodal and containerized shipping, is designed to work with electronic documentation, allows use of the terms for domestic (as well as international) transactions, and clearly delineates waterway transit from other forms.

As a formalization of the *lex mercatoria*, the Incoterms are neither a statute nor an international treaty. Thus, an Incoterm definition will be applicable only if the contract incorporates that term, or the entire Incoterms, expressly or by implication (the introduction to Incoterms 2010 makes this clear by stating: "If you want the Incoterms 2010 rules to apply to your contract, you should make this clear in the contract"). Use in a contract of the term "CIF Philadelphia (Incoterms 2010)," for example, is normally sufficient for express application. U.S. courts do not hesitate to apply Incoterms when parties expressly agree upon their application.[1]

Parties to a sales contract may use Incoterms as a short-hand form of agreeing to the division of responsibilities (between seller and buyer) associated with delivery of the goods. Each of the Incoterms allocates these responsibilities—customs documentation, transportation and insurance costs, moment when risk of loss passes, etc.—in a different pattern. If the seller, for example, wishes to minimize its delivery responsibilities it may ask the buyer to agree to delivery EXW (ex works), a term that requires the buyer to pick up the goods at seller's plant at the buyer's risk and expense. The 2010 Incoterms clearly divide terms between rules for any mode of transport

---

1. *See, e.g., Phillips Puerto Rico Core, Inc. v. Tradax Petroleum Ltd.*, 782 F.2d 314 (2d Cir. 1985) (application where C & F (Incoterms 1980) agreed upon by the parties).

(EXW, FCA, CPT, CIP, DAT, DAP, and DDP), and those applicable only to sea or inland waterway transport (FAS, FOB, CFR, and CIF).

Application of Incoterms may be implied where the law which is applicable to the dispute defers to international usage or custom. Article 9, paragraph 2 of the U.N. Convention on Contracts for the International Sale of Goods (CISG), for example, makes applicable to a sales contract "a[ny] usage of which the parties knew or ought to have known and which in international trade is widely known to, and regularly observed by, parties to contracts of the type involved in the particular trade concerned." It has been widely suggested that Incoterms qualify as such "usage."[2]

While Article 2 of the Uniform Commercial Code has been amended by the National Conference of Commissioners on Uniform State Laws to delete all specific definitions of price-delivery terms, many of those amendments have not made their way into state enactment. Thus, if the law of a U.S. state that has retained specific price-delivery term definitions in the UCC governs the contract, and the parties have not expressly incorporated the Incoterms as the source of definition of price-delivery terms, the court must decide whether the Uniform Commercial Code's definitions of trade terms govern or whether the Incoterms are applicable as a usage of trade. At some risk for confusion, the former UCC used some of the same shipping terms as Incoterms.[3] The UCC definitions of the terms may or may not coordinate with Incoterms. Since UCC § 1-201(3) considers usage of trade to be part of the parties' agreement, it is arguable that Incoterms, as usage of trade, should be looked to where the UCC makes no express provision. Usage of trade is defined in the UCC as "any practice or method of dealing having such regularity of observance in a place, vocation or trade as to justify an expectation that it will be observed with respect to the transaction in question."[4]

The following list provides a brief explanation of each term found in the Incoterms 2010:

> **EXW** — *EX WORKS* (. . . named place of delivery): This is the term entailing the least responsibility on the part of the seller. EXW simply requires that the goods be placed at the disposal of the buyer at the seller's premises. All other responsibilities, such as export documentation, freight, and insurance, fall on the buyer. Other terms, including ex mill, ex factory, or ex warehouse, have been used for the same results in the past, but the express use of the term EXW followed by the specific location is recommended in the Incoterms. Note that an EXW transaction does not create an export-import contract as between the buyer and the seller; when the transaction is international, the buyer is both the exporter and the importer.

---

2. *See, e.g.*, Ramberg, "INCOTERMS 1980," in The Transnational Law of International Commercial Transactions 137, at 151 (N. Horn & C. Schmitthoff eds., Deventer: Kluwer Law and Taxation Publishers, 1982).
3. UCC §§ 2-319 - 2-322. These sections define the terms F.O.B., F.A.S., C.I.F., C. & F., and "Ex Ship".
4. UCC § 1-205(2).

FAS — *FREE ALONGSIDE SHIP* (. . . named port of shipment): FAS goes beyond the EXW term, and does create an export-import contract between the buyer and seller. It requires the seller to deliver the goods alongside the vessel named by the buyer (*i.e.*, on a quay or a barge). The risk of loss or damage to the goods passes at that point, with the buyer bearing subsequent costs. The seller, however, is responsible for clearing the goods for export and thus for the costs of any export license and fees. This term is meant for use only when the goods will be shipped by sea. If the seller is to hand the goods over to the carrier at a terminal, and not alongside the vessel, the FCA term should be used.

FOB — *FREE ON BOARD* (. . . named port of shipment): The seller's primary duties under this term are to deliver the goods on board the vessel named by the buyer and to obtain the necessary export documents at the seller's expense. Risk transfers when the goods are onboard the vessel. This term is appropriate only for transit by sea or inland waterway. Otherwise, the FCA term may be a suitable alternative. FOB carries limited responsibility for the seller while at the same time being a true export-import contract. For the sake of convenience, the seller will likely arrange for shipment and insurance even though the cost of these items is the buyer's responsibility. All responsibilities associated with delivering the goods on board the vessel—inland transfer, export license, dock charges, etc.—are the responsibility of the seller.

FCA — *FREE CARRIER* (. . . named place of delivery): This term may be used for any mode of transport, including multi-modal transport. When the transaction is international, the seller is generally responsible for export clearance and costs, but this may vary depending on the point at which goods are handed over to the carrier. The risk passes to the buyer at the place of delivery to the carrier, so a clear designation of the exact place of delivery to the carrier is important.

CPT — *CARRIAGE PAID TO* (. . . named portplace of destination): This term may be used for any mode of transport. While the seller has the obligation to pay the cost of freight to the named place of destination, for purposes of passage of risk, this is a "shipment" contract, and risk passes when the goods have been delivered to the first carrier at the place chosen by the seller. The seller must obtain any export license, and the buyer is responsible for any necessary import license and fees. The buyer bears the cost of insurance.

CIP — *CARRIAGE AND INSURANCE PAID TO* (. . . named place of destination): This term is similar to the CPT term, except that the seller bears the cost of insurance. Delivery is complete, and risk transfers when the goods are placed into the custody of the first carrier.

CFR — *COST AND FREIGHT* (. . . named port of destination): Under this term, risk transfers when the goods are on board the vessel at the port of shipment. This term allocates responsibility to the parties in the same way as the FOB and FCA terms, except that the seller is responsible for the cost of freight. While the contract must always specify the destination, this is a "shipment" contract, and the place of shipment is where the risk passes.

CIF — *COST, INSURANCE AND FREIGHT* (. . . named port of destination): The CIF term allocates responsibilities the same as under the CFR term, except that the insurance cost is the responsibility of the seller. This is a "shipment" contract, even though the words will designate the port of destination. Risk transfers at the port of shipment, when the goods are on board the vessel.

DAT — *DELIVERED AT TERMINAL* (. . . named terminal at port or place of destination): This term means that seller's delivery obligation is completed once the goods are unloaded from the arriving means of transport and placed at the disposal of the buyer at the named port or place of destination. The seller bears all risks in getting the goods to the terminal or place of destination. The seller is responsible for the export license and costs and the buyer is responsible for the import license and costs. The seller must pay the freight costs to the terminal, and must unload the goods from the arriving means of transport and place them at the disposal of the buyer.

DAP — *DELIVERED AT PLACE* (. . . named place of destination): This term means that seller's delivery obligation is completed once the goods are placed at the disposal of the buyer on the arriving means of transport (ready to be unloaded) at the named place. The seller bears risks prior to reaching the named place, and the buyer bears risks after delivery onboard at the named place. The seller bears costs of export, and the buyer bears costs of import.

DDP — *DELIVERED DUTY PAID* (. . . named place of destination): This term represents the opposite end of the continuum of responsibility from the EXW term. The seller must deliver the goods at the buyer's disposal on the arriving means of transport ready for unloading. The seller is both the exporter (responsible for export licenses and fees) and the importer (responsible for import licenses and fees). Risk passes when the goods are placed at the buyer's disposal.

B. INTERNATIONAL CHAMBER OF COMMERCE UNIFORM CUSTOMS AND PRACTICE FOR DOCUMENTARY CREDITS (UCP)

Source: ICC Publication No. 600 (2007)

Website information:

http://www.iccwbo.org

This is the website of the International Chamber of Commerce (ICC). It provides a general introduction to the ICC, and contains information on the work, structure and role of the ICC. The website does not contain the text of the Uniform Customs and Practice (UCP), but does provide details on purchasing information about the UCP from the ICC.

Introduction

Like the Incoterms, the UCP is neither legislation nor international treaty, but rather a set of rules that may be incorporated as part of the chosen substantive law in the contract. While the parties to a sales contract may choose Incoterms to govern aspects of the performance of the contract itself, UCP is generally chosen by the bank which issues a letter of credit in favor of one of the parties. As a general rule, the UCP is applicable to a documentary credit when an issuing bank expressly incorporates the UCP. Since the UCP is a set of rules developed by the banking community, it has become a popular addition to letter of credit agreements.

The first version of the UCP was published in 1933. Revisions came in 1951, 1962, 1974, 1983 1993, and, most recently, 2007 (Publication No. 600). The last two revisions provide a focus on electronic transactions.

Text

The text of the UCP 600 is available only by purchase from the ICC.

UNITED STATES FEDERAL LAWS, REGULATIONS AND OTHER DOCUMENTS

A. FEDERAL ARBITRATION ACT (SELECTED PROVISIONS)

9 U.S. Code - ARBITRATION
(FEDERAL ARBITRATION ACT OF 1925)
CHAPTER 1. GENERAL PROVISIONS

§ 1. "Maritime transactions and "commerce" defined; exceptions to operation of title

"Maritime transactions", as herein defined, means charter parties, bills of lading of water carriers, agreements relating to wharfage, supplies furnished vessels or repairs to vessels, collisions, or any other matters in foreign commerce which, if the subject of controversy, would be embraced within admiralty jurisdiction; "commerce", as herein defined, means commerce among the several States or with foreign nations, or in any Territory of the United States or in the District of Columbia, or between any such Territory and another, or between any such Territory and any State or foreign nation, or between the District of Columbia and any State or Territory or foreign nation, but nothing herein contained shall apply to contracts of employment of seamen, railroad employees, or any other class of workers engaged in foreign or interstate commerce.

HISTORY: (July 30, 1947, ch 392, § 1, 61 Stat. 670.)

§ 2. Validity, irrevocability, and enforcement of agreements to arbitrate

A written provision in any maritime transaction or a contract evidencing a transaction involving commerce to settle by arbitration a controversy thereafter arising out of such contract or transaction, or the refusal to perform the whole or any part thereof, or an agreement in writing to submit to arbitration an existing controversy arising out of such a contract, transaction, or refusal, shall be valid, irrevocable, and enforceable, save upon such grounds as exist at law or in equity for the revocation of any contract.

HISTORY: (July 30, 1947, ch 392, § 1, 61 Stat. 670.)

§ 3. Stay of proceedings where issue therein referable to arbitration

If any suit or proceeding be brought in any of the courts of the United States upon any issue referable to arbitration under an agreement in writing for such arbitration, the court in which such suit is pending, upon being satisfied that the issue involved in such suit or proceeding is referable to arbitration under such an agreement, shall on application of one of the parties stay the trial of the action until such arbitration has been had in accordance with the terms of the agreement, providing the applicant for the stay is not in default in proceeding with such arbitration.

HISTORY: (July 30, 1947, ch 392, § 1, 61 Stat. 670.)

§ 4. Failure to arbitrate under agreement; petition to United States court having jurisdiction for order to compel arbitration; notice and service thereof; hearing and determination

A party aggrieved by the alleged failure, neglect, or refusal of another to arbitrate under a written agreement for arbitration may petition any United States district court which, save for such agreement, would have jurisdiction under Title 28 [28 USC §§ 1 et seq.], in a civil action or in admiralty of the subject matter of a suit arising out of the controversy between the parties, for an order directing that such arbitration proceed in the manner provided for in such agreement. Five days' notice in writing of such application shall be served upon the party in default. Service thereof shall be made in the manner provided by the Federal Rules of Civil Procedure [USC Rules of Civil Procedure]. The court shall hear the parties, and upon being satisfied that the making of the agreement for arbitration or the failure to comply therewith is not in issue, the court shall make an order directing the parties to proceed to arbitration in accordance with the terms of the agreement. The hearing and proceedings, under such agreement, shall be within the district in which the petition for an order directing such arbitration is filed. If the making of the arbitration agreement or the failure, neglect, or refusal to perform the same be in issue, the court shall proceed summarily to the trial thereof. If no jury trial be demanded by the party alleged to be in default, or if the matter in dispute is within admiralty jurisdiction, the court shall hear and determine such issue. Where such an issue is raised, the party alleged to be in default may, except in cases of admiralty, on or before the return day of the notice of application, demand a jury trial of such issue, and upon such demand the court shall make an order referring the issue or issues to a jury in the manner provided by the Federal Rules of Civil Procedure [USC Rules of Civil Procedure], or may specially call a jury for that purpose. If the jury find that no agreement in writing for arbitration was made or that there is no default in proceeding thereunder, the proceeding shall be dismissed. If the jury find that an agreement for arbitration was made in writing and that there is a default in proceeding thereunder, the court shall make an order summarily directing the parties to proceed with the arbitration in accordance with the terms thereof.

HISTORY: (July 30, 1947, ch 392, § 1, 61 Stat. 671; Sept. 3, 1954, ch 1263, § 19, 68 Stat. 1233.)

§ 5. Appointment of arbitrators or umpire

If in the agreement provision be made for a method of naming or appointing an arbitrator or arbitrators or an umpire, such method shall be followed; but if no method be provided therein, or if a method be provided and any party thereto shall fail to avail himself of such method, or if for any other reason there shall be a lapse in the naming of an arbitrator or arbitrators or umpire, or in filling a vacancy, then upon the application of either party to the controversy the court shall designate and appoint an arbitrator or arbitrators or umpire, as the case may require, who shall act under the said agreement with the same force and effect as if he or they had been specifically named therein; and unless otherwise provided in the agreement the arbitration shall be by a single arbitrator.

HISTORY: (July 30, 1947, ch 392, § 1, 61 Stat. 671.)

§ 6. Application heard as motion

Any application to the court hereunder shall be made and heard in the manner provided by law for the making and hearing of motions, except as otherwise herein expressly provided.

HISTORY: (July 30, 1947, ch 392, § 1, 61 Stat. 671.)

§ 7. Witnesses before arbitrators; fees; compelling attendance

The arbitrators selected either as prescribed in this title [9 USC §§ 1 et seq.] or otherwise, or a majority of them, may summon in writing any person to attend before them or any of them as a witness and in a proper case to bring with him or them any book, record, document, or paper which may be deemed material as evidence in the case. The fees for such attendance shall be the same as the fees of witnesses before masters of the United States courts. Said summons shall issue in the name of the arbitrator or arbitrators, or a majority of them, and shall be signed by the arbitrators, or a majority of them, and shall be directed to the said person and shall be served in the same manner as subpoenas to appear and testify before the court; if any person or persons so summoned to testify shall refuse or neglect to obey said summons, upon petition the United States district court for the district in which such arbitrators, or a majority of them, are sitting may compel the attendance of such person or persons before said arbitrator or arbitrators, or punish said person or persons for contempt in the same manner provided by law for securing the attendance of witnesses or their punishment for neglect or refusal to attend in the courts of the United States.

HISTORY: (July 30, 1947, ch 392, § 1, 61 Stat. 672: Oct. 31, 1951, ch 655, § 14, 65 Stat. 715.)

§ 8. Proceedings begun by libel in admiralty and seizure of vessel or property

If the basis of jurisdiction be a cause of action otherwise justiciable in admiralty, then, notwithstanding anything herein to the contrary, the party claiming to be aggrieved may begin his proceeding hereunder by libel and seizure of the vessel or other property of the other party according to the usual course of admiralty proceedings, and the court shall then have jurisdiction to direct the parties to proceed with the arbitration and shall retain jurisdiction to enter its decree upon the award.

HISTORY: (July 30, 1947, ch 392, § 1, 61 Stat. 672.)

§ 9. Award of arbitrators; confirmation; jurisdiction; procedure

If the parties in their agreement have agreed that a judgment of the court shall be entered upon the award made pursuant to the arbitration, and shall specify the court, then at any time within one year after the award is made any party to the arbitration may apply to the court so specified for an order confirming the award, and thereupon the court must grant such an order unless the award is vacated, modified, or corrected as prescribed in sections 10 and 11 of this title [9 USC §§ 10, 11]. If no court is specified in the agreement of the parties, then such application may be made to the United States court in and for the district within which such award was made. Notice of the application shall be served upon the adverse party, and thereupon the court shall have jurisdiction of such party as though he had appeared generally in the proceeding. If the adverse party is a resident of the district within which the award was made, such service shall be made upon the adverse party or his attorney as prescribed by law for service of notice of motion in an action in the same court. If the adverse party shall be a nonresident, then the notice of the application shall be served by the marshal of any district within which the adverse party may be found in like manner as other process of the court.

HISTORY: (July 30, 1947, ch 392, § 1, 61 Stat. 672.)

§ 10. Same; vacation; grounds; rehearing

(a) In any of the following cases the United States court in and for the district wherein the award was made may make an order vacating the award upon the application of any party to the arbitration—
   (1) Where the award was procured by corruption, fraud, or undue means.
   (2) Where there was evident partiality or corruption in the arbitrators, or either of them.
   (3) Where the arbitrators were guilty of misconduct in refusing to postpone the hearing, upon sufficient cause shown, or in refusing to hear evidence pertinent and material to the controversy; or of any other misbehavior by which the rights of any party have been prejudiced.
   (4) Where the arbitrators exceeded their powers, or so imperfectly executed them that a mutual, final, and definite award upon the subject matter submitted was not made.
   (5) Where an award is vacated and the time within which the agreement required the award to be made has not expired the court may, in its discretion, direct a rehearing by the arbitrators.

(b) The United States district court for the district wherein an award was made that was issued pursuant to section 580 of title 5 may make an order vacating the award upon the application of a person, other than a party to the arbitration, who is adversely affected or aggrieved by the award, if the use of arbitration or the award is clearly inconsistent with the factors set forth in section 572 of title 5.

HISTORY: (July 30, 1947, ch 392, § 1, 61 Stat. 672; as amended Nov. 15, 1990, P .L. 101-552, § 5, 104 Stat. 2745; Aug. 26, 1992, Pub. L. 102-354, § 5(b)(4), 106 Stat. 946.)

§ 11. Same; modification or correction; grounds; order

In either of the following cases the United States court in and for the district wherein the award was made may make an order modifying or correcting the award upon the application of any party to the arbitration—

(a) Where there was an evident material miscalculation of figures or an evident material mistake in the description of any person, thing, or property referred to in the award.

(b) Where the arbitrators have awarded upon a matter not submitted to them, unless it is a matter not affecting the merits of the decision upon the matter submitted.

(c) Where the award is imperfect in matter of form not affecting the merits of the controversy.

The order may modify and correct the award, so as to effect the intent thereof and promote justice between the parties.

HISTORY: (July 30, 1947, ch 392, § 1, 61 Stat. 673.)

§ 12. Notice of motions to vacate or modify; service; stay of proceedings

Notice of a motion to vacate, modify, or correct an award must be served upon the adverse party or his attorney within three months after the award is filed or delivered. If the adverse party is a resident of the district within which the award was made, such service shall be made upon the adverse party or his attorney as prescribed by law for service of notice of motion in an action in the same court. If the adverse party shall be a nonresident then the notice of the application shall be served by the marshal of any district within which the adverse party may be found in like manner as other process of the court. For the purposes of the motion any judge who might make an order to stay the proceedings in an action brought in the same court may make an order, to be served with the notice of motion, staying the proceedings of the adverse party to enforce the award.

HISTORY: (July 30, 1947, ch 392, § 1, 61 Stat. 673.)

§ 13. Papers filed with order on motions; judgment; docketing; force and effect; enforcement

The party moving for an order confirming, modifying, or correcting an award shall, at the time such order is filed with the clerk for the entry of judgment thereon, also file the following papers with the clerk:

(a) The agreement; the selection or appointment, if any, of an additional arbitrator or umpire; and each written extension of the time, if any, within which to make the award.

(b) The award.

(c) Each notice, affidavit, or other paper used upon an application to confirm, modify, or correct the award, and a copy of each order of the court upon such an application.

The judgment shall be docketed as if it was rendered in an action.

The judgment so entered shall have the same force and effect, in all respects, as, and be subject to all the provisions of law relating to, a judgment in an action; and it may be enforced as if it had been rendered in an action in the court in which it is entered.

HISTORY: (July 30, 1947, ch 392, § 1, 61 Stat. 673.)

§ 14. Contracts not affected

This title [9 USC §§ 1 et seq.] shall not apply to contracts made prior to January 1, 1926.

HISTORY: (July 30, 1947, ch 392, § 1, 61 Stat. 674.)

§ 15. Inapplicability of the Act of State doctrine

Enforcement of arbitral agreements, confirmation of arbitral awards, and execution upon judgments based on orders confirming such awards shall not be refused on the basis of the Act of State doctrine.

HISTORY: (Added Nov. 16, 1988, P.L. 100-669, § 1, 102 Stat. 3969.)

§ 16. Appeals

(a) An appeal may be taken from—

(1) an order—

(A) refusing a stay of any action under section 3 of this title,

(B) denying a petition under section 4 of this title to order arbitration to proceed,

      (C) denying an application under section 206 of this title to compel arbitration,

      (D) confirming or denying confirmation of an award of partial award, or

      (E) modifying, correcting, or vacating an award;

    (2) an interlocutory order granting, continuing, or modifying an injunction against an arbitration that is subject to this title; or

    (3) a final decision with respect to an arbitration that is subject to this title.

  (b) Except as otherwise provided in section 1292(b) of title 28, an appeal may not be taken from an interlocutory order—

    (1) granting a stay of any action under section 3 of this title;

    (2) directing arbitration to proceed under section 4 of this title;

    (3) compelling arbitration under section 206 of this title; or

    (4) refusing to enjoin an arbitration that is subject to this title.

HISTORY: (Added Nov. 19, 1988, P.L. 100-702, Title X, § 1019(a), 102 Stat. 4671; Dec. 1, 1990, P.L. 101-650, Title III, § 325(a)(1), 104 Stat. 5120.)

CHAPTER 2. CONVENTION ON THE RECOGNITION AND ENFORCEMENT OF FOREIGN ARBITRAL AWARDS

§ 201. Enforcement of Convention

The Convention on the Recognition and Enforcement of Foreign Arbitral Awards of June 10, 1958, shall be enforced in United States courts in accordance with this chapter [9 USC §§ 201 et seq.].

HISTORY: (Added July 31, 1970, P.L. 91-368, § 1, 84 Stat. 692.)

§ 202. Agreement or award falling under the Convention

An arbitration agreement or arbitral award arising out of a legal relationship, whether contractual or not, which is considered as commercial, including a transaction, contract, or agreement described in section 2 of this title [9 USC § 2], falls under the Convention. An agreement or award arising out of such a relationship which is entirely between citizens of the United States shall be deemed not to fall under the Convention unless that relationship involves property located abroad, envisages performance or enforcement abroad, or has some other reasonable relation with one or more foreign states. For the purpose of this section a corporation is a citizen of the United States if it is incorporated or has its principal place of business in the United States.

HISTORY: (Added July 31, 1970, P.L. 91-368, § 1, 84 Stat. 692.)

§ 203. Jurisdiction; amount in controversy

An action or proceeding falling under the Convention shall be deemed to arise under the laws and treaties of the United States. The district courts of the United States (including the courts enumerated in section 460 of title 28 [28 USC § 460]) shall have original jurisdiction over such an action or proceeding, regardless of the amount in controversy.

HISTORY: (Added July 31, 1970, P.L. 91-368, § 1, 84 Stat. 692.)

§ 204. Venue

An action or proceeding over which the district courts have jurisdiction pursuant to section 203 of this title [9 USC § 203] may be brought in any such court in which save for the arbitration agreement an action or proceeding with respect to the controversy between the parties could be brought, or in such court for the district and division which embraces the place designated in the agreement as the place of arbitration if such place is within the United States.

HISTORY: (Added July 31, 1970, P.L. 91-368, § 1, 84 Stat. 692.)

§ 205. Removal of cases from State courts

Where the subject matter of an action or proceeding pending in a State court relates to an arbitration agreement or award falling under the Convention, the defendant or the defendants may, at any time before the trial thereof, remove such action or proceeding to the district court of the United States for the district and division embracing the place where the action or proceeding is pending. The procedure for removal of causes otherwise provided by law shall apply, except that the ground for removal provided in this section need not appear on the face of the complaint but may be shown in the petition for removal. For the purposes of Chapter 1 of this title [9 USC §§ 1 et seq.] any action or proceeding removed under this section shall be deemed to have been brought in the district court to which it is removed.

HISTORY: (Added July 31, 1970, P.L. 91-368, § 1, 84 Stat. 692.)

§ 206. Order to compel arbitration; appointment of arbitrators

A court having jurisdiction under this chapter [9 USC §§ 201 et seq.] may direct that arbitration be held in accordance with the agreement at any place therein provided for, whether that place is within or without the United States. Such court may also appoint arbitrators in accordance with the provisions of the agreement.

HISTORY: (Added July 31, 1970, P.L. 91-368, § 1, 84 Stat. 693.)

§ 207. Award of arbitrators; confirmation; jurisdiction; proceeding

Within three years after an arbitral award falling under the Convention is made, any party to the arbitration may apply to any court having jurisdiction under this chapter [9 USC §§ 201 et seq.] for an order confirming the award as against any other party to the arbitration. The court shall confirm the award unless it finds one of the grounds for refusal or deferral of recognition or enforcement of the award specified in the said Convention.

HISTORY: (Added July 31, 1970, P.L. 91-368, § 1, 84 Stat. 693.)

§ 208. Chapter 1; residual application

Chapter 1 [9 USC §§ 1 et seq.] applies to actions and proceedings brought under this chapter [9 USC §§ 201 et seq.] to the extent that chapter is not in conflict with this chapter [9 USC §§ 201 et seq.] or the Convention as ratified by the United States.

HISTORY: (Added July 31, 1970, P.L. 91-368, § 1, 84 Stat. 693.)

CHAPTER 3. INTER-AMERICAN CONVENTION ON INTERNATIONAL COMMERCIAL ARBITRATION

§ 301. Enforcement of Convention

The Inter-American Convention on International Commercial Arbitration of January 30, 1975, shall be enforced in United States courts in accordance with this chapter [9 USC §§ 301 et seq.].

HISTORY: (Added Aug. 15, 1990, P.L. 101-369, § 1, 104 Stat. 448.)

§ 302. Incorporation by reference

Sections 202, 203, 204, 205, and 207 of this title shall apply to this chapter [9 USC §§ 301 et seq.] as if specifically set forth herein, except that for the purposes of this chapter [9 USC §§ 301 et seq.] "the Convention" shall mean the Inter-American Convention.

HISTORY: (Added Aug. 15, 1990, P.L. 101-369, § 1, 104 Stat. 448.)

§ 303. Order to compel arbitration; appointment of arbitrators; locale

(a) A court having jurisdiction under this chapter [9 USC §§ 301 et seq.] may direct that arbitration be held in accordance with the agreement at any place therein provided for, whether that place is within or without the United States. The court may also appoint arbitrators in accordance with the provisions of the agreement.

(b) In the event the agreement does not make provision for the place of arbitration or the appointment of arbitrators, the court shall direct that the arbitration shall be held and the arbitrators be appointed in accordance with Article 3 of the Inter-American Convention.

HISTORY: (Added Aug. 15, 1990, P.L. 101-369, § 1, 104 Stat. 448.)

§ 304. Recognition and enforcement of foreign arbitral decisions and awards; reciprocity

Arbitral decisions or awards made in the territory of a foreign State shall, on the basis of reciprocity, be recognized and enforced under this chapter [9 USC §§ 301 et seq.] only if that State has ratified or acceded to the Inter-American Convention.

HISTORY: (Added Aug. 15, 1990, P.L. 101-369, § 1, 104 Stat. 449.)

§ 305. Relationship between the Inter-American Convention and the Convention on the Recognition and Enforcement of Foreign Arbitral Awards of June 10, 1958

When the requirements for application of both the Inter-American Convention and the Convention on the Recognition and Enforcement of Foreign Arbitral Awards of June 10, 1958, are met, determination as to which Convention applies shall, unless otherwise expressly agreed, be made as follows:

(1) If a majority of the parties to the arbitration agreement are citizens of a State or States that have ratified or acceded to the Inter-American Convention and are member States of the Organization of American States, the Inter-American Convention shall apply.

(2) In all other cases the Convention on the Recognition and Enforcement of Foreign Arbitral Awards of June 10, 1958, shall apply.

HISTORY: (Added Aug. 15, 1990, P.L. 101-369, § 1, 104 Stat. 449.)

§ 306. Applicable rules of Inter-American Commercial Arbitration Commission

(a) For the purposes of this chapter [9 USC §§ 301 et seq.] the rules of procedure of the Inter-American Commercial Arbitration Commission referred to in Article 3 of the Inter-American Convention shall, subject to subsection (b) of this section, be those rules as promulgated by the Commission on July 1, 1988.

(b) In the event the rules of procedure of the Inter-American Commercial Arbitration Commission are modified or amended in accordance with the procedures for amendment of the rules of that Commission, the Secretary of State, by regulation in accordance with section 553 of title 5, consistent with the aims and purposes of this Convention, may prescribe that such modifications or amendments shall be effective for purposes of this chapter [9 USC §§ 301 et seq.].

HISTORY: (Added Aug. 15, 1990, P.L. 101-369, § 1, 104 Stat. 449.)

§ 307. Chapter 1; residual application

Chapter 1 [9 USC §§ 1 et seq.] applies to actions and proceedings brought under this chapter [9 USC §§ 301 et seq.] to the extent chapter 1 [9 USC §§ 1 et seq.] is not in conflict with this chapter [9 USC §§ 301 et seq.] or the Inter-American Convention as ratified by the United States.

HISTORY: (Added Aug. 15, 1990, P.L. 101-369, § 1, 104 Stat. 449.)

B. JURISDICTIONAL PROVISIONS OF TITLE 28 OF THE U.S. CODE

Introduction

Article III of the U.S. Constitution provides that "[t]he judicial Power of the United States, shall be vested in one supreme Court, and in such inferior Courts as the Congress may from time to time establish." Congress has exercised its power to create the system of District Courts at the trial level, and Courts of Appeal at the intermediate appellate level, as well as special courts with exclusive jurisdiction over certain matters. Federal District Courts have limited "subject matter" jurisdiction. Thus, cases brought to them must fall within the Constitution and statutory authorization provided by Congress. The rules of subject matter jurisdiction are found in Title 28 of the United States Code. The most important of these rules are § 1331, providing for "federal question" jurisdiction, and thus allowing actions based on federal law; and § 1332, providing for "diversity jurisdiction," and thus giving the federal courts authority to hear cases involving "citizens" of different states of the United States, as well as cases involving foreign citizens on one side and "citizens" of U.S. states on the other. Title 28 also contains sections providing District Court subject matter jurisdiction over cases suits dealing with admiralty (§ 1333), bankruptcy (§ 1334), antitrust (§ 1337), and intellectual property rights (§ 1338). Special provisions exist for tort claims involving violations of international law (§ 1350), and cases against "consuls or vice consuls of foreign states" and "members of a mission or members of their families." (§ 1351)

Title 28 also has sections dealing with service of process in international litigation (§ 1696), transmittal of letters rogatory to and from foreign courts (§ 1781), and assistance to foreign and international tribunals. (§ 1782).

28 U.S. Code - JUDICIARY AND JUDICIAL PROCEDURE
PART IV. JURISDICTION AND VENUE
CHAPTER 85. DISTRICT COURTS; JURISDICTION

§ 1330. Actions against foreign states

(a) The district courts shall have original jurisdiction without regard to amount in controversy of any nonjury civil action against a foreign state as defined in section 1603(a) of this title [28 USC § 1603(a)] as to any claim for relief in personam with respect to which the foreign state is not entitled to immunity either under sections 1605-1607 of this title [28 USC §§ 1605-1607] or under any applicable international agreement.

(b) Personal jurisdiction over a foreign state shall exist as to every claim for relief over which the district courts have jurisdiction under subsection (a) where service has been made under section 1608 of this title [28 USC § 1608].

(c) For purposes of subsection (b), an appearance by a foreign state does not confer personal jurisdiction with respect to any claim for relief not arising out of any transaction or occurrence enumerated in sections 1605-1607 of this title [28 USC §§ 1605-1607].

HISTORY: (Added Oct. 21, 1976, P.L. 94-583, § 2(a), 90 Stat. 2891.)

§ 1331. Federal question

The district courts shall have original jurisdiction of all civil actions arising under the Constitution, laws, or treaties of the United States.

HISTORY: (June 25, 1948, ch 646, § 1, 62 Stat. 930; July 25, 1958, P.L. 85-554, § 1, 72 Stat. 415; Oct. 21, 1976, P.L. 94-574, § 2, 90 Stat. 2721; Dec. 1, 1980, P.L. 96-486, § 2(a), 94 Stat. 2369.)

§ 1332. Diversity of citizenship; amount in controversy; costs

(a) The district courts shall have original jurisdiction of all civil actions where the matter in controversy exceeds the sum or value of $75,000, exclusive of interest and costs, and is between—

(1) citizens of different States;

(2) citizens of a State and citizens or subjects of a foreign state;

(3) citizens of different States and in which citizens or subjects of a foreign state are additional parties; and

(4) a foreign state, defined in section 1603(a) of this title [28 USC § 1603(a)], as plaintiff and citizens of a State or of different States.

For the purposes of this section, section 1335, and section 1441, an alien admitted to the United States for permanent residence shall be deemed a citizen of the State in which such alien is domiciled.

(b) Except when express provision therefor is otherwise made in a statute of the United States, where the plaintiff who files the case originally in the Federal courts is finally adjudged to be entitled to recover less than the sum or value of $75,000, computed without regard to any setoff or counterclaim to which the defendant may be adjudged to be entitled, and exclusive of interest and costs, the district court may deny costs to the plaintiff and, in addition, may impose costs on the plaintiff.

(c) For the purposes of this section and section 1441 of this title—

    (1) a corporation shall be deemed to be a citizen of any State by which it has been incorporated and of the State where it has its principal place of business, except that in any direct action against the insurer of a policy or contract of liability insurance, whether incorporated or unincorporated, to which action the insured is not joined as a party-defendant, such insurer shall be deemed a citizen of the state of which the insured is a citizen, as well as of any State by which the insurer has been incorporated and of the State where it has its principal place of business; and

    (2) the legal representative of the estate of a decedent shall be deemed to be a citizen only of the same State as the decedent, and the legal representative of an infant or incompetent shall be deemed to be a citizen only of the same State as the infant or incompetent.

(d) The word "States", as used in this section, includes the Territories, the District of Columbia, and the Commonwealth of Puerto Rico.

HISTORY: (June 25, 1948, ch 646, § 1, 62 Stat. 930; July 26, 1956, ch 740, 70 Stat. 658; July 25, 1958, P.L. 85-554, § 2, 72 Stat. 415; Aug. 14, 1964, P.L. 88-439, § 1, 78 Stat. 445; Oct. 21, 1976, P.L. 94-583, § 3, 90 Stat. 2891; Nov. 19, 1988, Pub. L. 100-702, Title II, §§ 201(a), 202(a), 203(a), 102 Stat. 4646.) (As amended Oct. 19, 1996, Pub. L. 104-317, Title II, § 205(a), 110 Stat. 3850.)

§ 1333. Admiralty, maritime and prize cases

The district courts shall have original jurisdiction, exclusive of the courts of the States, of:

    (1) Any civil case of admiralty or maritime jurisdiction, saving to suitors in all cases all other remedies to which they are otherwise entitled.

    (2) Any prize brought into the United States and all proceedings for the condemnation of property taken as prize.

HISTORY: (June 25, 1948, ch 646, § 1, 62 Stat. 931; May 24, 1949, ch 139, § 79, 63 Stat. 101.)

§ 1334. Bankruptcy cases and proceedings

(a) Except as provided in subsection (b) of this section, the district courts shall have original and exclusive jurisdiction of all cases under title 11 [11 USC §§ 101 et seq.].

(b) Notwithstanding any Act of Congress that confers exclusive jurisdiction on a court or courts other than the district courts, the district courts shall have original but not exclusive jurisdiction of all civil proceedings arising under title 11 [11 USC §§ 101 et seq.], or arising in or related to cases under title 11 [11 USC §§ 101 et seq.].

(c) (1) Nothing in this section prevents a district court in the interest of justice, or in the interest of comity with State courts or respect for State law, from abstaining from hearing a particular proceeding arising under title 11 [11 USC §§ 101 et seq.] or arising in or related to a case under title 11 [11 USC §§ 101 et seq.].

(2) Upon timely motion of a party in a proceeding based upon a State law claim or State law cause of action, related to a case under title 11 [11 USC §§ 101 et seq.] but not arising under title 11 [11 USC §§ 101 et seq.], with respect to which an action could not have been commenced in a court of the United States absent jurisdiction under this section, the district court shall abstain from hearing such proceeding if an action is commenced, and can be timely adjudicated, in a State forum of appropriate jurisdiction.

(d) Any decision to abstain or not to abstain made under this subsection (other than a decision not to abstain in a proceeding described in subsection (c)(2)), is not reviewable by appeal or otherwise by the court of appeals under section 158(d), 1291, or 1292 of this title or by the Supreme Court of the United States under section 1254 of this title. This subsection shall not be construed to limit the applicability of the stay provided for by section 362 of title 11, United States Code [11 USC § 362], as such section applies to an action affecting the property of the estate in bankruptcy.

(e) The district court in which a case under title 11 [11 USC §§ 101 et seq.] is commenced or is pending shall have exclusive jurisdiction of all of the property, wherever located, of the debtor as of the commencement of such case, and of property of the estate.

HISTORY: (June 25, 1948, ch 646, § 1, 62 Stat. 931; Nov. 6, 1978, P.L. 95-598, Title II, § 238(a), 92 Stat. 2667; July 10, 1984, P.L. 98-353, Title I, § 101(a), 98 Stat. 333; Oct. 27, 1986, P.L. 99-554, Title I, Subtitle C, § 144(e), 100 Stat. 3096; Dec. 1, 1990, P.L. 101-650, Title III, § 309(b), 104 Stat. 5113; Oct. 22, 1994, P.L. 103-394, Title I, § 104(b), 108 Stat. 4109.)

§ 1337. Commerce and antitrust regulations; amount in controversy, costs

(a) The district courts shall have original jurisdiction of any civil action or proceeding arising under any Act of Congress regulating commerce or protecting trade and commerce against restraints and monopolies: Provided, however, That the district courts shall have original jurisdiction of an action brought under section 11707 or 14706 of title 49 [49 USC § 11707], only if the matter in controversy for each receipt or bill of lading exceeds $10,000, exclusive of interest and costs.

(b) Except when express provision therefor is otherwise made in a statute of the United States, where a plaintiff who files the case under section 11707 or 14706 of title 49 [49 USC § 11707], originally in the Federal courts is finally adjudged to be entitled to recover less than the sum or value of $10,000, computed without regard to any setoff or counterclaim to which the defendant may be adjudged to be entitled, and exclusive of any interest and costs, the district court may deny costs to the plaintiff and, in addition, may impose costs on the plaintiff.

(c) The district courts shall not have jurisdiction under this section of any matter within the exclusive jurisdiction of the Court of International Trade under chapter 95 of this title [28 USC §§ 1581 et seq.].

HISTORY: (June 25, 1948, ch 646, § 1, 62 Stat. 931; Oct. 20, 1978, P.L. 95-486, § 9(a), 92 Stat. 1633; Oct. 10, 1980, P.L. 96-417, Title V, § 505, 94 Stat. 1743; Jan. 12, 1983, P.L. 97-449, § 5(f), 96 Stat. 2442; Dec. 29, 1995, P.L. 104-88, Title III, Subtitle A, § 305(a)(3), 109 Stat. 944.)

§ 1338. Patents, plant variety protection, copyrights, mask works, designs, trademarks, and unfair competition

(a) The district courts shall have original jurisdiction of any civil action arising under any Act of Congress relating to patents, plant variety protection, copyrights and trade-marks. Such jurisdiction shall be exclusive of the courts of the states in patent, plant variety protection and copyright cases.

(b) The district courts shall have original jurisdiction of any civil action asserting a claim of unfair competition when joined with a substantial and related claim under the copyright, patent, plant variety protection or trade-mark laws.

(c) Subsections (a) and (b) apply to exclusive rights in mask works under chapter 9 of title 17 [17 USC §§ 901 et seq.] and to exclusive rights in designs under chapter 13 of title 17 [19 USC § 1301 et seq.], to the same extent as such subsections apply to copyrights.

HISTORY: (June 25, 1948, ch 646, § 1, 62 Stat. 931; Dec. 24, 1970, P.L. 91-577, Title III, § 143(b), 84 Stat. 1559.) (As amended Nov. 19, 1988, P.L. 100-702, Title X, § 1020(a)(4), 102 Stat. 4671; Oct. 28, 1998, P.L. 105-304, Title V, § 503(b)(1), (2)(A), 112 Stat. 2917.)

§ 1350. Alien's action for tort

The district courts shall have original jurisdiction of any civil action by an alien for a tort only, committed in violation of the law of nations or a treaty of the United States.
HISTORY: (June 25, 1948, ch 646, § 1, 62 Stat. 934.)

§ 1351. Consuls, vice consuls, and members of a diplomatic mission as defendant

The district courts shall have original jurisdiction, exclusive of the courts of the States, of all civil actions and proceedings against—

   (1) consuls or vice consuls of foreign states; or
   (2) members of a mission or members of their families (as such terms are defined in section 2 of the Diplomatic Relations Act [22 USC § 254a]).
   HISTORY: (June 25, 1948, ch 646, § 1, 62 Stat. 934; May 24, 1949, ch 139, § 80(c), 63 Stat. 101; Sept. 30, 1978, P.L. 95-393, § 8(a)(1), 92 Stat. 810.)

CHAPTER 87. DISTRICT COURTS; VENUE

§ 1391. Venue generally

   . . . .

   (f) A civil action against a foreign state as defined in section 1603(a) of this title may be brought—
      (1) in any judicial district in which a substantial part of the events or omissions giving rise to the claim occurred, or a substantial part of property that is the subject of the action is situated;
      (2) in any judicial district in which the vessel or cargo of a foreign state is situated, if the claim is asserted under section 1605(b) of this title;
      (3) in any judicial district in which the agency or instrumentality is licensed to do business or is doing business, if the action is brought against an agency or instrumentality of a foreign state as defined in section 1603(b) of this title; or
      (4) in the United States District Court for the District of Columbia if the action is brought against a foreign state or political subdivision thereof.
   HISTORY: (June 25, 1948, ch. 646, § 1, 62 Stat. 935; Oct. 5, 1962, P.L. 87-748, § 2, 76 Stat. 744; Dec. 23, 1963, P.L. 88-234, 77 Stat. 473; Nov. 2, 1966, P.L. 89-714, §§ 1, 2, 80 Stat. 1111; Oct. 21, 1976, P.L. 94-583, §§ 3, 5, 90 Stat. 2721, 2897; Nov. 19, 1988, P.L. 100-702, Title X, § 1013(a), 102 Stat. 4669; Dec. 1, 1990, P.L. 101-650, Title III, § 311, 104 Stat. 5114; Dec. 9, 1991, Pub. L. 102-198, § 3, 105 Stat. 1623; Oct. 29, 1992, Pub. L. 102-572, Title V, § 504, 106 Stat. 4513; Oct. 3, 1995, Pub. L. 104-34, § 1, 109 Stat. 293.)

CHAPTER 89. DISTRICT COURTS; REMOVAL OF CASES FROM STATE COURTS

§ 1441. Actions removable generally

(a) Except as otherwise expressly provided by Act of Congress, any civil action brought in a State court of which the district courts of the United States have original jurisdiction, may be removed by the defendant or the defendants, to the district court of the United States for the district and division embracing the place where such action is pending. For purposes of removal under this chapter [28 USC §§ 1441 et seq.], the citizenship of defendants sued under fictitious names shall be disregarded.

(b) Any civil action of which the district courts have original jurisdiction founded on a claim or right arising under the Constitution, treaties or laws of the United States shall be removable without regard to the citizenship or residence of the parties. Any other such action shall be removable only if none of the parties in interest properly joined and served as defendants is a citizen of the State in which such action is brought.

(c) Whenever a separate and independent claim or cause of action within the jurisdiction conferred by section 1331 of this title is joined with one or more otherwise nonremovable claims or causes of action, the entire case may be removed and the district court may determine all issues therein, or, in its discretion, may remand all matters in which State law predominates.

(d) Any civil action brought in a State court against a foreign state as defined in section 1603(a) of this title may be removed by the foreign state to the district court of the United States for the district and division embracing the place where such action is pending. Upon removal the action shall be tried by the court without jury. Where removal is based upon this subsection, the time limitations of section 1446(b) of this chapter may be enlarged at any time for cause shown.

(e) The court to which such civil action is removed is not precluded from hearing and determining any claim in such civil action because the State court from which such civil action is removed did not have jurisdiction over that claim.

HISTORY: (June 25, 1948, ch 646, § 1, 62 Stat. 937; Oct. 21, 1976, P.L. 94-583, § 6, 90 Stat. 2898; June 19, 1986, P.L. 99-336, § 3(a), 100 Stat. 637; Nov. 19, 1988, P.L. 100-702, Title X, § 1016(a), 102 Stat. 4669; Dec. 1, 1990, P.L. 101-650, Title III, § 312, 104 Stat. 5114; Dec. 9, 1991, Pub. L. 102-198, § 4, 105 Stat. 1623.)

PART V. PROCEDURE

CHAPTER 113. PROCESS

§ 1696. Service in foreign and international litigation

(a) The district court of the district in which a person resides or is found may order service upon him of any document issued in connection with a proceeding in a foreign or international tribunal. The order may be made pursuant to a letter rogatory issued, or request made, by a foreign or international tribunal or upon application of any interested person and shall direct the manner of service. Service pursuant to this subsection does not, of itself, require the recognition or enforcement in the United States of a judgment, decree, or order rendered by a foreign or international tribunal.

(b) This section does not preclude service of such a document without an order of court.

HISTORY: (Added Oct. 3, 1964, P.L. 88-619, § 4(a), 78 Stat. 995.)

CHAPTER 117. EVIDENCE; DEPOSITIONS

§ 1781. Transmittal of letter rogatory or request

(a) The Department of State has power, directly, or through suitable channels—

(1) to receive a letter rogatory issued, or request made, by a foreign or international tribunal, to transmit it to the tribunal, officer, or agency in the United States to whom it is addressed, and to receive and return it after execution; and

(2) to receive a letter rogatory issued, or request made, by a tribunal in the United States, to transmit it to the foreign or international tribunal, officer, or agency to whom it is addressed, and to receive and return it after execution.

(b) This section does not preclude—

(1) the transmittal of a letter rogatory or request directly from a foreign or international tribunal to the tribunal, officer, or agency in the United States to whom it is addressed and its return in the same manner; or

(2) the transmittal of a letter rogatory or request directly from a tribunal in the United States to the foreign or international tribunal, officer, or agency to whom it is addressed and its return in the same manner.

HISTORY: (June 25, 1945, c. 646, § 1, 62 Stat. 949; Oct. 3, 1964, P.L. 88-619, § 8(a), 78 Stat. 996.)

§ 1782. Assistance to foreign and international tribunals and to litigants before such tribunals

(a) The district court of the district in which a person resides or is found may order him to give his testimony or statement or to produce a document or other thing for use in a proceeding in a foreign or international tribunal, including criminal investigations conducted before formal accusation. The order may be made pursuant to a letter rogatory issued, or request made, by a foreign or international tribunal or upon the application of any interested person and may direct that the testimony or statement be given, or the document or other thing be produced, before a person appointed by the court. By virtue of his appointment, the person appointed has power to administer any necessary oath and take the testimony or statement. The order may prescribe the practice and procedure, which may be in whole or part the practice and procedure of the foreign country or the international tribunal, for taking the testimony or statement or producing the document or other thing. To the extent that the order does not prescribe otherwise, the testimony or statement shall be taken, and the document or other thing produced, in accordance with the Federal Rules of Civil Procedure.

A person may not be compelled to give his testimony or statement or to produce a document or other thing in violation of any legally applicable privilege.

(b) This chapter [28 USC §§ 1781 et seq.] does not preclude a person within the United States from voluntarily giving his testimony or statement, or producing a document or other thing, for use in a proceeding in a foreign or international tribunal before any person and in any manner acceptable to him.

HISTORY: (June 25, 1948, c. 646, § 1, 62 Stat. 949; May 24, 1949, c. 139, § 93, 63 Stat. 103; Oct. 3, 1964, P.L. 88-619, § 9(a), 78 Stat. 997; Feb. 10, 1996, P.L. 104-106, Div. A., Title XII, Subtitle E, § 1342(b), 110 Stat. 486.)

§ 1783. Subpoena of person in foreign country

(a) A court of the United States may order the issuance of a subpoena requiring the appearance as a witness before it, or before a person or body designated by it, of a national or resident of the United States who is in a foreign country, or requiring the production of a specified document or other thing by him, if the court finds that particular testimony or the production of the document or other thing by him is necessary in the interest of justice, and, in other than a criminal action or proceeding, if the court finds, in addition, that it is not possible to obtain his testimony in admissible form without his personal appearance or to obtain the production of the document or other thing in any other manner.

(b) The subpoena shall designate the time and place for the appearance or for the production of the document or other thing. Service of the subpoena and any order to show cause, rule, judgment, or decree authorized by this section or by section 1784 of this title [28 USC § 1784] shall be effected in accordance with the provisions of the Federal Rules of Civil Procedure relating to service of process on a person in a foreign country. The person serving the subpoena shall tender to the person to whom the subpoena is addressed his estimated necessary travel and attendance expenses, the amount of which shall be determined by the court and stated in the order directing the issuance of the subpoena.

HISTORY: (June 25, 1948, c. 646, § 1, 62 Stat. 949; Oct. 3, 1964, P.L. 88-619, § 10(a), 78 Stat. 997.)

§ 1784. Contempt

(a) The court of the United States which has issued a subpoena served in a foreign country may order the person who has failed to appear or who has failed to produce a document or other thing as directed therein to show cause before it at a designated time why he should not be punished for contempt.

(b) The court, in the order to show cause, may direct that any of the person's property within the United States be levied upon or seized, in the manner provided by law or court rules governing levy or seizure under execution, and held to satisfy any judgment that may be rendered against him pursuant to subsection (d) of this section if adequate security, in such amount as the court may direct in the order, be given for any damage that he might suffer should he not be found in contempt. Security under this subsection may not be required of the United States.

(c) A copy of the order to show cause shall be served on the person in accordance with section 1783(b) of this title [28 USC § 1783 (b)].

(d) On the return day of the order to show cause or any later day to which the hearing may be continued, proof shall be taken. If the person is found in contempt, the court, notwithstanding any limitation upon its power generally to punish for contempt, may fine him not more than $100,000 and direct that the fine and costs of the proceedings be satisfied by a sale of the property levied upon or seized, conducted upon the notice required and in the manner provided for sales upon execution.

HISTORY: (June 25, 1948, c. 646, § 1, 62 Stat. 949; Oct. 3, 1964, P.L. 88-619, § 11, 78 Stat. 998.)

C. FOREIGN SOVEREIGN IMMUNITIES ACT (SELECTED PROVISIONS)

Foreign Sovereign Immunities Act

Introduction

The Foreign Sovereign Immunities Act of 1976 (FSIA), as amended and codified at 28 U.S.C. § 1603, *et seq.*, specifies the circumstances and procedures by which plaintiffs may sue foreign states, their agents or instrumentalities in United States courts. This act of Congress codifies the modern "restrictive theory" of the principle of sovereign immunity, and supplants the traditional role of the executive branch with that of the judiciary in determining state immunity. Under the restrictive theory of sovereign immunity, a state or state instrumentality remains immune from the jurisdiction of the courts of another state in claims arising out of public matters. However, it is not immune from claims arising out of commercial and non-governmental activities that may be carried on by private persons.

The Act provides specific exceptions to the jurisdictional immunity of a foreign state beyond the limited realm of "commercial activity." Immunity to suit will not exist under § 1605(a) when:

(1) it has been explicitly or implicitly waived by the foreign state;

(2) the suit arises out of commercial activity carried on in the United States that causes a direct effect in the United States;

(3) property has been taken in violation of international law;

(4) property rights in the United States are acquired in immovable property, or by succession or gift;

(5) the claim is for money damages against a foreign state for personal injury or death, damage to or loss of property, occurring in the United States and caused by the tortious act or omission of a foreign state;

(6) the action is brought to enforce an arbitration agreement made by a foreign state with or for the benefit of a private party; or

(7) where the action is for money damages for personal injury or death that was caused by an act of torture, extrajudicial killing, aircraft sabotage, or hostage taking, if the foreign state is designated as a state sponsor of terrorism under § 6(j) of the Export Administration Act of 1979 (50 U.S.C. App 2405(j)) or § 620A of the Foreign Assistance Act of 1961 (22 U.S.C. 2371).

In addition to immunity from suit, the FSIA also contains rules dealing with immunity from attachment and execution of property of a foreign state (§§ 1609-1610), including specific rules on prejudgment attachment (§ 1610(d)), and rules dealing with immunity from attachment and execution of property of a foreign central bank or monetary authority.

28 U.S. Code - JUDICIARY AND JUDICIAL PROCEDURE
CHAPTER 97. JURISDICTIONAL IMMUNITIES OF FOREIGN STATES

§ 1602. Findings and declaration of purpose

The Congress finds that the determination by United States courts of the claims of foreign states to immunity from the jurisdiction of such courts would serve the interests of justice and would protect the rights of both foreign states and litigants in United States courts. Under international law, states are not immune from the jurisdiction of foreign courts insofar as their commercial activities are concerned, and their commercial property may be levied upon for the satisfaction of judgments rendered against them in connection with their commercial activities. Claims of foreign states to immunity should henceforth be decided by courts of the United States and of the States in conformity with the principles set forth in this chapter.

HISTORY: (Added Oct. 21, 1976, P.L. 94-583, § 4(a), 90 Stat. 2892.)

§ 1603. Definitions

For purposes of this chapter—

(a) A "foreign state", except as used in section 1608 of this title [28 USC § 1608], includes a political subdivision of a foreign state or an agency or instrumentality of a foreign state as defined in subsection (b).

(b) An "agency or instrumentality of a foreign state" means any entity—
   (1) which is a separate legal person, corporate or otherwise, and
   (2) which is an organ of a foreign state or political subdivision thereof, or a majority of whose shares or other ownership interest is owned by a foreign state or political subdivision thereof, and
   (3) which is neither a citizen of a State of the United States as defined in section 1332(c) and (d) of this title [28 USC § 1332(c), (d)], nor created under the laws of any third country.

(c) The "United States" includes all territory and waters, continental or insular, subject to the jurisdiction of the United States.

(d) A "commercial activity" means either a regular course of commercial conduct or a particular commercial transaction or act. The commercial character of an activity shall be determined by reference to the nature of the course of conduct or particular transaction or act, rather than by reference to its purpose.

236

(e) A "commercial activity carried on in the United States by a foreign state" means commercial activity carried on by such state and having substantial contact with the United States.

HISTORY: (Added Oct. 21, 1976, P.L. 94-583, § 4(a), 90 Stat. 2892.)

§ 1604. Immunity of a foreign state from jurisdiction

Subject to existing international agreements to which the United States is a party at the time of enactment of this Act [enacted Oct. 21, 1976] a foreign state shall be immune from the jurisdiction of the courts of the United States and of the States except as provided in sections 1605 to 1607 of this chapter [28 USC §§ 1605-1607].

HISTORY: (Added Oct. 21, 1976, P.L. 94-583, § 4(a), 90 Stat. 2892.)

§ 1605. General exceptions to the jurisdictional immunity of a foreign state

(a) A foreign state shall not be immune from the jurisdiction of courts of the United States or of the States in any case—

(1) in which the foreign state has waived its immunity either explicitly or by implication, notwithstanding any withdrawal of the waiver which the foreign state may purport to effect except in accordance with the terms of the waiver;

(2) in which the action is based upon a commercial activity carried on in the United States by the foreign state; or upon an act performed in the United States in connection with a commercial activity of the foreign state elsewhere; or upon an act outside the territory of the United States in connection with a commercial activity of the foreign state elsewhere and that act causes a direct effect in the United States;

(3) in which rights in property taken in violation of international law are in issue and that property or any property exchanged for such property is present in the United States in connection with a commercial activity carried on in the United States by the foreign state; or that property or any property exchanged for such property is owned or operated by an agency or instrumentality of the foreign state and that agency or instrumentality is engaged in a commercial activity in the United States;

(4) in which rights in property in the United States acquired by succession or gift or rights in immovable property situated in the United States are in issue;

(5) not otherwise encompassed in paragraph (2) above, in which money damages are sought against a foreign state for personal injury or death, or damage to or loss of property, occurring in the United States and caused by the tortious act or omission of that foreign state or of any official or employee of that foreign state while acting within the scope of his office or employment; except this paragraph shall not apply to—

    (A) any claim based upon the exercise or performance or the failure to exercise or perform a discretionary function regardless of whether the discretion be abused, or

    (B) any claim arising out of malicious prosecution, abuse of process, libel, slander, misrepresentation, deceit, or interference with contract rights;

(6) in which the action is brought, either to enforce an agreement made by the foreign state with or for the benefit of a private party to submit to arbitration all or any differences which have arisen or which may arise between the parties with respect to a defined legal relationship, whether contractual or not, concerning a subject matter capable of settlement by arbitration under the laws of the United States, or to confirm an award made pursuant to such an agreement to arbitrate, if (A) the arbitration takes place or is intended to take place in the United States, (B) the agreement or award is or may be governed by a treaty or other international agreement in force for the United States calling for the recognition and enforcement of arbitral awards, (C) the underlying claim, save for the agreement to arbitrate, could have been brought in a United States court under this section or section 1607 [28 USC § 1607], or (D) paragraph (1) of this subsection is otherwise applicable.

(7) Repealed. Pub. L. 110-181, Div. A, § 1083(b)(1)(A)(iii), Jan. 28, 2008, 122 Stat. 341

(b) A foreign state shall not be immune from the jurisdiction of the courts of the United States in any case in which a suit in admiralty is brought to enforce a maritime lien against a vessel or cargo of the foreign state, which maritime lien is based upon a commercial activity of the foreign state: Provided, That—

(1) notice of the suit is given by delivery of a copy of the summons and of the complaint to the person, or his agent, having possession of the vessel or cargo against which the maritime lien is asserted; and if the vessel or cargo is arrested pursuant to process obtained on behalf of the party bringing the suit, the service of process of arrest shall be deemed to constitute valid delivery of such notice, but the party bringing the suit shall be liable for any damages sustained by the foreign state as a result of the arrest if the party bringing the suit had actual or constructive knowledge that the vessel or cargo of a foreign state was involved; and

    (2) notice to the foreign state of the commencement of suit as provided in section 1608 of this title [28 USC § 1608] is initiated within ten days either of the delivery of notice as provided in paragraph (1) of this subsection or, in the case of a party who was unaware that the vessel or cargo of a foreign state was involved, of the date such party determined the existence of the foreign state's interest.

(c) Whenever notice is delivered, under subsection (b)(1), the suit to enforce a maritime lien shall thereafter proceed and shall be heard and determined according to the principles of law and rules of practice of suits in rem whenever it appears that, had the vessel been privately owned and possessed, a suit in rem might have been maintained. A decree against the foreign state may include costs of the suit and, if the decree is for a money judgment, interest as ordered by the court, except that the court may not award judgment against the foreign state in an amount greater than the value of the vessel or cargo upon which the maritime lien arose. Such value shall be determined as of the time notice is served under subsection (b)(1). Decrees shall be subject to appeal and revision as provided in other cases of admiralty and maritime jurisdiction. Nothing shall preclude the plaintiff in any proper case from seeking relief in personam in the same action brought to enforce a maritime lien as provided in this section.

(d) A foreign state shall not be immune from the jurisdiction of the courts of the United States in any action brought to foreclose a preferred mortgage, as defined in the Ship Mortgage Act, 1920 (46 U.S.C. 911 and following). Such action shall be brought, heard, and determined in accordance with the provisions of that Act and in accordance with the principles of law and rules of practice of suits in rem, whenever it appears that had the vessel been privately owned and possessed a suit in rem might have been maintained.

    [(e)(f) Repealed 2008, 122 Stat. 341]

(g) Limitation on discovery.

    (1) In general.

        (A) Subject to paragraph (2), if an action is filed that would otherwise be barred by section 1604, but for subsection (a)(7), the court, upon request of the Attorney General, shall stay any request, demand, or order for discovery on the United States that the Attorney General certifies would significantly interfere with a criminal investigation or prosecution, or a national security operation, related to the incident that gave rise to the cause of action, until such time as the Attorney General advises the court that such request, demand, or order will no longer so interfere.

    (B) A stay under this paragraph shall be in effect during the 12-month period beginning on the date on which the court issues the order to stay discovery. The court shall renew the order to stay discovery for additional 12-month periods upon motion by the United States if the Attorney General certifies that discovery would significantly interfere with a criminal investigation or prosecution, or a national security operation, related to the incident that gave rise to the cause of action.

(2) Sunset.

    (A) Subject to subparagraph (B), no stay shall be granted or continued in effect under paragraph (1) after the date that is 10 years after the date on which the incident that gave rise to the cause of action occurred.

    (B) After the period referred to in subparagraph (A), the court, upon request of the Attorney General, may stay any request, demand, or order for discovery on the United States that the court finds a substantial likelihood would—

        (i) create a serious threat of death or serious bodily injury to any person;

        (ii) adversely affect the ability of the United States to work in cooperation with foreign and international law enforcement agencies in investigating violations of United States law; or

        (iii) obstruct the criminal case related to the incident that gave rise to the cause of action or undermine the potential for a conviction in such case.

(3) Evaluation of evidence. The court's evaluation of any request for a stay under this subsection filed by the Attorney General shall be conducted ex parte and in camera.

(4) Bar on motions to dismiss. A stay of discovery under this subsection shall constitute a bar to the granting of a motion to dismiss under rules 12(b)(6) and 56 of the Federal Rules of Civil Procedure.

(5) Construction. Nothing in this subsection shall prevent the United States from seeking protective orders or asserting privileges ordinarily available to the United States.

HISTORY: (Added Oct. 21, 1976, P.L. 94-583, § 4(a), 90 Stat. 2892; Nov. 9, 1988, P.L. 100-640, § 1, 102 Stat. 3333; Nov. 16, 1988, P.L. 100-669, § 2, 102 Stat. 3969.) (As amended Dec. 1, 1990, P.L. 101-650, Title III, § 325(b)(8), 104 Stat. 5121; April 24, 1996, P.L. 104-132, Title II, Subtitle B, § 221(a), 110 Stat. 1241; April 25, 1997, P.L. 105-11, 111 Stat. 22.)

§ 1605A. Terrorism exception to the jurisdictional immunity of a foreign state

(a) In general.—

    (1) No immunity.—A foreign state shall not be immune from the jurisdiction of courts of the United States or of the States in any case not otherwise covered by this chapter in which money damages are sought against a foreign state for personal injury or death that was caused by an act of torture, extrajudicial killing, aircraft sabotage, hostage taking, or the provision of material support or resources for such an act if such act or provision of material support or resources is engaged in by an official, employee, or agent of such foreign state while acting within the scope of his or her office, employment, or agency.

    (2) Claim heard.—The court shall hear a claim under this section if—

        (A)(i) (I) the foreign state was designated as a state sponsor of terrorism at the time the act described in paragraph (1) occurred, or was so designated as a result of such act, and, subject to subclause (II), either remains so designated when the claim is filed under this section or was so designated within the 6-month period before the claim is filed under this section; or

            (II) in the case of an action that is refiled under this section by reason of section 1083(c)(2)(A) of the National Defense Authorization Act for Fiscal Year 2008 or is filed under this section by reason of section 1083(c)(3) of that Act, the foreign state was designated as a state sponsor of terrorism when the original action or the related action under section 1605(a)(7) (as in effect before the enactment of this section) or section 589 of the Foreign Operations, Export Financing, and Related Programs Appropriations Act, 1997 (as contained in section 101(c) of division A of Public Law 104-208) was filed;

        (ii) the claimant or the victim was, at the time the act described in paragraph (1) occurred—

            (I) a national of the United States;

            (II) a member of the armed forces; or

            (III) otherwise an employee of the Government of the United States, or of an individual performing a contract awarded by the United States Government, acting within the scope of the employee's employment; and

        (iii) in a case in which the act occurred in the foreign state against which the claim has been brought, the claimant has afforded the foreign state a reasonable opportunity to arbitrate the claim in accordance with the accepted international rules of arbitration; or

241

  (B) the act described in paragraph (1) is related to Case Number 1:00CV03110 (EGS) in the United States District Court for the District of Columbia.

(b) Limitations.—An action may be brought or maintained under this section if the action is commenced, or a related action was commenced under section 1605(a)(7) (before the date of the enactment of this section) or section 589 of the Foreign Operations, Export Financing, and Related Programs Appropriations Act, 1997 (as contained in section 101(c) of division A of Public Law 104-208) not later than the latter of—

  (1) 10 years after April 24, 1996; or

  (2) 10 years after the date on which the cause of action arose.

(c) Private right of action.—A foreign state that is or was a state sponsor of terrorism as described in subsection (a)(2)(A)(i), and any official, employee, or agent of that foreign state while acting within the scope of his or her office, employment, or agency, shall be liable to—

  (1) a national of the United States,

  (2) a member of the armed forces,

  (3) an employee of the Government of the United States, or of an individual performing a contract awarded by the United States Government, acting within the scope of the employee's employment, or

  (4) the legal representative of a person described in paragraph (1), (2), or (3), for personal injury or death caused by acts described in subsection (a) (1) of that foreign state, or of an official, employee, or agent of that foreign state, for which the courts of the United States may maintain jurisdiction under this section for money damages. In any such action, damages may include economic damages, solatium, pain and suffering, and punitive damages. In any such action, a foreign state shall be vicariously liable for the acts of its officials, employees, or agents.

(d) Additional damages.—After an action has been brought under subsection (c), actions may also be brought for reasonably foreseeable property loss, whether insured or uninsured, third party liability, and loss claims under life and property insurance policies, by reason of the same acts on which the action under subsection (c) is based.

(e) Special masters.—

  (1) In general.—The courts of the United States may appoint special masters to hear damage claims brought under this section.

(2) Transfer of funds.—The Attorney General shall transfer, from funds available for the program under section 1404C of the Victims of Crime Act of 1984 (42 U.S.C. 10603c), to the Administrator of the United States district court in which any case is pending which has been brought or maintained under this section such funds as may be required to cover the costs of special masters appointed under paragraph (1). Any amount paid in compensation to any such special master shall constitute an item of court costs.

(f) Appeal.—In an action brought under this section, appeals from orders not conclusively ending the litigation may only be taken pursuant to section 1292(b) of this title.

(g) Property disposition.—

(1) In general.—In every action filed in a United States district court in which jurisdiction is alleged under this section, the filing of a notice of pending action pursuant to this section, to which is attached a copy of the complaint filed in the action, shall have the effect of establishing a lien of lis pendens upon any real property or tangible personal property that is—

(A) subject to attachment in aid of execution, or execution, under section 1610;

(B) located within that judicial district; and

(C) titled in the name of any defendant, or titled in the name of any entity controlled by any defendant if such notice contains a statement listing such controlled entity.

(2) Notice.—A notice of pending action pursuant to this section shall be filed by the clerk of the district court in the same manner as any pending action and shall be indexed by listing as defendants all named defendants and all entities listed as controlled by any defendant.

(3) Enforceability.—Liens established by reason of this subsection shall be enforceable as provided in chapter 111 of this title.

(h) Definitions.—For purposes of this section—

(1) the term "aircraft sabotage" has the meaning given that term in Article 1 of the Convention for the Suppression of Unlawful Acts Against the Safety of Civil Aviation;

(2) the term "hostage taking" has the meaning given that term in Article 1 of the International Convention Against the Taking of Hostages;

(3) the term "material support or resources" has the meaning given that term in section 2339A of title 18;

(4) the term "armed forces" has the meaning given that term in section 101 of title 10;

(5) the term "national of the United States" has the meaning given that term in section 101(a)(22) of the Immigration and Nationality Act (8 U.S.C. 1101(a)(22));

(6) the term "state sponsor of terrorism" means a country the government of which the Secretary of State has determined, for purposes of section 6(j) of the Export Administration Act of 1979 (50 U.S.C. App. 2405(j)), section 620A of the Foreign Assistance Act of 1961 (22 U.S.C. 2371), section 40 of the Arms Export Control Act (22 U.S.C. 2780), or any other provision of law, is a government that has repeatedly provided support for acts of international terrorism; and

(7) the terms "torture" and "extrajudicial killing" have the meaning given those terms in section 3 of the Torture Victim Protection Act of 1991 (28 U.S.C. 1350 note).

HISTORY: Added Pub. L. 110-181, Div. A, Title X, § 1083(a)(1), Jan. 28, 2008, 122 Stat. 338.

§ 1606. Extent of liability

As to any claim for relief with respect to which a foreign state is not entitled to immunity under section 1605 or 1607 of this chapter [28 USC §§ 1605, 1607], the foreign state shall be liable in the same manner and to the same extent as a private individual under like circumstances; but a foreign state except for an agency or instrumentality thereof shall not be liable for punitive damages, except any action under section 1605(a)(7) or 1610(f); if, however, in any case wherein death was caused, the law of the place where the action or omission occurred provides, or has been construed to provide, for damages only punitive in nature, the foreign state shall be liable for actual or compensatory damages measured by the pecuniary injuries resulting from such death which were incurred by the persons for whose benefit the action was brought.

HISTORY: (Added Oct. 21, 1976, P.L. 94-583, § 4(a), 90 Stat. 2894.) (As amended Oct. 21, 1998, P.L. 105-277, Div A, § 101(h) [Title I, § 117(b)], 112 Stat. 2681-491.)

§ 1607. Counterclaims

In any action brought by a foreign state, or in which a foreign state intervenes, in a court of the United States or of a State, the foreign state shall not be accorded immunity with respect to any counterclaim—

(a) for which a foreign state would not be entitled to immunity under section 1605 of this chapter [28 USC § 1605] had such claim been brought in a separate action against the foreign state; or

(b) arising out of the transaction or occurrence that is the subject matter of the claim of the foreign state; or

(c) to the extent that the counterclaim does not seek relief exceeding in amount or differing in kind from that sought by the foreign state.

HISTORY: (Added Oct. 21, 1976, P.L. 94-583, § 4(a), 90 Stat. 2894.)

§ 1608. Service; time to answer; default

(a) Service in the courts of the United States and of the States shall be made upon a foreign state or political subdivision of a foreign state:

    (1) by delivery of a copy of the summons and complaint in accordance with any special arrangement for service between the plaintiff and the foreign state or political subdivision; or

    (2) if no special arrangement exists, by delivery of a copy of the summons and complaint in accordance with an applicable international convention on service of judicial documents; or

    (3) if service cannot be made under paragraphs (1) or (2), by sending a copy of the summons and complaint and a notice of suit, together with a translation of each into the official language of the foreign state, by any form of mail requiring a signed receipt, to be addressed and dispatched by the clerk of the court to the head of the ministry of foreign affairs of the foreign state concerned, or

    (4) if service cannot be made within 30 days under paragraph (3), by sending two copies of the summons and complaint and a notice of suit, together with a translation of each into the official language of the foreign state, by any form of mail requiring a signed receipt, to be addressed and dispatched by the clerk of the court to the Secretary of State in Washington, District of Columbia, to the attention of the Director of Special Consular Services—and the Secretary shall transmit one copy of the papers through diplomatic channels to the foreign state and shall send to the clerk of the court a certified copy of the diplomatic note indicating when the papers were transmitted.

    As used in this subsection, a "notice of suit" shall mean a notice addressed to a foreign state and in a form prescribed by the Secretary of State by regulation.

(b) Service in the courts of the United States and of the States shall be made upon an agency or instrumentality of a foreign state:

    (1) by delivery of a copy of the summons and complaint in accordance with any special arrangement for service between the plaintiff and the agency or instrumentality; or

    (2) if no special arrangement exists, by delivery of a copy of the summons and complaint either to an officer, a managing or general agent, or to any other agent authorized by appointment or by law to receive service of process in the United States; or in accordance with an applicable international convention on service of judicial documents; or

    (3) if service cannot be made under paragraphs (1) or (2), and if reasonably calculated to give actual notice, by delivery of a copy of the summons and complaint, together with a translation of each into the official language of the foreign state—

245

(A) as directed by an authority of the foreign state or political subdivision in response to a letter rogatory or request or

(B) by any form of mail requiring a signed receipt, to be addressed and dispatched by the clerk of the court to the agency or instrumentality to be served, or

(C) as directed by order of the court consistent with the law of the place where service is to be made.

(c) Service shall be deemed to have been made—

(1) in the case of service under subsection (a)(4), as of the date of transmittal indicated in the certified copy of the diplomatic note; and

(2) in any other case under this section, as of the date of receipt indicated in the certification, signed and returned postal receipt, or other proof of service applicable to the method of service employed.

(d) In any action brought in a court of the United States or of a State, a foreign state, a political subdivision thereof, or an agency or instrumentality of a foreign state shall serve an answer or other responsive pleading to the complaint within sixty days after service has been made under this section.

(e) No judgment by default shall be entered by a court of the United States or of a State against a foreign state, a political subdivision thereof, or an agency or instrumentality of a foreign state, unless the claimant establishes his claim or right to relief by evidence satisfactory to the court. A copy of any such default judgment shall be sent to the foreign state or political subdivision in the manner prescribed for service in this section.

HISTORY: (Added Oct. 21, 1976, P.L. 94-583, § 4(a), 90 Stat. 2894.)

§ 1609. Immunity from attachment and execution of property of a foreign state

Subject to existing international agreements to which the United States is a party at the time of enactment of this Act [enacted Oct. 21, 1976] the property in the United States of a foreign state shall be immune from attachment arrest and execution except as provided in sections 1610 and 1611 of this chapter [28 USC §§ 1610, 1611].

HISTORY: (Added Oct. 21, 1976, P.L. 94-583, § 4(a), 90 Stat. 2895.)

§ 1610. Exceptions to the immunity from attachment or execution

(a) The property in the United States of a foreign state, as defined in section 1603(a) of this chapter [28 USC § 1603(a)], used for a commercial activity in the United States, shall not be immune from attachment in aid of execution, or from execution, upon a judgment entered by a court of the United States or of a State after the effective date of this Act [see effective date note to 28 USC § 1602], if—

(1) the foreign state has waived its immunity from attachment in aid of execution or from execution either explicitly or by implication, notwithstanding any withdrawal of the waiver the foreign state may purport to effect except in accordance with the terms of the waiver, or

246

(2) the property is or was used for the commercial activity upon which the claim is based, or

(3) the execution relates to a judgment establishing rights in property which has been taken in violation of international law or which has been exchanged for property taken in violation of international law, or

(4) the execution relates to a judgment establishing rights in property—

    (A) which is acquired by succession or gift, or

    (B) which is immovable and situated in the United States: Provided, That such property is not used for purposes of maintaining a diplomatic or consular mission or the residence of the Chief of such mission, or

(5) the property consists of any contractual obligation or any proceeds from such a contractual obligation to indemnify or hold harmless the foreign state or its employees under a policy of automobile or other liability or casualty insurance covering the claim which merged into the judgment, or

(6) the judgment is based on an order confirming an arbitral award rendered against the foreign state, provided that attachment in aid of execution, or execution, would not be inconsistent with any provision in the arbitral agreement, or

(7) the judgment relates to a claim for which the foreign state is not immune under section 1605(a)(7), regardless of whether the property is or was involved with the act upon which the claim is based.

(b) In addition to subsection (a), any property in the United States of an agency or instrumentality of a foreign state engaged in commercial activity in the United States shall not be immune from attachment in aid of execution, or from execution, upon a judgment entered by a court of the United States or of a State after the effective date of this Act [see effective date note to 28 USC § 1062], if—

(1) the agency or instrumentality has waived its immunity from attachment in aid of execution or from execution either explicitly or implicitly, notwithstanding any withdrawal of the waiver the agency or instrumentality may purport to effect except in accordance with the terms of the waiver, or

(2) the judgment relates to a claim for which the agency or instrumentality is not immune by virtue of section 1605(a)(2), (3), (5) or (7), or 1605(b) of this chapter [28 USC § 1605 (a)(2), (3), (5), (b)], regardless of whether the property is or was involved in the act upon which the claim is based.

(c) No attachment or execution referred to in subsections (a) and (b) of this section shall be permitted until the court has ordered such attachment and execution after having determined that a reasonable period of time has elapsed following the entry of judgment and the giving of any notice required under section 1608(e) of this chapter [28 USC § 1608(e)].

(d) The property of a foreign state, as defined in section 1603(a) of this chapter [28 USC § 1603(a)], used for a commercial activity in the United States, shall not be immune from attachment prior to the entry of judgment in any action brought in a court of the United States or of a State, or prior to the elapse of the period of time provided in subsection (c) of this section, if—

    (1) the foreign state has explicitly waived its immunity from attachment prior to judgment, notwithstanding any withdrawal of the waiver the foreign state may purport to effect except in accordance with the terms of the waiver, and

    (2) the purpose of the attachment is to secure satisfaction of a judgment that has been or may ultimately be entered against the foreign state, and not to obtain jurisdiction.

(e) The vessels of a foreign state shall not be immune from arrest in rem, interlocutory sale, and execution in actions brought to foreclose a preferred mortgage as provided in section 1605(d).

(f) (1) (A) Notwithstanding any other provision of law, including but not limited to section 208(f) of the Foreign Missions Act (22 U.S.C. 4308(f)), and except as provided in subparagraph (B), any property with respect to which financial transactions are prohibited or regulated pursuant to section 5(b) of the Trading with the Enemy Act (50 U.S.C. App. 5(b)), section 620(a) of the Foreign Assistance Act of 1961 (22 U.S.C. 2370(a)), sections 202 and 203 of the International Emergency Economic Powers Act (50 U.S.C. 1701-1702), or any other proclamation, order, regulation, or license issued pursuant thereto, shall be subject to execution or attachment in aid of execution of any judgment relating to a claim for which a foreign state (including any agency or instrumentality or such state) claiming such property is not immune under section 1605(a)(7).

       (B) Subparagraph (A) shall not apply if, at the time the property is expropriated or seized by the foreign state, the property has been held in title by a natural person or, if held in trust, has been held for the benefit of a natural person or persons.

    (2) (A) At the request of any party in whose favor a judgment has been issued with respect to a claim for which the foreign state is not immune under section 1605(a)(7), the Secretary of the Treasury and the Secretary of State shall fully, promptly, and effectively assist any judgment creditor or any court that has issued any such judgment in identifying, locating, and executing against the property of that foreign state or any agency or instrumentality of such state.

    (B) In providing such assistance, the Secretaries—

        (i) may provide such information to the court under seal; and

        (ii) shall provide the information in a manner sufficient to allow the court to direct the United States Marshall's office to promptly and effectively execute against that property.

    (3) Waiver.—The President may waive any provision of paragraph (1) in the interest of national security.

(g) Property in Certain Actions.—

    (1) In general.—Subject to paragraph (3), the property of a foreign state against which a judgment is entered under section 1605A, and the property of an agency or instrumentality of such a state, including property that is a separate juridical entity or is an interest held directly or indirectly in a separate juridical entity, is subject to attachment in aid of execution, and execution, upon that judgment as provided in this section, regardless of—

      (A) the level of economic control over the property by the government of the foreign state;

      (B) whether the profits of the property go to that government;

      (C) the degree to which officials of that government manage the property or otherwise control its daily affairs;

      (D) whether that government is the sole beneficiary in interest of the property; or

      (E) whether establishing the property as a separate entity would entitle the foreign state to benefits in United States courts while avoiding its obligations.

    (2) United states sovereign immunity inapplicable.—Any property of a foreign state, or agency or instrumentality of a foreign state, to which paragraph (1) applies shall not be immune from attachment in aid of execution, or execution, upon a judgment entered under section 1605A because the property is regulated by the United States Government by reason of action taken against that foreign state under the Trading With the Enemy Act or the International Emergency Economic Powers Act.

    (3) Third-party joint property holders.—Nothing in this subsection shall be construed to supersede the authority of a court to prevent appropriately the impairment of an interest held by a person who is not liable in the action giving rise to a judgment in property subject to attachment in aid of execution, or execution, upon such judgment.

HISTORY: (Added Pub. L. 94–583, § 4(a), Oct. 21, 1976, 90 Stat. 2896; amended Pub. L. 100–640, § 2, Nov. 9, 1988, 102 Stat. 3333; Pub. L. 100–669, § 3, Nov. 16, 1988, 102 Stat. 3969; Pub. L. 101–650, title III, § 325(b)(9), Dec. 1, 1990, 104 Stat. 5121; Pub. L. 104–132, title II, § 221(b), Apr. 24, 1996, 110 Stat. 1242; Pub. L. 105–277, div. A, § 101(h) [title I, § 117(a)], Oct. 21, 1998, 112 Stat. 2681–480, 2681–491; Pub. L. 106–386, div. C, § 2002(g)(1), formerly § 2002(f)(1), Oct. 28, 2000, 114 Stat. 1543, renumbered § 2002(g)(1), Pub. L. 107–297, title II, § 201(c)(3), Nov. 26, 2002, 116 Stat. 2337; Pub. L. 110–181, div. A, title X, § 1083(b)(3), Jan. 28, 2008, 122 Stat. 341.)

§ 1611. Certain types of property immune from execution

(a) Notwithstanding the provisions of section 1610 of this chapter [28 USC § 1610], the property of those organizations designated by the President as being entitled to enjoy the privileges, exemptions, and immunities provided by the International Organizations Immunities Act [22 USC §§ 288 et seq.] shall not be subject to attachment or any other judicial process impeding the disbursement of funds to, or on the order of, a foreign state as the result of an action brought in the courts of the United States or of the States.

(b) Notwithstanding the provisions of section 1610 of this chapter [28 USC § 1610], the property of a foreign state shall be immune from attachment and from execution, if—

    (1) the property is that of a foreign central bank or monetary authority held for its own account, unless such bank or authority, or its parent foreign government, has explicitly waived its immunity from attachment in aid of execution, or from execution, notwithstanding any withdrawal of the waiver which the bank, authority or government may purport to effect except in accordance with the terms of the waiver; or

    (2) the property is, or is intended to be, used in connection with a military activity and

        (A) is of a military character, or

        (B) is under the control of a military authority or defense agency.

(c) Notwithstanding the provisions of section 1610 of this chapter, the property of a foreign state shall be immune from attachment and from execution in an action brought under section 302 of the Cuban Liberty and Democratic Solidarity (LIBERTAD) Act of 1996 [22 USC § 6082] to the extent that the property is a facility or installation used by an accredited diplomatic mission for official purposes.

HISTORY: (Added Oct. 21, 1976, P.L. 94-583, § 4(a), 90 Stat. 2897.) (As amended March 12, 1996, P.L. 104-114, Title III, § 302(e), 110 Stat. 818.)

D. FOREIGN CORRUPT PRACTICES ACT

Introduction

The Foreign Corrupt Practices Act, originally enacted in 1977, was amended in 1988 and 1998. It contains both accounting provisions requiring careful record-keeping by public companies regarding disposition of assets, and "anti-bribery" provisions prohibiting payments to foreign officials. Under the anti-bribery provisions, there are six principal elements of a violation, providing that it is unlawful to:

(1) make use of interstate commerce
(2) corruptly
(3) in furtherance of an offer of anything of value
(4) to (a) a foreign official, (b) a foreign political party, party official, or candidate for office or (c) to any person while knowing that all or any portion of such thing of value will be offered or given to a foreign official, political party or candidate
(5) for the purpose of inducing a foreign official to use his influence to affect any act or decision of his government or governmental instrumentality
(6) in order to obtain or retain business, or direct business to any person.[1]

The Act provides an exception to liability for "any facilitating or expediting payment to a foreign official, political party, or party official the purpose of which is to expedite or to secure the performance of a routine governmental action by a foreign official, political party, or party official."[2] Two affirmative defenses exist to a violation of the Act: (1) where the payment was "lawful under the written laws and regulations of the foreign . . . country," and (2) where the payment "was a reasonable and bonafide expenditure, such as travel and lodging expenses . . . directly related to (A) the promotion, demonstration or explanation of products or services; or (b) the execution or performance of a contract."[3]

---

1. 15 U.S.C. § 78dd-1(a) and § 78dd-2(a). Item (5) of this list can further be broken down per the language of the statute, prohibiting a payment to the target individual for purposes of:

   (A) (i) influencing any act or decision of such foreign official in his official capacity, (ii) inducing such foreign official to do or omit to do any act in violation of the lawful duty of such official [political party or candidate], to do or omit to do any act in violation of the lawful duty of such official, or (iii) securing any improper advantage; or
   (B) inducing such foreign official to use his influence with a foreign government or instrumentality thereof to affect or influence any act or decision of such government or instrumentality . . . .

   Id. at § 78dd-1(a)(1). *See also* §§ 78dd-1(a)(2) & (3) and 78dd-2(a)(1), (2) & (3). The "securing any improper advantage" language was added in 1998 to conform to the requirements o the OECD Convention on Combating Bribery of Foreign Public Official in International Business Transactions.
2. 15 U.S.C. §§ 78dd-1(b) and 78dd-2(b).
3. 15 U.S.C. §§ 78dd-1(c) and 78dd-2(c).

The Act also provides for vicarious liability when a person knows that a payment to another person will be offered or given to a foreign official or political party.[4]

The 1998 amendments to the Act, contained in the International Anti-Bribery and Fair Competition Act,[5] implemented changes agreed to in the OECD Convention on Combating Bribery of Foreign Public Officials in International Business Transactions.

15 U.S. Code - COMMERCE AND TRADE
Chapter 2B–1 SECURITIES INVESTOR PROTECTION (FOREIGN CORRUPT PRACTICES ACT)

§ 78m. Periodical and other reports

(a) **Reports by issuer of security; contents.** Every issuer of a security registered pursuant to section 12 of this title [15 USC § 78l] shall file with the Commission, in accordance with such rules and regulations as the Commission may prescribe as necessary or appropriate for the proper protection of investors and to insure fair dealing in the security—

(1) such information and documents (and such copies thereof) as the Commission shall require to keep reasonably current the information and documents required to be included in or filed with an application or registration statement filed pursuant to section 12 [15 USC § 78l], except that the Commission may not require the filing of any material contract wholly executed before July 1, 1962.

(2) such annual reports (and such copies thereof), certified if required by the rules and regulations of the Commission by independent public accountants, and such quarterly reports (and such copies thereof), as the Commission may prescribe.

   Every issuer of a security registered on a national securities exchange shall also file a duplicate original of such information, documents, and reports with the exchange.

---

4. 15 U.S.C. §§ 78dd-1(a)(3) and 78dd-2(a)(3).
5. Pub. L. 105-366; 112 Stat. 3202 (1998).

(b) Form of report; books, records, and internal accounting; directives.

(1) The Commission may prescribe, in regard to reports made pursuant to this title, the form or forms in which the required information shall be set forth, the items or details to be shown in the balance sheet and the earning statement, and the methods to be followed in the preparation of reports, in the appraisal or valuation of assets and liabilities, in the determination of depreciation and depletion, in the differentiation of recurring and nonrecurring income, in the differentiation of investment and operating income, and in the preparation, where the Commission deems it necessary or desirable, of separate and/or consolidated balance sheets or income accounts of any person directly or indirectly controlling or controlled by the issuer, or any person under direct or indirect common control with the issuer; but in the case of the reports of any person whose methods of accounting are prescribed under the provisions of any law of the United States, or any rule or regulation thereunder, the rules and regulations of the Commission with respect to reports shall not be inconsistent with the requirements imposed by such law or rule or regulation in respect of the same subject matter (except that such rules and regulations of the Commission may be inconsistent with such requirements to the extent that the Commission determines that the public interest or the protection of investors so requires).

(2) Every issuer which has a class of securities registered pursuant to section 12 of this title [15 USC § 78l] and every issuer which is required to file reports pursuant to section 15(d) of this title [15 USC § 78o(d)] shall—

(A) make and keep books, records, and accounts, which, in reasonable detail, accurately and fairly reflect the transactions and dispositions of the assets of the issuer; and

(B) devise and maintain a system of internal accounting controls sufficient to provide reasonable assurances that—

(i) transactions are executed in accordance with management's general or specific authorization;

(ii) transactions are recorded as necessary (I) to permit preparation of financial statements in conformity with generally accepted accounting principles or any other criteria applicable to such statements, and (II) to maintain accountability for assets;

(iii) access to assets is permitted only in accordance with management's general or specific authorization; and

(iv) the recorded accountability for assets is compared with the existing assets at reasonable intervals and appropriate action is taken with respect to any differences.

(3) (A) With respect to matters concerning the national security of the United States, no duty or liability under paragraph (2) of this subsection shall be imposed upon any person acting in cooperation with the head of any Federal department or agency responsible for such matters if such act in cooperation with such head of a department or agency was done upon the specific, written directive of the head of such department or agency pursuant to Presidential authority to issue such directives. Each directive issued under this paragraph shall set forth the specific facts and circumstances with respect to which the provisions of this paragraph are to be invoked. Each such directive shall, unless renewed in writing, expire one year after the date of issuance.

(B) Each head of a Federal department or agency of the United States who issues a directive pursuant to this paragraph shall maintain a complete file of all such directives and shall, on October 1 of each year, transmit a summary of matters covered by such directives in force at any time during the previous year to the Permanent Select Committee on Intelligence of the House of Representatives and the Select Committee on Intelligence of the Senate.

(4) No criminal liability shall be imposed for failing to comply with the requirements of paragraph (2) of this subsection except as provided in paragraph (5) of this subsection.

(5) No person shall knowingly circumvent or knowingly fail to implement a system of internal accounting controls or knowingly falsify any book, record, or account described in paragraph (2).

(6) Where an issuer which has a class of securities registered pursuant to section 12 of this title [15 USC § 78l] or an issuer which is required to file reports pursuant to section 15(d) of this title [15 USC § 78o(d)] holds 50 per centum or less of the voting power with respect to a domestic or foreign firm, the provisions of paragraph (2) require only that the issuer proceed in good faith to use its influence, to the extent reasonable under the issuer's circumstances, to cause such domestic or foreign firm to devise and maintain a system of internal accounting controls consistent with paragraph (2). Such circumstances include the relative degree of the issuer's ownership of the domestic or foreign firm and the laws and practices governing the business operations of the country in which such firm is located. An issuer which demonstrates good faith efforts to use such influence shall be conclusively presumed to have complied with the requirements of paragraph (2).

(7) For the purpose of paragraph (2) of this subsection, the terms "reasonable assurances" and "reasonable detail" mean such level of detail and degree of assurance as would satisfy prudent officials in the conduct of their own affairs.

(c) Alternative reports. If in the judgment of the Commission any report required under subsection (a) is inapplicable to any specified class or classes of issuers, the Commission shall require in lieu thereof the submission of such reports of comparable character as it may deem applicable to such class or classes of issuers.

(d) Reports by persons acquiring more than five per centum of certain classes of securities.

(1) Any person who, after acquiring directly or indirectly the beneficial ownership of any equity security of a class which is registered pursuant to section 12 of this title [15 USC § 78l], or any equity security of an insurance company which would have been required to be so registered except for the exemption contained in section 12(g)(2)(G) of this title [15 USC § 78l(g)(2)(G)], or any equity security issued by a closed-end investment company registered under the Investment Company Act of 1940 [15 USC §§ 80a-1 *et seq.*] or any equity security issued by a Native Corporation pursuant to section 37(d)(6) of the Alaska Native Claims Settlement Act [43 USC § 1629c(d)(6)], is directly or indirectly the beneficial owner of more than 5 per centum of such class shall, within ten days after such acquisition, send to the issuer of the security at its principal executive office, by registered or certified mail, send to each exchange where the security is traded, and file with the Commission, a statement containing such of the following information, and such additional information, as the Commission may by rules and regulations, prescribe as necessary or appropriate in the public interest or for the protection of investors—

  (A) the background, and identity, residence, and citizenship of, and the nature of such beneficial ownership by, such person and all other persons by whom or on whose behalf the purchases have been or are to be effected;

  (B) the source and amount of the funds or other consideration used or to be used in making the purchases, and if any part of the purchase price is represented or is to be represented by funds or other consideration borrowed or otherwise obtained for the purpose of acquiring, holding, or trading such security, a description of the transaction and the names of the parties thereto, except that where a source of funds is a loan made in the ordinary course of business by a bank, as defined in section 3(a)(6) of this title [15 USC § 78c(a)(6)], if the person filing such statement so requests, the name of the bank shall not be made available to the public;

  (C) if the purpose of the purchases or prospective purchases is to acquire control of the business of the issuer of the securities, any plans or proposals which such persons may have to liquidate such issuer, to sell its assets to or merge it with any other persons, or to make any other major change in its business or corporate structure;

(D) the number of shares of such security which are beneficially owned, and the number of shares concerning which there is a right to acquire, directly or indirectly, by (i) such person, and (ii) by each associate of such person, giving the background, identity, residence, and citizenship of each such associate; and

(E) information as to any contracts, arrangements, or understandings with any person with respect to any securities of the issuer, including but not limited to transfer of any of the securities, joint ventures, loan or option arrangements, puts or calls, guaranties of loans, guaranties against loss or guaranties of profits, division of losses or profits, or the giving or withholding of proxies, naming the persons with whom such contracts, arrangements, or understandings have been entered into, and giving the details thereof.

(2) If any material change occurs in the facts set forth in the statements to the issuer and the exchange, and in the statement filed with the Commission, an amendment shall be transmitted to the issuer and the exchange and shall be filed with the Commission, in accordance with such rules and regulations as the Commission may prescribe as necessary or appropriate in the public interest or for the protection of investors.

(3) When two or more persons act as a partnership, limited partnership, syndicate, or other group for the purpose of acquiring, holding, or disposing of securities of an issuer, such syndicate or group shall be deemed a "person" for the purposes of this subsection.

(4) In determining, for purposes of this subsection, any percentage of a class of any security, such class shall be deemed to consist of the amount of the outstanding securities of such class, exclusive of any securities of such class held by or for the account of the issuer or a subsidiary of the issuer.

(5) The Commission, by rule or regulation or by order, may permit any person to file in lieu of the statement required by paragraph (1) of this subsection or the rules and regulations thereunder, a notice stating the name of such person, the number of shares of any equity securities subject to paragraph (1) which are owned by him, the date of their acquisition and such other information as the Commission may specify, if it appears to the Commission that such securities were acquired by such person in the ordinary course of his business and were not acquired for the purpose of and do not have the effect of changing or influencing the control of the issuer nor in connection with or as a participant having such purpose or effect.

(6) The provisions of this subsection shall not apply to—

(A) any acquisition or offer to acquire securities made or proposed to be made by means of a registration statement under the Securities Act of 1933;

(B) any acquisition of the beneficial ownership of a security which, together with all other acquisitions by the same person of securities of the same class during the preceding twelve months, does not exceed 2 per centum of that class;

(C) any acquisition of an equity security by the issuer of such security;

(D) any acquisition or proposed acquisition of a security which the Commission, by rules or regulations or by order, shall exempt from the provisions of this subsection as not entered into for the purpose of, and not having the effect of, changing or influencing the control of the issuer or otherwise as not comprehended within the purposes of this subsection.

(e) Purchase of securities by issuer.

(1) It shall be unlawful for an issuer which has a class of equity securities registered pursuant to section 12 of this title [15 USC § 78l], or which is a closed-end investment company registered under the Investment Company Act of 1940 [15 USC §§ 80a-1 *et seq.*], to purchase any equity security issued by it if such purchase is in contravention of such rules and regulations as the Commission, in the public interest or for the protection of investors, may adopt (A) to define acts and practices which are fraudulent, deceptive, or manipulative, and (B) to prescribe means reasonably designed to prevent such acts and practices. Such rules and regulations may require such issuer to provide holders of equity securities of such class with such information relating to the reasons for such purchase, the source of funds, the number of shares to be purchased, the price to be paid for such securities, the method of purchase, and such additional information, as the Commission deems necessary or appropriate in the public interest or for the protection of investors, or which the Commission deems to be material to a determination whether such security should be sold.

(2) For the purpose of this subsection, a purchase by or for the issuer or any person controlling, controlled by, or under common control with the issuer, or a purchase subject to control of the issuer or any such person, shall be deemed to be a purchase by the issuer. The Commission shall have power to make rules and regulations implementing this paragraph in the public interest and for the protection of investors, including exemptive rules and regulations covering situations in which the Commission deems it unnecessary or inappropriate that a purchase of the type described in this paragraph shall be deemed to be a purchase by the issuer for purposes of some or all of the provisions of paragraph (1) of this subsection.

(3) At the time of filing such statement as the Commission may require by rule pursuant to paragraph (1) of this subsection, the person making the filing shall pay to the Commission a fee of 1/50 of 1 per centum of the value of securities proposed to be purchased. The fee shall be reduced with respect to securities in an amount equal to any fee paid with respect to any securities issued in connection with the proposed transaction under section 6(b) of the Securities Act of 1933 [15 USC § 77f(b)], or the fee paid under that section [15 USC § 77f(b)] shall be reduced in an amount equal to the fee paid to the Commission in connection with such transaction under this paragraph.

(f) Reports by institutional investment managers.

(1) Every institutional investment manager which uses the mails, or any means or instrumentality of interstate commerce in the course of its business as an institutional investment manager and which exercises investment discretion with respect to accounts holding equity securities of a class described in section 13(d)(1) of this title [subsec. (d)(1) of this section] having an aggregate fair market value on the last trading day in any of the preceding twelve months of at least $100,000,000 or such lesser amount (but in no case less than $10,000,000) as the Commission, by rule, may determine, shall file reports with the Commission in such form, for such periods, and at such times after the end of such periods as the Commission, by rule, may prescribe, but in no event shall such reports be filed for periods longer than one year or shorter than one quarter. Such reports shall include for each such equity security held on the last day of the reporting period by accounts (in aggregate or by type as the Commission, by rule, may prescribe) with respect to which the institutional investment manager exercises investment discretion (other than securities held in amounts which the Commission, by rule, determines to be insignificant for purposes of this subsection), the name of the issuer and the title, class, CUSIP number, number of shares or principal amount, and aggregate fair market value of each such security. Such reports may also include for accounts (in aggregate or by type) with respect to which the institutional investment manager exercises investment discretion such of the following information as the Commission, by rule, prescribes—

(A) the name of the issuer and the title, class, CUSIP number, number of shares or principal amount, and aggregate fair market value or cost or amortized cost of each other security (other than an exempted security) held on the last day of the reporting period by such accounts;

(B) the aggregate fair market value or cost or amortized cost of exempted securities (in aggregate or by class) held on the last day of the reporting period by such accounts;

(C) the number of shares of each equity security of a class described in section 13(d)(1) of this title [subsec. (d)(1) of this section] held on the last day of the reporting period by such accounts with respect to which the institutional investment manager possesses sole or shared authority to exercise the voting rights evidenced by such securities;

(D) the aggregate purchases and aggregate sales during the reporting period of each security (other than an exempted security) effected by or for such accounts; and

(E) with respect to any transaction or series of transactions having a market value of at least $500,000 or such other amount as the Commission, by rule, may determine, effected during the reporting period by or for such accounts in any equity security of a class described in section 13(d)(1) of this title [subsec. (d)(1) of this section]—

    (i) the name of the issuer and the title, class, and CUSIP number of the security;

    (ii) the number of shares or principal amount of the security involved in the transaction;

    (iii) whether the transaction was a purchase or sale;

    (iv) the per share price or prices at which the transaction was effected;

    (v) the date or dates of the transaction;

    (vi) the date or dates of the settlement of the transaction;

    (vii) the broker or dealer through whom the transaction was effected;

    (viii) the market or markets in which the transaction was effected; and

    (ix) such other related information as the Commission, by rule, may prescribe.

(2) The Commission, by rule or order, may exempt, conditionally or unconditionally, any institutional investment manager or security or any class of institutional investment managers or securities from any or all of the provisions of this subsection or the rules thereunder.

(3) The Commission shall make available to the public for a reasonable fee a list of all equity securities of a class described in section 13(d)(1) of this title [subsec. (d)(1) of this section], updated no less frequently than reports are required to be filed pursuant to paragraph (1) of this subsection. The Commission shall tabulate the information contained in any report filed pursuant to this subsection in a manner which will, in the view of the Commission, maximize the usefulness of the information to other Federal and State authorities and the public. Promptly after the filing of any such report, the Commission shall make the information contained therein conveniently available to the public for a reasonable fee in such form as the Commission, by rule, may prescribe, except that the Commission, as it determines to be necessary or appropriate in the public interest or for the protection of investors, may delay or prevent public disclosure of any such information in accordance with section 552 of title 5, United States Code [5 USC § 552]. Notwithstanding the preceding sentence, any such information identifying the securities held by the account of a natural person or an estate or trust (other than a business trust or investment company) shall not be disclosed to the public.

(4) In exercising its authority under this subsection, the Commission shall determine (and so state) that its action is necessary or appropriate in the public interest and for the protection of investors or to maintain fair and orderly markets or, in granting an exemption, that its action is consistent with the protection of investors and the purposes of this subsection. In exercising such authority the Commission shall take such steps as are within its power, including consulting with the Comptroller General of the United States, the Director of the Office of Management and Budget, the appropriate regulatory agencies, Federal and State authorities which, directly or indirectly, require reports from institutional investment managers of information substantially similar to that called for by this subsection, national securities exchanges, and registered securities associations, (A) to achieve uniform, centralized reporting of information concerning the securities holdings of and transactions by or for accounts with respect to which institutional investment managers exercise investment discretion, and (B) consistently with the objective set forth in the preceding subparagraph, to avoid unnecessarily duplicative reporting by, and minimize the compliance burden on, institutional investment managers. Federal authorities which, directly or indirectly, require reports from institutional investment managers of information substantially similar to that called for by this subsection shall cooperate with the Commission in the performance of its responsibilities under the preceding sentence. An institutional investment manager which is a bank, the deposits of which are insured in accordance with the Federal Deposit Insurance Act, shall file with the appropriate regulatory agency a copy of every report filed with the Commission pursuant to this subsection.

(5)　(A) For purposes of this subsection the term "institutional investment manager" includes any person, other than a natural person, investing in or buying and selling securities for its own account, and any person exercising investment discretion with respect to the account of any other person.

(B) The Commission shall adopt such rules as it deems necessary or appropriate to prevent duplicative reporting pursuant to this subsection by two or more institutional investment managers exercising investment discretion with respect to the same amount [account].

(g) Statement of equity security ownership.

(1) Any person who is directly or indirectly the beneficial owner of more than 5 per centum of any security of a class described in subsection (d)(1) of this section shall send to the issuer of the security and shall file with the Commission a statement setting forth, in such form and at such time as the Commission may, by rule, prescribe—

(A) such person's identity, residence, and citizenship; and

(B) the number and description of the shares in which such person has an interest and the nature of such interest.

(2) If any material change occurs in the facts set forth in the statement sent to the issuer and filed with the Commission, an amendment shall be transmitted to the issuer and shall be filed with the Commission, in accordance with such rules and regulations as the Commission may prescribe as necessary or appropriate in the public interest or for the protection of investors.

(3) When two or more persons act as a partnership, limited partnership, syndicate, or other group for the purpose of acquiring, holding, or disposing of securities of an issuer, such syndicate or group shall be deemed a "person" for the purposes of this subsection.

(4) In determining, for purposes of this subsection, any percentage of a class of any security, such class shall be deemed to consist of the amount of the outstanding securities of such class, exclusive of any securities of such class held by or for the account of the issuer or a subsidiary of the issuer.

(5) In exercising its authority under this subsection, the Commission shall take such steps as it deems necessary or appropriate in the public interest or for the protection of investors (A) to achieve centralized reporting of information regarding ownership, (B) to avoid unnecessarily duplicative reporting by and minimize the compliance burden on persons required to report, and (C) to tabulate and promptly make available the information contained in any report filed pursuant to this subsection in a manner which will, in the view of the Commission, maximize the usefulness of the information to other Federal and State agencies and the public.

(6) The Commission may, by rule or order, exempt, in whole or in part, any person or class of persons from any or all of the reporting requirements of this subsection as it deems necessary or appropriate in the public interest or for the protection of investors.

(h) **Large trader reporting.**

(1) **Identification requirements for large traders.** For the purpose of monitoring the impact on the securities markets of securities transactions involving a substantial volume or a large fair market value or exercise value and for the purpose of otherwise assisting the Commission in the enforcement of this title, each large trader shall—

(A) provide such information to the Commission as the Commission may by rule or regulation prescribe as necessary or appropriate, identifying such large trader and all accounts in or through which such large trader effects such transactions; and

(B) identify, in accordance with such rules or regulations as the Commission may prescribe as necessary or appropriate, to any registered broker or dealer by or through whom such large trader directly or indirectly effects securities transactions, such large trader and all accounts directly or indirectly maintained with such broker or dealer by such large trader in or through which such transactions are effected.

(2) **Recordkeeping and reporting requirements for brokers and dealers.** Every registered broker or dealer shall make and keep for prescribed periods such records as the Commission by rule or regulation prescribes as necessary or appropriate in the public interest, for the protection of investors, or otherwise in furtherance of the purposes of this title, with respect to securities transactions that equal or exceed the reporting activity level effected directly or indirectly by or through such registered broker or dealer of or for any person that such broker or dealer knows is a large trader, or any person that such broker or dealer has reason to know is a large trader on the basis of transactions in securities effected by or through such broker or dealer. Such records shall be available for reporting to the Commission, or any self-regulatory organization that the Commission shall designate to receive such reports, on the morning of the day following the day the transactions were effected, and shall be reported to the Commission or a self-regulatory organization designated by the Commission immediately upon request by the Commission or such a self-regulatory organization. Such records and reports shall be in a format and transmitted in a manner prescribed by the Commission (including, but not limited to, machine readable form).

(3) **Aggregation rules.** The Commission may prescribe rules or regulations governing the manner in which transactions and accounts shall be aggregated for the purpose of this subsection, including aggregation on the basis of common ownership or control.

(4) Examination of broker and dealer records. All records required to be made and kept by registered brokers and dealers pursuant to this subsection with respect to transactions effected by large traders are subject at any time, or from time to time, to such reasonable periodic, special, or other examinations by representatives of the Commission as the Commission deems necessary or appropriate in the public interest, for the protection of investors, or otherwise in furtherance of the purposes of this title.

(5) Factors to be considered in Commission actions. In exercising its authority under this subsection, the Commission shall take into account—

    (A) existing reporting systems;

    (B) the costs associated with maintaining information with respect to transactions effected by large traders and reporting such information to the Commission or self-regulatory organizations; and

    (C) the relationship between the United States and international securities markets.

(6) Exemptions. The Commission, by rule, regulation, or order, consistent with the purposes of this title, may exempt any person or class of persons or any transaction or class of transactions, either conditionally or upon specified terms and conditions or for stated periods, from the operation of this subsection, and the rules and regulations thereunder.

(7) Authority of Commission to limit disclosure of information. Notwithstanding any other provision of law, the Commission shall not be compelled to disclose any information required to be kept or reported under this subsection. Nothing in this subsection shall authorize the Commission to withhold information from Congress, or prevent the Commission from complying with a request for information from any other Federal department or agency requesting information for purposes within the scope of its jurisdiction, or complying with an order of a court of the United States in an action brought by the United States or the Commission. For purposes of section 552 of title 5, United States Code, this subsection shall be considered a statute described in subsection (b)(3)(B) of such section 552.

(8) Definitions. For purposes of this subsection—

    (A) the term "large trader" means every person who, for his own account or an account for which he exercises investment discretion, effects transactions for the purchase or sale of any publicly traded security or securities by use of any means or instrumentality of interstate commerce or of the mails, or of any facility of a national securities exchange, directly or indirectly by or through a registered broker or dealer in an aggregate amount equal to or in excess of the identifying activity level;

(B) the term "publicly traded security" means any equity security (including an option on individual equity securities, and an option on a group or index of such securities) listed, or admitted to unlisted trading privileges, on a national securities exchange, or quoted in an automated interdealer quotation system;

(C) the term "identifying activity level" means transactions in publicly traded securities at or above a level of volume, fair market value, or exercise value as shall be fixed from time to time by the Commission by rule or regulation, specifying the time interval during which such transactions shall be aggregated;

(D) the term "reporting activity level" means transactions in publicly traded securities at or above a level of volume, fair market value, or exercise value as shall be fixed from time to time by the Commission by rule, regulation, or order, specifying the time interval during which such transactions shall be aggregated; and

(E) the term "person" has the meaning given in section 3(a)(9) of this title [15 USC § 78c(a)(9)] and also includes two or more persons acting as a partnership, limited partnership, syndicate, or other group, but does not include a foreign central bank.

HISTORY: (June 6, 1934, c. 404, Title I, § 13, 48 Stat. 894; Aug 20, 1964, Pub. L. 88-467, § 4, 78 Stat. 569; July 29, 1968, Pub. L. 90-439, § 2, 82 Stat. 454; Dec. 22, 1970, Pub. L. 91-567, §§ 1, 2, 84 Stat. 1497; June 4, 1975, Pub. L. 94-29, § 10, 89 Stat. 119; Feb. 5, 1976, Pub. L. 94-210, Title III, § 308(b), 90 Stat. 57; Dec. 19, 1977, Pub. L. 95-213, Title I, § 102, Title II, §§ 202, 203, 91 Stat. 1494, 1498, 1499; June 6, 1983, Pub. L. 98-38, § 2(a), 97 Stat. 205; Dec. 4, 1987, Pub. L. 100-181, Title III, §§ 315, 316, 101 Stat. 1256; Feb. 3, 1988, Pub. L. 100-241, § 12(d), 101 Stat. 1810; Aug. 23, 1988, Pub. L. 100-418, Title V, § 5002, 102 Stat. 1415; Oct. 16, 1990, Pub. L. 101-432, § 3, 104 Stat. 964.)

§ 78dd-1. Prohibited foreign trade practices by issuers

(a) **Prohibition.** It shall be unlawful for any issuer which has a class of securities registered pursuant to section 12 of this title [15 USC § 78 l] or which is required to file reports under section 15(d) of this title [15 USC § 78o(d)], or for any officer, director, employee, or agent of such issuer or any stockholder thereof acting on behalf of such issuer, to make use of the mails or any means or instrumentality of interstate commerce corruptly in furtherance of an offer, payment, promise to pay, or authorization of the payment of any money, or offer, gift, promise to give, or authorization of the giving of anything of value to—

(1) any foreign official for purposes of—

    (A)   (i) influencing any act or decision of such foreign official in his official capacity,

          (ii) inducing such foreign official to do or omit to do any act in violation of the lawful duty of such official, or

(iii) securing any improper advantage; or

(B) inducing such foreign official to use his influence with a foreign government or instrumentality thereof to affect or influence any act or decision of such government or instrumentality,

in order to assist such issuer in obtaining or retaining business for or with, or directing business to, any person;

(2) any foreign political party or official thereof or any candidate for foreign political office for purposes of—

(A) (i) influencing any act or decision of such party, official, or candidate in its or his official capacity,

(ii) inducing such party, official, or candidate to do or omit to do an act in violation of the lawful duty of such party, official, or candidate, or

(iii) securing any improper advantage; or

(B) inducing such party, official, or candidate to use its or his influence with a foreign government or instrumentality thereof to affect or influence any act or decision of such government or instrumentality,

in order to assist such issuer in obtaining or retaining business for or with, or directing business to, any person; or

(3) any person, while knowing that all or a portion of such money or thing of value will be offered, given, or promised, directly or indirectly, to any foreign official, to any foreign political party or official thereof, or to any candidate for foreign political office, for purposes of—

(A) (i) influencing any act or decision of such foreign official, political party, party official, or candidate in his or its official capacity,

(ii) inducing such foreign official, political party, party official, or candidate to do or omit to do any act in violation of the lawful duty of such foreign official, political party, party official, or candidate, or

(iii) securing any improper advantage; or

(B) inducing such foreign official, political party, party official, or candidate to use his or its influence with a foreign government or instrumentality thereof to affect or influence any act or decision of such government or instrumentality,

in order to assist such issuer in obtaining or retaining business for or with, or directing business to, any person.

(b) Exception for routine governmental action. Subsection (a) and (g) shall not apply to any facilitating or expediting payment to a foreign official, political party, or party official the purpose of which is to expedite or to secure the performance of a routine governmental action by a foreign official, political party, or party official.

(c) Affirmative defenses. It shall be an affirmative defense to actions under subsection (a) that—

(1) the payment, gift, offer, or promise of anything of value that was made, was lawful under the written laws and regulations of the foreign official's, political party's, party official's, or candidate's country; or

(2) the payment, gift, offer, or promise of anything of value that was made, was a reasonable and bona fide expenditure, such as travel and lodging expenses, incurred by or on behalf of a foreign official, party, party official, or candidate and was directly related to—

   (A) the promotion, demonstration, or explanation of products or services; or

   (B) the execution or performance of a contract with a foreign government or agency thereof.

(d) Guidelines by the Attorney General. Not later than one year after the date of the enactment of the Foreign Corrupt Practices Act Amendments of 1988 [enacted Aug. 23, 1988], the Attorney General, after consultation with the Commission, the Secretary of Commerce, the United States Trade Representative, the Secretary of State, and the Secretary of the Treasury, and after obtaining the views of all interested persons through public notice and comment procedures, shall determine to what extent compliance with this section would be enhanced and the business community would be assisted by further clarification of the preceding provisions of this section and may, based on such determination and to the extent necessary and appropriate, issue—

(1) guidelines describing specific types of conduct, associated with common types of export sales arrangements and business contracts, which for purposes of the Department of Justice's present enforcement policy, the Attorney General determines would be in conformance with the preceding provisions of this section; and

(2) general precautionary procedures which issuers may use on a voluntary basis to conform their conduct to the Department of Justice's present enforcement policy regarding the preceding provisions of this section.

The Attorney General shall issue the guidelines and procedures referred to in the preceding sentence in accordance with the provisions of subchapter II of chapter 5 of title 5, United States Code [5 USC §§ 551 *et seq.*], and those guidelines and procedures shall be subject to the provisions of chapter 7 of that title [5 USC §§ 701 *et seq.*].

(e) Opinions of the Attorney General.

    (1) The Attorney General, after consultation with appropriate departments and agencies of the United States and after obtaining the views of all interested persons through public notice and comment procedures, shall establish a procedure to provide responses to specific inquiries by issuers concerning conformance of their conduct with the Department of Justice's present enforcement policy regarding the preceding provisions of this section. The Attorney General shall, within 30 days after receiving such a request, issue an opinion in response to that request. The opinion shall state whether or not certain specified prospective conduct would, for purposes of the Department of Justice's present enforcement policy, violate the preceding provisions of this section. Additional requests for opinions may be filed with the Attorney General regarding other specified prospective conduct that is beyond the scope of conduct specified in previous requests. In any action brought under the applicable provisions of this section, there shall be a rebuttable presumption that conduct, which is specified in a request by an issuer and for which the Attorney General has issued an opinion that such conduct is in conformity with the Department of Justice's present enforcement policy, is in compliance with the preceding provisions of this section. Such a presumption may be rebutted by a preponderance of the evidence. In considering the presumption for purposes of this paragraph, a court shall weigh all relevant factors, including but not limited to whether the information submitted to the Attorney General was accurate and complete and whether it was within the scope of the conduct specified in any request received by the Attorney General. The Attorney General shall establish the procedure required by this paragraph in accordance with the provisions of subchapter II of chapter 5 of title 5, United States Code [5 USC §§ 551 *et seq.*], and that procedure shall be subject to the provisions of chapter 7 of that title [5 USC §§ 701 *et seq.*].

    (2) Any document or other material which is provided to, received by, or prepared in the Department of Justice or any other department or agency of the United States in connection with a request by an issuer under the procedure established under paragraph (1), shall be exempt from disclosure under section 552 of title 5, United States Code, and shall not, except with the consent of the issuer, be made publicly available, regardless of whether the Attorney General responds to such a request or the issuer withdraws such request before receiving a response.

    (3) Any issuer who has made a request to the Attorney General under paragraph (1) may withdraw such request prior to the time the Attorney General issues an opinion in response to such request. Any request so withdrawn shall have no force or effect.

(4) The Attorney General shall, to the maximum extent practicable, provide timely guidance concerning the Department of Justice's present enforcement policy with respect to the preceding provisions of this section to potential exporters and small businesses that are unable to obtain specialized counsel on issues pertaining to such provisions. Such guidance shall be limited to responses to requests under paragraph (1) concerning conformity of specified prospective conduct with the Department of Justice's present enforcement policy regarding the preceding provisions of this section and general explanations of compliance responsibilities and of potential liabilities under the preceding provisions of this section.

(f) Definitions. For purposes of this section:

(1) (A) The term "foreign official" means any officer or employee of a foreign government or any department, agency, or instrumentality thereof, or of a public international organization, or any person acting in an official capacity for or on behalf of any such government or department, agency, or instrumentality, or for or on behalf of any such public international organization.

(B) For purposes of subparagraph (A), the term "public international organization" means—

(i) an organization that is designated by Executive order pursuant to section 1 of the International Organizations Immunities Act (22 U.S.C. 288); or

(ii) any other international organization that is designated by the President by Executive order for the purposes of this section, effective as of the date of publication of such order in the Federal Register.

(2) (A) A person's state of mind is "knowing" with respect to conduct, a circumstance, or a result if—

(i) such person is aware that such person is engaging in such conduct, that such circumstance exists, or that such result is substantially certain to occur; or

(ii) such person has a firm belief that such circumstance exists or that such result is substantially certain to occur.

(B) When knowledge of the existence of a particular circumstance is required for an offense, such knowledge is established if a person is aware of a high probability of the existence of such circumstance, unless the person actually believes that such circumstance does not exist.

(3) (A) The term "routine governmental action" means only an action which is ordinarily and commonly performed by a foreign official in—

(i) obtaining permits, licenses, or other official documents to qualify a person to do business in a foreign country;

    (ii) processing governmental papers, such as visas and work orders;

    (iii) providing police protection, mail pick-up and delivery, or scheduling inspections associated with contract performance or inspections related to transit of goods across country;

    (iv) providing phone service, power and water supply, loading and unloading cargo, or protecting perishable products or commodities from deterioration; or

    (v) actions of a similar nature.

(B) The term "routine governmental action" does not include any decision by a foreign official whether, or on what terms, to award new business to or to continue business with a particular party, or any action taken by a foreign official involved in the decisionmaking process to encourage a decision to award new business to or continue business with a particular party.

(g) Alternative jurisdiction.

(1) It shall also be unlawful for any issuer organized under the laws of the United States, or a State, territory, possession, or commonwealth of the United States or a political subdivision thereof and which has a class of securities registered pursuant to section 12 of this title [15 USC § 78l] or which is required to file reports under section 15(d) of this title [15 USC § 78o(d)], or for any United States person that is an officer, director, employee, or agent of such issuer or a stockholder thereof acting on behalf of such issuer, to corruptly do any act outside the United States in furtherance of an offer, payment, promise to pay, or authorization of the payment of any money, or offer, gift, promise to give, or authorization of the giving of anything of value to any of the persons or entities set forth in paragraphs (1), (2), and (3) of subsection (a) of this section for the purposes set forth therein, irrespective of whether such issuer or such officer, director, employee, agent, or stockholder makes use of the mails or any means or instrumentality of interstate commerce in furtherance of such offer, gift, payment, promise, or authorization.

(2) As used in this subsection, the term "United States person" means a national of the United States (as defined in section 101 of the Immigration and Nationality Act (8 U.S.C. 1101)) or any corporation, partnership, association, joint-stock company, business trust, unincorporated organization, or sole proprietorship organized under the laws of the United States or any State, territory, possession, or commonwealth of the United States, or any political subdivision thereof.

HISTORY: (June 6, 1934, ch 404, Title I, § 30A, as added Dec. 19, 1977, P.L. 95-213, Title I, § 103(a), 91 Stat. 1495; Aug. 23, 1988, P.L. 100-418, Title V, Subtitle A, Part I, § 5003(a), 102 Stat. 1415.) (As amended Nov. 10, 1998, P.L. 105-366, §§ 2(a)-(c), 112 Stat. 3302.)

§ 78dd-2. Prohibited foreign trade practices by domestic concerns

(a) **Prohibition**. It shall be unlawful for any domestic concern, other than an issuer which is subject to section 30A of the Securities Exchange Act of 1934 [15 USC § 78dd-1], or for any officer, director, employee, or agent of such domestic concern or any stockholder thereof acting on behalf of such domestic concern, to make use of the mails or any means or instrumentality of interstate commerce corruptly in furtherance of an offer, payment, promise to pay, or authorization of the payment of any money, or offer, gift, promise to give, or authorization of the giving of anything of value to—

(1) any foreign official for purposes of—

    (A)   (i) influencing any act or decision of such foreign official in his official capacity,

          (ii) inducing such foreign official to do or omit to do any act in violation of the lawful duty of such official, or

          (iii) securing any improper advantage; or

    (B) inducing such foreign official to use his influence with a foreign government or instrumentality thereof to affect or influence any act or decision of such government or instrumentality,

in order to assist such domestic concern in obtaining or retaining business for or with, or directing business to, any person;

(2) any foreign political party or official thereof or any candidate for foreign political office for purposes of—

    (A)   (i) influencing any act or decision of such party, official, or candidate in its or his official capacity,

          (ii) inducing such party, official, or candidate to do or omit to do an act in violation of the lawful duty of such party, official, or candidate, or

          (iii) securing any improper advantage; or

    (B) inducing such party, official, or candidate to use its or his influence with a foreign government or instrumentality thereof to affect or influence any act or decision of such government or instrumentality,

in order to assist such domestic concern in obtaining or retaining business for or with, or directing business to, any person; or

(3) any person, while knowing that all or a portion of such money or thing of value will be offered, given, or promised, directly or indirectly, to any foreign official, to any foreign political party or official thereof, or to any candidate for foreign political office, for purposes of—

    (A)   (i) influencing any act or decision of such foreign official, political party, party official, or candidate in his or its official capacity,

      (ii) inducing such foreign official, political party, party official, or candidate to do or omit to do any act in violation of the lawful duty of such foreign official, political party, party official, or candidate, or

      (iii) securing any improper advantage; or

    (B) inducing such foreign official, political party, party official, or candidate to use his or its influence with a foreign government or instrumentality thereof to affect or influence any act or decision of such government or instrumentality,

in order to assist such domestic concern in obtaining or retaining business for or with, or directing business to, any person.

(b) Exception for routine governmental action. Subsection (a) and (i) shall not apply to any facilitating or expediting payment to a foreign official, political party, or party official the purpose of which is to expedite or to secure the performance of a routine governmental action by a foreign official, political party, or party official.

(c) Affirmative defenses. It shall be an affirmative defense to actions under subsection (a) that—

    (1) the payment, gift, offer, or promise of anything of value that was made, was lawful under the written laws and regulations of the foreign official's, political party's, party official's, or candidate's country; or

    (2) the payment, gift, offer, or promise of anything of value that was made, was a reasonable and bona fide expenditure, such as travel and lodging expenses, incurred by or on behalf of a foreign official, party, party official, or candidate and was directly related to—

      (A) the promotion, demonstration, or explanation of products or services; or

      (B) the execution or performance of a contract with a foreign government or agency thereof.

(d) Injunctive relief.

    (1) When it appears to the Attorney General that any domestic concern to which this section applies, or officer, director, employee, agent, or stockholder thereof, is engaged, or about to engage, in any act or practice constituting a violation of subsection (a) of this section, the Attorney General may, in his discretion, bring a civil action in an appropriate district court of the United States to enjoin such act or practice, and upon a proper showing, a permanent injunction or a temporary restraining order shall be granted without bond.

(2) For the purpose of any civil investigation which, in the opinion of the Attorney General, is necessary and proper to enforce this section, the Attorney General or his designee are empowered to administer oaths and affirmations, subpoena witnesses, take evidence, and require the production of any books, papers, or other documents which the Attorney General deems relevant or material to such investigation. The attendance of witnesses and the production of documentary evidence may be required from any place in the United States, or any territory, possession, or commonwealth of the United States, at any designated place of hearing.

(3) In case of contumacy by, or refusal to obey a subpoena issued to, any person, the Attorney General may invoke the aid of any court of the United States within the jurisdiction of which such investigation or proceeding is carried on, or where such person resides or carries on business, in requiring the attendance and testimony of witnesses and the production of books, papers, or other documents. Any such court may issue an order requiring such person to appear before the Attorney General or his designee, there to produce records, if so ordered, or to give testimony touching the matter under investigation. Any failure to obey such order of the court may be punished by such court as a contempt thereof. All process in any such case may be served in the judicial district in which such person resides or may be found. The Attorney General may make such rules relating to civil investigations as may be necessary or appropriate to implement the provisions of this subsection.

(e) Guidelines by the Attorney General. Not later than 6 months after the date of the enactment of the Foreign Corrupt Practices Act Amendments of 1988 [enacted Aug. 23, 1988], the Attorney General, after consultation with the Securities and Exchange Commission, the Secretary of Commerce, the United States Trade Representative, the Secretary of State, and the Secretary of the Treasury, and after obtaining the views of all interested persons through public notice and comment procedures, shall determine to what extent compliance with this section would be enhanced and the business community would be assisted by further clarification of the preceding provisions of this section and may, based on such determination and to the extent necessary and appropriate, issue—

(1) guidelines describing specific types of conduct, associated with common types of export sales arrangements and business contracts, which for purposes of the Department of Justice's present enforcement policy, the Attorney General determines would be in conformance with the preceding provisions of this section; and

(2) general precautionary procedures which domestic concerns may use on a voluntary basis to conform their conduct to the Department of Justice's present enforcement policy regarding the preceding provisions of this section.

The Attorney General shall issue the guidelines and procedures referred to in the preceding sentence in accordance with the provisions of subchapter II of chapter 5 of title 5, United States Code [5 USC §§ 551 *et seq.*], and those guidelines and procedures shall be subject to the provisions of chapter 7 of that title [5 USC §§ 701 *et seq.*].

(f) Opinions of the Attorney General.

(1) The Attorney General, after consultation with appropriate departments and agencies of the United States and after obtaining the views of all interested persons through public notice and comment procedures, shall establish a procedure to provide responses to specific inquiries by domestic concerns concerning conformance of their conduct with the Department of Justice's present enforcement policy regarding the preceding provisions of this section. The Attorney General shall, within 30 days after receiving such a request, issue an opinion in response to that request. The opinion shall state whether or not certain specified prospective conduct would, for purposes of the Department of Justice's present enforcement policy, violate the preceding provisions of this section. Additional requests for opinions may be filed with the Attorney General regarding other specified prospective conduct that is beyond the scope of conduct specified in previous requests. In any action brought under the applicable provisions of this section, there shall be a rebuttable presumption that conduct, which is specified in a request by a domestic concern and for which the Attorney General has issued an opinion that such conduct is in conformity with the Department of Justice's present enforcement policy, is in compliance with the preceding provisions of this section. Such a presumption may be rebutted by a preponderance of the evidence. In considering the presumption for purposes of this paragraph, a court shall weigh all relevant factors, including but not limited to whether the information submitted to the Attorney General was accurate and complete and whether it was within the scope of the conduct specified in any request received by the Attorney General. The Attorney General shall establish the procedure required by this paragraph in accordance with the provisions of subchapter II of chapter 5 of title 5, United States Code [5 USC §§ 551 *et seq.*], and that procedure shall be subject to the provisions of chapter 7 of that title [5 USC §§ 701 *et seq.*].

(2) Any document or other material which is provided to, received by, or prepared in the Department of Justice or any other department or agency of the United States in connection with a request by a domestic concern under the procedure established under paragraph (1), shall be exempt from disclosure under section 552 of title 5, United States Code, and shall not, except with the consent of the domestic concern, be made publicly available, regardless of whether the Attorney General responds to such a request or the domestic concern withdraws such request before receiving a response.

(3) Any domestic concern who has made a request to the Attorney General under paragraph (1) may withdraw such request prior to the time the Attorney General issues an opinion in response to such request. Any request so withdrawn shall have no force or effect.

(4) The Attorney General shall, to the maximum extent practicable, provide timely guidance concerning the Department of Justice's present enforcement policy with respect to the preceding provisions of this section to potential exporters and small businesses that are unable to obtain specialized counsel on issues pertaining to such provisions. Such guidance shall be limited to responses to requests under paragraph (1) concerning conformity of specified prospective conduct with the Department of Justice's present enforcement policy regarding the preceding provisions of this section and general explanations of compliance responsibilities and of potential liabilities under the preceding provisions of this section.

(g) Penalties.

(1) (A) Penalties. Any domestic concern that is not a natural person and that violates subsection (a) or (i) of this section shall be fined not more than $2,000,000.

(B) Any domestic concern that is not a natural person and that violates subsection (a) or (i) of this section shall be subject to a civil penalty of not more than $10,000 imposed in an action brought by the Attorney General.

(2) (A) Any natural person that is an officer, director, employee, or agent of a domestic concern, or stockholder acting on behalf of such domestic concern, who willfully violates subsection (a) or (i) of this section shall be fined not more than $100,000 or imprisoned not more than 5 years, or both.

(B) Any natural person that is an officer, director, employee, or agent of a domestic concern, or stockholder acting on behalf of such domestic concern, who violates subsection (a) or (i) of this section shall be subject to a civil penalty of not more than $10,000 imposed in an action brought by the Attorney General.

(3) Whenever a fine is imposed under paragraph (2) upon any officer, director, employee, agent, or stockholder of a domestic concern, such fine may not be paid, directly or indirectly, by such domestic concern.

(h) Definitions. For purposes of this section:

(1) The term "domestic concern" means—

(A) any individual who is a citizen, national, or resident of the United States; and

(B) any corporation, partnership, association, joint-stock company, business trust, unincorporated organization, or sole proprietorship which has its principal place of business in the United States, or which is organized under the laws of a State of the United States or a territory, possession, or commonwealth of the United States.

(2) The term "foreign official" means any officer or employee of a foreign government or any department, agency, or instrumentality thereof, or any person acting in an official capacity for or on behalf of any such government or department, agency, or instrumentality.

(3) (A) A person's state of mind is "knowing" with respect to conduct, a circumstance, or a result if—

   (i) such person is aware that such person is engaging in such conduct, that such circumstance exists, or that such result is substantially certain to occur; or

   (ii) such person has a firm belief that such circumstance exists or that such result is substantially certain to occur.

(B) When knowledge of the existence of a particular circumstance is required for an offense, such knowledge is established if a person is aware of a high probability of the existence of such circumstance, unless the person actually believes that such circumstance does not exist.

(4) (A) For purposes of paragraph (1), the term "routine governmental action" means only an action which is ordinarily and commonly performed by a foreign official in—

   (i) obtaining permits, licenses, or other official documents to qualify a person to do business in a foreign country;

   (ii) processing governmental papers, such as visas and work orders;

   (iii) providing police protection, mail pick-up and delivery, or scheduling inspections associated with contract performance or inspections related to transit of goods across country;

   (iv) providing phone service, power and water supply, loading and unloading cargo, or protecting perishable products or commodities from deterioration; or

   (v) actions of a similar nature.

(B) The term "routine governmental action" does not include any decision by a foreign official whether, or on what terms, to award new business to or to continue business with a particular party, or any action taken by a foreign official involved in the decision-making process to encourage a decision to award new business to or continue business with a particular party.

(5) The term "interstate commerce" means trade, commerce, transportation, or communication among the several States, or between any foreign country and any State or between any State and any place or ship outside thereof, and such term includes the intrastate use of—

(A) a telephone or other interstate means of communication, or

(B) any other interstate instrumentality.

(i) Alternative jurisdiction

(1) It shall also be unlawful for any United States person to corruptly do any act outside the United States in furtherance of an offer, payment, promise to pay, or authorization of the payment of any money, or offer, gift, promise to give, or authorization of the giving of anything of value to any of the persons or entities set forth in paragraphs (1), (2), and (3) of subsection (a), for the purposes set forth therein, irrespective of whether such United States person makes use of the mails or any means or instrumentality of interstate commerce in furtherance of such offer, gift, payment, promise, or authorization.

(2) As used in this subsection, the term "United States person" means a national of the United States (as defined in section 101 of the Immigration and Nationality Act (8 U.S.C. 1101)) or any corporation, partnership, association, joint-stock company, business trust, unincorporated organization, or sole proprietorship organized under the laws of the United States or any State, territory, possession, or commonwealth of the United States, or any political subdivision thereof."

HISTORY: (Dec. 19, 1977, P.L. 95-213, Title I, § 104, 91 Stat. 1496; Aug. 23, 1988, P.L. 100-418, Title V, Subtitle A, Part I, § 5003(c), 102 Stat. 1419; Sept. 13, 1994, P.L. 103-322, Title XXXIII, § 330005, 108 Stat. 2142.) (As amended Nov. 10, 1998, P.L. 105-366, § 3, 112 Stat. 3304.)

§ 78dd-3. Prohibited foreign trade practices by persons other than issuers or domestic concerns

(a) **Prohibition**. It shall be unlawful for any person other than an issuer that is subject to section 78dd-1 of this title or a domestic concern (as defined in section 78dd-2 of this title), or for any officer, director, employee, or agent of such person or any stockholder thereof acting on behalf of such person, while in the territory of the United States, corruptly to make use of the mails or any means or instrumentality of interstate commerce or to do any other act in furtherance of an offer, payment, promise to pay, or authorization of the payment of any money, or offer, gift, promise to give, or authorization of the giving of anything of value to—

(1) any foreign official for purposes of—

    (A)   (i) influencing any act or decision of such foreign official in his official capacity,

          (ii) inducing such foreign official to do or omit to do any act in violation of the lawful duty of such official, or

          (iii) securing any improper advantage; or

    (B) inducing such foreign official to use his influence with a foreign government or instrumentality thereof to affect or influence any act or decision of such government or instrumentality,

in order to assist such person in obtaining or retaining business for or with, or directing business to, any person;

(2) any foreign political party or official thereof or any candidate for foreign political office for purposes of—

(A) (i) influencing any act or decision of such party, official, or candidate in its or his official capacity,

(ii) inducing such party, official, or candidate to do or omit to do an act in violation of the lawful duty of such party, official, or candidate, or

(iii) securing any improper advantage; or

(B) inducing such party, official, or candidate to use its or his influence with a foreign government or instrumentality thereof to affect or influence any act or decision of such government or instrumentality,

in order to assist such person in obtaining or retaining business for or with, or directing business to, any person; or

(3) any person, while knowing that all or a portion of such money or thing of value will be offered, given, or promised, directly or indirectly, to any foreign official, to any foreign political party or official thereof, or to any candidate for foreign political office, for purposes of—

(A) (i) influencing any act or decision of such foreign official, political party, party official, or candidate in his or its official capacity,

(ii) inducing such foreign official, political party, party official, or candidate to do or omit to do any act in violation of the lawful duty of such foreign official, political party, party official, or candidate, or

(iii) securing any improper advantage; or

(B) inducing such foreign official, political party, party official, or candidate to use his or its influence with a foreign government or instrumentality thereof to affect or influence any act or decision of such government or instrumentality,

in order to assist such person in obtaining or retaining business for or with, or directing business to, any person.

(b) Exception for routine governmental action. Subsection (a) of this section shall not apply to any facilitating or expediting payment to a foreign official, political party, or party official the purpose of which is to expedite or to secure the performance of a routine governmental action by a foreign official, political party, or party official.

(c) Affirmative defenses. It shall be an affirmative defense to actions under subsection (a) of this section that—

(1) the payment, gift, offer, or promise of anything of value that was made, was lawful under the written laws and regulations of the foreign official's, political party's, party official's, or candidate's country; or

(2) the payment, gift, offer, or promise of anything of value that was made, was a reasonable and bona fide expenditure, such as travel and lodging expenses, incurred by or on behalf of a foreign official, party, party official, or candidate and was directly related to—

    (A) the promotion, demonstration, or explanation of products or services; or

    (B) the execution or performance of a contract with a foreign government or agency thereof.

(d) Injunctive relief.

(1) When it appears to the Attorney General that any person to which this section applies, or officer, director, employee, agent, or stockholder thereof, is engaged, or about to engage, in any act or practice constituting a violation of subsection (a) of this section, the Attorney General may, in his discretion, bring a civil action in an appropriate district court of the United States to enjoin such act or practice, and upon a proper showing, a permanent injunction or a temporary restraining order shall be granted without bond.

(2) For the purpose of any civil investigation which, in the opinion of the Attorney General, is necessary and proper to enforce this section, the Attorney General or his designee are empowered to administer oaths and affirmations, subpoena witnesses, take evidence, and require the production of any books, papers, or other documents which the Attorney General deems relevant or material to such investigation. The attendance of witnesses and the production of documentary evidence may be required from any place in the United States, or any territory, possession, or commonwealth of the United States, at any designated place of hearing.

(3) In case of contumacy by, or refusal to obey a subpoena issued to, any person, the Attorney General may invoke the aid of any court of the United States within the jurisdiction of which such investigation or proceeding is carried on, or where such person resides or carries on business, in requiring the attendance and testimony of witnesses and the production of books, papers, or other documents. Any such court may issue an order requiring such person to appear before the Attorney General or his designee, there to produce records, if so ordered, or to give testimony touching the matter under investigation. Any failure to obey such order of the court may be punished by such court as a contempt thereof.

(4) All process in any such case may be served in the judicial district in which such person resides or may be found. The Attorney General may make such rules relating to civil investigations as may be necessary or appropriate to implement the provisions of this subsection.

(e) Penalties.

(1) (A) Any juridical person that violates subsection (a) of this section shall be fined not more than $2,000,000.

      (B) Any juridical person that violates subsection (a) of this section shall be subject to a civil penalty of not more than $10,000 imposed in an action brought by the Attorney General.

(2) (A) Any natural person who willfully violates subsection (a) of this section shall be fined not more than $100,000 or imprisoned not more than 5 years, or both.

      (B) Any natural person who violates subsection (a) of this section shall be subject to a civil penalty of not more than $10,000 imposed in an action brought by the Attorney General.

(3) Whenever a fine is imposed under paragraph (2) upon any officer, director, employee, agent, or stockholder of a person, such fine may not be paid, directly or indirectly, by such person.

(f) Definitions. For purposes of this section:

(1) The term "person", when referring to an offender, means any natural person other than a national of the United States (as defined in section 101 of the Immigration and Nationality Act [8 U.S.C. § 1101] or any corporation, partnership, association, joint-stock company, business trust, unincorporated organization, or sole proprietorship organized under the law of a foreign nation or a political subdivision thereof.

(2) (A) The term "foreign official" means any officer or employee of a foreign government or any department, agency, or instrumentality thereof, or of a public international organization, or any person acting in an official capacity for or on behalf of any such government or department, agency, or instrumentality, or for or on behalf of any such public international organization.

      (B) For purposes of subparagraph (A), the term "public international organization" means—

          (i) an organization that is designated by Executive order pursuant to section 1 of the International Organizations Immunities Act [22 U.S.C. § 288]; or

         (ii) any other international organization that is designated by the President by Executive order for the purposes of this section, effective as of the date of publication of such order in the Federal Register.

(3) (A) A person's state of mind is knowing, with respect to conduct, a circumstance or a result if—

          (i) such person is aware that such person is engaging in such conduct, that such circumstance exists, or that such result is substantially certain to occur; or

         (ii) such person has a firm belief that such circumstance exists or that such result is substantially certain to occur.

(B) When knowledge of the existence of a particular circumstance is required for an offense, such knowledge is established if a person is aware of a high probability of the existence of such circumstance, unless the person actually believes that such circumstance does not exist.

(4) (A) The term "routine governmental action" means only an action which is ordinarily and commonly performed by a foreign official in—

(i) obtaining permits, licenses, or other official documents to qualify a person to do business in a foreign country;

(ii) processing governmental papers, such as visas and work orders;

(iii) providing police protection, mail pick-up and delivery, or scheduling inspections associated with contract performance or inspections related to transit of goods across country;

(iv) providing phone service, power and water supply, loading and unloading cargo, or protecting perishable products or commodities from deterioration; or

(v) actions of a similar nature.

(B) The term "routine governmental action" does not include any decision by a foreign official whether, or on what terms, to award new business to or to continue business with a particular party, or any action taken by a foreign official involved in the decision-making process to encourage a decision to award new business to or continue business with a particular party.

(5) The term "interstate commerce" means trade, commerce, transportation, or communication among the several States, or between any foreign country and any State or between any State and any place or ship outside thereof, and such term includes the intrastate use of—

(A) a telephone or other interstate means of communication, or

(B) any other interstate instrumentality.

HISTORY: (Pub. L. 95-213, Title I, S 104A, as added Pub. L. 105-366, S 3, Nov. 10, 1998, 112 Stat. 3306.)

§ 78ff. Penalties

(a) **Willful violations; false and misleading statements.** Any person who willfully violates any provision of this title (other than section 30A [15 USC § 78dd-1]), or any rule or regulation thereunder the violation of which is made unlawful or the observance of which is required under the terms of this title, or any person who willfully and knowingly makes, or causes to be made, any statement in any application, report, or document required to be filed under this title or any rule or regulation thereunder or any undertaking contained in a registration statement as provided in subsection (d) of section 15 of this title [15 USC § 78 o(d)] or by any self-regulatory organization in connection with an application for membership or participation therein or to become associated with a member thereof [,], which statement was false or misleading with respect to any material fact, shall upon conviction be fined not more than $1,000,000, or imprisoned not more than 10 years, or both, except that when such person is a person other than a natural person, a fine not exceeding $2,500,000 may be imposed; but no person shall be subject to imprisonment under this section for the violation of any rule or regulation if he proves that he had no knowledge of such rule or regulation.

(b) **Failure to file information, documents, or reports.** Any issuer which fails to file information, documents, or reports required to be filed under subsection (d) of section 15 of this title [15 USC § 78o(d)] or any rule or regulation thereunder shall forfeit to the United States the sum of $100 for each and every day such failure to file shall continue. Such forfeiture, which shall be in lieu of any criminal penalty for such failure to file which might be deemed to arise under subsection (a) of this section, shall be payable to the Treasury of the United States and shall be recoverable in a civil suit in the name of the United States.

(c) **Violations by issuers, officers, directors, stockholders, employees, or agents of issuers.**

    (1) (A) Any issuer that violates subsection (a) or (g) of section 30A [15 USC § 78dd-1] shall be fined not more than $2,000,000.

           (B) Any issuer that violates subsection (a) or (g) of section 30A [15 USC § 78dd-1] shall be subject to a civil penalty of not more than $10,000 imposed in an action brought by the Commission.

    (2) (A) Any officer, director, employee, or agent of an issuer, or stockholder acting on behalf of such issuer, who willfully violates subsection (a) or (g) of section 30A of this title [15 USC § 78dd-1] shall be fined not more than $100,000, or imprisoned not more than 5 years, or both.

           (B) Any officer, director, employee, or agent of an issuer, or stockholder acting on behalf of such issuer, who violates subsection (a) or (g) of section 30A of this title [15 USC § 78dd-1] shall be subject to a civil penalty of not more than $10,000 imposed in an action brought by the Commission.

    (3) Whenever a fine is imposed under paragraph (2) upon any officer, director, employee, agent, or stockholder of an issuer, such fine may not be paid, directly or indirectly, by such issuer.

HISTORY: (June 6, 1934, ch 404, Title I, § 32, 48 Stat. 904; May 27, 1936, ch 462, § 9, 49 Stat. 1380; June 25, 1938, ch 677, § 4, 52 Stat. 1076; Aug. 20, 1964, P.L. 88-467, § 11, 78 Stat. 580; June 4, 1975, P.L. 94-29, § 23, 27(b), 89 Stat. 162, 163; Dec. 19, 1977, P.L. 95-213, Title I, § 103(b), 91 Stat. 1496; Aug. 10, 1984, P.L. 98-376, § 3, 98 Stat. 1265; Aug. 23, 1988, P.L. 100-418, Title V, Subtitle A, Part I, § 5003(b), 102 Stat. 1419; Nov. 19, 1988, P.L. 100-704, § 4, 102 Stat. 4680.) (As amended Nov. 10, 1998, P.L. 105-366, § 2(d), 112 Stat. 3303.)

E. STATUTORY PROVISIONS GOVERNING THE OVERSEAS PRIVATE INVESTMENT CORPORATION

Introduction

The Overseas Private Investment Corporation (OPIC) is chartered by Congress to "mobilize and facilitate the participation of United States private capital and skills in the economic and social development of less developed countries and areas, and countries in transition from nonmarket to market economies." 22 U.S.C. § 2191. By providing insurance, financing and reinsurance for such investments, OPIC complements other foreign assistance programs through inducement of private sector investment in target economies.

OPIC carries out its functions through four types of activities:

1) It provides insurance against the following types of political risks for investments overseas:
   a) inability to convert foreign currencies into U.S. dollars.
   b) loss due to expropriation or confiscation by a foreign government,
   c) loss due to war, revolution, insurrection, or civil strife, and
   d) loss due to business interruption caused by any of the above risks. 22 U.S.C. § 2194(a).
2) It provides loans and loan guaranties for overseas investments. 22 U.S.C. § 2194(b).
3) It provides direct investment through equity participation in overseas investments. 22 U.S.C. § 2194(c).
4) It encourages investment by advocating the interests of the American business community overseas. 22 U.S.C. § 2194(d).

OPIC coverage of an investment involves a series of agreements. In the standard OPIC insurance arrangement, there is first an Investment Incentive Agreement between the United States and the host government. This agreement provides that OPIC may offer coverage of investors with projects in the host country, require that such projects be approved by the host government, recognize the U.S. government's right as transferee of the investor's rights should coverage be claimed, and provide for dispute resolution should it be necessary between the two governments.

The second agreement is between the investor and the host government, providing the requisite approval of the investment and acknowledgment that it is in accordance with the government-to-government agreement. This agreement, and the resulting approval of investments, help make certain that any covered investments are not objectionable to the host government. The third agreement is the insurance agreement between OPIC and the investor. This agreement provides in detail the covered investment, the risks covered, and the manner in which coverage will be realized should one of the risks occur.

283

OPIC has accumulated reserves of more than $3 billion, having recorded a positive net income in every year of its operation. It covers investments in nearly 140 countries worldwide.

22 U.S. Code - FOREIGN RELATIONS AND INTERCOURSE
CHAPTER 32 - FOREIGN ASSISTANCE

§ 2191. Congressional statement of purpose; creation and functions of Corporation

To mobilize and facilitate the participation of United States private capital and skills in the economic and social development of less developed countries and areas, and countries in transition from nonmarket to market economies, thereby complementing the development assistance objectives of the United States, there is hereby created the Overseas Private Investment Corporation (hereinafter called the "Corporation"), which shall be an agency of the United States under the policy guidance of the Secretary of State.

The Corporation, in determining whether to provide insurance, financing, or reinsurance for a project, shall especially—

(1) be guided by the economic and social development impact and benefits of such a project and the ways in which such a project complements, or is compatible with, other development assistance programs or projects of the United States or other donors;

(2) give preferential consideration to investment projects in less developed countries that have per capita incomes of $984 or less in 1986 United States dollars, and restrict its activities with respect to investment projects in less developed countries that have per capita incomes of $4,269 or more in 1986 United States dollars (other than countries designated as beneficiary countries under section 2702 of Title 19, Ireland, and Northern Ireland); and

(3) ensure that the project is consistent with the provisions of section 2151p of this title, section 2151p-1 of this title, and section 2151q of this title relating to the environment and natural resources of, and tropical forests and endangered species in, developing countries, and consistent with the intent of regulations issued pursuant to section 2151p of this title, section 2151p-1 of this title, and section 2151q of this title.

In carrying out its purpose, the Corporation, utilizing broad criteria, shall undertake—

(a) to conduct financing, insurance, and reinsurance operations on a self-sustaining basis, taking into account in its financing operations the economic and financial soundness of projects;

(b) to utilize private credit and investment institutions and the Corporation's guaranty authority as the principal means of mobilizing capital investment funds;

(c) to broaden private participation and revolve its funds through selling its direct investments to private investors whenever it can appropriately do so on satisfactory terms;

(d) to conduct its insurance operations with due regard to principles of risk management including efforts to share its insurance and reinsurance risks;

(e) to the maximum degree possible consistent with its purposes—

    (1) to give preferential consideration in its investment insurance, reinsurance, and guaranty activities to investment projects sponsored by or involving United States small business; and

    (2) to increase the proportion of projects sponsored by or significantly involving United States small business to at least 30 percent of all projects insured, reinsured, or guaranteed by the Corporation;

(f) to consider in the conduct of its operations the extent to which less developed country governments are receptive to private enterprise, domestic and foreign, and their willingness and ability to maintain conditions which enable private enterprise to make its full contribution to the development process;

(g) to foster private initiative and competition and discourage monopolistic practices;

(h) to further to the greatest degree possible, in a manner consistent with its goals, the balance-of-payments and employment objectives of the United States;

(i) to conduct its activities in consonance with the activities of the agency primarily responsible for administering subchapter I of this chapter and the international trade, investment, and financial policies of the United States Government, and to seek to support those developmental projects having positive trade benefits for the United States;

(j) to advise and assist, within its field of competence, interested agencies of the United States and other organizations, both public and private, national and international, with respect to projects and programs relating to the development of private enterprise in less developed countries and areas;

(k) (1) to decline to issue any contract of insurance or reinsurance, or any guaranty, or to enter into any agreement to provide financing for an eligible investor's proposed investment if the Corporation determines that such investment is likely to cause such investor (or the sponsor of an investment project in which such investor is involved) significantly to reduce the number of his employees in the United States because he is replacing his United States production with production from such investment which involves substantially the same product for substantially the same market as his United States production; and (2) to monitor conformance with the representations of the investor on which the Corporation relied in making the determination required by clause (1);

(l) to decline to issue any contract of insurance or reinsurance, or any guaranty, or to enter into any agreement to provide financing for an eligible investor's proposed investment if the Corporation determines that such investment is likely to cause a significant reduction in the number of employees in the United States;

(m) to refuse to insure, reinsure, or finance any investment subject to performance requirements which would reduce substantially the positive trade benefits likely to accrue to the United States from the investment; and

(n) to refuse to insure, reinsure, guarantee, or finance any investment in connection with a project which the Corporation determines will pose an unreasonable or major environmental, health, or safety hazard, or will result in the significant degradation of national parks or similar protected areas.

HISTORY: (Pub. L. 87-195, Pt. I, § 231, as added Pub. L. 91-175, Pt. I, § 105, Dec. 30, 1969, 83 Stat. 809, and amended Pub. L. 93-390, § 2(1), Aug. 27, 1974, 88 Stat. 763; Pub. L. 95-268, § 2, Apr. 24, 1978, 92 Stat. 213; Pub. L. 97-65, § 2, Oct. 16, 1981, 95 Stat. 1021; Pub. L. 99-204, § 3, 4(a), Dec. 23, 1985, 99 Stat. 1669; Pub. L. 100-461, Title V, § 555, Oct. 1, 1988, 102 Stat. 2268-36.) (As amended Pub. L. 102-549, Title I, § 101, Oct. 28, 1992, 106 Stat. 3651; Pub. L. 103-392, Title I, § 105, Oct. 22, 1994, 108 Stat. 4099.)

§ 2191a. Additional requirements

(a) Worker rights
   (1) Limitation on OPIC activities
      The Corporation may insure, reinsure, guarantee, or finance a project only if the country in which the project is to be undertaken is taking steps to adopt and implement laws that extend internationally recognized worker rights, as defined in section 2467(4) of Title 19, to workers in that country (including any designated zone in that country). The Corporation shall also include the following language, in substantially the following form, in all contracts which the Corporation enters into with eligible investors to provide financial support under this subpart:

"The investor agrees not to take actions to prevent employees of the foreign enterprise from lawfully exercising their right of association and their right to organize and bargain collectively. The investor further agrees to observe applicable laws relating to a minimum age for employment of children, acceptable conditions of work with respect to minimum wages, hours of work, and occupational health and safety, and not to use forced labor. The investor is not responsible under this paragraph for the actions of a foreign government."

(2) Use of annual reports on workers rights

The Corporation shall, in making its determinations under paragraph (1), use the reports submitted to the Congress pursuant to section 2464 of Title 19. The restriction set forth in paragraph (1) shall not apply until the first such report is submitted to the Congress.

(3) Waiver

Paragraph (1) shall not prohibit the Corporation from providing any insurance, reinsurance, guaranty, or financing with respect to a country if the President determines that such activities by the Corporation would be in the national economic interests of the United States. Any such determination shall be reported in writing to the Congress, together with the reasons for the determination.

(4) Operations of OPIC in the People's Republic of China

In making a determination under this section for the People's Republic of China, the Corporation shall discuss fully and completely the justification for making such determination with respect to each item set forth in subparagraphs (A) through (E) of section 2467(4) of Title 19.

(b) Environmental Impact

The Board of Directors of the Corporation shall not vote in favor of any action proposed to be taken by the Corporation that is likely to have significant adverse environmental impacts that are sensitive, diverse, or unprecedented, unless for at least 60 days before the date of the vote

(1) an environmental impact assessment or initial environmental audit, analyzing the environmental impacts of the proposed action and of alternatives to the proposed action has been completed by the project applicant and made available to the Board of Directors; and

(2) such assessment or audit has been made available to the public of the United States, locally affected groups in the host country, and host country nongovernmental organizations.

(c) Public hearings

(1) The Board shall hold at least one public hearing each year in order to afford an opportunity for any person to present views as to whether the Corporation is carrying out its activities in accordance with section 2191 of this title and this section or whether any investment in a particular country should have been or should be extended insurance, reinsurance, guarantees, or financing under this subpart.

(2) In conjunction with each meeting of its Board of Directors, the Corporation shall hold a public hearing in order to afford an opportunity for any person to present views regarding the activities of the Corporation. Such views shall be made part of the record.

HISTORY: (Pub. L. 87-195, Pt. 1, § 231A, as added Pub. L. 99-204, § 5(a), Dec. 23, 1985, 99 Stat. 1670, and amended Pub. L. 100-418, Title II, § 2203(c), Aug. 23, 1988, 102 Stat. 1328.) (As amended Pub. L. 102-549, Title I, § 102, Oct. 28, 1992, 106 Stat. 3651; Pub. L. 104-188, Title I, § 1954(b)(3), Aug. 20, 1996, 110 Stat. 1928.) (As amended PL 106-158, December 9, 1999, 113 Stat. 1745.)

§ 2192. Capital of the Corporation

The President is authorized to pay in as capital of the Corporation, out of dollar receipts made available through the appropriation process from loans made pursuant to subchapter I of this chapter and from loans made under the Mutual Security Act of 1954, as amended, for the fiscal year 1970 not to exceed $20,000,000 and for the fiscal year 1971 not to exceed $20,000,000. Upon the payment of such capital by the President, the Corporation shall issue an equivalent amount of capital stock to the Secretary of the Treasury.

HISTORY: (Pub. L. 87-195, Pt. I, § 232, as added Pub. L. 91-175, Pt. I, § 105, Dec. 30, 1969, 83 Stat. 810.)

§ 2193. Organization and management

(a) Structure

The Corporation shall have a Board of Directors, a President, an Executive Vice President, and such other officers and staff as the Board of Directors may determine.

(b) Board of directors

All powers of the Corporation shall vest in and be exercised by or under the authority of its Board of Directors ("the Board") which shall consist of fifteen Directors, including the Chairman, with eight Directors constituting a quorum for the transaction of business. Eight Directors shall be appointed by the President of the United States, by and with the advice and consent of the Senate, and shall not be officials or employees of the Government of the United States. At least two of the eight Directors appointed under the preceding sentence shall be experienced in small business, one in organized labor, and one in cooperatives. Each such Director shall be appointed for a term of no more than three years. The terms of no more than three such Directors shall expire in any one year. Such Directors shall serve until their successors are appointed and qualified and may be reappointed.

The other Directors shall be officials of the Government of the United States, including the President of the Corporation, the Administrator of the Agency for International Development, the United States Trade Representative, and an official of the Department of Labor, designated by and serving at the pleasure of the President of the United States. The United States Trade Representative may designate a Deputy United States Trade Representative to serve on the Board in place of the United States Trade Representative. There shall be a Chairman and a Vice Chairman of the Board, both of whom shall be designated by the President of the United States from among the Directors of the Board other than those appointed under the second sentence of the first paragraph of this subsection.

All Directors who are not officers of the Corporation or officials of the Government of the United States shall be compensated at a rate equivalent to that of level IV of the Executive Schedule when actually engaged in the business of the Corporation and may be paid per diem in lieu of subsistence at the applicable rate prescribed in the standardized Government travel regulations, as amended from time to time, while away from their homes or usual places of business.

(c) President

The President of the Corporation shall be appointed by the President of the United States, by and with the advice and consent of the Senate, and shall serve at the pleasure of the President. In making such appointment, the President shall take into account private business experience of the appointee. The President of the Corporation shall be its Chief Executive Officer and responsible for the operations and management of the Corporation, subject to bylaws and policies established by the Board.

(d) Officers and staff

The Executive Vice President of the Corporation shall be appointed by the President of the United States, by and with the advice and consent of the Senate, and shall serve at the pleasure of the President. Other officers, attorneys, employees, and agents shall be selected and appointed by the Corporation, and shall be vested with such powers and duties as the Corporation may determine. Of such persons employed by the Corporation, not to exceed twenty may be appointed, compensated, or removed without regard to the civil service laws and regulations: Provided, That under such regulations as the President of the United States may prescribe, officers and employees of the United States Government who are appointed to any of the above positions may be entitled, upon removal from such position, except for cause, to reinstatement to the position occupied at the time of appointment or to a position of comparable grade and salary. Such positions shall be in addition to those otherwise authorized by law, including those authorized by section 5108 of Title 5.

HISTORY: (Pub. L. 87-195, Pt. I, § 233, as added Pub. L. 91-175, Pt. I, § 105, Dec. 30, 1969, 83 Stat. 810, and amended 1979 Reorg. Plan No. 2, § 6(a)(1), eff. Oct. 1, 1979, 44 F.R. 41166, 93 Stat. 1379; Pub. L. 97-65, § 3(a), (b), Oct. 16, 1981, 95 Stat. 1021, 1022.) (As amended PL 106-158, December 9, 1999, 113 Stat. 1745.)

§ 2194. Investment insurance and other programs

The Corporation is hereby authorized to do the following:

(a) Investment insurance

(1) To issue insurance, upon such terms and conditions as the Corporation may determine, to eligible investors assuring protection in whole or in part against any or all of the following risks with respect to projects which the Corporation has approved—

(A) inability to convert into United States dollars other currencies, or credits in such currencies, received as earnings or profits from the approved project, as repayment or return of the investment therein, in whole or in part, or as compensation for the sale or disposition of all or any part thereof;

(B) loss of investment, in whole or in part, in the approved project due to expropriation or confiscation by action of a foreign government;

(C) loss due to war, revolution, insurrection, or civil strife; and

(D) loss due to business interruption caused by any of the risks set forth in subparagraphs (A), (B), and (C).

(2) Recognizing that major private investments in less developed friendly countries or areas are often made by enterprises in which there is multinational participation, including significant United States private participation, the Corporation may make arrangements with foreign governments (including agencies, instrumentalities, or political subdivisions thereof) or with multilateral organizations and institutions for sharing liabilities assumed under investment insurance for such investments and may in connection therewith issue insurance to investors not otherwise eligible hereunder, except that liabilities assumed by the Corporation under the authority of this subsection shall be consistent with the purposes of this subpart and that the maximum share of liabilities so assumed shall not exceed the proportionate participation by eligible investors in the project.

(3) Not more than 10 per centum of the maximum contingent liability of investment insurance which the Corporation is permitted to have outstanding under section 2195(a)(1) of this title shall be issued to a single investor.

(4) Before issuing insurance for the first time for loss due to business interruption, and in each subsequent instance in which a significant expansion is proposed in the type of risk to be insured under the definition of "civil strife" or "business interruption", the Corporation shall, at least sixty days before such insurance is issued, submit to the Committee on Foreign Relations of the Senate and the Committee on Foreign Affairs of the House of Representatives a report with respect to such insurance, including a thorough analysis of the risks to be covered, anticipated losses, and proposed rates and reserves and, in the case of insurance for loss due to business interruption, an explanation of the underwriting basis upon which the insurance is to be offered. Any such report with respect to insurance for loss due to business interruption shall be considered in accordance with the procedures applicable to reprogramming notifications pursuant to section 2394-1 of this title.

(b) Investment guaranties

To issue to eligible investors guaranties of loans and other investments made by such investors assuring against loss due to such risks and upon such terms and conditions as the Corporation may determine: Provided, however, That such guaranties on other than loan investments shall not exceed 75 per centum of such investment: Provided further, That except for loan investments for credit unions made by eligible credit unions or credit union associations, the aggregate amount of investment (exclusive of interest and earnings) so guaranteed with respect to any project shall not exceed, at the time of issuance of any such guaranty, 75 per centum of the total investment committed to any such project as determined by the Corporation, which determination shall be conclusive for purposes of the Corporation's authority to issue any such guaranty: Provided further, That not more than 15 per centum of the maximum contingent liability of investment guaranties which the Corporation is permitted to have outstanding under section 2195(a)(2) of this title shall be issued to a single investor.

(c) Direct investment

To make loans in United States dollars repayable in dollars or loans in foreign currencies (including, without regard to section 1306 of Title 31, such foreign currencies which the Secretary of the Treasury may determine to be excess to the normal requirements of the United States and the Director of the Office of Management and Budget may allocate) to firms privately owned or of mixed private and public ownership upon such terms and conditions as the Corporation may determine. Loans may be made under this subsection only for projects that are sponsored by or significantly involve United States small business or cooperatives.

The Corporation may designate up to 25 percent of any loan under this subsection for use in the development or adaptation in the United States of new technologies or new products or services that are to be used in the project for which the loan is made and are likely to contribute to the economic or social development of less developed countries.

No loan may be made under this subsection to finance any operation for the extraction of oil or gas. The aggregate amount of loans under this subsection to finance operations for the mining or other extraction of any deposit of ore or other nonfuel minerals may not in any fiscal year exceed $4,000,000.

(d) Investment encouragement

To initiate and support through financial participation, incentive grant, or otherwise, and on such terms and conditions as the Corporation may determine, the identification, assessment, surveying and promotion of private investment opportunities, utilizing wherever feasible and effective the facilities of private organizations or private investors, except that:

(1) the Corporation shall not finance any survey to ascertain the existence, location, extent, or quality of, or to determine the feasibility of undertaking operations for the extraction of, oil or gas; and

(2) expenditures financed by the Corporation during any fiscal year on surveys to ascertain the existence, location, extent, or quality of, or to determine the feasibility of undertaking operations for the extraction of nonfuel minerals may not exceed $200,000.

In carrying out this authority, the Corporation shall coordinate with such investment promotion activities as are carried out by the Department of Commerce.

(e) Special projects and programs

To administer and manage special projects and programs, including programs of financial and advisory support which provide private technical, professional, or managerial assistance in the development of human resources, skills, technology, capital savings and intermediate financial and investment institutions and cooperatives and including the initiation of incentives, grants, and studies for renewable energy and other small activities. The funds for these projects and programs may, with the Corporation's concurrence, be transferred to it for such purposes under the authority of section 2392(a) of this title or from other sources, public or private. Administrative funds may not be made available for incentives, grants, and studies for renewable energy and other small business activities.

(f) Additional insurance functions

(1) To make and carry out contracts of insurance or reinsurance, or agreements to associate or share risks, with insurance companies, financial institutions, any other persons, or groups thereof, and employing the same, where appropriate, as its agent, or acting as their agent, in the issuance and servicing of insurance, the adjustment of claims, the exercise of subrogation rights, the ceding and accepting of reinsurance, and in any other matter incident to an insurance business; except that such agreements and contracts shall be consistent with the purposes of the Corporation set forth in section 2191 of this title and shall be on equitable terms.

(2) To enter into pooling or other risk-sharing arrangements with multi-national insurance or financing agencies or groups of such agencies.

(3) To hold an ownership interest in any association or other entity established for the purposes of sharing risks under investment insurance.

(4) To issue, upon such terms and conditions as it may determine, reinsurance of liabilities assumed by other insurers or groups thereof in respect of risks referred to in subsection (a)(1) of this section.

The amount of reinsurance of liabilities under this subpart which the Corporation may issue shall not in the aggregate exceed at any one time an amount equal to the amount authorized for the maximum contingent liability outstanding at any one time under section 2195(a)(1) of this title. All reinsurance issued by the Corporation under this subsection shall require that the reinsured party retain for his own account specified portions of liability, whether first loss or otherwise.

(g) Pilot equity finance program

(1) Authority for pilot program. In order to study the feasibility and desirability of a program of equity financing, the Corporation is authorized to establish a 4-year pilot program under which it may, on the limited basis prescribed in paragraphs (2) through (5), purchase, invest in, or otherwise acquire equity or quasi-equity securities of any firm or entity, upon such terms and conditions as the Corporation may determine, for the purpose of providing capital for any project which is consistent with the provisions of this subpart, except that:

(A) the aggregate amount of the Corporation's equity investment with respect to any project shall not exceed 30 percent of the aggregate amount of all equity investment made with respect to such project at the time that the Corporation's equity investment is made, except for securities acquired through the enforcement of any lien, pledge, or contractual arrangement as a result of a default by any party under any agreement relating to the terms of the Corporation's investment; and

(B) the Corporation's equity investment under this subsection with respect to any project, when added to any other investments made or guaranteed by the Corporation under subsection (b) or (c) of this section with respect to such project, shall not cause the aggregate amount of all such investment to exceed, at the time any such investment is made or guaranteed by the Corporation, 75 percent of the total investment committed to such project as determined by the Corporation.

The determination of the Corporation under subparagraph (B) shall be conclusive for purposes of the Corporation's authority to make or guarantee any such investment.

293

(2) Equity authority limited to projects in sub-Saharan Africa and Caribbean basin and marine transportation projects globally. Equity investments may be made under this subsection only in projects in countries eligible for financing under this subpart that are countries in sub-Saharan Africa or countries designated as beneficiary countries under section 2702 of Title 19 and in marine transportation projects in countries and areas eligible for OPIC support worldwide using United States commercial maritime expertise.

(3) Additional criteria. In making investment decisions under this subsection, the Corporation shall give preferential consideration to projects sponsored by or significantly involving United States small business or cooperatives. The Corporation shall also consider the extent to which the Corporation's equity investment will assist in obtaining the financing required for the project.

(4) Disposition of equity interest. Taking into consideration, among other things, the Corporation's financial interests and the desirability of fostering the development of local capital markets in less developed countries, the Corporation shall endeavor to dispose of any equity interest it may acquire under this subsection within a period of 10 years from the date of acquisition of such interest.

(5) Implementation. To the extent provided in advance in appropriations Acts, the Corporation is authorized to create such legal vehicles as may be necessary for implementation of its authorities, which legal vehicles may be deemed non-Federal borrowers for purposes of the Federal Credit Reform Act of 1990. Income and proceeds of investments made pursuant to this subsection may be used to purchase equity or quasi-equity securities in accordance with the provisions of this section: Provided, however, That such purchases shall not be limited to the 4-year period of the pilot program: Provided further, That the limitations contained in paragraph (2) shall not apply to such purchases.

(6) Consultations with Congress. The Corporation shall consult annually with the Committee on Foreign Affairs of the House of Representatives and the Committee on Foreign Relations of the Senate on the implementation of the pilot equity finance program established under this subsection.

HISTORY: (Pub. L. 87-195, Pt. I, § 234, as added Pub. L. 91-175, Pt. I, § 105, Dec. 30, 1969, 83 Stat. 811, and amended 1970 Reorg. Plan No. 2, § 102, eff. July 1, 1970, 35 F.R. 7959, 84 Stat. 2085; Pub. L. 93-390, § 2(2), Aug. 27, 1974, 88 Stat. 764; Pub. L. 95-268, § 3, Apr. 24, 1978, 92 Stat. 214; Pub. L. 97-65, § 4, Oct. 16, 1981, 95 Stat. 1022; Pub. L. 99-204, §§ 6(a), 7, 8, Dec. 23, 1985, 99 Stat. 1671, 1672; Pub. L. 100-461, Title V, § 555, Oct. 1, 1988, 102 Stat. 2268-36; Pub. L. 101-218, § 8(c), Dec. 11, 1989, 103 Stat. 1868.) (As amended Pub. L. 102-549, Title I, § 103, Oct. 28, 1992, 106 Stat. 3651; Pub. L. 106-31, Title VI, § 6001, May 21, 1999, 113 Stat. 112; Pub. L. 106-31, Title VI, § 6001, May 21, 1999, 113 Stat. 112.)

§ 2194a. Contract authority of Corporation; specific authorization in appropriation Acts required

The authority of the Overseas Private Investment Corporation to enter into contracts under section 2194(a) of this title shall be effective for any fiscal year beginning after September 30, 1981, only to such extent or in such amounts as are provided in appropriation Acts.

HISTORY: (Pub. L. 97-65, § 5(b)(2), Oct. 16, 1981, 95 Stat. 1023.)

§ 2194b. Enhancing private political risk insurance industry

(a) Cooperative programs

In order to encourage greater availability of political risk insurance for eligible investors by enhancing the private political risk insurance industry in the United States, and to the extent consistent with this subpart, the Corporation shall undertake programs of cooperation with such industry, and in connection with such programs may engage in the following activities:

(1) Utilizing its statutory authorities, encourage the development of associations, pools, or consortia of United States private political risk insurers.

(2) Share insurance risks (through coinsurance, contingent insurance, or other means) in a manner that is conducive to the growth and development of the private political risk insurance industry in the United States.

(3) Notwithstanding section 2197(e) of this title, upon the expiration of insurance provided by the Corporation for an investment, enter into risk- sharing agreements with United States private political risk insurers to insure any such investment; except that, in cooperating in the offering of insurance under this paragraph, the Corporation shall not assume responsibility for more than 50 percent of the insurance being offered in each separate transaction.

(b) Advisory group

(1) Establishment and membership

The Corporation shall establish a group to advise the Corporation on the development and implementation of the cooperative programs under this section. The group shall be appointed by the Board and shall be composed of up to 12 members, including the following:

(A) Up to seven persons from the private political risk insurance industry, of whom no fewer than two shall represent private political risk insurers, one shall represent private political risk reinsurers, and one shall represent insurance or reinsurance brokerage firms.

295

(B) Up to four persons, other than persons described in subparagraph (A), who are purchasers of political risk insurance.

(2) Functions

The Corporation shall call upon members of the advisory group, either collectively or individually, to advise it regarding the capability of the private political risk insurance industry to meet the political risk insurance needs of United States investors, and regarding the development of cooperative programs to enhance such capability.

(3) Meetings

The advisory group shall meet not later than September 30, 1989, and at least annually thereafter. The Corporation may from time to time convene meetings of selected members of the advisory group to address particular questions requiring their specialized knowledge.

(4) Federal Advisory Committee Act

The advisory group shall not be subject to the Federal Advisory Committee Act (5 U.S.C. App.).

HISTORY: (Pub. L. 87-195, Pt. I, § 234A, as added Pub. L. 99-204, § 9(a), Dec. 23, 1985, 99 Stat. 1672, and amended Pub. L. 100-461, Title V, § 555, Oct. 1, 1988, 102 Stat. 2268-36.)

§ 2195. Issuing authority, direct investment authority and reserves

(a) Issuing authority

(1) Insurance and financing.

(A) The maximum contingent liability outstanding at any one time pursuant to insurance issued under section 2194(a) of this title, and the amount of financing issued under sections 2194(b) and (c) of this title, shall not exceed in the aggregate $29,000,000,000.

(B) Subject to spending authority provided in appropriations Acts pursuant to section 661c(b) of Title 2, the Corporation is authorized to transfer such sums as are necessary from its noncredit activities to pay for the subsidy cost of the investment guaranties and direct loan programs under subsections (b) and (c) of section 2194 of this title.

(2) Termination of authority

The authority of subsections (a), (b), and (c) of section 2194 of this title shall continue until November 1, 2000.

(b) Repealed. Pub. L. 102-549, Title I, § 104(a)(3), Oct. 28, 1992, 106 Stat. 3652

(c) Insurance Reserve; Guaranty Reserve

There shall be established in the Treasury of the United States an insurance and guaranty fund, which shall have separate accounts to be known as the Insurance Reserve and the Guaranty Reserve, which reserves shall be available for discharge of liabilities, as provided in subsection (d) of this section, until such time as all such liabilities have been discharged or have expired or until all such reserves have been expended in accordance with the provisions of this section. Such fund shall be funded by: (1) the funds heretofore available to discharge liabilities under predecessor guaranty authority (including housing guaranty authorities), less both the amount made available for housing guaranty programs pursuant to section 2183(b) of this title and the amount made available to the Corporation pursuant to subsection (e) of this section of this title; and (2) such sums as shall be appropriated pursuant to subsection (f) of this section for such purpose. The allocation of such funds to each such reserve shall be determined by the Board after consultation with the Secretary of the Treasury. Additional amounts may thereafter be transferred to such reserves pursuant to section 2196 of this title.

(d) Priority of funds used to discharge liabilities

Any payments made to discharge liabilities under investment insurance or reinsurance issued under section 2194 of this title, under similar predecessor guaranty authority, or under section 2194b of this title shall be paid first out of the Insurance Reserve, as long as such reserve remains available, and thereafter out of funds made available pursuant to subsection (f) of this section. Any payments made to discharge liabilities under guaranties issued under section 2194(b) of this title or under similar predecessor guaranty authority shall be paid first out of the Guaranty Reserve as long as such reserve remains available, and thereafter out of funds made available pursuant to subsection (f) of this section.

(e) Reserves from predecessor guaranty authority

There is hereby authorized to be transferred to the Corporation at its call, for the purposes specified in section 2196 of this title, all fees and other revenues collected under predecessor guaranty authority from December 31, 1968, available as of the date of such transfer.

(f) Authorization of appropriations; issuance, etc., of obligations by Corporation for purchase by Secretary of the Treasury

There are authorized to be appropriated to the Corporation, to remain available until expended, such amounts as may be necessary from time to time to replenish or increase the insurance and guaranty fund, to discharge the liabilities under insurance, reinsurance, or guaranties issued by the Corporation or issued under predecessor guaranty authority, or to discharge obligations of the Corporation purchased by the Secretary of the Treasury pursuant to this subsection. However, no appropriations shall be made to augment the Insurance Reserve until the amount of funds in the Insurance Reserve is less than $25,000,000. Any appropriations to augment the Insurance Reserve shall then only be made either pursuant to specific authorization enacted after August 27, 1974, or to satisfy the full faith and credit provision of section 2197(c) of this title. In order to discharge liabilities under investment insurance or reinsurance, the Corporation is authorized to issue from time to time for purchase by the Secretary of the Treasury its notes, debentures, bonds, or other obligations; but the aggregate amount of such obligations outstanding at any one time shall not exceed $100,000,000. Any such obligation shall be repaid to the Treasury within one year after the date of issue of such obligation. Any such obligation shall bear interest at a rate determined by the Secretary of the Treasury, taking into consideration the current average market yield on outstanding marketable obligations of the United States of comparable maturities during the month preceding the issuance of any obligation authorized by this subsection. The Secretary of the Treasury shall purchase any obligation of the Corporation issued under this subsection, and for such purchase he may use as a public debt transaction the proceeds of the sale of any securities issued under chapter 31 of Title 31 after August 27, 1974. The purpose for which securities may be issued under such chapter shall include any such purchase.

HISTORY: (Pub. L. 87-195, Pt. I, § 235, as added Pub. L. 91-175, Pt. I, § 105, Dec. 30, 1969, 83 Stat. 813, and amended Pub. L. 93-189, § 6(1), Dec. 17, 1973, 87 Stat. 717; Pub. L. 93-390, § 2(3), Aug. 27, 1974, 88 Stat. 766; Pub. L. 95-268, § 4, Apr. 24, 1978, 92 Stat. 214; Pub. L. 97-65, § 5(a), (b)(1), (c), Oct. 16, 1981, 95 Stat. 1022, 1023; Pub. L. 99-204, §§ 9(b)(1), 10, 17(b), Dec. 23, 1985, 99 Stat. 1673, 1676; Pub. L. 100-418, Title II, § 2203(b), Aug. 23, 1988, 102 Stat. 1328; Pub. L. 100-461, Title V, § 555, Oct. 1, 1988, 102 Stat. 2268-36.) (As amended Pub. L. 102-549, Title I, § 104, Oct. 28, 1992, 106 Stat. 3652; Pub. L. 103-392, Title I, §§ 101 to 104, Oct. 22, 1994, 108 Stat. 4098; Pub. L. 104-208, Div. A, Title I, § 101(c) [Title I], Sept. 30, 1996, 110 Stat. 3009-123; Pub. L. 105-118, Title V, § 581(a), Nov. 26, 1997, 111 Stat. 2435.) (As amended PL 106-113, November 29, 1999, 113 Stat. 1501.)

§ 2196. Income and revenues

In order to carry out the purposes of the Corporation, all revenues and income transferred to or earned by the Corporation, from whatever source derived, shall be held by the Corporation and shall be available to carry out its purposes, including without limitation

    (a) payment of all expenses of the Corporation, including investment promotion expenses;

    (b) transfers and additions to the insurance or guaranty reserves, the Direct Investment Fund established pursuant to section 2195 of this title, and such other funds or reserves as the Corporation may establish, at such time and in such amounts as the Board may determine; and

    (c) payment of dividends, on capital stock, which shall consist of and be paid from net earnings of the Corporation after payments, transfers, and additions under subsections (a) and (b) hereof.

HISTORY: (Pub. L. 87-195, Pt. I, § 236, as added Pub. L. 91-175, Pt. I, § 105, Dec. 30, 1969, 83 Stat. 814.)

§ 2197. General provisions relating to insurance, guaranty, financing and reinsurance programs

    (a) Scope

        Insurance, guaranties, and reinsurance issued under this subpart shall cover investment made in connection with projects in any less developed friendly country or area with the government of which the President of the United States has agreed to institute a program for insurance, guaranties, or reinsurance.

    (b) Protection of interest

        The Corporation shall determine that suitable arrangements exist for protecting the interest of the Corporation in connection with any insurance, guaranty or reinsurance issued under this subpart, including arrangements concerning ownership, use, and disposition of the currency, credits, assets, or investments on account of which payment under such insurance, guaranty or reinsurance is to be made, and any right, title, claim, or cause of action existing in connection therewith.

(c) Guaranties as obligations backed by full faith and credit of United States

All guaranties issued prior to July 1, 1956, all guaranties issued under sections 1872(b) and 1933(b) of this title, all guaranties heretofore issued pursuant to prior guaranty authorities repealed by the Foreign Assistance Act of 1969, and all insurance, reinsurance and guaranties issued pursuant to this subpart shall constitute obligations, in accordance with the terms of such insurance, reinsurance or guaranties, of the United States of America and the full faith and credit of the United States of America is hereby pledged for the full payment and performance of such obligations.

(d) Fees

(1) In general

Fees may be charged for providing insurance, reinsurance, financing, and other services under this subpart in amounts to be determined by the Corporation. In the event fees charged for insurance, reinsurance, financing, or other services are reduced, fees to be paid under existing contracts for the same type of insurance, reinsurance, financing, or services and for similar guarantees issued under predecessor guarantee authority may be reduced.

(2) Credit transaction costs

Project-specific transaction costs incurred by the Corporation relating to loan obligations or loan guarantee commitments covered by the provisions of the Federal Credit Reform Act of 1990 [2 U.S.C.A. § 661 et seq.], including the costs of project-related travel and expenses for legal representation provided by persons outside the Corporation and other similar expenses which are charged to the borrower, shall be paid out of the appropriate finance account established pursuant to section 505(b) of such Act [2 U.S.C.A. § 661d(b)].

(3) Noncredit transaction costs

Fees paid for the project-specific transaction costs and other direct costs associated with services provided to specific investors or potential investors pursuant to section 2194 of this title (other than those covered in paragraph (2)), including financing, insurance, reinsurance, missions, seminars, conferences, and other preinvestment services, shall be available for obligation for the purposes for which they were collected, notwithstanding any other provision of law.

(e) Maximum term of obligation

No insurance, guaranty, or reinsurance of any equity investment shall extend beyond twenty years from the date of issuance.

(f) Limitations on amounts

Compensation for insurance, reinsurance, or guaranties issued under this subpart shall not exceed the dollar value, as of the date of the investment, of the investment made in the project with the approval of the Corporation plus interest, earnings, or profits actually accrued on such investment to the extent provided by such insurance, reinsurance, or guaranty, except that the Corporation may provide that (1) appropriate adjustments in the insured dollar value be made to reflect the replacement cost of project assets, (2) compensation for a claim of loss under insurance of an equity investment may be computed on the basis of the net book value attributable to such equity investment on the date of loss, and (3) compensation for loss due to business interruption may be computed on a basis to be determined by the Corporation which reflects amounts lost. Notwithstanding the preceding sentence, the Corporation shall limit the amount of direct insurance and reinsurance issued by it under section 2194 or 2194b of this title so that risk of loss as to at least 10 per centum of the total investment of the insured and its affiliates in the project is borne by the insured and such affiliates, except that such limitation shall not apply to direct insurance or reinsurance of loans by banks or other financial institutions to unrelated parties.

(g) Fraud or misrepresentation

No payment may be made under any guaranty, insurance, or reinsurance issued pursuant to this subpart for any loss arising out of fraud or misrepresentation for which the party seeking payment is responsible.

(h) Limits of obligation

Insurance, guaranties, or reinsurance of a loan or equity investment of an eligible investor in a foreign bank, finance company, or other credit institution shall extend only to such loan or equity investment and not to any individual loan or equity investment made by such foreign bank, finance company, or other credit institution.

(i) Claims settlement

Claims arising as a result of insurance, reinsurance, or guaranty operations under this subpart or under predecessor guaranty authority may be settled, and disputes arising as a result thereof may be arbitrated with the consent of the parties, on such terms and conditions as the Corporation may determine. Payment made pursuant to any such settlement, or as a result of an arbitration award, shall be final and conclusive notwithstanding any other provision of law.

(j) Presumption of compliance

Each guaranty contract executed by such officer or officers as may be designated by the Board shall be conclusively presumed to be issued in compliance with the requirements of this chapter.

(k) Balance of payments

In making a determination to issue insurance, guaranties, or reinsurance under this subpart, the Corporation shall consider the possible adverse effect of the dollar investment under such insurance, guaranty, or reinsurance upon the balance of payments of the United States.

(l) Convictions under Foreign Corrupt Practices Act of 1977; prohibition on payments for losses resulting from unlawful activities; suspension from eligibility of receipt of financial support

(1) No payment may be made under any insurance or reinsurance which is issued under this subpart on or after April 24, 1978, for any loss occurring with respect to a project, if the preponderant cause of such loss was an act by the investor seeking payment under this subpart, by a person possessing majority ownership and control of the investor at the time of the act, or by any agent of such investor or controlling person, and a court of the United States has entered a final judgment that such act constituted a violation under the Foreign Corrupt Practices Act of 1977.

(2) Not later than 120 days after April 24, 1978, the Corporation shall adopt regulations setting forth appropriate conditions under which any person convicted under the Foreign Corrupt Practices Act of 1977 for an offense related to a project insured or otherwise supported by the Corporation shall be suspended, for a period of not more than five years, from eligibility to receive any insurance, reinsurance, guaranty, loan, or other financial support authorized by this subpart.

(m) Notification of countries of environmental restrictions on certain activities

(1) Before finally providing insurance, reinsurance, guarantees, or financing under this subpart for any environmentally sensitive investment in connection with a project in a country, the Corporation shall notify appropriate government officials of that country of

(A) all guidelines and other standards adopted by the International Bank for Reconstruction and Development and any other international organization relating to the public health or safety or the environment which are applicable to the project; and

(B) to the maximum extent practicable, any restriction under any law of the United States relating to public health or safety or the environment that would apply to the project if the project were undertaken in the United States.

The notification under the preceding sentence shall include a summary of the guidelines, standards, and restrictions referred to in subparagraphs (A) and (B), and may include any environmental impact statement, assessment, review, or study prepared with respect to the investment pursuant to section 2199(g) of this title.

(2) Before finally providing insurance, reinsurance, guarantees, or financing for any investment subject to paragraph (1), the Corporation shall take into account any comments it receives on the project involved.

(3) On or before September 30, 1986, the Corporation shall notify appropriate government officials of a country of the guidelines, standards, and legal restrictions described in paragraph (1) that apply to any project in that country—

 (A) which the Corporation identifies as potentially posing major hazards to public health and safety or the environment; and

 (B) for which the Corporation provided insurance, reinsurance, guarantees, or financing under this subpart before December 23, 1985, and which is in the Corporation's portfolio on that date.

(n) Penalties for fraud

Whoever knowingly makes any false statement or report, or willfully overvalues any land, property, or security, for the purpose of influencing in any way the action of the Corporation with respect to any insurance, reinsurance, guarantee, loan, equity investment, or other activity of the Corporation under section 2194 of this title or any change or extension of any such insurance, reinsurance, guarantee, loan, equity investment, or activity, by renewal, deferment of action or otherwise, or the acceptance, release, or substitution of security therefor, shall be fined not more than $1,000,000 or imprisoned not more than 30 years, or both.

(o) Use of local currencies

Direct loans or investments made in order to preserve the value of funds received in inconvertible foreign currency by the Corporation as a result of activities conducted pursuant to section 2194(a) of this title shall not be considered in determining whether the Corporation has made or has outstanding loans or investments to the extent of any limitation on obligations and equity investment imposed by or pursuant to this subpart. The provisions of section 504(b) of the Federal Credit Reform Act of 1990 [2 U.S.C.A. § 661c(b)] shall not apply to direct loan obligations made with funds described in this subsection.

HISTORY: (Pub. L. 87-195, Pt. I, § 237, as added Pub. L. 91-175, Pt. I, § 105, Dec. 30, 1969, 83 Stat. 814, and amended Pub. L. 93-390, § 2(4), Aug. 27, 1974, 88 Stat. 767; Pub. L. 95-268, §§ 5, 6, Apr. 24, 1978, 92 Stat. 215; Pub. L. 97-65, § 6, Oct. 16, 1981, 95 Stat. 1023; Pub. L. 99-204, §§ 4(b), 6(b), 9(b)(2), Dec. 23, 1985, 99 Stat. 1670, 1671, 1673; Pub. L. 100-461, Title V, § 555, Oct. 1, 1988, 102 Stat. 2268-36.) (As amended Pub. L. 102-549, Title I, § 105, Oct. 28, 1992, 106 Stat. 3652.)

§ 2198. Definitions

As used in this subpart—

(a) the term "investment" includes any contribution or commitment of funds, commodities, services, patents, processes, or techniques, in the form of (1) a loan or loans to an approved project, (2) the purchase of a share of ownership in any such project, (3) participation in royalties, earnings, or profits of any such project, and (4) the furnishing of commodities or services pursuant to a lease or other contract;

(b) the term "expropriation" includes, but is not limited to, any abrogation, repudiation, or impairment by a foreign government of its own contract with an investor with respect to a project, where such abrogation, repudiation, or impairment is not caused by the investor's own fault or misconduct, and materially adversely affects the continued operation of the project;

(c) the term "eligible investor" means: (1) United States citizens; (2) corporations, partnerships, or other associations including nonprofit associations, created under the laws of the United States, any State or territory thereof, or the District of Columbia, and substantially beneficially owned by United States citizens; and (3) foreign corporations, partnerships, of [FN1] other associations wholly owned by one or more such United States citizens, corporations, partnerships, or other associations: Provided, however, That the eligibility of such foreign corporation shall be determined without regard to any shares, in aggregate less than 5 per centum of the total of issued and subscribed share capital, held by other than the United States owners: Provided further, That in the case of any loan investment a final determination of eligibility may be made at the time the insurance or guaranty is issued; in all other cases, the investor must be eligible at the time a claim arises as well as at the time the insurance or guaranty is issued;

(d) the term "noncredit account revolving fund" means the account in which funds under section 2196 of this title and all funds from noncredit activities are held; and

(e) the term "noncredit activities" means all activities of the Corporation other than its loan guarantee program under section 2194(b) of this title and its direct loan program under section 2194(c) of this title;

(f) the term "predecessor guaranty authority" means prior guaranty authorities (other than housing guaranty authorities) repealed by the Foreign Assistance Act of 1969, and sections 1509(b)(3), 1872(b), and 1933(b) of this title (exclusive of authority relating to informational media guaranties).

HISTORY: (Pub. L. 87-195, Pt. I, § 238, as added Pub. L. 91-175, Pt. I, § 105, Dec. 30, 1969, 83 Stat. 815, and amended Pub. L. 92-226, Pt. I, § 104(a), Feb. 7, 1972, 86 Stat. 22; Pub. L. 97-65, § 7, Oct. 16, 1981, 95 Stat. 1024; Pub. L. 99-204, § 17(a), Dec. 23, 1985, 99 Stat. 1676.) (As amended Pub. L. 102-549, Title I, § 106, Oct. 28, 1992, 106 Stat. 3653.)

§ 2199. General provisions and powers

(a) Place of residence

The Corporation shall have its principal office in the District of Columbia and shall be deemed, for purposes of venue in civil actions, to be a resident thereof.

(b) Transfer of prior obligations, etc.; administration prior to transfer

The President shall transfer to the Corporation, at such time as he may determine, all obligations, assets and related rights and responsibilities arising out of, or related to, predecessor programs and authorities similar to those provided for in section 2194(a), (b), and (d) of this title. Until such transfer, the agency heretofore responsible for such predecessor programs shall continue to administer such assets and obligations, and such programs and activities authorized under this subpart as may be determined by the President.

(c) Audits of the Corporation

(1) The Corporation shall be subject to the applicable provisions of chapter 91 of Title 31, except as otherwise provided in this subpart.

(2) An independent certified public accountant shall perform a financial and compliance audit of the financial statements of the Corporation at least once every three years, in accordance with generally accepted Government auditing standards for a financial and compliance audit, as issued by the Comptroller General. The independent certified public accountant shall report the results of such audit to the Board. The financial statements of the Corporation shall be presented in accordance with generally accepted accounting principles. These financial statements and the report of the accountant shall be included in a report which contains, to the extent applicable, the information identified in section 9106 of Title 31 and which the Corporation shall submit to the Congress not later than six and one-half months after the end of the last fiscal year covered by the audit. The General Accounting Office may review the audit conducted by the accountant and the report to the Congress in the manner and at such times as the General Accounting Office considers necessary.

(3) In lieu of the financial and compliance audit required by paragraph (2), the General Accounting Office shall, if the Office considers it necessary or upon the request of the Congress, audit the financial statements of the Corporation in the manner provided in paragraph (2). The Corporation shall reimburse the General Accounting Office for the full cost of any audit conducted under this paragraph.

(4) All books, accounts, financial records, reports, files, workpapers, and property belonging to or in use by the Corporation and the accountant who conducts the audit under paragraph (2), which are necessary for purposes of this subsection, shall be made available to the representatives of the General Accounting Office.

(d) Powers of Corporation

To carry out the purposes of this subpart, the Corporation is authorized to adopt and use a corporate seal, which shall be judicially noticed; to sue and be sued in its corporate name; to adopt, amend, and repeal bylaws governing the conduct of its business and the performance of the powers and duties granted to or imposed upon it by law; to acquire, hold or dispose of, upon such terms and conditions as the Corporation may determine, any property, real, personal, or mixed, tangible or intangible, or any interest therein; to invest funds derived from fees and other revenues in obligations of the United States and to use the proceeds therefrom, including earnings and profits, as it shall deem appropriate; to indemnify directors, officers, employees and agents of the Corporation for liabilities and expenses incurred in connection with their Corporation activities; notwithstanding any other provision of law, to represent itself or to contract for representation in all legal and arbitral proceedings; to enter into limited-term contracts with nationals of the United States for personal services to carry out activities in the United States and abroad under subsections (d) and (e) of section 2194 of this title; to purchase, discount, rediscount, sell, and negotiate, with or without its endorsement or guaranty, and guarantee notes, participation certificates, and other evidence of indebtedness (provided that the Corporation shall not issue its own securities, except participation certificates for the purpose of carrying out section 2191(c) of this title or participation certificates as evidence of indebtedness held by the Corporation in connection with settlement of claims under section 2197(i) of this title); to make and carry out such contracts and agreements as are necessary and advisable in the conduct of its business; to exercise any priority of the Government of the United States in collecting debts from bankrupt, insolvent, or decedents' estates; to determine the character of and the necessity for its obligations and expenditures, and the manner in which they shall be incurred, allowed, and paid, subject to provisions of law specifically applicable to Government corporations; to collect or compromise any obligations assigned to or held by the Corporation, including any legal or equitable rights accruing to the Corporation; and to take such actions as may be necessary or appropriate to carry out the powers herein or hereafter specifically conferred upon it.

(e) Reviews, investigations, and inspections by Inspector General of Agency for International Development

The Inspector General of the Agency for International Development (1) may conduct reviews, investigations, and inspections of all phases of the Corporation's operations and activities and (2) shall conduct all security activities of the Corporation relating to personnel and the control of classified material. With respect to his responsibilities under this subsection, the Inspector General shall report to the Board. The agency primarily responsible for administering subchapter I of this chapter shall be reimbursed by the Corporation for all expenses incurred by the Inspector General in connection with his responsibilities under this subsection.

(f) Programs in Yugoslavia, Poland, Hungary, Romania, the People's Republic of China, or Pakistan; national interest

Except for the provisions of this subpart, no other provision of this chapter or any other law shall be construed to prohibit the operation in Yugoslavia, Poland, Hungary, or any other East European Country, or the People's Republic of China, or Pakistan of the programs authorized by this subpart, if the President determines that the operation of such program in such country is important to the national interest.

(g) Environmental impact assessments

The requirements of section 2151p(c) of this title relating to environmental impact statements and environmental assessments shall apply to any investment which the Corporation insures, reinsures, guarantees, or finances under this subpart in connection with a project in a country.

(h) Preparation, maintenance, and contents of development impact profile for investment projects; development of criteria for evaluating projects

In order to carry out the policy set forth in paragraph (1) of the second undesignated paragraph of section 2191 of this title, the Corporation shall prepare and maintain for each investment project it insures, finances, or reinsures, a development impact profile consisting of data appropriate to measure the projected and actual effects of such project on development. Criteria for evaluating projects shall be developed in consultation with the Director of the United States International Development Cooperation Agency.

(i) Observance of and respect for human rights and fundamental freedoms as considerations for conduct of assistance programs, etc.; provisions applicable for determinations; exceptions

The Corporation shall take into account in the conduct of its programs in a country, in consultation with the Secretary of State, all available information about observance of and respect for human rights and fundamental freedoms in such country and the effect the operation of such programs will have on human rights and fundamental freedoms in such country. The provisions of section 2151n of this title shall apply to any insurance, reinsurance, guaranty, or loan issued by the Corporation for projects in a country, except that in addition to the exception (with respect to benefiting needy people) set forth in subsection (a) of such section, the Corporation may support a project if the national security interest so requires.

(j) Exemption from taxation

The Corporation, including its franchise, capital, reserves, surplus, advances, intangible property, and income, shall be exempt from all taxation at any time imposed by the United States, by any territory, dependency, or possession of the United States, or by any State, the District of Columbia, or any county, municipality, or local taxing authority.

(k) Publication of policy guidelines

The Corporation shall publish, and make available to applicants for insurance, reinsurance, guarantees, financing, or other assistance made available by the Corporation under this subpart, the policy guidelines of the Corporation relating to its programs.

HISTORY: (Pub. L. 87-195, Pt. I, § 239, as added Pub. L. 91-175, Pt. I, § 105, Dec. 30, 1969, 83 Stat. 816, and amended Pub. L. 92-226, Pt. I, § 104(b), Feb. 7, 1972, 86 Stat. 22; Pub. L. 92-310, Title II, § 227(d), June 6, 1972, 86 Stat. 207; Pub. L. 93-390, § 2(5), Aug. 27, 1974, 88 Stat. 768; Pub. L. 95-268, §§ 7, 8, Apr. 24, 1978, 92 Stat. 215, 216; Pub. L. 95-598, Title III, § 318, Nov. 6, 1978, 92 Stat. 2678; 1979 Reorg. Plan No. 2, § 6(a)(1), eff. Oct. 1, 1979, 44 F.R. 41166, 93 Stat. 1379; Pub. L. 96-327, Aug. 8, 1980, 94 Stat. 1026; Pub. L. 97-65, § 8, Oct. 16, 1981, 95 Stat. 1024; Pub. L. 97-113, Title VII, § 705(b)(2), Dec. 29, 1981, 95 Stat. 1545; Pub. L. 99-204, §§ 4(c), 11 to 13, Dec. 23, 1985, 99 Stat. 1670, 1673, 1674; Pub. L. 100-461, Title V, § 555, Oct. 1, 1988, 102 Stat. 2268-36; Pub. L. 101-167, Title V, § 597(a), Nov. 21, 1989, 103 Stat. 1257; Pub. L. 101-179, Title III, § 302(a), Nov. 28, 1989, 103 Stat. 1311.) (As amended Pub. L. 101-513, Title V, § 576(a), Nov. 5, 1990, 104 Stat. 2044; Pub. L. 102-549, Title I, § 107, Oct. 28, 1992, 106 Stat. 3654; Pub. L. 105-118, Title V, § 579(a), Nov. 26, 1997, 111 Stat. 2435.)

§ 2200. Small business development in less developed friendly countries or areas; encouragement by other Federal departments, etc., of broadened participation by United States small business cooperatives and investors; project funding

The Corporation shall undertake, in cooperation with appropriate departments, agencies, and instrumentalities of the United States as well as private entities and others, to broaden the participation of United States small business, cooperatives, and other small United States investors in the development of small private enterprise in less developed friendly countries or areas. The Corporation shall allocate up to 50 per cent of its annual net income, after making suitable provision for transfers and additions to reserves, to assist and facilitate the development of projects consistent with the provisions of this section. Such funds may be expended, notwithstanding the requirements of section 2191(a) of this title, on such terms and conditions as the Corporation may determine, through loans, grants, or other programs authorized by section 2194 and section 2194b of this title.

HISTORY: (Pub. L. 87-195, Pt. I, § 240, as added Pub. L. 95-268, § 9, Apr. 24, 1978, 92 Stat. 216, and amended Pub. L. 99-204, § 9(b)(3), Dec. 23, 1985, 99 Stat. 1673.)

§ 2200a. Report to Congress

(a) Annual report

\\\After the end of each fiscal year, the Corporation shall submit to the Congress a complete and detailed report of its operations during such fiscal year. Such report shall include—

(1) an assessment, based upon the development impact profiles required by section 2199(h) of this title, of the economic and social development impact and benefits of the projects with respect to which such profiles are prepared, and of the extent to which the operations of the Corporation complement or are compatible with the development assistance programs of the United States and other donors; and

(2) a description of any project for which the Corporation—

(A) refused to provide any insurance, reinsurance, guaranty, financing, or other financial support, on account of violations of human rights referred to in section 2199(i) of this title; or

(B) notwithstanding such violations, provided such insurance, reinsurance, guaranty, financing, or financial support, on the basis of a determination (i) that the project will directly benefit the needy people in the country in which the project is located, or (ii) that the national security interest so requires.

309

(b) Effect of all projects on employment in United States to be included in annual report

   (1) Each annual report required by subsection (a) of this section shall contain projections of the effects on employment in the United States of all projects for which, during the preceding fiscal year, the Corporation initially issued any insurance, reinsurance, or guaranty or made any direct loan. Each such report shall include projections of

     (A) the amount of United States exports to be generated by those projects, both during the start-up phase and over a period of years;

     (B) the final destination of the products to be produced as a result of those projects; and

     (C) the impact such production will have on the production of similar products in the United States with regard to both domestic sales and exports.

   (2) The projections required by this subsection shall be based on an analysis of each of the projects described in paragraph (1).

   (3) In reporting the projections on employment required by this subsection, the Corporation shall specify, with respect to each project—

     (A) any loss of jobs in the United States caused by the project, whether or not the project itself creates other jobs;

     (B) any jobs created by the project; and

     (C) the country in which the project is located, and the economic sector involved in the project.

   No proprietary information may be disclosed under this paragraph.

(c) Repealed. Pub.L. 100-461, Title V, § 555, Oct. 1, 1988, 102 Stat. 2268-36

(d) Maintenance of records

  The Corporation shall maintain as part of its records

   (1) all information collected in preparing the report required by subsection (c) of this section (as in effect before October 1, 1988), whether the information was collected by the Corporation itself or by a contractor; and

   (2) a copy of the analysis of each project analyzed in preparing the reports required either by subsection (b) of this section, or by subsection (c) of this section (as in effect before October 1, 1988).

(e) Assessment of cooperative political risk insurance program

   Each annual report required by subsection (a) of this section shall include an assessment of programs implemented by the Corporation under section 2194b(a) of this title including the following information, to the extent such information is available to the Corporation:

   (1) The nature and dollar value of political risk insurance provided by private insurers in conjunction with the Corporation, which the Corporation was not permitted to provide under this subpart.

(2) The nature and dollar value of political risk insurance provided by private insurers in conjunction with the Corporation, which the Corporation was permitted to provide under this subpart.

(3) The manner in which such private insurers and the Corporation cooperated in recovery efforts and claims management.

(f) Information not required to be made available to public excluded from reports

Subsections (b) and (e) of this section do not require the inclusion in any report submitted pursuant to those subsections of any information which would not be required to be made available to the public pursuant to section 552 of Title 5 (relating to freedom of information).

HISTORY: (Pub. L. 87-195, Pt. I, § 240A, as added Pub. L. 91-175, Pt. I, § 105, Dec. 30, 1969, 83 Stat. 818, and amended Pub. L. 93-390, § 2(7), Aug. 27, 1974, 88 Stat. 768; Pub. L. 95-268, § 10, Apr. 24, 1978, 92 Stat. 216; Pub. L. 97-65, § 9, formerly S 9(a), Oct. 16, 1981, 95 Stat. 1024, renumbered § 9, Pub. L. 99-204, § 17(c)(1), Dec. 23, 1985, 99 Stat. 1677; Pub. L. 99-204, § 14(a), Dec. 23, 1985, 99 Stat. 1674; Pub. L. 100-461, Title V, § 555, Oct. 1, 1988, 102 Stat. 2268-36.) (As amended Pub. L. 102-549, Title I, § 108, Oct. 28, 1992, 106 Stat. 3654.)

§ 2200b. Prohibition on noncompetitive awarding of insurance contracts on OPIC supported exports

(a) Requirement for certification

(1) In general

Except as provided in paragraph (3), the investor on whose behalf insurance, reinsurance, guaranties, or other financing is provided under this title with respect to a project shall be required to certify to the Corporation that any contract for the export of goods as part of that project will include a clause requiring that United States insurance companies have a fair and open competitive opportunity to provide insurance against risk of loss of such export.

(2) When certification must be made

The investor shall be required, in every practicable case, to so certify before the insurance, reinsurance, guarantee, or other financing is provided. In any case in which such a certification is not made in advance, the investor shall include in the certification the reasons for the failure to make a certification in advance.

(3) Exception

Paragraph (1) does not apply with respect to an investor who does not, because of the nature of the investment, have a controlling interest in fact in the project in question.

(b) Reports by United States Trade Representative

The United States Trade Representative shall review the actions of the Corporation under subsection (a) of this section and, after consultation with representatives of United States insurance companies, shall report to the Congress in the report required by section 2241(b) of Title 19 with respect to such actions.

(c) Definitions

For purposes of this section—

(1) the term "United States insurance company" includes—

(A) an individual, partnership, corporation, holding company, or other legal entity which is authorized, or in the case of a holding company, subsidiaries of which are authorized, by a State to engage in the business of issuing insurance contracts or reinsuring the risk underwritten by insurance companies; and

(B) foreign operations, branches, agencies, subsidiaries, affiliates, or joint ventures of any entity described in subparagraph (A);

(2) United States insurance companies shall be considered to have had a "fair and open competitive opportunity to provide insurance" if they—

(A) have received notice of the opportunity to provide insurance; and

(B) have been evaluated on a nondiscriminatory basis; and

(3) the term "State" includes the District of Columbia and any commonwealth, territory, or possession of the United States.

HISTORY: (Pub. L. 87-195, Pt. I, § 240B, as added Pub. L. 102-549, Title I, § 109, Oct. 28, 1992, 106 Stat. 3654.)

F.   BASIC ANTITRUST STATUTES AND REGULATIONS

15 U.S. Code - COMMERCE AND TRADE
CHAPTER 1—MONOPOLIES AND COMBINATIONS IN RESTRAINT OF TRADE

§ 1. Trusts, etc., in restraint of trade illegal; penalty (Sherman Act, § 1)

Every contract, combination in the form of trust or otherwise, or conspiracy, in restraint of trade or commerce among the several States, or with foreign nations, is declared to be illegal. Every person who shall make any contract or engage in any combination or conspiracy hereby declared to be illegal shall be deemed guilty of a felony, and, on conviction thereof, shall be punished by fine not exceeding $10,000,000 if a corporation, or, if any other person, $350,000, or by imprisonment not exceeding three years, or by both said punishments, in the discretion of the court.

HISTORY: (July 2, 1890, c. 647, § 1, 26 Stat. 209; Aug. 17, 1937, c. 690, Title VIII, 50 Stat. 693; July 7, 1955, c. 281, 69 Stat. 282; Dec. 21, 1974, Pub. L. 93-528, § 3, 88 Stat. 1708; Dec. 12, 1975, Pub. L. 94-145, § 2, 89 Stat. 801; Nov. 16, 1990, Pub. L. 101-588, § 4(a), 104 Stat. 2880.)

§ 2. Monopolizing trade a felony; penalty (Sherman Act § 2)

Every person who shall monopolize, or attempt to monopolize, or combine or conspire with any other person or persons, to monopolize any part of the trade or commerce among the several States, or with foreign nations, shall be deemed guilty of a felony, and, on conviction thereof, shall be punished by fine not exceeding $10,000,000 if a corporation, or, if any other person, $350,000, or by imprisonment not exceeding three years, or by both said punishments, in the discretion of the court.

HISTORY: (July 2, 1890, c. 647, S 2, 26 Stat. 209; July 7, 1955, c. 281, 69 Stat. 282; Dec. 21, 1974, Pub. L. 93-528, § 3, 88 Stat. 1708; Nov. 16, 1990, Pub. L. 101-588, § 4(b), 104 Stat. 2880.)

§ 6a. Conduct involving trade or commerce with foreign nations (Foreign Trade Antitrust Improvements Act § 402)

Sections 1 to 7 of this title shall not apply to conduct involving trade or commerce (other than import trade or import commerce) with foreign nations unless—

(1) such conduct has a direct, substantial, and reasonably foreseeable effect—

    (A) on trade or commerce which is not trade or commerce with foreign nations, or on import trade or import commerce with foreign nations; or

    (B) on export trade or export commerce with foreign nations, of a person engaged in such trade or commerce in the United States; and

(2) such effect gives rise to a claim under the provisions of sections 1 to 7 of this title, other than this section.

If sections 1 to 7 of this title apply to such conduct only because of the operation of paragraph (1) (B), then sections 1 to 7 of this title shall apply to such conduct only for injury to export business in the United States.

HISTORY: (July 2, 1890, c. 647, S 7, as added Oct. 8, 1982, Pub. L. 97-290, Title IV, § 402, 96 Stat. 1246.)

§ 8. Trusts in restraint of import trade illegal; penalty (Wilson Tariff Act § 73)

Every combination, conspiracy, trust, agreement, or contract is declared to be contrary to public policy, illegal, and void when the same is made by or between two or more persons or corporations, either of whom, as agent or principal, is engaged in importing any article from any foreign country into the United States, and when such combination, conspiracy, trust, agreement, or contract is intended to operate in restraint of lawful trade, or free competition in lawful trade or commerce, or to increase the market price in any part of the United States of any article or articles imported or intended to be imported into the United States, or of any manufacture into which such imported article enters or is intended to enter. Every person who shall be engaged in the importation of goods or any commodity from any foreign country in violation of this section, or who shall combine or conspire with another to violate the same, is guilty of a misdemeanor, and on conviction thereof in any court of the United States such person shall be fined in a sum not less than $100 and not exceeding $5,000, and shall be further punished by imprisonment, in the discretion of the court, for a term not less than three months nor exceeding twelve months.

HISTORY: (Aug. 27, 1894, c. 349, § 73, 28 Stat. 570; Feb. 12, 1913, c. 40, 37 Stat. 667.)

§ 15. Suits by persons injured (Clayton Act § 4)

(a) Amount of recovery; prejudgment interest

Except as provided in subsection (b) of this section, any person who shall be injured in his business or property by reason of anything forbidden in the antitrust laws may sue therefor in any district court of the United States in the district in which the defendant resides or is found or has an agent, without respect to the amount in controversy, and shall recover threefold the damages by him sustained, and the cost of suit, including a reasonable attorney's fee. The court may award under this section, pursuant to a motion by such person promptly made, simple interest on actual damages for the period beginning on the date of service of such person's pleading setting forth a claim under the antitrust laws and ending on the date of judgment, or for any shorter period therein, if the court finds that the award of such interest for such period is just in the circumstances. In determining whether an award of interest under this section for any period is just in the circumstances, the court shall consider only—

(1) whether such person or the opposing party, or either party's representative, made motions or asserted claims or defenses so lacking in merit as to show that such party or representative acted intentionally for delay, or otherwise acted in bad faith;

(2) whether, in the course of the action involved, such person or the opposing party, or either party's representative, violated any applicable rule, statute, or court order providing for sanctions for dilatory behavior or otherwise providing for expeditious proceedings; and

(3) whether such person or the opposing party, or either party's representative, engaged in conduct primarily for the purpose of delaying the litigation or increasing the cost thereof.

(b) Amount of damages payable to foreign states and instrumentalities of foreign states

(1) Except as provided in paragraph (2), any person who is a foreign state may not recover under subsection (a) of this section an amount in excess of the actual damages sustained by it and the cost of suit, including a reasonable attorney's fee.

(2) Paragraph (1) shall not apply to a foreign state if—

(A) such foreign state would be denied, under section 1605(a)(2) of Title 28, immunity in a case in which the action is based upon a commercial activity, or an act, that is the subject matter of its claim under this section;

(B) such foreign state waives all defenses based upon or arising out of its status as a foreign state, to any claims brought against it in the same action;

(C) such foreign state engages primarily in commercial activities; and

(D) such foreign state does not function, with respect to the commercial activity, or the act, that is the subject matter of its claim under this section as a procurement entity for itself or for another foreign state.

(c) Definitions

For purposes of this section—

(1) the term "commercial activity" shall have the meaning given it in section 1603(d) of Title 28, and

(2) the term "foreign state" shall have the meaning given it in section 1603(a) of Title 28.

HISTORY: (Oct. 15, 1914, c. 323, § 4, 38 Stat. 731; Sept. 12, 1980, Pub. L. 96-349, § 4(a)(1), 94 Stat. 1156; Dec. 29, 1982, Pub. L. 97-393, 96 Stat. 1964.)

§ 18. Acquisition by one corporation of stock of another (Clayton Act § 7)

No person engaged in commerce or in any activity affecting commerce shall acquire, directly or indirectly, the whole or any part of the stock or other share capital and no person subject to the jurisdiction of the Federal Trade Commission shall acquire the whole or any part of the assets of another person engaged also in commerce or in any activity affecting commerce, where in any line of commerce or in any activity affecting commerce in any section of the country, the effect of such acquisition may be substantially to lessen competition, or to tend to create a monopoly.

No person shall acquire, directly or indirectly, the whole or any part of the stock or other share capital and no person subject to the jurisdiction of the Federal Trade Commission shall acquire the whole or any part of the assets of one or more persons engaged in commerce or in any activity affecting commerce, where in any line of commerce or in any activity affecting commerce in any section of the country, the effect of such acquisition, of such stocks or assets, or of the use of such stock by the voting or granting of proxies or otherwise, may be substantially to lessen competition, or to tend to create a monopoly.

This section shall not apply to persons purchasing such stock solely for investment and not using the same by voting or otherwise to bring about, or in attempting to bring about, the substantial lessening of competition. Nor shall anything contained in this section prevent a corporation engaged in commerce or in any activity affecting commerce from causing the formation of subsidiary corporations for the actual carrying on of their immediate lawful business, or the natural and legitimate branches or extensions thereof, or from owning and holding all or a part of the stock of such subsidiary corporations, when the effect of such formation is not to substantially lessen competition.

. . . .

HISTORY: (Oct. 15, 1914, c. 323, § 7, 38 Stat. 731; Dec. 29, 1950, c. 1184, 64 Stat. 1125; Sept. 12, 1980, Pub. L. 96-349, § 6(a), 94 Stat. 1157; Oct. 4, 1984, Pub. L. 98-443, § 9(l), 98 Stat. 1708; Dec. 29, 1995, Pub. L. 104-88, Title III, § 318(1), 109 Stat. 949; Feb. 8, 1996, Pub. L. 104-104, Title VI, § 601(b)(3), 110 Stat. 143.)

§ 26. Injunctive relief for private parties; exception; costs (Clayton Act § 16)

Any person, firm, corporation, or association shall be entitled to sue for and have injunctive relief, in any court of the United States having jurisdiction over the parties, against threatened loss or damage by a violation of the antitrust laws, including sections 13, 14, 18, and 19 of this title, when and under the same conditions and principles as injunctive relief against threatened conduct that will cause loss or damage is granted by courts of equity, under the rules governing such proceedings, and upon the execution of proper bond against damages for an injunction improvidently granted and a showing that the danger of irreparable loss or damage is immediate, a preliminary injunction may issue: Provided, That nothing herein contained shall be construed to entitle any person, firm, corporation, or association, except the United States, to bring suit for injunctive relief against any common carrier subject to the jurisdiction of the Surface Transportation Board under subtitle IV of Title 49. In any action under this section in which the plaintiff substantially prevails, the court shall award the cost of suit, including a reasonable attorney's fee, to such plaintiff.

HISTORY: (Oct. 15, 1914, c. 323, § 16, 38 Stat. 737; Sept. 30, 1976, Pub. L. 94-435, Title III, § 302(3), 90 Stat. 1396; Dec. 29, 1995, Pub. L. 104-88, Title III, § 318(3), 109 Stat. 949.)

§ 45. Unfair methods of competition unlawful; prevention by Commission (Federal Trade Commission Act § 5)

(a) **Declaration of unlawfulness; power to prohibit unfair practices; inapplicability to foreign trade**

(1) Unfair methods of competition in or affecting commerce, and unfair or deceptive acts or practices in or affecting commerce, are declared unlawful.

(2) The Commission is empowered and directed to prevent persons, partnerships, or corporations, except banks, savings and loan institutions described in section 57a(f)(3) of this title, Federal credit unions described in section 57a(f)(4) of this title, common carriers subject to the Acts to regulate commerce, air carriers and foreign air carriers subject to the Federal Aviation Act of 1958, and persons, partnerships, or corporations insofar as they are subject to the Packers and Stockyards Act, 1921, as amended [7 U.S.C.A. § 181 et seq.], except as provided in section 406(b) of said Act [7 U.S.C.A. § 227(a)], from using unfair methods of competition in or affecting commerce and unfair or deceptive acts or practices in or affecting commerce.

(3) This subsection shall not apply to unfair methods of competition involving commerce with foreign nations (other than import commerce) unless—

(A) such methods of competition have a direct, substantial, and reasonably foreseeable effect—

(i) on commerce which is not commerce with foreign nations, or on import commerce with foreign nations; or

(ii) on export commerce with foreign nations, of a person engaged in such commerce in the United States; and

(B) such effect gives rise to a claim under the provisions of this subsection, other than this paragraph.

If this subsection applies to such methods of competition only because of the operation of subparagraph (A) (ii), this subsection shall apply to such conduct only for injury to export business in the United States.

. . . .

HISTORY: (Sept. 26, 1914, c. 311, § 5, 38 Stat. 719; Mar. 21, 1938, c. 49, § 3, 52 Stat. 111; June 23, 1938, c. 601, Title XI, § 1107(f), 52 Stat. 1028; June 25, 1948, c. 646, § 32(a), 62 Stat. 991; May 24, 1949, c. 139, § 127, 63 Stat. 107; Mar. 16, 1950, c. 61, § 4(c), 64 Stat. 21; July 14, 1952, c. 745, § 2, 66 Stat. 632; Aug. 23, 1958, Pub. L. 85-726,

Title XIV, §§ 1401(b), 1411, 72 Stat. 806, 809; Aug. 28, 1958, Pub. L. 85-791, § 3, 72 Stat. 942; Sept. 2, 1958, Pub. L. 85-909, § 3, 72 Stat. 1750; June 11, 1960, Pub. L. 86-507, § 1(13), 74 Stat. 200; Nov. 16, 1973, Pub. L. 93-153, Title IV, § 408(c), (d), 87 Stat. 591, 592; Jan. 4, 1975, Pub. L. 93-637, Title II, §§ 201(a), 204(b), 205(a), 88 Stat. 2193, 2200; Dec. 12, 1975, Pub. L. 94-145, § 3, 89 Stat. 801; July 23, 1979, Pub. L. 96-37, § 1(a), 93 Stat. 95; May 28, 1980, Pub. L. 96-252, § 2, 94 Stat. 374; Oct. 8, 1982, Pub. L. 97-290, Title IV, § 403, 96 Stat. 1246; Nov. 8, 1984, Pub. L. 98-620, Title IV, § 655; Aug. 26, 1994, Pub. L. 103-312, §§ 4, 6, 9, 108 Stat. 1691, 1692, 1695.)

§ 62. Export trade and antitrust legislation (Webb-Pomerene Act § 2)

Nothing contained in sections 1 to 7 of this title shall be construed as declaring to be illegal an association entered into for the sole purpose of engaging in export trade and actually engaged solely in such export trade, or an agreement made or act done in the course of export trade by such association, provided such association, agreement, or act is not in restraint of trade within the United States, and is not in restraint of the export trade of any domestic competitor of such association: Provided, That such association does not, either in the United States or elsewhere, enter into any agreement, understanding, or conspiracy, or do any act which artificially or intentionally enhances or depresses prices within the United States of commodities of the class exported by such association, or which substantially lessens competition within the United States or otherwise restrains trade therein.

HISTORY: (Apr. 10, 1918, c. 50, § 2, 40 Stat. 517.)

CODE OF FEDERAL REGULATIONS

TITLE 28—JUDICIAL ADMINISTRATION

CHAPTER I—DEPARTMENT OF JUSTICE

PART 50—STATEMENTS OF POLICY

§ 50.6 Antitrust Division business review procedure.

Although the Department of Justice is not authorized to give advisory opinions to private parties, for several decades the Antitrust Division has been willing in certain circumstances to review proposed business conduct and state its enforcement intentions. This originated with a "railroad release" procedure under which the Division would forego the initiation of criminal antitrust proceedings. The procedure was subsequently expanded to encompass a "merger clearance" procedure under which the Division would state its present enforcement intention with respect to a merger or acquisition; and the Department issued a written statement entitled "Business Review Procedure." That statement has been revised several times.

1. A request for a business review letter must be submitted in writing to the Assistant Attorney General, Antitrust Division, Department of Justice, Washington, D.C. 20530.
2. The Division will consider only requests with respect to proposed business conduct, which may involve either domestic or foreign commerce.
3. The Division may, in its discretion, refuse to consider a request.
4. A business review letter shall have no application to any party which does not join in the request therefor.
5. The requesting parties are under an affirmative obligation to make full and true disclosure with respect to the business conduct for which review is requested. Each request must be accompanied by all relevant data including background information, complete copies of all operative documents and detailed statements of all collateral oral understandings, if any. All parties requesting the review letter must provide the Division with whatever additional information or documents the Division may thereafter request in order to review the matter. Such additional information, if furnished orally, shall be promptly confirmed in writing. In connection with any request for review the Division will also conduct whatever independent investigation it believes is appropriate.
6. No oral clearance, release or other statement purporting to bind the enforcement discretion of the Division may be given. The requesting party may rely upon only a written business review letter signed by the Assistant Attorney General in charge of the Antitrust Division or his delegate.
7. (a) If the business conduct for which review is requested is subject to approval by a regulatory agency, a review request may be considered before agency approval has been obtained only where it appears that exceptional and unnecessary burdens might otherwise be imposed on the party or parties requesting review, or where the agency specifically requests that a party or parties request review. However, any business review letter issued in these as in any other circumstances will state only the Department's present enforcement intentions under the antitrust laws. It shall in no way be taken to indicate the Department's views on the legal or factual issues that may be raised before the regulatory agency, or in an appeal from the regulatory agency's decision. In particular, the issuance of such a letter is not to be represented to mean that the Division believes that there are no anticompetitive consequences warranting agency consideration.
   (b) The submission of a request for a business review, or its pendency, shall in no way alter any responsibility of any party to comply with the Premerger Notification provisions of the Antitrust Improvements Act of 1976, 15 U.S.C. 18A, and the regulations promulgated thereunder, 16 CFR, Part 801.

8. After review of a request submitted hereunder the Division may: state its present enforcement intention with respect to the proposed business conduct; decline to pass on the request; or take such other position or action as it considers appropriate.

9. A business review letter states only the enforcement intention of the Division as of the date of the letter, and the Division remains completely free to bring whatever action or proceeding it subsequently comes to believe is required by the public interest. As to a stated present intention not to bring an action, however, the Division has never exercised its right to bring a criminal action where there has been full and true disclosure at the time of presenting the request.

10. (a) Simultaneously upon notifying the requesting party of and Division action described in paragraph 8, the business review request, and the Division's letter in response shall be indexed and placed in a file available to the public upon request.

(b) On that date or within thirty days after the date upon which the Division takes any action as described in paragraph 8, the information supplied to support the business review request and any other information supplied by the requesting party in connection with the transaction that is the subject of the business review request, shall be indexed and placed in a file with the request and the Division's letter, available to the public upon request. This file shall remain open for one year, after which time it shall be closed and the documents either returned to the requesting party or otherwise disposed of, at the discretion of the Antitrust Division.

(c) Prior to the time the information described in subparagraphs (a) and (b) is indexed and made publicly available in accordance with the terms of that subparagraph, the requesting party may ask the Division to delay making public some or all of such information. However the requesting party must: (1) Specify precisely the documents or parts thereof that he asks not be made public; (2) state the minimum period of time during which nondisclosure is considered necessary; and (3) justify the request for non-disclosure, both as to content and time, by showing good cause therefor, including a showing that disclosure would have a detrimental effect upon the requesting party's operations or relationships with actual or potential customers, employees, suppliers (including suppliers of credit), stockholders, or competitors. The Department of Justice, in its discretion, shall make the final determination as to whether good cause for non-disclosure has been shown.

(d) Nothing contained in subparagraphs (a), (b) and (c) shall limit the Division's right, in its discretion, to issue a press release describing generally the identity of the requesting party or parties and the nature of action taken by the Division upon the request.

(e) This paragraph reflects a policy determination by the Justice Department and is subject to any limitations on public disclosure arising from statutory restrictions, Executive Order, or the national interest.

11. Any requesting party may withdraw a request for review at any time. The Division remains free, however, to submit such comments to such requesting party as it deems appropriate. Failure to take action after receipt of documents or information whether submitted pursuant to this procedure or otherwise, does not in any way limit or stop the Division from taking such action at such time thereafter as it deems appropriate. The Division reserves the right to retain documents submitted to it under this procedure or otherwise and to use them for all governmental purposes.

[42 FR 11831, Mar. 1, 1977]

CODE OF FEDERAL REGULATIONS

TITLE 16—COMMERCIAL PRACTICES

CHAPTER I—FEDERAL TRADE COMMISSION

SUBCHAPTER A—ORGANIZATION, PROCEDURES AND RULES OF PRACTICE

PART 1—GENERAL PROCEDURES

SUBPART A—INDUSTRY GUIDANCE

ADVISORY OPINIONS

§ 1.1 Policy.

(a) Any person, partnership, or corporation may request advice from the Commission with respect to a course of action which the requesting party proposes to pursue. The Commission will consider such requests for advice and inform the requesting party of the Commission's views, where practicable, under the following circumstances.

(1) The matter involves a substantial or novel question of fact or law and there is no clear Commission or court precedent; or

(2) The subject matter of the request and consequent publication of Commission advice is of significant public interest.

(b) The Commission has authorized its staff to consider all requests for advice and to render advice, where practicable, in those circumstances in which a Commission opinion would not be warranted. Hypothetical questions will not be answered, and a request for advice will ordinarily be considered inappropriate where: (1) The same or substantially the same course of action is under investigation or is or has been the subject of a current proceeding involving the Commission or another governmental agency, or (2) an informed opinion cannot be made or could be made only after extensive investigation, clinical study, testing, or collateral inquiry.

[44 FR 21624, Apr. 11, 1979; 44 FR 23515, Apr. 20, 1979; 54 FR 14072, April 7, 1989]

§ 1.2 Procedure.

(a) Application. The request for advice or interpretation should be submitted in writing (one original and two copies) to the Secretary of the Commission and should: (1) State clearly the question(s) that the applicant wishes resolved; (2) cite the provision of law under which the question arises; and (3) state all facts which the applicant believes to be material. In addition, the identity of the companies and other persons involved should be disclosed. Letters relating to unnamed companies or persons may not be answered. Submittal of additional facts may be requested prior to the rendering of any advice.

(b) Compliance matters. If the request is for advice as to whether the proposed course of action may violate an outstanding order to cease and desist issued by the Commission, such request will be considered as provided for in § 2.41 of this chapter.

[44 FR 21624, Apr. 11, 1979, as amended at 44 FR 40638, July 12, 1979]

§ 1.3 Advice.

(a) On the basis of the materials submitted, as well as any other information available, and if practicable, the Commission or its staff will inform the requesting party of its views.

(b) Any advice given by the Commission is without prejudice to the right of the Commission to reconsider the questions involved and, where the public interest requires, to rescind or revoke the action. Notice of such rescission or revocation will be given to the requesting party so that he may discontinue the course of action taken pursuant to the Commission's advice. The Commission will not proceed against the requesting party with respect to any action taken in good faith reliance upon the Commission's advice under this section, where all the relevant facts were fully, completely, and accurately presented to the Commission and where such action was promptly discontinued upon notification of rescission or revocation of the Commission's approval.

(c) Advice rendered by the staff is without prejudice to the right of the Commission later to rescind the advice and, where appropriate, to commence an enforcement proceeding.

[44 FR 21624, Apr. 11, 1979]

§ 1.4 Public disclosure.

Written advice rendered pursuant to this Section and requests therefor, including names and details, will be placed in the Commission's public record immediately after the requesting party has received the advice, subject to any limitations on public disclosure arising from statutory restrictions, the Commission's rules, and the public interest. A request for confidential treatment of information submitted in connection with the questions should be made separately.

[44 FR 21624, Apr. 11, 1979]

The Export Trading Company Act of 1982 - 15 U.S.C. § 4001 *et seq.*

§ 4001. Congressional findings and declaration of purpose

(a) The Congress finds that—

(1) United States exports are responsible for creating and maintaining one out of every nine manufacturing jobs in the United States and for generating one out of every seven dollars of total United States goods produced;

(2) the rapidly growing service-related industries are vital to the well-being of the United States economy inasmuch as they create jobs for seven out of every ten Americans, provide 65 per centum of the Nation's gross national product, and offer the greatest potential for significantly increased industrial trade involving finished products;

(3) trade deficits contribute to the decline of the dollar on international currency markets and have an inflationary impact on the United States economy;

(4) tens of thousands of small- and medium-sized United States businesses produce exportable goods or services but do not engage in exporting;

(5) although the United States is the world's leading agricultural exporting nation, many farm products are not marketed as widely and effectively abroad as they could be through export trading companies;

(6) export trade services in the United States are fragmented into a multitude of separate functions, and companies attempting to offer export trade services lack financial leverage to reach a significant number of potential United States exporters;

(7) the United States needs well-developed export trade intermediaries which can achieve economies of scale and acquire expertise enabling them to export goods and services profitably, at low per unit cost to producers;

(8) the development of export trading companies in the United States has been hampered by business attitudes and by Government regulations;

(9) those activities of State and local governmental authorities which initiate, facilitate, or expand exports of goods and services can be an important source for expansion of total United States exports, as well as for experimentation in the development of innovative export programs keyed to local, State, and regional economic needs;

(10) if United States trading companies are to be successful in promoting United States exports and in competing with foreign trading companies, they should be able to draw on the resources, expertise, and knowledge of the United States banking system, both in the United States and abroad; and

(11) the Department of Commerce is responsible for the development and promotion of United States exports, and especially for facilitating the export of finished products by United States manufacturers.

(b) It is the purpose of this chapter to increase United States exports of products and services by encouraging more efficient provision of export trade services to United States producers and suppliers, in particular by establishing an office within the Department of Commerce to promote the formation of export trade associations and export trading companies, by permitting bank holding companies, bankers' banks, and Edge Act corporations and agreement corporations that are subsidiaries of bank holding companies to invest in export trading companies, by reducing restrictions on trade financing provided by financial institutions, and by modifying the application of the antitrust laws to certain export trade.

HISTORY: (Pub. L. 97-290, Title I, § 102, Oct. 8, 1982, 96 Stat. 1233.)

§ 4002. Definitions

(a) For purposes of this subchapter—

   (1) the term "export trade" means trade or commerce in goods or services produced in the United States which are exported, or in the course of being exported, from the United States to any other country;

   (2) the term "services" includes, but is not limited to, accounting, amusement, architectural, automatic data processing, business, communications, construction franchising and licensing, consulting, engineering, financial, insurance, legal, management, repair, tourism, training, and transportation services;

   (3) the term "export trade services" includes, but is not limited to, consulting, international market research, advertising, marketing, insurance, product research and design, legal assistance, transportation, including trade documentation and freight forwarding, communication and processing of foreign orders to and for exporters and foreign purchasers, warehousing, foreign exchange, financing, and taking title to goods, when provided in order to facilitate the export of goods or services produced in the United States;

   (4) the term "export trading company" means a person, partnership, association, or similar organization, whether operated for profit or as a nonprofit organization, which does business under the laws of the United States or any State and which is organized and operated principally for purposes of—

     (A) exporting goods or services produced in the United States; or

     (B) facilitating the exportation of goods or services produced in the United States by unaffiliated persons by providing one or more export trade services;

   (5) the term "State" means any of the several States of the United States, the District of Columbia, the Commonwealth of Puerto Rico, the Virgin Islands, American Samoa, Guam, the Commonwealth of the Northern Mariana Islands, and the Trust Territory of the Pacific Islands;

   (6) the term "United States" means the several States of the United States, the District of Columbia, the Commonwealth of Puerto Rico, the Virgin Islands, American Samoa, Guam, the Commonwealth of the Northern Mariana Islands, and the Trust Territory of the Pacific Islands; and

   (7) the term "antitrust laws" means the antitrust laws as defined in section 12(a) of this title, section 45 of this title to the extent that section 45 of this title applies to unfair methods of competition, and any State antitrust or unfair competition law.

(b) The Secretary of Commerce may by regulation further define any term defined in subsection (a) of this section, in order to carry out this subchapter.

      HISTORY: (Pub. L. 97-290, Title I, § 103, Oct. 8, 1982, 96 Stat. 1234.)

§ 4003. Office of Export Trade in Department of Commerce

The Secretary of Commerce shall establish within the Department of Commerce an office to promote and encourage to the greatest extent feasible the formation of export trade associations and export trading companies. Such office shall provide information and advice to interested persons and shall provide a referral service to facilitate contact between producers of exportable goods and services and firms offering export trade services. The office shall establish a program to encourage and assist the operation of other export intermediaries, including existing and newly formed export management companies.

> HISTORY: (Pub. L. 97-290, Title I, § 104, Oct. 8, 1982, 96 Stat. 1235; Pub. L. 100-418, Title II, § 2310, Aug. 23, 1988, 102 Stat. 1346.)

§ 4011. Export trade promotion; duties of Secretary of Commerce

To promote and encourage export trade, the Secretary may issue certificates of review and advise and assist any person with respect to applying for certificates of review.

> HISTORY: (Pub. L. 97-290, Title III, § 301, Oct. 8, 1982, 96 Stat. 1240.)

§ 4012. Application for issuance of certificate of review

(a) Written form; limitation to export trade; compliance with regulations
   To apply for a certificate of review, a person shall submit to the Secretary a written application which—
   (1) specifies conduct limited to export trade, and
   (2) is in a form and contains any information, including information pertaining to the overall market in which the applicant operates, required by rule or regulation promulgated under section 4020 of this title.
(b) Publication of notice of application; transmittal to Attorney General
   (1) Within ten days after an application submitted under subsection (a) of this section is received by the Secretary, the Secretary shall publish in the Federal Register a notice that announces that an application for a certificate of review has been submitted, identifies each person submitting the application, and describes the conduct for which the application is submitted.
   (2) Not later than seven days after an application submitted under subsection (a) of this section is received by the Secretary, the Secretary shall transmit to the Attorney General—
      (A) a copy of the application,
      (B) any information submitted to the Secretary in connection with the application, and

(C) any other relevant information (as determined by the Secretary) in the possession of the Secretary, including information regarding the market share of the applicant in the line of commerce to which the conduct specified in the application relates.

HISTORY: (Pub. L. 97-290, Title III, § 302, Oct. 8, 1982, 96 Stat. 1240.)

§ 4013. Issuance of certificate

(a) Requirements

A certificate of review shall be issued to any applicant that establishes that its specified export trade, export trade activities, and methods of operation will—

(1) result in neither a substantial lessening of competition or restraint of trade within the United States nor a substantial restraint of the export trade of any competitor of the applicant,

(2) not unreasonably enhance, stabilize, or depress prices within the United States of the goods, wares, merchandise, or services of the class exported by the applicant,

(3) not constitute unfair methods of competition against competitors engaged in the export of goods, wares, merchandise, or services of the class exported by the applicant, and

(4) not include any act that may reasonably be expected to result in the sale for consumption or resale within the United States of the goods, wares, merchandise, or services exported by the applicant.

(b) Time for determination; specification in certificate

Within ninety days after the Secretary receives an application for a certificate of review, the Secretary shall determine whether the applicant's export trade, export trade activities, and methods of operation meet the standards of subsection (a) of this section. If the Secretary, with the concurrence of the Attorney General, determines that such standards are met, the Secretary shall issue to the applicant a certificate of review. The certificate of review shall specify—

(1) the export trade, export trade activities, and methods of operation to which the certificate applies,

(2) the person to whom the certificate of review is issued, and

(3) any terms and conditions the Secretary or the Attorney General deems necessary to assure compliance with the standards of subsection (a) of this section.

(c) Expedited action

If the applicant indicates a special need for prompt disposition, the Secretary and the Attorney General may expedite action on the application, except that no certificate of review may be issued within thirty days of publication of notice in the Federal Register under section 4012(b)(1) of this title.

(d) Notification of denial; request for reconsideration

(1) If the Secretary denies in whole or in part an application for a certificate, he shall notify the applicant of his determination and the reasons for it.

(2) An applicant may, within thirty days of receipt of notification that the application has been denied in whole or in part, request the Secretary to reconsider the determination. The Secretary, with the concurrence of the Attorney General, shall notify the applicant of the determination upon reconsideration within thirty days of receipt of the request.

(e) Return of documents upon request after denial

If the Secretary denies an application for the issuance of a certificate of review and thereafter receives from the applicant a request for the return of documents submitted by the applicant in connection with the application for the certificate, the Secretary and the Attorney General shall return to the applicant, not later than thirty days after receipt of the request, the documents and all copies of the documents available to the Secretary and the Attorney General, except to the extent that the information contained in a document has been made available to the public.

(f) Fraudulent procurement of certificate

A certificate shall be void ab initio with respect to any export trade, export trade activities, or methods of operation for which a certificate was procured by fraud.

HISTORY: (Pub. L. 97-290, Title III, § 303, Oct. 8, 1982, 96 Stat. 1241.)

§ 4014. Reporting requirement; amendment of certificate; revocation

(a) Report of changes in matters specified; application to amend; treatment as application for issuance

(1) Any applicant who receives a certificate of review—

(A) shall promptly report to the Secretary any change relevant to the matters specified in the certificate, and

(B) may submit to the Secretary an application to amend the certificate to reflect the effect of the change on the conduct specified in the certificate.

(2) An application for an amendment to a certificate of review shall be treated as an application for the issuance of a certificate. The effective date of an amendment shall be the date on which the application for the amendment is submitted to the Secretary.

(b) Request for compliance information; failure to provide; notice of noncompliance; revocation or modification; antitrust investigation; no civil investigative demand

(1) If the Secretary or the Attorney General has reason to believe that the export trade, export trade activities, or methods of operation of a person holding a certificate of review no longer comply with the standards of section 4013(a) of this title, the Secretary shall request such information from such person as the Secretary or the Attorney General deems necessary to resolve the matter of compliance. Failure to comply with such request shall be grounds for revocation of the certificate under paragraph (2).

(2) If the Secretary or the Attorney General determines that the export trade, export trade activities, or methods of operation of a person holding a certificate no longer comply with the standards of section 4013(a) of this title, or that such person has failed to comply with a request made under paragraph (1), the Secretary shall give written notice of the determination to such person. The notice shall include a statement of the circumstances underlying, and the reasons in support of, the determination. In the 60-day period beginning 30 days after the notice is given, the Secretary shall revoke the certificate or modify it as the Secretary or the Attorney General deems necessary to cause the certificate to apply only to the export trade, export trade activities, or methods of operation which are in compliance with the standards of section 4013(a) of this title.

(3) For purposes of carrying out this subsection, the Attorney General, and the Assistant Attorney General in charge of the antitrust division of the Department of Justice, may conduct investigations in the same manner as the Attorney General and the Assistant Attorney General conduct investigations under section 1312 of this title, except that no civil investigative demand may be issued to a person to whom a certificate of review is issued if such person is the target of such investigation.

HISTORY: (Pub. L. 97-290, Title III, § 304, Oct. 8, 1982, 96 Stat. 1242.)

§ 4015. Judicial review; admissibility

(a) District court review of grants or denials; erroneous determination

If the Secretary grants or denies, in whole or in part, an application for a certificate of review or for an amendment to a certificate, or revokes or modifies a certificate pursuant to section 4014(b) of this title, any person aggrieved by such determination may, within 30 days of the determination, bring an action in any appropriate district court of the United States to set aside the determination on the ground that such determination is erroneous.

(b) Exclusive provision for review

Except as provided in subsection (a) of this section, no action by the Secretary or the Attorney General pursuant to this subchapter shall be subject to judicial review.

(c) Inadmissibility in antitrust proceedings

If the Secretary denies, in whole or in part, an application for a certificate of review or for an amendment to a certificate, or revokes or amends a certificate, neither the negative determination nor the statement of reasons therefor shall be admissible in evidence, in any administrative or judicial proceeding, in support of any claim under the antitrust laws.

HISTORY: (Pub. L. 97-290, Title III, § 305, Oct. 8, 1982, 96 Stat. 1243.)

§ 4016. Protection conferred by certificate of review

(a) Protection from civil or criminal antitrust actions

Except as provide in subsection (b) of this section, no criminal or civil action may be brought under the antitrust laws against a person to whom a certificate of review is issued which is based on conduct which is specified in, and complies with the terms of, a certificate issued under section 4013 of this title which certificate was in effect when the conduct occurred.

(b) Special restraint of trade civil actions; time limitations; certificate governed conduct presumed in compliance; award of costs to successful defendant; suit by Attorney General

(1) Any person who has been injured as a result of conduct engaged in under a certificate of review may bring a civil action for injunctive relief, actual damages, the loss of interest on actual damages, and the cost of suit (including a reasonable attorney's fee) for the failure to comply with the standards of section 4013(a) of this title. Any action commenced under this subchapter shall proceed as if it were an action commenced under section 15 or section 26 of this title, except that the standards of section 4013(a) of this title and the remedies provided in this paragraph shall be the exclusive standards and remedies applicable to such action.

(2) Any action brought under paragraph (1) shall be filed within two years of the date the plaintiff has notice of the failure to comply with the standards of section 4013(a) of this title but in any event within four years after the cause of action accrues.

(3) In any action brought under paragraph (1), there shall be a presumption that conduct which is specified in and complies with a certificate of review does comply with the standards of section 4013(a) of this title.

(4) In any action brought under paragraph (1), if the court finds that the conduct does comply with the standards of section 4013(a) of this title, the court shall award to the person against whom the claim is brought the cost of suit attributable to defending against the claim (including a reasonable attorney's fee).

(5) The Attorney General may file suit pursuant to section 25 of this title to enjoin conduct threatening clear and irreparable harm to the national interest.

HISTORY: (Pub. L. 97-290, Title III, § 306, Oct. 8, 1982, 96 Stat. 1243.)

§ 4017. Guidelines

(a) Issuance; content

To promote greater certainty regarding the application of the antitrust laws to export trade, the Secretary, with the concurrence of the Attorney General, may issue guidelines—

(1) describing specific types of conduct with respect to which the Secretary, with the concurrence of the Attorney General, has made or would make, determinations under sections 4013 and 4014 of this title, and

(2) summarizing the factual and legal bases in support of the determinations.

(b) Administrative rulemaking requirements not applicable

Section 553 of Title 5 shall not apply to the issuance of guidelines under subsection (a) of this section.

HISTORY: (Pub. L. 97-290, Title III, § 307, Oct. 8, 1982, 96 Stat. 1244.)

§ 4018. Annual reports

Every person to whom a certificate of review is issued shall submit to the Secretary an annual report, in such form and at such time as the Secretary may require, that updates where necessary the information required by section 4012(a) of this title.

HISTORY: (Pub. L. 97-290, Title III, § 308, Oct. 8, 1982, 96 Stat. 1244.)

§ 4019. Disclosure of information

(a) Exemption

Information submitted by any person in connection with the issuance, amendment, or revocation of a certificate of review shall be exempt from disclosure under section 552 of Title 5.

(b) Protection of potentially harmful confidential information; exceptions: Congress; judicial or administrative proceedings; consent; necessity for determination; Federal law; regulations

(1) Except as provided in paragraph (2), no officer or employee of the United States shall disclose commercial or financial information submitted in connection with the issuance, amendment, or revocation of a certificate of review if the information is privileged or confidential and if disclosure of the information would cause harm to the person who submitted the information.

(2) Paragraph (1) shall not apply with respect to information disclosed—

    (A) upon a request made by the Congress or any committee of the Congress,

    (B) in a judicial or administrative proceeding, subject to appropriate protective orders,

    (C) with the consent of the person who submitted the information,

    (D) in the course of making a determination with respect to the issuance, amendment, or revocation of a certificate of review, if the Secretary deems disclosure of the information to be necessary in connection with making the determination,

    (E) in accordance with any requirement imposed by a statute of the United States, or

    (F) in accordance with any rule or regulation promulgated under section 4020 of this title permitting the disclosure of the information to an agency of the United States or of a State on the condition that the agency will disclose the information only under the circumstances specified in subparagraphs (A) through (E).

HISTORY: (Pub. L. 97-290, Title III, § 309, Oct. 8, 1982, 96 Stat. 1244.)

§ 4020. Rules and regulations

The Secretary, with the concurrence of the Attorney General, shall promulgate such rules and regulations as are necessary to carry out the purposes of this chapter.

HISTORY: (Pub. L. 97-290, Title III, § 310, Oct. 8, 1982, 96 Stat. 1245.)

§ 4021. Definitions

As used in this subchapter—

(1) the term "export trade" means trade or commerce in goods, wares, merchandise, or services exported, or in the course of being exported, from the United States or any territory thereof to any foreign nation,

(2) the term "service" means intangible economic output, including, but not limited to—

    (A) business, repair, and amusement services,

    (B) management, legal, engineering, architectural, and other professional services, and

    (C) financial, insurance, transportation, informational and any other data-based services, and communication services,

(3) the term "export trade activities" means activities or agreements in the course of export trade,

(4) the term "methods of operation" means any method by which a person conducts or proposes to conduct export trade,

(5) the term "person" means an individual who is a resident of the United States; a partnership that is created under and exists pursuant to the laws of any State or of the United States; a State or local government entity; a corporation, whether organized as a profit or nonprofit corporation, that is created under and exists pursuant to the laws of any State or of the United States; or any association or combination, by contract or other arrangement, between or among such persons,

(6) the term "antitrust laws" means the antitrust laws, as such term is defined in section 12 of this title, and section 45 of this title (to the extent that section 45 of this title prohibits unfair methods of competition), and any State antitrust or unfair competition law,

(7) the term "Secretary" means the Secretary of Commerce or his designee, and

(8) the term "Attorney General" means the Attorney General of the United States or his designee.

HISTORY: (Pub. L. 97-290, Title III, § 311, Oct. 8, 1982, 96 Stat. 1245.)

§ 4051. Requirement of prior authorization

(a) General rule

Notwithstanding any other provision of law, money appropriated to the Department of Commerce for expenses to carry out any export promotion program may be obligated or expended only if—

(1) the appropriation thereof has been previously authorized by law enacted on or after July 12, 1985; or

(2) the amount of all such obligations and expenditures does not exceed an amount previously prescribed by law enacted on or after such date.

(b) Exception for later legislation authorizing obligations or expenditures

To the extent that legislation enacted after the making of an appropriation to carry out any export promotion program authorizes the obligation or expenditure thereof, the limitation contained in subsection (a) of this section shall have no effect.

(c) Provisions must be specifically superseded

The provisions of this section shall not be superseded except by a provision of law enacted after July 12, 1985, which specifically repeals, modifies, or supersedes the provisions of this section.

(d) "Export promotion program" defined

For purposes of this subchapter, the term "export promotion program" means any activity of the Department of Commerce designed to stimulate or assist United States businesses in marketing their goods and services abroad competitively with businesses from other countries, including, but not limited to—

(1) trade development (except for the trade adjustment assistance program) and dissemination of foreign marketing opportunities and other marketing information to United States producers of goods and services, including the expansion of foreign markets for United States textiles and apparel and any other United States products;

(2) the development of regional and multilateral economic policies which enhance United States trade and investment interests, and the provision of marketing services with respect to foreign countries and regions;

(3) the exhibition of United States goods in other countries;

(4) the operations of the United States and Foreign Commercial Service, or any successor agency; and

(5) the Market Development Cooperator Program established under section 4723 of this title, and assistance for trade shows provided under section 4724 of this title.

(e) Printing outside the United States

(1) Notwithstanding the provisions of section 501 of Title 44, and consistent with other applicable law, the Secretary of Commerce in carrying out any export promotion program, may authorize—

(A) the printing, distribution, and sale of documents outside the contiguous United States, if the Secretary finds that the implementation of such export promotion program would be more efficient, and if such documents will be distributed primarily and sold exclusively outside the United States; and

(B) the acceptance of private notices and advertisements in connection with the printing and distribution of such documents.

(2) Any fees received by the Secretary pursuant to paragraph (1) shall be deposited in a separate account or accounts which may be used to defray directly the costs incurred in conducting activities authorized by paragraph (1) or to repay or make advances to appropriations or other funds available for such activities.

HISTORY: (Pub. L. 99-64, Title II, § 201, July 12, 1985, 99 Stat. 157; Pub. L. 100-418, Title II, §§ 2305(a), 2308(a), Aug. 23, 1988, 102 Stat. 1344, 1346.)

§ 4052. Authorization of appropriations

There are authorized to be appropriated to the Department of Commerce to carry out export promotion programs such sums as are necessary for fiscal years 1995 and 1996.

HISTORY: (Pub. L. 99-64, Title II, § 202, July 12, 1985, 99 Stat. 158; Pub. L. 99-633, § 2, Nov. 7, 1986, 100 Stat. 3522; Pub. L. 100-418, Title II, § 2305(b)(1), Aug. 23, 1988, 102 Stat. 1344; Pub. L. 102-429, Title II, § 208, Oct. 21, 1992, 106 Stat. 2205; Pub. L. 103-392, Title III, § 301, Oct. 22, 1994, 108 Stat. 4099.)

§ 4053. Barter arrangements

(a) Report on status of Federal barter programs

The Secretary of Agriculture and the Secretary of Energy shall, not later than 90 days after July 12, 1985, submit to the Congress a report on the status of Federal programs relating to the barter or exchange of commodities owned by the Commodity Credit Corporation for materials and products produced in foreign countries. Such report shall include details of any changes necessary in existing law to allow the Department of Agriculture and, in the case of petroleum resources, the Department of Energy, to implement fully any barter program.

(b) Authorities of President

The President is authorized—

(1) to barter stocks of agricultural commodities acquired by the Government for petroleum and petroleum products, and for other materials vital to the national interest, which are produced abroad, in situations in which sales would otherwise not occur; and

(2) to purchase petroleum and petroleum products, and other materials vital to the national interest, which are produced abroad and acquired by persons in the United States through barter for agricultural commodities produced in and exported from the United States through normal commercial trade channels.

(c) Other provisions of law not affected

In the case of any petroleum, petroleum products, or other materials vital to the national interest, which are acquired under subsection (b) of this section, nothing in this section shall be construed to render inapplicable the provisions of any law then in effect which apply to the storage, distribution, or use of such petroleum, petroleum products, or other materials vital to the national interest.

(d) Conventional markets not to be displaced by barters

The President shall take steps to ensure that, in making any barter described in subsection (a) or (b)(1) of this section or any purchase authorized by subsection (b)(2) of this section, existing export markets for agricultural commodities operating on conventional business terms are safeguarded from displacement by the barter described in subsection (a), (b)(1), or (b)(2) of this section, as the case may be. In addition, the President shall ensure that any such barter is consistent with the international obligations of the United States, including the General Agreement on Tariffs and Trade.

(e) Report to the Congress

The Secretary of Energy shall report to the Congress on the effect on energy security and on domestic energy supplies of any action taken under this section which results in the acquisition by the Government of petroleum or petroleum products. Such report shall be submitted to the Congress not later than 90 days after such acquisition.

HISTORY: (Pub. L. 99-64, Title II, § 203, July 12, 1985, 99 Stat. 158.)

UNIFORM LAWS AND MODEL RULES

A. UNIFORM COMMERCIAL CODE (UCC) (SELECTED PROVISIONS)

§ 1-201 General Definitions.

Subject to additional definitions contained in the subsequent Articles of this Act which are applicable to specific Articles or Parts thereof, and unless the context otherwise requires, in this Act:

> (15) "Document of title" includes bill of lading, dock warrant, dock receipt, warehouse receipt or order for the delivery of goods, and also any other document which in the regular course of business or financing is treated as adequately evidencing that the person in possession of it is entitled to receive, hold and dispose of the document and the goods it covers. To be a document of title a document must purport to be issued by or addressed to a bailee and purport to cover goods in the bailee's possession which are either identified or are fungible portions of an identified mass.

OFFICIAL COMMENT

15. "Document of title". From Section 76, Uniform Sales Act, but rephrased to eliminate certain ambiguities. Thus, by making it explicit that the obligation or designation of a third party as "bailee" is essential to a document of title, this definition clearly rejects any such result as obtained in *Hixson v. Ward*, 254 Ill App 505 (1929), which treated a conditional sales contract as a document of title. Also the definition is left open so that new types of documents may be included. It is unforeseeable what documents may one day serve the essential purpose now filled by warehouse receipts and bills of lading. Truck transport has already opened up problems which do not fit the patterns of practice resting upon the assumption that a draft can move through banking channels faster than the goods themselves can reach their destination. There lie ahead air transport and such probabilities as teletype transmission of what may some day be regarded commercially as "Documents of Title". The definition is stated in terms of the function of the documents with the intention that any document which gains commercial recognition as accomplishing the desired result shall be included within its scope. Fungible goods are adequately identified within the language of the definition by identification of the mass of which they are a part.

Dock warrants were within the Sales Act definition of document of title apparently for the purpose of recognizing a valid tender by means of such paper. In current commercial practice a dock warrant or receipt is a kind of interim certificate issued by steamship companies upon delivery of the goods at the dock, entitling a designated person to have issued to him at the company's office a bill of lading. The receipt itself is invariably nonnegotiable in form although it may indicate that a negotiable bill is to be forthcoming. Such a document is not within the general compass of the definition, although trade usage may in some cases entitle such paper to be treated as a document of title. If the dock receipt actually represents a storage obligation undertaken by the shipping company, then it is a warehouse receipt within this Section regardless of the name given to the instrument.

The goods must be "described", but the description may be by marks or labels and may be qualified in such a way as to disclaim personal knowledge of the issuer regarding contents or condition. However, baggage and parcel checks and similar "tokens" of storage which identify stored goods only as those received in exchange for the token are not covered by this Article.

The definition is broad enough to include an airway bill.

§ 1-205 Course of Dealing and Usage of Trade.

(1) A course of dealing is a sequence of previous conduct between the parties to a particular transaction which is fairly to be regarded as establishing a common basis of understanding for interpreting their expressions and other conduct.

(2) A usage of trade is any practice or method of dealing having such regularity of observance in a place, vocation or trade as to justify an expectation that it will be observed with respect to the transaction in question. The existence and scope of such a usage are to be proved as facts. If it is established that such a usage is embodied in a written trade code or similar writing the interpretation of the writing is for the court.

(3) A course of dealing between parties and any usage of trade in the vocation or trade in which they are engaged or of which they are or should be aware give particular meaning to and supplement or qualify terms of an agreement.

(4) The express terms of an agreement and an applicable course of dealing or usage of trade shall be construed wherever reasonable as consistent with each other; but when such construction is unreasonable express terms control both course of dealing and usage of trade and course of dealing controls usage of trade.

(5) An applicable usage of trade in the place where any part of performance is to occur shall be used in interpreting the agreement as to that part of the performance.

(6) Evidence of a relevant usage of trade offered by one party is not admissible unless and until he has given the other party such notice as the court finds sufficient to prevent unfair surprise to the latter.

§ 2-105 Definitions: Transferability; "Goods"; "Future" Goods; "Lot"; "Commercial Unit".

(1) "Goods" means all things (including specially manufactured goods) which are movable at the time of identification to the contract for sale other than the money in which the price is to be paid, investment securities (Article 8) and things in action. "Goods" also includes the unborn young of animals and growing crops and other identified things attached to realty as described in the section on goods to be severed from realty (Section 2-107).

(2) Goods must be both existing and identified before any interest in them can pass. Goods which are not both existing and identified are "future" goods. A purported present sale of future goods or of any interest therein operates as a contract to sell.

(3) There may be a sale of a part interest in existing identified goods.

(4) An undivided share in an identified bulk of fungible goods is sufficiently identified to be sold although the quantity of the bulk is not determined. Any agreed proportion of such a bulk or any quantity thereof agreed upon by number, weight or other measure may to the extent of the seller's interest in the bulk be sold to the buyer who then becomes an owner in common.

(5) "Lot" means a parcel or a single article which is the subject matter of a separate sale or delivery, whether or not it is sufficient to perform the contract.

(6) "Commercial unit" means such a unit of goods as by commercial usage is a single whole for purposes of sale and division of which materially impairs its character or value on the market or in use. A commercial unit may be a single article (as a machine) or a set of articles (as a suite of furniture or an assortment of sizes) or a quantity (as a bale, gross, or carload) or any other unit treated in use or in the relevant market as a single whole.

§ 2-319 F.O.B. and F.A.S. Terms.

(1) Unless otherwise agreed the term F.O.B. (which means "free on board") at a named place, even though used only in connection with the stated price, is a delivery term under which

    (a) when the term is F.O.B. the place of shipment, the seller must at that place ship the goods in the manner provided in this Article (Section 2-504) and bear the expense and risk of putting them into the possession of the carrier; or

    (b) when the term is F.O.B. the place of destination, the seller must at his own expense and risk transport the goods to that place and there tender delivery of them in the manner provided in this Article (Section 2-503);

(c) when under either (a) or (b) the term is also F.O.B. vessel, car or other vehicle, the seller must in addition at his own expense and risk load the goods on board. If the term is F.O.B. vessel the buyer must name the vessel and in an appropriate case the seller must comply with the provisions of this Article on the form of bill of lading (Section 2-323).

(2) Unless otherwise agreed the term F.A.S. vessel (which means "free alongside") at a named port, even though used only in connection with the stated price, is a delivery term under which the seller must

(a) at his own expense and risk deliver the goods alongside the vessel in the manner usual in that port or on a dock designated and provided by the buyer; and

(b) obtain and tender a receipt for the goods in exchange for which the carrier is under a duty to issue a bill of lading.

(3) Unless otherwise agreed in any case falling within subsection (1)(a) or (c) or subsection (2) the buyer must seasonably give any needed instructions for making delivery, including when the term is F.A.S. or F.O.B. the loading berth of the vessel and in an appropriate case its name and sailing date. The seller may treat the failure of needed instructions as a failure of cooperation under this Article (Section 2-311). He may also at his option move the goods in any reasonable manner preparatory to delivery or shipment.

(4) Under the term F.O.B. vessel or F.A.S. unless otherwise agreed the buyer must make payment against tender of the required documents and the seller may not tender nor the buyer demand delivery of the goods in substitution for the documents.

OFFICIAL COMMENT

Purposes:

1. This section is intended to negate the uncommercial line of decision which treats an "F.O.B." term as "merely a price term." The distinctions taken in subsection (1) handle most of the issues which have on occasion led to the unfortunate judicial language just referred to. Other matters which have led to sound results being based on unhappy language in regard to F.O.B. clauses are dealt with in this Act by Section 2-311(2) (seller's option re arrangements relating to shipment) and Sections 2-614 and 615 (substituted performance and seller's excuse).

2. Subsection (1)(c) not only specifies the duties of a seller who engages to deliver "F.O.B. vessel," or the like, but ought to make clear that no agreement is soundly drawn when it looks to reshipment from San Francisco or New York, but speaks merely of "F.O.B." the place.

3. The buyer's obligations stated in subsection (1)(c) and subsection (3) are, as shown in the text, obligations of cooperation. The last sentence of subsection (3) expressly, though perhaps unnecessarily, authorizes the seller, pending instructions, to go ahead with such preparatory moves as shipment from the interior to the named point of delivery. The sentence presupposes the usual case in which instructions "fail"; a prior repudiation by the buyer, giving notice that breach was intended, would remove the reason for the sentence, and would normally bring into play, instead, the second sentence of Section 2-704, which duly calls for lessening damages.

4. The treatment of "F.O.B. vessel" in conjunction with F.A.S. fits, in regard to the need for payment against documents, with standard practice and case law; but "F.O.B. vessel" is a term which by its very language makes express the need for an "on board" document. In this respect, that term is stricter than the ordinary overseas "shipment" contract (C.I.F., etc., Section 2-320).

§ 2-320 C.I.F. and C. & F. Terms.

(1) The term C.I.F. means that the price includes in a lump sum the cost of the goods and the insurance and freight to the named destination. The term C. & F. or C.F. means that the price so includes cost and freight to the named destination.

(2) Unless otherwise agreed and even though used only in connection with the stated price and destination, the term C.I.F. destination or its equivalent requires the seller at his own expense and risk to

(a) put the goods into the possession of a carrier at the port for shipment and obtain a negotiable bill or bills of lading covering the entire transportation to the named destination; and

(b) load the goods and obtain a receipt from the carrier (which may be contained in the bill of lading) showing that the freight has been paid or provided for; and

(c) obtain a policy or certificate of insurance, including any war risk insurance, of a kind and on terms then current at the port of shipment in the usual amount, in the currency of the contract, shown to cover the same goods covered by the bill of lading and providing for payment of loss to the order of the buyer or for the account of whom it may concern; but the seller may add to the price the amount of the premium for any such war risk insurance; and

(d) prepare an invoice of the goods and procure any other documents required to effect shipment or to comply with the contract; and

(e) forward and tender with commercial promptness all the documents in due form and with any indorsement necessary to perfect the buyer's rights.

(3) Unless otherwise agreed the term C. & F. or its equivalent has the same effect and imposes upon the seller the same obligations and risks as a C.I.F. term except the obligation as to insurance.

(4) Under the term C.I.F. or C. & F. unless otherwise agreed the buyer must make payment against tender of the required documents and the seller may not tender nor the buyer demand delivery of the goods in substitution for the documents.

OFFICIAL COMMENT

Purposes: To make it clear that:

1. The C.I.F. contract is not a destination but a shipment contract with risk of subsequent loss or damage to the goods passing to the buyer upon shipment if the seller has properly performed all his obligations with respect to the goods. Delivery to the carrier is delivery to the buyer for purposes of risk and "title". Delivery of possession of the goods is accomplished by delivery of the bill of lading, and upon tender of the required documents the buyer must pay the agreed price without awaiting the arrival of the goods and if they have been lost or damaged after proper shipment he must seek his remedy against the carrier or insurer. The buyer has no right of inspection prior to payment or acceptance of the documents.
2. The seller's obligations remain the same even though the C.I.F. term is "used only in connection with the stated price and destination".
3. The insurance stipulated by the C.I.F. term is for the buyer's benefit, to protect him against the risk of loss or damage to the goods in transit. A clause in a C.I.F. contract "insurance—for the account of sellers" should be viewed in its ordinary mercantile meaning that the sellers must pay for the insurance and not that it is intended to run to the seller's benefit.
4. A bill of lading covering the entire transportation from the port of shipment is explicitly required but the provision on this point must be read in the light of its reason to assure the buyer of as full protection as the conditions of shipment reasonably permit, remembering always that this type of contract is designed to move the goods in the channels commercially available. To enable the buyer to deal with the goods while they are afloat the bill of lading must be one that covers only the quantity of goods called for by the contract. The buyer is not required to accept his part of the goods without a bill of lading because the latter covers a larger quantity, nor is he required to accept a bill of lading for the whole quantity under a stipulation to hold the excess for the owner. Although the buyer is not compelled to accept either goods or documents under such circumstances he may of course claim his rights in any goods which have been identified to his contract.
5. The seller is given the option of paying or providing for the payment of freight. He has no option to ship "freight collect" unless the agreement so provides. The rule of the common law that the buyer need not pay the freight if the goods do not arrive is preserved.

Unless the shipment has been sent "freight collect" the buyer is entitled to receive documentary evidence that he is not obligated to pay the freight; the seller is therefore required to obtain a receipt "showing that the freight has been paid or provided for." The usual notation in the appropriate space on the bill of lading that the freight has been prepaid is a sufficient receipt, as at common law. The phrase "provided for" is intended to cover the frequent situation in which the carrier extends credit to a shipper for the freight on successive shipments and receives periodical payments of the accrued freight charges from him.

6. The requirement that unless otherwise agreed the seller must procure insurance "of a kind and on terms then current at the port for shipment in the usual amount, in the currency of the contract, sufficiently shown to cover the same goods covered by the bill of lading", applies to both marine and war risk insurance. As applied to marine insurance, it means such insurance as is usual or customary at the port for shipment with reference to the particular kind of goods involved, the character and equipment of the vessel, the route of the voyage, the port of destination and any other considerations that affect the risk. It is the substantial equivalent of the ordinary insurance in the particular trade and on the particular voyage and is subject to agreed specifications of type or extent of coverage. The language does not mean that the insurance must be adequate to cover all risks to which the goods may be subject in transit. There are some types of loss or damage that are not covered by the usual marine insurance and are excepted in bills of lading or in applicable statutes from the causes of loss or damage for which the carrier or the vessel is liable. Such risks must be borne by the buyer under this Article.

Insurance secured in compliance with a C.I.F. term must cover the entire transportation of the goods to the named destination.

7. An additional obligation is imposed upon the seller in requiring him to procure customary war risk insurance at the buyer's expense. This changes the common law on the point. The seller is not required to assume the risk of including in the C.I.F. price the cost of such insurance, since it often fluctuates rapidly, but is required to treat it simply as a necessary for the buyer's account. What war risk insurance is "current" or usual turns on the standard forms of policy or rider in common use.

8. The C.I.F. contract calls for insurance covering the value of the goods at the time and place of shipment and does not include any increase in market value during transit or any anticipated profit to the buyer on a sale by him.

The contract contemplates that before the goods arrive at their destination they may be sold again and again on C.I.F. terms and that the original policy of insurance and bill of lading will run with the interest in the goods by being transferred to each successive buyer. A buyer who becomes the seller in such an intermediate contract for sale does not thereby, if his sub-buyer knows the circumstances, undertake to insure the goods again at an increased price fixed in the new contract or to cover the increase in price by additional insurance, and his buyer may not reject the documents on the ground that the original policy does not cover such higher price. If such a sub-buyer desires additional insurance he must procure it for himself.

Where the seller exercises an option to ship "freight collect" and to credit the buyer with the freight against the C.I.F. price, the insurance need not cover the freight since the freight is not at the buyer's risk. On the other hand, where the seller prepays the freight upon shipping under a bill of lading requiring prepayment and providing that the freight shall be deemed earned and shall be retained by the carrier "ship and/or cargo lost or not lost," or using words of similar import, he must procure insurance that will cover the freight, because notwithstanding that the goods are lost in transit the buyer is bound to pay the freight as part of the C.I.F. price and will be unable to recover it back from the carrier.

9. Insurance "for the account of whom it may concern" is usual and sufficient. However, for a valid tender the policy of insurance must be one which can be disposed of together with the bill of lading and so must be "sufficiently shown to cover the same goods covered by the bill of lading." It must cover separately the quantity of goods called for by the buyer's contract and not merely insure his goods as part of a larger quantity in which others are interested, a case provided for in American mercantile practice by the use of negotiable certificates of insurance which are expressly authorized by this section. By usage these certificates are treated as the equivalent of separate policies and are good tender under C.I.F. contracts. The term "certificate of insurance", however, does not of itself include certificates or "cover notes" issued by the insurance broker and stating that the goods are covered by a policy. Their sufficiency as substitutes for policies will depend upon proof of an established usage or course of dealing. The present section rejects the English rule that not only brokers' certificates and "cover notes" but also certain forms of American insurance certificates are not the equivalent of policies and are not good tender under a C.I.F. contract.

   The seller's failure to tender a proper insurance document is waived if the buyer refuses to make payment on other and untenable grounds at a time when proper insurance could have been obtained and tendered by the seller if timely objection had been made. Even a failure to insure on shipment may be cured by seasonable tender of a policy retroactive in effect; e.g., one insuring the goods "lost or not lost." The provisions of this Article on cure of improper tender and on waiver of buyer's objections by silence are applicable to insurance tenders under a C.I.F. term. Where there is no waiver by the buyer as described above, however, the fact that the goods arrive safely does not cure the seller's breach of his obligations to insure them and tender to the buyer a proper insurance document.

10. The seller's invoice of the goods shipped under a C.I.F. contract is regarded as a usual and necessary document upon which reliance may properly be placed. It is the document which evidences points of description, quality

and the like which do not readily appear in other documents. This Article rejects those statements to the effect that the invoice is a usual but not a necessary document under a C.I.F. term.

11. The buyer needs all of the documents required under a C.I.F. contract, in due form and with necessary endorsements, so that before the goods arrive he may deal with them by negotiating the documents or may obtain prompt possession of the goods after their arrival. If the goods are lost or damaged in transit the documents are necessary to enable him promptly to assert his remedy against the carrier or insurer. The seller is therefore obligated to do what is mercantilely reasonable in the circumstances and should make every reasonable exertion to send forward the documents as soon as possible after the shipment. The requirement that the documents be forwarded with "commercial promptness" expresses a more urgent need for action than that suggested by the phrase "reasonable time".

12. Under a C.I.F. contract the buyer, as under the common law, must pay the price upon tender of the required documents without first inspecting the goods, but his payment in these circumstances does not constitute an acceptance of the goods nor does it impair his right of subsequent inspection or his options and remedies in the case of improper delivery. All remedies and rights for the seller's breach are reserved to him. The buyer must pay before inspection and assert his remedy against the seller afterward unless the nonconformity of the goods amounts to a real failure of consideration, since the purpose of choosing this form of contract is to give the seller protection against the buyer's unjustifiable rejection of the goods at a distant port of destination which would necessitate taking possession of the goods and suing the buyer there.

13. A valid C.I.F. contract may be made which requires part of the transportation to be made on land and part on the sea, as where the goods are to be brought by rail from an inland point to a seaport and thence transported by vessel to the named destination under a "through" or combination bill of lading issued by the railroad company. In such a case shipment by rail from the inland point within the contract period is a timely shipment notwithstanding that the loading of the goods on the vessel is delayed by causes beyond the seller's control.

14. Although subsection (2) stating the legal effects of the C.I.F. term is an "unless otherwise agreed" provision, the express language used in an agreement is frequently a precautionary, fuller statement of the normal C.I.F. terms and hence not intended as a departure or variation from them. Moreover, the dominant outlines of the C.I.F. term are so well understood commercially that any variation should, whenever reasonably possible, be read as falling within those dominant outlines rather than as destroying the whole meaning of a term which essentially indicates a contract for proper shipment rather than one for delivery at destination. Particularly careful consideration is necessary before a printed form or clause is construed to mean agreement otherwise and where a C.I.F. contract is prepared on a

printed form designed for some other type of contract, the C.I.F. terms must prevail over printed clauses repugnant to them.

15. Under subsection (4) the fact that the seller knows at the time of the tender of the documents that the goods have been lost in transit does not affect his rights if he has performed his contractual obligations. Similarly, the seller cannot perform under a C.I.F. term by purchasing and tendering landed goods.

16. Under the C. & F. term, as under the C.I.F. term, title and risk of loss are intended to pass to the buyer on shipment. A stipulation in a C. & F. contract that the seller shall effect insurance on the goods and charge the buyer with the premium (in effect that he shall act as the buyer's agent for that purpose) is entirely in keeping with the pattern. On the other hand, it often happens that the buyer is in a more advantageous position than the seller to effect insurance on the goods or that he has in force an "open" or "floating" policy covering all shipments made by him or to him, in either of which events the C. & F. term is adequate without mention of insurance.

17. It is to be remembered that in a French contract the term "C.A.F." does not mean "Cost and Freight" but has exactly the same meaning as the term "C.I.F." since it is merely the French equivalent of that term. The "A" does not stand for "and" but for "assurance" which means insurance.

§ 2-321 C.I.F. or C. & F.: "Net Landed Weights"; "Payment on Arrival"; Warranty of Condition on Arrival.

Under a contract containing a term C.I.F. or C. & F.

(1) Where the price is based on or is to be adjusted according to "net landed weights", "delivered weights", "out turn" quantity or quality or the like, unless otherwise agreed the seller must reasonably estimate the price. The payment due on tender of the documents called for by the contract is the amount so estimated, but after final adjustment of the price a settlement must be made with commercial promptness.

(2) An agreement described in subsection (1) or any warranty of quality or condition of the goods on arrival places upon the seller the risk of ordinary deterioration, shrinkage and the like in transportation but has no effect on the place or time of identification to the contract for sale or delivery or on the passing of the risk of loss.

(3) Unless otherwise agreed where the contract provides for payment on or after arrival of the goods the seller must before payment allow such preliminary inspection as is feasible; but if the goods are lost delivery of the documents and payment are due when the goods should have arrived.

OFFICIAL COMMENT

Purposes:

This section deals with two variations of the C.I.F. contract which have evolved in mercantile practice but are entirely consistent with the basic C.I.F. pattern. Subsections (1) and (2), which provide for a shift to the seller of the risk of quality and weight deterioration during shipment, are designed to conform the law to the best mercantile practice and usage without changing the legal consequences of the C.I.F. or C. & F. term as to the passing of marine risks to the buyer at the point of shipment. Subsection (3) provides that where under the contract documents are to be presented for payment after arrival of the goods, this amounts merely to a postponement of the payment under the C.I.F. contract and is not to be confused with the "no arrival, no sale" contract. If the goods are lost, delivery of the documents and payment against them are due when the goods should have arrived. The clause for payment on or after arrival is not to be construed as such a condition precedent to payment that if the goods are lost in transit the buyer need never pay and the seller must bear the loss.

§ 2-322 Delivery "Ex-Ship".

(1) Unless otherwise agreed a term for delivery of goods "ex-ship" (which means from the carrying vessel) or in equivalent language is not restricted to a particular ship and requires delivery from a ship which has reached a place at the named port of destination where goods of the kind are usually discharged.

(2) Under such a term unless otherwise agreed
    (a) the seller must discharge all liens arising out of the carriage and furnish the buyer with a direction which puts the carrier under a duty to deliver the goods; and
    (b) the risk of loss does not pass to the buyer until the goods leave the ship's tackle or are otherwise properly unloaded.

OFFICIAL COMMENT

Purposes:

1. The delivery term, "ex ship", as between seller and buyer, is the reverse of the f.a.s. term covered.
2. Delivery need not be made from any particular vessel under a clause calling for delivery "ex ship", even though a vessel on which shipment is to be made originally is named in the contract, unless the agreement by appropriate language, restricts the clause to delivery from a named vessel.
3. The appropriate place and manner of unloading at the port of destination depend upon the nature of the goods and the facilities and usages of the port.

349

4. A contract fixing a price "ex ship" with payment "cash against documents" calls only for such documents as are appropriate to the contract. Tender of a delivery order and of a receipt for the freight after the arrival of the carrying vessel is adequate. The seller is not required to tender a bill of lading as a document of title nor is he required to insure the goods for the buyer's benefit, as the goods are not at the buyer's risk during the voyage.

§ 2-323 Form of Bill of Lading Required in Overseas Shipment; "Overseas".

(1) Where the contract contemplates overseas shipment and contains a term C.I.F. or C. & F. or F.O.B. vessel, the seller unless otherwise agreed must obtain a negotiable bill of lading stating that the goods have been loaded on board or, in the case of a term C.I.F. or C. & F., received for shipment.

(2) Where in a case within subsection (1) a bill of lading has been issued in a set of parts, unless otherwise agreed if the documents are not to be sent from abroad the buyer may demand tender of the full set; otherwise only one part of the bill of lading need be tendered. Even if the agreement expressly requires a full set

    (a) due tender of a single part is acceptable within the provisions of this Article on cure of improper delivery (subsection (1) of Section 2-508); and

    (b) even though the full set is demanded, if the documents are sent from abroad the person tendering an incomplete set may nevertheless require payment upon furnishing an indemnity which the buyer in good faith deems adequate.

(3) A shipment by water or by air or a contract contemplating such shipment is "overseas" insofar as by usage of trade or agreement it is subject to the commercial, financing or shipping practices characteristic of international deep water commerce.

OFFICIAL COMMENT

Purposes:

1. Subsection (1) follows the "American" rule that a regular bill of lading indicating delivery of the goods at the dock for shipment is sufficient, except under a term "F.O.B. vessel." See Section 2-319 and comment thereto.

2. Subsection (2) deals with the problem of bills of lading covering deep water shipments, issued not as a single bill of lading but in a set of parts, each part referring to the other parts and the entire set constituting in commercial practice and at law a single bill of lading. Commercial practice in international commerce is to accept and pay against presentation of the first part of a set if the part is sent from overseas even though the contract of the

buyer requires presentation of a full set of bills of lading provided adequate indemnity for the missing parts is forthcoming.

This subsection codifies that practice as between buyer and seller. Article 5 (Section 5-113) authorizes banks presenting drafts under letters of credit to give indemnities against the missing parts, and this subsection means that the buyer must accept and act on such indemnities if he in good faith deems them adequate. But neither this subsection nor Article 5 decides whether a bank which has issued a letter of credit is similarly bound. The issuing bank's obligation under a letter of credit is independent and depends on its own terms. See Article 5.

§ 2-324 "No Arrival, No Sale" Term.

(1) Under a term "no arrival, no sale" or terms of like meaning, unless otherwise agreed,
    (a) the seller must properly ship conforming goods and if they arrive by any means he must tender them on arrival but he assumes no obligation that the goods will arrive unless he has caused the non-arrival; and
    (b) where without fault of the seller the goods are in part lost or have so deteriorated as no longer to conform to the contract or arrive after the contract time, the buyer may proceed as if there had been casualty to identified goods (Section 2-613).

OFFICIAL COMMENT

Purposes:

1. The "no arrival, no sale" term in a "destination" overseas contract leaves risk of loss on the seller but gives him an exemption from liability for nondelivery. Both the nature of the case and the duty of good faith require that the seller must not interfere with the arrival of the goods in any way. If the circumstances impose upon him the responsibility for making or arranging the shipment, he must have a shipment made despite the exemption clause. Further, the shipment made must be a conforming one, for the exemption under a "no arrival, no sale" term applies only to the hazards of transportation and the goods must be proper in all other respects.

    The reason of this section is that where the seller is reselling goods bought by him as shipped by another and this fact is known to the buyer, so that the seller is not under any obligation to make the shipment himself, the seller is entitled under the "no arrival, no sale" clause to exemption from payment of damages for non-delivery if the goods do not arrive or if the goods which actually arrive are non-conforming. This does not extend to sellers who arrange shipment by their own agents, in which case the clause is limited to casualty due to marine hazards. But sellers who make known that they are contracting only with respect to what will be delivered to them by parties over whom they assume no control are entitled to the full quantum of the exemption.

2. The provisions of this Article on identification must be read together with the present section in order to bring the exemption into application. Until there is some designation of the goods in a particular shipment or on a particular ship as being those to which the contract refers there can be no application of an exemption for their non-arrival.

3. The seller's duty to tender the agreed or declared goods if they do arrive is not impaired because of their delay in arrival or by their arrival after transshipment.

4. The phrase "to arrive" is often employed in the same sense as "no arrival, no sale" and may then be given the same effect. But a "to arrive" term, added to a C.I.F. or C. & F. contract, does not have the full meaning given by this section to "no arrival, no sale". Such a "to arrive" term is usually intended to operate only to the extent that the risks are not covered by the agreed insurance and the loss or casualty is due to such uncovered hazards. In some instances the "to arrive" term may be regarded as a time of payment term, or, in the case of the reselling seller discussed in point 1 above, as negating responsibility for conformity of the goods, if they arrive, to any description which was based on his good faith belief of the quality. Whether this is the intention of the parties is a question of fact based on all the circumstances surrounding the resale and in case of ambiguity the rules of Sections 2-316 and 2-317 apply to preclude dishonor.

5. Paragraph (b) applies where goods arrive impaired by damage or partial loss during transportation and makes the policy of this Article on casualty to identified goods applicable to such a situation. For the term cannot be regarded as intending to give the seller an unforeseen profit through casualty; it is intended only to protect him from loss due to causes beyond his control.

§ 2-401 Passing of Title; Reservation for Security; Limited Application of This Section.

Each provision of this Article with regard to the rights, obligations and remedies of the seller, the buyer, purchasers or other third parties applies irrespective of title to the goods except where the provision refers to such title. Insofar as situations are not covered by the other provisions of this Article and matters concerning title become material the following rules apply:

(1) Title to goods cannot pass under a contract for sale prior to their identification to the contract (Section 2-501), and unless otherwise explicitly agreed the buyer acquires by their identification a special property as limited by this Act. Any retention or reservation by the seller of the title (property) in goods shipped or delivered to the buyer is limited in effect to

a reservation of a security interest. Subject to these provisions and to the provisions of the Article on Secured Transactions (Article 9), title to goods passes from the seller to the buyer in any manner and on any conditions explicitly agreed on by the parties.

(2) Unless otherwise explicitly agreed title passes to the buyer at the time and place at which the seller completes his performance with reference to the physical delivery of the goods, despite any reservation of a security interest and even though a document of title is to be delivered at a different time or place; and in particular and despite any reservation of a security interest by the bill of lading

    (a) if the contract requires or authorizes the seller to send the goods to the buyer but does not require him to deliver them at destination, title passes to the buyer at the time and place of shipment; but

    (b) if the contract requires delivery at destination, title passes on tender there.

(3) Unless otherwise explicitly agreed where delivery is to be made without moving the goods,

    (a) if the seller is to deliver a document of title, title passes at the time when and the place where he delivers such documents; or

    (b) if the goods are at the time of contracting already identified and no documents are to be delivered, title passes at the time and place of contracting.

(4) A rejection or other refusal by the buyer to receive or retain the goods, whether or not justified, or a justified revocation of acceptance revests title to the goods in the seller. Such revesting occurs by operation of law and is not a "sale".

OFFICIAL COMMENT

1. This Article deals with the issues between seller and buyer in terms of step by step performance or non-performance under the contract for sale and not in terms of whether or not "title" to the goods has passed. That the rules of this section in no way alter the rights of either the buyer, seller or third parties declared elsewhere in the Article is made clear by the preamble of this section. This section, however, in no way intends to indicate which line of interpretation should be followed in cases where the applicability of "public" regulation depends upon a "sale" or upon location of "title" without further definition. The basic policy of this Article that known purpose and reason should govern interpretation cannot extend beyond the scope of its own provisions. It is therefore necessary to state what a "sale" is and when title passes under this Article in case the courts deem any public regulation to incorporate the defined term of the "private" law.

2. "Future" goods cannot be the subject of a present sale. Before title can pass the goods must be identified in the manner set forth in Section 2-501. The

parties, however, have full liberty to arrange by specific terms for the passing of title to goods which are existing.

3. The "special property" of the buyer in goods identified to the contract is excluded from the definition of "security interest"; its incidents are defined in provisions of this Article such as those on the rights of the seller's creditors, on good faith purchase, on the buyer's right to goods on the seller's insolvency, and on the buyer's right to specific performance or replevin.

4. The factual situations in subsections (2) and (3) upon which passage of title turn actually base the test upon the time when the seller has finally committed himself in regard to specific goods. Thus in a "shipment" contract he commits himself by the act of making the shipment. If shipment is not contemplated subsection (3) turns on the seller's final commitment, i.e. the delivery of documents or the making of the contract.

§ 2-501 Insurable Interest in Goods; Manner of Identification of Goods.

(1) The buyer obtains a special property and an insurable interest in goods by identification of existing goods as goods to which the contract refers even though the goods so identified are non-conforming and he has an option to return or reject them. Such identification can be made at any time and in any manner explicitly agreed to by the parties. In the absence of explicit agreement identification occurs

   (a) when the contract is made if it is for the sale of goods already existing and identified;

   (b) if the contract is for the sale of future goods other than those described in paragraph (c), when goods are shipped, marked or otherwise designated by the seller as goods to which the contract refers;

   (c) when the crops are planted or otherwise become growing crops or the young are conceived if the contract is for the sale of unborn young to be born within twelve months after contracting or for the sale of crops to be harvested within twelve months or the next normal harvest season after contracting whichever is longer.

(2) The seller retains an insurable interest in goods so long as title to or any security interest in the goods remains in him and where the identification is by the seller alone he may until default or insolvency or notification to the buyer that the identification is final substitute other goods for those identified.

(3) Nothing in this section impairs any insurable interest recognized under any other statute or rule of law.

OFFICIAL COMMENT

1. The present section deals with the manner of identifying goods to the contract so that an insurable interest in the buyer and the rights set forth in

the next section will accrue. Generally speaking, identification may be made in any manner "explicitly agreed to" by the parties. The rules of paragraphs (a), (b) and (c) apply only in the absence of such "explicit agreement".

2. In the ordinary case identification of particular existing goods as goods to which the contract refers is unambiguous and may occur in one of many ways. It is possible, however, for the identification to be tentative or contingent. In view of the limited effect given to identification by this Article, the general policy is to resolve all doubts in favor of identification.

3. The provision of this section as to "explicit agreement" clarifies the present confusion in the law of sales which has arisen from the fact that under prior uniform legislation all rules of presumption with reference to the passing of title or to appropriation (which in turn depended upon identification) were regarded as subject to the contrary intention of the parties or of the party appropriating. Such uncertainty is reduced to a minimum under this section by requiring "explicit agreement" of the parties before the rules of paragraphs (a), (b) and (c) are displaced—as they would be by a term giving the buyer power to select the goods. An "explicit" agreement, however, need not necessarily be found in the terms used in the particular transaction. Thus, where a usage of the trade has previously been made explicit by reduction to a standard set of "rules and regulations" currently incorporated by reference into the contracts of the parties, a relevant provision of those "rules and regulations" is "explicit" within the meaning of this section.

4. In view of the limited function of identification there is no requirement in this section that the goods be in deliverable state or that all of the seller's duties with respect to the processing of the goods be completed in order that identification occur. For example, despite identification the risk of loss remains on the seller under the risk of loss provisions until completion of his duties as to the goods and all of his remedies remain dependent upon his not defaulting under the contract.

5. Undivided shares in an identified fungible bulk, such as grain in an elevator or oil in a storage tank, can be sold. The mere making of the contract with reference to an undivided share in an identified fungible bulk is enough under subsection (a) to effect an identification if there is no explicit agreement otherwise. The seller's duty, however, to segregate and deliver according to the contract is not affected by such an identification but is controlled by other provisions of this Article.

6. Identification of crops under paragraph (c) is made upon planting only if they are to be harvested within the year or within the next normal harvest season. The phrase "next normal harvest season" fairly includes nursery stock raised for normally quick "harvest," but plainly excludes a "timber" crop to which the concept of a harvest "season" is inapplicable.

Paragraph (c) is also applicable to a crop of wool or the young of animals to be born within twelve months after contracting. The product of

355

a lumbering, mining or fishing operation, though seasonal, is not within the concept of "growing". Identification under a contract for all or part of the output of such an operation can be effected early in the operation.

§ 2-503 Manner of Seller's Tender of Delivery.

(1) Tender of delivery requires that the seller put and hold conforming goods at the buyer's disposition and give the buyer any notification reasonably necessary to enable him to take delivery. The manner, time and place for tender are determined by the agreement and this Article, and in particular
   (a) tender must be at a reasonable hour, and if it is of goods they must be kept available for the period reasonably necessary to enable the buyer to take possession; but
   (b) unless otherwise agreed the buyer must furnish facilities reasonably suited to the receipt of the goods.

(2) Where the case is within the next section respecting shipment tender requires that the seller comply with its provisions.

(3) Where the seller is required to deliver at a particular destination tender requires that he comply with subsection (1) and also in any appropriate case tender documents as described in subsections (4) and (5) of this section.

(4) Where goods are in the possession of a bailee and are to be delivered without being moved
   (a) tender requires that the seller either tender a negotiable document of title covering such goods or procure acknowledgment by the bailee of the buyer's right to possession of the goods; but
   (b) tender to the buyer of a non-negotiable document of title or of a written direction to the bailee to deliver is sufficient tender unless the buyer seasonably objects, and receipt by the bailee of notification of the buyer's rights fixes those rights as against the bailee and all third persons; but risk of loss of the goods and of any failure by the bailee to honor the non-negotiable document of title or to obey the direction remains on the seller until the buyer has had a reasonable time to present the document or direction, and a refusal by the bailee to honor the document or to obey the direction defeats the tender.

(5) Where the contract requires the seller to deliver documents
   (a) he must tender all such documents in correct form, except as provided in this Article with respect to bills of lading in a set (subsection (2) of Section 2-323); and
   (b) tender through customary banking channels is sufficient and dishonor of a draft accompanying the documents constitutes non-acceptance or rejection.

OFFICIAL COMMENT

Changes: The general policy of the above sections is continued and supplemented but subsection (3) changes the rule of prior section 19(5) as to what constitutes a "destination" contract and subsection (4) incorporates a minor correction as to tender of delivery of goods in the possession of a bailee.

Purposes of Changes:

1. The major general rules governing the manner of proper or due tender of delivery are gathered in this section. The term "tender" is used in this Article in two different senses. In one sense it refers to "due tender" which contemplates an offer coupled with a present ability to fulfill all the conditions resting on the tendering party and must be followed by actual performance if the other party shows himself ready to proceed. Unless the context unmistakably indicates otherwise this is the meaning of "tender" in this Article and the occasional addition of the word "due" is only for clarity and emphasis. At other times it is used to refer to an offer of goods or documents under a contract as if in fulfillment of its conditions even though there is a defect when measured against the contract obligation. Used in either sense, however, "tender" connotes such performance by the tendering party as puts the other party in default if he fails to proceed in some manner.

2. The seller's general duty to tender and deliver is laid down in Section 2-301 and more particularly in Section 2-507. The seller's right to a receipt if he demands one and receipts are customary is governed by Section 2-205. Subsection (1) of the present section proceeds to set forth two primary requirements of tender: first, that the seller "put and hold conforming goods at the buyer's disposition" and, second, that he "give the buyer any notice reasonably necessary to enable him to take delivery."

   In case in which payment is due and demanded upon delivery the "buyer's disposition" is qualified by the seller's right to retain control of the goods until payment by the provision of this Article on delivery on condition. However, where the seller is demanding payment on delivery he must first allow the buyer to inspect the goods in order to avoid impairing his tender unless the contract for sale is on C.I.F., C.O.D., cash against documents or similar terms negating the privilege of inspection before payment.

   In the case of contracts involving documents the seller can "put and hold conforming goods at the buyer's disposition" under subsection (1) by tendering documents which give the buyer complete control of the goods under the provisions of Article 7 on due negotiation.

3. Under paragraph (a) of subsection (1) usage of the trade and the circumstances of the particular case determine what is a reasonable hour for tender and what constitutes a reasonable period of holding the goods available.

4. The buyer must furnish reasonable facilities for the receipt of the goods tendered by the seller under subsection (1), paragraph (b). This obligation of the buyer is no part of the seller's tender.

5. For the purposes of subsections (2) and (3) there is omitted from this Article the rule under prior uniform legislation that a term requiring the seller to pay the freight or cost of transportation to the buyer is equivalent to an agreement by the seller to deliver to the buyer or at an agreed destination. This omission is with the specific intention of negating the rule, for under this Article the "shipment" contract is regarded as the normal one and the "destination" contract as the variant type. The seller is not obligated to deliver at a named destination and bear the concurrent risk of loss until arrival, unless he has specifically agreed so to deliver or the commercial understanding of the terms used by the parties contemplates such delivery.

6. Paragraph (a) of subsection (4) continues the rule of the prior uniform legislation as to acknowledgment by the bailee. Paragraph (b) of subsection (4) adopts the rule that between the buyer and the seller the risk of loss remains on the seller during a period reasonable for securing acknowledgment of the transfer from the bailee, while as against all other parties the buyer's rights are fixed as of the time the bailee receives notice of the transfer.

7. Under subsection (5) documents are never "required" except where there is an express contract term or it is plainly implicit in the peculiar circumstances of the case or in a usage of trade. Documents may, of course, be "authorized" although not required, but such cases are not within the scope of this subsection. When documents are required, there are three main requirements of this subsection: (1) "All": each required document is essential to a proper tender; (2) "Such": the documents must be the ones actually required by the contract in terms of source and substance; (3) "Correct form": All documents must be in correct form.

When a prescribed document cannot be procured, a question of fact arises under the provision of this Article on substituted performance as to whether the agreed manner of delivery is actually commercially impracticable and whether the substitute is commercially reasonable.

§ 2-504 Shipment by Seller.

Where the seller is required or authorized to send the goods to the buyer and the contract does not require him to deliver them at a particular destination, then unless otherwise agreed he must

(a) put the goods in the possession of such a carrier and make such a contract for their transportation as may be reasonable having regard to the nature of the goods and other circumstances of the case; and

(b) obtain and promptly deliver or tender in due form any document necessary to enable the buyer to obtain possession of the goods or otherwise required by the agreement or by usage of trade; and

(c) promptly notify the buyer of the shipment.

Failure to notify the buyer under paragraph (c) or to make a proper contract under paragraph (a) is a ground for rejection only if material delay or loss ensues.

OFFICIAL COMMENT

Changes: Rewritten.

Purposes of Changes: To continue the general policy of the prior uniform statutory provision while incorporating certain modifications with respect to the requirement that the contract with the carrier be made expressly on behalf of the buyer and as to the necessity of giving notice of the shipment to the buyer, so that:

1. The section is limited to "shipment" contracts as contrasted with "destination" contracts or contracts for delivery at the place where the goods are located. The general principles embodied in this section cover the special cases of F.O.B. point of shipment contracts and C.I.F. and C. & F. contracts. Under the preceding section on manner of tender of delivery, due tender by the seller requires that he comply with the requirements of this section in appropriate cases.

2. The contract to be made with the carrier under paragraph (a) must conform to all express terms of the agreement, subject to any substitution necessary because of failure of agreed facilities as provided in the later provision on substituted performance. However, under the policies of this Article on good faith and commercial standards and on buyer's rights on improper delivery, the requirements of explicit provisions must be read in terms of their commercial and not their literal meaning. This policy is made express with respect to bills of lading in a set in the provision of this Article on form of bills of lading required in overseas shipment.

3. In the absence of agreement, the provision of this Article on options and cooperation respecting performance gives the seller the choice of any reasonable carrier, routing and other arrangements. Whether or not the shipment is at the buyer's expense the seller must see to any arrangements, reasonable in the circumstances, such as refrigeration, watering of live stock, protection against cold, the sending along of any necessary help, selection of specialized cars and the like for paragraph (a) is intended to cover all necessary arrangements whether made by contract with the carrier or otherwise. There is, however, a proper relaxation of such

requirements if the buyer is himself in a position to make the appropriate arrangements and the seller gives him reasonable notice of the need to do so. It is an improper contract under paragraph (a) for the seller to agree with the carrier to a limited valuation below the true value and thus cut off the buyer's opportunity to recover from the carrier in the event of loss, when the risk of shipment is placed on the buyer by his contract with the seller.

4. Both the language of paragraph (b) and the nature of the situation it concerns indicate that the requirement that the seller must obtain and deliver promptly to the buyer in due form any document necessary to enable him to obtain possession of the goods is intended to cumulate with the other duties of the seller such as those covered in paragraph (a).

   In this connection, in the case of pool car shipments a delivery order furnished by the seller on the pool car consignee, or on the carrier for delivery out of a larger quantity, satisfies the requirements of paragraph (b) unless the contract requires some other form of document.

5. This Article, unlike the prior uniform statutory provision, makes it the seller's duty to notify the buyer of shipment in all cases. The consequences of his failure to do so, however, are limited in that the buyer may reject on this ground only where material delay or loss ensues.

   A standard and acceptable manner of notification in open credit shipments is the sending of an invoice and in the case of documentary contracts is the prompt forwarding of the documents as under paragraph (b) of this section. It is also usual to send on a straight bill of lading but this is not necessary to the required notification. However, should such a document prove necessary or convenient to the buyer, as in the case of loss and claim against the carrier, good faith would require the seller to send it on request.

   Frequently the agreement expressly requires prompt notification as by wire or cable. Such a term may be of the essence and the final clause of paragraph (c) does not prevent the parties from making this a particular ground for rejection. To have this vital and irreparable effect upon the seller's duties, such a term should be part of the "dickered" terms written in any "form," or should otherwise be called seasonably and sharply to the seller's attention.

6. Generally, under the final sentence of the section, rejection by the buyer is justified only when the seller's dereliction as to any of the requirements of this section in fact is followed by material delay or damage. It rests on the seller, so far as concerns matters not within the peculiar knowledge of the buyer, to establish that his error has not been followed by events which justify rejection.

360

§ 2-513 Buyer's Right to Inspection of Goods.

(1) Unless otherwise agreed and subject to subsection (3), where goods are tendered or delivered or identified to the contract for sale, the buyer has a right before payment or acceptance to inspect them at any reasonable place and time and in any reasonable manner. When the seller is required or authorized to send the goods to the buyer, the inspection may be after their arrival.

(2) Expenses of inspection must be borne by the buyer but may be recovered from the seller if the goods do not conform and are rejected.

(3) Unless otherwise agreed and subject to the provisions of this Article on C.I.F. contracts (subsection (3) of Section 2-321), the buyer is not entitled to inspect the goods before payment of the price when the contract provides

(a) for delivery "C.O.D." or on other like terms; or

(b) for payment against documents of title, except where such payment is due only after the goods are to become available for inspection.

(4) A place or method of inspection fixed by the parties is presumed to be exclusive but unless otherwise expressly agreed it does not postpone identification or shift the place for delivery or for passing the risk of loss. If compliance becomes impossible, inspection shall be as provided in this section unless the place or method fixed was clearly intended as an indispensable condition failure of which avoids the contract.

OFFICIAL COMMENT

Purposes of Changes and New Matter: To correspond in substance with the prior uniform statutory provision and to incorporate in addition some of the results of the better case law so that:

1. The buyer is entitled to inspect goods as provided in subsection (1) unless it has been otherwise agreed by the parties. The phrase "unless otherwise agreed" is intended principally to cover such situations as those outlined in subsections (3) and (4) and those in which the agreement of the parties negates inspection before tender of delivery. However, no agreement by the parties can displace the entire right of inspection except where the contract is simply for the sale of "this thing." Even in a sale of boxed goods "as is" inspection is a right of the buyer, since if the boxes prove to contain some other merchandise altogether the price can be recovered back; nor do the limitations of the provision on effect of acceptance apply in such a case.

2. The buyer's right of inspection is available to him upon tender, delivery or appropriation of the goods with notice to him. Since inspection is available to him on tender, where payment is due against delivery he may, unless otherwise agreed, make his inspection before payment of the price. It is also available to him after receipt of the goods and so may be postponed

after receipt for a reasonable time. Failure to inspect before payment does not impair the right to inspect after receipt of the goods unless the case falls within subsection (4) on agreed and exclusive inspection provisions. The right to inspect goods which have been appropriated with notice to the buyer holds whether or not the sale was by sample.

3. The buyer may exercise his right of inspection at any reasonable time or place and in any reasonable manner. It is not necessary that he select the most appropriate time, place or manner to inspect or that his selection be the customary one in the trade or locality. Any reasonable time, place or manner is available to him and the reasonableness will be determined by trade usages, past practices between the parties and the other circumstances of the case.

The last sentence of subsection (1) makes it clear that the place of arrival of shipped goods is a reasonable place for their inspection.

4. Expenses of an inspection made to satisfy the buyer of the seller's performance must be assumed by the buyer in the first instance. Since the rule provides merely for an allocation of expense there is no policy to prevent the parties from providing otherwise in the agreement. Where the buyer would normally bear the expenses of the inspection but the goods are rightly rejected because of what the inspection reveals, demonstrable and reasonable costs of the inspection are part of his incidental damage caused by the seller's breach.

5. In the case of payment against documents, subsection (3) requires payment before inspection, since shipping documents against which payment is to be made will commonly arrive and be tendered while the goods are still in transit. This Article recognizes no exception in any peculiar case in which the goods happen to arrive before the documents. However, where by the agreement payment is to await the arrival of the goods, inspection before payment becomes proper since the goods are then "available for inspection."

Where by the agreement the documents are to be held until arrival the buyer is entitled to inspect before payment since the goods are then "available for inspection". Proof of usage is not necessary to establish this right, but if inspection before payment is disputed the contrary must be established by usage or by an explicit contract term to that effect.

For the same reason, that the goods are available for inspection, a term calling for payment against storage documents or a delivery order does not normally bar the buyer's right to inspection before payment under subsection (3)(b). This result is reinforced by the buyer's right under subsection (1) to inspect goods which have been appropriated with notice to him.

6. Under subsection (4) an agreed place or method of inspection is generally held to be intended as exclusive. However, where compliance with such an agreed inspection term becomes impossible, the question is basically one of intention. If the parties clearly intend that the method of inspection named

is to be a necessary condition without which the entire deal is to fail, the contract is at an end if that method becomes impossible. On the other hand, if the parties merely seek to indicate a convenient and reliable method but do not intend to give up the deal in the event of its failure, any reasonable method of inspection may be substituted under this Article.

Since the purpose of an agreed place of inspection is only to make sure at that point whether or not the goods will be thrown back, the "exclusive" feature of the named place is satisfied under this Article if the buyer's failure to inspect there is held to be an acceptance with the knowledge of such defects as inspection would have revealed within the section on waiver of buyer's objections by failure to particularize. Revocation of the acceptance is limited to the situations stated in the section pertaining to that subject. The reasonable time within which to give notice of defects within the section on notice of breach begins to run from the point of the "acceptance."

7. Clauses on time of inspection are commonly clauses which limit the time in which the buyer must inspect and give notice of defects. Such clauses are therefore governed by the section of this Article which requires that such a time limitation must be reasonable.

8. Inspection under this Article is not to be regarded as a "condition precedent to the passing of title" so that risk until inspection remains on the seller. Under subsection (4) such an approach cannot be sustained. Issues between the buyer and seller are settled in this Article almost wholly by special provisions and not by the technical determination of the locus of the title. Thus "inspection as a condition to the passing of title" becomes a concept almost without meaning. However, in peculiar circumstances inspection may still have some of the consequences hitherto sought and obtained under that concept.

9. "Inspection" under this section has to do with the buyer's check-up on whether the seller's performance is in accordance with a contract previously made and is not to be confused with the "examination" of the goods or of a sample or model of them at the time of contracting which may affect the warranties involved in the contract.

§ 2-613 Casualty to Identified Goods.

Where the contract requires for its performance goods identified when the contract is made, and the goods suffer casualty without fault of either party before the risk of loss passes to the buyer, or in a proper case under a "no arrival, no sale" term (Section 2-324) then

(a) if the loss is total the contract is avoided; and

(b) if the loss is partial or the goods have so deteriorated as no longer to conform to the contract the buyer may nevertheless demand inspection and at his option either treat the contract as avoided or accept the goods with due allowance from the contract price for the deterioration or the deficiency in quantity but without further right against the seller.

OFFICIAL COMMENT

Purposes of Changes:

1. Where goods whose continued existence is presupposed by the agreement are destroyed without fault of either party, the buyer is relieved from his obligation but may at his option take the surviving goods at a fair adjustment. "Fault" is intended to include negligence and not merely wilful wrong. The buyer is expressly given the right to inspect the goods in order to determine whether he wishes to avoid the contract entirely or to take the goods with a price adjustment.

2. The section applies whether the goods were already destroyed at the time of contracting without the knowledge of either party or whether they are destroyed subsequently but before the risk of loss passes to the buyer. Where under the agreement, including of course usage of trade, the risk has passed to the buyer before the casualty, the section has no application. Beyond this, the essential question in determining whether the rules of this section are to be applied is whether the seller has or has not undertaken the responsibility for the continued existence of the goods in proper condition through the time of agreed or expected delivery.

3. The section on the term "no arrival, no sale" makes clear that delay in arrival, quite as much as physical change in the goods, gives the buyer the options set forth in this section.

§ 2-615 Excuse by Failure of Presupposed Conditions.

Except so far as a seller may have assumed a greater obligation and subject to the preceding section on substituted performance:

(a) Delay in delivery or non-delivery in whole or in part by a seller who complies with paragraphs (b) and (c) is not a breach of his duty under a contract for sale if performance as agreed has been made impracticable by the occurrence of a contingency the non-occurrence of which was a basic assumption on which the contract was made or by compliance in good faith with any applicable foreign or domestic governmental regulation or order whether or not it later proves to be invalid.

(b) Where the causes mentioned in paragraph (a) affect only a part of the seller's capacity to perform, he must allocate production and deliveries among his customers but may at his option include regular customers not then under contract as well as his own requirements for further manufacture. He may so allocate in any manner which is fair and reasonable.

364

(c) The seller must notify the buyer seasonably that there will be delay or non-delivery and, when allocation is required under paragraph (b), of the estimated quota thus made available for the buyer.

OFFICIAL COMMENT

Purposes:

1. This section excuses a seller from timely delivery of goods contracted for, where his performance has become commercially impracticable because of unforeseen supervening circumstances not within the contemplation of the parties at the time of contracting. The destruction of specific goods and the problem of the use of substituted performance on points other than delay or quantity, treated elsewhere in this Article, must be distinguished from the matter covered by this section.

2. The present section deliberately refrains from any effort at an exhaustive expression of contingencies and is to be interpreted in all cases sought to be brought within its scope in terms of its underlying reason and purpose.

3. The first test for excuse under this Article in terms of basic assumption is a familiar one. The additional test of commercial impracticability (as contrasted with "impossibility," "frustration of performance" or "frustration of the venture") has been adopted in order to call attention to the commercial character of the criterion chosen by this Article.

4. Increased cost alone does not excuse performance unless the rise in cost is due to some unforeseen contingency which alters the essential nature of the performance. Neither is a rise or a collapse in the market in itself a justification, for that is exactly the type of business risk which business contracts made at fixed prices are intended to cover. But a severe shortage of raw materials or of supplies due to a contingency such as war, embargo, local crop failure, unforeseen shutdown of major sources of supply or the like, which either causes a marked increase in cost or altogether prevents the seller from securing supplies necessary to his performance, is within the contemplation of this section. (See *Ford & Sons, Ltd., v. Henry Leetham & Sons, Ltd.*, 21 Com Cas 55 (1915, KBD)).

5. Where a particular source of supply is exclusive under the agreement and fails through casualty, the present section applies rather than the provision on destruction or deterioration of specific goods. The same holds true where a particular source of supply is shown by the circumstances to have been contemplated or assumed by the parties at the time of contracting. (See *Davis Co. v. Hoffman-La Roche Chemical Works*, 178 App Div 855, 166 NYS 179 (1917) and *International Paper Co. v. Rockefeller*, 161 App Div 180, 146 NYS 371 (1914)). There is no excuse under this section, however, unless the seller has employed all due measures to assure himself that his source will not fail. (See *Canadian Industrial Alcohol Co., Ltd. v. Dunbar*

Molasses Co., 258 NY 194, 179 NE 383, 80 ALR 1173 (1932) and *Washington Mfg. Co. v. Midland Lumber Co.*, 113 Wash 593, 194 P 777 (1921)).

In the case of failure of production by an agreed source for causes beyond the seller's control, the seller should, if possible, be excused since production by an agreed source is without more a basic assumption of the contract. Such excuse should not result in relieving the defaulting supplier from liability nor in dropping into the seller's lap an unearned bonus of damages over. The flexible adjustment machinery of this Article provides the solution under the provision on the obligation of good faith. A condition to his making good the claim of excuse is the turning over to the buyer of his rights against the defaulting source of supply to the extent of the buyer's contract in relation to which excuse is being claimed.

6. In situations in which neither sense nor justice is served by either answer when the issue is posed in flat terms of "excuse" or "no excuse," adjustment under the various provisions of this Article is necessary, especially the sections on good faith, on insecurity and assurance and on the reading of all provisions in the light of their purposes, and the general policy of this Act to use equitable principles in furtherance of commercial standards and good faith.

7. The failure of conditions which go to convenience or collateral values rather than to the commercial practicability of the main performance does not amount to a complete excuse. However, good faith and the reason of the present section and of the preceding one may properly be held to justify and even to require any needed delay involved in a good faith inquiry seeking a readjustment of the contract terms to meet the new conditions.

8. The provisions of this section are made subject to assumption of greater liability by agreement and such agreement is to be found not only in the expressed terms of the contract but in the circumstances surrounding the contracting, in trade usage and the like. Thus the exemptions of this section do not apply when the contingency in question is sufficiently foreshadowed at the time of contracting to be included among the business risks which are fairly to be regarded as part of the dickered terms, either consciously or as a matter of reasonable, commercial interpretation from the circumstances. (See *Madeirense Do Brasil, S.A. v. Stulman-Emrick Lumber Co.*, 147 F2d 399 (CCA, 2 Cir. 1945).) The exemption otherwise present through usage of trade under the present section may also be expressly negated by the language of the agreement. Generally, express agreements as to exemptions designed to enlarge upon or supplant the provisions of this section are to be read in the light of mercantile sense and reason, for this section itself sets up the commercial standard for normal and reasonable interpretation and provides a minimum beyond which agreement may not go.

Agreement can also be made in regard to the consequences of exemption as laid down in paragraphs (b) and (c) and the next section on procedure on notice claiming excuse.

9. The case of a farmer who has contracted to sell crops to be grown on designated land may be regarded as falling either within the section on casualty to identified goods or this section, and he may be excused, when there is a failure of the specific crop, either on the basis of the destruction of identified goods or because of the failure of a basic assumption of the contract.

Exemption of the buyer in the case of a "requirements" contract is covered by the "Output and Requirements" section both as to assumption and allocation of the relevant risks. But when a contract by a manufacturer to buy fuel or raw material makes no specific reference to a particular venture and no such reference may be drawn from the circumstances, commercial understanding views it as a general deal in the general market and not conditioned on any assumption of the continuing operation of the buyer's plant. Even when notice is given by the buyer that the supplies are needed to fill a specific contract of a normal commercial kind, commercial understanding does not see such a supply contract as conditioned on the continuance of the buyer's further contract for outlet. On the other hand, where the buyer's contract is in reasonable commercial understanding conditioned on a definite and specific venture or assumption as, for instance, a war procurement subcontract known to be based on a prime contract which is subject to termination, or a supply contract for a particular construction venture, the reason of the present section may well apply and entitle the buyer to the exemption.

10. Following its basic policy of using commercial practicability as a test for excuse, this section recognizes as of equal significance either a foreign or domestic regulation and disregards any technical distinctions between "law," "regulation," "order" and the like. Nor does it make the present action of the seller depend upon the eventual judicial determination of the legality of the particular governmental action. The seller's good faith belief in the validity of the regulation is the test under this Article and the best evidence of his good faith is the general commercial acceptance of the regulation. However, governmental interference cannot excuse unless it truly "supervenes" in such a manner as to be beyond the seller's assumption of risk. And any action by the party claiming excuse which causes or colludes in inducing the governmental action preventing his performance would be in breach of good faith and would destroy his exemption.

11. An excused seller must fulfill his contract to the extent which the supervening contingency permits, and if the situation is such that his customers are generally affected he must take account of all in supplying one. Subsections (a) and (b), therefore, explicitly permit in any proration a fair and reasonable attention to the needs of regular customers who are probably relying on spot orders for supplies. Customers at different stages of the manufacturing process may be fairly treated by including the seller's manufacturing requirements. A fortiori, the seller may also take account of contracts later in date than the one in question. The fact that such spot

orders may be closed at an advanced price causes no difficulty, since any allocation which exceeds normal past requirements will not be reasonable. However, good faith requires, when prices have advanced, that the seller exercise real care in making his allocations, and in case of doubt his contract customers should be favored and supplies prorated evenly among them regardless of price. Save for the extra care thus required by changes in the market, this section seeks to leave every reasonable business leeway to the seller.

§ 2-616 Procedure on Notice Claiming Excuse.

(1) Where the buyer receives notification of a material or indefinite delay or an allocation justified under the preceding section he may by written notification to the seller as to any delivery concerned, and where the prospective deficiency substantially impairs the value of the whole contract under the provisions of this Article relating to breach of installment contracts (Section 2-612), then also as to the whole,

    (a) terminate and thereby discharge any unexecuted portion of the contract; or

    (b) modify the contract by agreeing to take his available quota in substitution.

(2) If after receipt of such notification from the seller the buyer fails so to modify the contract within a reasonable time not exceeding thirty days the contract lapses with respect to any deliveries affected.

(3) The provisions of this section may not be negated by agreement except in so far as the seller has assumed a greater obligation under the preceding section.

OFFICIAL COMMENT

Purposes:

This section seeks to establish simple and workable machinery for providing certainty as to when a supervening and excusing contingency "excuses" the delay, "discharges" the contract, or may result in a waiver of the delay by the buyer. When the seller notifies, in accordance with the preceding section, claiming excuse, the buyer may acquiesce, in which case the contract is so modified. No consideration is necessary in a case of this kind to support such a modification. If the buyer does not elect so to modify the contract, he may terminate it and under subsection (2) his silence after receiving the seller's claim of excuse operates as such a termination. Subsection (3) denies effect to any contract clause made in advance of trouble which would require the buyer to stand ready to take delivery whenever the seller is excused from delivery by unforeseen circumstances.

§ 2-708 Seller's Damages for Non-acceptance or Repudiation.

(1) Subject to subsection (2) and to the provisions of this Article with respect to proof of market price (Section 2-723), the measure of damages for non-acceptance or repudiation by the buyer is the difference between the market price at the time and place for tender and the unpaid contract price together with any incidental damages provided in this Article (Section 2-710), but less expenses saved in consequence of the buyer's breach.

(2) If the measure of damages provided in subsection (1) is inadequate to put the seller in as good a position as performance would have done then the measure of damages is the profit (including reasonable overhead) which the seller would have made from full performance by the buyer, together with any incidental damages provided in this Article (Section 2-710), due allowance for costs reasonably incurred and due credit for payments or proceeds of resale.

OFFICIAL COMMENT

Purposes of Changes: To make it clear that:

1. The prior uniform statutory provision is followed generally in setting the current market price at the time and place for tender as the standard by which damages for non-acceptance are to be determined. The time and place of tender is determined by reference to the section on manner of tender of delivery, and to the sections on the effect of such terms as FOB, FAS, CIF, C&F, Ex Ship and No Arrival, No Sale.

   In the event that there is no evidence available of the current market price at the time and place of tender, proof of a substitute market may be made under the section on determination and proof of market price. Furthermore, the section on the admissibility of market quotations is intended to ease materially the problem of providing competent evidence.

2. The provision of this section permitting recovery of expected profit including reasonable overhead where the standard measure of damages is inadequate, together with the new requirement that price actions may be sustained only where resale is impractical, are designed to eliminate the unfair and economically wasteful results arising under the older law when fixed price articles were involved. This section permits the recovery of lost profits in all appropriate cases, which would include all standard priced goods. The normal measure there would be list price less cost to the dealer or list price less manufacturing cost to the manufacturer. It is not necessary to a recovery of "profit" to show a history of earnings, especially if a new venture is involved.

3. In all cases the seller may recover incidental damages.

§ 2-713 Buyer's Damages for Non-Delivery or Repudiation.

(1) Subject to the provisions of this Article with respect to proof of market price (Section 2-723), the measure of damages for non-delivery or repudiation by the seller is the difference between the market price at the time when the buyer learned of the breach and the contract price together with any incidental and consequential damages provided in this Article (Section 2-715), but less expenses saved in consequence of the seller's breach.

(2) Market price is to be determined as of the place for tender or, in cases of rejection after arrival or revocation of acceptance, as of the place of arrival.

OFFICIAL COMMENT

Purposes of Changes: To clarify the former rule so that:

1. The general baseline adopted in this section uses as a yardstick the market in which the buyer would have obtained cover had he sought that relief. So the place for measuring damages is the place of tender (or the place of arrival if the goods are rejected or their acceptance is revoked after reaching their destination) and the crucial time is the time at which the buyer learns of the breach.

2. The market or current price to be used in comparison with the contract price under this section is the price for goods of the same kind and in the same branch of trade.

3. When the current market price under this section is difficult to prove the section on determination and proof of market price is available to permit a showing of a comparable market price or, where no market price is available, evidence of spot sale prices is proper. Where the unavailability of a market price is caused by a scarcity of goods of the type involved, a good case is normally made for specific performance under this Article. Such scarcity conditions, moreover, indicate that the price has risen and under the section providing for liberal administration of remedies, opinion evidence as to the value of the goods would be admissible in the absence of a market price and a liberal construction of allowable consequential damages should also result.

4. This section carries forward the standard rule that the buyer must deduct from his damages any expenses saved as a result of the breach.

5. The present section provides a remedy which is completely alternative to cover under the preceding section and applies only when and to the extent that the buyer has not covered.

§ 2-714 Buyer's Damages for Breach in Regard to Accepted Goods.

(1) Where the buyer has accepted goods and given notification (subsection (3) of Section 2-607) he may recover as damages for any non-conformity of

tender the loss resulting in the ordinary course of events from the seller's breach as determined in any manner which is reasonable.

(2) The measure of damages for breach of warranty is the difference at the time and place of acceptance between the value of the goods accepted and the value they would have had if they had been as warranted, unless special circumstances show proximate damages of a different amount.

(3) In a proper case any incidental and consequential damages under the next section may also be recovered.

OFFICIAL COMMENT

Purposes of Changes:

1. This section deals with the remedies available to the buyer after the goods have been accepted and the time for revocation of acceptance has gone by. In general this section adopts the rule of the prior uniform statutory provision for measuring damages where there has been a breach of warranty as to goods accepted, but goes further to lay down an explicit provision as to the time and place for determining the loss.

    The section on deduction of damages from price provides an additional remedy for a buyer who still owes part of the purchase price, and frequently the two remedies will be available concurrently. The buyer's failure to notify of his claim under the section on effects of acceptance, however, operates to bar his remedies under either that section or the present section.

2. The "non-conformity" referred to in subsection (1) includes not only breaches of warranties but also any failure of the seller to perform according to his obligations under the contract. In the case of such non-conformity, the buyer is permitted to recover for his loss "in any manner which is reasonable."

3. Subsection (2) describes the usual, standard and reasonable method of ascertaining damages in the case of breach of warranty but it is not intended as an exclusive measure. It departs from the measure of damages for non-delivery in utilizing the place of acceptance rather than the place of tender. In some cases the two may coincide, as where the buyer signifies his acceptance upon the tender. If, however, the non-conformity is such as would justify revocation of acceptance, the time and place of acceptance under this section is determined as of the buyer's decision not to revoke.

4. The incidental and consequential damages referred to in subsection (3), which will usually accompany an action brought under this section, are discussed in detail in the comment on the next section.

§ 2-715 Buyer's Incidental and Consequential Damages.

(1) Incidental damages resulting from the seller's breach include expenses reasonably incurred in inspection, receipt, transportation and care and custody of goods rightfully rejected, any commercially reasonable charges, expenses or commissions in connection with effecting cover and any other reasonable expense incident to the delay or other breach.

(2) Consequential damages resulting from the seller's breach include

    (a) any loss resulting from general or particular requirements and needs of which the seller at the time of contracting had reason to know and which could not reasonably be prevented by cover or otherwise; and

    (b) injury to person or property proximately resulting from any breach of warranty.

OFFICIAL COMMENT

Purposes of Changes and New Matter:

1. Subsection (1) is intended to provide reimbursement for the buyer who incurs reasonable expenses in connection with the handling of rightfully rejected goods or goods whose acceptance may be justifiably revoked, or in connection with effecting cover where the breach of the contract lies in non-conformity or non-delivery of the goods. The incidental damages listed are not intended to be exhaustive but are merely illustrative of the typical kinds of incidental damage.

2. Subsection (2) operates to allow the buyer, in an appropriate case, any consequential damages which are the result of the seller's breach. The "tacit agreement" test for the recovery of consequential damages is rejected. Although the older rule at common law which made the seller liable for all consequential damages of which he had "reason to know" in advance is followed, the liberality of that rule is modified by refusing to permit recovery unless the buyer could not reasonably have prevented the loss by cover or otherwise. Subparagraph (2) carries forward the provisions of the prior uniform statutory provision as to consequential damages resulting from breach of warranty, but modifies the rule by requiring first that the buyer attempt to minimize his damages in good faith, either by cover or otherwise.

3. In the absence of excuse under the section on merchant's excuse by failure of presupposed conditions, the seller is liable for consequential damages in all cases where he had reason to know of the buyer's general or particular requirements at the time of contracting. It is not necessary that there be a conscious acceptance of an insurer's liability on the seller's part, nor is his obligation for consequential damages limited to cases in which he fails to use due effort in good faith.

Particular needs of the buyer must generally be made known to the seller while general needs must rarely be made known to charge the seller with knowledge.

Any seller who does not wish to take the risk of consequential damages has available the section on contractual limitation on remedy.

4. The burden of proving the extent of loss incurred by way of consequential damage is on the buyer, but the section on liberal administration of remedies rejects any doctrine of certainty which requires almost mathematical precision in the proof of loss. Loss may be determined in any manner which is reasonable under the circumstances.

5. Subsection (2)(b) states the usual rule as to breach of warranty, allowing recovery for injuries "proximately" resulting from the breach. Where the injury involved follows the use of goods without discovery of the defect causing the damage, the question of "proximate" cause turns on whether it was reasonable for the buyer to use the goods without such inspection as would have revealed the defect. If it was not reasonable for him to do so, or if he did in fact discover the defect prior to his use, the injury would not proximately result from the breach of warranty.

6. In the case of sale of wares to one in the business of reselling them, resale is one of the requirements of which the seller has reason to know within the meaning of subsection (2)(a).

2-719 Contractual Modification or Limitation of Remedy.

(1) Subject to the provisions of subsections (2) and (3) of this section and of the preceding section on liquidation and limitation of damages,

   (a) the agreement may provide for remedies in addition to or in substitution for those provided in this Article and may limit or alter the measure of damages recoverable under this Article, as by limiting the buyer's remedies to return of the goods and repayment of the price or to repair and replacement of non-conforming goods or parts; and

   (b) resort to a remedy as provided is optional unless the remedy is expressly agreed to be exclusive, in which case it is the sole remedy.

(2) Where circumstances cause an exclusive or limited remedy to fail of its essential purpose, remedy may be had as provided in this Act.

(3) Consequential damages may be limited or excluded unless the limitation or exclusion is unconscionable. Limitation of consequential damages for injury to the person in the case of consumer goods is prima facie unconscionable but limitation of damages where the loss is commercial is not.

Purposes:

1. Under this section parties are left free to shape their remedies to their particular requirements and reasonable agreements limiting or modifying remedies are to be given effect.

   However, it is of the very essence of a sales contract that at least minimum adequate remedies be available. If the parties intend to conclude a contract for sale within this Article they must accept the legal consequence that there be at least a fair quantum of remedy for breach of the obligations or duties outlined in the contract. Thus any clause purporting to modify or limit the remedial provisions of this Article in an unconscionable manner is subject to deletion and in that event the remedies made available by this Article are applicable as if the stricken clause had never existed. Similarly, under subsection (2), where an apparently fair and reasonable clause because of circumstances fails in its purpose or operates to deprive either party of the substantial value of the bargain, it must give way to the general remedy provisions of this Article.

2. Subsection (1)(b) creates a presumption that clauses prescribing remedies are cumulative rather than exclusive. If the parties intend the term to describe the sole remedy under the contract, this must be clearly expressed.

3. Subsection (3) recognizes the validity of clauses limiting or excluding consequential damages but makes it clear that they may not operate in an unconscionable manner. Actually such terms are merely an allocation of unknown or undeterminable risks. The seller in all cases is free to disclaim warranties in the manner provided in Section 2-316.

§ 3-301 Rights of a Holder.

The holder of an instrument whether or not he is the owner may transfer or negotiate it and, except as otherwise provided in Section 3-603 on payment or satisfaction, discharge it or enforce payment in his own name.

OFFICIAL COMMENT

Purposes of Changes: The section is revised to state in one provision all the rights of a holder, and to make it clear that every holder has such rights. The only limitations are those found in Section 3-603 on payment or satisfaction. That section provides (with stated exceptions) that payment to a holder discharges the liability of the party paying even though made with knowledge of a claim of another person to the instrument, unless the adverse claimant posts indemnity or procures the issuance of appropriate legal process restraining the payment. Thus payment to a holder in an adverse claim situation would not give discharge if the adverse claimant had followed either of the procedures provided for in the "unless" clause of Section 3-603; nor would a discharge result from payment in two other specific situations described in Section 3-603.

§ 3-302 Holder in Due Course.

(1) A holder in due course is a holder who takes the instrument
    (a) for value; and
    (b) in good faith; and
    (c) without notice that it is overdue or has been dishonored or of any defense against or claim to it on the part of any person.
(2) A payee may be a holder in due course.
(3) A holder does not become a holder in due course of an instrument:
    (a) by purchase of it at judicial sale or by taking it under legal process; or
    (b) by acquiring it in taking over an estate; or
    (c) by purchasing it as part of a bulk transaction not in regular course of business of the transferor.
(4) A purchaser of a limited interest can be a holder in due course only to the extent of the interest purchased.

OFFICIAL COMMENT

Purposes of Changes and New Matter: The changes are intended to remove uncertainties arising under the original section.

1. The language "without notice that it is overdue" is substituted for that of the original subsection (2) in order to make it clear that the purchaser of an instrument which is in fact overdue may be a holder in due course if he takes it without notice that it is overdue. Such notice is covered by the section on notice to purchaser (Section 3-304).

2. Subsection (2) is intended to settle the long continued conflict over the status of the payee as a holder in due course. This conflict has turned very largely upon the word "negotiated" in the original Section 52(4), which is now eliminated. The position here taken is that the payee may become a holder in due course to the same extent and under the same circumstances as any other holder. This is true whether he takes the instrument by purchase from a third person or directly from the obligor. All that is necessary is that the payee meet the requirements of this section. In the following cases, among others, the payee is a holder in due course:
   a. A remitter, purchasing goods from P, obtains a bank draft payable to P and forwards it to P, who takes it for value, in good faith and without notice as required by this section.
   b. The remitter buys the bank draft payable to P, but it is forwarded by the bank directly to P, who takes it in good faith and without notice in payment of the remitter's obligation to him.
   c. A and B sign a note as co-makers. A induces B to sign by fraud, and without authority from B delivers the note to P, who takes it for value, in good faith and without notice.

    d. A defrauds the maker into signing an instrument payable to P. P pays A for it in good faith and without notice, and the maker delivers the instrument directly to P.

    e. D draws a check payable to P and gives it to his agent to be delivered to P in payment of D's debt. The agent delivers it to P, who takes it in good faith and without notice in payment of the agent's debt to P. But as to this case see Section 3-304(2), which may apply.

    f. D draws a check payable to P but blank as to the amount, and gives it to his agent to be delivered to P. The agent fills in the check with an excessive amount, and P takes it for value, in good faith and without notice.

    g. D draws a check blank as to the name of the payee, and gives it to his agent to be filled in with the name of A and delivered to A. The agent fills in the name of P, and P takes the check in good faith, for value and without notice.

3. Subsection (3) is intended to state existing case law. It covers a few situations in which the purchaser takes the instrument under unusual circumstances which indicate that he is merely a successor in interest to the prior holder and can acquire no better rights. (If such prior holder was himself a holder in due course, the purchaser succeeds to that status under Section 3-201 on Transfer.) The provision applies to a purchaser at an execution sale, a sale in bankruptcy or a sale by a state bank commissioner of the assets of an insolvent bank. It applies equally to an attaching creditor or any other person who acquires the instrument by legal process, even under an antecedent claim; and equally to a representative, such as an executor, administrator, receiver or assignee for the benefit of creditors, who takes over the instrument as part of an estate, even though he is representing antecedent creditors.

    Subsection (3)(c) applies to bulk purchases lying outside of the ordinary course of business of the seller. It applies, for example, when a new partnership takes over for value all of the assets of an old one after a new member has entered the firm, or to a reorganized or consolidated corporation taking over in bulk the assets of a predecessor. It has particular application to the purchase by one bank of a substantial part of the paper held by another bank which is threatened with insolvency and seeking to liquidate its assets.

4. A purchaser of a limited interest—as a pledgee in a security transaction—may become a holder in due course, but he may enforce the instrument over defenses only to the extent of his interest, and defenses good against the pledgor remain available insofar as the pledgor retains an equity in the instrument. This is merely a special application of the general rule (Section 1-201) that a purchaser of a limited interest acquires rights only to the extent of the interest purchased. Section 27 of the original Act contained a similar provision.

§ 3-307 Burden of Establishing Signatures, Defenses and Due Course.

(1) Unless specifically denied in the pleadings each signature on an instrument is admitted. When the effectiveness of a signature is put in issue
   (a) the burden of establishing it is on the party claiming under the signature; but
   (b) the signature is presumed to be genuine or authorized except where the action is to enforce the obligation of a purported signer who has died or become incompetent before proof is required.

(2) When signatures are admitted or established, production of the instrument entitles a holder to recover on it unless the defendant establishes a defense.

(3) After it is shown that a defense exists a person claiming the rights of a holder in due course has the burden of establishing that he or some person under whom he claims is in all respects a holder in due course.

OFFICIAL COMMENT

Purposes of Changes and New Matter:

1. Subsection (1) is new, although similar provisions are found in a number of states. The purpose of the requirement of a specific denial in the pleadings is to give the plaintiff notice that he must meet a claim of forgery or lack of authority as to the particular signature, and to afford him an opportunity to investigate and obtain evidence. Where local rules of pleading permit, the denial may be on information and belief, or it may be a denial of knowledge or information sufficient to form a belief. It need not be under oath unless the local statutes or rules require verification. In the absence of such specific denial the signature stands admitted, and is not in issue. Nothing in this section is intended, however, to prevent amendment of the pleading in a proper case.

   The question of the burden of establishing the signature arises only when it has been put in issue by specific denial. "Burden of establishing" is defined in the definitions section of this Act (Section 1-201). The burden is on the party claiming under the signature, but he is aided by the presumption that it is genuine or authorized stated in paragraph (b). "Presumption" is also defined in this Act (Section 1-201). It means that until some evidence is introduced which would support a finding that the signature is forged or unauthorized the plaintiff is not required to prove that it is authentic. The presumption rests upon the fact that in ordinary experience forged or unauthorized signatures are very uncommon, and normally any evidence is within the control of the defendant or more accessible to him. He is therefore required to make some sufficient showing of the grounds for his denial before the plaintiff is put to his proof. His evidence need not be sufficient to require a directed verdict in his favor, but it must be enough to support his denial by permitting a finding in his favor. Until he introduces such evidence the presumption requires a finding for the plaintiff. Once such evidence is introduced the burden of establishing the signature by a preponderance of the total evidence is on the plaintiff.

Under paragraph (b) this presumption does not arise where the action is to enforce the obligation of a purported signer who has died or become incompetent before the evidence is required, and so is disabled from obtaining or introducing it. "Action" of course includes a claim asserted against the estate of a deceased or an incompetent.

2. Subsection (2) is substituted for the first clause of the original Section 59. Once signatures are proved or admitted, a holder makes out his case by mere production of the instrument, and is entitled to recover in the absence of any further evidence. The defendant has the burden of establishing any and all defenses, not only in the first instance but by a preponderance of the total evidence. The provision applies only to a holder, as defined in this Act (Section 1-201). Any other person in possession of an instrument must prove his right to it and account for the absence of any necessary indorsement. If he establishes a transfer which gives him the rights of a holder (Section 3-201), this provision becomes applicable, and he is then entitled to recover unless the defendant establishes a defense.

3. Subsection (3) rephrases the last clause of the first sentence of the original Section 59. Until it is shown that a defense exists the issue as to whether the holder is a holder in due course does not arise. In the absence of a defense any holder is entitled to recover and there is no occasion to say that he is deemed prima facie to be a holder in due course. When it is shown that a defense exists the plaintiff may, if he so elects, seek to cut off the defense by establishing that he is himself a holder in due course, or that he has acquired the rights of a prior holder in due course (Section 3-201). On this issue he has the full burden of proof by a preponderance of the total evidence. "In all respects" means that he must sustain this burden by affirmative proof that the instrument was taken for value, that it was taken in good faith, and that it was taken without notice (Section 3-302).

Nothing in this section is intended to say that the plaintiff must necessarily prove that he is a holder in due course. He may elect to introduce no further evidence, in which case a verdict may be directed for the plaintiff or the defendant, or the issue of the defense may be left to the jury, according to the weight and sufficiency of the defendant's evidence. He may elect to rebut the defense itself by proof to the contrary, in which case again a verdict may be directed for either party or the issue may be for the jury. This subsection means only that if the plaintiff claims the rights of a holder in due course against the defense he has the burden of proof upon that issue.

§ 3-301 Person Entitled To Enforce Instrument.

"Person entitled to enforce" an instrument means (i) the holder of the instrument, (ii) a nonholder in possession of the instrument who has the rights of a holder, or (iii) a person not in possession of the instrument who is entitled to enforce the instrument pursuant to Section 3-309 or 3-418(d). A person may be a person entitled to enforce the instrument even though the person is not the owner of the instrument or is in wrongful possession of the instrument.

OFFICIAL COMMENT

This section replaces former Section 3-301 that stated the rights of a holder. The rights stated in former Section 3-301 to transfer, negotiate, enforce, or discharge an instrument are stated in other sections of Article 3. In revised Article 3, Section 3-301 defines "person entitled to enforce" an instrument. The definition recognizes that enforcement is not limited to holders. The quoted phrase includes a person enforcing a lost or stolen instrument. Section 3-309. It also includes a person in possession of an instrument who is not a holder. A nonholder in possession of an instrument includes a person that acquired rights of a holder by subrogation or under Section 3-203(a). It also includes any other person who under applicable law is a successor to the holder or otherwise acquires the holder's rights.

§ 3-302 Holder in Due Course.

(a) Subject to subsection (c) and Section 3-106(d), "holder in due course" means the holder of an instrument if:
  (1) the instrument when issued or negotiated to the holder does not bear such apparent evidence of forgery or alteration or is not otherwise so irregular or incomplete as to call into question its authenticity; and
  (2) the holder took the instrument (i) for value, (ii) in good faith, (iii) without notice that the instrument is overdue or has been dishonored or that there is an uncured default with respect to payment of another instrument issued as part of the same series, (iv) without notice that the instrument contains an unauthorized signature or has been altered, (v) without notice of any claim to the instrument described in Section 3-306, and (vi) without notice that any party has a defense or claim in recoupment described in Section 3-305(a).
(b) Notice of discharge of a party, other than discharge in an insolvency proceeding, is not notice of a defense under subsection (a), but discharge is effective against a person who became a holder in due course with notice of the discharge. Public filing or recording of a document does not of itself constitute notice of a defense, claim in recoupment, or claim to the instrument.
(c) Except to the extent a transferor or predecessor in interest has rights as a holder in due course, a person does not acquire rights of a holder in due

course of an instrument taken (i) by legal process or by purchase in an execution, bankruptcy, or creditor's sale or similar proceeding, (ii) by purchase as part of a bulk transaction not in ordinary course of business of the transferor, or (iii) as the successor in interest to an estate or other organization.

(d) If, under Section 3-303(a)(1), the promise of performance that is the consideration for an instrument has been partially performed, the holder may assert rights as a holder in due course of the instrument only to the fraction of the amount payable under the instrument equal to the value of the partial performance divided by the value of the promised performance.

(e) If (i) the person entitled to enforce an instrument has only a security interest in the instrument and (ii) the person obliged to pay the instrument has a defense, claim in recoupment, or claim to the instrument that may be asserted against the person who granted the security interest, the person entitled to enforce the instrument may assert rights as a holder in due course only to an amount payable under the instrument which, at the time of enforcement of the instrument, does not exceed the amount of the unpaid obligation secured.

(f) To be effective, notice must be received at a time and in a manner that gives a reasonable opportunity to act on it.

(g) This section is subject to any law limiting status as a holder in due course in particular classes of transactions.

OFFICIAL COMMENT

1. Subsection (a)(1) is a return to the N.I.L. rule that the taker of an irregular or incomplete instrument is not a person the law should protect against defenses of the obligor or claims of prior owners. This reflects a policy choice against extending the holder in due course doctrine to an instrument that is so incomplete or irregular "as to call into question its authenticity." The term "authenticity" is used to make it clear that the irregularity or incompleteness must indicate that the instrument may not be what it purports to be. Persons who purchase or pay such instruments should do so at their own risk. Under subsection (1) of former Section 3-304, irregularity or incompleteness gave a purchaser notice of a claim or defense. But it was not clear from that provision whether the claim or defense had to be related to the irregularity or incomplete aspect of the instrument. This ambiguity is not present in subsection (a)(1).

2. Subsection (a)(2) restates subsection (1) of former Section 3-302. Section 3-305(a) makes a distinction between defenses to the obligation to pay an instrument and claims in recoupment by the maker or drawer that may be asserted to reduce the amount payable on the instrument. Because of this distinction, which was not made in former Article 3, the reference in subsection (a)(2)(vi) is to both a defense and a claim in recoupment. Notice

of forgery or alteration is stated separately because forgery and alteration are not technically defenses under subsection (a) of Section 3-305.

3. Discharge is also separately treated in the first sentence of subsection (b). Except for discharge in an insolvency proceeding, which is specifically stated to be a real defense in Section 3-305(a)(1), discharge is not expressed in Article 3 as a defense and is not included in Section 3-305(a)(2). Discharge is effective against anybody except a person having rights of a holder in due course who took the instrument without notice of the discharge. Notice of discharge does not disqualify a person from becoming a holder in due course. For example, a check certified after it is negotiated by the payee may subsequently be negotiated to a holder. If the holder had notice that the certification occurred after negotiation by the payee, the holder necessarily had notice of the discharge of the payee as indorser. Section 3-415(d). Notice of that discharge does not prevent the holder from becoming a holder in due course, but the discharge is effective against the holder. Section 3-601(b). Notice of a defense under Section 3-305(a)(1) of a maker, drawer or acceptor based on a bankruptcy discharge is different. There is no reason to give holder in due course status to a person with notice of that defense. The second sentence of subsection (b) is from former Section 3-304(5).

4. Professor Britton in his treatise Bills and Notes 309 (1961) stated: "A substantial number of decisions before the [N.I.L.] indicates that at common law there was nothing in the position of the payee as such which made it impossible for him to be a holder in due course." The courts were divided, however, about whether the payee of an instrument could be a holder in due course under the N.I.L. Some courts read N.I.L. § 52(4) to mean that a person could be a holder in due course only if the instrument was "negotiated" to that person. N.I.L. § 30 stated that "an instrument is negotiated when it is transferred from one person to another in such manner as to constitute the transferee the holder thereof." Normally, an instrument is "issued" to the payee; it is not transferred to the payee. N.I.L. § 191 defined "issue" as the "first delivery of the instrument . . . to a person who takes it as a holder." Thus, some courts concluded that the payee never could be a holder in due course. Other courts concluded that there was no evidence that the N.I.L. was intended to change the common law rule that the payee could be a holder in due course. Professor Britton states on p.318: "The typical situations which raise the [issue] are those where the defense of a maker is interposed because of fraud by a [maker who is] principal debtor . . . against a surety co-maker, or where the defense of fraud by a purchasing remitter is interposed by the drawer of the instrument against the good faith purchasing payee."

Former Section 3-302(2) stated: "A payee may be a holder in due course." This provision was intended to resolve the split of authority under the N.I.L. It made clear that there was no intent to change the common-law rule that allowed a payee to become a holder in due course. See Comment

2 to former Section 3-302. But there was no need to put subsection (2) in former Section 3-302 because the split in authority under the N.I.L. was caused by the particular wording of N.I.L. § 52(4). The troublesome language in that section was not repeated in former Article 3 nor is it repeated in revised Article 3. Former Section 3-302(2) has been omitted in revised Article 3 because it is surplusage and may be misleading. The payee of an instrument can be a holder in due course, but use of the holder-in-due-course doctrine by the payee of an instrument is not the normal situation.

The primary importance of the concept of holder in due course is with respect to assertion of defenses or claims in recoupment (Section 3-305) and of claims to the instrument (Section 3-306). The holder-in-due-course doctrine assumes the following case as typical. Obligor issues a note or check to Obligee. Obligor is the maker of the note or drawer of the check. Obligee is the payee. Obligor has some defense to Obligor's obligation to pay the instrument. For example,

> Obligor issued the instrument for goods that Obligee promised to deliver. Obligee never delivered the goods. The failure of Obligee to deliver the goods is a defense. Section 3-303(b). Although Obligor has a defense against Obligee, if the instrument is negotiated to Holder and the requirements of subsection (a) are met, Holder may enforce the instrument against Obligor free of the defense. Section 3-305(b). In the typical case the holder in due course is not the payee of the instrument. Rather, the holder in due course is an immediate or remote transferee of the payee. If Obligor in our example is the only obligor on the check or note, the holder-in-due-course doctrine is irrelevant in determining rights between Obligor and Obligee with respect to the instrument.

But in a small percentage of cases it is appropriate to allow the payee of an instrument to assert rights as a holder in due course. The cases are like those referred to in the quotation from Professor Britton referred to above, or other cases in which conduct of some third party is the basis of the defense of the issuer of the instrument. The following are examples:

Case No. 1. Buyer pays for goods bought from Seller by giving to Seller a cashier's check bought from Bank. Bank has a defense to its obligation to pay the check because Buyer bought the check from Bank with a check known to be drawn on an account with insufficient funds to cover the check. If Bank issued the check to Buyer as payee and Buyer indorsed it over to Seller, it is clear that Seller can be a holder in due course taking free of the defense if Seller had no notice of the defense. Seller is a transferee of the check. There is no good reason why Seller's position should be any different if Bank drew the check to the order of Seller as payee. In that case, when Buyer took delivery of the check from Bank, Buyer became the owner of the check even though Buyer was not the holder. Buyer was a remitter. Section 3-103(a)(11). At that point nobody was the holder. When Buyer delivered the check to Seller, ownership of the check was transferred to Seller who also became the holder. This is a negotiation. Section 3-201. The rights of Seller should not be affected by the fact that in one case the negotiation to Seller was by a holder and in the other case the negotiation was by a remitter. Moreover, it should be irrelevant whether Bank delivered the check to Buyer and Buyer delivered it to Seller or whether Bank delivered it directly to Seller. In either case Seller can be a holder in due course that takes free of Bank's defense.

Case No. 2. X fraudulently induces Y to join X in a spurious venture to purchase a business. The purchase is to be financed by a bank loan for part of the price. Bank lends money to X and Y by deposit in a joint account of X and Y who sign a note payable to Bank for the amount of the loan. X then withdraws the money from the joint account and absconds. Bank acted in good faith and without notice of the fraud of X against Y. Bank is payee of the note executed by Y, but its right to enforce the note against Y should not be affected by the fact that Y was induced to execute the note by the fraud of X. Bank can be a holder in due course that takes free of the defense of Y. Case No. 2 is similar to Case No. 1. In each case the payee of the instrument has given value to the person committing the fraud in exchange for the obligation of the person against whom the fraud was committed. In each case the payee was not party to the fraud and had no notice of it.

Suppose in Case No. 2 that the note does not meet the requirements of Section 3-104(a) and thus is not a negotiable instrument covered by Article 3. In that case, Bank cannot be a holder in due course but the result should be the same. Bank's rights are determined by general principles of contract law.

Restatement Second, Contracts § 164(2) governs the case. If Y is induced to enter into a contract with Bank by a fraudulent misrepresentation by X, the contract is voidable by Y unless Bank "in good faith and without reason to know of the misrepresentation either gives value or relies materially on the transaction." Comment e to § 164(2) states:

> "This is the same principle that protects an innocent person who purchases goods or commercial paper in good faith, without notice and for value from one who obtained them from the original owner by a misrepresentation. See Uniform Commercial Code §§ 2-403(1), 3-305. In the cases that fall within [§ 164(2)], however, the innocent person deals directly with the recipient of the misrepresentation, which is made by one not a party to the contract."

The same result follows in Case No. 2 if Y had been induced to sign the note as an accommodation party (Section 3-419). If Y signs as co-maker of a note for the benefit of X, Y is a surety with respect to the obligation of X to pay the note but is liable as maker of the note to pay Bank. Section 3-419(b). If Bank is a holder in due course, the fraud of X cannot be asserted against Bank under Section 3-305(b). But the result is the same without resort to holder-in-due-course doctrine. If the note is not a negotiable instrument governed by Article 3, general rules of suretyship apply. Restatement, Security § 119 states that the surety (Y) cannot assert a defense against the creditor (Bank) based on the fraud of the principal (X) if the creditor "without knowledge of the fraud . . . extended credit to the principal on the security of the surety's promise . . . ." The underlying principle of § 119 is the same as that of § 164(2) of Restatement Second, Contracts.

Case No. 3. Corporation draws a check payable to Bank. The check is given to an officer of Corporation who is instructed to deliver it to Bank in payment of a debt owed by Corporation to Bank. Instead, the officer, intending to defraud Corporation, delivers the check to Bank in payment of the officer's personal debt, or the check is delivered to Bank for deposit to the officer's personal account. If Bank obtains payment of the check, Bank has received funds of Corporation which have been used for the personal benefit of the officer. Corporation in this case will assert a claim to the proceeds of the check against Bank. If Bank was a holder in due course of the check it took the check free of Corporation's claim. Section 3-306. The issue in this case is whether Bank had notice of the claim when it took the check. If Bank knew that the officer was a fiduciary with respect to the check, the issue is governed by Section 3-307.

Case No. 4. Employer, who owed money to X, signed a blank check and delivered it to Secretary with instructions to complete the check by typing in X's name and the amount owed to X. Secretary fraudulently completed the check by typing in the name of Y, a creditor to whom Secretary owed money. Secretary then delivered the check to Y in payment of Secretary's debt. Y obtained payment of the check. This case is similar to Case No. 3. Since Secretary was authorized to complete the check, Employer is bound by Secretary's act in making the check payable to Y. The drawee bank properly paid the check. Y received funds of Employer which were used for the personal benefit of Secretary. Employer asserts a claim to these funds against Y. If Y is a holder in due course, Y takes free of the claim. Whether Y is a holder in due course depends upon whether Y had notice of Employer's claim.

5. Subsection (c) is based on former Section 3-302(3). Like former Section 3-302(3), subsection (c) is intended to state existing case law. It covers a few situations in which the purchaser takes an instrument under unusual circumstances. The purchaser is treated as a successor in interest to the prior holder and can acquire no better rights. But if the prior holder was a holder in due course, the purchaser obtains rights of a holder in due course.

Subsection (c) applies to a purchaser in an execution sale or sale in bankruptcy. It applies equally to an attaching creditor or any other person who acquires the instrument by legal process or to a representative, such as an executor, administrator, receiver or assignee for the benefit of creditors, who takes the instrument as part of an estate. Subsection (c) applies to bulk purchases lying outside of the ordinary course of business of the seller. For example, it applies to the purchase by one bank of a substantial part of the paper held by another bank which is threatened with insolvency and seeking to liquidate its assets. Subsection (c) would also apply when a new partnership takes over for value all of the assets of an old one after a new member has entered the firm, or to a reorganized or consolidated corporation taking over the assets of a predecessor.

In the absence of controlling state law to the contrary, subsection (c) applies to a sale by a state bank commissioner of the assets of an insolvent bank. However, subsection (c) may be preempted by federal law if the Federal Deposit Insurance Corporation takes over an insolvent bank. Under the governing federal law, the FDIC and similar financial institution insurers are given holder in due course status and that status is also acquired by their assignees under the shelter doctrine.

6. Subsection (d) and (e) clarify two matters not specifically addressed by former Article 3:

Case No. 5. Payee negotiates a $1,000 note to Holder who agrees to pay $900 for it. After paying $500, Holder learns that Payee defrauded Maker in the transaction giving rise to the note. Under subsection (d) Holder may assert rights as a holder in due course to the extent of $555.55 ($500/$900 = .555 x $1,000 = $555.55). This formula rewards Holder with a ratable portion of the bargained for profit.

Case No. 6. Payee negotiates a note of Maker for $1,000 to Holder as security for payment of Payee's debt to Holder of $600. Maker has a defense which is good against Payee but of which Holder has no notice. Subsection (e) applies. Holder may assert rights as a holder in due course only to the extent of $600. Payee does not get the benefit of the holder-in-due-course status of Holder. With respect to $400 of the note, Maker may assert any rights that Maker has against Payee. A different result follows if the payee of a note negotiated it to a person who took it as a holder in due course and that person pledged the note as security for a debt. Because the defense cannot be asserted against the pledgor, the pledgee can assert rights as a holder in due course for the full amount of the note for the benefit of both the pledgor and the pledgee.

7. There is a large body of state statutory and case law restricting the use of the holder in due course doctrine in consumer transactions as well as some business transactions that raise similar issues. Subsection (g) subordinates Article 3 to that law and any other similar law that may evolve in the future. Section 3-106(d) also relates to statutory or administrative law intended to restrict use of the holder-in-due-course doctrine. See Comment 3 to Section 3-106.

§ 3-307 Notice of Breach of Fiduciary Duty.

(a) In this section:
   (1) "Fiduciary" means an agent, trustee, partner, corporate officer or director, or other representative owing a fiduciary duty with respect to an instrument.
   (2) "Represented person" means the principal, beneficiary, partnership, corporation, or other person to whom the duty stated in paragraph (1) is owed.

(b) If (i) an instrument is taken from a fiduciary for payment or collection or for value, (ii) the taker has knowledge of the fiduciary status of the fiduciary, and (iii) the represented person makes a claim to the instrument or its proceeds on the basis that the transaction of the fiduciary is a breach of fiduciary duty, the following rules apply:

(1) Notice of breach of fiduciary duty by the fiduciary is notice of the claim of the represented person.

(2) In the case of an instrument payable to the represented person or the fiduciary as such, the taker has notice of the breach of fiduciary duty if the instrument is (i) taken in payment of or as security for a debt known by the taker to be the personal debt of the fiduciary, (ii) taken in a transaction known by the taker to be for the personal benefit of the fiduciary, or (iii) deposited to an account other than an account of the fiduciary, as such, or an account of the represented person.

(3) If an instrument is issued by the represented person or the fiduciary as such, and made payable to the fiduciary personally, the taker does not have notice of the breach of fiduciary duty unless the taker knows of the breach of fiduciary duty.

(4) If an instrument is issued by the represented person or the fiduciary as such, to the taker as payee, the taker has notice of the breach of fiduciary duty if the instrument is (i) taken in payment of or as security for a debt known by the taker to be the personal debt of the fiduciary, (ii) taken in a transaction known by the taker to be for the personal benefit of the fiduciary, or (iii) deposited to an account other than an account of the fiduciary, as such, or an account of the represented person.

OFFICIAL COMMENT

1. This section states rules for determining when a person who has taken an instrument from a fiduciary has notice of a breach of fiduciary duty that occurs as a result of the transaction with the fiduciary. Former Section 3-304(2) and (4)(e) related to this issue, but those provisions were unclear in their meaning. Section 3-307 is intended to clarify the law by stating rules that comprehensively cover the issue of when the taker of an instrument has notice of breach of a fiduciary duty and thus notice of a claim to the instrument or its proceeds.

2. Subsection (a) defines the terms "fiduciary" and "represented person" and the introductory paragraph of subsection (b) describes the transaction to which the section applies. The basic scenario is one in which the fiduciary in effect embezzles money of the represented person by applying the proceeds of an instrument that belongs to the represented person to the personal use of the fiduciary. The person dealing with the fiduciary may be a depositary bank that takes the instrument for collection or a bank or other person that pays value for the instrument. The section also covers a

transaction in which an instrument is presented for payment to a payor bank that pays the instrument by giving value to the fiduciary. Subsections (b)(2), (3), and (4) state rules for determining when the person dealing with the fiduciary has notice of breach of fiduciary duty. Subsection (b)(1) states that notice of breach of fiduciary duty is notice of the represented person's claim to the instrument or its proceeds.

Under Section 3-306, a person taking an instrument is subject to a claim to the instrument or its proceeds, unless the taker has rights of a holder in due course. Under Section 3-302(a)(2)(v), the taker cannot be a holder in due course if the instrument was taken with notice of a claim under Section 3-306. Section 3-307 applies to cases in which a represented person is asserting a claim because a breach of fiduciary duty resulted in a misapplication of the proceeds of an instrument. The claim of the represented person is a claim described in Section 3-306. Section 3-307 states rules for determining when a person taking an instrument has notice of the claim which will prevent assertion of rights as a holder in due course. It also states rules for determining when a payor bank pays an instrument with notice of breach of fiduciary duty.

Section 3-307(b) applies only if the person dealing with the fiduciary "has knowledge of the fiduciary status of the fiduciary." Notice which does not amount to knowledge is not enough to cause Section 3-307 to apply. "Knowledge" is defined in Section 1-201(25). In most cases, the "taker" referred to in Section 3-307 will be a bank or other organization. Knowledge of an organization is determined by the rules stated in Section 1-201(27). In many cases, the individual who receives and processes an instrument on behalf of the organization that is the taker of the instrument "for payment or collection or for value" is a clerk who has no knowledge of any fiduciary status of the person from whom the instrument is received. In such cases, Section 3-307 doesn't apply because, under Section 1-201(27), knowledge of the organization is determined by the knowledge of the "individual conducting that transaction," i.e. the clerk who receives and processes the instrument. Furthermore, paragraphs (2) and (4) each require that the person acting for the organization have knowledge of facts that indicate a breach of fiduciary duty. In the case of an instrument taken for deposit to an account, the knowledge is found in the fact that the deposit is made to an account other than that of the represented person or a fiduciary account for benefit of that person. In other cases the person acting for the organization must know that the instrument is taken in payment or as security for a personal debt of the fiduciary or for the personal benefit of the fiduciary. For example, if the instrument is being used to buy goods or services, the person acting for the organization must know that the goods or services are for the personal benefit of the fiduciary. The requirement that the taker have knowledge rather than notice is meant to limit Section 3-307 to relatively uncommon cases in which the person who deals with the fiduciary knows all the relevant facts: the fiduciary status and that the proceeds of the instrument are being used for the personal debt or benefit of the fiduciary or are being paid to an account that is not an account of the represented person or of the fiduciary, as such. Mere notice of these facts is not enough to put the taker on notice of the breach of fiduciary duty and does not give rise to any duty of investigation by the taker.

3. Subsection (b)(2) applies to instruments payable to the represented person or the fiduciary as such. For example, a check payable to Corporation is indorsed in the name of Corporation by Doe as its President. Doe gives the check to Bank as partial repayment of a personal loan that Bank had made to Doe. The check was indorsed either in blank or to Bank. Bank collects the check and applies the proceeds to reduce the amount owed on Doe's loan. If the person acting for Bank in the transaction knows that Doe is a fiduciary and that the check is being used to pay a personal obligation of Doe, subsection (b)(2) applies. If Corporation has a claim to the proceeds of the check because the use of the check by Doe was a breach of fiduciary duty, Bank has notice of the claim and did not take the check as a holder in due course. The same result follows if Doe had indorsed the check to himself before giving it to Bank. Subsection (b)(2) follows Uniform Fiduciaries Act § 4 in providing that if the instrument is payable to the fiduciary, as such, or to the represented person, the taker has notice of a claim if the instrument is negotiated for the fiduciary's personal debt. If fiduciary funds are deposited to a personal account of the fiduciary or to an account that is not an account of the represented person or of the fiduciary, as such, there is a split of authority concerning whether the bank is on notice of a breach of fiduciary duty. Subsection (b)(2)(iii) states that the bank is given notice of breach of fiduciary duty because of the deposit. The Uniform Fiduciaries Act § 9 states that the bank is not on notice unless it has knowledge of facts that makes its receipt of the deposit an act of bad faith.

The rationale of subsection (b)(2) is that it is not normal for an instrument payable to the represented person or the fiduciary, as such, to be used for the personal benefit of the fiduciary. It is likely that such use reflects an unlawful use of the proceeds of the instrument. If the fiduciary is entitled to compensation from the represented person for services rendered or for expenses incurred by the fiduciary the normal mode of payment is by a check drawn on the fiduciary account to the order of the fiduciary.

4. Subsection (b)(3) is based on Uniform Fiduciaries Act § 6 and applies when the instrument is drawn by the represented person or the fiduciary as such to the fiduciary personally. The term "personally" is used as it is used in the Uniform Fiduciaries Act to mean that the instrument is payable to the payee as an individual and not as a fiduciary. For example, Doe as President of Corporation writes a check on Corporation's account to the order of Doe personally. The check is then indorsed over to Bank as in Comment 3. In this case there is no notice of breach of fiduciary duty because there is nothing unusual about the transaction. Corporation may have owed Doe

money for salary, reimbursement for expenses incurred for the benefit of Corporation, or for any other reason. If Doe is authorized to write checks on behalf of Corporation to pay debts of Corporation, the check is a normal way of paying a debt owed to Doe. Bank may assume that Doe may use the instrument for his personal benefit.

5. Subsection (b)(4) can be illustrated by a hypothetical case. Corporation draws a check payable to an organization. X, an officer or employee of Corporation, delivers the check to a person acting for the organization. The person signing the check on behalf of Corporation is X or another person. If the person acting for the organization in the transaction knows that X is a fiduciary, the organization is on notice of a claim by Corporation if it takes the instrument under the same circumstances stated in subsection (b)(2). If the organization is a bank and the check is taken in repayment of a personal loan of the bank to X, the case is like the case discussed in Comment 3. It is unusual for Corporation, the represented person, to pay a personal debt of Doe by issuing a check to the bank. It is more likely that the use of the check by Doe reflects an unlawful use of the proceeds of the check. The same analysis applies if the check is made payable to an organization in payment of goods or services. If the person acting for the organization knew of the fiduciary status of X and that the goods or services were for X's personal benefit, the organization is on notice of a claim by Corporation to the proceeds of the check. See the discussion in the last paragraph of Comment 2.

§ 5-101 Short Title.

This article may be cited as Uniform Commercial Code—Letters of Credit.

OFFICIAL COMMENT

The Official Comment to the original Section 5-101 was a remarkably brief inaugural address. Noting that letters of credit had not been the subject of statutory enactment and that the law concerning them had been developed in the cases, the Comment stated that Article 5 was intended "within its limited scope" to set an independent theoretical frame for the further development of letters of credit. That statement addressed accurately conditions as they existed when the statement was made, nearly half a century ago. Since Article 5 was originally drafted, the use of letters of credit has expanded and developed, and the case law concerning these developments is, in some respects, discordant.

Revision of Article 5 therefore has required reappraisal both of the statutory goals and of the extent to which particular statutory provisions further or adversely affect achievement of those goals.

The statutory goal of Article 5 was originally stated to be: (1) to set a substantive theoretical frame that describes the function and legal nature of letters of credit; and (2) to preserve procedural flexibility in order to accommodate further development of the efficient use of letters of credit. A letter of credit is an idiosyncratic form of undertaking that supports performance of an obligation incurred in a separate financial, mercantile, or other transaction or arrangement. The objectives of the original and revised Article 5 are best achieved (1) by defining the peculiar characteristics of a letter of credit that distinguish it and the legal consequences of its use from other forms of assurance such as secondary guarantees, performance bonds, and insurance policies, and from ordinary contracts, fiduciary engagements, and escrow arrangements; and (2) by preserving flexibility through variation by agreement in order to respond to and accommodate developments in custom and usage that are not inconsistent with the essential definitions and substantive mandates of the statute. No statute can, however, prescribe the manner in which such substantive rights and duties are to be enforced or imposed without risking stultification of wholesome developments in the letter of credit mechanism. Letter of credit law should remain responsive to commercial reality and in particular to the customs and expectations of the international banking and mercantile community. Courts should read the terms of this article in a manner consistent with these customs and expectations.

The subject matter in Article 5, letters of credit, may also be governed by an international convention that is now being drafted by UNCITRAL, the draft Convention on Independent Guarantees and Standby Letters of Credit. The Uniform Customs and Practice is an international body of trade practice that is commonly adopted by international and domestic letters of credit and as such is the "law of the transaction" by agreement of the parties. Article 5 is consistent with and was influenced by the rules in the existing version of the UCP. In addition to the UCP and the international convention, other bodies of law apply to letters of credit. For example, the federal bankruptcy law applies to letters of credit with respect to applicants and beneficiaries that are in bankruptcy; regulations of the Federal Reserve Board and the Comptroller of the Currency lay out requirements for banks that issue letters of credit and describe how letters of credit are to be treated for calculating asset risk and for the purpose of loan limitations. In addition there is an array of anti-boycott and other similar laws that may affect the issuance and performance of letters of credit. All of these laws are beyond the scope of Article 5, but in certain circumstances they will override Article 5.

§ 5-102 Definitions.

(a) In this article:
  (1) "Adviser" means a person who, at the request of the issuer, a confirmer, or another adviser, notifies or requests another adviser to notify the beneficiary that a letter of credit has been issued, confirmed, or amended.
  (2) "Applicant" means a person at whose request or for whose account a letter of credit is issued. The term includes a person who requests an issuer to issue a letter of credit on behalf of another if the person making the request undertakes an obligation to reimburse the issuer.
  (3) "Beneficiary" means a person who under the terms of a letter of credit is entitled to have its complying presentation honored. The term

includes a person to whom drawing rights have been transferred under a transferable letter of credit.

(4) "Confirmer" means a nominated person who undertakes, at the request or with the consent of the issuer, to honor a presentation under a letter of credit issued by another.

(5) "Dishonor" of a letter of credit means failure timely to honor or to take an interim action, such as acceptance of a draft, that may be required by the letter of credit.

(6) "Document" means a draft or other demand, document of title, investment security, certificate, invoice, or other record, statement, or representation of fact, law, right, or opinion (i) which is presented in a written or other medium permitted by the letter of credit or, unless prohibited by the letter of credit, by the standard practice referred to in Section 5-108(e) and (ii) which is capable of being examined for compliance with the terms and conditions of the letter of credit. A document may not be oral.

(7) "Good faith" means honesty in fact in the conduct or transaction concerned.

(8) "Honor" of a letter of credit means performance of the issuer's undertaking in the letter of credit to pay or deliver an item of value. Unless the letter of credit otherwise provides, "honor" occurs

(i) upon payment,

(ii) if the letter of credit provides for acceptance, upon acceptance of a draft and, at maturity, its payment, or

(iii) if the letter of credit provides for incurring a deferred obligation, upon incurring the obligation and, at maturity, its performance.

(9) "Issuer" means a bank or other person that issues a letter of credit, but does not include an individual who makes an engagement for personal, family, or household purposes.

(10) "Letter of credit" means a definite undertaking that satisfies the requirements of Section 5-104 by an issuer to a beneficiary at the request or for the account of an applicant or, in the case of a financial institution, to itself or for its own account, to honor a documentary presentation by payment or delivery of an item of value.

(11) "Nominated person" means a person whom the issuer (i) designates or authorizes to pay, accept, negotiate, or otherwise give value under a letter of credit and (ii) undertakes by agreement or custom and practice to reimburse.

(12) "Presentation" means delivery of a document to an issuer or nominated person for honor or giving of value under a letter of credit.

(13) "Presenter" means a person making a presentation as or on behalf of a beneficiary or nominated person.

(14) "Record" means information that is inscribed on a tangible medium, or that is stored in an electronic or other medium and is retrievable in perceivable form.

(15) "Successor of a beneficiary" means a person who succeeds to substantially all of the rights of a beneficiary by operation of law, including a corporation with or into which the beneficiary has been merged or consolidated, an administrator, executor, personal representative, trustee in bankruptcy, debtor in possession, liquidator, and receiver.

(b) Definitions in other Articles applying to this article and the sections in which they appear are:

"Accept" or "Acceptance"   Section 3-409
"Value"   Sections 3-303, 4-211

(c) Article 1 contains certain additional general definitions and principles of construction and interpretation applicable throughout this article.

OFFICIAL COMMENT

1. Since no one can be a confirmer unless that person is a nominated person as defined in Section 5-102(a)(11), those who agree to "confirm" without the designation or authorization of the issuer are not confirmers under Article 5. Nonetheless, the undertakings to the beneficiary of such persons may be enforceable by the beneficiary as letters of credit issued by the "confirmer" for its own account or as guarantees or contracts outside of Article 5.

2. The definition of "document" contemplates and facilitates the growing recognition of electronic and other nonpaper media as "documents," however, for the time being, data in those media constitute documents only in certain circumstances. For example, a facsimile received by an issuer would be a document only if the letter of credit explicitly permitted it, if the standard practice authorized it and the letter did not prohibit it, or the agreement of the issuer and beneficiary permitted it. The fact that data transmitted in a nonpaper (unwritten) medium can be recorded on paper by a recipient's computer printer, facsimile machine, or the like does not under current practice render the data so transmitted a "document." A facsimile or S.W.I.F.T. message received directly by the issuer is in an electronic medium when it crosses the boundary of the issuer's place of business. One wishing to make a presentation by facsimile (an electronic medium) will have to procure the explicit agreement of the issuer (assuming that the standard practice does not authorize it). Where electronic transmissions are authorized neither by the letter of credit nor by the practice, the beneficiary may transmit the data electronically to its agent who may be able to put it in written form and make a conforming presentation.

3. "Good faith" continues in revised Article 5 to be defined as "honesty in fact." "Observance of reasonable standards of fair dealing" has not been added to the definition. The narrower definition of "honesty in fact" reinforces the "independence principle" in the treatment of "fraud," "strict compliance," "preclusion," and other tests affecting the performance of obligations that are unique to letters of credit. This narrower definition—which does not include "fair dealing"—is appropriate to the decision to honor or dishonor a presentation of documents specified in a letter of credit. The narrower definition is also appropriate for other parts of revised Article 5 where greater certainty of obligations is necessary and is consistent with the goals of speed and low cost. It is important that U.S. letters of credit have continuing vitality and competitiveness in international transactions.

For example, it would be inconsistent with the "independence" principle if any of the following occurred: (i) the beneficiary's failure to adhere to the standard of "fair dealing" in the underlying transaction or otherwise in presenting documents were to provide applicants and issuers with an "unfairness" defense to dishonor even when the documents complied with the terms of the letter of credit; (ii) the issuer's obligation to honor in "strict compliance in accordance with standard practice" were changed to "reasonable compliance" by use of the "fair dealing" standard, or (iii) the preclusion against the issuer (Section 5-108(d)) were modified under the "fair dealing" standard to enable the issuer later to raise additional deficiencies in the presentation. The rights and obligations arising from presentation, honor, dishonor and reimbursement, are independent and strict, and thus "honesty in fact" is an appropriate standard.

The contract between the applicant and beneficiary is not governed by Article 5, but by applicable contract law, such as Article 2 or the general law of contracts. "Good faith" in that contract is defined by other law, such as Section 2-103(1)(b) or Restatement of Contracts 2d, § 205, which incorporate the principle of "fair dealing" in most cases, or a State's common law or other statutory provisions that may apply to that contract.

The contract between the applicant and the issuer (sometimes called the "reimbursement" agreement) is governed in part by this article (e.g., Sections 5-108(i), 5-111(b), and 5-103(c)) and partly by other law (e.g., the general law of contracts). The definition of good faith in Section 5-102(a)(7) applies only to the extent that the reimbursement contract is governed by provisions in this article; for other purposes good faith is defined by other law.

4. Payment and acceptance are familiar modes of honor. A third mode of honor, incurring an unconditional obligation, has legal effects similar to an acceptance of a time draft but does not technically constitute an acceptance. The practice of making letters of credit available by "deferred

payment undertaking" as now provided in UCP 500 has grown up in other countries and spread to the United States. The definition of "honor" will accommodate that practice.

5. The exclusion of consumers from the definition of "issuer" is to keep creditors from using a letter of credit in consumer transactions in which the consumer might be made the issuer and the creditor would be the beneficiary. If that transaction were recognized under Article 5, the effect would be to leave the consumer without defenses against the creditor. That outcome would violate the policy behind the Federal Trade Commission Rule in 16 CFR Part 433. In a consumer transaction, an individual cannot be an issuer where that person would otherwise be either the principal debtor or a guarantor.

6. The label on a document is not conclusive; certain documents labelled "guarantees" in accordance with European (and occasionally, American) practice are letters of credit. On the other hand, even documents that are labelled "letter of credit" may not constitute letters of credit under the definition in Section 5-102(a). When a document labelled a letter of credit requires the issuer to pay not upon the presentation of documents, but upon the determination of an extrinsic fact such as applicant's failure to perform a construction contract, and where that condition appears on its face to be fundamental and would, if ignored, leave no obligation to the issuer under the document labelled letter of credit, the issuer's undertaking is not a letter of credit. It is probably some form of suretyship or other contractual arrangement and may be enforceable as such. See Sections 5-102(a)(10) and 5-103(d). Therefore, undertakings whose fundamental term requires an issuer to look beyond documents and beyond conventional reference to the clock, calendar, and practices concerning the form of various documents are not governed by Article 5. Although Section 5-108(g) recognizes that certain nondocumentary conditions can be included in a letter of credit without denying the undertaking the status of letter of credit, that section does not apply to cases where the nondocumentary condition is fundamental to the issuer's obligation. The rules in Sections 5-102(a)(10), 5-103(d), and 5-108(g) approve the conclusion in Wichita Eagle & Beacon Publishing Co. v. Pacific Nat. Bank, 493 F.2d 1285 (9th Cir.1974).

The adjective "definite" is taken from the UCP. It approves cases that deny letter of credit status to documents that are unduly vague or incomplete. See, e.g., *Transparent Products Corp. v. Paysaver Credit Union*, 864 F.2d 60 (7th Cir.1988). Note, however, that no particular phrase or label is necessary to establish a letter of credit. It is sufficient if the undertaking of the issuer shows that it is intended to be a letter of credit. In most cases the parties' intention will be indicated by a label on the undertaking itself indicating that it is a "letter of credit," but no such language is necessary.

A financial institution may be both the issuer and the applicant or the issuer and the beneficiary. Such letters are sometimes issued by a bank in support of the bank's own lease obligations or on behalf of one of its divisions as an applicant or to one of its divisions as beneficiary, such as an overseas branch. Because wide use of letters of credit in which the issuer and the applicant or the issuer and the beneficiary are the same would endanger the unique status of letters of credit, only financial institutions are authorized to issue them.

In almost all cases the ultimate performance of the issuer under a letter of credit is the payment of money. In rare cases the issuer's obligation is to deliver stock certificates or the like. The definition of letter of credit in Section 5-102(a)(10) contemplates those cases.

7. Under the UCP any bank is a nominated bank where the letter of credit is "freely negotiable." A letter of credit might also nominate by the following: "We hereby engage with the drawer, indorsers, and bona fide holders of drafts drawn under and in compliance with the terms of this credit that the same will be duly honored on due presentation" or "available with any bank by negotiation." A restricted negotiation credit might be "available with x bank by negotiation" or the like.

In several legal consequences may attach to the status of nominated person. First, when the issuer nominates a person, it is authorizing that person to pay or give value and is authorizing the beneficiary to make presentation to that person. Unless the letter of credit provides otherwise, the beneficiary need not present the documents to the issuer before the letter of credit expires; it need only present those documents to the nominated person. Secondly, a nominated person that gives value in good faith has a right to payment from the issuer despite fraud. Section 5-109(a)(1).

8. A "record" must be in or capable of being converted to a perceivable form. For example, an electronic message recorded in a computer memory that could be printed from that memory could constitute a record. Similarly, a tape recording of an oral conversation could be a record.

9. Absent a specific agreement to the contrary, documents of a beneficiary delivered to an issuer or nominated person are considered to be presented under the letter of credit to which they refer, and any payment or value given for them is considered to be made under that letter of credit. As the court held in *Alaska Textile Co. v. Chase Manhattan Bank, N.A.*, 982 F.2d 813, 820 (2d Cir.1992), it takes a "significant showing" to make the presentation of a beneficiary's documents for "collection only" or otherwise outside letter of credit law and practice.

10. Although a successor of a beneficiary is one who succeeds "by operation of law," some of the successions contemplated by Section 5-102(a)(15) will have resulted from voluntary action of the beneficiary such as merger of a corporation. Any merger makes the successor corporation the "successor of a beneficiary" even though the transfer occurs partly by operation of law and partly by the voluntary action of the parties. The definition excludes

certain transfers, where no part of the transfer is "by operation of law"—such as the sale of assets by one company to another.

11. "Draft" in Article 5 does not have the same meaning it has in Article 3. For example, a document may be a draft under Article 5 even though it would not be a negotiable instrument, and therefore would not qualify as a draft under Section 3-104(e).

§ 5-103 Scope.

(a) This article applies to letters of credit and to certain rights and obligations arising out of transactions involving letters of credit.

(b) The statement of a rule in this article does not by itself require, imply, or negate application of the same or a different rule to a situation not provided for, or to a person not specified, in this article.

(c) With the exception of this subsection, subsections (a) and (d), Sections 5-102(a)(9) and (10), 5-106(d), and 5-114(d), and except to the extent prohibited in Sections 1-102(3) and 5-117(d), the effect of this article may be varied by agreement or by a provision stated or incorporated by reference in an undertaking. A term in an agreement or undertaking generally excusing liability or generally limiting remedies for failure to perform obligations is not sufficient to vary obligations prescribed by this article.

(d) Rights and obligations of an issuer to a beneficiary or a nominated person under a letter of credit are independent of the existence, performance, or nonperformance of a contract or arrangement out of which the letter of credit arises or which underlies it, including contracts or arrangements between the issuer and the applicant and between the applicant and the beneficiary.

OFFICIAL COMMENT

1. Sections 5-102(a)(10) and 5-103 are the principal limits on the scope of Article 5. Many undertakings in commerce and contract are similar, but not identical to the letter of credit. Principal among those are "secondary," "accessory," or "suretyship" guarantees. Although the word "guarantee" is sometimes used to describe an independent obligation like that of the issuer of a letter of credit (most often in the case of European bank undertakings but occasionally in the case of undertakings of American banks), in the United States the word "guarantee" is more typically used to describe a suretyship transaction in which the "guarantor" is only second-arily liable and has the right to assert the underlying debtor's defenses. This article does not apply to secondary or accessory guarantees and it is important to recognize the distinction between letters of credit and those guarantees. It is often a defense to a secondary or accessory guarantor's

liability that the underlying debt has been discharged or that the debtor has other defenses to the underlying liability. In letter of credit law, on the other hand, the independence principle recognized throughout Article 5 states that the issuer's liability is independent of the underlying obligation. That the beneficiary may have breached the underlying contract and thus have given a good defense on that contract to the applicant against the beneficiary is no defense for the issuer's refusal to honor. Only staunch recognition of this principle by the issuers and the courts will give letters of credit the continuing vitality that arises from the certainty and speed of payment under letters of credit. To that end, it is important that the law not carry into letter of credit transactions rules that properly apply only to secondary guarantees or to other forms of engagement.

2. Like all of the provisions of the Uniform Commercial Code, Article 5 is supplemented by Section 1-103 and, through it, by many rules of statutory and common law. Because this article is quite short and has no rules on many issues that will affect liability with respect to a letter of credit transaction, law beyond Article 5 will often determine rights and liabilities in letter of credit transactions. Even within letter of credit law, the article is far from comprehensive; it deals only with "certain" rights of the parties. Particularly with respect to the standards of performance that are set out in Section 5-108, it is appropriate for the parties and the courts to turn to customs and practice such as the Uniform Customs and Practice for Documentary Credits, currently published by the International Chamber of Commerce as I.C.C. Pub. No. 500 (hereafter UCP). Many letters of credit specifically adopt the UCP as applicable to the particular transaction. Where the UCP are adopted but conflict with Article 5 and except where variation is prohibited, the UCP terms are permissible contractual modifications under Sections 1-102(3) and 5-103(c). See Section 5-116(c). Normally Article 5 should not be considered to conflict with practice except when a rule explicitly stated in the UCP or other practice is different from a rule explicitly stated in Article 5.

Except by choosing the law of a jurisdiction that has not adopted the Uniform Commercial Code, it is not possible entirely to escape the Uniform Commercial Code. Since incorporation of the UCP avoids only "conflicting" Article 5 rules, parties who do not wish to be governed by the nonconflicting provisions of Article 5 must normally either adopt the law of a jurisdiction other than a State of the United States or state explicitly the rule that is to govern. When rules of custom and practice are incorporated by reference, they are considered to be explicit terms of the agreement or undertaking.

Neither the obligation of an issuer under Section 5-108 nor that of an adviser under Section 5-107 is an obligation of the kind that is invariable under Section 1-102(3). Section 5-103(c) and Comment 1 to Section 5-108 make it clear that the applicant and the issuer may agree to almost any provision establishing the obligations of the issuer to the applicant. The last sentence of subsection (c) limits the power of the issuer to achieve that result by a nonnegotiated disclaimer or limitation of remedy.

What the issuer could achieve by an explicit agreement with its applicant or by a term that explicitly defines its duty, it cannot accomplish by a general disclaimer. The restriction on disclaimers in the last sentence of subsection (c) is based more on procedural than on substantive unfairness. Where, for example, the reimbursement agreement provides explicitly that the issuer need not examine any documents, the applicant understands the risk it has undertaken. A term in a reimbursement agreement which states generally that an issuer will not be liable unless it has acted in "bad faith" or committed "gross negligence" is ineffective under Section 5-103(c). On the other hand, less general terms such as terms that permit issuer reliance on an oral or electronic message believed in good faith to have been received from the applicant or terms that entitle an issuer to reimbursement when it honors a "substantially" though not "strictly" complying presentation, are effective. In each case the question is whether the disclaimer or limitation is sufficiently clear and explicit in reallocating a liability or risk that is allocated differently under a variable Article 5 provision.

Of course, no term in a letter of credit, whether incorporated by reference to practice rules or stated specifically, can free an issuer from a conflicting contractual obligation to its applicant. If, for example, an issuer promised its applicant that it would pay only against an inspection certificate of a particular company but failed to require such a certificate in its letter of credit or made the requirement only a nondocumentary condition that had to be disregarded, the issuer might be obliged to pay the beneficiary even though its payment might violate its contract with its applicant.

3. Parties should generally avoid modifying the definitions in Section 5-102. The effect of such an agreement is almost inevitably unclear. To say that something is a "guarantee" in the typical domestic transaction is to say that the parties intend that particular legal rules apply to it. By acknowledging that something is a guarantee, but asserting that it is to be treated as a "letter of credit," the parties leave a court uncertain about where the rules on guarantees stop and those concerning letters of credit begin.

4. Section 5-102(2) and (3) of Article 5 are omitted as unneeded; the omission does not change the law.

§ 5-104 Formal Requirements.

A letter of credit, confirmation, advice, transfer, amendment, or cancellation may be issued in any form that is a record and is authenticated (i) by a signature or (ii) in accordance with the agreement of the parties or the standard practice referred to in Section 5-108(e).

OFFICIAL COMMENT

1. Neither Section 5-104 nor the definition of letter of credit in Section 5-102(a)(10) requires inclusion of all the terms that are normally contained in a letter of credit in order for an undertaking to be recognized as a letter of credit under Article 5. For example, a letter of credit will typically specify the amount available, the expiration date, the place where presentation should be made, and the documents that must be presented to entitle a person to honor. Undertakings that have the formalities required by Section 5-104 and meet the conditions specified in Section 5-102(a)(10) will be recognized as letters of credit even though they omit one or more of the items usually contained in a letter of credit.

2. The authentication specified in this section is authentication only of the identity of the issuer, confirmer, or adviser.

   An authentication agreement may be by system rule, by standard practice, or by direct agreement between the parties. The reference to practice is intended to incorporate future developments in the UCP and other practice rules as well as those that may arise spontaneously in commercial practice.

3. Many banking transactions, including the issuance of many letters of credit, are now conducted mostly by electronic means. For example, S.W.I.F.T. is currently used to transmit letters of credit from issuing to advising banks. The letter of credit text so transmitted may be printed at the advising bank, stamped "original" and provided to the beneficiary in that form. The printed document may then be used as a way of controlling and recording payments and of recording and authorizing assignments of proceeds or transfers of rights under the letter of credit. Nothing in this section should be construed to conflict with that practice.

   To be a record sufficient to serve as a letter of credit or other undertaking under this section, data must have a durability consistent with that function. Because consideration is not required for a binding letter of credit or similar undertaking (Section 5-105) yet those undertakings are to be strictly construed (Section 5-108), parties to a letter of credit transaction are especially dependent on the continued availability of the terms and conditions of the letter of credit or other undertaking. By declining to specify any particular medium in which the letter of credit must be established or communicated, Section 5-104 leaves room for future developments.

§ 5-105 Consideration.

Consideration is not required to issue, amend, transfer, or cancel a letter of credit, advice, or confirmation.

OFFICIAL COMMENT

It is not to be expected that any issuer will issue its letter of credit without some form of remuneration. But it is not expected that the beneficiary will know what the issuer's remuneration was or whether in fact there was any identifiable remuneration in a given case. And it might be difficult for the beneficiary to prove the issuer's remuneration. This section dispenses with this proof and is consistent with the position of Lord Mansfield in *Pillans v. Van Mierop*, 97 Eng.Rep. 1035 (K.B. 1765) in making consideration irrelevant.

§ 5-106 Issuance, Amendment, Cancellation, and Duration.

(a) A letter of credit is issued and becomes enforceable according to its terms against the issuer when the issuer sends or otherwise transmits it to the person requested to advise or to the beneficiary. A letter of credit is revocable only if it so provides.

(b) After a letter of credit is issued, rights and obligations of a beneficiary, applicant, confirmer, and issuer are not affected by an amendment or cancellation to which that person has not consented except to the extent the letter of credit provides that it is revocable or that the issuer may amend or cancel the letter of credit without that consent.

(c) If there is no stated expiration date or other provision that determines its duration, a letter of credit expires one year after its stated date of issuance or, if none is stated, after the date on which it is issued.

(d) A letter of credit that states that it is perpetual expires five years after its stated date of issuance, or if none is stated, after the date on which it is issued.

OFFICIAL COMMENT

1. This section adopts the position taken by several courts, namely that letters of credit that are silent as to revocability are irrevocable. See, e.g., *Weyerhaeuser Co. v. First Nat. Bank*, 27 UCC Rep.Serv. 777 (S.D. Iowa 1979); *West Va. Hous. Dev. Fund v. Sroka*, 415 F.Supp. 1107 (W.D.Pa.1976). This is the position of the current UCP (500). Given the usual commercial understanding and purpose of letters of credit, revocable letters of credit offer unhappy possibilities for misleading the parties who deal with them.

2. A person can consent to an amendment by implication. For example, a beneficiary that tenders documents for honor that conform to an amended letter of credit but not to the original letter of credit has probably consented to the amendment. By the same token an applicant that has procured the issuance of a transferable letter of credit has consented to its transfer and to performance under the letter of credit by a person to whom the beneficiary's rights are duly transferred. If some, but not all of the persons involved

in a letter of credit transaction consent to performance that does not strictly conform to the original letter of credit, those persons assume the risk that other nonconsenting persons may insist on strict compliance with the original letter of credit. Under subsection (b) those not consenting are not bound. For example, an issuer might agree to amend its letter of credit or honor documents presented after the expiration date in the belief that the applicant has consented or will consent to the amendment or will waive presentation after the original expiration date. If that belief is mistaken, the issuer is bound to the beneficiary by the terms of the letter of credit as amended or waived, even though it may be unable to recover from the applicant.

In general, the rights of a recognized transferee beneficiary cannot be altered without the transferee's consent, but the same is not true of the rights of assignees of proceeds from the beneficiary. When the beneficiary makes a complete transfer of its interest that is effective under the terms for transfer established by the issuer, adviser, or other party controlling transfers, the beneficiary no longer has an interest in the letter of credit, and the transferee steps into the shoes of the beneficiary as the one with rights under the letter of credit. Section 5-102(a)(3). When there is a partial transfer, both the original beneficiary and the transferee beneficiary have an interest in performance of the letter of credit and each expects that its rights will not be altered by amendment unless it consents.

The assignee of proceeds under a letter of credit from the beneficiary enjoys no such expectation. Notwithstanding an assignee's notice to the issuer of the assignment of proceeds, the assignee is not a person protected by subsection (b). An assignee of proceeds should understand that its rights can be changed or completely extinguished by amendment or cancellation of the letter of credit. An assignee's claim is precarious, for it depends entirely upon the continued existence of the letter of credit and upon the beneficiary's preparation and presentation of documents that would entitle the beneficiary to honor under Section 5-108.

3. The issuer's right to cancel a revocable letter of credit does not free it from a duty to reimburse a nominated person who has honored, accepted, or undertaken a deferred obligation prior to receiving notice of the amendment or cancellation. Compare UCP Article 8.

4. Although all letters of credit should specify the date on which the issuer's engagement expires, the failure to specify an expiration date does not invalidate the letter of credit, or diminish or relieve the obligation of any party with respect to the letter of credit. A letter of credit that may be revoked or terminated at the discretion of the issuer by notice to the beneficiary is not "perpetual."

§ 5-107 Confirmer, Nominated Person, and Adviser.

(a) A confirmer is directly obligated on a letter of credit and has the rights and obligations of an issuer to the extent of its confirmation. The confirmer also has rights against and obligations to the issuer as if the issuer were an applicant and the confirmer had issued the letter of credit at the request and for the account of the issuer.

(b) A nominated person who is not a confirmer is not obligated to honor or otherwise give value for a presentation.

(c) A person requested to advise may decline to act as an adviser. An adviser that is not a confirmer is not obligated to honor or give value for a presentation. An adviser undertakes to the issuer and to the beneficiary accurately to advise the terms of the letter of credit, confirmation, amendment, or advice received by that person and undertakes to the beneficiary to check the apparent authenticity of the request to advise. Even if the advice is inaccurate, the letter of credit, confirmation, or amendment is enforceable as issued.

(d) A person who notifies a transferee beneficiary of the terms of a letter of credit, confirmation, amendment, or advice has the rights and obligations of an adviser under subsection (c). The terms in the notice to the transferee beneficiary may differ from the terms in any notice to the transferor beneficiary to the extent permitted by the letter of credit, confirmation, amendment, or advice received by the person who so notifies.

OFFICIAL COMMENT

1. A confirmer has the rights and obligations identified in Section 5-108. Accordingly, unless the context otherwise requires, the terms "confirmer" and "confirmation" should be read into this article wherever the terms "issuer" and "letter of credit" appear.

   A confirmer that has paid in accordance with the terms and conditions of the letter of credit is entitled to reimbursement by the issuer even if the beneficiary committed fraud (see Section 5-109(a)(1)(ii)) and, in that sense, has greater rights against the issuer than the beneficiary has. To be entitled to reimbursement from the issuer under the typical confirmed letter of credit, the confirmer must submit conforming documents, but the confirmer's presentation to the issuer need not be made before the expiration date of the letter of credit.

   A letter of credit confirmation has been analogized to a guarantee of issuer performance, to a parallel letter of credit issued by the confirmer for the account of the issuer or the letter of credit applicant or both, and to a back-to-back letter of credit in which the confirmer is a kind of beneficiary of the original issuer's letter of credit. Like letter of credit undertakings, confirmations are both unique and flexible, so that no one of these analogies is perfect, but unless otherwise indicated in the letter of credit or confirmation, a confirmer should be viewed by the letter of credit issuer and the beneficiary as an issuer of a parallel letter of credit for the account of the original letter of credit issuer. Absent a direct agreement between the applicant and a confirmer, normally the obligations of a confirmer are to the issuer not the applicant, but the applicant might have a right to injunction against a confirmer under Section 5-109 or warranty claim under Section 5-110, and either might have claims against the other under Section 5-117.

2. No one has a duty to advise until that person agrees to be an adviser or undertakes to act in accordance with the instructions of the issuer. Except where there is a prior agreement to serve or where the silence of the adviser would be an acceptance of an offer to contract, a person's failure to respond to a request to advise a letter of credit does not in and of itself create any liability, nor does it establish a relationship of issuer and adviser between the two. Since there is no duty to advise a letter of credit in the absence of a prior agreement, there can be no duty to advise it timely or at any particular time. When the adviser manifests its agreement to advise by actually doing so (as is normally the case), the adviser cannot have violated any duty to advise in a timely way. This analysis is consistent with the result of *Sound of Market Street v. Continental Bank International*, 819 F.2d 384 (3d Cir.1987) which held that there is no such duty. This section takes no position on the reasoning of that case, but does not overrule the result. By advising or agreeing to advise a letter of credit, the adviser assumes a duty to the issuer and to the beneficiary accurately to report what it has received from the issuer, but, beyond determining the apparent authenticity of the letter, an adviser has no duty to investigate the accuracy of the message it has received from the issuer. "Checking" the apparent authenticity of the request to advise means only that the prospective adviser must attempt to authenticate the message (e.g., by "testing" the telex that comes from the purported issuer), and if it is unable to authenticate the message must report that fact to the issuer and, if it chooses to advise the message, to the beneficiary. By proper agreement, an adviser may disclaim its obligation under this section.

3. An issuer may issue a letter of credit which the adviser may advise with different terms. The issuer may then believe that it has undertaken a certain engagement, yet the text in the hands of the beneficiary will contain different terms, and the beneficiary would not be entitled to honor if the documents it submitted did not comply with the terms of the letter of credit as originally issued. On the other hand, if the adviser also confirmed the letter of credit, then as a confirmer it will be independently liable on the letter of credit as advised and confirmed. If in that situation the beneficiary's ultimate presentation entitled it to honor under the terms of the

confirmation but not under those in the original letter of credit, the confirmer would have to honor but might not be entitled to reimbursement from the issuer.

4. When the issuer nominates another person to "pay," "negotiate," or otherwise to take up the documents and give value, there can be confusion about the legal status of the nominated person. In rare cases the person might actually be an agent of the issuer and its act might be the act of the issuer itself. In most cases the nominated person is not an agent of the issuer and has no authority to act on the issuer's behalf. Its "nomination" allows the beneficiary to present to it and earns it certain rights to payment under Section 5-109 that others do not enjoy. For example, when an issuer issues a "freely negotiable credit," it contemplates that banks or others might take up documents under that credit and advance value against them, and it is agreeing to pay those persons but only if the presentation to the issuer made by the nominated person complies with the credit. Usually there will be no agreement to pay, negotiate, or to serve in any other capacity by the nominated person, therefore the nominated person will have the right to decline to take the documents. It may return them or agree merely to act as a forwarding agent for the documents but without giving value against them or taking any responsibility for their conformity to the letter of credit.

§ 5-108 Issuer's Rights and Obligations.

(a) Except as otherwise provided in Section 5-109, an issuer shall honor a presentation that, as determined by the standard practice referred to in subsection (e), appears on its face strictly to comply with the terms and conditions of the letter of credit. Except as otherwise provided in Section 5-113 and unless otherwise agreed with the applicant, an issuer shall dishonor a presentation that does not appear so to comply.

(b) An issuer has a reasonable time after presentation, but not beyond the end of the seventh business day of the issuer after the day of its receipt of documents:
    (1) to honor,
    (2) if the letter of credit provides for honor to be completed more than seven business days after presentation, to accept a draft or incur a deferred obligation, or
    (3) to give notice to the presenter of discrepancies in the presentation.

(c) Except as otherwise provided in subsection (d), an issuer is precluded from asserting as a basis for dishonor any discrepancy if timely notice is not given, or any discrepancy not stated in the notice if timely notice is given.

(d) Failure to give the notice specified in subsection (b) or to mention fraud, forgery, or expiration in the notice does not preclude the issuer from asserting as a basis for dishonor fraud or forgery as described in Section 5-109(a) or expiration of the letter of credit before presentation.

(e) An issuer shall observe standard practice of financial institutions that regularly issue letters of credit. Determination of the issuer's observance of the standard practice is a matter of interpretation for the court. The court shall offer the parties a reasonable opportunity to present evidence of the standard practice.

(f) An issuer is not responsible for:

(1) the performance or nonperformance of the underlying contract, arrangement, or transaction,

(2) an act or omission of others, or

(3) observance or knowledge of the usage of a particular trade other than the standard practice referred to in subsection (e).

(g) If an undertaking constituting a letter of credit under Section 5-102(a)(10) contains nondocumentary conditions, an issuer shall disregard the nondocumentary conditions and treat them as if they were not stated.

(h) An issuer that has dishonored a presentation shall return the documents or hold them at the disposal of, and send advice to that effect to, the presenter.

(i) An issuer that has honored a presentation as permitted or required by this article:

(1) is entitled to be reimbursed by the applicant in immediately available funds not later than the date of its payment of funds;

(2) takes the documents free of claims of the beneficiary or presenter;

(3) is precluded from asserting a right of recourse on a draft under Sections 3-414 and 3-415;

(4) except as otherwise provided in Sections 5-110 and 5-117, is precluded from restitution of money paid or other value given by mistake to the extent the mistake concerns discrepancies in the documents or tender which are apparent on the face of the presentation; and

(5) is discharged to the extent of its performance under the letter of credit unless the issuer honored a presentation in which a required signature of a beneficiary was forged.

OFFICIAL COMMENT

1. This section combines some of the duties previously included in Sections 5-114 and 5-109. Because a confirmer has the rights and duties of an issuer, this section applies equally to a confirmer and an issuer. See Section 5-107(a).

The standard of strict compliance governs the issuer's obligation to the beneficiary and to the applicant. By requiring that a "presentation" appear strictly to comply, the section requires not only that the documents themselves appear on their face strictly to comply, but also that the other terms of the letter of credit such as those dealing with the time and place of presentation are strictly complied with. Typically, a letter of credit will provide that presentation is timely if made to the issuer, confirmer, or any other nominated person prior to expiration of the letter of credit. Accordingly, a nominated person that has honored a demand or otherwise given value before expiration will have a right to reimbursement from the issuer even though presentation to the issuer is made after the expiration of the letter of credit. Conversely, where the beneficiary negotiates documents to one who is not a nominated person, the beneficiary or that person acting on behalf of the beneficiary must make presentation to a nominated person, confirmer, or issuer prior to the expiration date.

This section does not impose a bifurcated standard under which an issuer's right to reimbursement might be broader than a beneficiary's right to honor. However, the explicit deference to standard practice in Section 5-108(a) and (e) and elsewhere expands issuers' rights of reimbursement where that practice so provides. Also, issuers can and often do contract with their applicants for expanded rights of reimbursement. Where that is done, the beneficiary will have to meet a more stringent standard of compliance as to the issuer than the issuer will have to meet as to the applicant. Similarly, a nominated person may have reimbursement and other rights against the issuer based on this article, the UCP, bank-to-bank reimbursement rules, or other agreement or undertaking of the issuer. These rights may allow the nominated person to recover from the issuer even when the nominated person would have no right to obtain honor under the letter of credit.

The section adopts strict compliance, rather than the standard that commentators have called "substantial compliance," the standard arguably applied in *Banco Espanol de Credito v. State Street Bank and Trust Company*, 385 F.2d 230 (1st Cir.1967) and *Flagship Cruises Ltd. v. New England Merchants Nat. Bank*, 569 F.2d 699 (1st Cir.1978). Strict compliance does not mean slavish conformity to the terms of the letter of credit. For example, standard practice (what issuers do) may recognize certain presentations as complying that an unschooled layman would regard as discrepant. By adopting standard practice as a way of measuring strict compliance, this article indorses the conclusion of the court in *New Braunfels Nat. Bank v. Odiorne*, 780 S.W.2d 313 (Tex.Ct.App. 1989) (beneficiary could collect when draft requested payment on "Letter of Credit No. 86-122-5" and letter of credit specified "Letter of Credit No. 86-122-S" holding strict compliance does not demand oppressive perfectionism). The section also indorses the result in *Tosco Corp. v. Federal Deposit Insurance Corp.*, 723 F.2d 1242 (6th Cir.1983). The letter of credit in that case called for "drafts Drawn under Bank of Clarksville Letter of Credit Number 105." The draft presented stated "drawn under Bank of Clarksville, Clarksville, Tennessee letter of Credit No. 105." The court correctly found that despite the change of upper case "L" to a lower case "l" and the use of the word "No." instead of "Number," and despite the addition of the words "Clarksville, Tennessee," the presentation conformed. Similarly a document addressed by a foreign person to General Motors as "Jeneral Motors" would strictly conform in the absence of other defects.

Identifying and determining compliance with standard practice are matters of interpretation for the court, not for the jury. As with similar rules in Sections 4A-202(c) and 2-302, it is hoped that there will be more consistency in the outcomes and speedier resolution of disputes if the responsibility for determining the nature and scope of standard practice is granted to the court, not to a jury. Granting the court authority to make these decisions will also encourage the salutary practice of courts' granting summary judgment in circumstances where there are no significant factual disputes. The statute encourages outcomes such as *American Coleman Co. v. Intrawest Bank*, 887 F.2d 1382 (10th Cir.1989), where summary judgment was granted.

In some circumstances standards may be established between the issuer and the applicant by agreement or by custom that would free the issuer from liability that it might otherwise have. For example, an applicant might agree that the issuer would have no duty whatsoever to examine documents on certain presentations (e.g., those below a certain dollar amount). Where the transaction depended upon the issuer's payment in a very short time period (e.g., on the same day or within a few hours of presentation), the issuer and the applicant might agree to reduce the issuer's responsibility for failure to discover discrepancies. By the same token, an agreement between the applicant and the issuer might permit the issuer to examine documents exclusively by electronic or electro-optical means. Neither those agreements nor others like them explicitly made by issuers and applicants violate the terms of Section 5-108(a) or (b) or Section 5-103(c).

2. Section 5-108(a) balances the need of the issuer for time to examine the documents against the possibility that the examiner (at the urging of the applicant or for fear that it will not be reimbursed) will take excessive time to search for defects. What is a "reasonable time" is not extended to accommodate an issuer's procuring a waiver from the applicant. See Article 14c of the UCP.

Under both the UCC and the UCP the issuer has a reasonable time to honor or give notice. The outside limit of that time is measured in business days under the UCC and in banking days under the UCP, a difference that will rarely be significant. Neither business nor banking days are defined in

Article 5, but a court may find useful analogies in Regulation CC, 12 CFR 229.2, in state law outside of the Uniform Commercial Code, and in Article 4.

Examiners must note that the seven-day period is not a safe harbor. The time within which the issuer must give notice is the lesser of a reasonable time or seven business days. Where there are few documents (as, for example, with the mine run standby letter of credit), the reasonable time would be less than seven days. If more than a reasonable time is consumed in examination, no timely notice is possible. What is a "reasonable time" is to be determined by examining the behavior of those in the business of examining documents, mostly banks. Absent prior agreement of the issuer, one could not expect a bank issuer to examine documents while the beneficiary waited in the lobby if the normal practice was to give the documents to a person who had the opportunity to examine those together with many others in an orderly process. That the applicant has not yet paid the issuer or that the applicant's account with the issuer is insufficient to cover the amount of the draft is not a basis for extension of the time period.

This section does not preclude the issuer from contacting the applicant during its examination; however, the decision to honor rests with the issuer, and it has no duty to seek a waiver from the applicant or to notify the applicant of receipt of the documents. If the issuer dishonors a conforming presentation, the beneficiary will be entitled to the remedies under Section 5-111, irrespective of the applicant's views.

Even though the person to whom presentation is made cannot conduct a reasonable examination of documents within the time after presentation and before the expiration date, presentation establishes the parties' rights. The beneficiary's right to honor or the issuer's right to dishonor arises upon presentation at the place provided in the letter of credit even though it might take the person to whom presentation has been made several days to determine whether honor or dishonor is the proper course. The issuer's time for honor or giving notice of dishonor may be extended or shortened by a term in the letter of credit. The time for the issuer's performance may be otherwise modified or waived in accordance with Section 5-106.

The issuer's time to inspect runs from the time of its "receipt of documents." Documents are considered to be received only when they are received at the place specified for presentation by the issuer or other party to whom presentation is made.

Failure of the issuer to act within the time permitted by subsection (b) constitutes dishonor. Because of the preclusion in subsection (c) and the liability that the issuer may incur under Section 5-111 for wrongful dishonor, the effect of such a silent dishonor may ultimately be the same as though the issuer had honored, i.e., it may owe damages in the amount drawn but unpaid under the letter of credit.

3. The requirement that the issuer send notice of the discrepancies or be precluded from asserting discrepancies is new to Article 5. It is taken from the similar provision in the UCP and is intended to promote certainty and finality.

   The section thus substitutes a strict preclusion principle for the doctrines of waiver and estoppel that might otherwise apply under Section 1-103. It rejects the reasoning in *Flagship Cruises Ltd. v. New England Merchants' Nat. Bank*, 569 F.2d 699 (1st Cir.1978) and *Wing On Bank Ltd. v. American Nat. Bank & Trust Co.*, 457 F.2d 328 (5th Cir.1972) where the issuer was held to be estopped only if the beneficiary relied on the issuer's failure to give notice.

   Assume, for example, that the beneficiary presented documents to the issuer shortly before the letter of credit expired, in circumstances in which the beneficiary could not have cured any discrepancy before expiration. Under the reasoning of *Flagship* and *Wing On*, the beneficiary's inability to cure, even if it had received notice, would absolve the issuer of its failure to give notice. The virtue of the preclusion obligation adopted in this section is that it forecloses litigation about reliance and detriment.

   Even though issuers typically give notice of the discrepancy of tardy presentation when presentation is made after the expiration of a credit, they are not required to give that notice and the section permits them to raise late presentation as a defect despite their failure to give that notice.

4. To act within a reasonable time, the issuer must normally give notice without delay after the examining party makes its decision. If the examiner decides to dishonor on the first day, it would be obliged to notify the beneficiary shortly thereafter, perhaps on the same business day. This rule accepts the reasoning in cases such as *Datapoint Corp. v. M & I Bank*, 665 F.Supp. 722 (W.D.Wis.1987) and *Esso Petroleum Canada, Div. of Imperial Oil, Ltd. v. Security Pacific Bank*, 710 F.Supp. 275 (D.Or.1989).

   The section deprives the examining party of the right simply to sit on a presentation that is made within seven days of expiration. The section requires the examiner to examine the documents and make a decision and, having made a decision to dishonor, to communicate promptly with the presenter. Nevertheless, a beneficiary who presents documents shortly before the expiration of a letter of credit runs the risk that it will never have the opportunity to cure any discrepancies.

5. Confirmers, other nominated persons, and collecting banks acting for beneficiaries can be presenters and, when so, are entitled to the notice provided in subsection (b). Even nominated persons who have honored or given value against an earlier presentation of the beneficiary and are themselves seeking reimbursement or honor need notice of discrepancies in the hope that they may be able to procure complying documents. The issuer has the obligations imposed by this section whether the issuer's performance is characterized as "reimbursement" of a nominated person or as "honor."

6. In many cases a letter of credit authorizes presentation by the beneficiary to someone other than the issuer. Sometimes that person is identified as a "payor" or "paying bank," or as an "acceptor" or "accepting bank," in other cases as a "negotiating bank," and in other cases there will be no specific designation. The section does not impose any duties on a person other than the issuer or confirmer, however a nominated person or other person may have liability under this article or at common law if it fails to perform an express or implied agreement with the beneficiary.

7. The issuer's obligation to honor runs not only to the beneficiary but also to the applicant. It is possible that an applicant who has made a favorable contract with the beneficiary will be injured by the issuer's wrongful dishonor. Except to the extent that the contract between the issuer and the applicant limits that liability, the issuer will have liability to the applicant for wrongful dishonor under Section 5-111 as a matter of contract law. A good faith extension of the time in Section 5-108(b) by agreement between the issuer and beneficiary binds the applicant even if the applicant is not consulted or does not consent to the extension.

   The issuer's obligation to dishonor when there is no apparent compliance with the letter of credit runs only to the applicant. No other party to the transaction can complain if the applicant waives compliance with terms or conditions of the letter of credit or agrees to a less stringent standard for compliance than that supplied by this article. Except as otherwise agreed with the applicant, an issuer may dishonor a noncomplying presentation despite an applicant's waiver.

   Waiver of discrepancies by an issuer or an applicant in one or more presentations does not waive similar discrepancies in a future presentation. Neither the issuer nor the beneficiary can reasonably rely upon honor over past waivers as a basis for concluding that a future defective presentation will justify honor. The reasoning of *Courtaulds of North America Inc. v. North Carolina Nat. Bank*, 528 F.2d 802 (4th Cir.1975) is accepted and that expressed in *Schweibish v. Pontchartrain State Bank*, 389 So.2d 731 (La.App.1980) and *Titanium Metals Corp. v. Space Metals, Inc.*, 529 P.2d 431 (Utah 1974) is rejected.

8. The standard practice referred to in subsection (e) includes (i) international practice set forth in or referenced by the Uniform Customs and Practice, (ii) other practice rules published by associations of financial institutions, and (iii) local and regional practice. It is possible that standard practice will vary from one place to another. Where there are conflicting practices, the parties should indicate which practice governs their rights. A practice may be overridden by agreement or course of dealing. See Section 1-205(4).

9. The responsibility of the issuer under a letter of credit is to examine documents and to make a prompt decision to honor or dishonor based upon that examination. Nondocumentary conditions have no place in this regime and are better accommodated under contract or suretyship law and practice. In requiring that nondocumentary conditions in letters of credit be

ignored as surplusage, Article 5 remains aligned with the UCP (see UCP 500 Article 13c), approves cases like *Pringle-Associated Mortgage Corp. v. Southern National Bank*, 571 F.2d 871, 874 (5th Cir.1978), and rejects the reasoning in cases such as *Sherwood & Roberts, Inc. v. First Security Bank*, 682 P.2d 149 (Mont. 1984).

Subsection (g) recognizes that letters of credit sometimes contain nondocumentary terms or conditions. Conditions such as a term prohibiting "shipment on vessels more than 15 years old," are to be disregarded and treated as surplusage. Similarly, a requirement that there be an award by a "duly appointed arbitrator" would not require the issuer to determine whether the arbitrator had been "duly appointed." Likewise a term in a standby letter of credit that provided for differing forms of certification depending upon the particular type of default does not oblige the issuer independently to determine which kind of default has occurred. These conditions must be disregarded by the issuer. Where the nondocumentary conditions are central and fundamental to the issuer's obligation (as for example a condition that would require the issuer to determine in fact whether the beneficiary had performed the underlying contract or whether the applicant had defaulted) their inclusion may remove the undertaking from the scope of Article 5 entirely. See Section 5-102(a)(10) and Comment 6 to Section 5-102.

Subsection (g) would not permit the beneficiary or the issuer to disregard terms in the letter of credit such as place, time, and mode of presentation. The rule in subsection (g) is intended to prevent an issuer from deciding or even investigating extrinsic facts, but not from consulting the clock, the calendar, the relevant law and practice, or its own general knowledge of documentation or transactions of the type underlying a particular letter of credit.

Even though nondocumentary conditions must be disregarded in determining compliance of a presentation (and thus in determining the issuer's duty to the beneficiary), an issuer that has promised its applicant that it will honor only on the occurrence of those nondocumentary conditions may have liability to its applicant for disregarding the conditions.

10. Subsection (f) condones an issuer's ignorance of "any usage of a particular trade"; that trade is the trade of the applicant, beneficiary, or others who may be involved in the underlying transaction. The issuer is expected to know usage that is commonly encountered in the course of document examination. For example, an issuer should know the common usage with respect to documents in the maritime shipping trade but would not be expected to understand synonyms used in a particular trade for product descriptions appearing in a letter of credit or an invoice.

11. Where the issuer's performance is the delivery of an item of value other than money, the applicant's reimbursement obligation would be to make the "item of value" available to the issuer.

12. An issuer is entitled to reimbursement from the applicant after honor of a forged or fraudulent drawing if honor was permitted under Section 5-109(a).
13. The last clause of Section 5-108(i)(5) deals with a special case in which the fraud is not committed by the beneficiary, but is committed by a stranger to the transaction who forges the beneficiary's signature. If the issuer pays against documents on which a required signature of the beneficiary is forged, it remains liable to the true beneficiary.

§ 5-109 Fraud and Forgery.

(a) If a presentation is made that appears on its face strictly to comply with the terms and conditions of the letter of credit, but a required document is forged or materially fraudulent, or honor of the presentation would facilitate a material fraud by the beneficiary on the issuer or applicant:
  (1) the issuer shall honor the presentation, if honor is demanded by (i) a nominated person who has given value in good faith and without notice of forgery or material fraud, (ii) a confirmer who has honored its confirmation in good faith, (iii) a holder in due course of a draft drawn under the letter of credit which was taken after acceptance by the issuer or nominated person, or (iv) an assignee of the issuer's or nominated person's deferred obligation that was taken for value and without notice of forgery or material fraud after the obligation was incurred by the issuer or nominated person; and
  (2) the issuer, acting in good faith, may honor or dishonor the presentation in any other case.
(b) If an applicant claims that a required document is forged or materially fraudulent or that honor of the presentation would facilitate a material fraud by the beneficiary on the issuer or applicant, a court of competent jurisdiction may temporarily or permanently enjoin the issuer from honoring a presentation or grant similar relief against the issuer or other persons only if the court finds that:
  (1) the relief is not prohibited under the law applicable to an accepted draft or deferred obligation incurred by the issuer;
  (2) a beneficiary, issuer, or nominated person who may be adversely affected is adequately protected against loss that it may suffer because the relief is granted;
  (3) all of the conditions to entitle a person to the relief under the law of this State have been met; and
  (4) on the basis of the information submitted to the court, the applicant is more likely than not to succeed under its claim of forgery or material fraud and the person demanding honor does not qualify for protection under subsection (a)(1).

OFFICIAL COMMENT

1. This recodification makes clear that fraud must be found either in the documents or must have been committed by the beneficiary on the issuer or applicant. See *Cromwell v. Commerce & Energy Bank*, 464 So.2d 721 (La.1985).

   Secondly, it makes clear that fraud must be "material." Necessarily courts must decide the breadth and width of "materiality." The use of the word requires that the fraudulent aspect of a document be material to a purchaser of that document or that the fraudulent act be significant to the participants in the underlying transaction. Assume, for example, that the beneficiary has a contract to deliver 1,000 barrels of salad oil. Knowing that it has delivered only 998, the beneficiary nevertheless submits an invoice showing 1,000 barrels. If two barrels in a 1,000 barrel shipment would be an insubstantial and immaterial breach of the underlying contract, the beneficiary's act, though possibly fraudulent, is not materially so and would not justify an injunction. Conversely, the knowing submission of those invoices upon delivery of only five barrels would be materially fraudulent. The courts must examine the underlying transaction when there is an allegation of material fraud, for only by examining that transaction can one determine whether a document is fraudulent or the beneficiary has committed fraud and, if so, whether the fraud was material.

   Material fraud by the beneficiary occurs only when the beneficiary has no colorable right to expect honor and where there is no basis in fact to support such a right to honor. The section indorses articulations such as those stated in *Intraworld Indus. v. Girard Trust Bank*, 336 A.2d 316 (Pa.1975), *Roman Ceramics Corp. v. People's Nat. Bank*, 714 F.2d 1207 (3d Cir.1983), and similar decisions and embraces certain decisions under Section 5-114 that relied upon the phrase "fraud in the transaction." Some of these decisions have been summarized as follows in *Ground Air Transfer, Inc. v. Westate's Airlines, Inc.*, 899 F.2d 1269, 1272-73 (1st Cir.1990):

   > We have said throughout that courts may not "normally" issue an injunction because of an important exception to the general "no injunction" rule. The exception, as we also explained in Itek, 730 F.2d at 24-25, concerns "fraud" so serious as to make it obviously pointless and unjust to permit the beneficiary to obtain the money. Where the circumstances "plainly" show that the underlying contract forbids the beneficiary to call a letter of credit, *Itek*, 730 F.2d at 24; where they show that the contract deprives the beneficiary of even a "colorable" right to do so, id., at 25; where the contract and circumstances reveal that the beneficiary's demand for payment has "absolutely no basis in fact," id.; see *Dynamics Corp. of America*, 356 F.Supp. at 999; where the beneficiary's conduct has "so vitiated the entire transaction that the legitimate purposes of the independence of the issuer's obligation would no longer be served," *Itek*, 730 F.2d at 25 (quoting *Roman Ceramics Corp. v. Peoples National Bank*, 714 F.2d

413

1207, 1212 n.12, 1215 (3d Cir.1983) (quoting *Intraworld Indus.*, 336 A.2d at 324-25)); then a court may enjoin payment.

2. Subsection (a)(2) makes clear that the issuer may honor in the face of the applicant's claim of fraud. The subsection also makes clear what was not stated in former Section 5-114, that the issuer may dishonor and defend that dishonor by showing fraud or forgery of the kind stated in subsection (a). Because issuers may be liable for wrongful dishonor if they are unable to prove forgery or material fraud, presumably most issuers will choose to honor despite applicant's claims of fraud or forgery unless the applicant procures an injunction. Merely because the issuer has a right to dishonor and to defend that dishonor by showing forgery or material fraud does not mean it has a duty to the applicant to dishonor. The applicant's normal recourse is to procure an injunction, if the applicant is unable to procure an injunction, it will have a claim against the issuer only in the rare case in which it can show that the issuer did not honor in good faith.

3. Whether a beneficiary can commit fraud by presenting a draft under a clean letter of credit (one calling only for a draft and no other documents) has been much debated. Under the current formulation it would be possible but difficult for there to be fraud in such a presentation. If the applicant were able to show that the beneficiary were committing material fraud on the applicant in the underlying transaction, then payment would facilitate a material fraud by the beneficiary on the applicant and honor could be enjoined. The courts should be skeptical of claims of fraud by one who has signed a "suicide" or clean credit and thus granted a beneficiary the right to draw by mere presentation of a draft.

4. The standard for injunctive relief is high, and the burden remains on the applicant to show, by evidence and not by mere allegation, that such relief is warranted. Some courts have enjoined payments on letters of credit on insufficient showing by the applicant. For example, in *Griffin Cos. v. First Nat. Bank*, 374 N.W.2d 768 (Minn.App.1985), the court enjoined payment under a standby letter of credit, basing its decision on plaintiff's allegation, rather than competent evidence, of fraud.

   There are at least two ways to prohibit injunctions against honor under this section after acceptance of a draft by the issuer. First is to define honor (see Section 5-102(a)(8)) in the particular letter of credit to occur upon acceptance and without regard to later payment of the acceptance. Second is explicitly to agree that the applicant has no right to an injunction after acceptance—whether or not the acceptance constitutes honor.

5. Although the statute deals principally with injunctions against honor, it also cautions against granting "similar relief" and the same principles apply when the applicant or issuer attempts to achieve the same legal outcome by injunction against presentation (see *Ground Air Transfer, Inc. v. Westates Airlines, Inc.*, 899 F.2d 1269 (1st Cir.1990)), interpleader, declaratory judgment, or attachment. These attempts should face the same obstacles

that face efforts to enjoin the issuer from paying. Expanded use of any of these devices could threaten the independence principle just as much as injunctions against honor. For that reason courts should have the same hostility to them and place the same restrictions on their use as would be applied to injunctions against honor. Courts should not allow the "sacred cow of equity to trample the tender vines of letter of credit law."

6. Section 5-109(a)(1) also protects specified third parties against the risk of fraud. By issuing a letter of credit that nominates a person to negotiate or pay, the issuer (ultimately the applicant) induces that nominated person to give value and thereby assumes the risk that a draft drawn under the letter of credit will be transferred to one with a status like that of a holder in due course who deserves to be protected against a fraud defense.

7. The "loss" to be protected against—by bond or otherwise under subsection (b)(2)—includes incidental damages. Among those are legal fees that might be incurred by the beneficiary or issuer in defending against an injunction action.

§ 5-110 Warranties.

(a) If its presentation is honored, the beneficiary warrants:
   (1) to the issuer, any other person to whom presentation is made, and the applicant that there is no fraud or forgery of the kind described in Section 5-109(a); and
   (2) to the applicant that the drawing does not violate any agreement between the applicant and beneficiary or any other agreement intended by them to be augmented by the letter of credit.

(b) The warranties in subsection (a) are in addition to warranties arising under Articles 3, 4, 7, and 8 because of the presentation or transfer of documents covered by any of those articles.

OFFICIAL COMMENT

1. Since the warranties in subsection (a) are not given unless a letter of credit has been honored, no breach of warranty under this subsection can be a defense to dishonor by the issuer. Any defense must be based on Section 5-108 or 5-109 and not on this section. Also, breach of the warranties by the beneficiary in subsection (a) cannot excuse the applicant's duty to reimburse.

2. The warranty in Section 5-110(a)(2) assumes that payment under the letter of credit is final. It does not run to the issuer, only to the applicant. In most cases the applicant will have a direct cause of action for breach of the underlying contract. This warranty has primary application in standby letters of credit or other circumstances where the applicant is not a party to an underlying contract with the beneficiary. It is not a warranty that the

statements made on the presentation of the documents presented are truthful nor is it a warranty that the documents strictly comply under Section 5-108(a). It is a warranty that the beneficiary has performed all the acts expressly and implicitly necessary under any underlying agreement to entitle the beneficiary to honor. If, for example, an underlying sales contract authorized the beneficiary to draw only upon "due performance" and the beneficiary drew even though it had breached the underlying contract by delivering defective goods, honor of its draw would break the warranty. By the same token, if the underlying contract authorized the beneficiary to draw only upon actual default or upon its or a third party's determination of default by the applicant and if the beneficiary drew in violation of its authorization, then upon honor of its draw the warranty would be breached. In many cases, therefore, the documents presented to the issuer will contain inaccurate statements (concerning the goods delivered or concerning default or other matters), but the breach of warranty arises not because the statements are untrue but because the beneficiary's drawing violated its express or implied obligations in the underlying transaction.

3. The damages for breach of warranty are not specified in Section 5-111. Courts may find damage analogies in Section 2-714 in Article 2 and in warranty decisions under Articles 3 and 4.

   Unlike wrongful dishonor cases—where the damages usually equal the amount of the draw—the damages for breach of warranty will often be much less than the amount of the draw, sometimes zero. Assume a seller entitled to draw only on proper performance of its sales contract. Assume it breaches the sales contract in a way that gives the buyer a right to damages but no right to reject. The applicant's damages for breach of the warranty in subsection (a)(2) are limited to the damages it could recover for breach of the contract of sale. Alternatively assume an underlying agreement that authorizes a beneficiary to draw only the "amount in default." Assume a default of $200,000 and a draw of $500,000. The damages for breach of warranty would be no more than $300,000.

§ 5-111 Remedies.

(a) If an issuer wrongfully dishonors or repudiates its obligation to pay money under a letter of credit before presentation, the beneficiary, successor, or nominated person presenting on its own behalf may recover from the issuer the amount that is the subject of the dishonor or repudiation. If the issuer's obligation under the letter of credit is not for the payment of money, the claimant may obtain specific performance or, at the claimant's election, recover an amount equal to the value of performance from the issuer. In either case, the claimant may also recover incidental but not consequential damages. The claimant is not obligated to take action to avoid damages that might be due from the issuer under this subsection. If, although not obligated to do so, the claimant avoids damages, the claimant's recovery from the issuer must be reduced by the amount of damages avoided. The issuer has the burden of proving the amount of damages avoided. In the case of repudiation the claimant need not present any document.

(b) If an issuer wrongfully dishonors a draft or demand presented under a letter of credit or honors a draft or demand in breach of its obligation to the applicant, the applicant may recover damages resulting from the breach, including incidental but not consequential damages, less any amount saved as a result of the breach.

(c) If an adviser or nominated person other than a confirmer breaches an obligation under this article or an issuer breaches an obligation not covered in subsection (a) or (b), a person to whom the obligation is owed may recover damages resulting from the breach, including incidental but not consequential damages, less any amount saved as a result of the breach. To the extent of the confirmation, a confirmer has the liability of an issuer specified in this subsection and subsections (a) and (b).

(d) An issuer, nominated person, or adviser who is found liable under subsection (a), (b), or (c) shall pay interest on the amount owed there-under from the date of wrongful dishonor or other appropriate date.

(e) Reasonable attorney's fees and other expenses of litigation must be awarded to the prevailing party in an action in which a remedy is sought under this article.

(f) Damages that would otherwise be payable by a party for breach of an obligation under this article may be liquidated by agreement or undertaking, but only in an amount or by a formula that is reasonable in light of the harm anticipated.

OFFICIAL COMMENT

1. The right to specific performance is new. The express limitation on the duty of the beneficiary to mitigate damages adopts the position of certain courts and commentators. Because the letter of credit depends upon speed and certainty of payment, it is important that the issuer not be given an incentive to dishonor. The issuer might have an incentive to dishonor if it could rely on the burden of mitigation falling on the beneficiary, (to sell goods and sue only for the difference between the price of the goods sold and the amount due under the letter of credit). Under the scheme contemplated by Section 5-111(a), the beneficiary would present the documents to the issuer. If the issuer wrongfully dishonored, the beneficiary would have no further duty to the issuer with respect to the goods covered by documents that the issuer dishonored and returned. The issuer thus takes the risk that the beneficiary will let the goods rot or be destroyed. Of course the beneficiary may have a duty of mitigation to the applicant arising from the underlying agreement, but the issuer would not have the right to assert

that duty by way of defense or setoff. See Section 5-117(d). If the beneficiary sells the goods covered by dishonored documents or if the beneficiary sells a draft after acceptance but before dishonor by the issuer, the net amount so gained should be subtracted from the amount of the beneficiary's damages—at least where the damage claim against the issuer equals or exceeds the damage suffered by the beneficiary. If, on the other hand, the beneficiary suffers damages in an underlying transaction in an amount that exceeds the amount of the wrongfully dishonored demand (e.g., where the letter of credit does not cover 100 percent of the underlying obligation), the damages avoided should not necessarily be deducted from the beneficiary's claim against the issuer. In such a case, the damages would be the lesser of (i) the amount recoverable in the absence of mitigation (that is, the amount that is subject to the dishonor or repudiation plus any incidental damages) and (ii) the damages remaining after deduction for the amount of damages actually avoided.

A beneficiary need not present documents as a condition of suit for anticipatory repudiation, but if a beneficiary could never have obtained documents necessary for a presentation conforming to the letter of credit, the beneficiary cannot recover for anticipatory repudiation of the letter of credit. *Doelger v. Battery Park Bank*, 201 A.D. 515, 194 N.Y.S. 582 (1922) and *Decor by Nikkei Int'l, Inc. v. Federal Republic of Nigeria*, 497 F.Supp. 893 (S.D.N.Y.1980), *aff'd*, 647 F.2d 300 (2d Cir.1981), *cert. denied*, 454 U.S. 1148 (1982). The last sentence of subsection (c) does not expand the liability of a confirmer to persons to whom the confirmer would not otherwise be liable under Section 5-107.

Almost all letters of credit, including those that call for an acceptance, are "obligations to pay money" as that term is used in Section 5-111(a).

2. What damages "result" from improper honor is for the courts to decide. Even though an issuer pays a beneficiary in violation of Section 5-108(a) or of its contract with the applicant, it may have no liability to an applicant. If the underlying contract has been fully performed, the applicant may not have been damaged by the issuer's breach. Such a case would occur when A contracts for goods at $100 per ton, but, upon delivery, the market value of conforming goods has decreased to $25 per ton. If the issuer pays over discrepancies, there should be no recovery by A for the price differential if the issuer's breach did not alter the applicant's obligation under the underlying contract, i.e., to pay $100 per ton for goods now worth $25 per ton. On the other hand, if the applicant intends to resell the goods and must itself satisfy the strict compliance requirements under a second letter of credit in connection with its sale, the applicant may be damaged by the issuer's payment despite discrepancies because the applicant itself may then be unable to procure honor on the letter of credit where it is the beneficiary, and may be unable to mitigate its damages by enforcing its rights against others in the underlying transaction. Note that an issuer

found liable to its applicant may have recourse under Section 5-117 by subrogation to the applicant's claim against the beneficiary or other persons.

One who inaccurately advises a letter of credit breaches its obligation to the beneficiary, but may cause no damage. If the beneficiary knows the terms of the letter of credit and understands the advice to be inaccurate, the beneficiary will have suffered no damage as a result of the adviser's breach.

3. Since the confirmer has the rights and duties of an issuer, in general it has an issuer's liability, see subsection (c). The confirmer is usually a confirming bank. A confirming bank often also plays the role of an adviser. If it breaks its obligation to the beneficiary, the confirming bank may have liability as an issuer or, depending upon the obligation that was broken, as an adviser. For example, a wrongful dishonor would give it liability as an issuer under Section 5-111(a). On the other hand a confirming bank that broke its obligation to advise the credit but did not commit wrongful dishonor would be treated under Section 5-111(c).

4. Consequential damages for breach of obligations under this article are excluded in the belief that these damages can best be avoided by the beneficiary or the applicant and out of the fear that imposing consequential damages on issuers would raise the cost of the letter of credit to a level that might render it uneconomic. *A fortiori* punitive and exemplary damages are excluded, however, this section does not bar recovery of consequential or even punitive damages for breach of statutory or common law duties arising outside of this article.

5. The section does not specify a rate of interest. It leaves the setting of the rate to the court. It would be appropriate for a court to use the rate that would normally apply in that court in other situations where interest is imposed by law.

6. The court must award attorney's fees to the prevailing party, whether that party is an applicant, a beneficiary, an issuer, a nominated person, or adviser. Since the issuer may be entitled to recover its legal fees and costs from the applicant under the reimbursement agreement, allowing the issuer to recover those fees from a losing beneficiary may also protect the applicant against undeserved losses. The party entitled to attorneys' fees has been described as the "prevailing party." Sometimes it will be unclear which party "prevailed," for example, where there are multiple issues and one party wins on some and the other party wins on others. Determining which is the prevailing party is in the discretion of the court. Subsection (e) authorizes attorney's fees in all actions where a remedy is sought "under this article." It applies even when the remedy might be an injunction under Section 5-109 or when the claimed remedy is otherwise outside of Section 5-111. Neither an issuer nor a confirmer should be treated as a "losing" party when an injunction is granted to the applicant over the objection of the issuer or confirmer; accordingly neither should be liable for fees and expenses in that case.

"Expenses of litigation" is intended to be broader than "costs." For example, expense of litigation would include travel expenses of witnesses, fees for expert witnesses, and expenses associated with taking depositions.

7. For the purposes of Section 5-111(f) "harm anticipated" must be anticipated at the time when the agreement that includes the liquidated damage clause is executed or at the time when the undertaking that includes the clause is issued. See Section 2A-504.

§ 5-112 Transfer of Letter of Credit.

(a) Except as otherwise provided in Section 5-113, unless a letter of credit provides that it is transferable, the right of a beneficiary to draw or otherwise demand performance under a letter of credit may not be transferred.

(b) Even if a letter of credit provides that it is transferable, the issuer may refuse to recognize or carry out a transfer if:

(1) the transfer would violate applicable law; or

(2) the transferor or transferee has failed to comply with any requirement stated in the letter of credit or any other requirement relating to transfer imposed by the issuer which is within the standard practice referred to in Section 5-108(e) or is otherwise reasonable under the circumstances.

OFFICIAL COMMENT

1. In order to protect the applicant's reliance on the designated beneficiary, letter of credit law traditionally has forbidden the beneficiary to convey to third parties its right to draw or demand payment under the letter of credit. Subsection (a) codifies that rule. The term "transfer" refers to the beneficiary's conveyance of that right. Absent incorporation of the UCP (which make elaborate provision for partial transfer of a commercial letter of credit) or similar trade practice and absent other express indication in the letter of credit that the term is used to mean something else, a term in the letter of credit indicating that the beneficiary has the right to transfer should be taken to mean that the beneficiary may convey to a third party its right to draw or demand payment. Even in that case, the issuer or other person controlling the transfer may make the beneficiary's right to transfer subject to conditions, such as timely notification, payment of a fee, delivery of the letter of credit to the issuer or other person controlling the transfer, or execution of appropriate forms to document the transfer. A nominated person who is not a confirmer has no obligation to recognize a transfer.

The power to establish "requirements" does not include the right absolutely to refuse to recognize transfers under a transferable letter of credit. An issuer who wishes to retain the right to deny all transfers should not issue transferable letters of credit or should incorporate the UCP. By stating its requirements in the letter of credit an issuer may impose any requirement without regard to its conformity to practice or reasonableness. Transfer requirements of issuers and nominated persons must be made known to potential transferors and transferees to enable those parties to comply with the requirements. A common method of making such requirements known is to use a form that indicates the information that must be provided and the instructions that must be given to enable the issuer or nominated person to comply with a request to transfer.

2. The issuance of a transferable letter of credit with the concurrence of the applicant is ipso facto an agreement by the issuer and applicant to permit a beneficiary to transfer its drawing right and permit a nominated person to recognize and carry out that transfer without further notice to them. In international commerce, transferable letters of credit are often issued under circumstances in which a nominated person or adviser is expected to facilitate the transfer from the original beneficiary to a transferee and to deal with that transferee. In those circumstances it is the responsibility of the nominated person or adviser to establish procedures satisfactory to protect itself against double presentation or dispute about the right to draw under the letter of credit. Commonly such a person will control the transfer by requiring that the original letter of credit be given to it or by causing a paper copy marked as an original to be issued where the original letter of credit was electronic. By keeping possession of the original letter of credit the nominated person or adviser can minimize or entirely exclude the possibility that the original beneficiary could properly procure payment from another bank. If the letter of credit requires presentation of the original letter of credit itself, no other payment could be procured. In addition to imposing whatever requirements it considers appropriate to protect itself against double payment the person that is facilitating the transfer has a right to charge an appropriate fee for its activity.

"Transfer" of a letter of credit should be distinguished from "assignment of proceeds." The former is analogous to a novation or a substitution of beneficiaries. It contemplates not merely payment to but also performance by the transferee. For example, under the typical terms of transfer for a commercial letter of credit, a transferee could comply with a letter of credit transferred to it by signing and presenting its own draft and invoice. An assignee of proceeds, on the other hand, is wholly dependent on the presentation of a draft and invoice signed by the beneficiary.

By agreeing to the issuance of a transferable letter of credit, which is not qualified or limited, the applicant may lose control over the identity of the person whose performance will earn payment under the letter of credit.

§ 5-113 Transfer by Operation of Law.

(a) A successor of a beneficiary may consent to amendments, sign and present documents, and receive payment or other items of value in the name of the beneficiary without disclosing its status as a successor.

(b) A successor of a beneficiary may consent to amendments, sign and present documents, and receive payment or other items of value in its own name as the disclosed successor of the beneficiary. Except as otherwise provided in subsection (e), an issuer shall recognize a disclosed successor of a beneficiary as beneficiary in full substitution for its predecessor upon compliance with the requirements for recognition by the issuer of a transfer of drawing rights by operation of law under the standard practice referred to in Section 5-108(e) or, in the absence of such a practice, compliance with other reasonable procedures sufficient to protect the issuer.

(c) An issuer is not obliged to determine whether a purported successor is a successor of a beneficiary or whether the signature of a purported successor is genuine or authorized.

(d) Honor of a purported successor's apparently complying presentation under subsection (a) or (b) has the consequences specified in Section 5-108(i) even if the purported successor is not the successor of a beneficiary. Documents signed in the name of the beneficiary or of a disclosed successor by a person who is neither the beneficiary nor the successor of the beneficiary are forged documents for the purposes of Section 5-109.

(e) An issuer whose rights of reimbursement are not covered by subsection (d) or substantially similar law and any confirmer or nominated person may decline to recognize a presentation under subsection (b).

(f) A beneficiary whose name is changed after the issuance of a letter of credit has the same rights and obligations as a successor of a beneficiary under this section.

OFFICIAL COMMENT

This section affirms the result in *Pastor v. Nat. Republic Bank of Chicago*, 76 Ill.2d 139, 390 N.E.2d 894 (Ill.1979) and *Federal Deposit Insurance Co. v. Bank of Boulder*, 911 F.2d 1466 (10th Cir.1990).

An issuer's requirements for recognition of a successor's status might include presentation of a certificate of merger, a court order appointing a bankruptcy trustee or receiver, a certificate of appointment as bankruptcy trustee, or the like. The issuer is entitled to rely upon such documents which on their face demonstrate that presentation is made by a successor of a beneficiary. It is not obliged to make an independent investigation to determine the fact of succession.

§ 5-114 Assignment of Proceeds.

(a) In this section, "proceeds of a letter of credit" means the cash, check, accepted draft, or other item of value paid or delivered upon honor or giving of value by the issuer or any nominated person under the letter of credit. The term does not include a beneficiary's drawing rights or documents presented by the beneficiary.

(b) A beneficiary may assign its right to part or all of the proceeds of a letter of credit. The beneficiary may do so before presentation as a present assignment of its right to receive proceeds contingent upon its compliance with the terms and conditions of the letter of credit.

(c) An issuer or nominated person need not recognize an assignment of proceeds of a letter of credit until it consents to the assignment.

(d) An issuer or nominated person has no obligation to give or withhold its consent to an assignment of proceeds of a letter of credit, but consent may not be unreasonably withheld if the assignee possesses and exhibits the letter of credit and presentation of the letter of credit is a condition to honor.

(e) Rights of a transferee beneficiary or nominated person are independent of the beneficiary's assignment of the proceeds of a letter of credit and are superior to the assignee's right to the proceeds.

(f) Neither the rights recognized by this section between an assignee and an issuer, transferee beneficiary, or nominated person nor the issuer's or nominated person's payment of proceeds to an assignee or a third person affect the rights between the assignee and any person other than the issuer, transferee beneficiary, or nominated person. The mode of creating and perfecting a security interest in or granting an assignment of a beneficiary's rights to proceeds is governed by Article 9 or other law. Against persons other than the issuer, transferee beneficiary, or nominated person, the rights and obligations arising upon the creation of a security interest or other assignment of a beneficiary's right to proceeds and its perfection are governed by Article 9 or other law.

OFFICIAL COMMENT

1. Subsection (b) expressly validates the beneficiary's present assignment of letter of credit proceeds if made after the credit is established but before the proceeds are realized. This section adopts the prevailing usage—"assignment of proceeds"—to an assignee. That terminology carries with it no implication, however, that an assignee acquires no interest until the proceeds are paid by the issuer. For example, an "assignment of the right to proceeds" of a letter of credit for purposes of security that meets the requirements of Section 9-203(1) would constitute the present creation of a security interest in that right. This security interest can be perfected by

possession (Section 9-305) if the letter of credit is in written form. Although subsection (a) explains the meaning of "'proceeds' of a letter of credit," it should be emphasized that those proceeds also may be Article 9 proceeds of other collateral. For example, if a seller of inventory receives a letter of credit to support the account that arises upon the sale, payments made under the letter of credit are Article 9 proceeds of the inventory, account, and any document of title covering the inventory. Thus, the secured party who had a perfected security interest in that inventory, account, or document has a perfected security interest in the proceeds collected under the letter of credit, so long as they are identifiable cash proceeds (Section 9-306(2), (3)). This perfection is continuous, regardless of whether the secured party perfected a security interest in the right to letter of credit proceeds.

2. An assignee's rights to enforce an assignment of proceeds against an issuer and the priority of the assignee's rights against a nominated person or transferee beneficiary are governed by Article 5. Those rights and that priority are stated in subsections (c), (d), and (e). Note also that Section 4-210 gives first priority to a collecting bank that has given value for a documentary draft.

3. By requiring that an issuer or nominated person consent to the assignment of proceeds of a letter of credit, subsections (c) and (d) follow more closely recognized national and international letter of credit practices than did prior law. In most circumstances, it has always been advisable for the assignee to obtain the consent of the issuer in order better to safeguard its right to the proceeds. When notice of an assignment has been received, issuers normally have required signatures on a consent form. This practice is reflected in the revision. By unconditionally consenting to such an assignment, the issuer or nominated person becomes bound, subject to the rights of the superior parties specified in subsection (e), to pay to the assignee the assigned letter of credit proceeds that the issuer or nominated person would otherwise pay to the beneficiary or another assignee.

Where the letter of credit must be presented as a condition to honor and the assignee holds and exhibits the letter of credit to the issuer or nominated person, the risk to the issuer or nominated person of having to pay twice is minimized. In such a situation, subsection (d) provides that the issuer or nominated person may not unreasonably withhold its consent to the assignment.

§ 5-115 Statute of Limitations.

An action to enforce a right or obligation arising under this article must be commenced within one year after the expiration date of the relevant letter of credit or one year after the [claim for relief] [cause of action] accrues, whichever occurs later. A [claim for relief] [cause of action] accrues when the breach occurs, regardless of the aggrieved party's lack of knowledge of the breach.

OFFICIAL COMMENT

1. This section is based upon Sections 4-111 and 2-725(2).

2. This section applies to all claims for which there are remedies under Section 5-111 and to other claims made under this article, such as claims for breach of warranty under Section 5-110. Because it covers all claims under Section 5-111, the statute of limitations applies not only to wrongful dishonor claims against the issuer but also to claims between the issuer and the applicant arising from the reimbursement agreement. These might be for reimbursement (issuer v. applicant) or for breach of the reimbursement contract by wrongful honor (applicant v. issuer).

3. The statute of limitations, like the rest of the statute, applies only to a letter of credit issued on or after the effective date and only to transactions, events, obligations, or duties arising out of or associated with such a letter. If a letter of credit was issued before the effective date and an obligation on that letter of credit was breached after the effective date, the complaining party could bring its suit within the time that would have been permitted prior to the adoption of Section 5-115 and would not be limited by the terms of Section 5-115.

§ 5-116 Choice of Law and Forum.

(a) The liability of an issuer, nominated person, or adviser for action or omission is governed by the law of the jurisdiction chosen by an agreement in the form of a record signed or otherwise authenticated by the affected parties in the manner provided in Section 5-104 or by a provision in the person's letter of credit, confirmation, or other undertaking. The jurisdiction whose law is chosen need not bear any relation to the transaction.

(b) Unless subsection (a) applies, the liability of an issuer, nominated person, or adviser for action or omission is governed by the law of the jurisdiction in which the person is located. The person is considered to be located at the address indicated in the person's undertaking. If more than one address is indicated, the person is considered to be located at the address from which the person's undertaking was issued. For the purpose of jurisdiction, choice of law, and recognition of interbranch letters of credit, but not enforcement of a judgment, all branches of a bank are considered separate juridical entities and a bank is considered to be located at the place where its relevant branch is considered to be located under this subsection.

(c) Except as otherwise provided in this subsection, the liability of an issuer, nominated person, or adviser is governed by any rules of custom or practice, such as the Uniform Customs and Practice for Documentary Credits, to which the letter of credit, confirmation, or other undertaking is expressly made subject. If (i) this article would govern the liability of an issuer, nominated person, or adviser under subsection (a) or (b), (ii) the relevant undertaking incorporates rules of custom or practice, and (iii) there is conflict between this article and those rules as applied to that undertaking, those rules govern except to the extent of any conflict with the nonvariable provisions specified in Section 5-103(c).

(d) If there is conflict between this article and Article 3, 4, 4A, or 9, this article governs.

(e) The forum for settling disputes arising out of an undertaking within this article may be chosen in the manner and with the binding effect that governing law may be chosen in accordance with subsection (a).

OFFICIAL COMMENT

1. Although it would be possible for the parties to agree otherwise, the law normally chosen by agreement under subsection (a) and that provided in the absence of agreement under subsection (b) is the substantive law of a particular jurisdiction not including the choice of law principles of that jurisdiction. Thus, two parties, an issuer and an applicant, both located in Oklahoma might choose the law of New York. Unless they agree otherwise, the section anticipates that they wish the substantive law of New York to apply to their transaction and they do not intend that a New York choice of law principle might direct a court to Oklahoma law. By the same token, the liability of an issuer located in New York is governed by New York substantive law—in the absence of agreement—even in circumstances in which choice of law principles found in the common law of New York might direct one to the law of another State. Subsection (b) states the relevant choice of law principles and it should not be subordinated to some other choice of law rule. Within the States of the United States renvoi will not be a problem once every jurisdiction has enacted Section 5-116 because every jurisdiction will then have the same choice of law rule and in a particular case all choice of law rules will point to the same substantive law.

Subsection (b) does not state a choice of law rule for the "liability of an applicant." However, subsection (b) does state a choice of law rule for the liability of an issuer, nominated person, or adviser, and since some of the issues in suits by applicants against those persons involve the "liability of an issuer, nominated person, or adviser," subsection (b) states the choice of law rule for those issues. Because an issuer may have liability to a confirmer both as an issuer (Section 5-108(a), Comment 5 to Section 5-108) and as an applicant (Section 5-107(a), Comment 1 to Section 5-107, Section 5-108(i)), subsection (b) may state the choice of law rule for some but not all of the issuer's liability in a suit by a confirmer.

2. Because the confirmer or other nominated person may choose different law from that chosen by the issuer or may be located in a different jurisdiction

and fail to choose law, it is possible that a confirmer or nominated person may be obligated to pay (under their law) but will not be entitled to payment from the issuer (under its law). Similarly, the rights of an unreimbursed issuer, confirmer, or nominated person against a beneficiary under Section 5-109, 5-110, or 5-117, will not necessarily be governed by the same law that applies to the issuer's or confirmer's obligation upon presentation. Because the UCP and other practice are incorporated in most international letters of credit, disputes arising from different legal obligations to honor have not been frequent. Since Section 5-108 incorporates standard practice, these problems should be further minimized—at least to the extent that the same practice is and continues to be widely followed.

3. This section does not permit what is now authorized by the nonuniform Section 5-102(4) in New York. Under the current law in New York a letter of credit that incorporates the UCP is not governed in any respect by Article 5. Under revised Section 5-116 letters of credit that incorporate the UCP or similar practice will still be subject to Article 5 in certain respects. First, incorporation of the UCP or other practice does not override the nonvariable terms of Article 5. Second, where there is no conflict between Article 5 and the relevant provision of the UCP or other practice, both apply. Third, practice provisions incorporated in a letter of credit will not be effective if they fail to comply with Section 5-103(c). Assume, for example, that a practice provision purported to free a party from any liability unless it were "grossly negligent" or that the practice generally limited the remedies that one party might have against another. Depending upon the circumstances, that disclaimer or limitation of liability might be ineffective because of Section 5-103(c).

Even though Article 5 is generally consistent with UCP 500, it is not necessarily consistent with other rules or with versions of the UCP that may be adopted after Article 5's revision, or with other practices that may develop. Rules of practice incorporated in the letter of credit or other undertaking are those in effect when the letter of credit or other undertaking is issued. Except in the unusual cases discussed in the immediately preceding paragraph, practice adopted in a letter of credit will override the rules of Article 5 and the parties to letter of credit transactions must be familiar with practice (such as future versions of the UCP) that is explicitly adopted in letters of credit.

4. In several ways Article 5 conflicts with and overrides similar matters governed by Articles 3 and 4. For example, "draft" is more broadly defined in letter of credit practice than under Section 3-104. The time allowed for honor and the required notification of reasons for dishonor are different in letter of credit practice than in the handling of documentary and other drafts under Articles 3 and 4.

5. Subsection (e) must be read in conjunction with existing law governing subject matter jurisdiction. If the local law restricts a court to certain subject matter jurisdiction not including letter of credit disputes,

subsection (e) does not authorize parties to choose that forum. For example, the parties' agreement under Section 5-116(e) would not confer jurisdiction on a probate court to decide a letter of credit case.

If the parties choose a forum under subsection (e) and if—because of other law—that forum will not take jurisdiction, the parties' agreement or undertaking should then be construed (for the purpose of forum selection) as though it did not contain a clause choosing a particular forum. That result is necessary to avoid sentencing the parties to eternal purgatory where neither the chosen State nor the State which would have jurisdiction but for the clause will take jurisdiction—the former in disregard of the clause and the latter in honor of the clause.

§ 5-117 Subrogation of Issuer, Applicant, and Nominated Person.

(a) An issuer that honors a beneficiary's presentation is subrogated to the rights of the beneficiary to the same extent as if the issuer were a secondary obligor of the underlying obligation owed to the beneficiary and of the applicant to the same extent as if the issuer were the secondary obligor of the underlying obligation owed to the applicant.

(b) An applicant that reimburses an issuer is subrogated to the rights of the issuer against any beneficiary, presenter, or nominated person to the same extent as if the applicant were the secondary obligor of the obligations owed to the issuer and has the rights of subrogation of the issuer to the rights of the beneficiary stated in subsection (a).

(c) A nominated person who pays or gives value against a draft or demand presented under a letter of credit is subrogated to the rights of:

    (1) the issuer against the applicant to the same extent as if the nominated person were a secondary obligor of the obligation owed to the issuer by the applicant;

    (2) the beneficiary to the same extent as if the nominated person were a secondary obligor of the underlying obligation owed to the beneficiary; and

    (3) the applicant to same extent as if the nominated person were a secondary obligor of the underlying obligation owed to the applicant.

(d) Notwithstanding any agreement or term to the contrary, the rights of subrogation stated in subsections (a) and (b) do not arise until the issuer honors the letter of credit or otherwise pays and the rights in subsection (c) do not arise until the nominated person pays or otherwise gives value. Until then, the issuer, nominated person, and the applicant do not derive under this section present or prospective rights forming the basis of a claim, defense, or excuse.

OFFICIAL COMMENT

1. By itself this section does not grant any right of subrogation. It grants only the right that would exist if the person seeking subrogation "were a secondary obligor." (The term "secondary obligor" refers to a surety, guarantor, or other person against whom or whose property an obligee has recourse with respect to the obligation of a third party. See Restatement of the Law Third, Suretyship and Guaranty § 1 (1996).) If the secondary obligor would not have a right to subrogation in the circumstances in which one is claimed under this section, none is granted by this section. In effect, the section does no more than to remove an impediment that some courts have found to subrogation because they conclude that the issuer's or other claimant's rights are "independent" of the underlying obligation. If, for example, a secondary obligor would not have a subrogation right because its payment did not fully satisfy the underlying obligation, none would be available under this section. The section indorses the position of Judge Becker in *Tudor Development Group, Inc. v. United States Fidelity and Guaranty*, 968 F.2d 357 (3rd Cir.1991).

2. To preserve the independence of the letter of credit obligation and to insure that subrogation not be used as an offensive weapon by an issuer or others, the admonition in subsection (d) must be carefully observed. Only one who has completed its performance in a letter of credit transaction can have a right to subrogation. For example, an issuer may not dishonor and then defend its dishonor or assert a setoff on the ground that it is subrogated to another person's rights. Nor may the issuer complain after honor that its subrogation rights have been impaired by any good faith dealings between the beneficiary and the applicant or any other person. Assume, for example, that the beneficiary under a standby letter of credit is a mortgagee. If the mortgagee were obliged to issue a release of the mortgage upon payment of the underlying debt (by the issuer under the letter of credit), that release might impair the issuer's rights of subrogation, but the beneficiary would have no liability to the issuer for having granted that release.

§ 7-102 Definitions and Index of Definitions.

(1) In this Article, unless the context otherwise requires:
   (a) "Bailee" means the person who by a warehouse receipt, bill of lading or other document of title acknowledges possession of goods and contracts to deliver them.
   (b) "Consignee" means the person named in a bill to whom or to whose order the bill promises delivery.
   (c) "Consignor" means the person named in a bill as the person from whom the goods have been received for shipment.

429

(d) "Delivery order" means a written order to deliver goods directed to a warehouseman, carrier or other person who in the ordinary course of business issues warehouse receipts or bills of lading.

(e) "Document" means document of title as defined in the general definitions in Article 1 (Section 1-201).

(f) "Goods" means all things which are treated as movable for the purposes of a contract of storage or transportation.

(g) "Issuer" means a bailee who issues a document except that in relation to an unaccepted delivery order it means the person who orders the possessor of goods to deliver. Issuer includes any person for whom an agent or employee purports to act in issuing a document if the agent or employee has real or apparent authority to issue documents, notwithstanding that the issuer received no goods or that the goods were misdescribed or that in any other respect the agent or employee violated his instructions.

(h) "Warehouseman" is a person engaged in the business of storing goods for hire.

(2) Other definitions applying to this Article or to specified Parts thereof, and the sections in which they appear are:

"Duly negotiate". Section 7-501.

"Person entitled under the document". Section 7-403(4).

(3) Definitions in other Articles applying to this Article and the sections in which they appear are:

"Contract for sale". Section 2-106.

"Overseas". Section 2-323.

"Receipt" of goods. Section 2-103.

(4) In addition Article 1 contains general definitions and principles of construction and interpretation applicable throughout this Article.

OFFICIAL COMMENT

Purposes of Changes and New Matter:

1. "Bailee" was not defined in the old uniform acts. It is used in this Article as a blanket term to designate carriers, warehousemen and others who normally issue documents of title on the basis of goods which they have received. The definition does not, however, require actual possession of the goods. If a bailee acknowledges possession when he does not have it he is bound by sections of this Article which declare the "bailee's" obligations. (See definition of "Issuer" in this section and Sections 7-203 and 7-301 on liability in case of non-receipt.)

2. The definition of warehouse receipt contained in the general definitions section of this Act (Section 1-201) eliminates the requirement of the Uniform Warehouse Receipts Act that the issuing warehouseman be "lawfully engaged" in business. The warehouseman's compliance with

430

applicable state regulations such as the filing of a bond has no bearing on the substantive issues dealt with in this Article. Certainly the issuer's violations of law should not diminish his responsibility on documents he has put in commercial circulation. The Uniform Warehouse Receipts Act requirement that the warehouseman be engaged "for profit" has also been eliminated in view of the existence of state operated and cooperative warehouses. But it is still essential that the business be storing goods "for hire" (Section 1-201 and this section). A person does not become a warehouseman by storing his own goods.

3. Delivery orders, which were included without qualification in the Uniform Sales Act definition of document of title, must be treated differently in this consolidation of provisions from the three uniform acts. When a delivery order has been accepted by the bailee it is for practical purposes indistinguishable from a warehouse receipt. Prior to such acceptance there is no basis for imposing obligations on the bailee other than the ordinary obligation of contract which the bailee may have assumed to the depositor of the goods.

§ 7-304 Bills of Lading in a Set.

(1) Except where customary in overseas transportation, a bill of lading must not be issued in a set of parts. The issuer is liable for damages caused by violation of this subsection.

(2) Where a bill of lading is lawfully drawn in a set of parts, each of which is numbered and expressed to be valid only if the goods have not been delivered against any other part, the whole of the parts constitute one bill.

(3) Where a bill of lading is lawfully issued in a set of parts and different parts are negotiated to different persons, the title of the holder to whom the first due negotiation is made prevails as to both the document and the goods even though any later holder may have received the goods from the carrier in good faith and discharged the carrier's obligation by surrender of his part.

(4) Any person who negotiates or transfers a single part of a bill of lading drawn in a set is liable to holders of that part as if it were the whole set.

(5) The bailee is obliged to deliver in accordance with Part 4 of this Article against the first presented part of a bill of lading lawfully drawn in a set. Such delivery discharges the bailee's obligation on the whole bill.

OFFICIAL COMMENT

Purposes of Changes:

The statement of the legal effect of a lawfully issued set is in accord with existing commercial law relating to maritime and other overseas bills. This law has been codified in the Hague and Warsaw Conventions and in the Carriage of Goods by Sea Act, the provisions of which would ordinarily govern in situations where bills in a set are recognized by this Article.

§ 7-503 Document of Title to Goods Defeated in Certain Cases.

(1) A document of title confers no right in goods against a person who before issuance of the document had a legal interest or a perfected security interest in them and who neither

    (a) delivered or entrusted them or any document of title covering them to the bailor or his nominee with actual or apparent authority to ship, store or sell or with power to obtain delivery under this Article (Section 7-403) or with power of disposition under this Act (Sections 2-403 and 9-307) or other statute or rule of law; nor

    (b) acquiesced in the procurement by the bailor or his nominee of any document of title.

(2) Title to goods based upon an unaccepted delivery order is subject to the rights of anyone to whom a negotiable warehouse receipt or bill of lading covering the goods has been duly negotiated. Such a title may be defeated under the next section to the same extent as the rights of the issuer or a transferee from the issuer.

(3) Title to goods based upon a bill of lading issued to a freight forwarder is subject to the rights of anyone to whom a bill issued by the freight forwarder is duly negotiated; but delivery by the carrier in accordance with Part 4 of this Article pursuant to its own bill of lading discharges the carrier's obligation to deliver.

OFFICIAL COMMENT

Purposes of Changes:

1. In general it may be said that the title of a purchaser by due negotiation prevails over almost any interest in the goods which existed prior to the procurement of the document of title if the possession of the goods by the person obtaining the document derived from any action by the prior claimant which introduced the goods into the stream of commerce or carried them along that stream. A thief of the goods cannot indeed by shipping or storing them to his own order acquire power to transfer them to a good faith purchaser. Nor can a tenant or mortgagor defeat any rights of a landlord or mortgagee which have been perfected under the local law merely by wrongfully shipping or storing a portion of the crop or other goods. However, "acquiescence" by the landlord or tenant does not require active consent under subsection (1)(b) and knowledge of the likelihood of

storage or shipment with no objection or effort to control it is sufficient to defeat his rights as against one who takes by "due" negotiation of a negotiable document.

On the other hand, where goods are delivered to a factor for sale, even though the factor has made no advances and is limited in his duty to sell for cash, the goods are "entrusted" to him "with actual . . . authority . . . to sell" under subsection (1)(a), and if he procures a negotiable document of title he can transfer the owner's interest to a purchaser by due negotiation. Further, where the factor is in the business of selling, goods entrusted to him simply for safekeeping or storage may be entrusted under circumstances which give him "apparent authority to ship, store or sell" under subsection (1)(a), or power of disposition under Section 2-403, 7-205 or 9-307, or under a statute such as the earlier Factors Acts, or under a rule of law giving effect to apparent ownership. See Section 1-103.

Persons having an interest in goods also frequently deliver or entrust them to agents or servants other than factors for the purpose of shipping or warehousing or under circumstances reasonably contemplating such action. Rounding out the case law development under the prior Acts, this Act is clear that such persons assume full risk that the agent to whom the goods are so delivered may ship or store in breach of duty, take a document to his own order and then proceed to misappropriate it. This Act makes no distinction between possession or mere custody in such situations and finds no exception in the case of larceny by a bailee or the like. The safeguard in such situations lies in the requirement that a due negotiation can occur only "in the regular course of business or financing" and that the purchase be in good faith and without notice. See Section 7-501. Documents of title have no market among the commercially inexperienced and the commercially experienced do not take them without inquiry from persons known to be truck drivers or petty clerks even though such persons purport to be operating in their own names.

Again, where the seller allows a buyer to receive goods under a contract for sale, though as a "conditional delivery" or under "cash sale" terms and on explicit agreement for immediate payment, the buyer thereby acquires power to defeat the seller's interest by transfer of the goods to certain good faith purchasers. See Section 2-403. Both in policy and under the language of subsection (1)(a) that same power must be extended to accomplish the same result if the buyer procures a negotiable document of title to the goods and duly negotiates it.

2. Under subsection (1) a delivery order issued by a person having no right in or power over the goods is ineffective unless the owner acts as provided in subsection (1)(a) or (b). Thus the rights of a transferee of a non-negotiable warehouse receipt can be defeated by a delivery order subsequently issued by the transferor only if the transferee "delivers or entrusts" to the "person procuring" the delivery order or "acquiesces" in his procurement. Similarly, a second delivery order issued by the same issuer for the same goods

will ordinarily be subject to the first, both under this section and under Section 7-402. After a delivery order is validly issued but before it is accepted, it may nevertheless be defeated under subsection (2) in much the same way that the rights of a transferee may be defeated under Section 7-504. For example, a buyer in ordinary course from the issuer may defeat the rights of the holder of a prior delivery order if the bailee receives notification of the buyer's rights before notification of the holder's rights. Section 7-504(2)(b). But an accepted delivery order has the same effect as a document issued by the bailee.

3. Under subsection (3) a bill of lading issued to a freight forwarder is subordinated to the freight forwarder's certificate, since the bill on its face gives notice of the fact that a freight forwarder is in the picture and has in all probability issued a certificate. But the carrier is protected in following the terms of its own bill of lading.

Sec. 7-504 Rights Acquired in the Absence of Due Negotiation; Effect of Diversion; Seller's Stoppage of Delivery.

(1) A transferee of a document, whether negotiable or nonnegotiable, to whom the document has been delivered but not duly negotiated, acquires the title and rights which his transferor had or had actual authority to convey.

(2) In the case of a non-negotiable document, until but not after the bailee receives notification of the transfer, the rights of the transferee may be defeated
   (a) by those creditors of the transferor who could treat the sale as void under Section 2-402; or
   (b) by a buyer from the transferor in ordinary course of business if the bailee has delivered the goods to the buyer or received notification of his rights; or
   (c) as against the bailee by good faith dealings of the bailee with the transferor.

(3) A diversion or other change of shipping instructions by the consignor in a non-negotiable bill of lading which causes the bailee not to deliver to the consignee defeats the consignee's title to the goods if they have been delivered to a buyer in ordinary course of business and in any event defeats the consignee's rights against the bailee.

(4) Delivery pursuant to a non-negotiable document may be stopped by a seller under Section 2-705, and subject to the requirement of due notification there provided. A bailee honoring the seller's instructions is entitled to be indemnified by the seller against any resulting loss or expense.

OFFICIAL COMMENT

Purposes of Changes and New Matter:

1. Under the general principles controlling negotiable documents, it is clear that in the absence of due negotiation a transferor cannot convey greater rights than he himself has, even when the negotiation is formally perfect. This section recognizes the transferor's power to transfer rights which he himself has or has "actual authority to convey." Thus, where a negotiable document of title is being transferred the operation of the principle of estoppel is not recognized, as contrasted with situations involving the transfer of the goods themselves. (Compare Section 2-403 on good faith purchase of goods.)

   A necessary part of the price for the protection of regular dealings with negotiable documents of title is an insistence that no dealing which is in any way irregular shall be recognized as a good faith purchase of the document or of any rights pertaining to it. So, where the transfer of a negotiable document fails as a negotiation because a requisite indorsement is forged or otherwise missing, the purchaser in good faith and for value may be in the anomalous position of having less rights, in part, than if he had purchased the goods themselves. True, his rights are not subject to defeat by attachment of the goods or surrender of them to his transferor [contrast subsection (2)]; but on the other hand, he cannot acquire enforceable rights to control or receive the goods over the bailee's objection merely by giving notice to the bailee. Similarly, a consignee who makes payment to his consignor against a straight bill of lading can thereby acquire the position of a good faith purchaser of goods under provisions of the Article of this Act on Sales (Section 2-403), whereas the same payment made in good faith against an unindorsed order bill would not have such effect. The appropriate remedy of a purchaser in such a situation is to regularize his status by compelling indorsement of the document (see Section 7-506).

2. As in the case of transfer—as opposed to "due negotiation"—of negotiable documents, subsection (1) empowers the transferor of a nonnegotiable document to transfer only such rights as he himself has or has "actual authority" to convey. In contrast to situations involving the goods themselves the operation of estoppel or agency principles is not here recognized to enable the transferor to convey greater rights than he actually has. Subsection (2) makes it clear, however, that the transferee of a nonnegotiable document may acquire rights greater in some respects than those of his transferor by giving notice of the transfer to the bailee.

3. Subsection (3) is in part a reiteration of the carrier's immunity from liability if it honors instructions of the consignor to divert, but there is added a provision protecting the title of the substituted consignee if the latter is a buyer in ordinary course of business. A typical situation would be where a

manufacturer, having shipped a lot of standardized goods to A on nonne-gotiable bill of lading, diverts the goods to customer B who pays for them. Under orthodox passage-of-title-by-appropriation doctrine A might reclaim the goods from B. However, no consideration of commercial policy supports this involvement of an innocent third party in the default of the manufacturer on his contract to A; and the common commercial practice of diverting goods in transit suggests a trade understanding in accordance with this subsection.

4. Subsection (4) gives the carrier an express right to indemnity where he honors a seller's request to stop delivery.

5. Section 1-201(27) gives the bailee protection, if due diligence is exercised, similar to that found in the third paragraph of Section 33, Uniform Bills of Lading Act, where the bailee's organization has not had time to act on a notification.

B. UNIFORM FOREIGN-COUNTRY MONEY JUDGMENTS RECOGNITION ACT

UNIFORM FOREIGN-COUNTRY MONEY JUDGMENTS RECOGNITION ACT

drafted by the

NATIONAL CONFERENCE OF COMMISSIONERS

ON UNIFORM STATE LAWS

and by it

APPROVED AND RECOMMENDED FOR ENACTMENT

IN ALL THE STATES

at its

ANNUAL CONFERENCE

MEETING IN ITS ONE-HUNDRED-AND-FOURTEENTH YEAR

PITTSBURGH, PENNSYLVANIA

July 21-28, 2005

WITH PREFATORY NOTE AND COMMENTS

Copyright ©2005

By

NATIONAL CONFERENCE OF COMMISSIONERS

ON UNIFORM STATE LAWS

February 10, 2006

UNIFORM FOREIGN-COUNTRY MONEY JUDGMENTS RECOGNITION ACT

PREFATORY NOTE

This Act is a revision of the Uniform Foreign Money-Judgments Recognition Act of 1962. That Act codified the most prevalent common law rules with regard to the recognition of money judgments rendered in other countries. The hope was that codification by a state of its rules on the recognition of foreign-country money judgments, by satisfying reciprocity concerns of foreign courts, would make it more likely that money judgments rendered in that state would be recognized in other countries. Towards this end, the Act sets out the circumstances in which the courts in states that have adopted the Act must recognize foreign-country money judgments. It delineates a minimum of foreign-country judgments that must be recognized by the courts of adopting states, leaving those courts free to recognize other foreign-country judgments not covered by the Act under principles of comity or otherwise. Since its promulgation over forty years ago, the 1962 Act has been adopted in a majority of the states and has been in large part successful in carrying out it purpose of establishing uniform and clear standards under which state courts will enforce the foreign-country money judgments that come within its scope.

This Act continues the basic policies and approach of the 1962 Act. Its purpose is not to depart from the basic rules or approach of the 1962 Act, which have withstood well the test of time, but rather to update the 1962 Act, to clarify its provisions, and to correct problems created by the interpretation of the provisions of that Act by the courts over the years since its promulgation. Among the more significant issues that have arisen under the 1962 Act which are addressed in this Revised Act are (1) the need to update and clarify the definitions section; (2) the need to reorganize and clarify the scope provisions, and to allocate the burden of proof with regard to establishing application of the Act; (3) the need to set out the procedure by which recognition of a foreign-country money judgment under the Act must be sought; (4) the need to clarify and, to a limited extent, expand upon the grounds for denying recognition in light of differing interpretations of those provisions in the current case law; (5) the need to expressly allocate the burden of proof with regard to the grounds for denying recognition; and (6) the need to establish a statute of limitations for recognition actions.

In the course of drafting this Act, the drafters revisited the decision made in the 1962 Act not to require reciprocity as a condition to recognition of the foreign-country money judgments covered by the Act. After much discussion, the drafters decided that the approach of the 1962 Act continues to be the wisest course with regard to this issue. While recognition of U.S. judgments continues to be problematic in a number of foreign countries, there was insufficient evidence to establish that a reciprocity requirement would have a greater effect on encouraging foreign recognition of U.S. judgments than does the approach taken by the Act. At the same time, the certainty and uniformity provided by the approach of the 1962 Act, and continued in this Act, creates a stability in this area that facilitates international commercial transactions.

UNIFORM FOREIGN-COUNTRY MONEY JUDGMENTS RECOGNITION ACT

SECTION 1. SHORT TITLE. This [act] may be cited as the [Uniform Foreign-Country Money Judgments Recognition Act].

Comment

Source: This section is an updated version of Section 9 of the Uniform Foreign Money-Judgments Recognition Act of 1962.

SECTION 2. DEFINITIONS. In this [act]:

(1) "Foreign country" means a government other than:
    (A) the United States;
    (B) a state, district, commonwealth, territory, or insular possession of the United States; or
    (C) any other government with regard to which the decision in this state as to whether to recognize a judgment of that government's courts is initially subject to determination under the Full Faith and Credit Clause of the United States Constitution.
(2) "Foreign-country judgment" means a judgment of a court of a foreign country.

Comment

Source: This section is derived from Section 1 of the Uniform Foreign Money-Judgments Recognition Act of 1962.

1. The defined terms "foreign state" and "foreign judgment" in the 1962 Act have been changed to "foreign country" and "foreign-country judgment" in order to make it clear that the Act does not apply to recognition of sister-state judgments. Some courts have noted that the "foreign state" and "foreign judgment" definitions of the 1962 Act have caused confusion as to whether the Act should apply to sister-state judgments because "foreign state" and "foreign judgment" are terms of art generally used in connection with recognition and enforcement of sister-state judgments. *See, e.g.,* Eagle Leasing v. Amandus, 476 N.W.2d 35 (S.Ct. Iowa 1991) (reversing lower court's application of UFMJRA to a sister-state judgment, but noting lower court's confusion was understandable as "foreign judgment" is term of art normally applied to sister-state judgments). *See also,* Uniform Enforcement of Foreign Judgments Act § 1 (defining "foreign judgment" as the judgment of a sister state or federal court).

    The 1962 Act defines a "foreign state" as "any governmental unit other than the United States, or any state, district, commonwealth, territory, insular possession thereof, or the Panama Canal Zone, the Trust Territory of the Pacific Islands, or the Ryuku Islands." Rather than simply updating the list in the 1962 Act's definition of "foreign state," the new definition of "foreign country" in this Act combines the "listing" approach of the 1962 Act's "foreign state" definition with a provision that defines "foreign country" in terms of whether the judgments of the particular government's courts are initially subject to the Full Faith and Credit Clause standards for determining whether those judgments will be recognized. Under this new definition, a governmental unit is a "foreign country" if it is (1) not the United States or a state, district, commonwealth, territory or insular possession of the United States; and (2) its judgments are not initially subject to Full Faith and Credit Clause standards.

The Full Faith and Credit Clause, Art. IV, section 1, provides that "Full Faith and Credit shall be given in each State to the public Acts, Records, and judicial Proceedings of every other State. And the Congress may by general Laws prescribe the Manner in which such Acts, Records, and Proceedings shall be proved, and the Effect thereof." Whether the judgments of a governmental unit are subject to the Full Faith and Credit Clause may be determined by judicial interpretation of the Full Faith and Credit Clause or by statute, or by a combination of these two sources. For example, pursuant to the authority granted by the second sentence of the Full Faith and Credit Clause, Congress has passed 28 U.S.C.A. § 1738, which provides *inter alia* that court records from "any State, Territory, or Possession of the United States" are entitled to full faith and credit under the Full Faith and Credit Clause. In *Stoll v. Gottlieb*, 305 U.S. 165, 170 (1938), the United States Supreme Court held that this statute also requires that full faith and credit be given to judgments of federal courts. States also have made determinations as to whether certain types of judgments are subject to the Full Faith and Credit Clause. *E.g.* Day v. Montana Dept. Of Social & Rehab. Servs., 900 P.2d 296 (Mont. 1995) (tribal court judgment not subject to Full Faith and Credit, and should be treated with same deference shown foreign-country judgments). Under the definition of "foreign country" in this Act, the determination as to whether a governmental unit's judgments are subject to full faith and credit standards should be made by reference to any relevant law, whether statutory or decisional, that is applicable "in this state."

The definition of "foreign country" in terms of those judgments not subject to Full Faith and Credit standards also has the advantage of more effectively coordinating the Act with the Uniform Enforcement of Foreign Judgments Act. That Act, which establishes a registration procedure for the enforcement of sister state and equivalent judgments, defines a "foreign judgment" as "any judgment, decree, or order of a court of the United States or of any other court which is entitled to full faith and credit in this state." Uniform Enforcement of Foreign Judgments Act, § 1 (1964). By defining "foreign country" in the Recognition Act in terms of those judgments not subject to full faith and credit standards, this Act makes it clear that the Enforcement Act and the Recognition Act are mutually exclusive – if a foreign money judgment is subject to full faith and credit standards, then the Enforcement Act's registration procedure is available with regard to its enforcement; if the foreign money judgment is not subject to full faith and credit standards, then the foreign money judgment may not be enforced until recognition of it has been obtained in accordance with the provisions of the Recognition Act.

2. The definition of "foreign-country judgment" in this Act differs significantly from the 1962 Act's definition of "foreign judgment." The 1962 Act's

definition served in large part as a scope provision for the Act. The part of the definition defining the scope of the Act has been moved to section 3, which is the scope section.

3. The definition of "foreign-country judgment" in this Act refers to "a judgment" of "a court" of the foreign country. The foreign-country judgment need not take a particular form – any order or decree that meets the requirements of this section and comes within the scope of the Act under Section 3 is subject to the Act. Similarly, any competent government tribunal that issues such a "judgment" comes within the term "court" for purposes of this Act. The judgment, however, must be a judgment of an adjudicative body of the foreign country, and not the result of an alternative dispute mechanism chosen by the parties. Thus, foreign arbitral awards and agreements to arbitrate are not covered by this Act. They are governed instead by federal law, Chapter 2 of the U.S. Arbitration Act, 9 U.S.C. §§ 201-208, implementing the United Nations Convention on the Recognition and Enforcement of Foreign Arbitral Awards and Chapter 3 of the U.S. Arbitration Act, 9 U.S.C. §§ 301-307, implementing the Inter-American Convention on International Commercial Arbitration. A judgment of a foreign court confirming or setting aside an arbitral award, however, would be covered by this Act.

4. The definition of "foreign-country judgment" does not limit foreign-country judgments to those rendered in litigation between private parties. Judgments in which a governmental entity is a party also are included, and are subject to this Act if they meet the requirements of this section and are within the scope of the Act under Section 3.

SECTION 3. APPLICABILITY.

(a) Except as otherwise provided in subsection (b), this [act] applies to a foreign-country judgment to the extent that the judgment:
  (1) grants or denies recovery of a sum of money; and
  (2) under the law of the foreign country where rendered, is final, conclusive, and enforceable.
(b) This [act] does not apply to a foreign-country judgment, even if the judgment grants or denies recovery of a sum of money, to the extent that the judgment is:
  (1) a judgment for taxes;
  (2) a fine or other penalty; or
  (3) a judgment for divorce, support, or maintenance, or other judgment rendered in connection with domestic relations.
(c) A party seeking recognition of a foreign-country judgment has the burden of establishing that this [act] applies to the foreign-country judgment.

Comment

Source: This section is based on Section 2 of the 1962 Act. Subsection (b) contains material that was included as part of the definition of "foreign judgment" in Section 1(2) of the 1962 Act. Subsection (c) is new.

1. Like the 1962 Act, this Act sets out in subsection 3(a) two basic requirements that a foreign-country judgment must meet before it comes within the scope of this Act – the foreign-country judgment must (1) grant or deny recovery of a sum of money and (2) be final, conclusive and enforceable under the law of the foreign country where it was rendered. Subsection 3(b) then sets out three types of foreign-country judgments that are excluded from the coverage of this Act, even though they meet the criteria of subsection 3(a) – judgments for taxes, judgments constituting fines and other penalties, and judgments in domestic relations matters. These exclusions are comparable to those contained in Section 1(2) of the 1962 Act.

2. This Act applies to a foreign-country judgment only to the extent the foreign-country judgment grants or denies recovery of a sum of money. If a foreign-country judgment both grants or denies recovery of a sum money and provides for some other form of relief, this Act would apply to the portion of the judgment that grants or denies monetary relief, but not to the portion that provides for some other form of relief. The U.S. court, however, would be left free to decide to recognize and enforce the non-monetary portion of the judgment under principles of comity or other applicable law. See Section 11.

3. In order to come within the scope of this Act, a foreign-country judgment must be final, conclusive, and enforceable under the law of the foreign country in which it was rendered. This requirement contains three distinct, although inter-related concepts. A judgment is final when it is not subject to additional proceedings in the rendering court other than execution. A judgment is conclusive when it is given effect between the parties as a determination of their legal rights and obligations. A judgment is enforceable when the legal procedures of the state to ensure that the judgment debtor complies with the judgment are available to the judgment creditor to assist in collection of the judgment.

   While the first two of these requirements – finality and conclusiveness – will apply with regard to every foreign-country money judgment, the requirement of enforceability is only relevant when the judgment is one granting recovery of a sum of money. A judgment denying a sum of money obviously is not subject to enforcement procedures, as there is no monetary award to enforce. This Act, however, covers both judgments granting and those denying recovery of a sum of money. Thus, the fact that a foreign-country judgment denying recovery of a sum of money is not enforceable does not mean that such judgments are not within the scope of the Act. Instead, the requirement that the judgment be enforceable should be read to mean that, if the foreign-country judgment grants recovery of a sum of money, it must be enforceable in the foreign country in order to be within the scope of the Act.

Like the 1962 Act, subsection 3(b) requires that the determinations as to finality, conclusiveness and enforceability be made using the law of the foreign country in which the judgment was rendered. Unless the foreign-country judgment is final, conclusive, and (to the extent it grants recovery of a sum of money) enforceable in the foreign country where it was rendered, it will not be within the scope of this Act.

4. Subsection 3(b) follows the 1962 Act by excluding three categories of foreign-country money judgments from the scope of the Act – judgments for taxes, judgments that constitute fines and penalties, and judgments in domestic relations matters. The domestic relations exclusion has been redrafted to make it clear that all judgments in domestic relations matters are excluded from the Act, not just judgments "for support" as provided in the 1962 Act. This is consistent with interpretation of the 1962 Act by the courts, which extended the "support" exclusion in the 1962 Act beyond its literal wording to exclude other money judgments in connection with domestic matters. *E.g.*, Wolff v. Wolff, 389 A.2d 413 (My. App. 1978) ("support" includes alimony).

Recognition and enforcement of domestic relations judgments traditionally has been treated differently from recognition and enforcement of other judgments. The considerations with regard to those judgments, particularly with regard to jurisdiction and finality, differ from those with regard to other money judgments. Further, national laws with regard to domestic relations vary widely, and recognition and enforcement of such judgments thus is more appropriately handled through comity than through use of this uniform Act. Finally, other statutes, such as the Uniform Interstate Family Support Act and the federal International Child Support Enforcement Act, 42 U.S.C. § 659a (1996), address various aspects of the recognition and enforcement of domestic relations awards. Under Section 11 of this Act, courts are free to recognize money judgments in domestic relations matters under principles of comity or otherwise, and U.S. courts routinely enforce money judgments in domestic relations matters under comity principles.

Foreign-country judgments for taxes and judgments that constitute fines or penalties traditionally have not been recognized and enforced in U.S. courts. *See, e.g.*, Restatement Third of the Foreign Relations Law of the United States § 483 (1986). Both the "revenue rule," under which the courts of one country will not enforce the revenue laws of another country, and the prohibition on enforcement of penal judgments seem to be grounded in the idea that one country does not enforce the public laws of another. *See id.* Reporters' Note 2. The exclusion of tax judgments and judgments constituting fines or penalties from the scope of the Act reflects this tradition. Under Section 11, however, courts remain free to consider whether such judgments should be recognized and enforced under comity or other principles.

A judgment for taxes is a judgment in favor of a foreign country or one of its subdivisions based on a claim for an assessment of a tax. Thus, a judgment awarding a plaintiff restitution of the purchase price paid for an item would not be considered in any part a judgment for taxes, even though one element of the recovery was the sales tax paid by the plaintiff at the time of purchase. Such a judgment would not be one designed to enforce the revenue laws of the foreign country, but rather one designed to compensate the plaintiff. Courts generally hold that the test for whether a judgment is a fine or penalty is determined by whether its purpose is remedial in nature, with its benefits accruing to private individuals, or it is penal in nature, punishing an offense against public justice. *E.g.*, Chase Manhattan Bank, N.A. v. Hoffman, 665 F.Supp 73 (D. Mass. 1987) (finding that Belgium judgment was not penal even though the proceeding forming the basis of the suit was primarily criminal where Belgium court considered damage petition a civil remedy, the judgment did not constitute punishment for an offense against public justice of Belgium, and benefit of the judgment accrued to private judgment creditor, not Belgium). Thus, a judgment that awards compensation or restitution for the benefit of private individuals should not automatically be considered penal in nature and therefore outside the scope of the Act simply because the action is brought on behalf of the private individuals by a government entity. *Cf.* U.S.-Australia Free Trade Agreement, art.14.7.2, U.S.-Austl., May 18, 2004 (providing that when government agency obtains a civil monetary judgment for purpose of providing restitution to consumers, investors, or customers who suffered economic harm due to fraud, judgment generally should not be denied recognition and enforcement on ground that it is penal or revenue in nature, or based on other foreign public law).

5. Under subsection 3(b), a foreign-country money judgment is not within the scope of this Act "to the extent" that it comes within one of the excluded categories. Therefore, if a foreign-country money judgment is only partially within one of the excluded categories, the non-excluded portion will be subject to this Act.

6. Subsection 3(c) is new. The 1962 Act does not expressly allocate the burden of proof with regard to establishing whether a foreign-country judgment is within the scope of the Act. Courts applying the 1962 Act generally have held that the burden of proof is on the person seeking recognition to establish that the judgment is final, conclusive and enforceable where rendered. *E.g.*, Mayekawa Mfg. Co. Ltd. v. Sasaki, 888 P.2d 183, 189 (Wash. App. 1995) (burden of proof on creditor to establish judgment is final, conclusive, and enforceable where rendered); Bridgeway Corp. v. Citibank, 45 F.Supp.2d 276, 285 (S.D.N.Y. 1999) (party seeking recognition must establish that there is a final judgment, conclusive and enforceable where rendered); S.C.Chimexim S.A. v. Velco Enterprises,

Ltd., 36 F. Supp.2d 206, 212 (S.D.N.Y. 1999) (Plaintiff has the burden of establishing conclusive effect). Subsection (3)(c) places the burden of proof to establish whether a foreign-country judgment is within the scope of the Act on the party seeking recognition of the foreign-country judgment with regard to both subsection (a) and subsection (b).

SECTION 4. STANDARDS FOR RECOGNITION OF FOREIGN-COUNTRY JUDGMENT.

(a) Except as otherwise provided in subsections (b) and (c), a court of this state shall recognize a foreign-country judgment to which this [act] applies.

(b) A court of this state may not recognize a foreign-country judgment if:

  (1) the judgment was rendered under a judicial system that does not provide impartial tribunals or procedures compatible with the requirements of due process of law;

  (2) the foreign court did not have personal jurisdiction over the defendant; or

  (3) the foreign court did not have jurisdiction over the subject matter.

(c) A court of this state need not recognize a foreign-country judgment if:

  (1) the defendant in the proceeding in the foreign court did not receive notice of the proceeding in sufficient time to enable the defendant to defend;

  (2) the judgment was obtained by fraud that deprived the losing party of an adequate opportunity to present its case;

  (3) the judgment or the [cause of action] [claim for relief] on which the judgment is based is repugnant to the public policy of this state or of the United States;

  (4) the judgment conflicts with another final and conclusive judgment;

  (5) the proceeding in the foreign court was contrary to an agreement between the parties under which the dispute in question was to be determined otherwise than by proceedings in that foreign court;

  (6) in the case of jurisdiction based only on personal service, the foreign court was a seriously inconvenient forum for the trial of the action;

  (7) the judgment was rendered in circumstances that raise substantial doubt about the integrity of the rendering court with respect to the judgment; or

  (8) the specific proceeding in the foreign court leading to the judgment was not compatible with the requirements of due process of law.

(d) A party resisting recognition of a foreign-country judgment has the burden of establishing that a ground for nonrecognition stated in subsection (b) or (c) exists.

Comment

Source: This section is based on Section 4 of the 1962 Act.

1. This Section provides the standards for recognition of a foreign-country money judgment. Section 7 sets out the effect of recognition of a foreign-country money judgment under this Act.

2. Recognition of a judgment means that the forum court accepts the determination of legal rights and obligations made by the rendering court in the foreign country. *See, e.g.* Restatement (Second) of Conflicts of Laws, Ch. 5, Topic 3, Introductory Note (recognition of foreign judgment occurs to the extent the forum court gives the judgment "the same effect with respect to the parties, the subject matter of the action and the issues involved that it has in the state where it was rendered.") Recognition of a foreign-country judgment must be distinguished from enforcement of that judgment. Enforcement of the foreign-country judgment involves the application of the legal procedures of the state to ensure that the judgment debtor obeys the foreign-country judgment. Recognition of a foreign-country money judgment often is associated with enforcement of the judgment, as the judgment creditor usually seeks recognition of the foreign-country judgment primarily for the purpose of invoking the enforcement procedures of the forum state to assist the judgment creditor's collection of the judgment from the judgment debtor. Because the forum court cannot enforce the foreign-country judgment until it has determined that the judgment will be given effect, recognition is a prerequisite to enforcement of the foreign-country judgment. Recognition, however, also has significance outside the enforcement context because a foreign-country judgment also must be recognized before it can be given preclusive effect under res judicata and collateral estoppel principles. The issue of whether a foreign-country judgment will be recognized is distinct from both the issue of whether the judgment will be enforced, and the issue of the extent to which it will be given preclusive effect.

3. Subsection 4(a) places an affirmative duty on the forum court to recognize a foreign-country money judgment unless one of the grounds for nonrecognition stated in subsection (b) or (c) applies. Subsection (b) states three mandatory grounds for denying recognition to a foreign-country money judgment. If the forum court finds that one of the grounds listed in subsection (b) exists, then it must deny recognition to the foreign-country money judgment. Subsection (c) states eight nonmandatory grounds for denying recognition. The forum court has discretion to decide whether or not to refuse recognition based on one of these grounds. Subsection (d) places the burden of proof on the party resisting recognition of the foreign-country judgment to establish that one of the grounds for nonrecognition exists.

4. The mandatory grounds for nonrecognition stated in subsection (b) are identical to the mandatory grounds stated in Section 4 of the 1962 Act. The discretionary grounds stated in subsection 4(c)(1) through (6) are based on subsection 4(b)(1) through (6) of the 1962 Act. The discretionary grounds stated in subsection 4(c)(7) and (8) are new.

5. Under subsection (b)(1), the forum court must deny recognition to the foreign-country money judgment if that judgment was "rendered under a judicial system that does not provide impartial tribunals or procedures compatible with the requirements of due process of law." The standard for this ground for nonrecognition "has been stated authoritatively by the Supreme Court of the United States in *Hilton v. Guyot*, 159 U.S.113, 205 (1895). As indicated in that decision, a mere difference in the procedural system is not a sufficient basis for nonrecognition. A case of serious injustice must be involved." Cmt § 4, Uniform Foreign Money-Judgment Recognition Act (1962). The focus of inquiry is not whether the procedure in the rendering country is similar to U.S. procedure, but rather on the basic fairness of the foreign-country procedure. Kam-Tech Systems, Ltd. V. Yardeni, 74 A.2d 644, 649 (N.J. App. 2001) (interpreting the comparable provision in the 1962 Act); *accord*, Society of Lloyd's v. Ashenden, 233 F.3d 473 (7th Cir. 2000) (procedures need not meet all the intricacies of the complex concept of due process that has emerged from U.S. case law, but rather must be fair in the broader international sense) (interpreting comparable provision in the 1962 Act). Procedural differences, such as absence of jury trial or different evidentiary rules are not sufficient to justify denying recognition under subsection (b)(1), so long as the essential elements of impartial administration and basic procedural fairness have been provided in the foreign proceeding. As the U.S. Supreme Court stated in *Hilton*:

> Where there has been opportunity for a full and fair trial abroad before a court of competent jurisdiction conducting the trial upon regular proceedings, after due citation or voluntary appearance of the defendant, and under a system of jurisprudence likely to secure an impartial administration of justice between the citizens of its own country and those of other countries, and there is nothing to show either prejudice in the court, or in the system of laws under which it was sitting, or fraud in procuring the judgment, or any other special reason why the comity of this nation should not allow it full effect then a foreign-country judgment should be recognized. *Hilton*, 159 U.S. at 202.

6. Under section 4(b)(2), the forum court must deny recognition to the foreign-country judgment if the foreign court did not have personal jurisdiction over the defendant. Section 5(a) lists six bases for personal jurisdiction that are adequate as a matter of law to establish that the foreign court had personal jurisdiction. Section 5(b) makes clear that other grounds for personal jurisdiction may be found sufficient.

7. Subsection 4(c)(2) limits the type of fraud that will serve as a ground for denying recognition to extrinsic fraud. This provision is consistent with the

interpretation of the comparable provision in subsection 4(b)(2) of the 1962 Act by the courts, which have found that only extrinsic fraud — conduct of the prevailing party that deprived the losing party of an adequate opportunity to present its case — is sufficient under the 1962 Act. Examples of extrinsic fraud would be when the plaintiff deliberately had the initiating process served on the defendant at the wrong address, deliberately gave the defendant wrong information as to the time and place of the hearing, or obtained a default judgment against the defendant based on a forged confession of judgment. When this type of fraudulent action by the plaintiff deprives the defendant of an adequate opportunity to present its case, then it provides grounds for denying recognition of the foreign-country judgment. Extrinsic fraud should be distinguished from intrinsic fraud, such as false testimony of a witness or admission of a forged document into evidence during the foreign proceeding. Intrinsic fraud does not provide a basis for denying recognition under subsection 4(c)(2), as the assertion that intrinsic fraud has occurred should be raised and dealt with in the rendering court.

8. The public policy exception in subsection 4(c)(3) is based on the public policy exception in subsection 4(b)(3) of the 1962 Act, with one difference. The public policy exception in the 1962 Act states that the relevant inquiry is whether "the [cause of action] [claim for relief] on which the judgment is based" is repugnant to public policy. Based on this "cause of action" language, some courts interpreting the 1962 Act have refused to find that a public policy challenge based on something other than repugnancy of the foreign cause of action comes within this exception. *E.g.*, Southwest Livestock & Trucking Co., Inc. v. Ramon, 169 F.3d 317 (5th Cir. 1999) (refusing to deny recognition to Mexican judgment on promissory note with interest rate of 48% because cause of action to collect on promissory note does not violate public policy); Guinness PLC v. Ward, 955 F.2d 875 (4th Cir. 1992) (challenge to recognition based on post-judgment settlement could not be asserted under public policy exception); The Society of Lloyd's v. Turner, 303 F.3d 325 (5th Cir. 2002) (rejecting argument legal standards applied to establish elements of breach of contract violated public policy because cause of action for breach of contract itself is not contrary to state public policy); *cf.* Bachchan v. India Abroad Publications, Inc., 585 N.Y.S.2d 661 (N.Y. Sup. Ct. 1992) (judgment creditor argued British libel judgment should be recognized despite argument it violated First Amendment because New York recognizes a cause of action for libel). Subsection 4(c)(3) rejects this narrow focus by providing that the forum court may deny recognition if either the cause of action or the judgment itself violates public policy. *Cf.* Restatement (Third) of the Foreign Relations Law of the United States, § 482(2)(d) (1986) (containing a similarly-worded public policy exception to recognition).

Although subsection 4(c)(3) of this Act rejects the narrow focus on the cause of action under the 1962 Act, it retains the stringent test for finding a public policy violation applied by courts interpreting the 1962 Act. Under that test, a difference in law, even a marked one, is not sufficient to raise a public policy issue. Nor is it relevant that the foreign law allows a recovery that the forum state would not allow. Public policy is violated only if recognition or enforcement of the foreign-country judgment would tend clearly to injure the public health, the public morals, or the public confidence in the administration of law, or would undermine "that sense of security for individual rights, whether of personal liberty or of private property, which any citizen ought to feel." Hunt v. BP Exploration Co. (Libya) Ltd., 492 F. Supp. 885, 901 (N.D. Tex. 1980).

The language "or of the United States" in subsection 4(c)(3), which does not appear in the 1962 Act provision, makes it clear that the relevant public policy is that of both the State in which recognition is sought and that of the United States. This is the position taken by the vast majority of cases interpreting the 1962 public policy provision. *E.g.,* Bachchan v. India Abroad Publications, Inc., 585 N.Y.S.2d 661 (Sup.Ct. N.Y. 1992) (British libel judgment denied recognition because it violates First Amendment).

9. Subsection 4(c)(5) allows the forum court to refuse recognition of a foreign-country judgment when the parties had a valid agreement, such as a valid forum selection clause or agreement to arbitrate, providing that the relevant dispute would be resolved in a forum other than the forum issuing the foreign-country judgment. Under this provision, the forum court must find both the existence of a valid agreement and that the agreement covered the subject matter involved in the foreign litigation resulting in the foreign-country judgment.

10. Subsection 4(c)(6) authorizes the forum court to refuse recognition of a foreign-country judgment that was rendered in the foreign country solely on the basis of personal service when the forum court believes the original action should have been dismissed by the court in the foreign country on grounds of *forum non conveniens.*

11. Subsection 4(c)(7) is new. Under this subsection, the forum court may deny recognition to a foreign-country judgment if there are circumstances that raise substantial doubt about the integrity of the rendering court with respect to that judgment. It requires a showing of corruption in the particular case that had an impact on the judgment that was rendered. This provision may be contrasted with subsection 4(b)(1), which requires that the forum court refuse recognition to the foreign-country judgment if it was rendered under a judicial system that does not provide impartial tribunals. Like the comparable provision in subsection 4(a)(1) of the 1962 Act, subsection 4(b)(1) focuses on the judicial system of the foreign country as a whole, rather than on whether the particular judicial proceeding leading to the foreign-country judgment was impartial and fair. *See, e.g.,* The Society of Lloyd's v. Turner, 303 F.3d 325, 330 (5th Cir. 2002) (interpreting the 1962 Act); CIBC Mellon Trust Co. v. Mora Hotel Corp,. N.V., 743 N.Y.S.2d 408, 415 (N.Y. App. 2002) (interpreting the 1962 Act); Society of

Lloyd's v. Ashenden, 233 F.3d 473, 477 (7th Cir. 2000) (interpreting the 1962 Act). On the other hand, subsection 4(c)(7) allows the court to deny recognition to the foreign-country judgment if it finds a lack of impartiality and fairness of the tribunal in the individual proceeding leading to the foreign-country judgment. Thus, the difference is that between showing, for example, that corruption and bribery is so prevalent throughout the judicial system of the foreign country as to make that entire judicial system one that does not provide impartial tribunals versus showing that bribery of the judge in the proceeding that resulted in the particular foreign-country judgment under consideration had a sufficient impact on the ultimate judgment as to call it into question.

12. Subsection 4(c)(8) also is new. It allows the forum court to deny recognition to the foreign-country judgment if the court finds that the specific proceeding in the foreign court was not compatible with the requirements of fundamental fairness. Like subsection 4(c)(7), it can be contrasted with subsection 4(b)(1), which requires the forum court to deny recognition to the foreign-country judgment if the forum court finds that the entire judicial system in the foreign country where the foreign-country judgment was rendered does not provide procedures compatible with the requirements of fundamental fairness. While the focus of subsection 4(b)(1) is on the foreign country's judicial system as a whole, the focus of subsection 4(c)(8) is on the particular proceeding that resulted in the specific foreign-country judgment under consideration. Thus, the difference is that between showing, for example, that there has been such a breakdown of law and order in the particular foreign country that judgments are rendered on the basis of political decisions rather than the rule of law throughout the judicial system versus a showing that for political reasons the particular party against whom the foreign-country judgment was entered was denied fundamental fairness in the particular proceedings leading to the foreign-country judgment.

Subsections 4(c)(7) and (8) both are discretionary grounds for denying recognition, while subsection 4(b)(1) is mandatory. Obviously, if the entire judicial system in the foreign country fails to satisfy the requirements of impartiality and fundamental fairness, a judgment rendered in that foreign country would be so compromised that the forum court should refuse to recognize it as a matter of course. On the other hand, if the problem is evidence of a lack of integrity or fundamental fairness with regard to the particular proceeding leading to the foreign-country judgment, then there may or may not be other factors in the particular case that would cause the forum court to decide to recognize the foreign-country judgment. For example, a forum court might decide not to exercise its discretion to deny recognition despite evidence of corruption or procedural unfairness in a particular case because the party resisting recognition failed to raise the issue on appeal from the foreign-country judgment in the foreign country, and the evidence establishes that, if the party had done so, appeal would have been an adequate mechanism for correcting the transgressions of the lower court.

13. Under subsection 4(d), the party opposing recognition of the foreign-country judgment has the burden of establishing that one of the grounds for nonrecognition set out in subsection 4(b) or (c) applies. The 1962 Act was silent as to who had the burden of proof to establish a ground for nonrecognition and courts applying the 1962 Act took different positions on the issue. *Compare* Bridgeway Corp. v. Citibank, 45 F.Supp. 2d 276, 285 (S.D.N.Y. 1999) (plaintiff has burden to show no mandatory basis under 4(a) for nonrecognition exists; defendant has burden regarding discretionary bases) *with* The Courage Co. LLC v. The ChemShare Corp., 93 S.W.3d 323, 331 (Tex. App. 2002) (party seeking to avoid recognition has burden to prove ground for nonrecognition). Because the grounds for nonrecognition in Section 4 are in the nature of defenses to recognition, the burden of proof is most appropriately allocated to the party opposing recognition of the foreign-country judgment.

SECTION 5. PERSONAL JURISDICTION.

(a) A foreign-country judgment may not be refused recognition for lack of personal jurisdiction if:
   (1) the defendant was served with process personally in the foreign country;
   (2) the defendant voluntarily appeared in the proceeding, other than for the purpose of protecting property seized or threatened with seizure in the proceeding or of contesting the jurisdiction of the court over the defendant;
   (3) the defendant, before the commencement of the proceeding, had agreed to submit to the jurisdiction of the foreign court with respect to the subject matter involved;
   (4) the defendant was domiciled in the foreign country when the proceeding was instituted or was a corporation or other form of business organization that had its principal place of business in, or was organized under the laws of, the foreign country;
   (5) the defendant had a business office in the foreign country and the proceeding in the foreign court involved a [cause of action] [claim for relief] arising out of business done by the defendant through that office in the foreign country; or
   (6) the defendant operated a motor vehicle or airplane in the foreign country and the proceeding involved a [cause of action] [claim for relief] arising out of that operation.

(b) The list of bases for personal jurisdiction in subsection (a) is not exclusive. The courts of this state may recognize bases of personal jurisdiction other than those listed in subsection (a) as sufficient to support a foreign-country judgment.

Comment

Source: This provision is based on Section 5 of the 1962 Act. Its substance is the same as that of Section 5 of the 1962 Act, except as noted in Comment 2 below with regard to subsection 5(a)(4).

1. Under section 4(b)(2), the forum court must deny recognition to the foreign-country judgment if the foreign court did not have personal jurisdiction over the defendant. Section 5(a) lists six bases for personal jurisdiction that are adequate as a matter of law to establish that the foreign court had personal jurisdiction. Section 5(b) makes it clear that these bases of personal jurisdiction are not exclusive. The forum court may find that the foreign court had personal jurisdiction over the defendant on some other basis.

2. Subsection 5(a)(4) of the 1962 Act provides that the foreign court had personal jurisdiction over the defendant if the defendant was "a body corporate" that "had its principal place of business, was incorporated, or had otherwise acquired corporate status, in the foreign state." Subsection 5(a)(4) of this Act extends that concept to forms of business organization other than corporations.

3. Subsection 5(a)(3) provides that the foreign court has personal jurisdiction over the defendant if the defendant agreed before commencement of the proceeding leading to the foreign-country judgment to submit to the jurisdiction of the foreign court with regard to the subject matter involved. Under this provision, the forum court must find both the existence of a valid agreement to submit to the foreign court's jurisdiction and that the agreement covered the subject matter involved in the foreign litigation resulting in the foreign-country judgment.

SECTION 6. PROCEDURE FOR RECOGNITION OF FOREIGN-COUNTRY JUDGMENT. (a) If recognition of a foreign-country judgment is sought as an original matter, the issue of recognition shall be raised by filing an action seeking recognition of the foreign-country judgment.

(b) If recognition of a foreign-country judgment is sought in a pending action, the issue of recognition may be raised by counterclaim, cross-claim, or affirmative defense.

Comment

Source: This section is new.

1. Unlike the 1962 Act, which was silent as to the proper procedure for seeking recognition of a foreign-country judgment, Section 6 of this Act expressly sets out the ways in which the issue of recognition may be raised. Under section 6, the issue of recognition always must be raised in a court proceeding. Thus, section 6 rejects decisions under the 1962 Act holding that the registration procedure found in the Uniform Enforcement of Foreign Judgments Act could be utilized with regard to recognition of a foreign-country judgment. *E.g.* Society of Lloyd's v. Ashenden, 233 F.3d 473 (7th Cir. 2000). The Enforcement Act deals solely with the *enforcement* of sister-state judgments and other judgments entitled to full faith and credit, not with the *recognition* of foreign-country judgments.

   More broadly, section 6 rejects the use of any registration procedure in the context of the foreign-country judgments covered by this Act. A registration procedure represents a balance between the interest of the judgment creditor in obtaining quick and efficient recognition and enforcement of a judgment when the judgment debtor has already been provided with an opportunity to litigate the underlying issues, and the interest of the judgment debtor in being provided an adequate opportunity to raise and litigate issues regarding whether the foreign-country judgment should be recognized. In the context of sister-state judgments, this balance favors use of a truncated procedure such as that found in the Enforcement Act. Recognition of sister-state judgments normally is mandated by the Full Faith and Credit Clause. Courts recognize only a very limited number of grounds for denying full faith and credit to a sister-state judgment – that the rendering court lacked jurisdiction, that the judgment was procured by fraud, that the judgment has been satisfied, or that the limitations period has expired. Thus, the judgment debtor with regard to a sister-state judgment normally does not have any grounds for opposing recognition and enforcement of the judgment. The extremely limited grounds for denying full faith and credit to a sister-state judgment reflect the fact such judgments will have been rendered by a court that is subject to the same due process limitations and the same overlap of federal statutory and constitutional law as the forum state's courts, and, to a large extent, the same body of court precedent and socio-economic ideas as those shaping the law of the forum state. Therefore, there is a strong presumption of fairness and competence attached to a sister-state judgment that justifies use of a registration procedure.

   The balance between the benefits and costs of a registration procedure is significantly different, however, in the context of recognition and enforcement of foreign-country judgments. Unlike the limited grounds for denying full faith and credit to a sister-state judgment, this Act provides a number of grounds upon which recognition of a foreign-country judgment may be denied. Determination of whether these grounds apply requires the forum court to look behind the foreign-country judgment to evaluate the law and the judicial system under which the foreign-country judgment was rendered. The existence of these grounds for nonrecognition reflects the fact there is less expectation that foreign-country courts will follow procedures comporting with U.S. notions of fundamental fairness and jurisdiction or that those courts will apply laws viewed as substantively tolerable by U.S. standards than there is with regard to sister-state courts. In some situations, there also may be suspicions of corruption or fraud in the foreign-country proceedings. These differences between sister-state judgments and foreign-country judgments provide a justification for requiring judicial involvement in the decision whether to recognize a foreign-country judgment in all cases in which that issue is raised. Although the threshold for establishing that a foreign-country judgment is not entitled to recognition under Section 4 is high, there is a sufficiently greater likelihood that significant recognition issues will be raised so as to require a judicial proceeding.

2. This Section contemplates that the issue of recognition may be raised either as an original matter or in the context of a pending proceeding. Subsection 6(a) provides that in order to raise the issue of recognition of a foreign-country judgment as an initial matter, the party seeking recognition must file an action for recognition of the foreign-country judgment. Subsection 6(b) provides that when the recognition issue is raised in a pending proceeding, it may be raised by counterclaim, cross-claim or affirmative defense, depending on the context in which it is raised. These rules are consistent with the way the issue of recognition most often was raised in most states under the 1962 Act.

3. An action seeking recognition of a foreign-country judgment under this Section is an action on the foreign-country judgment itself, not an action on the underlying cause of action that gave rise to that judgment. The parties to an action under Section 6 may not relitigate the merits of the underlying dispute that gave rise to the foreign-country judgment.

4. While this Section sets out the ways in which the issue of recognition of a foreign-country judgment may be raised, it is not intended to create any new procedure not currently existing in the state or to otherwise effect existing state procedural requirements. The parties to an action in which recognition of a foreign-country judgment is sought under Section 6 must comply with all state procedural rules with regard to that type of action. Nor does this Act address the question of what constitutes a sufficient basis for jurisdiction to adjudicate with regard to an action under Section 6. Courts have split over the issue of whether the presence of assets of the debtor in a state is a sufficient basis for jurisdiction in light of footnote 36 of the U.S. Supreme Court decision in Shaffer v. Heitner, 433 U.S. 186, 210 n.36 (1977). This Act takes no position on that issue.

5. In states that have adopted the Uniform Foreign-Money Claims Act, that Act will apply to the determination of the amount of a money judgment recognized under this Act.

SECTION 7. EFFECT OF RECOGNITION OF FOREIGN-COUNTRY JUDGMENT. If the court in a proceeding under Section 6 finds that the foreign-country judgment is entitled to recognition under this [act] then, to the extent that the foreign-country judgment grants or denies recovery of a sum of money, the foreign-country judgment is:

(1) conclusive between the parties to the same extent as the judgment of a sister state entitled to full faith and credit in this state would be conclusive; and

(2) enforceable in the same manner and to the same extent as a judgment rendered in this state.

Comment

Source: The substance of subsection 7(1) is based on Section 3 of the 1962 Act. Subsection 7(2) is new.

1. Section 5 of this Act sets out the standards for the recognition of foreign-country judgments within the scope of this Act, and places an affirmative duty on the forum court to recognize any foreign-country judgment that meets those standards. Section 6 of this Act sets out the procedures by which the issue of recognition may be raised. This Section sets out the consequences of the decision by the forum court that the foreign-country judgment is entitled to recognition.

2. Under subsection 7(1), the first consequence of recognition of a foreign-country judgment is that it is treated as conclusive between the parties in the forum state. Section 7(1) does not attempt to establish directly the extent of that conclusiveness. Instead, it provides that the foreign-country judgment is treated as conclusive to the same extent that a judgment of a sister state that had been determined to be entitled to full faith and credit would be conclusive. This means that the foreign-country judgment generally will be given the same effect in the forum state that it has in the foreign country where it was rendered. Subsection 7(1), however, sets out the minimum effect that must be given to the foreign-country judgment once recognized. The forum court remains free to give the foreign-country judgment a greater preclusive effect in the forum state than the judgment would have in the foreign country where it was rendered. *Cf.* Restatement (Third) of the Foreign Relations Law of the United States, § 481 cmt *c* (1986).

3. Under subsection 7(2), the second consequence of recognition of a foreign-country judgment is that, to the extent it grants a sum of money, it is

enforceable in the forum state in accordance with the procedures for enforcement in the forum state and to the same extent that a judgment of the forum state would be enforceable. *Cf.* Restatement (Third) of the Foreign Relations Law of the United States § 481 (1986) (judgment entitled to recognition is enforceable in accordance with the procedure for enforcement of judgments applicable where enforcement is sought). Thus, under subsection 7(2), once recognized, the foreign-country judgment has the same effect and is subject to the same procedures, defenses and proceedings for reopening, vacating, or staying a judgment of a comparable court in the forum state, and can be enforced or satisfied in the same manner as such a judgment of the forum state.

SECTION 8. STAY OF PROCEEDINGS PENDING APPEAL OF FOREIGN-COUNTRY JUDGMENT. If a party establishes that an appeal from a foreign-country judgment is pending or will be taken, the court may stay any proceedings with regard to the foreign-country judgment until the appeal is concluded, the time for appeal expires, or the appellant has had sufficient time to prosecute the appeal and has failed to do so.

Comment

Source: This section is the same substantively as section 6 of the 1962 Act, except that it adds as an additional measure for the duration of the stay "the time for appeal expires."

1. Under Section 3 of this Act, a foreign-country judgment is not within the scope of this Act unless it is conclusive and enforceable where rendered. Thus, if the effect of appeal under the law of the foreign country in which the judgment was rendered is to prevent it from being conclusive or enforceable between the parties, the existence of a pending appeal in the foreign country would prevent the application of this Act. Section 8 addresses a different situation. It deals with the situation in which either (1) the party seeking a stay has demonstrated that it intends to file an appeal in the foreign country, although the appeal has not yet been filed or (2) an appeal has been filed in the foreign country, but under the law of the foreign country filing of an appeal does not affect the conclusiveness or enforceability of the judgment. Section 8 allows the forum court in those situations to determine in its discretion that a stay of proceedings is appropriate.

SECTION 9. STATUTE OF LIMITATIONS. An action to recognize a foreign-country judgment must be commenced within the earlier of the time during which the foreign-country judgment is effective in the foreign country or 15 years from the date that the foreign-country judgment became effective in the foreign country.

Comment

Source: This Section is new. The 1962 Act did not contain a statute of limitations. Some courts applying the 1962 Act have used the state's general statute of limitations, *e.g.*, Vrozos v. Sarantopoulos, 552 N.E.2d 1053 (Ill. App. 1990) (as Recognition Act contains no statute of limitations, general five-year statute of limitations applies), while others have used the statute of limitations applicable with regard to enforcement of a domestic judgment, *e.g.*, La Societe Anonyme Goro v. Conveyor Accessories, Inc., 677 N.E. 2d 30 (Ill. App. 1997).

1. Under Section 3 of this Act, this Act only applies to foreign-country judgments that are conclusive, and if the judgment grants recovery of a sum of money, enforceable where rendered. Thus, if the period of effectiveness of the foreign-country judgment has expired in the foreign country where the judgment was rendered, the foreign-country judgment would not be subject to this Act. This means that the period of time during which a foreign-country judgment may be recognized under this Act normally is measured by the period of time during which that judgment is effective (that is, conclusive and, if applicable, enforceable) in the foreign country that rendered the judgment. If, however, the foreign-country judgment remains effective for more than fifteen years after the date on which it became effective in the foreign country, Section 9 places an additional time limit on recognition of a foreign-country judgment. It provides that, if the foreign-country judgment remains effective between the parties for more than fifteen years, then an action to recognize the foreign-country judgment under this Act must be commenced within that fifteen year period.

2. Section 9 does not address the issue of whether a foreign-country judgment that can no longer be the basis of a recognition action under this Act because of the application of the fifteen-year limitations period in Section 9 may be used for other purposes. For example, a common rule with regard to judgments barred by a statute of limitations is that they still may be used defensively for purposes of offset and for their preclusive effect. The extent to which a foreign-country judgment with regard to which a recognition action is barred by Section 9 may be used for these or other purposes is left to the other law of the forum state.

SECTION 10. UNIFORMITY OF INTERPRETATION.

In applying and construing this uniform act, consideration must be given to the need to promote uniformity of the law with respect to its subject matter among states that enact it.

Comment

Source: This Section is substantively the same as Section 8 of the 1962 Act. The section has been rewritten to reflect current NCCUSL practice.

SECTION 11. SAVING CLAUSE. This [act] does not prevent the recognition under principles of comity or otherwise of a foreign-country judgment not within the scope of this [act].

Comment

Source: This section is based on Section 7 of the 1962 Act.

1. Section 3 of this Act provides that this Act applies only to certain foreign-country judgments that grant or deny recovery of a sum of money. The purpose of this Act is to establish the minimum standards for recognition of those judgments. Section 11 makes clear that no negative implication should be read from the fact that this Act does not provide for recognition of other foreign-country judgments. Rather, this Act simply does not address the issue of whether foreign-country judgments not within its scope under Section 3 should be recognized. Courts are free to recognize those foreign-country judgments not within the scope of this Act under common law principles of comity or other applicable law.

SECTION 12. EFFECTIVE DATE.

[(a) This [act] takes effect … .
[(b) This [act] applies to all actions commenced on or after the effective date of this [act] in which the issue of recognition of a foreign-country judgment is raised.]

Comment

Source: Subsection 12(a) is the same as Section 11 of the 1962 Act. Subsection 12(b) is new.

1. Subsection 12(b) provides that this Act will apply to all actions in which the issue of recognition of a foreign-country judgment is raised that are commenced on or after the effective date of this Act. Thus, the application of this Act is measured not from the time the original action leading to the foreign-country judgment was commenced in the foreign country, but rather from the time the action in which the issue of recognition is raised is commenced in the forum court. Subsection 12(b) does not distinguish between whether the purpose of the action commenced in the forum court

was to seek recognition as an original matter under Subsection 6(a) or was an action that was already pending when the issue of recognition was raised under Subsection 6(b).

SECTION 13. REPEAL. The following [acts] are repealed:

(a) Uniform Foreign Money-Judgments Recognition Act,
(b) .]

Comment

Source: This Section is an updated version of Section 10 of the 1962 Act.

C. UNIFORM ENFORCEMENT OF FOREIGN JUDGMENTS ACT

(1964 Revised Act)

§ 1. Definition.

In this Act "foreign judgment" means any judgment, decree, or order of a court of the United States or of any other court which is entitled to full faith and credit in this state.

§ 2. Filing and Status of Foreign Judgments.

A copy of any foreign judgment authenticated in accordance with the act of Congress or the statutes of this state may be filed in the office of the Clerk of any [District Court of any city or county] of this state. The Clerk shall treat the foreign judgment in the same manner as a judgment of the [District Court of any city or county] of this state. A judgment so filed has the same effect and is subject to the same procedures, defenses and proceedings for reopening, vacating, or staying as a judgment of a [District Court of any city or county] of this state and may be enforced or satisfied in like manner.

§ 3. Notice of Filing.

(a) At the time of the filing of the foreign judgment, the judgment creditor or his lawyer shall make and file with the Clerk of Court an affidavit setting forth the name and last known post office address of the judgment debtor, and the judgment creditor.

(b) Promptly upon the filing of the foreign judgment and the affidavit, the Clerk shall mail notice of the filing of the foreign judgment to the judgment debtor at the address given and shall make a note of the mailing in the docket. The notice shall include the name and post office address of the judgment creditor and the judgment creditor's lawyer, if any, in this state. In addition, the judgment creditor may mail a notice of the filing of the judgment to the judgment debtor and may file proof of mailing with the Clerk.

§ 4. Stay.

(a) If the judgment debtor shows the [District Court of any city or county] that an appeal from the foreign judgment is pending or will be taken, or that a stay of execution has been granted, the court shall stay enforcement of the foreign judgment until the appeal is concluded, the time for appeal expires, or the stay of execution expires or is vacated, upon proof that the judgment debtor has furnished the security for the satisfaction of the judgment required by the state in which it was rendered.

(b) If the judgment debtor shows the [District Court of any city or county] any ground upon which enforcement of a judgment of any [District Court of any city or county] of this state would be stayed, the court shall stay enforcement of the foreign judgment for an appropriate period, upon requiring the same security for satisfaction of the judgment which is required in this state.

§ 5. Fees.

Any person filing a foreign judgment shall pay to the Clerk of Court _____ dollars. Fees for docketing, transcription or other enforcement proceedings shall be as provided for judgments of the [District Court of any city or county of this state].

§ 6. Optional Procedure.

The right of a judgment creditor to bring an action to enforce his judgment instead of proceeding under this Act remains unimpaired.

§ 7. Uniformity of Interpretation.

This Act shall be so interpreted and construed as to effectuate its general purpose to make uniform the law of those states which enact it.

§ 8. Short Title.

This Act may be cited as the Uniform Enforcement of Foreign Judgments Act.

§ 9. Repeal.

The following Acts and parts of Acts are repealed:

(1)
(2)
(3)

§ 10. Taking Effect.

This Act takes effect on _____

D. UNIFORM FOREIGN-MONEY CLAIMS ACT

PREFATORY NOTE

This Act facilitates uniform judicial determination of claims expressed in the money of foreign countries. It requires judgments and arbitration awards in these cases to be entered in the foreign money rather than in United States dollars. The debtor may pay the judgment in dollars on the basis of the rate of exchange prevailing at the time of payment.

A Uniform Act governing foreign-money claims has become desirable because:

These claims have increased greatly as a result of the growth in international trade.

Values of foreign moneys as compared to the United States dollar fluctuate more over shorter periods of time than was formerly the case.

United States jurisdictions treat recoveries on foreign-money claims differently than most of our major trading partners.

A lack of uniformity among the states in resolving foreign-money claims stimulates forum shopping and creates a lack of certainty in the law.

American courts historically follow one of two different rules in selecting a time during litigation for converting foreign money into United States dollars. These are called the "breach day rule"—the date the money should have been paid—and the "judgment date rule"—when judgment is entered. Many other countries use the "payment day rule"—when the judgment is paid. *See Miliangos v. George Frank (Textiles) Ltd.*, (1976) A.C. 1007. The merits of this approach have begun to be recognized in this country. The payment day rule is endorsed by this Act.

The three rules produce wildly disparate results in terms of making an injured person whole. This is illustrated by the following example:

An American citizen (A) owes 18,790 pounds sterling to a British corporation (BCo) suing in New York, and the pound is falling against the dollar. Due to the declining value of the pound, the three rules worked out as follows:

Date	Rate of Exchange	BCo Gets
Breach day	Pound = $2.20	$41,338
Judgment day	Pound = $1.50	$28,185
Payment day	Pound = $1.20	$22,548

A judgment of $41,338 may be entered based on the breach day rule. However, the payment in dollars was worth 34,449 pounds ($41,338 divided by $1.20) when eventually received, an excess of L15,659 over the actual loss.

This example is adapted from an actual case. See *Comptex v. LaBow*, 783 F.2d 333 (2d Cir. 1986). The facts are simplified.

463

If conversion is delayed until the date of actual payment, the creditor is recompensed with its own money or the financial equivalent in United States dollars; the debtor bears the risk of a fall in the debtor's money or reaps the benefit of a rise therein. If conversion is made at breach or judgment date, the risk of fluctuation in value of a money not of its selection falls on the creditor.

The real issue is where the risk of exchange rate fluctuation should be placed. This Act recognizes the right of the parties to agree upon the money that governs their relationship. In the absence of an agreement, the Act adopts the rule of giving the aggrieved party the amount to which it is entitled in its own money or the money in which the loss was suffered.

The principle of the Act is to restore the aggrieved party to the economic position it would have been in had the wrong not occurred. Thus, for example, if oil is spilled on the coast of France by an American ship, the loss is felt by the French in francs and a judgment of an American court for damages should reflect this fact. Courts should enter judgments in the money customarily used by the injured person.

The payment day rule, on which the Act is based, meets the reasonable expectations of the parties involved. It places the aggrieved party in the position it would have been in financially but for the wrong that gave rise to the claim. States which adopt it will align themselves with most of the major civilized countries of the world.

The Act also covers other issues that may arise in connection with foreign-money claims. These include revalorization and interest. In order to determine aliquot shares for distributions from funds created in insolvency and estate proceedings, the Act specifies use of the date the distribution proceeding was initiated for conversion of foreign money into United States dollars.

UNIFORM FOREIGN-MONEY CLAIMS ACT

SECTION 1. DEFINITIONS.

In this [Act]:

(1) "Action" means a judicial proceeding or arbitration in which a payment in money may be awarded or enforced with respect to a foreign-money claim.

(2) "Bank-offered spot rate" means the spot rate of exchange at which a bank will sell foreign money at a spot rate.

(3) "Conversion date" means the banking day next preceding the date on which money, in accordance with this [Act], is:

(i) paid to a claimant in an action or distribution proceeding;

(ii) paid to the official designated by law to enforce a judgment or award on behalf of a claimant; or

(iii) used to recoup, set-off, or counterclaim in different moneys in an action or distribution proceeding.

464

(4) "Distribution proceeding" means a judicial or nonjudicial proceeding for the distribution of a fund in which one or more foreign-money claims is asserted and includes an accounting, an assignment for the benefit of creditors, a foreclosure, the liquidation or rehabilitation of a corporation or other entity, and the distribution of an estate, trust, or other fund.

(5) "Foreign-money" means money other than money of the United States of America.

(6) "Foreign-money claim" means a claim upon an obligation to pay, or a claim for recovery of a loss, expressed in or measured by a foreign money.

(7) "Money" means a medium of exchange for the payment of obligations or a store of value authorized or adopted by a government or by inter-governmental agreement.

(8) "Money of the claim" means the money determined as proper pursuant to Section 4.

(9) "Person" means an individual, a corporation, government or governmental subdivision or agency, business trust, estate, trust, joint venture, partner-ship, association, two or more persons having a joint or common interest, or any other legal or commercial entity.

(10) "Rate of exchange" means the rate at which money of one country may be converted into money of another country in a free financial market convenient to or reasonably usable by a person obligated to pay or to state a rate of conversion. If separate rates of exchange apply to different kinds of transactions, the term means the rate applicable to the particular transaction giving rise to the foreign-money claim.

(11) "Spot rate" means the rate of exchange at which foreign money is sold by a bank or other dealer in foreign exchange for immediate or next day availability or for settlement by immediate payment in cash or equivalent, by charge to an account, or by an agreed delayed settlement not exceeding two days.

(12) "State" means a State of the United States, the District of Columbia, the Commonwealth of Puerto Rico, or a territory or insular possession subject to the jurisdiction of the United States.

COMMENT

1. "Action." A suit or arbitration may be legal or equitable in nature, but it must be based on a pecuniary claim.

2. "Bank-offered spot rate" is the rate at which a bank will sell the requisite amount of foreign money for immediate or nearly immediate use by the buyer.

3. "Conversion date." Exchange rates may fluctuate from day to day. A date must be picked for calculating the value of foreign money in terms of United States dollars. As used in the Act, "conversion date" means the day before a foreign-money claim is paid or set-off. The day refers to the time period of the place of the payor, not necessarily that of the recipient. The

exchange rate prevailing at or near the close of business on the banking day before the day payment is made will be well known at the time of payment. See Comment 2 to Section 7.

4. "Distribution proceeding." In keeping with the concept underlying Section 2, the coverage of this statute is limited to judicial actions and nonjudicial proceedings which involve the creation of a fund from which pro-rata distributions are made to claimants. As provided in Section 8, a different conversion date is required where either input to or outgo from a fund involves two or more different moneys. Thus, the term includes a mortgage foreclosure proceeding, judicial or under a trust deed, distribution of property in divorce and child support proceedings, distributions in the administration of a trust or a decedent's estate, an assignment for the benefit of creditors, an equity receivership, a liquidation by a statutory successor, a voluntary dissolution of a business or a nonprofit enterprise or the like when in each case a fund must be shared among claimants and where, usually, the fund will not satisfy all claimants of the same class. An asset or a liability of the fund must also involve one or more foreign-money claims, but not all of the claims can be in the same money.

5. "Foreign money." Since only the federal government has the power to coin money and regulate the value thereof, the term "foreign" means a government other than that of the United States of America. Special Drawing Rights of the International Monetary Fund are foreign money even though the United States is a member of the Fund. Foreign governments included are all those whose moneys are, in the currency markets of the world, exchangeable for the money of other currencies even though the government is not recognized by the United States.

6. "Foreign-money claim." The term "claim" is not limited to any one party to an action or a distribution proceeding and may be asserted by a plaintiff or a defendant or by a party to an arbitration or distribution proceeding. It may be based on a foreign judgment, or sound in contract, quasi-contract, or tort.

7. "Money." The definition includes composite currencies such as European Currency Units created by agreement of the governments that are members of the European Monetary System or the Special Drawing Rights created under the auspices of the International Money Fund. These are "stores of value" used to determine the quantity of payment in some international transactions.

8. "Money of the claim." See Section 4 and the Comment thereto.

9. "Party." This combines the Uniform Commercial Code's definitions of "person" and "organization," but is limited to those who are parties to transactions or involved in events which could give rise to a foreign-money claim.

10. "Rate of Exchange." A free market rate is to be used rather than an official rate if both exist. Some countries have transactional differences in exchange rates with slightly different rates; for example, in Belgium one rate

prevails for commercial and another for financial transactions. Both rates are recognized in money market transactions. The last sentence of the definition indicates that the rate appropriate to the transaction is the rate to be used.

11. "Spot rate" is the term used in the financial markets of the United States for the rate of exchange for immediate or nearly immediate transfers from one money to another, as distinguished from the rates for future options or future deliveries.

In the foreign exchange markets, as in the stock markets, quotations are either "bid" or "ask," and the spread between is where the dealer makes a profit. An "offered spot rate" is the rate at which the offeror will sell the particular money. It is, of course, higher than the rate at which that person will buy the same money. "Spot" refers to the time the trade is made, not the time for settlement, which in spot transactions is often two days after the date of the trade.

12. "State." The definition, as in other Uniform Laws, is extended to include areas given the same, or nearly the same, treatment in law as the states.

SECTION 2. SCOPE.

(a) This [Act] applies only to a foreign-money claim in an action or distribution proceeding.

(b) This [Act] applies to foreign-money issues even if other law under the conflict of laws rules of this State applies to other issues in the action or distribution proceeding.

COMMENT

Under the rules of the conflict of laws, the determination of when a foreign money is converted to United States dollars is generally considered a procedural matter for the law of the forum. Subsection (b) removes any doubt.

SECTION 3. VARIATION BY AGREEMENT.

(a) The effect of this [Act] may be varied by agreement of the parties made before or after commencement of an action or distribution proceeding or the entry of judgment.

(b) Parties to a transaction may agree upon the money to be used in a transaction giving rise to a foreign-money claim and may agree to use different moneys for different aspects of the transaction. Stating the price in a foreign money for one aspect of a transaction does not alone require the use of that money for other aspects of the transaction.

COMMENT

1. A basic policy of the Act is to preserve freedom of contract and to permit parties to resolve disputed matters by contract at any time, even as to choice of law problems. The parties may agree upon the date and time for conversion. After entry of judgment the parties may agree upon how the judgment is to be satisfied.

2. Subsection (b) covers cases where, for example, claims for petroleum may be settled in United States dollars but settlement for joint costs of exploration may be in pounds sterling. The parties also may agree on the money to be used for damages. The second sentence recognizes that a price stated in a particular money does to indicate, without more evidence, an intent that all damages from breach are to be in the same money. The principle of freedom of contract allows the parties to allocate the risks of currency fluctuations between foreign moneys as they desire. Sections 4 and 5 provide rules in the absence of special agreements by the parties for determining the money to be used. Parties may by agreement select a particular market or foreign exchange dealer to be used for exchange purposes.

SECTION 4. DETERMINING MONEY OF THE CLAIM.

(a) The money in which the parties to a transaction have agreed that payment is to be made is the proper money of the claim for payment.

(b) If the parties to a transaction have not otherwise agreed, the proper money of the claim, as in each case may be appropriate, is the money:

    (1) regularly used between the parties as a matter of usage or course of dealing;

    (2) used at the time of a transaction in international trade, by trade usage or common practice, for valuing or settling transactions in the particular commodity or service involved; or

    (3) in which the loss was ultimately felt or will be incurred by the party claimant.

COMMENT

1. Subsection (a) uses "payment" in a broad sense not related to just the price, but to any obligation arising out of a contract to transfer money. See also Section 3(b).

2. Subsection (b) states rules to fill gaps in the agreement of the parties with rules as to the allocation of risks of fluctuations in exchange rates. The three rules will normally apply in the order stated. Prior dealings may indicate the desired money. If there are none, it is appropriate to use the money indicated by trade usage or custom for transactions of like kind. The final rule of subsection (a) is one established in English cases. See *The*

Despina R and *The Folias*, (1979) A.C. 685. An example is the use of an operating account in United States dollars by a French company to buy Japanese yen for ship repairs; the loss is felt in the depletion of the dollar bank account. Appropriateness of a rule is to be determined by the judge from the facts of the case. See Section 6(d).

SECTION 5. DETERMINING AMOUNT OF THE MONEY OF CERTAIN CONTRACT CLAIMS.

(a) If an amount contracted to be paid in a foreign money is measured by a specified amount of a different money, the amount to be paid is determined on the conversion date.

(b) If an amount contracted to be paid in a foreign money is to be measured by a different money at the rate of exchange prevailing on a date before default, that rate of exchange applies only to payments made within a reasonable time after default, not exceeding 30 days. Thereafter, conversion is made at the bank-offered spot rate on the conversion date.

(c) A monetary claim is neither usurious nor unconscionable because the agreement on which it is based provides that the amount of the debtor's obligation to be paid in the debtor's money, when received by the creditor, must equal a specified amount of the foreign money of the country of the creditor. If, because of unexcused delay in payment of a judgment or award, the amount received by the creditor does not equal the amount of the foreign money specified in the agreement, the court or arbitrator shall amend the judgment or award accordingly.

COMMENT

1. Subsections (a) and (b) cover different interpretation problems. One arises where the amount of the money to be paid is measured by another money, one of which is foreign. An example is "pay 5,000 Swiss francs in pounds sterling." The issue is the time at which the rate of exchange into pounds sterling is to be applied. Subsection (a) says in a "measured by" situation with no rate specified, the rate of exchange that controls is the one prevailing at or near the close of business on the day before the day of payment. See Section 1(2), the definition of "conversion date."

2. Another problem arises when an exchange rate in effect before a default is used, as in "pay on November 30, 1989, 5,000 Swiss francs in pounds sterling at the exchange rate prevailing on June 30, 1989." In this case, the issue is how long does the specified exchange rate control in the absence of a clear expression of intent?

3. The most common application of subsection (c) will be found in international loan transactions. For example, a loan by a Japanese bank to an American company could be made with dollars purchased by yen for the purpose. The loan agreement could provide for repayment in dollars of an

amount which, when received by the lender, would repurchase the amount of yen used to acquire the dollars advanced.

Inclusion of a fixed rate as of a date before default, under subsection (b), remains effective only if payment is made within a reasonable time after default, not to exceed 30 days. The 30-day limitation accords usually with the expectation of the parties. Parties may agree to a longer time.

An exemption is needed from the application of usury laws that may be interpreted to hold that the indexing of the principal amount creates additional interest. See *Aztec Properties, Inc. v. Union Planters National Bank*, 530 S.W.2d 756 (Tenn. Sup. Ct. 1975). The subsection removes all doubts as to the legal enforceability of such agreements under theories such as usury, merger in a judgment, unconscionability, or the like.

SECTION 6. ASSERTING AND DEFENDING FOREIGN-MONEY CLAIM.

(a) A person may assert a claim in a specified foreign money. If a foreign-money claim is not asserted, the claimant makes the claim in United States dollars.

(b) An opposing party may allege and prove that a claim, in whole or in part, is in a different money than that asserted by the claimant.

(c) A person may assert a defense, set-off, recoupment, or counterclaim in any money without regard to the money of other claims.

(d) The determination of the proper money of the claim is a question of law.

COMMENT

1. Subsection (a) covers not only the claim of a plaintiff but also the assertion by a defendant of a defense, set-off, or counterclaim. Subsection (b) provides that the money asserted as the money of its defenses by the defendant need not be the same as that of the plaintiff.

2. The money to be used as the money of the claim is a threshold issue to be determined, if contested, by the court after any factual issues as to expenditures, custom, usage, or course of dealing or decided. See subsection (b). If a payment is made or a debt incurred in a money other than that in which the loss was felt, the party asserting the foreign-money claim should establish the amount of the money of the claim used to procure the money of expenditure and the applicable exchange rate used.

3. Judgments may be entered in more than one money when dealings impact on more than one area. An inn-keeper in Mexico, for example, in taking in customers from many countries, should be held to foresee that treatment for injuries at the inn would occur not only in Mexico, but also in the native land of the injured party or in a third country.

SECTION 7. JUDGMENTS AND AWARDS ON FOREIGN-MONEY CLAIMS; TIMES OF MONEY CONVERSION; FORM OF JUDGMENT.

(a) Except as provided in subsection (c), a judgment or award on a foreign-money claim must be stated in an amount of the money of the claim.

(b) A judgment or award on a foreign-money claim is payable in that foreign money or, at the option of the debtor, in the amount of United States dollars which will purchase that foreign money on the conversion date at a bank-offered spot rate.

(c) Assessed costs must be entered in United States dollars.

(d) Each payment in United States dollars must be accepted and credited on a judgment or award on a foreign-money claim in the amount of the foreign money that could be purchased by the dollars at a bank-offered spot rate of exchange at or near the close of business on the conversion date for that payment.

(e) A judgment or award made in an action or distribution proceeding on both (i) a defense, set-off, recoupment, or counterclaim and (ii) the adverse party's claim, must be netted by converting the money of the smaller into the money of the larger, and by subtracting the smaller from the larger, and specify the rates of exchange used.

(f) A judgment substantially in the following form complies with subsection (a);

[IT IS ADJUDGED AND ORDERED, that Defendant (insert name) pay to the Plaintiff (insert name) the sum of (insert amount in foreign money) plus interest on that sum at the rate of (insert rate - see Section 9) percent a year or, at the option of the judgment debtor, the number of United States dollars which will purchase the (insert name of foreign money) with interest due, at a bank-offered spot rate at or near the close of business on the banking day next before the day of payment, together with assessed costs of (insert amount) United States dollars.] [Note: States should insert their customary forms of judgment with appropriate modifications.]

(g) If a contract claim is of the type covered by Section 5(a) or (b), the judgment or award must be entered for the amount of money stated to measure the obligation to be paid in the money specified for payment or, at the option of the debtor, the number of United States dollars which will purchase the computed amount of the money of payment on the conversion date at a bank-offered spot rate.

(h) A judgment must be [filed] [docketed] [recorded] and indexed in foreign money in the same manner, and has the same effect as a lien, as other judgments. It may be discharged by payment.

COMMENT

1. Subsection (a) changes a number of statutes in the states which can be construed to require all values in legal proceedings to be expressed in United States dollars. Professor Brand, in his article in the Yale Journal of International Law, Vol. 11:139 at page 169, identified 18 states having statutes which could require all judgments to be entered in dollars. They are Arkansas, California, Idaho, Iowa, Louisiana, Maryland, Michigan, Montana, Nevada, New Jersey, New Mexico, New York, South Carolina, Tennessee, Vermont, Virginia, West Virginia, and Wisconsin. Brand, ibid. fn. 166. Hence, direct statutory authority must be given the courts in those states, and will be helpful in other states. In some states other statutes may need amendments. *See, e.g.,* Wisc. Stats. §§ 138.01, 138.02, 138.03, and 779.05.

2. Subsection (d) gives defendants the option of paying in dollars which are, at the payment date, practically the economic equivalent of the foreign money awarded. The judgment creditor should be indifferent to whether the debtor exercises the right to pay in dollars as the only difference is a small bank charge for exchanging the dollars for the foreign money. The concept of the rate of the banking day next before the payment day is taken from Section 131 of the Province of Ontario, Canada, Courts of Justice Act (Ch. 11 Ont. Stats. (1984) as recently amended). It gives the defendant and the sheriff conducting the sale the necessary conversion rate comfortably ahead of its use. Newspaper quotations are usually said to be "at or near the close of business" on the stated date, so that phrase is used in this Act.

3. Subsection (e) provides for netting the affirmative recoveries of a defendant and plaintiff, whether in the same money or in different moneys, but preserving the quantum of each for appellate purposes. The theory is that when claims are reduced to money, they become mutual debts and should be set-off, so that a person's exchange rate fluctuation risk continues only for the surplus in its money of the claim. The set-off is made by the judge or arbitrator.

4. The form of judgment in subsection (f) should be varied appropriately where the money to be paid is measured by a foreign money. See Section 5.

SECTION 8. CONVERSIONS OF FOREIGN MONEY IN DISTRIBUTION PROCEEDING.

The rate of exchange prevailing at or near the close of business on the day the distribution proceeding is initiated governs all exchanges of foreign money in a distribution proceeding. A foreign-money claimant in a distribution proceeding shall assert its claim in the named foreign money and show the amount of United States dollars resulting from a conversion as of the date the proceeding was initiated.

COMMENT

All claims must be in the same money when determining aliquot shares in a distribution proceeding. The Act requires use of the date the proceeding was initiated for applying the exchange rate to convert foreign-money claims into United States dollars. *See Re Lines Bros. Ltd.*, (1982) 2 All E.R. 99. A claim may be amended to show the proper conversion rate and the proper amount of United States dollars.

SECTION 9. PRE-JUDGMENT AND JUDGMENT INTEREST.

(a) With respect to a foreign-money claim, recovery of pre-judgment or pre-award interest and the rate of interest to be applied in the action or distribution proceeding, except as provided in subsection (b), are matters of the substantive law governing the right to recovery under the conflict-of-laws rules of this State.

(b) The court or arbitrator shall increase or decrease the amount of pre-judgment or pre-award interest otherwise payable in a judgment or award in foreign-money to the extent required by the law of this State governing a failure to make or accept an offer of settlement or offer of judgment, or conduct by a party or its attorney causing undue delay or expense.

(c) A judgment or award on a foreign-money claim bears interest at the rate applicable to judgments of this State.

COMMENT

1. As to pre-judgment interest, the Act adopts the majority rule in the United States that pre-judgment interest follows the substantive law of the case under conflict of laws rules, both as to the right to recover and the rate. English courts use a different rule, *i.e.*, the borrowing rate used by plaintiff or prevailing in the country issuing the money of the judgment. *See Helmsing Schiffarts G.M.B.H. v. Malta Drydock Corp.* (1977) 2 Lloyd's Rep. 44 (Maltese money but borrowed in West Germany; German rate); *Miliangos v. George Frank (Textiles) Ltd. (No. 2)*, (1976) 1 QB 487 at 489 (Swiss money, Swiss interest rate). Although pre-judgment interest is one form of damages, provision for pre-judgment interest is not to be taken as indicating that no other damages for delay in payment can be awarded under the substantive law applicable to the determination of damages. *Cf. Isaac Naylor & Sons, Ltd. v. New Zealand Co-operative Wool Marketing Association, Ltd.* (1981) 1 N.Z.L.R. 361 (exchange loss due to delay as additional damages).

2. Allowances of pre-judgment interest in some states depend upon a party's conduct with respect to settlement or delay of the proceeding. Subsection

(b) treats these state laws as either procedural in nature or expressions of a significant policy, in either case to be governed by the law of the forum state.

3. Interest on a judgment is considered to be procedural and also goes by the law of the forum. There is a problem here in that there is great discrepancy among the states in the rates for judgment interest. When a judgment is in a foreign money, United States interest rates may result in some overcompensation or undercompensation as compared to what would be awarded in the jurisdiction issuing the foreign money. But in both the United States and in foreign countries, most jurisdictions have fixed statutory rates that do not readily respond to the inflation or deflation of the value of their money in the world market. Hence it was decided to apply the usual rules of the conflict of laws.

SECTION 10. ENFORCEMENT OF FOREIGN JUDGMENTS.

(a) If an action is brought to enforce a judgment of another jurisdiction expressed in a foreign money and the judgment is recognized in this State as enforceable, the enforcing judgment must be entered as provided in Section 7, whether or not the foreign judgment confers an option to pay in an equivalent amount of United States dollars.

(b) A foreign judgment may be [filed] [docketed] [recorded] in accordance with any rule or statute of this State providing a procedure for its recognition and enforcement.

(c) A satisfaction or partial payment made upon the foreign judgment, on proof thereof, must be credited against the amount of foreign money specified in the judgment, notwithstanding the entry of judgment in this State.

(d) A judgment entered on a foreign-money claim only in United States dollars in another state must be enforced in this State in United States dollars only.

COMMENT

1. Some states have special acts that simply cover the recognition, entry, and enforcement of foreign judgments. Common law enforcement is by action. Subsection (a) refers to the common law method; it is subject to subsection (b) which refers to statutory procedures. Subsection (c) applies to both procedures.

2. Subsection (d) avoids constitutional issues under the full faith and credit clause by requiring that judgments of sister states be enforced as entered in the sister state.

SECTION 11. DETERMINING UNITED STATES DOLLAR VALUE OF FOREIGN-MONEY CLAIMS FOR LIMITED PURPOSES.

(a) Computations under this section are for the limited purposes of the section and do not affect computation of the United States dollar equivalent of the money of the judgment for the purpose of payment.

(b) For the limited purpose of facilitating the enforcement of provisional remedies in an action, the value in United States dollars of assets to be seized or restrained pursuant to a writ of attachment, garnishment, execution, or other process, the amount of United States dollars at issue for assessing costs, or the amount of United States dollars involved for a surety bond or other court-required undertaking, must be ascertained as provided in subsections (c) and (d).

(c) A party seeking process, costs, bond, or other undertaking under subsection (b) shall compute in United States dollars the amount of the foreign money claimed from a bank-offered spot rate prevailing at or near the close of business on the banking day next preceding the filing of a request or application for the issuance of process or for the determination of costs, or an application for a bond or other court-required undertaking.

(d) A party seeking process, costs, bond, or other undertaking under subsection (b) shall file with each request or application an affidavit or certificate executed in good faith by its counsel or a bank officer, stating the market quotation used and how it was obtained, and setting forth the calculation. Affected court officials incur no liability, after a filing of the affidavit or certificate, for acting as if the judgment were in the amount of United States dollars stated in the affidavit or certificate.

COMMENT

This section protects those who must determine how much should be held subject to a levy or other collection process or what the dollar amount of a supersedeas or other surety bond should be. If the judgment debtor is damaged by a gross overstatement of the dollar amount in the affidavit or certificate of counsel for the judgment creditor or the bank officer, recovery should be against that person.

SECTION 12. EFFECT OF CURRENCY REVALORIZATION.

(a) If, after an obligation is expressed or a loss is incurred in a foreign money, the country issuing or adopting that money substitutes a new money in place of that money, the obligation or the loss is treated as if expressed or incurred in the new money at a rate of conversion the issuing country establishes for the payment of like obligations or losses denominated in the former money.

(b) If substitution under subsection (a) occurs after a judgment or award is entered on a foreign-money claim, the court or arbitrator shall amend the judgment or award by a like conversion of the former money.

COMMENT

1. Subsection (a) refers to situations in which a country authorizes the issue of a new money to take the place of the old money at a stated ratio. An example is Brazil's recent abolition of cruzieros for cruzados. The subsection mandates that foreign money claims should be subjected to the same ratio.
2. The Act takes no position on the effect of money repudiations or revalorizations so drastic as to be, in effect, confiscations. Remedy, if any, for these is usually found through diplomatic channels. Equally, the Act takes no position on the effect of exchange control laws. The effect, if any, on obligations to pay is left to other law.

SECTION 13. SUPPLEMENTARY GENERAL PRINCIPLES OF LAW.

Unless displaced by particular provisions of this [Act], the principles of law and equity, including the law merchant, and the law relative to capacity to contract, principal and agent, estoppel, fraud, misrepresentation, duress, coercion, mistake, bankruptcy, or other validating or invalidating causes supplement its provisions.

COMMENT

The section is taken from Section 1-103 of the Uniform Commercial Code.

SECTION 14. UNIFORMITY OF APPLICATION AND CONSTRUCTION.

This [Act] shall be applied and construed to effectuate its general purpose to make uniform the law with respect to the subject of this [Act] among states enacting it.

SECTION 15. SHORT TITLE.

This [Act] may be cited as the Uniform Foreign-Money Claims Act.

SECTION 16. SEVERABILITY CLAUSE.

If any provision of this [Act] or its application to any person or circumstance is held invalid, the invalidity does not affect other provisions or applications of this [Act] which can be given effect without the invalid provision or application, and to this end the provisions of this [Act] are severable.

SECTION 17. EFFECTIVE DATE.

This [Act] becomes effective on January 1st following its enactment.

SECTION 18. TRANSITIONAL PROVISION.

This [Act] applies to actions and distribution proceedings commenced after its effective date.

[SECTION 19. REPEALS.

The following acts and parts of acts are repealed:

(1) [Any statute requiring judgments to be entered in United States dollars.]
(2) _____.
(3) _____.]

E. ABA MODEL RULE FOR THE LICENSING AND PRACTICE OF FOREIGN LEGAL CONSULTANTS

MODEL RULE FOR THE LICENSING AND PRACTICE OF FOREIGN LEGAL CONSULTANTS

(August 2006)

§ 1. General Regulation as to Licensing

In its discretion, the [name of court] may license to practice in this United States jurisdiction as a foreign legal consultant, without examination, an applicant who:

(a) is, and for at least five years has been, a member in good standing of a recognized legal profession in a foreign country, the members of which are admitted to practice as lawyers or counselors at law or the equivalent and are subject to effective regulation and discipline by a duly constituted professional body or a public authority;

(b) for at least five years preceding his or her application has been a member in good standing of such legal profession and has been lawfully engaged in the practice of law in the foreign country or elsewhere substantially involving or relating to the rendering of advice or the provision of legal services concerning the law of the foreign country;

(c) possesses the good moral character and general fitness requisite for a member of the bar of this jurisdiction; and

(d) intends to practice as a foreign legal consultant in this jurisdiction and to maintain an office in this jurisdiction for that purpose.

§ 2. Application

An applicant under this Rule shall file an application for a foreign legal consultant license, which shall include all of the following:

(a) a certificate from the professional body or public authority having final jurisdiction over professional discipline in the foreign country in which the applicant is admitted, certifying the applicant's admission to practice, date of admission, and good standing as a lawyer or counselor at law or the equivalent;

(b) a letter of recommendation from one of the members of the executive body of such professional body or public authority or from one of the judges of the highest law court or court of original jurisdiction in the foreign country in which the applicant is admitted;

(c) duly authenticated English translations of the certificate required by Section 2(a) of this Rule and the letter required by Section 2(b) of this Rule if they are not in English;

(d) other evidence as the [name of court] may require regarding the applicant's educational and professional qualifications, good moral character and general fitness, and compliance with the requirements of Section 1 of this Rule;

(e) an application fee as set by the [name of court].

§ 3. Scope of Practice

A person licensed to practice as a foreign legal consultant under this Rule may render legal services in this jurisdiction but shall not be considered admitted to practice law in this jurisdiction, or in any way hold himself or herself out as a member of the bar of this jurisdiction, or, do any of the following:

(a) appear as a lawyer on behalf of another person in any court, or before any magistrate or other judicial officer, in this jurisdiction (except when admitted pro hac vice pursuant to [citation of applicable rule]);

(b) prepare any instrument effecting the transfer or registration of title to real estate located in the United States of America;

(c) prepare:
   (i) any will or trust instrument effecting the disposition on death of any property located in and owned by a resident of the United States of America, or
   (ii) any instrument relating to the administration of a decedent's estate in the United States of America;

(d) prepare any instrument in respect of the marital or parental relations, rights or duties of a resident of the United States of America, or the custody or care of the children of such a resident;

(e) render professional legal advice on the law of this jurisdiction or of the United States of America (whether rendered incident to the preparation of legal instruments or otherwise) except on the basis of advice from a person duly qualified and entitled (other than by virtue of having been licensed under this Rule) to render professional legal advice in this jurisdiction;

(f) carry on a practice under, or utilize in connection with such practice, any name, title or designation other than one or more of the following:
   (i) the foreign legal consultant's own name;
   (ii) the name of the law firm with which the foreign legal consultant is affiliated;
   (iii) the foreign legal consultant's authorized title in the foreign country of his or her admission to practice, which may be used in conjunction with the name of that country; and

480

(iv) the title "foreign legal consultant," which may be used in conjunction with the words "admitted to the practice of law in [name of the foreign country of his or her admission to practice]".

(g) render legal services in this State pursuant to the Model Rule for the Temporary Practice by Foreign Lawyers.]

§ 4. Practice by a Foreign Legal Consultant Licensed in Another United States Jurisdiction

[A person licensed as a foreign legal consultant in another United States jurisdiction may provide legal services in this State on a temporary basis pursuant to the Model Rule for Temporary Practice by Foreign Lawyers. A person licensed as a foreign legal consultant in another United States jurisdiction shall not establish an office or otherwise engage in a systematic and continuous practice in this jurisdiction or hold out to the public or otherwise represent that the foreign legal consultant is licensed as a foreign legal consultant in this jurisdiction.]

§ 5. Rights and Obligations

Subject to the limitations listed in Section 3 of this Rule, a person licensed under this Rule shall be considered a foreign legal consultant affiliated with the bar of this State and shall be entitled and subject to:

(a) the rights and obligations set forth in the [Rules] [Code] of Professional [Conduct] [Responsibility] of [citation] or arising from the other conditions and requirements that apply to a member of the bar of this jurisdiction under the [rules of court governing members of the bar, including ethics]; and

(b) the rights and obligations of a member of the bar of this jurisdiction with respect to:

(i) affiliation in the same law firm with one or more members of the bar of this jurisdiction, including by:

(A) employing one or more members of the bar of this jurisdiction;

(B) being employed by one or more members of the bar of this jurisdiction or by any partnership [or professional corporation] that includes members of the bar of this jurisdiction or that maintains an office in this jurisdiction; and

(C) being a partner in any partnership [or shareholder in any professional corporation] that includes members of the bar of this jurisdiction or that maintains an office in this jurisdiction; and

(ii) attorney-client privilege, work-product privilege, and similar professional privileges.

§ 6. Discipline

A person licensed to practice as a foreign legal consultant under this Rule shall be subject to professional discipline in the same manner and to the same extent as members of the bar of this jurisdiction. To this end:

(a) Every person licensed to practice as a foreign legal consultant under this Rule:

    (i) shall be subject to the jurisdiction of the [name of court] and to censure, suspension, removal, or revocation of his or her license to practice by the [name of court] and shall otherwise be governed by [citation of applicable rules]; and

    (ii) shall execute and file with the [name of court], in the form and manner as the court may prescribe:

        (A) a commitment to observe the [Rules] [Code] of Professional [Conduct] [Responsibility] of [citation] and the [rules of court governing members of the bar] to the extent applicable to the legal services authorized under Section 3 of this Rule;

        (B) an undertaking or appropriate evidence of professional liability insurance, in an amount as the court may prescribe, to assure the foreign legal consultant's proper professional conduct and responsibility;

        (C) a written undertaking to notify the court of any change in the foreign legal consultant's good standing as a member of the foreign legal profession referred to in Section 1(a) of this Rule and of any final action of the professional body or public authority referred to in Section 2(a) of this Rule imposing any disciplinary censure, suspension, or other sanction upon the foreign legal consultant; and

        (D) a duly acknowledged instrument, in writing, providing the foreign legal consultant's address in this jurisdiction and designating the clerk of [name of court] as his or her agent for service of process. The foreign legal consultant shall keep the clerk advised in writing of any changes of address in this jurisdiction. In any action or proceeding brought against the foreign legal consultant and arising out of or based upon any legal services rendered or offered to be rendered by the foreign legal consultant within or to residents of this jurisdiction, service shall first be attempted upon the foreign legal consultant at the most recent address filed with the clerk. Whenever after due diligence service cannot be made upon the foreign legal consultant at that address, service may be made upon the clerk. Service made upon the clerk in accordance with this provision is effective as if service had been made personally upon the foreign legal consultant.

(b) Service of process on the clerk under Section 5(a)(ii)(D) of this Rule shall be made by personally delivering to the clerk's office, and leaving with the clerk or with a deputy or assistant authorized by the clerk to receive service, duplicate copies of the process together with a fee as set by the [name of court]. The clerk shall promptly send one copy of the process to the foreign legal consultant to whom the process is directed, by certified mail, return receipt requested, addressed to the foreign legal consultant at the most recent address provided in accordance with Section 5(a)(ii)(D).

§ 7. Annual Fee

A person licensed as a foreign legal consultant shall pay an annual fee as set by the [name of court].

§ 8. Revocation of License

If the [name of court] determines that a person licensed as a foreign legal consultant under this Rule no longer meets the requirements for licensure set forth in Section 1(a) or Section 1(b) of this Rule, it shall revoke the foreign legal consultant's license.

§ 9. Admission to Bar

If a person licensed as a foreign legal consultant under this Rule is subsequently admitted as a member of the bar of this jurisdiction under the Rules governing admission, that person's foreign legal consultant license shall be deemed superseded by the license to practice law as a member of the bar of this jurisdiction.

§ 10. Application for Waiver of Provisions

The [name of court], upon written application, may waive any provision or vary the application of this Rule where strict compliance will cause undue hardship to the applicant. An application for waiver shall be in the form of a verified petition setting forth the applicant's name, age, and residence address; the facts relied upon; and a prayer for relief.

LAWS OF OTHER NATIONS

A. SELECTED PROVISIONS OF THE ENGLISH SALE OF GOODS ACT

Source: Sale of Goods Act 1979 (c 54), 6 December 1979

Introduction

The English Sale of Goods Act 1979 (ESGA) replaced the Sale of Goods Act, 1893,[1] and parts of other statutes.[2] Representing a convenient way to consolidate and update some of the law of the intervening period, the 1979 Act is very similar to the 1893 Act, and applies retroactively to all contracts for the sale of goods made on or after 1 January 1894 (the date the original Act entered into force).[3] Because the Act is a so called "consolidating act," precedents interpreting the superseded statute are still good law.[4] Section 20 of the Act received significant amendments in 1995.

The Sale of Goods Bill was drafted in 1888 by Sir Mackenzie Chalmers. As enacted, it formed the basis for a number statutes in other common law jurisdictions, including the Uniform Sales Act (U.S.A.), which was the predecessor to the Uniform Commercial Code.[5] The ESGA was adopted with very little modification in most of the jurisdictions of the British Commonwealth, including Australia, New Zealand and India.[6]

The ESGA generally applies to all types of contracts for the sale of goods.[7] It was considered both a virtue and a fault of the 1893 Act that "virtually no distinctions were made between commercial sales and private sales, between merchants' sales and retail sales, or between sales of new and of second-hand goods."[8] The 1979 Act does away with the sweeping application of every provision; while it remains generally applicable to all sales of goods, the introduction into the Act of parts of other legislation (and the fact that other pieces of legislation are expressly saved by the new Act) makes particular parts of the Act applicable to one type of sale but not to others. For example, if a contract has an international element, several statutory provisions outside the context of the Act may come into play.[9] Section 62(2) saves "the rules of the common law, including the law merchant, except in so far as they are inconsistent with the provisions of this Act."

---

1. 56 & 57 Vict. c. 71.
2. *E.g.*, Misrepresentation Act, 1967, § 4; Misrepresentation (Northern Ireland) Act, 1967, § 4; Supply of Goods (Implied Terms) Act, 1973, §§ 1-7, 18(2).
3. § 1(1). *See* Chalmer's Sale of Goods Act, 1893 (Michael Mark, ed., 15th ed. 1967).
4. "There is a presumption in construing a consolidating act that no alteration of the previous law was intended. . . . The presumption applies even if the language of the two provisions is not identical; but this view must yield to plain words to the contrary." Benjamin's Sale of Goods, 7 (A. G. Guest et al. eds., 3d ed. 1987) *citing* MacConnell v. E. Prill & Co. [1916] 2 Ch. 57, 63.
5. It is important to note the substantial differences between the U.S.A. and U.C.C. The U.C.C.—and, therefore, American law—is significantly different in many respects to the Sale of Goods Act.
6. Benjamin's Sale of Goods, *supra* note 4, at 4.
7. *Id.* at 7.
8. *Id.*
9. *See id.* at 8; The Uniform Laws on International Sales Act, 1967 was enabling legislation for the two predecessors (ULF and ULIS) to the U.N. Convention on Contracts for the International Sales

The basic scope of the Act was stated by Lord Diplock in *Ashington Piggeries Ltd. v. Christopher Hill Ltd.*:[10]

> The provisions of the Act are in the main confined to statements of what promises are to be implied on the part of the buyer and the seller in respect of matters upon which the contract is silent, and to statements of the consequences of performance or non-performance of promises, whether express or implied, where the contract does not state what those consequences are to be.

Thus, Lord Diplock clearly implies that freedom of contract is an essential feature of the Act.[11]

The Act covers five broad topics: contract formation (Part I); transfer of property/title (Part II); contract performance (Part III); rights of the unpaid seller against the goods (Part IV); and, actions for breach of contract (Part V). It contains over 60 sections, most of which are not reproduced here.

SALE OF GOODS ACT 1979 (C 54)

6 DECEMBER 1979

Part I: Contracts to Which Act Applies
   1. Contracts to which Act applies
Part II: Formation of the Contract: Contract of Sale
   2. Contract of sale
   3. Capacity to buy and sell
   4. How contract of sale is made
   5. Existing or future goods
   6. Goods which have perished
   7. Goods perishing before sale but after agreement to sell
   8. Ascertainment of price
   9. Agreement to sell at valuation
   10. Stipulations about time
   11. When condition to be treated as warranty
   12. Implied terms about title, etc.
   13. Sale by description
   14. Implied terms about quality or fitness
   15. Sale by sample
   15A. Modification of remedies for breach of condition in non-consumer cases
Part III: Effects of the Contract: Transfer of property as between seller and buyer

---

of Goods (CISG). The United Kingdom has not become party to the CISG; therefore, even though the Uniform Laws Act remains in force, it would presumably not be applied.
10. [1972] A.C. 441, 501.
11. § 55(1).

16. Goods must be ascertained

[Subject to section 20A below] where there is a contract for the sale of unascertained goods no property in the goods is transferred to the buyer unless and until the goods are ascertained.

ANNOTATIONS: This section derived from the Sale of Goods Act 1893, § 16. Words in square brackets added by the Sale of Goods (Amendment) Act 1995, § 1(1).

17. Property passes when intended to pass

(1) Where there is a contract for the sale of specific or ascertained goods the property in them is transferred to the buyer at such time as the parties to the contract intend it to be transferred.

(2) For the purpose of ascertaining the intention of the parties regard shall be had to the terms of the contract, the conduct of the parties and the circumstances of the case.

ANNOTATIONS: This section derived from the Sale of Goods Act 1893, § 17.

18. Rules for ascertaining intention

Unless a different intention appears, the following are rules for ascertaining the intention of the parties as to the time at which the property in the goods is to pass to the buyer.

Rule 1.—Where there is an unconditional contract for the sale of specific goods in a deliverable state the property in the goods passes to the buyer when the contract is made, and it is immaterial whether the time of payment or the time of delivery, or both, be postponed.

Rule 2.—Where there is a contract for the sale of specific goods and the seller is bound to do something to the goods for the purpose of putting them into a deliverable state, the property does not pass until the thing is done and the buyer has notice that it has been done.

Rule 3.—Where there is a contract for the sale of specific goods in a deliverable state but the seller is bound to weigh, measure, test, or do some other act or thing with reference to the goods for the purpose of ascertaining the price, the property does not pass until the act or thing is done and the buyer has notice that it has been done.

Rule 4.—When goods are delivered to the buyer on approval or on sale or return or other similar terms the property in the goods passes to the buyer:—

(a) when he signifies his approval or acceptance to the seller or does any other act adopting the transaction;

(b) if he does not signify his approval or acceptance to the seller but retains the goods without giving notice of rejection, then, if a time has been fixed for the return of the goods, on the expiration of that time, and, if no time has been fixed, on the expiration of a reasonable time.

Rule 5.—(1) Where there is a contract for the sale of unascertained or future goods by description, and goods of that description and in a deliverable state are unconditionally appropriated to the contract, either by the seller with the assent of the buyer or by the buyer with the assent of the seller, the property in the goods then passes to the buyer; and the assent may be express or implied, and may be given either before or after the appropriation is made.

(2) Where, in pursuance of the contract, the seller delivers the goods to the buyer or to a carrier or other bailee or custodier (whether named by the buyer or not) for the purpose of transmission to the buyer, and does not reserve the right of disposal, he is to be taken to have unconditionally appropriated the goods to the contract.

(3) Where there is a contract for the sale of a specified quantity of unascertained goods in a deliverable state forming part of a bulk which is identified either in the contract or by subsequent agreement between the parties and the bulk is reduced to (or to less than) that quantity, then, if the buyer under that contract is the only buyer to whom goods are then due out of the bulk—

    (a) the remaining goods are to be taken as appropriated to that contract at the time when the bulk is so reduced; and

    (b) the property in those goods then passes to that buyer.

(4) Paragraph (3) above applies also (with the necessary modifications) where a bulk is reduced to (or to less than) the aggregate of the quantities due to a single buyer under separate contracts relating to that bulk and he is the only buyer to whom goods are then due out of that bulk.

ANNOTATIONS: This section derived from the Sale of Goods Act 1893, § 18. Rule 5: paras. (3), (4) added by the Sale of Goods (Amendment) Act 1995, § 1(2).

19. Reservation of right of disposal

(1) Where there is a contract for the sale of specific goods or where goods are subsequently appropriated to the contract, the seller may, by the terms of the contract or appropriation, reserve the right of disposal of the goods until certain conditions are fulfilled; and in such a case, notwithstanding the delivery of the goods to the buyer, or to a carrier or other bailee or custodier for the purpose of transmission to the buyer, the property in the goods does not pass to the buyer until the conditions imposed by the seller are fulfilled.

(2) Where goods are shipped, and by the bill of lading the goods are deliverable to the order of the seller or his agent, the seller is prima facie to be taken to reserve the right of disposal.

(3) Where the seller of goods draws on the buyer for the price, and transmits the bill of exchange and bill of lading to the buyer together to secure acceptance or payment of the bill of exchange, the buyer is bound to return the bill of lading if he does not honour the bill of exchange, and if he wrongfully retains the bill of lading the property in the goods does not pass to him.

ANNOTATIONS: This section derived from the Sale of Goods Act 1893, § 19.

20. Risk prima facie passes with property

(1) Unless otherwise agreed, the goods remain at the seller's risk until the property in them is transferred to the buyer, but when the property in them is transferred to the buyer the goods are at the buyer's risk whether delivery has been made or not.

(2) But where delivery has been delayed through the fault of either buyer or seller the goods are at the risk of the party at fault as regards any loss which might not have occurred but for such fault.

(3) Nothing in this section affects the duties or liabilities of either seller or buyer as a bailee or custodier of the goods of the other party.

ANNOTATIONS: This section derived from the Sale of Goods Act 1893, § 20.

20A. Undivided shares in goods forming part of a bulk

(1) This section applies to a contract for the sale of a specified quantity of unascertained goods if the following conditions are met—
  (a) the goods or some of them form part of a bulk which is identified either in the contract or by subsequent agreement between the parties; and
  (b) the buyer has paid the price for some or all of the goods which are the subject of the contract and which form part of the bulk.

(2) Where this section applies, then (unless the parties agree otherwise), as soon as the conditions specified in paragraphs (a) and (b) of subsection (1) above are met or at such later time as the parties may agree—
  (a) property in an undivided share in the bulk is transferred to the buyer, and
  (b) the buyer becomes an owner in common of the bulk.

(3) Subject to subsection (4) below, for the purposes of this section, the undivided share of a buyer in a bulk at any time shall be such share as the quantity of goods paid for and due to the buyer out of the bulk bears to the quantity of goods in the bulk at that time.

(4) Where the aggregate of the undivided shares of buyers in a bulk determined under subsection (3) above would at any time exceed the whole of the bulk at that time, the undivided share in the bulk of each buyer shall be reduced proportionately so that the aggregate of the undivided shares is equal to the whole bulk.

(5) Where a buyer has paid the price for only some of the goods due to him out of a bulk, any delivery to the buyer out of the bulk shall, for the purposes of this section, be ascribed in the first place to the goods in respect of which payment has been made.

(6) For the purposes of this section payment of part of the price for any goods shall be treated as payment for a corresponding part of the goods.]

ANNOTATIONS: This section was added by the Sale of Goods (Amendment) Act 1995, § 1(3).

20B. Deemed consent by co-owner to dealings in bulk goods

(1) A person who has become an owner in common of a bulk by virtue of section 20A above shall be deemed to have consented to—
  (a) any delivery of goods out of the bulk to any other owner in common of the bulk, being goods which are due to him under his contract;
  (b) any dealing with or removal, delivery or disposal of goods in the bulk by any other person who is an owner in common of the bulk in so far as the goods fall within that co-owner's undivided share in the bulk at the time of the dealing, removal, delivery or disposal.

(2) No cause of action shall accrue to anyone against a person by reason of that person having acted in accordance with paragraph (a) or (b) of subsection (1) above in reliance on any consent deemed to have been given under that subsection.

(3) Nothing in this section or section 20A above shall—
  (a) impose an obligation on a buyer of goods out of a bulk to compensate any other buyer of goods out of that bulk for any shortfall in the goods received by that other buyer;
  (b) affect any contractual arrangement between buyers of goods out of a bulk for adjustments between themselves; or
  (c) affect the rights of any buyer under his contract.]

ANNOTATIONS: This section was added by the Sale of Goods (Amendment) Act 1995, § 1(3).

27. Duties of seller and buyer

It is the duty of the seller to deliver the goods, and of the buyer to accept and pay for them, in accordance with the terms of the contract of sale.

ANNOTATIONS: This section derived from the Sale of Goods Act 1893, § 27.

28. Payment and delivery are concurrent conditions

Unless otherwise agreed, delivery of the goods and payment of the price are concurrent conditions, that is to say, the seller must be ready and willing to give possession of the goods to the buyer in exchange for the price and the buyer must be ready and willing to pay the price in exchange for possession of the goods.

ANNOTATIONS: This section derived from the Sale of Goods Act 1893, § 28.

29. Rules about delivery

(1) Whether it is for the buyer to take possession of the goods or for the seller to send them to the buyer is a question depending in each case on the contract, express or implied, between the parties.
(2) Apart from any such contract, express or implied, the place of delivery is the seller's place of business if he has one, and if not, his residence; except that, if the contract is for the sale of specific goods, which to the knowledge of the parties when the contract is made are in some other place, then that place is the place of delivery.
(3) Where under the contract of sale the seller is bound to send the goods to the buyer, but no time for sending them is fixed, the seller is bound to send them within a reasonable time.
(4) Where the goods at the time of sale are in the possession of a third person, there is no delivery by seller to buyer unless and until the third person acknowledges to the buyer that he holds the goods on his behalf; but nothing in this section affects the operation of the issue or transfer of any document of title to goods.
(5) Demand or tender of delivery may be treated as ineffectual unless made at a reasonable hour; and what is a reasonable hour is a question of fact.
(6) Unless otherwise agreed, the expenses of and incidental to putting the goods into a deliverable state must be borne by the seller.

ANNOTATIONS: This section derived from the Sale of Goods Act 1893, § 29.

30. Delivery of wrong quantity

31. Instalment deliveries

32. Delivery to Carrier

(1) Where, in pursuance of a contract of sale, the seller is authorised or required to send the goods to the buyer, delivery of the goods to a carrier (whether named by the buyer or not) for the purpose of transmission to the buyer is prima facie deemed to be a delivery of the goods to the buyer.

(2) Unless otherwise authorised by the buyer, the seller must make such contract with the carrier on behalf of the buyer as may be reasonable having regard to the nature of the goods and the other circumstances of the case; and if the seller omits to do so, and the goods are lost or damaged in course of transit, the buyer may decline to treat the delivery to the carrier as a delivery to himself or may hold the seller responsible in damages.

(3) Unless otherwise agreed, where goods are sent by the seller to the buyer by a route involving sea transit, under circumstances in which it is usual to insure, the seller must give such notice to the buyer as may enable him to insure them during their sea transit; and if the seller fails to do so, the goods are at his risk during such sea transit.

ANNOTATIONS: This section derived from the Sale of Goods Act 1893, § 32.

33. Risk where goods are delivered at distant place

Where the seller of goods agrees to deliver them at his own risk at a place other than that where they are when sold, the buyer must nevertheless (unless otherwise agreed) take any risk of deterioration in the goods necessarily incident to the course of transit.

ANNOTATIONS: This section derived from the Sale of Goods Act 1893, § 33.

34. Buyer's right of examining the goods

. . . Unless otherwise agreed, when the seller tenders delivery of goods to the buyer, he is bound on request to afford the buyer a reasonable opportunity of examining the goods for the purpose of ascertaining whether they are in conformity with the contract [and, in the case of a contract for sale by sample, of comparing the bulk with the sample.]

ANNOTATIONS: This section derived from the Sale of Goods Act 1893, § 34. Words omitted repealed, and words in square brackets added, by the Sale and Supply of Goods Act 1994, §§ 2(2), 7, Sch 3.

SECTION 35. ACCEPTANCE

(1) The buyer is deemed to have accepted the goods [subject to subsection (2) below—
  (a) when he intimates to the seller that he has accepted them, or
  (b) when the goods have been delivered to him and he does any act in relation to them which is inconsistent with the ownership of the seller.

(2) Where goods are delivered to the buyer, and he has not previously examined them, he is not deemed to have accepted them under subsection (1) above until he has had a reasonable opportunity of examining them for the purpose—
  (a) of ascertaining whether they are in conformity with the contract, and
  (b) in the case of a contract for sale by sample, of comparing the bulk with the sample.

(3) Where the buyer deals as consumer or (in Scotland) the contract of sale is a consumer contract, the buyer cannot lose his right to rely on subsection (2) above by agreement, waiver or otherwise.

(4) The buyer is also deemed to have accepted the goods when after the lapse of a reasonable time he retains the goods without intimating to the seller that he has rejected them.

(5) The questions that are material in determining for the purposes of subsection (4) above whether a reasonable time has elapsed include whether the buyer has had a reasonable opportunity of examining the goods for the purpose mentioned in subsection (2) above.

(6) The buyer is not by virtue of this section deemed to have accepted the goods merely because—
  (a) he asks for, or agrees to, their repair by or under an arrangement with the seller, or
  (b) the goods are delivered to another under a sub-sale or other disposition.

(7) Where the contract is for the sale of goods making one or more commercial units, a buyer accepting any goods included in a unit is deemed to have accepted all the goods making the unit; and in this subsection "commercial unit" means a unit division of which would materially impair the value of the goods or the character of the unit.

Sub-§ (1) derived from the Sale of Goods Act 1893, § 35. Words in square brackets substituted by the Sale and Supply of Goods Act 1994, § 2(l).

35A. Right of partial rejection
36. Buyer not bound to return rejected goods
37. Buyer's liability for not taking delivery of goods
Part V: Rights of Unpaid Seller Against the Goods: Preliminary
38. Unpaid seller defined
39. Unpaid seller's rights
40.

49. Action for price

(1) Where, under a contract of sale, the property in the goods has passed to the buyer and he wrongfully neglects or refuses to pay for the goods according to the terms of the contract, the seller may maintain an action against him for the price of the goods.

(2) Where, under a contract of sale, the price is payable on a day certain irrespective of delivery and the buyer wrongfully neglects or refuses to pay such price, the seller may maintain an action for the price, although the property in the goods has not passed and the goods have not been appropriated to the contract.

(3) . . .

ANNOTATIONS: This section derived from the Sale of Goods Act 1893, § 49. Sub-§ (3): applies to Scotland only.

50. Damages for non-acceptance

(1) Where the buyer wrongfully neglects or refuses to accept and pay for the goods, the seller may maintain an action against him for damages for non-acceptance.

(2) The measure of damages is the estimated loss directly and naturally resulting, in the ordinary course of events, from the buyer's breach of contract.

(3) Where there is an available market for the goods in question the measure of damages is prima facie to be ascertained by the difference between the contract price and the market or current price at the time or times when the goods ought to have been accepted or (if no time was fixed for acceptance) at the time of the refusal to accept.

ANNOTATIONS: This section derived from the Sale of Goods Act 1893, § 50.

Part   VI: Actions for Breach of the Contract: Buyer's remedies

51. Damages for non-delivery

(1) Where the seller wrongfully neglects or refuses to deliver the goods to the buyer, the buyer may maintain an action against the seller for damages for non-delivery.

(2) The measure of damages is the estimated loss directly and naturally resulting, in the ordinary course of events, from the seller's breach of contract.

(3) Where there is an available market for the goods in question the measure of damages is prima facie to be ascertained by the difference between the contract price and the market or current price of the goods at the time or times when they ought to have been delivered or (if no time was fixed) at the time of the refusal to deliver.

ANNOTATIONS: This section derived from the Sale of Goods Act 1893, § 51.

52. Specific performance

(1) In any action for breach of contract to deliver specific or ascertained goods the court may, if it thinks fit, on the plaintiff's application, by its judgment or decree direct that the contract shall be performed specifically, without giving the defendant the option of retaining the goods on payment of damages.

(2) The plaintiff's application may be made at any time before judgment or decree.

(3) The judgment or decree may be unconditional, or on such terms and conditions as to damages, payment of the price and otherwise as seem just to the court.

(4) . . .

ANNOTATIONS: This section derived from the Sale of Goods Act 1893, § 52. Sub-§ (4): applies to Scotland only.

61. Interpretation

(1) In this Act, unless the context or subject matter otherwise requires—

. . . .

"delivery" means voluntary transfer of possession from one person to another [except that in relation to sections 20A and 20B above it includes such appropriation of goods to the contract as results in property in the goods being transferred to the buyer;]

. . . .

"property" means the general property in goods, and not merely a special property;

B. U.K. PROTECTION OF TRADING INTERESTS ACT 1980

Source: Protection of Trading Interests Act 1980 (c 11) 20 March 1980

Introduction

The British Protection of Trading Interests Act 1980 is an example of "blocking legislation" enacted largely in response to the *Westinghouse Uranium Litigation* that took place in the United States in the 1970's. That litigation involved allegations of antitrust violations on the part of non-U.S. companies engaged in the mining and sale or uranium, after the world market price had increased dramatically and Westinghouse was unable to continue profitably to supply uranium for nuclear reactors it had constructed. The Act combines attacks on the process of discovery with limitations on the enforcement of foreign court damage awards.

Section 2 of the Act allows the Secretary of State to order prohibition of compliance with discovery orders issued from overseas courts, tribunals or authorities for purposes of protecting the interests of the United Kingdom, and § 3 makes failure to comply with such an order punishable by a fine. Sections 5 and 6 deal with the enforcement of multiple damages judgments in U.K. courts. Section 5 limits enforcement of a foreign award to actual damages. Section 6 provides a "clawback" remedy, allowing a U.K. citizen or business organization to recover back the excess of damages paid in foreign litigation over the amount of actual damages, thus neutralizing any foreign court award of multiple damages.

PROTECTION OF TRADING INTERESTS ACT 1980

An Act to provide protection from requirements, prohibitions and judgments imposed or given under the laws of countries outside the United Kingdom and affecting the trading or other interests of persons in the United Kingdom

1. Overseas measures affecting United Kingdom trading interests

(1) If it appears to the Secretary of State—
   (a) that measures have been or are proposed to be taken by or under the law of any overseas country for regulating or controlling international trade; and
   (b) that those measures, in so far as they apply or would apply to things done or to be done outside the territorial jurisdiction of that country by persons carrying on business in the United Kingdom, are damaging or threaten to damage the trading interests of the United Kingdom,

   the Secretary of State may by order direct that this section shall apply to those measures either generally or in their application to such cases as may be specified in the order.

(2) The Secretary of State may by order make provision for requiring, or enabling the Secretary of State to require, a person in the United Kingdom who carries on business there to give notice to the Secretary of State of any requirement or prohibition imposed or threatened to be imposed on that person pursuant to any measures in so far as this section applies to them by virtue of an order under subsection (1) above.

(3) The Secretary of State may give to any person in the United Kingdom who carries on business there such directions for prohibiting compliance with any such requirement or prohibition as aforesaid as he considers appropriate for avoiding damage to the trading interests of the United Kingdom.

(4) The power of the Secretary of State to make orders under subsection (1) or (2) above shall be exercisable by statutory instrument subject to annulment in pursuance of a resolution of either House of Parliament.

(5) Direction under subsection (3) above may be either general or special and may prohibit compliance with any requirement or prohibition either absolutely or in such cases or subject to such conditions as to consent or otherwise as may be specified in the directions; and general directions under that subsection shall be published in such manner as appears to the Secretary of State to be appropriate.

(6) In this section "trade" includes any activity carried on in the course of a business of any description and "trading interests" shall be construed accordingly.

ANNOTATIONS: See further, in relation to the disapplication of sub-§§ (1), (3) above: the Extraterritorial US Legislation (Sanctions against Cuba, Iran and Libya) (Protection of Trading Interests) Order 1996, SI 1996 No 3171, art. 3(1).

2. Documents and information required by overseas courts and authorities

(1) If it appears to the Secretary of State—
   (a) that a requirement has been or may be imposed on a person or persons in the United Kingdom to produce to any court, tribunal or authority of an overseas country any commercial document which is not within the territorial jurisdiction of that country or to furnish any commercial information to any such court, tribunal or authority; or
   (b) that any such authority has imposed or may impose a requirement on a person or persons in the United Kingdom to publish any such document or information,
   the Secretary of State may, if it appears to him that the requirement is inadmissible by virtue of subsection (2) or (3) below, give directions for prohibiting compliance with the requirement.

(2) A requirement such as is mentioned in subsection (1)(a) or (b) above is inadmissible—

    (a) if it infringes the jurisdiction of the United Kingdom or is otherwise prejudicial to the sovereignty of the United Kingdom; or

    (b) if compliance with the requirement would be prejudicial to the security of the United Kingdom or to the relations of the government of the United Kingdom with the government of any other country.

(3) A requirement such as is mentioned in subsection (1)(a) above is also inadmissible—

    (a) if it is made otherwise than for the purposes of civil or criminal proceedings which have been instituted in the overseas country; or

    (b) if it requires a person to state what documents relevant to any such proceedings are or have been in his possession, custody or power or to produce for the purposes of any such proceedings any documents other than particular documents specified in the requirement.

(4) Directions under subsection (1) above may be either general or special and may prohibit compliance with any requirement either absolutely or in such cases or subject to such conditions as to consent or otherwise as may be specified in the directions; and general directions under that subsection shall be published in such manner as appears to the Secretary of State to be appropriate.

(5) For the purposes of this section the making of a request or demand shall be treated as the imposition of a requirement if it is made in circumstances in which a requirement to the same effect could be or could have been imposed; and

    (a) any request or demand for the supply of a document or information which, pursuant to the requirement of any court, tribunal or authority of an overseas country, is addressed to a person in the United Kingdom; or

    (b) any requirement imposed by such a court, tribunal or authority to produce or furnish any document or information to a person specified in the requirement,

    shall be treated as a requirement to produce or furnish that document or information to that court, tribunal or authority.

(6) In this section "commercial document" and "commercial information" mean respectively a document or information relating to a business of any description and "document" includes any record or device by means of which material is recorded or stored.

ANNOTATIONS: See further, in relation to the disapplication of this section: the Extraterritorial US Legislation (Sanctions against Cuba, Iran and Libya) (Protection of Trading Interests) Order 1996, SI 1996 No 3171, art. 3(1).

3. Offences under §§ 1 and 2

(1) Subject to subsection (2) below, any person who without reasonable excuse fails to comply with any requirement imposed under subsection (2) of section 1 above or knowingly contravenes any directions given under subsection (3) of that section or section 2(1) above shall be guilty of an offence and liable—
   (a) on conviction on indictment, to a fine;
   (b) on summary conviction, to a fine not exceeding the statutory maximum.

(2) A person who is neither a citizen of the United Kingdom and Colonies nor a body corporate incorporated in the United Kingdom shall not be guilty of an offence under subsection (1) above by reason of anything done or omitted outside the United Kingdom in contravention of directions under section 1(3) or 2(1) above.

(3) No proceedings for an offence under subsection (1) above shall be instituted in England, Wales or Northern Ireland except by the Secretary of State or with the consent of the Attorney General or, as the case may be, the Attorney General for Northern Ireland.

(4) Proceedings against any person for an offence under this section may be taken before the appropriate court in the United Kingdom having jurisdiction in the place where that person is for the time being.
   (5) . . .

ANNOTATIONS: Sub-§ (5): repealed by the Statute Law (Repeals) Act 1993.

4. Restriction of Evidence (Proceedings in Other Jurisdictions) Act 1975

A court in the United Kingdom shall not make an order under section 2 of the Evidence (Proceedings in Other Jurisdictions) Act 1975 for giving effect to a request issued by or on behalf of a court or tribunal of an overseas country if it is shown that the request infringes the jurisdiction of the United Kingdom or is otherwise prejudicial to the sovereignty of the United Kingdom; and a certificate signed by or on behalf of the Secretary of State to the effect that it infringes that jurisdiction or is so prejudicial shall be conclusive evidence of that fact.

5. Restriction on enforcement of certain overseas judgments

(1) A judgment to which this section applies shall not be registered under Part II of the Administration of Justice Act 1920 or Part I of the Foreign Judgments (Reciprocal Enforcement) Act 1933 and no court in the United Kingdom shall entertain proceedings at common law for the recovery of any sum payable under such a judgment.

(2) This section applies to any judgment given by a court of an overseas country, being—

   (a) a judgment for multiple damages within the meaning of subsection (3) below;

   (b) a judgment based on a provision or rule of law specified or described in an order under subsection (4) below and given after the coming into force of the order; or

   (c) a judgment on a claim for contribution in respect of damages awarded by a judgment falling within paragraph (a) or (b) above.

(3) In subsection (2)(a) above a judgment for multiple damages means a judgment for an amount arrived at by doubling, trebling or otherwise multiplying a sum assessed as compensation for the loss or damage sustained by the person in whose favour the judgment is given.

(4) The Secretary of State may for the purposes of subsection (2)(b) above make an order in respect of any provision or rule of law which appears to him to be concerned with the prohibition or regulation of agreements, arrangements or practices designed to restrain, distort or restrict competition in the carrying on of business of any description or to be otherwise concerned with the promotion of such competition as aforesaid.

(5) The power of the Secretary of State to make orders under subsection (4) above shall be exercisable by statutory instrument subject to annulment in pursuance of a resolution of either House of Parliament.

(6) Subsection (2)(a) above applies to a judgement given before the date of the passing of this Act as well as to a judgment given on or after that date but this section does not affect any judgment which has been registered before that date under the provisions mentioned in subsection (1) above or in respect of which such proceedings as are there mentioned have been finally determined before that date.

6. Recovery of awards of multiple damages

(1) This section applies where a court of an overseas country has given a judgment for multiple damages with the meaning of section 5(3) above against—

   (a) a citizen of the United Kingdom and Colonies; or

   (b) a body corporate incorporated in the United Kingdom or in a territory outside the United Kingdom for whose international relations Her Majesty's Government in the United Kingdom are responsible; or

   (c) a person carrying on business in the United Kingdom,
(in this section referred to as a "qualifying defendant") and an amount on account of the damages has been paid by the qualifying defendant either to the party in whose favour the judgment was given or to another party who is entitled as against the qualifying defendant to contribution in respect of the damages.

(2) Subject to subsections (3) and (4) below, the qualifying defendant shall be entitled to recover from the party in whose favour the judgment was given so much of the amount referred to in subsection (1) above as exceeds the part attributable to compensation; and that part shall be taken to be such part of the amount as bears to the whole of it the same proportion as the sum assessed by the court that gave the judgment as compensation for the loss or damage sustained by that party bears to the whole of the damages awarded to that party.

(3) Subsection (2) above does not apply where the qualifying defendant is an individual who was ordinarily resident in the overseas country at the time when the proceedings in which the judgment was given were instituted or a body corporate which had its principal place of business there at that time.

(4) Subsection (2) above does not apply where the qualifying defendant carried on business in the overseas country and the proceedings in which the judgment was given were concerned with activities exclusively carried on in that country.

(5) A court in the United Kingdom may entertain proceedings on a claim under this section notwithstanding that the person against whom the proceedings are brought is not within the jurisdiction of the court.

(6) The reference in subsection (1) above to an amount paid by the qualifying defendant includes a reference to an amount obtained by execution against his property or against the property of a company which (directly or indirectly) is wholly owned by him; and references in that subsection and subsection (2) above to the party in whose favour the judgment was given or to a party entitled to contribution include references to any person in whom the rights of any such party have become vested by succession or assignment or otherwise.

(7) This section shall, with the necessary modifications, apply also in relation to any order which is made by a tribunal or authority of an overseas country and would, if that tribunal or authority were a court, be a judgment for multiple damages within the meaning of section 5(3) above.

(8) This section does not apply to any judgment given or order made before the passing of this Act.

ANNOTATIONS: See further, in relation to the disapplication of this section: the Extraterritorial US Legislation (Sanctions against Cuba, Iran and Libya) (Protection of Trading Interests) Order 1996, SI 1996 No 3171, art. 3(2).

7. Enforcement of overseas judgment under provision corresponding to § 6

(1) If it appears to Her Majesty that the law of an overseas country provides or will provide for the enforcement in that country of judgments given under section 6 above, Her Majesty may by Order in Council provide for the enforcement in the United Kingdom of [judgments of any description specified in the Order which are given under any provision of the law of that country relating to the recovery of sums paid or obtained pursuant to a judgment for multiple damages within the meaning of section 5(3) above, whether or not that provision corresponds to section 6 above].

[(1A) Such an Order in Council may, as respects judgments to which it relates—

(a) make different provisions for different descriptions of judgment; and

(b) impose conditions or restrictions on the enforcement of judgments of any description.]

(2) An Order under this section may apply, with or without modification, any of the provisions of the Foreign Judgments (Reciprocal Enforcement) Act 1933.

ANNOTATIONS: Amended by the Civil Jurisdiction and Judgments Act 1982, § 38.

8. Short title, interpretation, repeals and extent

(1) This Act may be cited as the Protection of Trading Interests Act 1980.

(2) In this Act "overseas country" means any country or territory outside the United Kingdom other than one for whose international relations Her Majesty's Government in the United Kingdom are responsible.

(3) References in this Act to the law or a court, tribunal or authority of an overseas country include, in the case of a federal state, references to the law or a court, tribunal or authority of any constituent part of that country.

(4) References in this Act to a claim for, or to entitlement to, contribution are references to a claim or entitlement based on an enactment or rule of law.

(5), (6) . . .

(7) This Act extends to Northern Ireland.

(8) Her Majesty may by Order in Council direct that this Act shall extend with such exceptions, adaptations and modifications, if any, as may be specified in the Order to any territory outside the United Kingdom, being a territory for the international relations of which Her Majesty's Government in the United Kingdom are responsible.

ANNOTATIONS: Sub-§§ (5), (6): repeal the Shipping Contracts and Commercial Documents Act 1964.

C. PRACTICE DIRECTION 6B, SUPPLEMENTING SECTION IV OF THE CIVIL PROCEDURE RULES (CPR) OF THE SUPREME COURT OF ENGLAND AND WALES

PRACTICE DIRECTION 6B – SERVICE OUT OF THE JURISDICTION

This Practice Direction supplements Section IV of CPR Part 6

. . . . .

Service out of the jurisdiction where permission is required

3.1 The claimant may serve a claim form out of the jurisdiction with the permission of the court under rule 6.36 where –

General Grounds

(1) A claim is made for a remedy against a person domiciled within the jurisdiction.

(2) A claim is made for an injunction(GL) ordering the defendant to do or refrain from doing an act within the jurisdiction.

(3) A claim is made against a person ('the defendant') on whom the claim form has been or will be served (otherwise than in reliance on this paragraph) and –

(a) there is between the claimant and the defendant a real issue which it is reasonable for the court to try; and

(b) the claimant wishes to serve the claim form on another person who is a necessary or proper party to that claim.

(4) A claim is an additional claim under Part 20 and the person to be served is a necessary or proper party to the claim or additional claim.

(4A) A claim is made against the defendant in reliance on one or more of paragraphs (2), (6) to (16), (19) or (21) and a further claim is made against the same defendant which arises out of the same or closely connected facts.

Claims for interim remedies

(5) A claim is made for an interim remedy under section 25(1) of the Civil Jurisdiction and Judgments Act 1982.

Claims in relation to contracts

(6) A claim is made in respect of a contract where the contract –

(a) was made within the jurisdiction;

(b) was made by or through an agent trading or residing within the jurisdiction;

(c) is governed by English law; or

507

(d) contains a term to the effect that the court shall have jurisdiction to determine any claim in respect of the contract.

(7) A claim is made in respect of a breach of contract committed within the jurisdiction.

(8) A claim is made for a declaration that no contract exists where, if the contract was found to exist, it would comply with the conditions set out in paragraph (6).

Claims in tort

(9) A claim is made in tort where –
(a) damage was sustained, or will be sustained, within the jurisdiction; or
(b) damage which has been or will be sustained results from an act committed, or likely to be committed, within the jurisdiction.

Enforcement

(10) A claim is made to enforce any judgment or arbitral award.

Claims about property within the jurisdiction

(11) The subject matter of the claim relates wholly or principally to property within the jurisdiction, provided that nothing under this paragraph shall render justiciable the title to or the right to possession of immovable property outside England and Wales.

Claims about trusts etc.

(12) A claim is made in respect of a trust which is created by the operation of a statute, or by a written instrument, or created orally and evidenced in writing, and which is governed by the law of England and Wales.

(12A) A claim is made in respect of a trust which is created by the operation of a statute, or by a written instrument, or created orally and evidenced in writing, and which provides that jurisdiction in respect of such a claim shall be conferred upon the courts of England and Wales.

(13) A claim is made for any remedy which might be obtained in proceedings for the administration of the estate of a person who died domiciled within the jurisdiction or whose estate includes assets within the jurisdiction.

(14) A probate claim or a claim for the rectification of a will.

(15) A claim is made against the defendant as constructive trustee, or as trustee of a resulting trust, where the claim arises out of acts committed or events occurring within the jurisdiction or relates to assets within the jurisdiction.

(16) A claim is made for restitution where –
(a) the defendant's alleged liability arises out of acts committed within the jurisdiction; or

(b) the enrichment is obtained within the jurisdiction; or

(c) the claim is governed by the law of England and Wales.

Claims by HM Revenue and Customs

(17) A claim is made by the Commissioners for H.M. Revenue and Customs relating to duties or taxes against a defendant not domiciled in Scotland or Northern Ireland.

Claim for costs order in favour of or against third parties

(18) A claim is made by a party to proceedings for an order that the court exercise its power under section 51 of the Senior Courts Act 1981 to make a costs order in favour of or against a person who is not a party to those proceedings.

(Rule 46.2 sets out the procedure where the court is considering whether to exercise its discretion to make a costs order in favour of or against a non-party.)

Admiralty claims

(19) A claim is –

(a) in the nature of salvage and any part of the services took place within the jurisdiction; or

(b) to enforce a claim under section 153, 154,175 or 176A of the Merchant Shipping Act 1995.

Claims under various enactments

(20) A claim is made –

(a) under an enactment which allows proceedings to be brought and those proceedings are not covered by any of the other grounds referred to in this paragraph; or

(b) under the Directive of the Council of the European Communities dated 15 March 1976 No. 76/308/EEC, where service is to be effected in a Member State of the European Union.

Claims for breach of confidence or misuse of private information

(21) A claim is made for breach of confidence or misuse of private information where –

(a) detriment was suffered, or will be suffered, within the jurisdiction; or

(b) detriment which has been, or will be, suffered results from an act committed, or likely to be committed, within the jurisdiction.

D. U.K. BRIBERY ACT 2010

Bribery Act 2010

CHAPTER 23

CONTENTS

General bribery offences

Bribery of foreign public officials

Failure of commercial organisations to prevent bribery

Prosecution and penalties

Other provisions about offences

Supplementary and final provisions

ELIZABETH II

Bribery Act 2010

2010 CHAPTER 23

An Act to make provision about offences relating to bribery; and for connected purposes. [8th April 2010]

BE IT ENACTED by the Queen's most Excellent Majesty, by and with the advice and consent of the Lords Spiritual and Temporal, and Commons, in this present Parliament assembled, and by the authority of the same, as follows: –

General bribery offences

1 Offences of bribing another person

(1) A person ("P") is guilty of an offence if either of the following cases applies.

(2) Case 1 is where –

    (a) P offers, promises or gives a financial or other advantage to another person, and

    (b) P intends the advantage –

        (i) to induce a person to perform improperly a relevant function or activity, or

        (ii) to reward a person for the improper performance of such a function or activity.

(3) Case 2 is where –

    (a) P offers, promises or gives a financial or other advantage to another person, and

(b) P knows or believes that the acceptance of the advantage would itself constitute the improper performance of a relevant function or activity.

(4) In case 1 it does not matter whether the person to whom the advantage is offered, promised or given is the same person as the person who is to perform, or has performed, the function or activity concerned.

(5) In cases 1 and 2 it does not matter whether the advantage is offered, promised or given by P directly or through a third party.

2 Offences relating to being bribed

(1) A person ("R") is guilty of an offence if any of the following cases applies.

(2) Case 3 is where R requests, agrees to receive or accepts a financial or other advantage intending that, in consequence, a relevant function or activity should be performed improperly (whether by R or another person).

(3) Case 4 is where –

(a) R requests, agrees to receive or accepts a financial or other advantage, and

(b) the request, agreement or acceptance itself constitutes the improper performance by R of a relevant function or activity.

(4) Case 5 is where R requests, agrees to receive or accepts a financial or other advantage as a reward for the improper performance (whether by R or another person) of a relevant function or activity.

(5) Case 6 is where, in anticipation of or in consequence of R requesting, agreeing to receive or accepting a financial or other advantage, a relevant function or activity is performed improperly –

(a) by R, or

(b) by another person at R's request or with R's assent or acquiescence.

(6) In cases 3 to 6 it does not matter –

(a) whether R requests, agrees to receive or accepts (or is to request, agree to receive or accept) the advantage directly or through a third party,

(b) whether the advantage is (or is to be) for the benefit of R or another person.

(7) In cases 4 to 6 it does not matter whether R knows or believes that the performance of the function or activity is improper.

(8) In case 6, where a person other than R is performing the function or activity, it also does not matter whether that person knows or believes that the performance of the function or activity is improper.

3 Function or activity to which bribe relates

(1) For the purposes of this Act a function or activity is a relevant function or activity if –
    (a) it falls within subsection (2), and
    (b) meets one or more of conditions A to C.

(2) The following functions and activities fall within this subsection –
    (a) any function of a public nature,
    (b) any activity connected with a business,
    (c) any activity performed in the course of a person's employment,
    (d) any activity performed by or on behalf of a body of persons (whether corporate or unincorporate).

(3) Condition A is that a person performing the function or activity is expected to perform it in good faith.

(4) Condition B is that a person performing the function or activity is expected to perform it impartially.

(5) Condition C is that a person performing the function or activity is in a position of trust by virtue of performing it.

(6) A function or activity is a relevant function or activity even if it –
    (a) has no connection with the United Kingdom, and
    (b) is performed in a country or territory outside the United Kingdom.

(7) In this section "business" includes trade or profession.

4 Improper performance to which bribe relates

(1) For the purposes of this Act a relevant function or activity –
    (a) is performed improperly if it is performed in breach of a relevant expectation, and
    (b) is to be treated as being performed improperly if there is a failure to perform the function or activity and that failure is itself a breach of a relevant expectation.

(2) In subsection (1) "relevant expectation" –
    (a) in relation to a function or activity which meets condition A or B, means the expectation mentioned in the condition concerned, and
    (b) in relation to a function or activity which meets condition C, means any expectation as to the manner in which, or the reasons for which, the function or activity will be performed that arises from the position of trust mentioned in that condition.

(3) Anything that a person does (or omits to do) arising from or in connection with that person's past performance of a relevant function or activity is to be treated for the purposes of this Act as being done (or omitted) by that person in the performance of that function or activity.

5 Expectation test

(1) For the purposes of sections 3 and 4, the test of what is expected is a test of what a reasonable person in the United Kingdom would expect in relation to the performance of the type of function or activity concerned.

(2) In deciding what such a person would expect in relation to the performance of a function or activity where the performance is not subject to the law of any part of the United Kingdom, any local custom or practice is to be disregarded unless it is permitted or required by the written law applicable to the country or territory concerned.

(3) In subsection (2) "written law" means law contained in –

(a) any written constitution, or provision made by or under legislation, applicable to the country or territory concerned, or

(b) any judicial decision which is so applicable and is evidenced in published written sources.

Bribery of foreign public officials

6 Bribery of foreign public officials

(1) A person ("P") who bribes a foreign public official ("F") is guilty of an offence if P's intention is to influence F in F's capacity as a foreign public official.

(2) P must also intend to obtain or retain –

(a) business, or

(b) an advantage in the conduct of business.

(3) P bribes F if, and only if –

(a) directly or through a third party, P offers, promises or gives any financial or other advantage –

(i) to F, or

(ii) to another person at F's request or with F's assent or acquiescence, and

(b) F is neither permitted nor required by the written law applicable to F to be influenced in F's capacity as a foreign public official by the offer, promise or gift.

(4) References in this section to influencing F in F's capacity as a foreign public official mean influencing F in the performance of F's functions as such an official, which includes –

(a) any omission to exercise those functions, and

(b) any use of F's position as such an official, even if not within F's authority.

(5) "Foreign public official" means an individual who –

(a) holds a legislative, administrative or judicial position of any kind, whether appointed or elected, of a country or territory outside the United Kingdom (or any subdivision of such a country or territory),

(b) exercises a public function –

    (i) for or on behalf of a country or territory outside the United Kingdom (or any subdivision of such a country or territory), or

    (ii) for any public agency or public enterprise of that country or territory (or subdivision), or

  (c) is an official or agent of a public international organisation.

(6) "Public international organisation" means an organisation whose members are any of the following –

  (a) countries or territories,

  (b) governments of countries or territories,

  (c) other public international organisations,

  (d) a mixture of any of the above.

(7) For the purposes of subsection (3)(b), the written law applicable to F is –

  (a) where the performance of the functions of F which P intends to influence would be subject to the law of any part of the United Kingdom, the law of that part of the United Kingdom,

  (b) where paragraph (a) does not apply and F is an official or agent of a public international organisation, the applicable written rules of that organisation,

  (c) where paragraphs (a) and (b) do not apply, the law of the country or territory in relation to which F is a foreign public official so far as that law is contained in –

    (i) any written constitution, or provision made by or under legislation, applicable to the country or territory concerned, or

    (ii) any judicial decision which is so applicable and is evidenced in published written sources.

(8) For the purposes of this section, a trade or profession is a business.

Failure of commercial organisations to prevent bribery

7 Failure of commercial organisations to prevent bribery

(1) A relevant commercial organisation ("C") is guilty of an offence under this section if a person ("A") associated with C bribes another person intending –

  (a) to obtain or retain business for C, or

  (b) to obtain or retain an advantage in the conduct of business for C.

(2) But it is a defence for C to prove that C had in place adequate procedures designed to prevent persons associated with C from undertaking such conduct.

(3) For the purposes of this section, A bribes another person if, and only if, A –

  (a) is, or would be, guilty of an offence under section 1 or 6 (whether or not A has been prosecuted for such an offence), or

  (b) would be guilty of such an offence if section 12(2)(c) and (4) were omitted.

(4) See section 8 for the meaning of a person associated with C and see section 9 for a duty on the Secretary of State to publish guidance.

(5) In this section –

"partnership" means –

(a) a partnership within the Partnership Act 1890, or

(b) a limited partnership registered under the Limited Partnerships Act 1907, or a firm or entity of a similar character formed under the law of a country or territory outside the United Kingdom,

"relevant commercial organisation" means –

(a) a body which is incorporated under the law of any part of the United Kingdom and which carries on a business (whether there or elsewhere),

(b) any other body corporate (wherever incorporated) which carries on a business, or part of a business, in any part of the United Kingdom,

(c) a partnership which is formed under the law of any part of the United Kingdom and which carries on a business (whether there or elsewhere), or

(d) any other partnership (wherever formed) which carries on a business, or part of a business, in any part of the United Kingdom,

and, for the purposes of this section, a trade or profession is a business.

8 Meaning of associated person

(1) For the purposes of section 7, a person ("A") is associated with C if (disregarding any bribe under consideration) A is a person who performs services for or on behalf of C.

(2) The capacity in which A performs services for or on behalf of C does not matter.

(3) Accordingly A may (for example) be C's employee, agent or subsidiary.

(4) Whether or not A is a person who performs services for or on behalf of C is to be determined by reference to all the relevant circumstances and not merely by reference to the nature of the relationship between A and C.

(5) But if A is an employee of C, it is to be presumed unless the contrary is shown that A is a person who performs services for or on behalf of C.

9 Guidance about commercial organisations preventing bribery

(1) The Secretary of State must publish guidance about procedures that relevant commercial organisations can put in place to prevent persons associated with them from bribing as mentioned in section 7(1).

(2) The Secretary of State may, from time to time, publish revisions to guidance under this section or revised guidance.

(3) The Secretary of State must consult the Scottish Ministers before publishing anything under this section.

(4) Publication under this section is to be in such manner as the Secretary of State considers appropriate.

(5) Expressions used in this section have the same meaning as in section 7.

Prosecution and penalties

10 Consent to prosecution

(1) No proceedings for an offence under this Act may be instituted in England and Wales except by or with the consent of –
   (a) the Director of Public Prosecutions,
   (b) the Director of the Serious Fraud Office, or
   (c) the Director of Revenue and Customs Prosecutions.

(2) No proceedings for an offence under this Act may be instituted in Northern Ireland except by or with the consent of –
   (a) the Director of Public Prosecutions for Northern Ireland, or
   (b) the Director of the Serious Fraud Office.

(3) No proceedings for an offence under this Act may be instituted in England and Wales or Northern Ireland by a person –
   (a) who is acting –
      (i) under the direction or instruction of the Director of Public Prosecutions, the Director of the Serious Fraud Office or the Director of Revenue and Customs Prosecutions, or
      (ii) on behalf of such a Director, or
   (b) to whom such a function has been assigned by such a Director, except with the consent of the Director concerned to the institution of the proceedings.

(4) The Director of Public Prosecutions, the Director of the Serious Fraud Office and the Director of Revenue and Customs Prosecutions must exercise personally any function under subsection (1), (2)or (3) of giving consent.

(5) The only exception is if –
   (a) the Director concerned is unavailable, and
   (b) there is another person who is designated in writing by the Director acting personally as the person who is authorised to exercise any such function when the Director is unavailable.

(6) In that case, the other person may exercise the function but must do so personally.

(7) Subsections (4) to (6) apply instead of any other provisions which would otherwise have enabled any function of the Director of Public Prosecutions, the Director of the Serious Fraud Office or the Director of Revenue and Customs Prosecutions under subsection (1), (2) or (3) of giving consent to be exercised by a person other than the Director concerned.

(8) No proceedings for an offence under this Act may be instituted in Northern Ireland by virtue of section 36 of the Justice (Northern Ireland) Act 2002 (delegation of the functions of the Director of Public Prosecutions for Northern Ireland to persons other than the Deputy Director) except with the consent of the Director of Public Prosecutions for Northern Ireland to the institution of the proceedings.

(9) The Director of Public Prosecutions for Northern Ireland must exercise personally any function under subsection (2) or (8) of giving consent unless the function is exercised personally by the Deputy Director of Public Prosecutions for Northern Ireland by virtue of section 30(4) or (7) of the Act of 2002 (powers of Deputy Director to exercise functions of Director).

(10) Subsection (9) applies instead of section 36 of the Act of 2002 in relation to the functions of the Director of Public Prosecutions for Northern Ireland and the Deputy Director of Public Prosecutions for Northern Ireland under, or (as the case may be) by virtue of, subsections (2) and (8) above of giving consent.

11 Penalties

(1) An individual guilty of an offence under section 1, 2 or 6 is liable –
   (a) on summary conviction, to imprisonment for a term not exceeding 12 months, or to a fine not exceeding the statutory maximum, or to both,
   (b) on conviction on indictment, to imprisonment for a term not exceeding 10 years, or to a fine, or to both.

(2) Any other person guilty of an offence under section 1, 2 or 6 is liable –
   (a) on summary conviction, to a fine not exceeding the statutory maximum,
   (b) on conviction on indictment, to a fine.

(3) A person guilty of an offence under section 7 is liable on conviction on indictment to a fine.

(4) The reference in subsection (1)(a) to 12 months is to be read –
   (a) in its application to England and Wales in relation to an offence committed before the commencement of section 154(1) of the Criminal Justice Act 2003, and
   (b) in its application to Northern Ireland,
   as a reference to 6 months.

Other provisions about offences

12 Offences under this Act: territorial application

(1) An offence is committed under section 1, 2 or 6 in England and Wales, Scotland or Northern Ireland if any act or omission which forms part of the offence takes place in that part of the United Kingdom.

(2) Subsection (3) applies if –
   (a) no act or omission which forms part of an offence under section 1, 2 or 6 takes place in the United Kingdom,
   (b) a person's acts or omissions done or made outside the United Kingdom would form part of such an offence if done or made in the United Kingdom, and
   (c) that person has a close connection with the United Kingdom.

(3) In such a case –

    (a) the acts or omissions form part of the offence referred to in subsection (2)(a), and

    (b) proceedings for the offence may be taken at any place in the United Kingdom.

(4) For the purposes of subsection (2)(c) a person has a close connection with the United Kingdom if, and only if, the person was one of the following at the time the acts or omissions concerned were done or made –

    (a) a British citizen,

    (b) a British overseas territories citizen,

    (c) a British National (Overseas),

    (d) a British Overseas citizen,

    (e) a person who under the British Nationality Act 1981 was a British subject,

    (f) a British protected person within the meaning of that Act,

    (g) an individual ordinarily resident in the United Kingdom,

    (h) a body incorporated under the law of any part of the United Kingdom,

    (i) a Scottish partnership.

(5) An offence is committed under section 7 irrespective of whether the acts or omissions which form part of the offence take place in the United Kingdom or elsewhere.

(6) Where no act or omission which forms part of an offence under section 7 takes place in the United Kingdom, proceedings for the offence may be taken at any place in the United Kingdom.

(7) Subsection (8) applies if, by virtue of this section, proceedings for an offence are to be taken in Scotland against a person.

(8) Such proceedings may be taken –

    (a) in any sheriff court district in which the person is apprehended or in custody, or

    (b) in such sheriff court district as the Lord Advocate may determine.

(9) In subsection (8) "sheriff court district" is to be read in accordance with section 307(1) of the Criminal Procedure (Scotland) Act 1995.

13 Defence for certain bribery offences etc.

(1) It is a defence for a person charged with a relevant bribery offence to prove that the person's conduct was necessary for –

    (a) the proper exercise of any function of an intelligence service, or

    (b) the proper exercise of any function of the armed forces when engaged on active service.

(2) The head of each intelligence service must ensure that the service has in place arrangements designed to ensure that any conduct of a member of the service which would otherwise be a relevant bribery offence is necessary for a purpose falling within subsection (1)(a).

(3) The Defence Council must ensure that the armed forces have in place arrangements designed to ensure that any conduct of –

    (a) a member of the armed forces who is engaged on active service, or

    (b) a civilian subject to service discipline when working in support of any person falling within paragraph (a),

which would otherwise be a relevant bribery offence is necessary for a purpose falling within subsection (1)(b).

(4) The arrangements which are in place by virtue of subsection (2) or (3) must be arrangements which the Secretary of State considers to be satisfactory.

(5) For the purposes of this section, the circumstances in which a person's conduct is necessary for a purpose falling within subsection (1)(a) or (b) are to be treated as including any circumstances in which the person's conduct –

    (a) would otherwise be an offence under section 2, and

    (b) involves conduct by another person which, but for subsection (1)(a) or (b), would be an offence under section 1.

(6) In this section –

"active service" means service in –

    (a) an action or operation against an enemy,

    (b) an operation outside the British Islands for the protection of life or property, or

    (c) the military occupation of a foreign country or territory,

"armed forces" means Her Majesty's forces (within the meaning of the Armed Forces Act 2006),

"civilian subject to service discipline" and "enemy" have the same meaning as in the Act of 2006,

"GCHQ" has the meaning given by section 3(3) of the Intelligence Services Act 1994,

"head" means –

    (a) in relation to the Security Service, the Director General of the Security Service,

    (b) in relation to the Secret Intelligence Service, the Chief of the Secret Intelligence Service, and

    (c) in relation to GCHQ, the Director of GCHQ,

"intelligence service" means the Security Service, the Secret Intelligence Service or GCHQ,

"relevant bribery offence" means –

    (a) an offence under section 1 which would not also be an offence under section 6,

    (b) an offence under section 2,

    (c) an offence committed by aiding, abetting, counselling or procuring the commission of an offence falling within paragraph (a) or (b),

(d) an offence of attempting or conspiring to commit, or of inciting the commission of, an offence falling within paragraph (a) or (b), or

(e) an offence under Part 2 of the Serious Crime Act 2007 (encouraging or assisting crime) in relation to an offence falling within paragraph (a) or (b).

14 Offences under sections 1, 2 and 6 by bodies corporate etc.

(1) This section applies if an offence under section 1, 2 or 6 is committed by a body corporate or a Scottish partnership.

(2) If the offence is proved to have been committed with the consent or connivance of –

(a) a senior officer of the body corporate or Scottish partnership, or

(b) a person purporting to act in such a capacity,

the senior officer or person (as well as the body corporate or partnership) is guilty of the offence and liable to be proceeded against and punished accordingly.

(3) But subsection (2) does not apply, in the case of an offence which is committed under section 1, 2 or 6 by virtue of section 12(2) to (4), to a senior officer or person purporting to act in such a capacity unless the senior officer or person has a close connection with the United Kingdom (within the meaning given by section 12(4)).

(4) In this section –

"director", in relation to a body corporate whose affairs are managed by its members, means a member of the body corporate,

"senior officer" means –

(a) in relation to a body corporate, a director, manager, secretary or other similar officer of the body corporate, and

(b) in relation to a Scottish partnership, a partner in the partnership.

15 Offences under section 7 by partnerships

(1) Proceedings for an offence under section 7 alleged to have been committed by a partnership must be brought in the name of the partnership (and not in that of any of the partners).

(2) For the purposes of such proceedings –

(a) rules of court relating to the service of documents have effect as if the partnership were a body corporate, and

(b) the following provisions apply as they apply in relation to a body corporate –

(i) section 33 of the Criminal Justice Act 1925 and Schedule 3 to the Magistrates' Courts Act 1980,

      (ii) section 18 of the Criminal Justice Act (Northern Ireland) 1945 (c.15 (N.I.)) and Schedule 4 to the Magistrates' Courts (Northern Ireland) Order 1981 (S.I. 1981/1675 (N.I.26)),

      (iii) section 70 of the Criminal Procedure (Scotland) Act 1995.

(3) A fine imposed on the partnership on its conviction for an offence under section 7 is to be paid out of the partnership assets.

(4) In this section "partnership" has the same meaning as in section 7.

Supplementary and final provisions

16 Application to Crown

This Act applies to individuals in the public service of the Crown as it applies to other individuals.

17 Consequential provision

(1) The following common law offences are abolished –
    (a) the offences under the law of England and Wales and Northern Ireland of bribery and embracery,
    (b) the offences under the law of Scotland of bribery and accepting a bribe.

(2) Schedule 1 (which contains consequential amendments) has effect.

(3) Schedule 2 (which contains repeals and revocations) has effect.

(4) The relevant national authority may by order make such supplementary, incidental or consequential provision as the relevant national authority considers appropriate for the purposes of this Act or in consequence of this Act.

(5) The power to make an order under this section –
    (a) is exercisable by statutory instrument,
    (b) includes power to make transitional, transitory or saving provision,
    (c) may, in particular, be exercised by amending, repealing, revoking or otherwise modifying any provision made by or under an enactment (including any Act passed in the same Session as this Act).

(6) Subject to subsection (7), a statutory instrument containing an order of the Secretary of State under this section may not be made unless a draft of the instrument has been laid before, and approved by a resolution of, each House of Parliament.

(7) A statutory instrument containing an order of the Secretary of State under this section which does not amend or repeal a provision of a public general Act or of devolved legislation is subject to annulment in pursuance of a resolution of either House of Parliament.

(8) Subject to subsection (9), a statutory instrument containing an order of the Scottish Ministers under this section may not be made unless a draft of the instrument has been laid before, and approved by a resolution of, the Scottish Parliament.

(9) A statutory instrument containing an order of the Scottish Ministers under this section which does not amend or repeal a provision of an Act of the Scottish Parliament or of a public general Act is subject to annulment in pursuance of a resolution of the Scottish Parliament.

(10) In this section –

"devolved legislation" means an Act of the Scottish Parliament, a Measure of the National Assembly for Wales or an Act of the Northern Ireland Assembly,

"enactment" includes an Act of the Scottish Parliament and Northern Ireland legislation,

"relevant national authority" means –

(a) in the case of provision which would be within the legislative competence of the Scottish Parliament if it were contained in an Act of that Parliament, the Scottish Ministers, and

(b) in any other case, the Secretary of State.

18 Extent

(1) Subject as follows, this Act extends to England and Wales, Scotland and Northern Ireland.

(2) Subject to subsections (3) to (5), any amendment, repeal or revocation made by Schedule 1 or 2 has the same extent as the provision amended, repealed or revoked.

(3) The amendment of, and repeals in, the Armed Forces Act 2006 do not extend to the Channel Islands.

(4) The amendments of the International Criminal Court Act 2001 extend to England and Wales and Northern Ireland only.

(5) Subsection (2) does not apply to the repeal in the Civil Aviation Act 1982.

19 Commencement and transitional provision etc.

(1) Subject to subsection (2), this Act comes into force on such day as the Secretary of State may by order made by statutory instrument appoint.

(2) Sections 16, 17(4) to (10) and 18, this section (other than subsections (5) to (7)) and section 20 come into force on the day on which this Act is passed.

(3) An order under subsection (1) may –

(a) appoint different days for different purposes,

(b) make such transitional, transitory or saving provision as the Secretary of State considers appropriate in connection with the coming into force of any provision of this Act.

(4) The Secretary of State must consult the Scottish Ministers before making an order under this section in connection with any provision of this Act which would be within the legislative competence of the Scottish Parliament if it were contained in an Act of that Parliament.

(5) This Act does not affect any liability, investigation, legal proceeding or penalty for or in respect of –

   (a) a common law offence mentioned in subsection (1) of section 17 which is committed wholly or partly before the coming into force of that subsection in relation to such an offence, or

   (b) an offence under the Public Bodies Corrupt Practices Act 1889 or the Prevention of Corruption Act 1906 committed wholly or partly before the coming into force of the repeal of the Act by Schedule 2 to this Act.

(6) For the purposes of subsection (5) an offence is partly committed before a particular time if any act or omission which forms part of the offence takes place before that time.

(7) Subsections (5) and (6) are without prejudice to section 16 of the Interpretation Act 1978 (general savings on repeal).

20 Short title

This Act may be cited as the Bribery Act 2010.

SCHEDULES

SCHEDULE 1 Section 17(2)

CONSEQUENTIAL AMENDMENTS

Ministry of Defence Police Act 1987 (c. 4)

1 In section 2(3)(ba) of the Ministry of Defence Police Act 1987 (jurisdiction of members of Ministry of Defence Police Force) for "Prevention of Corruption Acts 1889 to 1916" substitute "Bribery Act 2010".

Criminal Justice Act 1987 (c. 38)

2 In section 2A of the Criminal Justice Act 1987 (Director of SFO's preinvestigation powers in relation to bribery and corruption: foreign officers etc.) for subsections (5) and (6) substitute –

   "(5) This section applies to any conduct –

   (a) which, as a result of section 3(6) of the Bribery Act 2010, constitutes an offence under section 1 or 2 of that Act under the law of England and Wales or Northern Ireland, or

   (b) which constitutes an offence under section 6 of that Act under the law of England and Wales or Northern Ireland."

International Criminal Court Act 2001 (c. 17)

3 The International Criminal Court Act 2001 is amended as follows.
4 In section 54(3) (offences in relation to the ICC: England and Wales) –
   (a) in paragraph (b) for "or" substitute ", an offence under the Bribery Act 2010 or (as the case may be) an offence", and
   (b) in paragraph (c) after "common law" insert "or (as the case may be) under the Bribery Act 2010".
5 In section 61(3)(b) (offences in relation to the ICC: Northern Ireland) after "common law" insert "or (as the case may be) under the Bribery Act 2010".

International Criminal Court (Scotland) Act 2001 (asp 13)

6 In section 4(2) of the International Criminal Court (Scotland) Act 2001 (offences in relation to the ICC) –
   (a) in paragraph (b) after "common law" insert "or (as the case may be) under the Bribery Act 2010", and
   (b) in paragraph (c) for "section 1 of the Prevention of Corruption Act 1906 (c.34) or at common law" substitute "the Bribery Act 2010".

Serious Organised Crime and Police Act 2005 (c. 15)

7 The Serious Organised Crime and Police Act 2005 is amended as follows.
8 In section 61(1) (offences in respect of which investigatory powers apply) for paragraph (h) substitute –
   "(h) any offence under the Bribery Act 2010."
9 In section 76(3) (financial reporting orders: making) for paragraphs (d) to (f) substitute –
   "(da) an offence under any of the following provisions of the Bribery Act 2010 –
      section 1 (offences of bribing another person),
      section 2 (offences relating to being bribed),
      section 6 (bribery of foreign public officials),".
10 In section 77(3) (financial reporting orders: making in Scotland) after paragraph (b) insert –
   "(c) an offence under section 1, 2 or 6 of the Bribery Act 2010."

Armed Forces Act 2006 (c. 52)

11 In Schedule 2 to the Armed Forces Act 2006 (which lists serious offences the possible commission of which, if suspected, must be referred to a service police force), in paragraph 12, at the end insert –
   "(aw) an offence under section 1, 2 or 6 of the Bribery Act 2010."

Serious Crime Act 2007 (c. 27)

12 The Serious Crime Act 2007 is amended as follows.

13 (1) Section 53 of that Act (certain extra-territorial offences to be prosecuted only by, or with the consent of, the Attorney General or the Advocate General for Northern Ireland) is amended as follows.

    (2) The existing words in that section become the first subsection of the section.

    (3) After that subsection insert –

    "(2) Subsection (1) does not apply to an offence under this Part to which section 10 of the Bribery Act 2010 applies by virtue of section 54(1) and (2) below (encouraging or assisting bribery)."

14 (1) Schedule 1 to that Act (list of serious offences) is amended as follows.

    (2) For paragraph 9 and the heading before it (corruption and bribery: England and Wales) substitute –

"Bribery

9 An offence under any of the following provisions of the Bribery Act 2010 –
   (a) section 1 (offences of bribing another person);
   (b) section 2 (offences relating to being bribed);
   (c) section 6 (bribery of foreign public officials)."

    (3) For paragraph 25 and the heading before it (corruption and bribery: Northern Ireland) substitute –

"Bribery

25 An offence under any of the following provisions of the Bribery Act 2010 –
   (a) section 1 (offences of bribing another person);
   (b) section 2 (offences relating to being bribed);
   (c) section 6 (bribery of foreign public officials)."

SCHEDULE 2 Section 17(3)

Repeals and Revocations *Short title and chapter*	*Extent of repeal or revocation*
Public Bodies Corrupt Practices Act 1889 (c. 69)	The whole Act.
Prevention of Corruption Act 1906 (c. 34)	The whole Act.
Prevention of Corruption Act 1916 (c. 64)	The whole Act.
Criminal Justice Act (Northern Ireland) 1945 (c. 15 (N.I.))	Section 22.
Electoral Law Act (Northern Ireland) 1962 (c. 14 (N.I.))	Section 112(3).
Increase of Fines Act (Northern Ireland) 1967 (c. 29 (N.I.))	Section 1(8)(a) and (b).

Repeals and Revocations *Short title and chapter*	*Extent of repeal or revocation*
Criminal Justice (Miscellaneous Provisions) Act (Northern Ireland) 1968 (c. 28 (N.I.))	In Schedule 2, the entry in the table relating to the Prevention of Corruption Act 1906.
Local Government Act (Northern Ireland) 1972 (c. 9 (N.I.))	In Schedule 8, paragraphs 1 and 3.
Civil Aviation Act 1982 (c. 16)	Section 19(1).
Representation of the People Act 1983 (c. 2)	In section 165(1), paragraph (b) and the word "or" immediately before it.
Housing Associations Act 1985 (c. 69)	In Schedule 6, paragraph 1(2).
Criminal Justice Act 1988 (c. 33)	Section 47.
Criminal Justice (Evidence etc.) (Northern Ireland) Order 1988 (S.I. 1988/1847 (N.I.17))	Article 14.
Enterprise and New Towns (Scotland) Act 1990 (c. 35)	In Schedule 1, paragraph 2.
Scotland Act 1998 (c. 46)	Section 43.
Anti-terrorism, Crime and Security Act 2001 (c. 24)	Sections 108 to 110.
Criminal Justice (Scotland) Act 2003 (asp 7)	Sections 68 and 69.
Government of Wales Act 2006 (c. 32)	Section 44.
Armed Forces Act 2006 (c. 52)	In Schedule 2, paragraph 12(l) and (m).
Local Government and Public Involvement in Health Act 2007 (c. 28)	Section 217(1)(a). Section 244(4). In Schedule 14, paragraph 1.
Housing and Regeneration Act 2008 (c. 17)	In Schedule 1, paragraph 16.